Female Monasticism in Medieval Ireland: An archaeology

Female Monasticism in Medieval Ireland: An archaeology

TRACY COLLINS

CORK UNIVERSITY PRESS

First published in 2021 by
Cork University Press
Boole Library
University College Cork
CORK
T12 ND89
Ireland

Library of Congress Control Number 2021932851
Distribution in the USA: Longleaf Services, Chapel Hill, NC, USA

British Library Cataloguing in Publication Data
A CIP record for this book is available from the British Library.

ISBN: 978-1-78205-456-6

Printed by Gutenberg in Malta.
Print origination & design by Carrigboy Typesetting Services
www.carrigboy.co.uk

COVER IMAGES – Front Cover: Killone Abbey, County Clare. Image Frank Coyne.
Flap: West doorway of church, St Catherine's, County Limerick. Image: Tracy Collins.

www.corkuniversitypress.com

IRISH RESEARCH COUNCIL
An Chomhairle um Thaighde in Éirinn

ÆGIS

Contents

Acknowledgements

This book originated in my PhD thesis. A post-doctoral fellowship from the Irish Research Council in 2018, for which I am very grateful, allowed me the time and space to make it publication-ready. Throughout the entire course of this journey I have benefited from the knowledge, support and guidance of many generous colleagues and friends. First, I am very grateful to Professor William O'Brien, Department of Archaeology, University College Cork for facilitating the pursuit of my PhD and for hosting me during my year's fellowship. I thank Dr Colin Rynne and Dr Leonie Hicks (Canterbury Christ Church University), as my PhD examiners, who both actively encouraged me towards publication. Sincere thanks to my supervisor and mentor Dr Tomás Ó Carragáin, whose suggestions, critical eye and perseverance has seen this project to final fruition. I also thank other UCC departmental staff who assisted me in various ways: Nick Hogan, Mick Monk, Joy O'Callaghan, Barra O'Donnabhain and Denise Sheehan.

Many colleagues kindly provided advice, data, answered queries, or drew information to my attention, and I would like to specifically thank: Karl Brady, Nick Brannon, Martin Byrne, Christy Cunniffe, Audrey Horning, Linda Lynch, Conor MacDermott, Con Manning, Griffin Murray, Paul Murray, Ruairí Ó Baoill, Elizabeth O'Brien, Sheila Ronan, Robin Turk, Paul Walsh and Michelle O'Dea. I thank all the institutions and their staff and those who gave permission to re-produce images; they are credited individually throughout. I would like to acknowledge previous scholarship, particularly the work of antiquarians like T.J. Westropp, and the Archaeological Survey of Ireland: this book inevitably stands 'on the shoulders of giants'.

I am an archaeologist by profession, and not a historian, and I was struck by the genuine generosity and support shown by historian colleagues and friends. Thanks go to Edel Bhreathnach, Janet Burton, Kimm Curran, Marie Therese Flanagan, Brian Golding, Dianne Hall, Christina Harrington, Gillian Kenny, Paul MacCotter, Margaret MacCurtain, Bronagh McShane and Karen Stöber. A special note of gratitude goes to Colmán Ó Clabaigh OSB, who generously shared his particular insight into all things medieval religious with me. Many thanks to Mother Marie Fahy, abbess of St Mary's Abbey, Glencairn, Lismore, County Waterford, who generously discussed vocation and religious life with me and helped me gain some valuable insights. I am sincerely grateful to all the landowners who gave permission for site visits, especially the Guiney family, who allowed the excavations at St Catherine's, and who facilitated numerous visits and larger field trip groups. I would like to acknowledge the assistance and support of Aegis Archaeology Limited in funding the radiocarbon dates and specialist reports from the St Catherine excavations. Sincere thanks to my supportive family, and friends, too numerous to mention, but you know who you are! I am very grateful to Maria O'Donovan, Mike Collins, Aonghus Meaney, their colleagues and the academic board of Cork University Press for accepting this book and bringing it to final publication. I would specifically like to acknowledge the input of the two anonymous readers, whose comments and suggestions have greatly improved the final result. Of course, all errors and omissions are entirely my own.

Last, but by no means least, I would like to thank our daughter Sabina and, most especially, my archaeologist husband, Frank Coyne, for the images in this book, all his selfless support and the various sacrifices he has made which enabled me to complete this research.

Go raibh míle maith agaibh go léir.

List of Figures

List of Tables

CHAPTER I

Introduction

This book is the first comprehensive archaeological study of female monasticism in medieval Ireland. Historical accounts of medieval Ireland suggest that there was a substantial population of female religious in both the early and later medieval periods.[1] Despite this, however, there remains a lack of archaeological syntheses on medieval women generally and, in particular, female religious.[2] This is due to a number of factors many of which are a legacy of the past, and certainly not unique to Ireland. For example, male dominance in the discipline of archaeology and related disciplines, or the perceived paucity of documentary sources and material culture relating to this section of medieval society. A bias towards medieval male religious houses is evident in the published literature – though some do mention female religious houses – in part because of the better level of preservation at such sites, which makes them more suited to the architectural approach that has dominated monastic studies.[3]

The British and continental evidence for female religious has not been neglected to quite the same extent as the Irish evidence. Roberta Gilchrist has led the field in Britain and indeed globally, with a number of seminal publications on religious women, and wider gender issues, against a backdrop of monasticism.[4] In Ireland, by contrast, religious women are still largely invisible archaeologically, with very few archaeological books discussing them in any detail.[5] An archaeological study of female religious in medieval Ireland is therefore overdue. In this book, I take a nuanced approach to situate female religious in the monastic landscape of medieval Ireland, and attempt to elucidate the lives of these religious women through their material culture. I challenge perceived and accepted popular truths about medieval female religious in Ireland. For instance, the nature of enclosure and the relationships between female religious and wider society in the early medieval period, and especially in the later medieval period, are addressed. In the later medieval period, while some female religious houses did employ a claustral plan – the standard template for male monasteries – this book shows that many female religious houses did not conform to this classic arrangement; instead, we are confronted with a diversity of layouts that helped to structure the lives of female religious. Furthermore, a common assumption in relation to female religious houses is that they were deliberately isolated from male religious houses and secular society more generally. But contrary to this, I have found that medieval female religious and their houses were usually situated close to their patron's secular establishments, and were commonly within range of male religious houses or secular settlements. From this, coupled with the historical evidence, it can be inferred that the nuns likely maintained close ties with their locality and kin.

Based on the archaeological research discussed in this book, an alternative view of female monasticism in medieval Ireland is presented. A consideration of the early medieval evidence relating to female monasticism is made, though currently there is insufficient archaeological evidence from which to draw any firm conclusions. A comprehensive study has been made of the later medieval evidence of female monasticism. The alternative view taken in this book has been facilitated by various theoretical approaches, which have revealed that female monasticism in medieval Ireland was particularly fluid and diverse. It has elements in common with female monasticism in Britain and on the continent but there are also factors that are distinct and peculiar to Ireland.

SCOPE AND STRUCTURE

This book considers female monasticism in both the early and later periods of medieval Ireland, comprising a general study of the archaeology of female monasticism in Ireland, *c.*AD 500–1540, with a more detailed emphasis on the later medieval period *c.*AD 1100–1540. This emphasis is mainly due to the relative dearth of archaeological evidence for the earlier period. Yet I felt it was important in a book on medieval female monasticism in Ireland that the early medieval period be included due to its richness in other sources of evidence, especially hagiography.[6] As such, the early medieval material presented in Chapter 2 is intended as background context to what comes later in the period, while also highlighting where future archaeological research may prove fruitful.

The period of time under consideration in this book is bracketed by what might be considered processes rather than events: Ireland's conversion to Christianity, which is thought to have started early in the fifth century,[7] and the dissolution of its religious houses, beginning in the 1530s.[8] The archaeological division of the middle ages in Ireland into 'early' medieval and 'later' medieval is somewhat arbitrary, and not wholly agreed upon. For instance, it is common practice that the medieval period is subdivided into an early period *c.*AD 400–1169 and a later period *c.*AD 1169–1540.[9] The date of 1169 marks the coming of the Anglo-Normans to Ireland and has been traditionally used as a watershed in Irish history and archaeology.[10] However, when considering the organisation of the church in medieval Ireland, this subdivision does not make sense and is too late, in that the long process of church reform began *before* the coming of the Anglo-Normans in 1169, and was actually instigated by the Gaelic Irish, with the first synod recorded in 1101.[11] Hall in her historical study of the period thus uses *c.*1140–1540, 1144 being the traditional date when it is believed a number of nunneries within the reformed church were founded.[12] I have chosen the slightly earlier date of *c.*1100, having benefited greatly from Flanagan's comprehensive history of Ireland's church reform, in order to bracket the process that began early in the twelfth century, if not before.[13] The end of the period *c.*1540 marks the infamous event of the 'dissolution of the monasteries', when religious houses were suppressed by the crown, first under Henry VIII. However, again in this case, this was a protracted process rather than a single event, officially beginning in Ireland in 1539 and lasting until at least 1546, with many references and anecdotes of religious remaining in their houses long after this date, particularly in Gaelic and Gaelicised areas of the country.[14]

Desk-based research, archaeological fieldwork and archaeological excavation[15] were undertaken to collate existing information and create new knowledge.[16] I have created an archaeological catalogue with individual entries of all sites associated with early medieval female religious, later medieval nunneries, and possible sites, and my discussion and conclusions are based on this catalogue. Many of the individual sites have been used as examples throughout this book.[17] From the outset, I felt that it was insufficient to merely identify, or make visible, female religious in the archaeological record without trying to explore their lives and contribution to medieval society through their material culture. I have used approaches which have attempted to integrate all of the evidence, as it is currently known and in its broadest sense, to reach some meaningful conclusions.

Five principal questions are posed in the book. First, what are the theoretical perspectives that might elucidate the archaeology of medieval female religious in Ireland? Second, what is the archaeological evidence for female religious in medieval Ireland? Third, how did female religious, particularly of the later medieval period, construct their identity as religious women and negotiate religious life within nunneries? Fourth, where were female religious communities positioned in later medieval landscapes and what impact (if any) did they have on these landscapes? Finally, what can an archaeology of female monasticism in medieval Ireland contribute to the wider understanding of female medieval monasticism in a European context? These questions are not explicitly answered individually in the chapters of this book, nor are individual chapters exclusively focused on a single question. Rather these questions are intended to highlight ideas and are implicit threads that loosely guide the discussion and are resolved in the concluding chapter.

Following this introduction, the structure of the book is as follows: Chapter 2 provides an overview of the character of early medieval female religious communities in Ireland with some reference to British and continental evidence. Early medieval archaeological evidence relating to religious women is currently quite sparse and somewhat problematic, but nevertheless is crucial to an understanding of, and as a point of comparison with, the later medieval material that follows. As such, the discussion of early female religious and holy women and their associated places is primarily to provide a background context and a contrast to the nuns and nunneries of the later medieval period, illustrating the transformation (or otherwise) of the structure of the church throughout the twelfth century.

Chapter 3 considers first the historical evidence for women and their relationship with the church in later medieval Ireland, including as female religious and ordered nuns living under a rule. This chapter draws on the comprehensive histories of women and female religious, especially those by Hall, and Kenny.[18] This historical foundation then provides a context for the documentary and material evidence, which includes dates of establishment, founders, affiliation, dedications, and a list of the known nunneries. This is in effect a review of what is known to date. The chapters that follow then present the archaeological evidence for later medieval nunneries more fully. Chapter 4 situates nunneries in the landscape, discussing themes of distribution and topography, including water sources and land capability, and the nunneries' relationship to associated contemporary settlement. Chapter 5 explores nunnery enclosure and layout, comparing the evidence with that elsewhere, primarily through the concept of space and how it may have been perceived in the later medieval period. Chapter 6 focuses on the nunnery church, and considers its form – shape, proportion and architecture – and the ritual practices that took place within this most important structure in any monastic complex. Many nunnery churches were parish churches and as such were shared spaces with parishioners; how was this sharing of space achieved in practice? We are reminded in this chapter that professed nuns were just one form of religious women among many in medieval Europe, which included Beguines, mystics and anchorites. How might we expect these types of religious women to be represented in the archaeological record?

Chapter 7 attempts to broaden the discussion and is an exploration of daily life within the confines of the nunnery. It also explores how the identities of medieval nuns were constructed, especially through a consideration of the performance of daily routines and practices. Chapter 8 is a discussion of nuns' health, well-being, death and burial. As there is currently little if any evidence relating to the health and diet of nuns in medieval Ireland, archaeological evidence from Britain has been relied upon. There are only two nunneries in Ireland which have so far produced human remains and this archaeological evidence is discussed in detail. Notwithstanding the small sample, the results of analyses seem to challenge the notion that nuns came exclusively from the elite in medieval society. Chapter 9 considers nunneries in their guise as corporate entities that managed sometimes relatively large estates comprising landholdings and 'real estate' of different types, rights and benefices. This section uses St Catherine's, County Limerick as a micro case study to explore nunnery estates and discuss some of the current issues surrounding them. Finally, Chapter 10 returns to the five broad research questions posed in the first chapter and tries to resolve them in turn, offering a conclusion and synthesis of findings, and ending with suggestions for future research.

Notes on archaeology and terminology

The archaeology, monuments and material culture dating to the middle ages in Ireland has been found to differ significantly between the early and later periods. This has led the discipline of archaeology to subdivide it into two broad periods – early medieval and later medieval – which is more or less in line with the historical chronology previously outlined. Church archaeology and the ecclesiastical sites of the early medieval period (*c.*400–1100) are characterised by a circular or sub-circular enclosure formed by an earthen bank and fosse (ditch), and are of similar morphology to contemporary secular ringforts.[19] Depending on geographic location, these enclosures were constructed of earth or stone. Complexes of higher status may have had several concentric enclosures, demarcating sacred spaces, the most sacred being the innermost enclosure where the primary church was usually located. These ecclesiastical sites may have had one or a multiple of relatively small rectangular churches, many of which were replaced over time on the same site. Excavation has shown that in many cases the earliest church was made of timber, with later replacements in stone.[20] While having a religious function, these sites were also lived in by religious men and women – sometimes perhaps together in mixed communities – and the excavated archaeology has demonstrated that such mixed groups would also have carried out a variety of more specialist activities such as weaving and metalworking.[21] It is now agreed that most of these early medieval ecclesiastical sites were established as proprietary churches by important family groups. Many remained small and were relatively short-lived, though some became very important religious and political centres, for example Clonmacnoise in County Offaly, Glendalough in County Wicklow, and Kildare.[22]

The ecclesiastical archaeology of the later medieval period (*c.*1100–1540) is significantly different from the earlier period.[23] Most starkly, the claustral arrangement of the religious orders – a church and ranges of buildings set around a central cloister and garth – was first constructed at the Cistercian monastery of Mellifont, County Louth in 1142.[24] The idea of a claustral plan was adopted by all the religious orders introduced into Ireland – though importantly there was a flexibility in how it was employed at individual houses, and at some religious houses, particularly some nunneries, it was absent. As the parish system was embedded over time, stone parish churches were constructed.[25] These were relatively larger than the stone churches of the early medieval period in Ireland, though are small when compared to contemporary parish churches in Britain or the continent. Earthen ecclesiastical concentric enclosures were not constructed in this period – though some may have been reused (see Chapter 5). Secular living also changed, from earthen ringforts and stone cashels to castles, moated sites, increased urban and village settlement and, later, at the end of the period, to tower houses and fortified houses. It is thought that the lower strata of society may have employed timber and/or sod structures, though these are much more difficult to identify in the archaeological record.[26]

The main archaeological issue which relates to both the ecclesiastical enclosures and churches of the early medieval period, and the religious houses and their churches of the later period, is that neither monument type manifest any physical indicators that show what gender their original religious community was. That is to say, it is impossible to now look at a monument and conclude that it was used exclusively by religious women, men, or indeed a mixed community of the early medieval period. So, it is very important to realise from the outset that both male and female religious communities used the same 'vocabulary' of architecture and layout in both periods, and we are thus currently dependent on recorded history to elucidate – where it can – what gender a religious community was in a particular place. Despite this limitation, these sites associated with women religious are worthy of study in their own right, so that this section of medieval society might be represented in the Irish archaeological record to a greater extent than is currently the case.

Terminology in respect of female religious in both the early and later medieval periods can sometimes be a limitation or even misleading, particularly when several disciplines, such as archaeology, anthropology, historical geography, and history intersect.[27] Even the term 'nunnery' is contextually loaded, and implies a religious female community living enclosed under a rule, and in a particular style of dress. Current knowledge suggests that for Ireland this was considered the typical arrangement of later medieval female religious communities, but some early medieval female religious communities are likely to have been much more flexible in their organisation. Therefore, in an attempt to avoid anachronism in this book, early medieval establishments are referred to as female religious monasteries, communities or ecclesiastical sites, while the members thereof are termed women/female religious, rather than nuns. The terms 'nun' and 'nunnery' are applied only to the later medieval material. It is acknowledged that there were female religious in the later medieval period who lived in situations other than nunneries, but none of these female religious have, as yet, been identified in the archaeology of medieval Ireland. Furthermore, female religious in the later medieval period in the Augustinian order and Augustinian of Arroasian observance are regularly referred to as canonesses, after their male counterparts, the canons (ordained clerics living under a rule).[28] However, in this book it is preferred to term them nuns, along with the female religious of the other orders, as in reality they were not a female form of canons, in that they were not ordained.

The terms monastery and monasticism are used in this book in their widest sense in both periods. Monasticism being a regulated communal life embraced by men and women devoted to the contemplation, worship and service of God and to the pursuit of their own spiritual perfection;[29] and a monastery the location for such a communal life. However, when specifically referring to male houses of the later medieval period, monastery specifically denotes a house of monks, friary is used for friars, and religious house is used for canons. Female monasticism has been used as an umbrella term for the female religious communities of both the early and later medieval period in Ireland, which elsewhere is broadly termed the middle ages.

Another potential source of confusion arises from the use of the term 'convent'. While convent is synonymous with sisters and nuns in the modern period, the word denoted conventual buildings in earlier times and was used to describe both male and female religious houses. The Ordnance Survey of the 1830s to 1840s in Ireland annotated many monastic sites on its maps as 'convent'. For instance, Carnaun, near Athenry, County Galway was labelled 'convent', which has subsequently been suggested by some as a possible nunnery. However, based on the archaeological remains and other information, this is unlikely to have been the case. Indeed, many of the antiquities marked on the first-edition Ordnance Survey six-inch maps were based on local information gathered by the surveyors, which, while a great archaeological resource, was not always reliable.

Other religious terms that I use in this book may not be familiar, and where they first occur I have provided explanations.[30] For example, in the later medieval period, a Beguine was a member of a lay sisterhood mainly in the urban centres of the Low Countries, who lived in unenclosed communities (beguinages) but were not bound by vows.[31] None is known from medieval Ireland, but some beguinages are still in existence, most famously at Bruges in modern Belgium. A vowess was also a religious woman who took vows and dedicated herself to the church but was not a professed nun and was not enclosed. She was usually a widow and may have had children. Vowesses are mentioned in early and later medieval sources. This type of religious woman, particularly in the early medieval period, may have lived in her own home, and as such is very difficult to identify in the archaeological record. An anchorite was a man or a woman who lived a completely enclosed life within a small cell known as an anchorhold, which was attached to a church or religious house. A person needed permission to become an anchorite and there was a special ritual which was undertaken prior to their enclosure (see Chapter 6). In the later medieval period, a corrodian was a lay person who paid, or was sponsored, to lodge in private accommodation within a religious house's precinct. This could be a temporary arrangement but was often more permanent and served as a form of pension.

In this book, a number of theoretical perspectives are explored, and these are discussed in the sections below. Many of these perspectives are interdisciplinary, though nuances may be different when these perspectives are viewed through the lens of the discipline of archaeology. Medieval archaeology in Ireland has been relatively slow to engage with theory, though is catching-up,[32] so some concepts and terms require explicit definition. Two seminal theoretical archaeological texts which I have used extensively are Matthew Johnson's *Archaeological Theory: An introduction*[33] and Roberta Gilchrist's *Gender and Archaeology: Contesting the past*.[34]

Three key concepts in this regard are outlined here. The first is 'engendered' archaeology. This means the use of gender as an analytical category in archaeology. Gender in this context can be succinctly defined as the cultural interpretation of sexual difference, that results in the categorisation of individuals, artefacts, spaces and bodies, and is dependent on personal and historical circumstances. The origins of engendered studies lie in the second important concept, feminism and its 'three waves' – the political conviction to challenge existing power relations between men and women. The third concept is postmodernism – a movement of the later twentieth century – which has permeated through many if not all disciplines, and rejected single linear explanations of culture. Throughout the 1980s, history and, later, archaeology connected with this concept and slowly moved away from more traditional forms of single narrative interpretation of the evidence, to more multi-narrative interpretations, and this became known as the 'linguistic turn'.[35]

HISTORIOGRAPHY

There are several gaps in the current knowledge of female religious in medieval Ireland, which has in turn informed some of the research questions posed. It is first necessary to contextualise the Irish medieval written primary sources and highlight their limitations. The survival of Irish later medieval written sources is relatively poor, when compared to the early medieval written sources in Ireland, and written medieval sources elsewhere. Indeed, it could be argued that Ireland has the poorest survival rate in Europe for later medieval written historical sources associated with religious houses. This is due to a number of factors, not least the destruction of the Public Records Office at the Four Courts in 1922 during Ireland's civil war, when a substantial number of records were lost. Some which were lost are available in calendar form or as summaries, having been recorded prior to the destruction of the original manuscripts. Other documents remain in the Public Record Office in London as many of the sources relate to the official documentation of the English, created through government and administration, for example rolls, fiants, wills and deeds. These are certainly not known in the quantities that survive elsewhere due to the upheavals in Ireland of the sixteenth and seventeenth centuries, such as the dissolution and reformation,[36] and later the various plantations,[37] all of which brought about profound changes, culturally, socially and economically.

Medieval record sources that are available in Ireland for monastic and religious houses have been summarised by Philomena Connolly,[38] and for Gaelic Ireland in particular by Katherine Simms,[39] which includes, for example, the Annals, genealogies, literary works in prose and verse, religious writings such as saints' lives, and Brehon law. While primary contemporary sources for male religious houses are considered scant, similar sources for female religious houses in medieval Ireland are almost entirely lacking.[40] For instance, there is no cartulary extant for a medieval nunnery in Ireland, and there are only a few very short accounts of visitations to nunneries: two in Dublin dated to the fifteenth century, and one in Limerick of uncertain date. Similarly, no internal documents survive which might shed light on a nunnery's day-to-day activities.

Moreover, the processes of dissolution, reformation and plantation felt in Ireland in the sixteenth and seventeenth centuries had in turn dire consequences for the country's later medieval material culture. Religious buildings and traditional places of worship were abandoned, demolished or later re-used, and much of the material culture and portable artefacts associated with later medieval religious and monastic practice were destroyed or lost. Therefore, as will become apparent, secondary sources such as later surveys may contain the only extant historical evidence of many nunneries, and in many cases their medieval fabric is relatively poorly preserved.

Previous historical research

> Recovering information about the role of women religious in the medieval period is notoriously difficult ... given the overall paucity of evidence.[41]

The earliest descriptions of female religious houses were those included in lists of monastic and religious houses in Ireland written in the seventeenth century.[42] Many of the historical accounts that followed were based on these earlier publications, some of which reproduced misunderstandings and misidentifications.[43] Later works included female religious communities as part of wider religious and monastic house accounts rather than in their own right, for example *Onomasticon Goedelicum*,[44] or as part of edited primary sources such as *Extents of Irish Monastic Possessions 1540–'41*.[45] *Medieval Religious Houses Ireland* listed information from primary sources on houses of nuns, including them for both the early medieval and later medieval periods.[46] It was acknowledged in that publication that the lack of documentary evidence relating to female houses, coupled with their re-use through time, hindered their identification both in history, and archaeologically in the field.[47] Though not without its critics and subsequent amendments,[48] *Medieval Religious Houses Ireland* remains a good information source for medieval religious communities and various ecclesiastical sites in Ireland for archaeologists and historians alike, though it has now been somewhat superseded by online repositories.[49]

General histories on medieval monasticism and the church have mentioned female religious but never to the same degree as their male counterparts.[50] There have been several more specific historical studies which included aspects of female monasticism in medieval Ireland, for example hagiography,[51] annalistic and chronicle sources,[52] burial,[53] and specific important ecclesiastical sites that had associated female religious, for example Armagh.[54] There have been several studies of specific places associated with female religious,[55] and of religious orders that accommodated women.[56] Dianne Hall has listed all later medieval nuns and other religious women named in the currently available historical documents for the later medieval period.[57] Others have considered places associated with female religious, for example in studies on monastic topography.[58] Avril Thomas' *The Walled Towns of Ireland* included information on nunneries where they were known to have existed,[59] as did several volumes of the *Irish Historic Towns Atlas* series.[60] Most individual histories of cities and counties, including various gazetteers, the Down,[61] and civil surveys, books of survey and distribution, Ordnance Survey letters and name books also made reference to various houses of nuns when they existed or were thought to have existed, although little attention has been paid to them when compared to their contemporary male religious houses.[62]

From the late 1970s onwards, historians – predominantly but not exclusively female – began to consider women in Ireland in their own right,[63] as did folklorists as part of wider debates on terminology and gendered perspectives.[64] An internationally significant history of religious women, *Sisters in Arms: Catholic nuns through two millennia*, included accounts of religious women in Ireland, placing them in their wider European historical context.[65] An agenda for women's history in Ireland stressed the urgent need for an engendered approach in the discipline. The authors hoped that theirs would not go the way of other previous research agendas, 'interesting in theory but ignored in practice'.[66]

In 2000, to mark the end of the twentieth century, the discipline of medieval Irish history was reviewed and the potential of interdisciplinary approaches, such as that of history and archaeology, was discussed at length.[67] The rejection of stereotypes in history, and by extension archaeology, was stressed, which could be achieved through micro-studies.[68] This approach took root and culminated in several historical monographs being published on female religious in medieval Ireland.[69] Two in particular have influenced the writing of this book. The first was by Christina Harrington, *Women in a Celtic Church: Ireland 450–1150*, published in 2002. It adopted a more theoretical and nuanced approach to the history of female religious in early medieval Ireland than had previously been the case, through a chronological narrative from conversion to Christianity in the fifth and sixth centuries; the zenith of female religious establishments in the seventh to the ninth century; and then towards decline and reform in the tenth to the twelfth centuries. This publication was useful to the non-historian in that it provided detail of historical sources that had never been rigorously investigated, or were unknown to the non-specialist, while drawing together all the sources of the early medieval period that mentioned female religious.

The second of the histories published at this time and arguably the more influential of the two was Dianne Hall's *Women and the Church in Medieval Ireland* c.*1140–1540*, published in 2003. It continues to be an invaluable source to anyone interested in women religious of later medieval Ireland. This book detailed, in a very readable though nonetheless scholarly way, all the references in the available historical sources relating to nuns, female religious, women connected to nunneries and their wider families. Hall weaved this historical evidence into an engaging and sometimes intricate narrative of religious women in later medieval Ireland, culminating in a case study chapter on the interesting life of Elicia Butler, abbess of Kilculliheen. Through this evidence she considered themes of lay women's piety and patronage, nunnery foundation, management, buildings and estates, and engagement of religious communities through what Hall termed their 'permeable cloister' with neighbours and relations. She also provided a list of names of the women she encountered in the documents and a list of nunneries.[70] Hall's chapter on the buildings – with a sprinkling of architecture and archaeology – provided a summary overview of what remained, and a tantalising glimpse into what archaeology might reveal, if it was investigated.

From these publications onwards attempts were made to consider religious women as actors in narratives of important historical events, for example twelfth-century church reform.[71] Edited volumes and thematic monographs which considered Irish women in wider medieval and early modern European contexts also emerged;[72] and four important edited volumes which included contributions on Ireland were exclusively dedicated to aspects of female monasticism in Europe.[73]

Previous archaeological and architectural research

In Ireland, archaeological research and architectural research have a shared trajectory, with both disciplines developing from antiquarianism.[74] Until now, there has not been an architectural or archaeological synthesis of female monasticism in Ireland, and few individual site studies have been published. In the early days of antiquarian research, female religious ecclesiastical sites and nunneries received attention when they were well preserved in the field, for example the Nuns' Church, Clonmacnoise, County Offaly,[75] St Catherine's, Old Abbey, County Limerick,[76] Inishmaine, County Mayo,[77] or Killone, County Clare.[78] Interestingly, the Nuns' Church, restored in the 1860s, was the first example of monument conservation in Ireland.[79] All these studies looked at particular aspects of architecture and archaeology rather than female monasticism *per se*. For example, Arthur Champneys, writing in 1910, discussed the Nuns' Church and Temple Finghin at Clonmacnoise, County Offaly as examples of Romanesque architecture rather than churches associated with nuns.[80] Harold Leask in his three-volume *Irish Churches and Monastic Buildings* continued this methodology, including female religious ecclesiastical sites and nunneries on the basis of their architectural form and not their female association, for example St Mary's in Glendalough, County Wicklow and the Nuns' Church and Temple Finghin in County Offaly.[81] More recent studies also discuss monuments related to nuns on this basis; for example Killone and Inishmaine have been highlighted as being typical of 'School of the West' architecture, rather than being nunneries.[82]

Overall, then, it is relatively rare that medieval women and specifically female religious are considered in an Irish archaeological context, although there are notable exceptions. For instance, Nancy Edwards made a call some time ago for further research on early medieval women, including female religious.[83] Conleth Manning's identification of a second nunnery at Clonmacnoise, County Offaly, at Temple Finghin, proves the success that academic detective work and inquiry can achieve, while also highlighting that if current archaeological evidence is interpreted from a different perspective, different narratives might emerge.[84] Furthermore, Jenifer Ní Ghrádaigh's research on early medieval women, from primarily an art historical perspective, has shown them to have more agency in the patronage and manufacture of religious art and architecture than was previously thought.[85] Scholars have explored the possibility that female segregated burial may perhaps highlight the presence of a community of female religious.[86] There has been archaeological discussion of female religious communities as part of the diversity of the early medieval church in Ireland,[87] though there is yet no similar discourse for nuns of the later period.

A probable cause for the oversight of female religious in the archaeological record dating to the early medieval period in Ireland is the current dearth of extant and excavated evidence clearly related to them. It is surprising though that later medieval nunneries are also poorly represented in the published architectural and archaeological literature, despite their upstanding remains. This may be because of the relatively late flowering of later medieval archaeology in Ireland more generally, in part due to an ambivalence about this period among cultural nationalists. Briefly, cultural nationalists viewed the later medieval era as one of invasion, colonial expansion and religious suppression during the periods of reformation and plantation – a view which is now considered to have been somewhat simplistic. The period was subsequently viewed through the lenses of later political events such as the 1916 rising and the guerrilla war of independence with Britain (1919–21), which was closely followed by the Irish civil war (1922–3). Furthermore, the later medieval period in Ireland was not considered worthy of study when compared to the material culture of the earlier periods, which were thought of as more 'purely Irish'. For example, the Bronze Age period had produced a wealth of sophisticated gold objects, and early medieval Ireland, then Christian, was culturally rich and distinctive, dubbed the 'land of saints and scholars' by the Gaelic and Celtic Revival movements. All these factors combined to portray later medieval Ireland as a time of invasion and ethnic dilution that, in the modern nascent nation's history, was one which was best forgotten.[88]

Thomas J. Westropp's work still remains the largest body of detailed research on specific examples of medieval nunneries in Ireland.[89] More recent studies on later medieval architecture and archaeology have briefly mentioned nunneries.[90] The Archaeological Survey of Ireland, in the Department of Housing, Local Government and Heritage, and Northern Ireland's Historic Environment Division in the Department for Communities manage the monument databases of the Sites and Monuments Record and the Record of Monuments and Places.[91] These archives classify both early medieval ecclesiastical sites related to female religious communities and later nunneries, but those classifications are sometimes ambiguous. There have been a few archaeological geophysical surveys,[92] and excavations undertaken at or adjacent to monuments associated with female religious.[93] However, intrusive investigations have in the main been limited and results disappointing, particularly for those investigations at early medieval sites.

There remains a particular gap in knowledge in relation to the archaeology of monastic estates of both male and female religious communities.[94] The first published discussion of the archaeology of early medieval ecclesiastical estates in Ireland, which included an ecclesiastical estate related to a female religious community, was published in 2014.[95] Archaeologists in Ireland have also not considered the estates and precincts of any later medieval religious house, either male or female, until very recently, and the subject was largely left to historians.[96] Archaeologists have only just begun to consider monastic and religious house granges,[97] precincts and estates, such as that of the precinct of St John's Priory in Kilkenny,[98] and of St Mary's, Dublin.[99] Excavations at the Cistercian monastery of Bective, County Meath go some way to fill the gap in the archaeological record of monastic precincts.[100] Very little to no archaeological attention had been paid to nunnery precincts or estates before that of the nunnery estate of Timolin, County Kildare in 2014.[101]

A relatively new development in the disciplines of archaeology and history is the creation of web-based databases, in which large quantities of data can be managed and updated. The most recent in Ireland is the 'Monastic Ireland: landscape and settlement' project. A joint venture between the Discovery Programme, Trinity College Dublin, and University College Cork, this digital humanities project seeks to create a comprehensive baseline database of up to 300 medieval religious houses, including female religious houses.[102]

An overview of research in Britain and the continent

The historical and archaeological study of female monasticism in Britain and the continent is much more progressed than in Ireland. This is partly due to the better preservation of the documentary and physical evidence related to female religious in these regions, though this preservation is still considered not as good as that of the contemporary male religious houses. It has been suggested that mid-twentieth-century, predominantly male scholarship in Britain, such as the work of Knowles,[103] downplayed the history of female monasticism by not using earlier published material relating to nuns in England,[104] such as *Medieval English Nunneries* by Eileen Power published in 1922,[105] and other early scholarly works – all of which were undertaken by women – on female monasticism,[106] double monasteries,[107] hospitals,[108] anchorites[109] and minoresses.[110]

More recently, many studies have explored aspects of medieval female monasticism in Britain on a national or regional basis,[111] or in associated places such as Normandy, France.[112] The annual *Monastic Research Bulletin* was a very important resource for Britain and elsewhere, but was unfortunately discontinued in 2013.[113] Notwithstanding the excellent scholarship already highlighted, it can be argued that the research of Roberta Gilchrist, begun in the late 1980s, has transformed the way in which female monastic archaeology and monastic archaeology more generally are considered in many disciplines, not just archaeology. She has rigorously applied gender and social theory to monastic and secular archaeological evidence, producing several seminal publications which have created a watershed in medieval research globally.[114]

There have been a number of excavations of early medieval ecclesiastical sites and nunneries in Britain, and Gilchrist has summarised the archaeological data to the early 1990s.[115] More recently, several seasons of excavation were carried out at the Anglo-Saxon minster at Lyminge,[116] and published excavations of later medieval nunneries in Britain include Chester, Romsey Abbey, Holywell Priory, St Mary Clerkenwell, and Grovebury Priory.[117] Excavations have been undertaken by Jemma Bezant on one of the few Cistercian nunneries known in Wales at Llanllŷr,[118] and excavations have recently been completed at Littlemore Priory, Oxford.[119] Due to the relative wealth of documentary sources in Britain, themes such as nuns' literacy can be explored, for example the Barking Abbey community.[120] In contrast to Ireland, archaeological landscape studies in Britain have made significant contributions to the study of monastic precincts and estates including granges, of both male and female religious houses.[121]

Female monastic studies on continental Europe have progressed significantly in the past twenty years or so and overviews of the current state of knowledge have been recently published.[122] There have been several European-wide studies which were predominantly historical,[123] with those of the Cistercian order dominating the literature.[124] Architecture of the mendicant orders, including Clarissan (Order of St Clare) houses, has been discussed by Caroline Bruzelius.[125] German archaeological and architectural evidence has led the field in female monastic studies,[126] while two important collected works have also emanated from Germany: proceedings of a conference on female *vita religiosa* at the Research Centre for Comparative History of Religious Orders at the Catholic University of Eichstätt,[127] and a collection of essays translated from the catalogue of an extensive museum exhibition entitled 'Crown and Veil' of medieval female monastic material culture curated at Essen and Bonn in 2005.[128]

Studies of female monasticism, including some archaeological excavation, have also been undertaken in Belgium and the Netherlands,[129] France,[130] Spain,[131] Italy,[132] Switzerland,[133] Scandinavia,[134] and Eastern Europe.[135] The critical evaluation of the uses of monastic space in male and female houses – showing the continued influence of Roberta Gilchrist – is emerging as a popular theme,[136] though wider landscape and comparative studies are not as yet common.[137] Very useful web-based monastic databases have also been established, for example the Monastic Matrix, a scholarly resource for the study of women's religious communities from 400 to 1600 curated by Alison Beach;[138] the Monastic Wales project,[139] which includes data on the nunneries of Wales; and FemMoData,[140] a database of all European female monastic sites, which was a daughter project of the 'Crown and Veil' exhibition.[141] The benefit of such databases is that information can be updated and links created to new projects in all disciplines interested in female monasticism. Furthermore, there are a number of web-based groups which are dedicated to the study of female monasticism, for example the History of Women Religious of Britain and Ireland,[142] or medieval studies more generally, for example the Forum for Medieval and Renaissance Studies in Ireland.[143] The establishment of the

Journal of Medieval Monastic Studies in 2012 is indicative of the upsurge in female monastic studies, which to date has included reviews and essays on several diverse aspects of female monasticism.[144]

THEORETICAL PERSPECTIVES

The engagement with archaeological theory in Ireland began as late as the 1990s,[145] and was relatively slow to progress, improving in more recent years with publications on medieval archaeology employing theoretical approaches.[146] The search for new archaeological data was at fever pitch, fuelled by Ireland's development-driven economy of the early to mid-2000s. It has been suggested that archaeologists gather archaeological information without ever realising for the most part that they themselves are actively forming that information: their archaeological interpretations are inextricably linked to their own background and experiences.[147] With this in mind, this section sets out the theoretical perspectives that have influenced this book, particularly those formulated by Gilchrist. Due to the nature of the current archaeological evidence of female monasticism in early medieval Ireland, it is difficult at the moment to employ an engendered approach that would yield meaningful outcomes (see Chapter 2). As a result, the theoretical perspectives set out are mainly employed in Chapters 3 to 10.

Engendering archaeology: an overview

> Archaeology is uniquely situated to reveal aspects of the deep history of sex and gender relations in ways no other discipline can address.[148]

Feminist approaches are varied in archaeology and cannot be perceived as a single school of thought. Indeed, the movement of archaeological thought towards more engendered approaches is one that is still progressing.[149] When archaeology was grappling with 'new archaeology' in the 1960s and '70s, feminism became a force greater than just a women's rights movement, which influenced several disciplines.[150] Feminism facilitated the study of social relation and gender – the social construction of sexual difference between men and women.[151] Its first wave highlighted androcentrism, which portrayed women as 'Other' – deviant to a standard set by the male in every sphere of life.[152] Pioneering females attempted to redress gender imbalances.[153] This second wave exploded the traditional meta-narrative of history, but was criticised for merely making women visible by only considering traditional roles.[154]

Post-processual archaeology, which superseded 'new archaeology', was influenced by feminist thinking, rejecting dichotomies such as individual/society as being artificial binary creations.[155] It was also strongly influenced by postmodernism and the linguistic turn and its perceived lack of objectivity – hence the predilection of presentism in many archaeological narratives.[156] Just over thirty years ago, the first truly archaeological feminist critique of male bias was written, and was a tipping point in the discipline of archaeology between the second and third waves of feminism.[157] After this, gender was considered with other factors.[158] Archaeology was slow to adopt this approach because the discipline emphasised the biological aspects of gender, at first reluctant to accept gender as a cultural trait.[159] It also favoured testing of empirical data, which worked against abstract concepts like gender.[160] Gender theory did ultimately influence archaeological thought,[161] and biological sex was no longer static but considered 'as historically created and contextually perceived'.[162]

Roberta Gilchrist successfully applied such an engendered framework to English medieval nunneries, and demonstrated that there are varied theoretical approaches open to an archaeological study of female monasticism.[163] It has been established that female monasticism in medieval Ireland has been under-studied. A trend noted elsewhere is that early researchers of female monasticism tended to be women,[164] but over the history of archaeology in Ireland there were few females in academia to undertake such studies.[165] In the nineteenth and early twentieth centuries there was no female lecturer in archaeology, and though there were female historians, at that time none chose to undertake a historical study in Ireland, as was done in Britain by Eileen Power.[166] Therefore, in Ireland there were not the same opportunities for 'remedial works' – studies that related specifically to women.[167] Furthermore, it could be argued that the hierarchy in Ireland was androcentric at that time, in that mostly male academics (with a few exceptions) chose not to study female religious, though it is likely that this gender bias was unconscious.[168]

'Man as the measure' has long been considered the standard in archaeological discourse.[169] This status quo has been categorically rejected as it suggested that 'women, their behaviour and material culture, can be recognised only as a deviant pattern to a standard which is male'.[170] Previous studies and excavations of male religious houses in Ireland have assisted in setting this artificial standard.[171] It appears from the evidence that female religious houses have been compared, probably unconsciously, to this male standard and have been found wanting. This inappropriate comparison of female religious houses with their male counterparts is a primary reason why the archaeology of female monasticism has remained under-studied in Ireland. Gilchrist's work has proven that the comparison of nunneries with male houses is unjust; nunneries did not have the same functions as male houses, and therefore any direct comparison is otiose.[172] Female monasticism requires critical analysis on its own archaeological merits, and in comparison to a female standard comprising female religious houses elsewhere, so that new archaeological interpretations can be presented. The female religious sites included in this book are considered in this way and are deliberately not directly compared to a male monastic template.

An engendered study is justified by three connected arguments: first, in order to have comprehensive histories and archaeologies, women must be included in a scholarly way; second, if archaeology does not undertake this type of research then other disciplines, such as history, will; and third, feminist archaeology has the potential to transform ideas about the past and lead to a re-evaluation of social attitudes.[173] Gilchrist's strategy has been adopted in this book and it has been applied to the Irish data, in order to interpret the evidence in new ways, reach new conclusions, and generate debate and new ideas. Other theoretical perspectives have also influenced my thinking which has informed this book: the twin dangers of presentism and relativism; social archaeologies, experience, performance and personhood; space, place and time; and landscape. And each is now discussed.

Presentism and relativism

A pitfall in any study of the medieval past is the bias of presentism and the danger of being anachronistic. Archaeologists inhabit the archaeological landscape in the present[174] and it has been suggested that archaeology is the most recent form of dwelling on any ancient site.[175] The act of researching and investigating a place is a valid part of that site's history, and this should be duly acknowledged. It is also recognised that there may have been presentist biases in older studies undertaken, and it could be suggested that to some extent all archaeological discourses are inherently presentist. Indeed, Miri Rubin has recently written that an informed presentism can bring some scholarly advantages to studies of the past.[176]

Modern Ireland retains a legacy of dominant Roman Catholicism and has been shaped by that church in its widest sense, not least in education.[177] Indeed, the majority of Irish women of a certain age – and many men – were at one point educated at convent schools and taught by nuns. This is yet another mental template through which the nunneries of medieval Ireland might be viewed. What it means to be a modern sister in a convent is sometimes incorrectly projected onto the medieval past, producing an erroneous narrative. Furthermore, it has been highlighted that understanding medieval monastic identity in its *own* time and place can be complicated, 'most notably in the backward-projections that monastic orders made of their own collective identities and the tendency to tell their histories without recognition of the changes and developments in their own orders'.[178] It is thus important to realise that modern enclosed nuns, and other monastic orders for that matter, while certainly having their origins in the medieval period cannot be viewed as living the *same lives* as medieval nuns, despite following what is perceived as the same rule. However, their modern enclosed lives can certainly be used as a starting point to gain understandings of the past.

As such, it is fully acknowledged that modern archaeologists cannot read the thoughts of people in the past or get 'inside their heads'. However, present-day understandings which represent those past meanings can be established and interesting conclusions about the past can be arrived at.[179] Furthermore, the 'past' is not available for objective inspection, and so it follows that there can never be a universal consensus on a single narrative. This is but one of the results of the impact of modernity on archaeology internationally.[180]

A second pitfall to archaeological enquiry is relativism. The accusation of relativism is frequently levelled at post-processual approaches, which suggests that all interpretations are equally valid.[181] However, the nature of archaeological data as evidence must mitigate interpretation.[182] Interpretations must be constrained by the evidence, which itself cannot be taken as a given, nor be infinitely plastic.[183] In this study various archaeological interpretations are considered in relation to the sum of the evidence for female monasticism in medieval Ireland – some of which might be at odds with earlier conclusions – such as layout, the nature of enclosure, location, function and organisation of nunneries in medieval Ireland. However, interpretations suggested are at all times firmly supported by the archaeological evidence.

Interpretive and social archaeologies

From the 1990s, post-processual or interpretive archaeology has had a significant impact on Irish archaeologists. Exposure to the post-processual theories of Hodder,[184] Shanks and Tilley,[185] among others, provided a strong understanding of context, archaeological interpretation and a multi-narrative approach. This has led to a generation of archaeologists with the ability to analyse an archaeological site or excavation on a number of levels, and the confidence to present a number of valid interpretations, in so far as those interpretations are supported by the archaeological evidence.

Post-processual archaeology has been criticised for remaining largely androcentric and that, as a consequence, it has done little to advance the archaeological method of feminist analysis.[186] However, post-processual archaeology does owe a great deal to the strides made earlier by feminist and gender approaches. But 'gender archaeology will prove to be no more than a chimera ... if it merely reorders the dominant subject as female to a silent male "other"',[187] and so the multi-interpretive leanings of many archaeologists now encompass both masculinist and feminist approaches.

Exploration of personhood is useful in this regard as it breaks down binary oppositions highlighted through the lens of gender, such as woman/female/feminist and man/male/masculinist. Therefore, it is important that this book does not *exclude* religious men and the male. Rather, I attempt to, first, allow space to consider female monasticism in medieval Ireland in its own right and, second, to explore interactions with other groups through patronage, relations, celebration of the sacraments, servants, tenants and architecture. The interpretive approach adopted here towards female monasticism in medieval Ireland has stressed the specific rather than the general. I have embraced this approach due to the nature of the archaeology under consideration. A crucial strength of this interpretive approach is that it can focus on the individual, their active engagement or agency with their surroundings, while attempting to elucidate their lives.[188]

Experience, performance, personhood and being-in-the-world

A phenomenological perspective stresses 'experiences of thinking and knowing'.[189] Phenomenology is both a philosophical and methodological approach to past understandings of the material world, which can be equally applied to a medieval landscape and a prehistoric one. Phenomenology emphasises the intertwining of subject and object, things and person, mind and body, places, lived experience and being-in-the-world. Meanings and fresh understandings of place and landscape can be derived from an engaged perceiver and the structures of what is perceived. It involves the archaeologist – the effect of the researcher on things and those things around them. Persons do not passively receive information and knowledge about the world but always act in accordance with practical projects, values, needs, desires and interests. The benefit of a phenomenological stance in archaeology is that it protects the subjective view of experience 'as a necessary part of any full understanding of the nature of knowledge'.[190] It also encourages an encounter between the archaeologist and the places and monuments under study. The encounter may be real, in a physical sense, or imagined.[191] The approach acknowledges the archaeologist in the present as experiencing the landscape as it is perceived. It aims to describe the character of human experience, specifically via the understanding of the material world through intervention with the surroundings.[192]

Therefore, a phenomenological approach places the individual, through their experiences – in this case female religious – at centre stage, while at the same time acknowledging the input of the researcher. While this is a positive development in the archaeological study of the past, there are inherent difficulties with a purely phenomenological approach. First, it is impossible to realise the true past significance of characteristics such as intervisibility and proximity of monuments, which are identified as important or unimportant in the present. Of course, location in a landscape was likely important but may have been for reasons which are no longer apparent – a distinction between association and causation must be made.[193] Second, contemporary encounters with landscapes and monuments cannot fully embody actual experiences of people in the past, as it anachronistically assumes that past and modern people are essentially the same beings, at all stages of their life courses. This is clearly not the case, as the body itself is a product of social relations and contested meanings through time, and so 'our own bodily encounters with ancient monuments are therefore unlikely to match those of past peoples'.[194] Phenomenology then does not take account of the diversity of human experience. Third, monuments and landscapes are not static and can change seasonally and indeed over the course of a single day through light and weather. Therefore, the experiences and perceptions of those places are also likely to be variable. Moreover, it has been argued that perception itself is an act of interpretation and experience which is historically constituted.[195] So while phenomenology has certainly introduced a new way of exploring relationships of the past, it cannot reveal what those various relationships and experiences may have meant.

Returning to an engendered approach, it is never merely concerned with putting 'the people back'.[196] In this book, the medieval nuns themselves are considered significant agents in the study of female monasticism in Ireland. It is known that their lives and places would have been structured and timetabled,[197] though for the early medieval period in Ireland rules at female religious houses can only be inferred as none is extant.[198] In the later medieval period, different orders may also have had different paces of daily routine, following a rule and, though none is now extant for a nunnery in Ireland, rules are known from elsewhere.[199] Furthermore, the spiritual environment of the nunneries, as well as the materiality of the buildings themselves and the material culture, shaped the *habitus* of the religious communities: they provided 'a practical logic and sense of order that is learned unconsciously through the enactment of everyday life'.[200]

Habitus and performance through ritual leads to a discussion of agency: how individuals in the past are actively engaged, consciously and unconsciously, with their material culture.[201] It is through human agency that material culture is given meaning(s). They have 'intention' and these intentions can be interpreted by an archaeologist. There is a danger, though, that intention may be interpreted as society acting as a whole, when in fact only one section of that society, such as the elite, may have a particular intention.[202] Indeed, agency is not an innate characteristic of an individual but 'a product of the network of social relationships that constitute the person'.[203] The agency of nuns at medieval nunneries in Ireland can be considered in this way. What is their material culture revealing about their lives, individual and communal, both inside and outside the nunnery complexes? Agency can also facilitate the exploration of difference in the use of medieval material culture and architecture at Irish nunneries, when compared to that of their male religious counterparts, in a similar way to the interesting results of Brumfiel's study where she explored how indigenous peoples interacted and used the intrusive material culture of a coloniser.[204]

Furthermore, in such an engendered approach biological sex can no longer be considered fixed, as through performance or the repetition of cultural acts associated with gender, it becomes 'natural'.[205] The study of performance leads to a stress on material culture – settings, objects, dress and suchlike – and has much in common with the experience of phenomenology. Repetition of performance defines and structures who an individual is, leading to identity formation. Furthermore, performativity applies in the present as much as it does to the past, so this leads to the concept of reflexivity, the back-and-forth movement of academic inquiry.[206] Again, the breakdown of binary categories of male and female has led to explorations of a 'third gender', such as eunuchs, and notions of chastity in religious contexts.[207] For example, it has allowed Nancy Partner to explore the ambiguities of sex and gender through the record of a cross-dressed man in the nunnery church of St Radegund's at Poitiers, as a metaphor for multiple gender questions.[208]

An engendered archaeology has had the 'happy effect' of opening up avenues into identity and the body in an archaeological context,[209] labelled 'personhood' – where the whole living person and their experiences over time might be investigated.[210] Personhood is a useful term as it encompasses relationships with others and so is not bounded by individual experience.[211] The concept of *habitus*,[212] and its application particularly by Gilchrist, is preferred in this book to a phenomenological approach, although they do share some common features.[213] These approaches resist the idea that men and women, or indeed a variety of binary pairs, are considered one category with the same intentions. Multiple differences in a group may be acknowledged: sexual orientation, status, age or class. The lens of gender can elucidate these multiple agencies. For example, the nuns of later medieval nunneries in Ireland are known from history to have come from higher-status families, and many nuns were related to their patrons,[214] although excavated archaeological evidence might suggest otherwise (see Chapter 8). It may be suggested therefore that the nunnery group was a hierarchy and mirrored the social strata of the secular world – having many of the social positions that the secular world possessed, such as abbess and nun (equivalent to medieval ladies), servant, patron or priest. By applying the concept of agency, these subtle differences in the nunnery communities might be revealed. Gilchrist has highlighted that individuals from the same community may have had quite different 'narratives of personal identity [as] each person would have moved through a range of different contexts in the course of their life'.[215] A key way of revealing human group agency is through the study of the individual and their intimate moments, such as loss of a cherished item or the burial of a relative.[216] The active individual and personhood are also key concepts in identity construction. It has been suggested that issues of power, domination and prestige, that pre-occupied medieval studies in the past, should now be joined by themes of experience, agency and individuals' views and values in order to explore archaeologies of identity.[217]

Furthermore, the experience of the individual explored through a phenomenological approach also goes some way to explaining the concept of 'materiality' and a basic question in any archaeological study – how do things come to carry meanings?[218] For the study of medieval nunneries and female monasticism in Ireland, this approach can be framed in a series of questions: how did the nuns use and negotiate their architecture? How were the nuns and the nunneries positioned in the medieval landscape of Ireland? How did the nunneries interact with other contemporary monuments such as castles, churches, male religious houses and towns? What can be said about the lifestyle and life course, the 'lived experience' of medieval nuns in Ireland? Can any conclusions be drawn as to the perceptions of the nuns who lived in these places?

The consideration of the individual in social archaeology – that of the female religious in this particular book – draws on concepts of time, space and the life course. The phenomenological approach has allowed archaeologists to investigate individuals' concepts of time, interaction with landscape, social memory and its interaction with material culture, and also natural places.[219]

Material culture can also be used as a metaphor for the life course, as it binds together people and objects.[220] Gilchrist has investigated architecture as a metaphor for the life course, and has demonstrated this to great effect in her discussion of the archaeology of the parish church.[221] The church itself 'provided a sense of temporal and spatial order that united cosmological and human time scales with public and private memory'.[222]

Space, place and time

> Space is neither inert nor neutral, nor is its organisation, articulation or the formulation of its boundaries a natural phenomenon. Rather spatial constructs are the historical and cultural products of an age. As metaphors and symbolic systems, they embody the most basic rules and meaning of a culture.[223]

Humanly created and occupied spaces have long been the subject of philosophical and architectural study.[224] Medieval female religious communities constructed specific spaces in which they worshipped and lived. Space would initially appear to be self-explanatory but a precise meaning remains elusive.[225] For example, it has been defined as a multi-dimensional zone 'in which substances, people and objects move'.[226] Space can be 'in between' zones or at interfaces; it can be the expanses of landscape or can be created within structures; it can be physical or metaphysical. Space is no longer considered absolute and empty, and the term 'place' is now recognised by some as a better guide to medieval thinking about the lived environment than modern abstract notions of space.[227] Archaeologists, historians and art historians have all drawn on various philosophical approaches to the study and meaning of space and have applied these approaches to ecclesiastical and monastic contexts in an attempt to tease out functional, liturgical and more symbolic aspects.[228] An understanding of the interactions of people and the places they inhabit is critical for an appreciation of how monastic spaces were transformed through ritual and performance. Drawing on the work of de Certeau,[229] Anne Müller concluded that 'space is practised place [as] spatial representations of the transcendental ideas of the *vita religiosa* only become possible through living people and human activity'.[230]

It has been suggested that in many cultural contexts, people perceive three main categories of space: daily experience, regular communication, and the world. Furthermore, it can be argued that space is an ordering principle through which human hierarchies are created and maintained.[231] As such, space is humanly created and can change over time and location, and it can possess various meanings for different individuals or groups. It is a medium through which social relationships are played out, regulated and negotiated, including monasteries.[232] Monasticism, despite its ideals and codified behaviour, or *habitus*, did not operate in a vacuum, and other aspects of society, particularly status, shaped how space was formed and used throughout the middle ages.[233] Male and female monastic space was different also.[234] This codified behaviour was formed, to some extent, of the norms and rules of the hierarchical class-divided society, the social norms of aristocratic men and women and the treatment they expected from the lower strata of society.[235] In particular for the later medieval period, most professed religious men and women are thought to have come from this elite background and their learned social norms were carried through into the monastic space.[236] Knowing one's place in medieval society was intrinsic to how all medieval spaces were negotiated.[237] The interplay between the enclosed spaces of a monastery or nunnery, its religious community and other necessary individuals within that space is an important theme. This theme is further embodied in notions of public and private spheres of space which had specific meanings for enclosed nuns of the later medieval period.[238]

Time depth is particularly pertinent to the archaeological study of space, temporality and the life course.[239] It has repercussions in all aspects of the discipline of archaeology, though the discipline has been particularly criticised for not yet fully engaging with age as a cultural issue.[240] Studies of age using the lens of gender have highlighted the lives of the very young in Ireland, using archaeological evidence from children's, famine and workhouse burial grounds.[241] Similar gender-focused studies, which may prove helpful in elucidating the lives of female religious, have not yet taken place in the consideration of burials from possible female monastic sites in Ireland (see Chapter 8).

Considerations of landscape

Landscape archaeology is 'central to the archaeological programme as a whole because the history of human life is about ways of inhabiting the world'.[242] Usefully, it is a domain where the perceived gap between theory and practice can be bridged.[243] While the origins of a theoretical approach to landscape lie in archaeologies of prehistoric periods, historical archaeology has now become centre stage,[244] though Ireland has been somewhat slow to pursue theoretical approaches to medieval landscapes.[245] Landscape archaeology as a sub-discipline has been dominated by two methodological approaches: a detailed landscape-specific approach, concentrating on palimpsests, which are visual and empirical; and a post-processual approach that produces broad statements about people in the landscape and provides the context for everyday conduct.[246]

Theoretical perspectives to landscape are crucial to any study of female monasticism in Ireland but it is no longer adequate to look at the palimpsest, as this just identifies what has happened to the land while discounting the people that lived there.[247] Wendy Ashmore has advocated social archaeologies of landscape where future dialogues between landscape, gender and the body are postulated through questioning: is landscape a palimpsest of events, or more socially fluid trajectories of inhabitation?[248] If engaging with landscapes of female monasticism in medieval Ireland, the latter must surely be the more correct. A theoretical consideration of landscape is explored in the micro case study of St Catherine's, County Limerick (see Chapter 9).

I have attempted a fluid movement between theoretical considerations of the wider landscapes of female monastic communities and the more specific life courses of women religious. A medieval woman may have entered a nunnery at any stage in her life course. She may have entered as a young novice, as an adult woman, as a corrodian on an intermittent basis, or as a widow becoming a vowess rather than a fully professed nun. She may have been a professed nun perhaps holding an office, or have been another member of the nunnery household such as a servant. All these aspects of an individual's life may be explored through the wide lens of gender. Indeed, many of these keystone events in a nunnery, such as entering religious life, taking of vows, celebrating the daily divine office, marking the annual liturgical calendar, celebrating a patron saint's feast day, or marking the birthday or anniversary of a patron would have been marked through ritual and ceremony. Some of these events might be recognised in the archaeological evidence, if the correct questions can be asked of that data. A broad gender approach, as outlined, is an ideal perspective from which to ask such new questions of the archaeological evidence for female monasticism in medieval Ireland. I have tried to make a conscious break from the meta-narrative of popular histories and archaeologies of female religious in medieval Ireland in this book. Hopefully, this will provide new 'angle[s] of vision',[249] angles and perspectives that have not yet been fully considered in the archaeological study of female monasticism in medieval Ireland.

CHAPTER 2

The Character of Female Religious in Early Medieval Ireland

In order to understand female monasticism in later medieval Ireland, an outline of the character of early female religious communities, as it is currently understood, is required. First, an overview of women and early society in Ireland is given, followed by some of the themes that are associated with female religious in this period – many of which continue into the later period. This is to provide a context for the second section of the chapter where the archaeological evidence is presented and current evidential issues are discussed. Third, a brief consideration of early female religious in Britain and Europe is made for comparison. The chapter concludes with an overview of those early sites associated with female religious that were also used in the later medieval period. From the sum of this evidence, it is slowly emerging that female religious were found in a variety of situations that were connected to the church and secular society.[1]

At least fifty-one sites of female religious communities dating to the early medieval period can currently be identified (Figure 2.1; Table 2.1). This is considered an absolute minimum number as there are many more sites which exhibit inconclusive evidence or association with early female religious.[2] While Harrington may have over-estimated numbers when she said that there were hundreds of thousands of nuns in Ireland from the seventh to the ninth century,[3] they may have indeed been common, as 'hagiographers took it for granted that nunneries littered the Irish landscape'.[4] Much of this less-conclusive evidence takes the form of female saintly dedications, and these are discussed later in this chapter.

WOMEN IN EARLY IRELAND: AN OVERVIEW

For Ireland, the early medieval period (fifth to twelfth centuries) is considered transformational as literacy and Christianity were first introduced,[5] as part of a Christian cultural package which reached Ireland's shores through

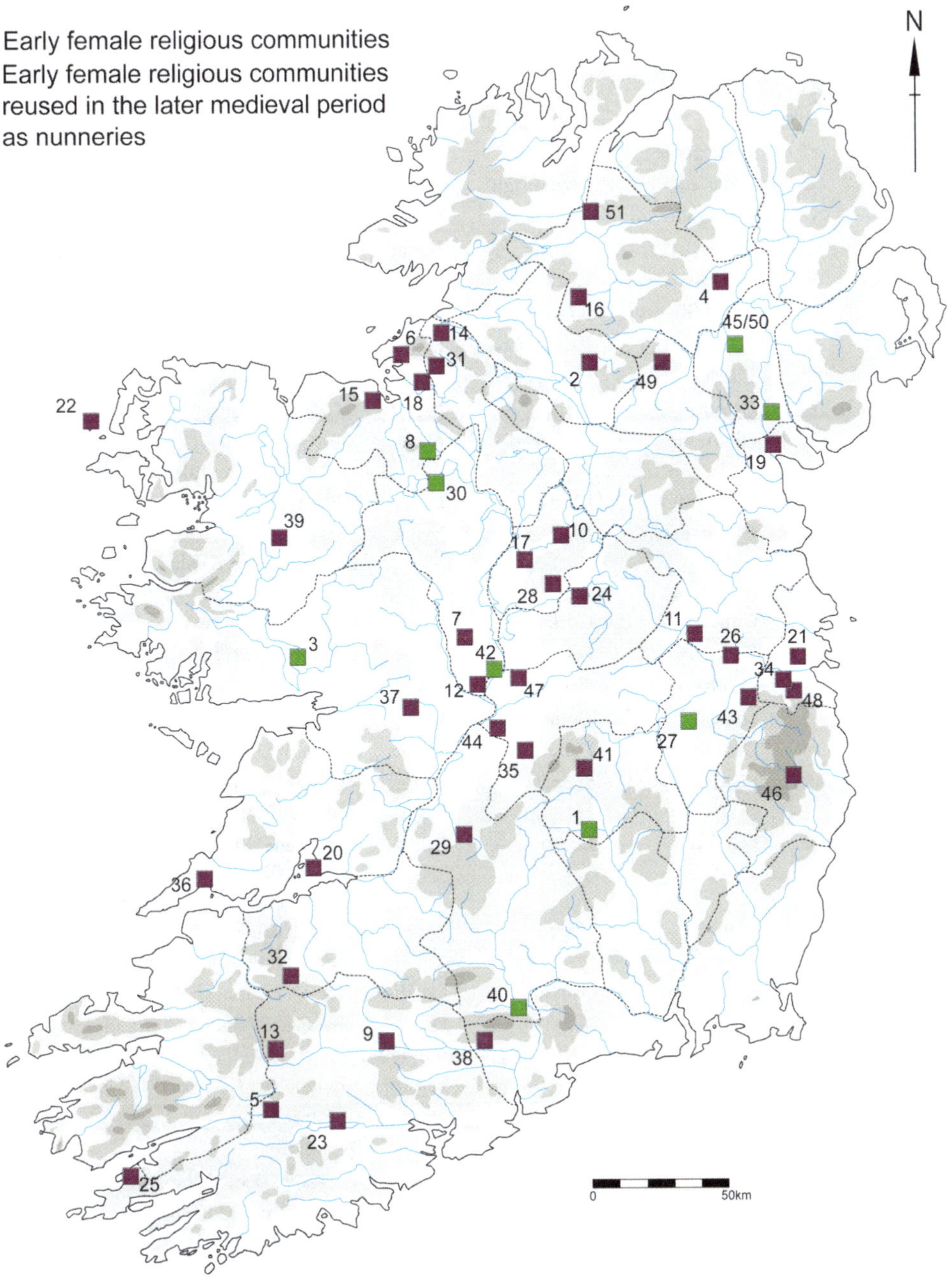

2.1 Female religious communities in early medieval Ireland. Image: Tracy Collins and Frank Coyne.

Table 2.1. List of early medieval female religious communities in Ireland (modern boundaries used throughout). Those sites marked with an asterisk* were re-used as nunneries in the later medieval period.

Map number	*Site Name*	*County*	*Category*	*Saintly Association(s)*
1*	Addrigoole	Laois	Lesser	Fionnbharr (Finnbarr) of Cork
2	Aghavea	Fermanagh	Lesser	Lasair and Molaise of Devenish
3*	Annaghdown	Galway	Satellite	Bréanainn (Brendan) of Clonfert
4	Artrea	Tyrone	Lesser	Trea, Patrick
5	Ballyvourney	Cork	Major	Gobnait (Gobnaid, Gobad)
6	Caille (Keelty)	Sligo	Lesser	Muadnata
7	Cam	Roscommon	Lesser	?Brigit (Brighid, Brigid, Bridget)
8*	Carricknahorna	Sligo	Lesser	Patrick
9	Clenor	Cork	Lesser	Cránaid (Cranat)
10	Clonbroney	Longford	Major	Patrick, 2 Emers, Fuinche, Samthann (Samhthann)
11	Clonguffin	Meath	Lesser	Fintana
12	Cloonburren	Roscommon	Major	Caoireach Dheargáin (Cairech Dergen), 'red or blush of Cloonburren'
13	Cullen	Cork	Lesser	Latiaran (Laitrian, Lasair Fiona)
14	Doiremelle	Leitrim	Lesser	Meall, Mealla (Mella)
15	Dromard	Sligo	Lesser	Patrick
16	Dromore	Tyrone	Lesser	Patrick
17	Druimcheo	Longford	Lesser	Lubaid (Lupita), Patrick, Mel (Meal)
18	Enachard	Sligo	Lesser	Osnad (Osnata), Talulla, Muadhnata, Molaise
19	Faughart	Louth	Lesser	Moninne (Monenna, Dairearca, Darerca), Brigit (Brighid, Brigid, Bridget), Patrick, Fiontan (Fintan)
20	Feenish	Clare	Lesser	Brigit (Brighid), Senán, Cainnear (Cainir) Chráibhtheach
21	Finglas	Dublin	Satellite	Canice (Cainnech)
22	Inishglora (Templenaman)	Mayo	Lesser/ ?satellite	Bréanainn (Brendan) of Clonfert
23	Inishleena	Cork	Lesser	Fionnbharr (Finnbarr) of Cork
24	Kilbixy	Westmeath	Lesser	Bigseach
25	Kilcatherine	Cork	Lesser	Caitiarn
26	Kilcock	Kildare	Lesser	Coga, ?Cóch, Ciarán (Sierkieran)
27*	Kildare	Kildare	Major	Brigit (Brighid, Brigid, Bridget)
28	Kilglass	Longford	Lesser	Eiche, Patrick, Mel, Lalloc
29	Kilkeary	Tipperary (North)	Lesser	Ciar (Cera, Ceara, Ciar Asgadh)
30*	Killaraght	Sligo	Major	Athracht (Attracta), Patrick
31	Killasnet	Leitrim	Lesser	Osnad (Osnata)

Table 2.1. (*continued*)

Map number	*Site Name*	*County*	*Category*	*Saintly Association(s)*
32	Killeedy	Limerick	Major	Íte (Íde, Ita)
33*	Killevy	Armagh	Major	Moninne (Monenna, Dairearca, Darerca)
34	Killiney	Dublin	Lesser	Brigit, Druighean, Luidhean, Lucella, Macha, Rinthacha
35	Killyon	Offaly	Lesser	Ciarán (Sierkieran), Liadhain
36	Kilnagallech	Clare	Lesser	Seanán (Senan)
37	Kilreekil	Galway	Lesser	Ríceall (Ríceann, Richella), Patrick, Finnian
38	Lismore	Waterford	Satellite	Mochuda (Carthach, Carthage, Cuddy)
39	Mayo	Mayo	Lesser/ ?satellite	Colmán, Garailt (Gerald), ?Segresia
40*	Molough	Tipperary (South)	Lesser	Déaglán (Declan)
41	Mountrath	Laois	Lesser	Brigit
42*	Nuns' Church	Offaly	Satellite	Ciarán (Clonmacnoise)
43	Oughterard	Kildare	Lesser/ ?major	Brigit (not of Kildare), Aodh of Killeenmore, Darchaorthainn daughter of Éanna
44	Reynagh	Offaly	Lesser	Ríceall (Ríceann, Richella)
45*	St Brigit's Armagh	Armagh	Satellite	Patrick
46	St Mary's Glendalough	Wicklow	Satellite	Caoimhghin (Kevin)
47	St Mella's	Offaly	Satellite	Manchán, Mella (Mealla)
48	Tallaght	Dublin	Satellite	Maol Ruain, Óengus (Aonghas)
49	Tedavnet	Monaghan	Lesser	Damhnat (Dympna)
50*	Temple na Ferta Armagh	Armagh	Satellite	Patrick
51	Urney (Ernaide)	Tyrone	Lesser	Samthann (Samhthann)

processes of acculturation.[6] There are severe limitations in the evidence on early medieval women, not least because sources are patchy, difficult to date, and often written to a traditional formula or topos. Moreover, terminology used can be inconsistent and contradictory,[7] and specific groups such as women, female religious, children and older people are not easily identified in either documentary sources or the archaeological record.[8] Notwithstanding these limitations, some light can be shed on women in this period,[9] and new archaeological studies are revealing the varied character of the church in early Ireland – once considered monolithic – from the civitates of Armagh, Clonmacnoise and Glendalough, to lesser ecclesiastical sites with pastoral roles and proprietary churches, including those associated with female religious.[10]

Society in early Ireland was based on principles of kinship, land tenure and clientship.[11] The primary determinant of class was land ownership, with the possession of cattle only permitted to free grades of society.[12] Noble kinship was the basis for everyday life in the upper classes, formed around a common great-grandfather, the *derb-fine*. In this arrangement, a female could inherit portable goods, but kin land only if no sons were present. She possessed land for her lifetime, after which it returned to the kin group. Women had little legal status, and while their rights were protected by law in property, marriage, divorce and the family, they were always in reference to the men in their lives.[13] The responsibility for women passed to their husband's kin group when they married, and for those who did not marry, her kin group retained responsibility for her. In such a society it made sense for women to marry, as it forged alliances and brought with it a substantial bride-price for the woman's family.

Therefore, if marriage was the primary kin group strategy, what possible advantages would there be to follow a religious life? Three reasons have been suggested: alliances with the church, containment of surplus females, and status and maintenance of kin group property. Through taking up the religious life a woman might forge ambitious alliances with the church, bringing prestige and protection to her kin group, ultimately leading to political success, such as the Uí Dúnlainge in Leinster, who eventually took control of Kildare.[14] Additionally, with the practice of bride-price and later dowry payments, entry to the religious life may have been an economic saving. However, it remains unclear if payment was made upon entering a female religious community.[15] Women, not being legally independent, may have been 'donated' to religious foundations, equating to a transfer of guardianship from father to church and, as Bitel has noted, 'the legal parallel to marriage in this practice is obvious'.[16]

The second advantage postulated was that entering a religious community solved the issue of surplus females in a kin group, when there were too many women to be married off. Moreover, females may have entered the religious life to limit the number of heirs in a particular kin group.[17] These scenarios, while possible, have not been substantiated for Ireland, and there is no evidence to suggest that religious provision had to be made for surpluses of eligible aristocratic women.[18] On the contrary, women were considered a precious resource, which may have worked against their choice of religious life.[19] Indeed, St Patrick's *Confessio* noted that several fathers were unhappy with their daughters' decision to dedicate their lives to the church.[20] Finally, a kin group may have established a proprietary church in which a religious woman might live and work – perhaps only for her lifetime or a single generation – while the kin group maintained control over its offices and property.[21] Indeed, on occasion women themselves may have established churches or made donations.[22] While this scenario of a plethora of propriety churches does not fit well with the older traditional model of the early Irish church and women's relationships with it,[23] it is wholly consistent with the more recent fully formed alternative interpretation of the church in Ireland.[24]

TYPES OF FEMALE RELIGIOUS COMMUNITIES

For the purpose of this book, early female establishments are divided into three very broad and sometimes overlapping categories. First, the major communities: by far the most important was Kildare, but a handful of other regionally important sites can be identified, including Clonbroney, Cloonburren, Killeedy and Killevy. Second is a category consisting of what might be termed lesser or other stand-alone communities, though the distinction between this relatively large group and the first is somewhat arbitrary, for some second-tier sites had important roles to play within their local polities. Furthermore, it is likely that their importance ebbed and flowed through time. For example, Faughart is included in this group, on the basis that it is neither a major nor satellite site, but recent archaeological research has shown that it was very important in its local and regional sphere.[25] Many of these other ecclesiastical sites were never more than a small church that may have had a female religious function for a generation or two.[26] Finally, the third category comprises satellite communities that were positioned adjacent to but at a remove from larger male ecclesiastical sites.[27] This also includes several male ecclesiastical sites where female religious were historically recorded.

Major communities

There were seven major female religious communities which were regionally – if not nationally – important at some stages of their use: Ballyvourney,[28] Clonbroney,[29] Cloonburren,[30] Kildare,[31] Killaraght,[32] Killeedy[33] and Killevy.[34] Oughterard might also be added to this list as the presence of a round tower there, dated to the eleventh century, suggests a site of status, at least in the latter part of the period.[35] Of this group, Clonbroney, Killaraght, Killeedy and Kildare have little if any extant early medieval remains. Kildare is worthy of some discussion, being the premier female religious community of the period and thought to have played an unusually important role in Leinster politics, as the only women's house to appear with frequency in the Annals.[36] It was presumably enclosed by several concentric enclosures with the most sacred at its centre, which contained the primary church, the position of which probably

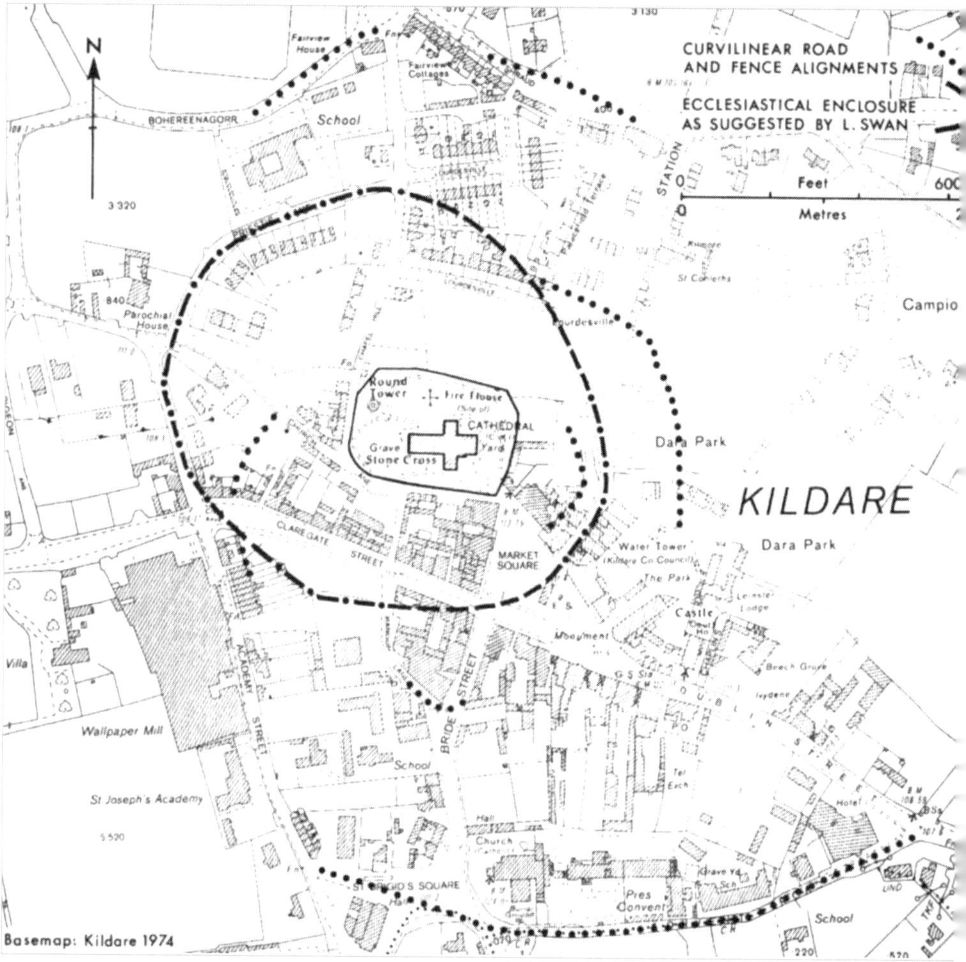

2.2 Kildare, showing conjectural outline of the early medieval ecclesiastical enclosure. Reproduced with permission of the IHTA.

lies beneath the later cathedral and likely close to the round tower (Figure 2.2). None of the other sites in this group retain any surface expression of their original enclosing element.

Of the remaining sites, Cloonburren is important due to its assemblage of cross slabs (Figure 2.3).[37] Ballyvourney is the only example in this group where a research excavation has taken place and remains an important regional pilgrimage destination to the present day.[38] Killevy is the only major female religious house to clearly retain early fabric.[39] Two churches are extant at Killevy, once about 11m apart but now peculiarly conjoined – the western example being considered the older of the two and not later than the eleventh to twelfth century. The eastern church is likely later medieval in date (Figure 2.4).

Cloonburren, Co. Roscommon; assemblage of fragmentary cross slabs. Image: Tracy Collins.

2.4 Killevy, Co. Armagh, conjoined churches, viewed from west. Image: Frank Coyne.

Lesser female religious communities

The historical evidence has numerous examples of holy women and female religious attached to churches, some of which likely had a laity-serving function. This group of thirty-three sites is represented by the various remains of smaller churches and ecclesiastical sites. The nature of these female religious communities at these places is considered very fluid. Many other possible early female religious communities, which number well over forty sites, could be added to this group, though in many of these cases the current evidence is at best putative.

For instance, ten of the thirty-three lesser sites are included on the basis of a historical reference alone, which in the majority of cases relates to a mention in the writings of St Patrick,[40] as at Carricknahorna, Dromore, Druimcheo and Kilreekil, or relates to other saints, as at Molough. Killabuonia, which is considered a possible female religious house, might be added, as St Buonia is a reputed sister of St Patrick.[41] Of this group, only Kilreekil and Molough have possible remains of early circular enclosures, both being preserved in the roadway around the sites (see Figure 2.16). Other lesser sites with remains of enclosing elements are Cam and Kilglass. Several other possible early female religious sites are based solely on local memory, like Templecashel, or Kilteel.[42] The majority of these lesser sites now manifest in the landscape as holy wells, churches and graveyards, for example Aghavea,[43] Clenor[44] or Faughart.[45]

Satellite female religious communities

There are perhaps ten larger ecclesiastical complexes where there is evidence of attached communities of female religious. The term satellite has been used as it most accurately describes the position of those extant female houses that can be considered archaeologically, notably Clonmacnoise, Glendalough and Lemanaghan. It can be concluded from the archaeological and historical evidence that female religious communities were in proximity to male ecclesiastical complexes, within their own discrete enclosure, and importantly were considered legitimate constituents of the religious population of those complexes. Those places are: Annaghdown,[46] Temple-na-Ferta and St Brigit's Armagh,[47] Clonmacnoise,[48] Lemanaghan,[49] Finglas and Tallaght,[50] Glendalough[51] and Lismore,[52] to which Mayo[53] might be tentatively added. Places where specific burial grounds or secondary churches for women are recorded might also be considered satellite groups of female religious.[54]

In six of these locations – Annaghdown, Finglas, Tallaght, the two female houses at Armagh, and Lismore – there is no upstanding archaeological evidence of the location of the female religious communities, though there is

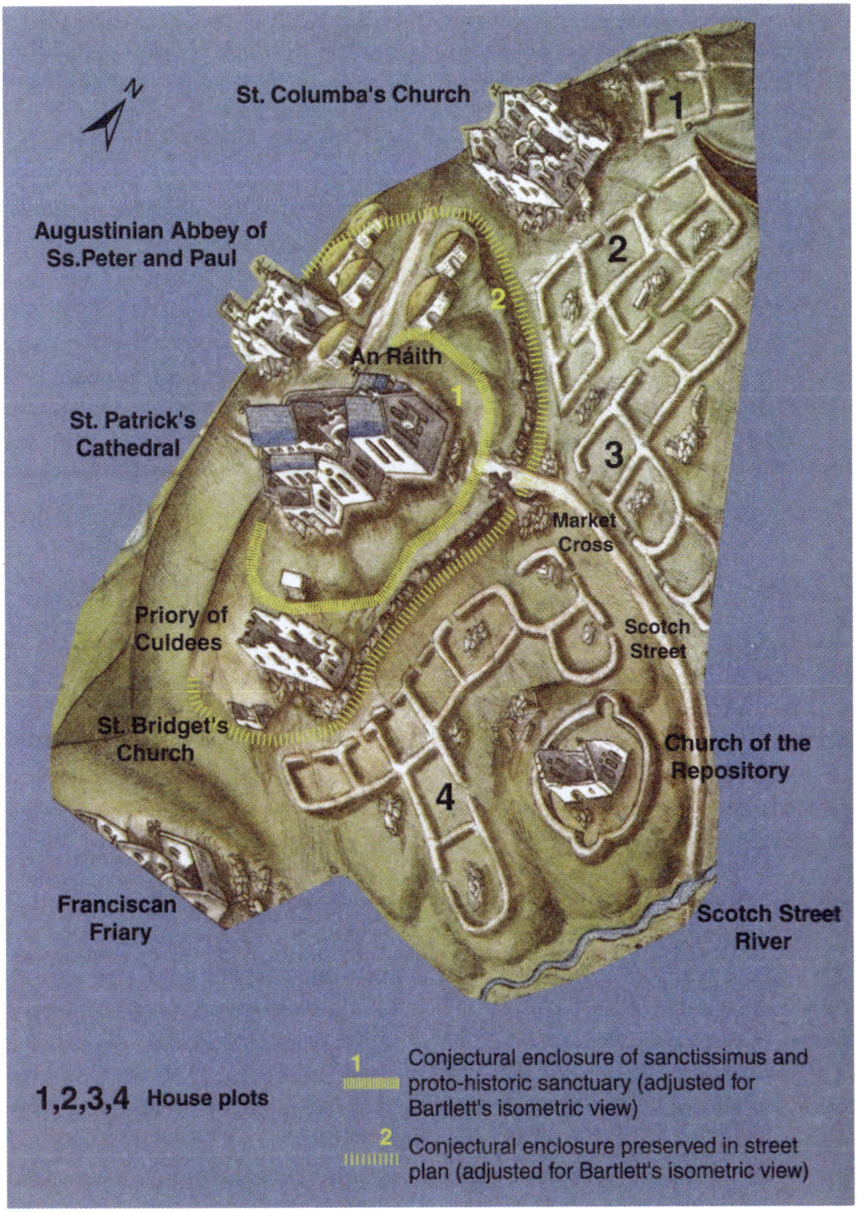

2.5 Armagh, Ms 2656 (3) Richard Bartlett. Plan of Armagh City and Mountjoy Fort on the Blackwater river, circa 1602. Courtesy of the National Library of Ireland. Annotation after FitzPatrick, reproduced with permission of the RIA.

excavated evidence from Armagh[55] and a 'nunnery' church at Annaghdown. Despite the caution of St Samthann, abbess of the female religious community at Clonbroney (d.739) to Mael Ruain of Tallaght on the counselling of women,[56] the Céli Dé sites of Finglas, Tallaght and Lismore do have historical evidence of female religious in proximity.[57] Tallaght possessed an oratory known as Cell-na-ingen and a female community lived around this church. These religious women were part of the religious *familia* there and were sympathetically accommodated. They were mentioned in the Tallaght rules concerning monks, which stipulated that menstruating nuns (female religious) were free from certain vigils and could eat a special gruel at tierce.[58] The female community at Finglas was mentioned in the *Customs of Tallaght* in an anecdote which has been interpreted as showing that female religious were not permitted into the inner (most sacred) enclosure, but retained their own enclosure within the larger ecclesiastical complex.[59]

Early female religious seem to have been at Lismore before the establishment of the male monastery there, as in the *Life of St Carthach*, the virgin Coemell donated her small church to him. Female religious subsequently re-used Coemell's site, but were not permitted to enter the monastic enclosure at Lismore.[60] The evidence of women religious at Mayo is very speculative, but its founder St Colmán is attested by Bede to have attended the Synod of Whitby in 664 – a large, important double/mixed house in Yorkshire – and would have seen at first hand the workings of an ecclesiastical community that included both female and male religious.[61] It is interesting to consider that Colmán may have returned with the idea of incorporating female religious into his new foundation, in addition to the Saxon monks that are known to have accompanied him back to Ireland, first to Inishbofin and later to Mayo. One of the few traces of the early medieval Mayo Abbey is an extant cross-head which has been identified as Anglo-Saxon.[62]

The locations of the two female communities at Armagh – Temple-na-Ferta and St Brigit's – are known. Temple-na-Ferta was situated outside the ecclesiastical complex to the southeast, while St Brigit's was also to the southeast of the centre. Temple-na-Ferta's circular enclosure is shown on Barlett's map dated to 1602, and is unusual in that it incorporates two 'lugs' along its northern and southern perimeter, the function of which is not clear but may be the remnants of circular huts.[63] A third church possibly associated with female religious at Armagh, Temple Muire, was located to the northwest within the Trian Mór (Figure 2.5).[64]

The best-preserved evidence of satellite female religious communities is at Clonmacnoise, St Mary's Glendalough, and St Mella's Lemanaghan (Figure 2.6). Their churches show a diversity of form, though they are all situated some distance outside the main ecclesiastical complex within their own discrete enclosures. The enclosing element in all three cases is now rectilinear rather

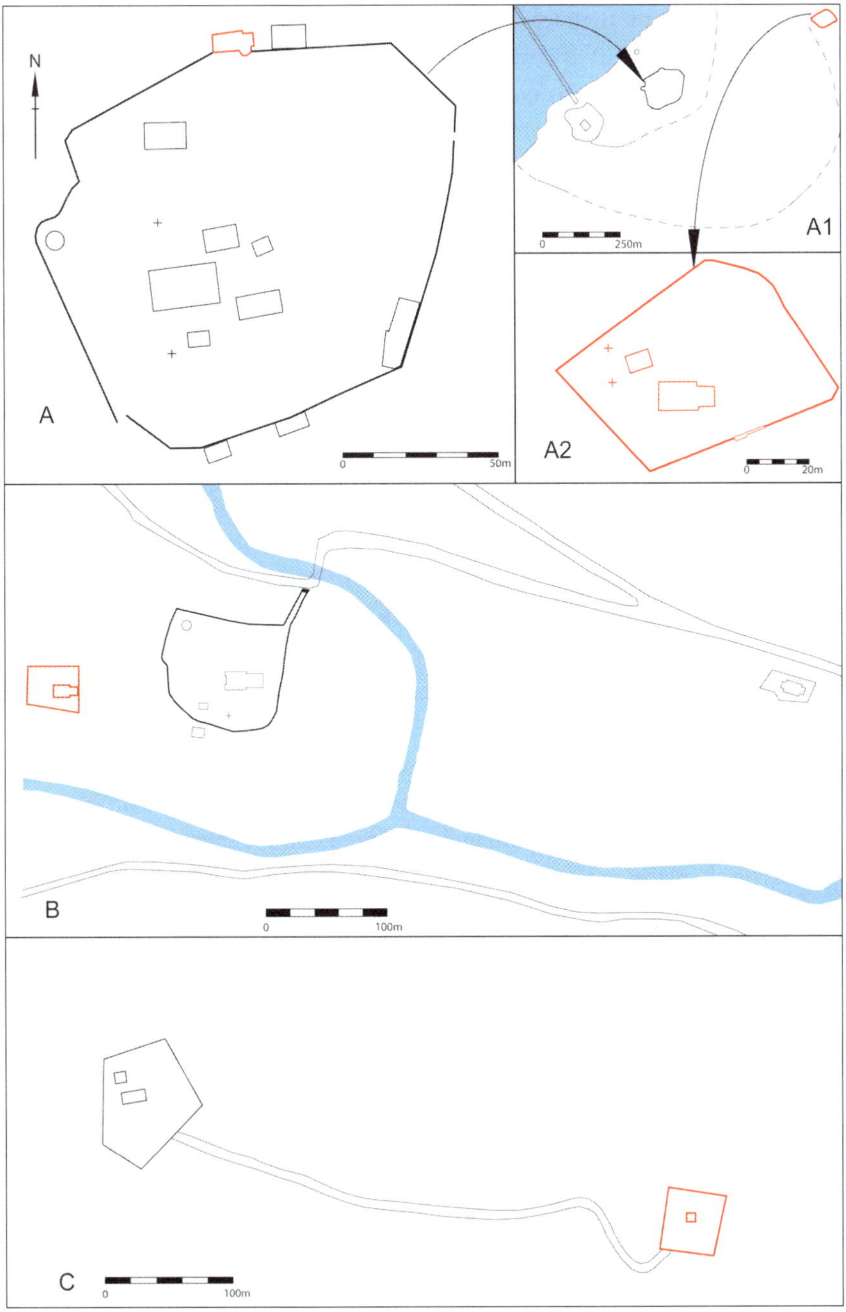

2.6 Locations of satellite female religious communities, shown in red. A: main complex at Clonmacnoise, Co. Offaly. A1: The Nuns' Church's position in relation to the main complex. A2: The layout of the Nuns' Church site. B: St Mary's, Glendalough, Co. Wicklow. C: St Mella's, Lemanaghan, Co. Offaly. After Ó Carragáin, reproduced with permission of the author.

than the more typical circular enclosures of the period. Without excavation it cannot be verified if this represents later re-modelling of the perimeters, and St Mella's enclosure is considered particularly unusual in its method of construction.[65] The female religious communities at these civitates were outside but connected to the main ecclesiastical complexes: Clonmacnoise, outside the outermost enclosure of the main complex and linked by a pavement from the Nuns' Church to the main complex now known as the Pilgrim's Road,[66] and St Mella's enclosure linked to the larger complex via a causeway.[67] A conjectured outline of the ecclesiastical enclosures at Glendalough suggests that St Mary's was located in the second (or middle) of three enclosures.[68]

Further putative female satellite houses might be added; for example, the ecclesiastical complex at Kells is thought to have had a small attached female religious community where several are named.[69] It is not known where these women lived at Kells, but based on the locations of known satellite female communities it is possible to speculate. The double-vaulted church of St Columba's House, Kells is outside the most sacred central enclosure, but within the outer perimeter of the complex. This structure has been identified as a church of recluses (persons living a solitary life) with a possible reliquary function.[70] It is interesting to postulate – although there is no historical evidence to support it – that at least some of these recluses were female religious. Other putative female satellite houses are on Iona and at Derry.[71] There is no historical evidence for early medieval female religious on Iona, but its later medieval nunnery is situated outside and at a distance from the main ecclesiastical enclosure in a location very reminiscent of the Nuns' Church at Clonmacnoise. At Derry there is a reference in the *Annals of the Four Masters* to the death of Bé Bhinn, a *banairchinnech*, which, it has been suggested, shows an earlier female religious community there rather than the Cistercian nunnery established in the thirteenth century.[72]

MATERIAL CULTURE OF EARLY FEMALE RELIGIOUS

Archaeological investigations

Considering the wealth of archaeological evidence from the early medieval period in Ireland as a whole,[73] the current dearth of material culture relating to female religious and the few archaeological investigations that have been undertaken at early medieval women's monasteries is somewhat surprising.[74] No intrusive excavations have been undertaken at the Nuns' Church, Clonmacnoise,[75] but there was a magnetometer survey, though results were somewhat disappointing (Figure 2.7).[76] Geophysical survey at Glendalough

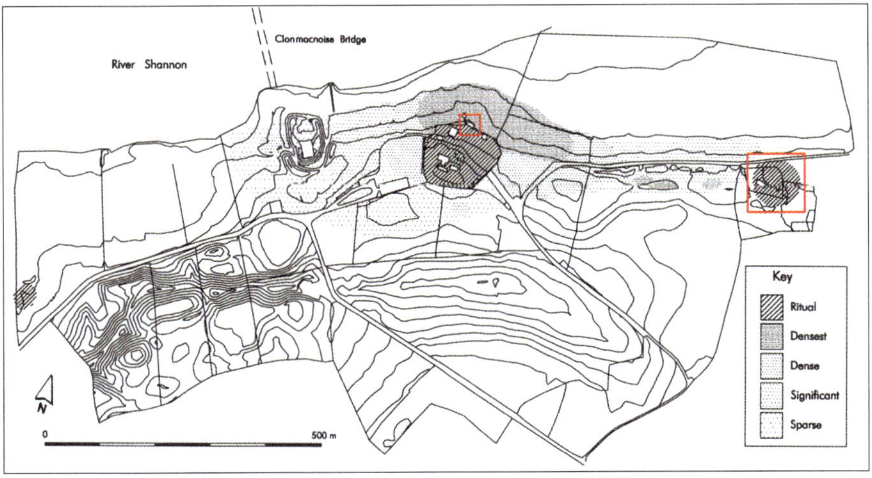

2.7 Interpretive map of geophysical surveys, Clonmacnoise, Co. Offaly. Temple Finghin and the Nuns' Church indicated. After Mytum, reproduced with permission of the author.

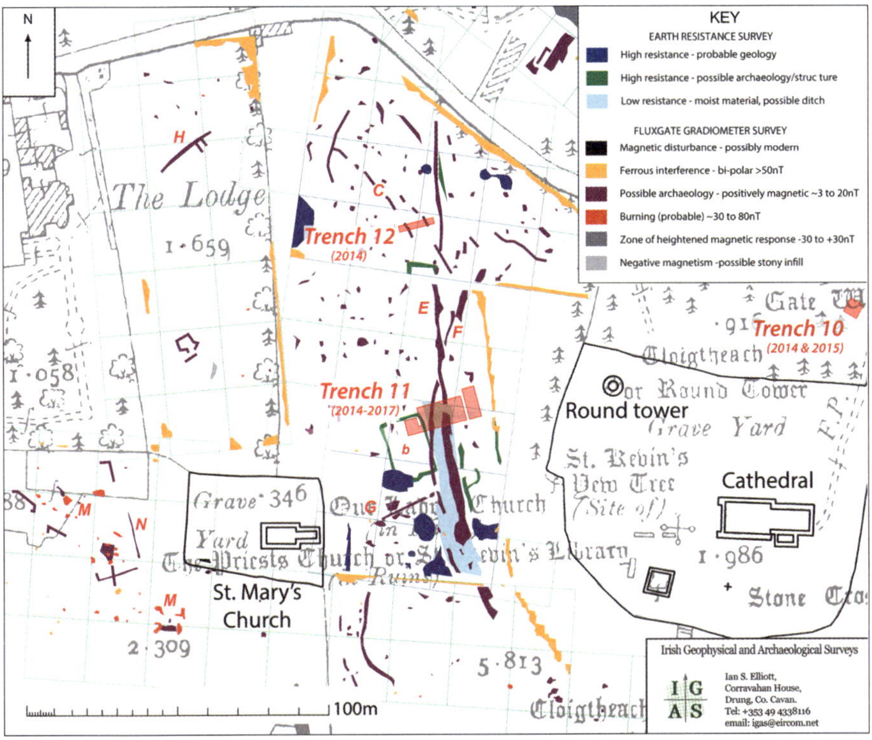

2.8 Interpretative plan of the 2011–12 geophysical surveys showing suggested archaeological features. 'F' curving monastic ditch; 'C' & 'H' possible earlier circular enclosure; 'E' & 'G' boundary ditches; 'M' possible metal or kiln works; 'N' & 'b' possible buildings. After Seaver et al., reproduced with permission of the authors.

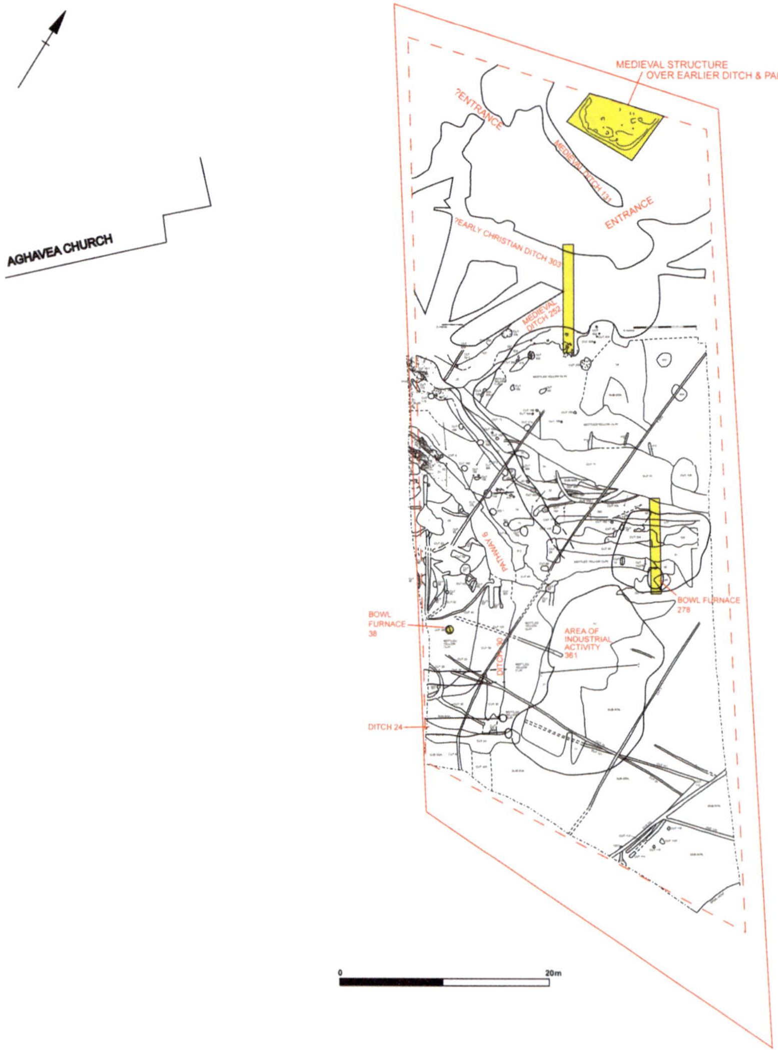

2.9 Excavation plan of features revealed at Aghavea, Co. Fermanagh, those in yellow fully excavated, in advance of development of a surface car park at Aghavea church. After Ó Baoill, reproduced with permission of the author.

revealed evidence of industrial activity to the west and southwest of St Mary's church there (Figure 2.8).[77]

Of those that have been excavated, as at Inishleena and Faughart, results were inconclusive.[78] Excavation at Ballyvourney was more fruitful, though the site of the early female foundation was unsuitable for excavation due to its continued use for burial. Evidence of extensive metalworking and occupation activity was recovered from a hut site known as 'St Gobnait's house', the first station in the modern penitential route at Ballyvourney.[79] The archaeological findings are particularly interesting as St Gobnait's name indicates an association with metalworking and possibly with the metalworking deity Goibhne.[80]

The body of St Lupita (Lubaid or Lupait),[81] sister of St Patrick, was reputedly discovered in 1633 at Temple-na-Ferta, Armagh.[82] Lynn's subsequent excavations revealed early medieval occupation, graves, and later activity. Occupation evidence included long linear features, which both pre-dated and post-dated the graves, which were tentatively interpreted as structures. Important information on early medieval burial was recovered, though none was identified as a female religious.[83] More recent excavations at Aghavea in 2000 also revealed intensive occupation and use in both the early and later medieval periods, including extensive industrial activity, but nothing clearly associated with early female religious (Figure 2.9).[84]

Burial

Early medieval burial evidence is currently unclear in regard to the positive identification of female religious. Indeed, the nature of burial evidence from this period is such that it may be difficult to ever conclusively reveal female religious human remains in the archaeological record. Traditionally, the presence of female burials has been interpreted as indicative of a lay cemetery, such as the female burial at Church Island, County Kerry.[85] Harrington has critiqued this assumption, suggesting that females buried on ecclesiastical sites may represent various types of women religious, such as vowed virgins or widows, family members of the patrons, female pilgrims, female religious in a mixed community or cleric's wives.[86] Furthermore, segregated burial that may indicate female religious has long been suggested by placename evidence, as the suffix 'na mban' and its derivatives is the Irish for women, as seen at Tempullnamban and Relicnamban on Inishmurray, County Sligo, Relignaman, County Tyrone and also on Inishglora, County Mayo (Figure 2.10).[87] Several of these sites were ecclesiastical and so it is possible that segregated burial was practised – though there is little contemporary historical evidence to show that it was.[88]

These segregated burial places are frequently on the edge of ecclesiastical sites, perhaps embodying liminal qualities, and are believed to have had a variety of functions. They may have been for the wider families and kin of ecclesiastics, who were not themselves part of the religious community, including lay women of status, and it may have been prestigious to be buried in such a cemetery.[89] Furthermore, it has been suggested that cemeteries which have a specific female placename indicate early female religious communities.

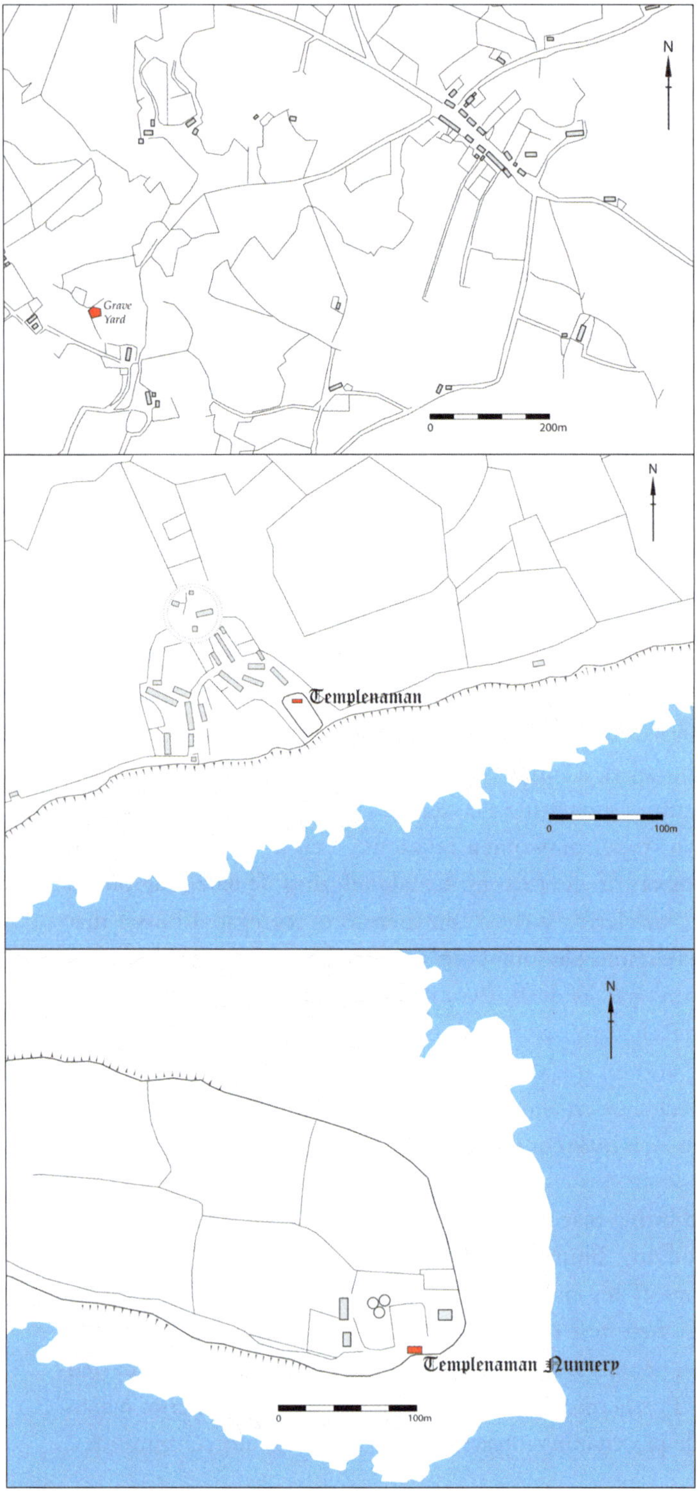

2.10 Placename evidence for the segregated burial of women, re-drawn frc first-edition six-inch Ordnance Survey ma (from top to bottom) Relignaman 'grave yard', locally known by its Irish name, nea Carrickmore, Co. Tyrone. Templemur or Templenamban, Inishmurray, Co. Slig on the southern edge the island ecclesiastic complex. Templenan Nunnery, Inishglora, Co. Mayo on the southeastern edge of the island ecclesiastic complex. Image: Fra Coyne.

There is not universal agreement on this interpretation, however, on the basis of the date of the placename itself – it may not be of early medieval date, and the placename may actually refer to lay women rather than female religious.[90] As such, these sites may represent satellite female religious communities, though currently the evidence is far from conclusive.

Over seventy excavated sites of early medieval date have yielded female human remains,[91] though just four are thought to be ecclesiastical: Collierstown 2, County Meath; Derry, County Down; Solar, County Antrim; and St John's Point, County Down.[92] In all cases, no obvious segregation in burial was noted during the excavation. Therefore, on the basis of current evidence female burials do not seem to occur in their own burial grounds or distinctly grouped within larger mixed cemeteries. However, four slab-lined cists in a non-ecclesiastical context at Ballymacaward, County Donegal, each containing a female dating to the fifth–sixth century, is an interesting exception.[93] In no case is it clear that those excavated might represent female religious at these sites. Several of the other sites which yielded female burials were previously unknown burial places or cemetery settlements, which are unlikely to be ecclesiastical in character, though some were sited on ecclesiastical land. Ó Carragáin has reviewed these site types, and he suggests that the dichotomy between secular and ecclesiastical may actually be anachronistic, particularly in relation to the period *c.*500–800.[94]

Artefacts

There are a small number of artefacts associated with early female saints or their ecclesiastical sites. Surprisingly, there are just two objects associated with St Brigit of Kildare, excluding her popular reed cross – a mantle[95] and a shoe[96] – with several possible relics at Glastonbury, England, Neustadt Cologne, Germany, and a skull fragment at Lisbon, Portugal.[97] There are four other early medieval female saints associated with artefacts: St Lasair with a reliquary book shrine, the *Domnach Airgid*;[98] St Dympna, with a crosier;[99] and St Attracta with a cross and cup,[100] while a rare survival is a timber statue of St Gobnait once retained by the O'Herlihys, who were *airchinnigh* (official keepers) of her church and custodians of her cult.[101] While the book shrine and the crosier originated in the latter portion of the early medieval period, they were substantially modified in the later medieval period, while the remainder of the objects mentioned are likely later medieval in date (see Chapter 7 and Figures 7.52, 7.53).

There are two early carved stones that may be interpreted as memorialising women, who may have been a *monachus* or an ecclesiastical wife;[102] one from

2.11 The cross slab from Clonmacnoise with the suffix 'igen' or daughter. Based on P. Lionard, 'Early Irish Grave-Slabs', *Proceedings of the Royal Irish Academy*, vol. 61C, 1961, pp. 95–169, at p. 113, figure 10, item 11, reproduced with permission.

Clonmacnoise with the suffix 'ingen' or daughter (Figure 2.11),[103] and the other from Inishmurray which includes the phrase *Mael Brigte* or 'servant of Brigit' and a female name Eileise, and may hint at the presence of female religious burials there (Figure 2.12).[104] None of the carved stones from Cloonburren is considered to be for female religious (see Figure 2.3).

I have now outlined the current archaeological evidence of early female religious communities in Ireland. It is clearly tentative, as from a historical perspective it is arguable if dedicated female religious communities following a rule over several generations were even commonplace in the early medieval period in Ireland.[105] Moreover, it remains debatable as to what extent

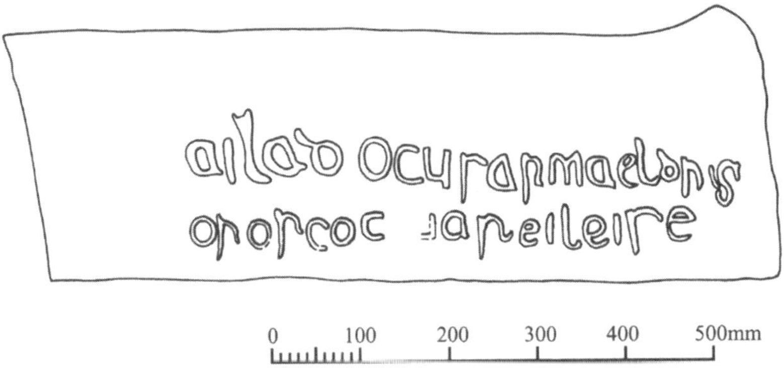

2.12 Carved stone from Inishmurray, Co. Sligo, which includes the phrase 'Mael Brigte' or 'servant of Brigit' and the female name Eileise. While Mael usually denotes a male, on occasion it can denote a female. After O'Sullivan and Ó Carragáin, reproduced with permission of the authors.

archaeology can ever specifically elucidate the lives of female religious, as none of the excavations indicated any gender bias in favour of females.[106] However, perhaps the archaeological record should not be expected to show such binary oppositions as male and female religious in this period. It has been suggested that a specific material culture, like spindle whorls, may point to a female religious presence, as spinning is considered a particular activity of women in the early medieval period.[107] It has been postulated that the early ecclesiastical site at Caherlehillan, County Kerry, which yielded thirty-nine spindle whorls from excavation, might be considered a female religious community on this basis, though on balance seems more likely to have been a proprietary church with both male and female residents.[108] Overall then, the current state of archaeological knowledge relating to early medieval female religious is slight, though is certainly suggestive of a varied character.

EVIDENTIAL ISSUES

There are currently a number of evidential issues in the archaeological study of early female religious communities. The primary issue in this early period is the sheer number of sites. It has been estimated that there are over 5,500 ecclesiastical settlements dating from the fifth to the twelfth centuries (pre-reform) in Ireland, many of which have female saint dedications.[109] Ó Carragáin notes that there is a peculiar density of minor church sites in Ireland at this time in comparison to contemporary England and, to a lesser extent, Frankia (parts of modern France and Germany). He suggests that this was primarily due to the diffuse nature of power structures in Ireland which permitted a higher proportion of the lay population to found their own churches.[110] This is a vexed issue, as it cannot be definitively concluded that a female saint dedication alone indicates a female religious community at a specific site. Furthermore, it cannot be presumed that these sites were continually occupied by religious females. The dedication may have simply indicated that a royal woman at a point in time donated her bride-price to the church, or that she was a female religious during her lifetime;[111] although the continued use of the saintly dedication through time might suggest a longer female religious relationship to the site.

Site names incorporating Brigit or its derivatives may also indicate a female religious use.[112] This is likely a simplification, however, of a much more complex reality of the transmission of the cult of Brigit of Kildare – and several other Brigits over time – in a similar manner to Finnbarr of Cork.[113] It has been demonstrated for parts of Leinster that ecclesiastical families aligned themselves with particular saintly cults,[114] and a saint's cult could be quite extensive.[115] Nevertheless, there may be an engendered aspect to the spread of a cult of a female saint, and secondary sites dedicated to female saints, for example St Brigit, might often have specifically housed female religious.

Furthermore, a distinction needs to be drawn between those female religious foundations established by a woman who lived a religious life, for example Brigit, Íte, Monenna and Samthann,[116] and those sites that are *dedicated* to those female saints but were clearly not founded by them. An example of the former is Clenor, dedicated to and believed to have been established by the female saint Cránaid/Cranat.[117] Historical and archaeological evidence from the early medieval kingdom in which Clenor was situated – Fir Maige – suggests that it was the centre of a female religious ecclesiastical estate, which had a demonstratable different settlement pattern to two contemporary male ecclesiastical estates in the region.[118]

A second evidential problem is that while there is a broadly consistent morphology of early ecclesiastical sites and churches in Ireland – one or more usually circular or sub-circular enclosing elements with one or more small rectangular churches – to date no particular features have been recognised in the archaeological record that distinguish female religious sites from the rest. The extant evidence suggests that site size and layout was broadly related to its status, as well as being influenced by regional variation. For example, Kildare, arguably the most important female religious house, was a large ecclesiastical complex in its own right, comparable to other contemporary major sites such as Armagh, Clonmacnoise, Glendalough or Kells (see Figure 2.2). It had similar archaeological features to these complexes and currently cannot be differentiated from them on the basis of the community's predominant gender.

A third, broader, evidential issue for female religious communities in the early medieval period is precisely what constituted a double house in an Irish context,[119] and how these so-called double houses, mixed or dual-sex communities, might have operated.[120] The group of satellite female religious communities may shed light on these mixed communities; or it may be that this satellite grouping is a distinct type in itself and that mixed communities may have operated in different situations and lived according to different rules.

THEMES ASSOCIATED WITH FEMALE RELIGIOUS

Any picture of early female religious would not be complete without a consideration of the themes of their enclosure, the segregation of male and female religious at ecclesiastical sites and in churches, and the monastic rules that were followed. Indeed, these are themes that are closely connected to female monasticism throughout the entire middle ages (for the later medieval period, see Chapter 3).

Enclosure was a method through which monastics could secure their symbolic removal from the world they wished to renounce, in order to get closer to God and fulfil the ideal of *fuga mundi* or flight from the world.[121] From earliest times monasticism thus required claustration, or the demarcation of spiritual space through detachment, which was conducive to contemplative prayer.[122] Therefore, enclosure was always part of the monastic life as a pre-requisite of all religious regardless of gender.[123] Earlier historical scholarship suggested that early female religious were strictly enclosed, particularly as Irish Christianity became more orthodox over time.[124] This view was based on the fact that some early rules did specify enclosure, particularly those intended for female communities in more urban environments. It was also noted that through the early medieval period enclosure of female religious was gradually more enforced and they were restricted to areas such as education.[125]

Recent scholarship has changed this view and concluded that for Ireland at least there is little or no historical evidence of strict enclosure. Indeed, there is ample evidence in the *Saints' Lives* to suggest that enclosure was not even an issue: 'that to have enclosed God's brides away from the world seems not to have crossed their minds'.[126] A second point was the high regard in which both the laity and church held female religious. If read with a more engendered perspective, some historians believe that the texts record, not misogyny, but rather collegiality, good relations and support, between female and male monasteries.[127]

Overall, early medieval female religious seemed to have had wide parameters, and where enclosures were used these demarcated sacred space and status rather than functioning as obstacles for access and egress. Furthermore, the locations of female religious varied, some of which could not be considered to be enclosed in a restrictive way. In the early part of the period it is highly likely that women lived with their kin group in 'household virginity' and as such were not enclosed.[128] They may have lived at a local church or with a priest in a household arrangement, in a small or large female monastic community, a smaller female community at a male house, or a nuns' residence serving the laity. As we have considered, this diversity is reflected in the archaeological record, which includes major independent female religious communities, satellite female communities adjacent to larger ecclesiastical complexes currently widely considered as male-only establishments, and various ecclesiastical sites associated with female religious.

In regard to segregation of male and female religious, all female religious communities required at least one priest to celebrate the sacraments.[129] Episcopal and other churches would have had male clerics already attached to perform pastoral duties, with which female religious may have assisted. Satellite female communities were likely served by clerics from the adjacent larger monasteries. Previous opinion has dictated that these female communities, as at Armagh, the Nuns' Church at Clonmacnoise or St Mary's Glendalough, for example, were set at a distance from the central complex in order to segregate the sexes and in some way isolate the female religious from the most sacred space. This may well have been the case, as female religious were not allowed into the inner sacred spaces at Finglas or Lismore, although at Tallaght its customs made provision for monks to regularly visit the female community as part of their pastoral care duties.[130] However, perceived peripheral female satellite communities might also be indicative of some specific function. For example, female religious and pilgrims is a strong motif in Irish hagiography,[131] and the early female community at Clonmacnoise is situated on the Pilgrim's Road which leads directly to the central complex. Perhaps the female religious offered the visiting pilgrims hospitality, sustenance and rest prior to their entry proper into the main ecclesiastical complex.

Cogitosus' seventh-century description and use of the supposed timber church at Kildare has been used as evidence for the strict separation of the sexes in an early medieval monastic context and is believed to be the earliest mention of a female religious community in Ireland (Figure 2.13).[132] However,

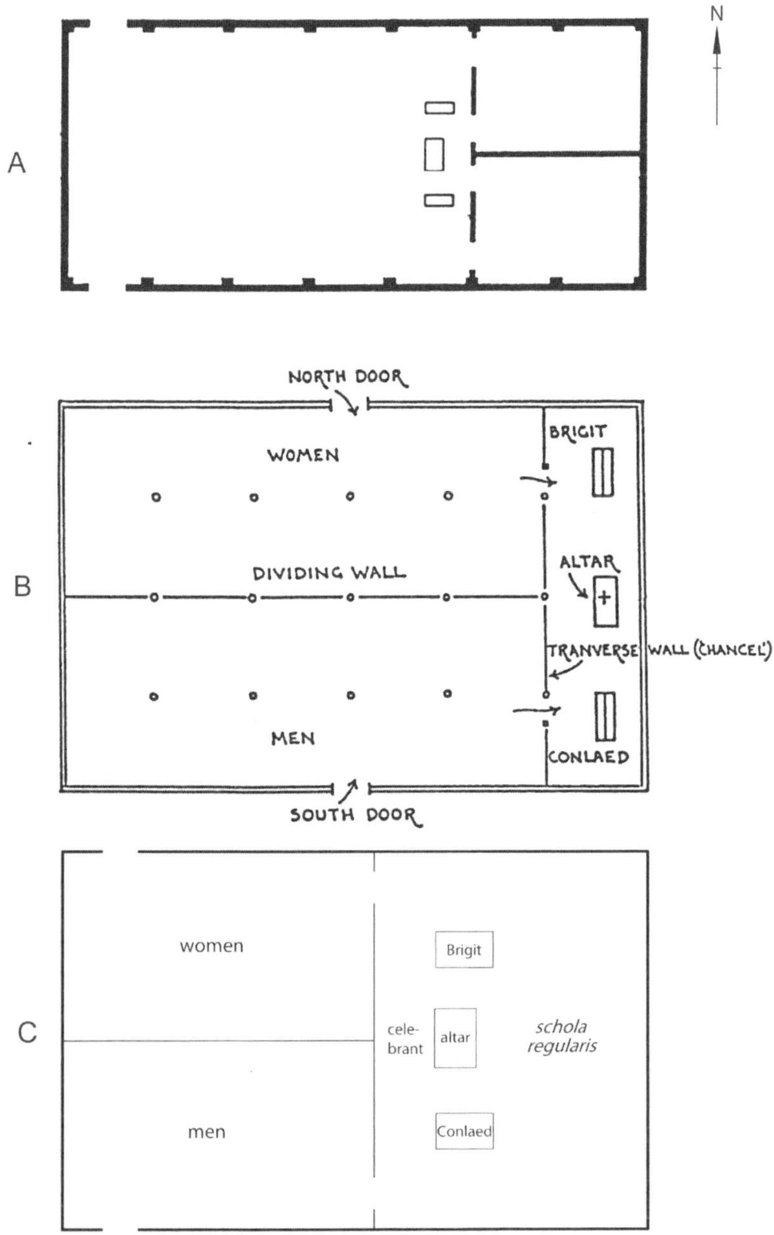

2.13 Representations of the 'great church at Kildare' from Cogitosus' seventh-century description. A. After Ralegh Radford, 1977, p. 6, reproduced with permission of the Ulster Archaeological Society. B. After Thomas, *The Early Christian Archaeology of North Britain* (Oxford: Oxford University Press, 1971), p. 145. Reproduced with permission of the licensor through PLSclear). C. After Ó Carragáin reproduced with permission of the author.

it cannot be known from this description if this was always the layout and form of this particular church at Kildare from St Brigit's time to his own, or if this arrangement was unique to the female community at Kildare or in operation at similar female communities elsewhere. Indeed, the interpretation of strict separation at Kildare can be viewed alternatively by suggesting that 'Cogitosus was not threatened by female sexuality, for he stressed not the separation of the sexes but their coming together [in church]'.[133] Moreover, the only reference to segregation prior to the eleventh century derives from a late seventh- or early eighth-century canonical collection which stated, '… it behoves women, as they accepted the fragility of their sex … to be segregated from the view of men and to live thus until death'.[134] However, the narrative presented elsewhere in the documentary sources 'was considerably different', according to Harrington.[135] Currently little is known of the segregation of religious females from the laity in early medieval Ireland, though judging from the wide variety of settings in which they were found in the sources, it can reasonably be suggested that female religious and laity interacted freely, at least in some contexts and on certain occasions.

Early monastic rules are known from the continent, for example that of St Benedict of Nursia (AD 480–547) which was the first to specify requirements of daily practice in a coenobitical or community environment.[136] The expectations of male monastic rules were never beyond the capabilities of women either spiritually or physically, and so it is possible that early female religious lived regular lives based on a 'male' rule.[137] The question of men and women religious living according to a rule in Ireland remains unanswered. Special instructions for both female religious and clerics have been noted in the sources but the texts of those rules are lost for female religious communities and it remains unknown specifically how, or if, they were administered universally.[138] The rule of Pachomius dating to the late third century is the earliest known monastic rule applicable to both male and female religious. Later Basil of Caesarea created a rule for his sister Macrina, based on Pachomius', which more strictly enclosed the females of the community.[139] Saint Augustine's letters, written about AD 397–423, perhaps to a female community at Hippo, are also considered early rules.[140] In about AD 503, Bishop Caesarius founded Saint Jean at Arles, France for his sister and provided a rule for the female community.[141] Early Irish ideas of monasticism likely influenced continental approaches. For example, Columbanus' monasticism was particularly influential among Frankish aristocratic families of the sixth and seventh centuries, as it permitted the retention of familial interests in property with which their foundations were endowed.[142]

Most of the evidence of rules in early England derives from Bede's *History of the English Church and People*.[143] Rules in England were influenced mainly by early female communities in Frankia, though northern England may also have been influenced by Ireland through Iona. There is no evidence for an early female religious community at Iona – though interestingly there is evidence of early segregated burial.[144] The Benedictine tradition probably arrived in England around AD 597, which eventually became the most popular rule.[145] It particularly stressed the need for the religious community to cut itself off from the outside world and suggested that the storehouse, bakehouse, garden and mill were situated within the monastic enclosure wherever possible. This rule was adopted as the preferred choice for all religious houses during the reform of the western church. Benedictine influence was felt later in Ireland, in the eleventh and twelfth centuries (see Chapter 3).[146]

Notwithstanding the lack of tangible material evidence for early monastic rules in Ireland, what is clear from the sheer numbers of female religious in the sources is that not all lived in the large female religious communities of Kildare, Killevy, Cloonburren or Clonbroney. Rather, they lived in a wide spectrum of locations which included satellites to large ecclesiastical complexes, regionally important churches and ecclesiastical sites, and at proprietary churches. Some of these churches may have held religious women's relics. Indeed, the definition of female religious in this period might be expanded to include additional roles such as priests' wives, hermits and recluses. Even married couples followed a particular path of religious life by being continent on particular days.[147] Therefore, the female religious visible in the historical evidence relating to early medieval Ireland can be described in a single word – diverse – which complements the current corpus of archaeological evidence already outlined.

THE WIDER EUROPEAN CONTEXT

Both men and women became hermits or joined dedicated communities from the outset of monasticism,[148] but for many women in Europe, until about the late sixth century, they followed their religious life at home, like St Genovefa.[149] That changed in the seventh century as a result of several councils, which concluded that female religious should be in monasteries.[150] These female religious houses tended to be urban in character and very little is known archaeologically of these early foundations.[151] In the Merovingian period (fifth to seventh centuries) it has been estimated that over one hundred female and double religious houses were founded on the continent.[152] Important women established many of these and usually became the first abbesses, for example

Radegund, Balthild, Burgundofara, Salaberga, Gertrude and Aldegund, although Radegund and Balthild were not the first abbesses of their monastic foundations.[153] Columbanus' Irish missionary influence on the continent was thought to have been a catalyst for a number of them.[154]

The seventh century is considered the zenith of early medieval female religious communities,[155] and their subsequent decline is traditionally explained through the onslaught of various marauders, not least the Vikings.[156] However, many female houses actually had no recorded history after foundation and their perceived ultimate demise or transformation may have had a variety of causes.[157] The Carolingian period (eighth and ninth centuries) became one of reform, which began in the ninth century.[158] After the Councils of Aachen in 813 and Chalons in 816, all male and female religious were subject of one of two rules. The Benedictine rule was preferred, but canonesses (in this earlier context religious women who maintained rights of property ownership, unenclosed living, and did not take full vows) were permitted as a separate category, under the Augustinian rule. These reforms were felt well beyond the Carolingian empire, for example in Catalonia where female religious houses flourished.[159] Further changes were made in the tenth century when new and reformed foundations were welcomed, the majority of which were Benedictine.[160]

In Wales several early female saints, some living as women religious, such as Gwenfrewy, Melangell and Dwynwen, are known. Their associated ecclesiastical sites have left some trace, such as Llanddwyn Island, Pennant Melangell, and Holywell in Flintshire.[161] It has been demonstrated for the Teifi Valley in mid Wales that earlier sites associated with particular saints and churches influenced later monastic land distribution and use.[162] For Scotland, its few early female religious houses do not seem to survive into the twelfth century,[163] though several nunneries may have been somehow connected to these earlier establishments.[164] England's Christianisation was a protracted process which continued long after the withdrawal of Rome in AD 410.[165] Anglo-Saxon monasticism, which included women, has been characterised by its diversity.[166] Royal women were responsible for several foundations in the seventh century, such as Folkestone, Lyminge and Barking, Ely, Whitby and Wimborne.[167] Many of these were royal double houses, once deemed typical of the period but which are now considered atypical of English early female monasticism.[168] The perceived decline of female monasteries in the ninth century in England is now attributed to a shift in devotion patterns from double-house communities to a single vowess or smaller groups,[169] with the majority of female religious, until at least the tenth century, living as vowesses or at least not fully professed religious living a communal life. Specific terms for these women have been identified in documents: cloistered nuns, *mynecena*, and non-cloistered secular vowesses, *nunnan*, from the Old English *nunne* and from the Latin *nonna*.[170] Monastic reform in England was manifested in the *Regularis Concordia*, a standardised rule compiled at Winchester in about 965–75.[171] This reform marked the end of early medieval double houses, replacing them with nunneries, and 'the character of women's religious communities [in England] had changed' forever.[172]

THE END OF AN ERA: THE LATER RE-USE OF EARLY MEDIEVAL SITES

In Ireland, ten early medieval female religious sites subsequently became nunneries in the later medieval period.[173] Was this a deliberate attempt to associate later nunneries with their earlier counterparts, thereby creating a perception of a long history at those locations? Indeed, further questions can be posed about nuns' possible acknowledgement of, or engagement with, even earlier prehistoric monuments near their nunneries. Several female religious sites, both from the earlier and later medieval periods, were situated on or very close to prehistoric monuments. This may be coincidental due to the preponderance of such monuments in the Irish landscape. But it may also have been a deliberate method of populating the land with Christianity, or creating a memory and historic connection to the chosen location. The deliberate use of the antique landscape has been identified elsewhere and so there is reason to suggest that it occurred in medieval Ireland.[174] Moreover, in two instances, at Inishmaine (Figure 2.14) and Killevy, earlier doorway fabric has been deliberately re-built into later churches (Figure 2.15).[175] Do these acts represent nunneries appropriating the past?

Older structures were sometimes deliberately retained and may have acquired the status of a relic.[176] It has been clearly demonstrated that early ecclesiastical sites were chosen as locations for later medieval male religious houses in Ireland, England and Wales and it is likely nunneries did likewise.[177] A particularly vexed issue though is that it remains unclear if re-use related to continuity of use from pre-reform female religious communities to post-reform nunneries throughout the twelfth century, or if there was an abandonment phase. It is likely that there was a combination of the re-purposing of ecclesiastical sites that had been abandoned over time; and at communities which continued without a break, certain changes in practice and ritual may have occurred.[178]

Excavations at Armagh may have revealed this continuity as early medieval material, and a large stone rectangular building measuring 8m by 9m, interpreted as part of the Augustinian nunnery, was found adjacent.[179] The archaeological

2.14 Inishmaine, Co. Mayo, re-use of earlier fabric, a trabeate doorway incorporated into the south wall of a later church, viewed from south. Image: Tracy Collins.

2.15 *(below)* Killevy, Co. Armagh, re-use of earlier fabric, a trabeate doorway and possibly an earlier west wall, incorporated into a later church, viewed from east. Image: Tracy Collins

2.16 Aerial view of Molough, Co. Tipperary, showing curving boundary indicative of the re-use of a possible early medieval circular enclosure. Image © Neil Jackman, Abarta Heritage.

evidence however did not clarify if the site had been continually occupied through the medieval period. It is possible that several ecclesiastical sites that were in use in the twelfth century at the time of reform made administrative changes and continued in use throughout the period of transformation.[180] One archaeologically attested example is Lorrha, County Tipperary, and with more archaeological excavations further continuity may be established elsewhere.[181] What is clearer from the extant archaeological evidence is that large-scale re-ordering and demolition of the layout of re-used sites after reform seems not to have occurred. Furthermore, a further fourteen nunneries can be identified that are associated with early medieval male foundations.[182] Having said this, it is possible that these so-called male foundations may have had small undocumented female religious communities attached, similar to the satellite houses previously discussed, such as perhaps Killeigh and Durrow, both County Offaly, and Kells, County Meath.

The frequency of re-use of earlier sites is suggestive of a conscious decision to re-use, rather than coincidence.[183] This is not a universal truth, however, as a deliberate decision seems to have been made to abandon older structures at

Clonmacnoise. The extant Nuns' Church was preceded by one, if not two, church structures, neither of which was used in the later period – the Nuns' Church dates to 1167.[184] However, the satellite position to the main complex was maintained, and perhaps this is evidence of re-use of place rather than structure. The decision was made to re-use earlier ecclesiastical sites (whether male or female) in well over a third of cases, and so this could be considered a fairly common occurrence (Figure 2.16).[185] Moreover, several later nunneries have associated features considered typical of the early medieval period, holy wells[186] and bullaun stones[187] being the most numerous associations.

This chapter has provided a concise overview of the current character of the archaeology of female religious in early medieval Ireland, primarily as a background context to nunneries of the later period. There are yet a number of gaps in the evidence, and the potential to increase knowledge of female religious through archaeological investigation is huge. Other forms of female religious, such as vowesses or recluses, should also be considered. It is apparent, as shown in the case of Clenor, that in some places the reconstruction of early ecclesiastical estates is possible. The current evidence suggests that only rarely were early medieval female religious communities strictly single-sexed or strictly enclosed, and it is possible that many ecclesiastical centres and smaller churches had a vowess or a community of female religious attached in some form. This situation was to change in the later medieval period (*c.*1100–1540) with church reform beginning in Ireland in the early twelfth century, which I now introduce in the following chapters.

CHAPTER 3

Women and Religious Life in Later Medieval Ireland: The documentary and material evidence

> It is obvious that women in medieval Ireland drew their attitudes not from their sex but from the times in which they lived … such diverse women cannot be viewed simply as representatives of their sex; they represented the whole medieval Irish society, with all its colour and contradictions.[1]

Turning to female monasticism in later medieval Ireland, we first need a historical context for women in that period. The status of native Gaelic and Anglo-Irish women outside of religious orders is important in order to inform the understanding of how religious life fitted into the range of trajectories that a woman's life may have taken. The church's interaction with women, through patronage and piety, and its responses to female vocation, enclosure and the *cura monialium*, are outlined. A brief section discusses monastic rules and the daily divine office which structured the nuns' lives throughout their life course. The final section gives details of the numbers, affiliation, founders and foundation dates and dedications of the nunneries. While mainly historical, this chapter is not divorced from archaeological evidence and makes use of it where pertinent, for example in the discussion of piety and in nunnery identification.

THE STATUS OF WOMEN

The population of Ireland in the middle ages is difficult to estimate. It has been suggested that it was low compared to modern demography, based on the low value of land in contemporary property deeds.[2] There is the further complication of having two ethnic groups in later medieval Ireland: Gaelic Irish and Anglo-Norman, the latter also known as Anglo-Irish[3] or English.[4] There is disagreement as to how divided the two groups actually were in reality,[5] as there was a familiarity, influence and interaction between the two communities' legal systems, customs and practices.[6] However, the Statutes of Kilkenny in 1366 represent an official attempt to prevent the Anglo-Irish from adopting Gaelic Irish ways.[7] There have been relatively few dedicated studies of Gaelic and Anglo-Irish women. Marital status tends to be used as a category as it was the marital position of a woman that defined her status legally, and permeated her entire life.[8] Elite women of both communities are visible primarily in records pertaining to marriage, and in particular its breakdown, and through ecclesiastical records of the church, which provided a court of appeal in such cases. These records, however, present a biased view, and there is evidence of successful marriages in both cultures in the period.[9]

Gaelic Irish women

Most of the current knowledge of the Gaelic Irish and their cultural identity comes from laws, annals and poetry.[10] Records kept by the colonists highlight both the Anglo-Norman and Gaelic cultures, as do some accounts of contemporary travellers.[11] While there is information on married Gaelic women,[12] there is surprisingly little information on Gaelic single women who were known as *banchomarba*. Their study is made doubly difficult as Gaelic Irish women, despite being married, were in many cases still referred to as 'daughter of'.[13] 'The idea of a single woman, as the Anglo-Irish would have understood the term, was unknown in Gaelic Ireland ... Gaelic single women are virtually invisible.'[14] Unlike Anglo-Irish women, who had some independence from males, Gaelic women were always under the authority of a male, whether it be father, husband, son or kin.[15] Land inheritance can sometimes reveal information about women. Inheritance of land was complicated in Gaelic Ireland and daughters could generally only hold life-interests in land and estates.[16] Gaelic women could hold portable property such as animals and gold and upon marriage could maintain some control over this property.[17] If the union ended in divorce, the woman was entitled to the return of her property, which was a key difference between the Gaelic and Anglo-Irish regulations. Widows were dependent on their sons. Children were excluded from their mother's family inheritance, as they were not considered to be of that lineage. Land could be held in pledge from father to daughter, for her dowry, for instance, which could then be re-possessed by male heirs in exchange for payment to her or her representatives.[18]

In Gaelic Ireland there were a number of families who held hereditary professions, thus forming the learned classes, studying medicine, history, poetry, music and law.[19] Poets appear to have been one of the earliest professional classes, originating in early Ireland and recorded from the eleventh century in Munster and the twelfth century in Connacht.[20] Other professional classes are recorded from the thirteenth century onwards. They were attached to different territories and lordships while a number were erenaghs (ecclesiastical tenants) on church land. Professional families also ran schools, and both students and masters would have travelled for study within the Gaelic world to places such as the isles of Scotland.[21] Women formed part of these professional classes; for example, women bards are included in a list dated to 1584 of poets, chroniclers and rhymers,[22] and a female physician and wright are recorded in the law tracts.[23] There are very few references to single Gaelic women working to support themselves, though several bardic poems of the thirteenth and fourteenth centuries mention, disparagingly, female fortune-tellers and balladeers, although it is unclear if these women were single or married.[24] The identification of Gaelic women in the professional classes suggests that at least some were educated, though Kenny has concluded that 'women were definitely barred ... schools of poets, historians, judges and physicians apparently had no place for female pupils in this period. The places where women could go to learn, the nunneries of Ireland, produced no great figures of female learning'. Therefore, the learned Gaelic women who are mentioned in the sources have been considered exceptions rather than the norm. Indeed, it has been suggested that female learning in Gaelic Ireland developed much later than in Anglo-Irish areas, perhaps not reaching some Gaelic areas until the early modern period.[25]

Anglo-Irish women

Those parts of Ireland that were under the control of the Anglo-Norman colonisers were ruled by English common law or feudal law.[26] In relation to women this law was similar to that found in other parts of Europe at the time,[27] and embodied attitudes that were very different to those in Gaelic parts of Ireland. For example, when there were no sons to inherit, a daughter might inherit her father's estate.[28] Anglo-Irish marriage rules were different to the Gaelic, and two distinct types of single Anglo-Irish woman were recognised: those who had yet to marry and those who would never marry.[29] These latter women were defined as *femmes soles*, and in Anglo-Irish areas could hold property, make a will without a man's consent, act as tenants and could work, although wages were on average half that of a man. *Femmes soles* were also associated with specific types of activities such as brewing, malting or baking, particularly in urban localities where economic opportunities were greater. For example, in 1461 Juliana Loghlin, apparently single, hired a vacant plot from the nuns of Hogges at Suto Street near Christ Church in Dublin, possibly for commercial activities: as a shop or warehouse.[30] Guilds were open to women, as apprentices and free citizens, but only men who were free citizens could vote in or be elected to municipal government, which clearly limited female roles in urban life.[31] Gaelic Irish were not allowed to enter Anglo-Irish merchant guilds, and though Gaelic traders did have their own guilds, it remains unknown if Gaelic women were allowed to join them.[32] Urban opportunities for single women may also have created difficulties such as sexual harassment, abuse and petty crime,[33] and prostitution was probably recognised as a profession in its own right, as in many other European urban centres.[34] Despite the opportunities for Anglo-Irish women, however, most who never married 'lived at or below the poverty level and were relegated to the poorer and despised sections of society, barely able to survive on their own. The very poor standard of living which many of these women had to endure was a consequence of not having the financial support of a husband and family'.[35]

The commercial activities of Anglo-Irish women that are recorded imply that at least some had been educated, and it has been suggested that this education was similar to their European counterparts: first girls were educated at home and when older moved to other wealthy families or to religious houses for further education.[36] Several nunneries within Anglo-Irish parts of Ireland were associated with education: an unidentified one in Cork; Lismullin, County Meath; Grace Dieu, County Dublin; and Graney, County Kildare.[37] Latin was only taught to those women who entered religious life – although the level of proficiency remains unknown – and secular women read and conversed in the vernacular. Latin was the language of power in the medieval period and the exclusion of secular women from a Latin education has been interpreted as a deliberate act intended to limit their social influence.[38]

WOMEN AND THE CHURCH

Parish formation and organisation began in the twelfth century, if not before, as part of the reform of existing church structures,[39] but was slow, and was still ongoing in Gaelic regions as late as the thirteenth century.[40] The synod of Rathbreasil in 1111 first set out a diocesan system, the synod of Kells in 1152 made modifications, and a number of minor synods were held.[41] It has been suggested that this reform was solely a native impetus, with papal endorsement for the changes not arriving until 1152 at the synod of Kells.[42] The parish structure provided for the spiritual well-being of the laity throughout medieval Ireland.[43] The Anglo-Normans, when they arrived in Ireland in 1169, were already very familiar with a church based on a parish structure.[44] After their settlement, the church in later medieval Ireland was divided along community lines – *inter Hibernicos* and *inter Anglicos* – although differences were not as clear-cut as these phrases might suggest.[45] For example, 'it was usual in some parishes within the English Pale to have a mixture of pastors, including clerics recruited from major erenagh [Gaelic] families'.[46] However, there were 'real discrepancies in ecclesiastical organisation' between the two jurisdictions which arose due to the unfinished and uneven nature of the twelfth-century reform.[47]

The church in Gaelic areas, despite having a parish structure, retained the older church offices such as that of erenagh. By this time, this was a lay guardian of a parish church, nominated by the bishop, and head of a hereditary family or families, who occupied church lands within the parish, and who had a say in some matters in the cathedral chapter. A coarb was a variant of the class of erenagh, but apparently more prestigious, although in some cases the terms were interchangeable. A coarb was guardian of a church which had jurisdiction over other smaller churches in the early medieval period, and at this time may have retained extensive property termed 'termon' or 'sanctuary' lands. Generally, in Gaelic lordships clergy were recruited from erenagh families.[48]

The fifteenth century heralded further reform. It was characterised by the Observantine movement of friars,[49] and erased the distinctions between Anglicised churchmen and those who continued the traditions of the pre-Norman church, distinctions which had been so obvious in the first reform movement of the twelfth century. The new division between these fifteenth-century reformers and what had gone before was the age-old issue of clerical celibacy. The Observant friars were strictly celibate, while most of the rest of the church at that time was not. Many fifteenth-century writings urged the laity to rise up against sinful churchmen and confiscate the dowries of their 'concubines'.[50]

The church occupied an important position and permeated all aspects of society and so people's fear of exclusion from it was very real.[51] The clergy of both communities in later medieval Ireland expected regular religious practice – though not necessarily religious understanding – from the laity: rest and attendance at mass on Sunday; participation in the sacraments of baptism, the Eucharist and penance; acknowledgement of the liturgical seasons of fasting and abstinence; almsgiving; payments of tithes; and compliance of canon law, not least in relation to the periods of sexual abstinence prescribed for married couples.[52]

The church had contradictory attitudes in relation to women. It held Mary as a woman and Mother of God in high esteem and protected some rights of women, for example making wills, and in certain circumstances facilitated their escape from unsuccessful marriages through separation, annulment or divorce.[53]

The church was also suspicious of women, however, and limited opportunities available to them. It completely excluded them from the sacrament of orders, although some acknowledged that women had the theoretical capacity for such a role. Aquinas suggested that women had a greater capacity for prophecy, thus providing a niche for female mysticism and religious consciousness throughout the medieval period, although there is currently little evidence of female mysticism in medieval Ireland.[54]

Officially, church authorities did not permit relationships between women and the clergy, both on moral grounds and for the more profane reason that church property should not be used to support a clerical wife and resulting children.[55] Gaelic and Anglo-Irish churches had very different attitudes to female partners of the clergy. In the Gaelic areas, perhaps because of its links with the early medieval church, and the structure of professional families from which coarbs and erenaghs were chosen, formal contracts of concubinage did exist between the parties, and in some cases there may have been a clandestine marriage.[56] These women would, in effect, have been priests' wives, although the situation was still not considered traditional, and difficulties with dowries and bride-prices must have occurred. Furthermore, it was an insecure position for the woman, who could have been forced out of her relationship and residence at any time.[57]

Clerical wives are also recorded at monasteries,[58] and just one example from the *Annals of Connacht* recorded that a candle carried by a canon's wife caused a fire at Holy Trinity, Lough Key, County Roscommon in 1466.[59] Moreover, applications for dispensations to enter the religious life sent to Rome came from men and women who themselves were the products of unions with priests, monks, canons or nuns, indicating indiscipline at Gaelic and Anglo-Irish churches and religious houses, as both groups are listed in those applications.[60] In Anglo-Irish areas priests did on occasion have relationships with women who had no status at all and were treated with contempt.[61] However, overall 'it was extremely rare for parishes *inter Anglicos* to develop hereditary incumbencies based on a family of English or Anglo-Norman extraction', with only three such families being noted in the records.[62]

Despite the suspicion, many women did legitimately engage with the church. Several married women became very involved upon the death of their husbands, perhaps because the church had an intense involvement in funerals and execution of wills.[63] Many women, following the settlement of their husbands' affairs – which may have been long and arduous, including collection and payment of debts – would make charitable donations of money and time to the church, and other institutions such as hospitals.[64] This was particularly true of Anglo-Irish women, many of whom had sole control over their property, portable items and the benefit of a dower – opportunities unavailable to Gaelic women.[65] As a result, re-marriage was probably a more common route for many Gaelic widows so that they did not become dependent on their own family or sons.[66]

Female piety and patronage

Devotion or piety is yet another area of women's lives in medieval Ireland that has been notoriously difficult to identify in the historical documents,[67] and has only relatively recently been brought to the fore.[68] Material culture relating to female piety in medieval Ireland remains sparse. For example, there have been a few finds of paternosters (equivalent to modern rosary beads). Initially, in the eleventh and twelfth centuries paternosters were permitted by religious orders, such as the Cistercians, to be used by those lay brethren and sisters who could not master the recitation of the 150 psalms and various lessons in Latin. The paternoster was used as a numerical aid to recite 150 Pater Nosters (Lord's Prayer) instead. Later, due to the increasing popularity of devotion to Mary, particularly among women, the Ave Maria (Hail Mary) prayer was added.[69] The use of paternosters was first documented in the 1250s, but by then was likely a well-established practice.[70] A particularly early example, interpreted as a paternoster, was found at Killeany, County Laois, associated with a female burial dated to the tenth century. This example is unusual because of its early date and that the beads are flat discs rather than in the round (Figure 3.1).[71] Most examples date to the later and post-medieval periods, though the earliest paternosters extant are of thirteenth-century date, are of amber, and have been found in Cork and Waterford.[72] Several paternosters have been found in excavations in Galway,[73] and a post-medieval sixteenth-century paternoster in bone was recovered from a burial at St Mary of the Isles Dominican Priory in Cork.[74]

Other material culture associated with medieval female piety included portable altars, private chapels, statuary, images and texts, unfortunately none of which has survived in great numbers for Ireland (Chapter 7). A number of surviving manuscripts containing religious texts were commissioned by women, sometimes with their husbands, for example *The Book of Lismore*[75] or the *Leabhar Clainne Suibhne*.[76] In addition to the material culture of devotion, piety was expressed in good deeds such as giving alms, which was rarely recorded; attending daily mass; fasting and other acts of charity, such as food donation; bequests in wills; and payments for masses at anniversaries and for special prayers to be said on behalf of the donor and for the souls of the departed.[77]

3.1 A possible early bone paternoster found at Killeany, Co. Laois. Reproduced with permission of Kenneth Wiggins and ACS Ltd.

Female piety extended to associations with religious houses. Widows of the elite sometimes chose to retire to a nunnery as a vowess – widows who took a vow of chastity in order to avoid re-marriage – or as a corrodian, a paying guest. There is some evidence of female corrodians at both male and female religious houses in Ireland.[78] Corrodians were not permitted to sit in the nuns' choir at church and likely had separate lodgings within the nunnery complex.[79] It is thought that vowesses and corrodians were not expected to be permanently enclosed.[80] Furthermore, elsewhere nunneries acted as a depository for unwanted surplus women,[81] but in Ireland they were not retirement homes for upper-class women and there is no evidence to show a surplus of elite females requiring nunnery placements. The Irish historical evidence shows that many widows did re-marry – even those beyond child-bearing age – and moreover, many elite female deaths are recorded at important ecclesiastical centres rather than nunneries. For instance, Derbforgaill, who had built (or re-built) the Nuns' Church at Clonmacnoise and whose relation, Agnes, was abbess of Clonard, County Meath, chose to live out her days and be buried at Mellifont, a male Cistercian house of which she was a patron.[82]

Female wills have provided excellent evidence for female piety and for nunneries more generally, through bequests to the church or religious houses.[83] Unfortunately, evidence of wills in Ireland generally is sparse and cannot be considered representative, and a single will written by a Gaelic woman survives.[84] She was Renalda O'Brien, a mistress as well as a wife, who had several children, both in and out of wedlock before becoming the abbess of Killone, County Clare in 1496, after her son's murder. The office of abbess was held by members of the O'Brien family, patrons of the nunnery. Catherine O'Brien, also a nun and relative, witnessed Renalda's will there in 1509. At her own request, Renalda was buried in 1510, at the Franciscan friary in Ennis, County Clare, burial place of her family.[85] In Renalda's case at least, family burial tradition was stronger than her position as abbess. Indeed, due to the lack of excavated evidence and synthesis, preferences of burial places for women in medieval Ireland cannot yet be estimated (Chapter 8).

Pilgrimage was another popular visual expression of piety in Ireland, as elsewhere in Europe.[86] It would have been expensive to make such journeys, so it was the elite of Irish society who would have travelled, especially abroad. The tradition of pilgrimage began as a practice in the early medieval period and continued to be popular in the later medieval period, continuing to the present day.[87] While more men travelled abroad, a significant minority of pilgrims were women.[88] For example, in 1186 Dervorgilla, daughter of Murchad Ó Maelsechlainn, travelled to Drogheda on pilgrimage; in 1188 at the death of Etain, daughter of Ó Cuinn, queen of Munster, it was recalled that she had gone to Doire (Derry) on pilgrimage; and Margaret O'Carroll travelled to Compostela in 1445.[89] Furthermore, even for those who could not travel, such as cloistered nuns, there is extant evidence for virtual pilgrimages within their enclosures (Chapter 7).[90]

Patronage was the key public expression of a donor's devotion to the church and highlighted medieval society's concern for the welfare of their souls. Women's patronage spanned a wide range of activities including support of religious houses, both male and female. Gaelic and Anglo-Irish wives, usually in partnership with their husbands, founded religious houses of all orders, for example the Franciscan male houses at Donegal town; Kilcrea, County Cork; Rathmullen, County Donegal; and Limerick.[91] Flanagan has suggested that female patronage may account for the substantial number of nunneries that were endowed in twelfth-century Ireland;[92] despite these numbers, only three nunneries are recorded as being instigated by women: the Nuns' Church, Clonmacnoise, County Offaly; a nunnery at Cork; and Lismullin, County Meath, by Derbforgaill, Agnes de Hareford, and Alice de la

Corner, respectively. In the latter two cases, the women did not act alone and male intervention was required. It is likely, however, that more women were nunnery patrons and their agency has been masked by husbands' and fathers' names in the documentary evidence.[93] There is no concrete evidence to suggest that women favoured nunneries over monasteries for men, even though it may have been thought more pious for a wealthy woman to support nuns,[94] but differences have been noted in patterns of patronage between Gaelic and Anglo-Irish women, primarily due to land holding rights, already mentioned.[95]

Patronage also included the commissioning of religious literature, church furnishings, vestments and church plate. A typical parish church required furnishings that included, at a minimum: a missal, silver chalice, alb, stole, chasuble, surplice, a font and vestries, three statues (Christ on the cross, the Virgin Mary and the patron saint), and a bell to be rung three times before service.[96] It was suggested that the laity would provide for their own parish church, as well as maintaining the nave, and so this was an opportunity to exercise one's piety by donating one or several of the items required. This was to ensure their own salvation and remembrance.[97] There are many examples in the historical evidence of women, sometimes along with their husbands, making such donations.[98] Religious patronage could also take the form of monuments and stone sculpture, such as the free-standing Killeen Cross, County Meath and others erected by the Plunketts, an Anglo-Irish family.[99]

Church responses to female vocation

While women may have patronised the church, several also entered religious life, both freely and perhaps under duress. Their motives were likely various: genuine vocation; as a career; or an unwillingness or lack of opportunity to marry. Others may have entered less willingly, for example women who were illegitimate, physically impaired, or with intellectual special needs; women forced to profess by relatives; or as a refuge for widows and occasionally wives.[100] More recent scholarship has identified instances of all these motivations.[101] While the Irish evidence reveals few such examples, it does include instances of widows entering religious life. For example, Fionnghuala retired to Killeigh, County Offaly in 1447, recorded in the *Annals of Connacht*, and Renalda O'Brien retired to Killone, County Clare in 1496.[102] It has been suggested that it was predominantly elite women who entered the religious life because a dowry, smaller than that required by a husband, was a pre-requisite for entering a nunnery. This practice was forbidden under monastic rule and canon law but was common nevertheless.[103] Therefore, due to a lack of means, women of lower social rank could not enter the religious life except as servants or, in the case of certain orders, as lay sisters (but see Chapter 8 for an alternative view).[104] Life as a nun at any life stage allowed a woman a professional career, possible advancement, and training in manuscript creation and illumination, embroidery and vestment-making, for instance.[105] The status of abbess was important both within the nunnery and in the wider local community, providing employment, while managing the estate of the nunnery. Many nunneries were associated with education and learning, such as Graney, County Kildare, which was granted a short reprieve at the dissolution in 1538 due to the educational services it provided in the region.[106]

The status of women religious had long been debated within the continental church, as, for example, the correspondence between Heloise and Abelard attested.[107] Gille and Malachy were the two most important male figures in the twelfth-century Irish church reform,[108] and have no known female counterpart.[109] From what is known of their lives and writings, an outline of the status of women religious in later medieval Ireland might be inferred. Gille wrote an important tract on the constitution of the reforming church, *De Statu Ecclesiae*,[110] and it has been postulated that this was a discussion document in advance of the synod of Rathbreasil of 1111.[111] In this document, Gille set out the church hierarchy in three grades, ruled over by the pope and Noah: first was the universal church – the bishops, archbishops, patriarchs and prophets; second, the local church or diocese which included seven grades of cleric headed by a priest;[112] and third was the laity, which were grouped into those who prayed, ploughed or fought. This schema would be easily understood in a society where everyone had an allotted place in the social order: 'an essential anchor in a world that was experiencing rapid change'.[113]

Women religious were excluded from Gille's schema of the seven grades of clergy and he accommodated them with the laity. Flanagan has undertaken a close reading of a manuscript copy of *De Statu Ecclesiae* in Cambridge,[114] and she has noted that Gille has written *moniales* between *canonicales* (clergy) and *universales* (laity). This suggested to her '… that [Gille] was conscious of the omission of women religious and the difficulty of accommodating them with the canonically recognised clerical grades in his diagrammatic scheme, but that he nonetheless felt the need to take account of them … [he] … therefore indubitably exhibited awareness of women religious in the guise of abbesses, dedicated virgins and vowed widows'.[115]

In comparison to Gille, much more is known of Malachy, through Bernard of Clairvaux who wrote a life of St Malachy.[116] His deep love of the monastic life originated in his visit to Clairvaux in 1140, where he died on 2 November 1148. Initially, he had requested of Pope Innocent II permission to join Clairvaux as a monk, though this was denied and instead Malachy introduced the Cistercian form of monasticism to Ireland.[117] *Fons Mellis*, Fount of Honey, Mellifont, County Louth was the first Cistercian house in Ireland, founded in 1142.[118] Malachy was also responsible for the introduction of the Augustinian order (of canons), specifically of Arroasian observance, after his visit to Arrouaise in Flanders, also in 1140. It has been suggested that the introduction of this religious order was to provide the dioceses in Ireland with cathedral chapters in the formation of a sub-diocesan administration.[119] Therefore, Malachy strategically introduced two orders to perform different functions in his dual reform of the church's clerical and monastic structures.[120]

Moreover, it is traditionally thought that Malachy made provision for nuns in Ireland and was probably influenced in this regard by his visit to Arrouaise.[121] Gervase, Arrouaise's third abbot, made provision for female religious about the time that Malachy made his visitation.[122] Gervase's first nunnery foundation was at Harrold in Bedfordshire, England in the 1130s.[123] There is further historical evidence in the twelfth-century *Vision of Tnugdal*, that described Malachy as founder of fifty-four congregations which included *sanctimoniales* or nuns.[124] This remains the traditional historical narrative of twelfth-century nunnery foundation in Ireland; and one which has only been recently challenged, as being more complex and earlier in date than has been portrayed.[125]

Interestingly, Malachy's motivation for female foundation could be interpreted negatively: that he was seeking to control previously autonomous female communities, by imposing the Arroasian observance of the Augustinian rule. This suggestion is supported by a decree of the second Lateran Council in 1139, which denounced the common practice of groups of women self-styling themselves as *sanctimoniales* without affiliation to an order, a decree about which Malachy, as papal legate, would have been well aware.[126] Nunneries may also have changed affiliation over time for a variety of reasons.[127] Therefore, although never explicitly described by either of the two twelfth-century church reformers, a picture of religious women and their treatment does emerge. Women religious were present in Ireland before (see Chapter 2) and at the onset of the church reform, and Gille included them, albeit with some difficulty, in his proposed schema, while Malachy also made provision for them by establishing and/or reforming several nunneries.

Periculoso: female enclosure by papal decree

> Intact boundaries with few points of access for laity or points of departure for nuns, was the guiding principal [sic] for this vision of enclosed spaces for nuns.[128]

Enclosure was used in monasticism to facilitate getting closer to God, both before and after church reforms. For example, the Cluniac nunnery of Marcigny, France, founded in the eleventh century, was to follow the customs of its male motherhouse of Cluny, with the addition that the nuns were to be strictly enclosed at all times, so much so that it was described as a 'jocund' or 'glorious' prison.[129] There was a two-fold purpose for this strict enclosure: first, outsiders seeing nuns beyond their cloister would desire them and, second, the nuns would see things they would desire for themselves. Even Abelard's rule for the Paraclete nunnery in Champagne, France, written at the request of Heloise in about 1129, proposed moderation in all things for the nuns, but stressed that strict enclosure, perpetual silence and a secluded location were essential to the religious life of women.[130] A twelfth-century German Cistercian monk, Idung of Prüfenig, discussed the discrepancies between male and female enclosure. Nuns were to be protected from four main terrors. Two were within herself: lust of the flesh and general female curiosity; while the other two were external: the lechery of men and envy of the devil. In addition, the threat of rape was always a danger. All these particular dangers needed protecting against.[131]

Thus, over time strict enclosure became synonymous with female religious. The terrors described, coupled with the widespread male distrust of women as 'weak vessels' and the originators of sin, were also prevalent among the medieval clergy and laity, which concluded that 'the only safe place for a woman who had no husband was behind the high walls of a nunnery or perpetually immured in an anchorhold'.[132] The strict enclosure advocated for women 'seems to reflect the underlying misogynism which one finds especially during periods of reform'.[133] The application of this strict active enclosure disadvantaged the nunneries in relation to their male counterparts in a number of ways, most obviously depriving the abbess of autonomy and control of the nunnery, as she now had to be totally dependent and under the authority of her bishop or abbot. The greater dependence on men in the church undermined and eroded the abbess' public role and forced the development of her private role within the confines of the nunnery.[134]

In 1298 strict and perpetual enclosure was imposed on all nuns regardless of order or location, through a papal decree promulgated by Pope Boniface VIII (1294–1303). The only exception made to strict enclosure were the contagiously ill, who might threaten the life of the entire community and were permitted to leave under those circumstances.[135] *Periculoso*, as the decree was called, was an unequal enforcement of monastic law along gender lines, and in regions such as Italy remained an integral part of a nun's life until the twentieth century.[136] The decree was concerned with isolating nuns from opportunities for sexual transgressions in order to protect their fragile virtue from overwhelming temptations to sin.[137] Many of the salacious scandals associated with nunneries might indicate that nuns were 'chafing under the burden of enclosure',[138] or were written by a biased reporter, such as Gerald of Wales.[139] Indeed, many of the narratives of 'naughty' nuns have become a motif of literary tradition, which may have exaggerated the negative, or may have just been untruths.[140]

Furthermore, under *Periculoso*, the nuns' communities were instructed to be solvent and self-sustaining. If not, they had to cease taking postulants (new entrants), and ultimately the community would wane. Any postulant admitted in contravention of the rule would have their religious profession declared void. Under the yoke of *Periculoso* abbesses and nuns were no longer permitted to carry out visitations on daughter houses and could no longer directly manage resources effectively.[141] *Periculoso* also allowed the papacy to draw a distinction between cloistered nuns officially attached to religious orders and those more autonomous – and perhaps less controllable – female religious communities such as the Beguines.[142] Indeed, the Beguines became so objectionable to the church that they were condemned as heretics at the Council of Vienne in 1312 and were almost forced out of existence.[143] *Periculoso* was another series of laws that discriminated on the grounds of gender difference, as it made religious life for nuns qualitatively different than it was for monks. So much so that, by the end of the fourteenth century, 'enclosure had become an end in itself to which other values of religious life were increasingly subordinated'.[144] *Periculoso* was known of in later medieval Ireland. For example, in 1427 the archbishop of Armagh John Swayne on visitation to Lismullin, County Meath ordered the nuns to obey the rules of enclosure and appended *Periculoso* to his order.[145]

Strict enclosure may have brought some benefits. Keeping has suggested that it might have protected nuns from many of the infectious diseases that less well enclosed male orders may have encountered, providing nuns with an enhanced health profile.[146] This suggests that though enclosure is often portrayed as something intensely negative in the lives of female religious, for them it may indeed have been a positive, further facilitating their rejection of the world and leading to a more contemplative life (see Chapter 7).[147] This may well be true, as there is not a single documented case of a medieval nun complaining of her enclosure.[148] Furthermore, the universal ideal of strict enclosure embodied in the *Periculoso* may never have been adhered to strictly on the ground,[149] and the continued repetition of the order that nuns should not leave their nunneries 'is the measure of its failure'.[150] Indeed, the decree was re-instated in 1563 at the Council of Trent, with far-reaching effects, suggesting that its thirteenth-century introduction was not a success.[151]

Attitudes of male religious orders to the *cura monialium*

With the strict enclosure of nuns came the *cura monialium* – the spiritual care of female religious – considered to be the joint responsibility of the papacy and male religious orders.[152] All religious orders first began with an open or at best neutral attitude to women religious, which slowly changed to one of exclusion.[153] Traditional scholarship on the Cistercians thought the order was initially opposed to female religious but recent research has revised this view, suggesting that Cistercian history with regard to nuns has been misread.[154] The *cura monialium* may have been considered an effective means of salvation for the religious men who advocated it,[155] but it remains generally accepted that it presented two main problems for the church hierarchy as women flocked to enter religious life within a church that was ill-prepared to accommodate them.[156]

First, the *cura monialium* was problematic in that the position of women religious had remained ambiguous.[157] In the later middle ages, monasticism was no longer primarily lay. The male Christian population had divided into those who were clerical (ordained) and the laity. Secular clergy were becoming more monastic in attitude, with celibacy and obedience being more rigidly followed. Regular clergy (under a rule) were becoming more clerical, and could be divided into those monks who were ordained and lay brothers who were not.[158] With these slight shifts, the lay brothers' position was being reduced to that of *conversi*. In this scheme, nuns and abbesses were thus part of the laity in that they could not be ordained; their position too became subordinated and even abbesses were equated with *conversi*. This shift in position left female religious at the very bottom of the religious scale, in effect excluded from the hierarchy of the church through 'institutional invisibility' and strict claustration.[159]

Second, while the onus of care of women religious was firmly placed on the male and double-house orders by the papacy, male religious orders were not pleased to shoulder the burden.[160] The papacy favoured the cloistered contemplative life of the Cistercian rule for women religious, as by the thirteenth century it had an effective mother/daughter house affiliated network established.[161] In other cases, local bishops became the male authority figure, particularly for the smaller female houses following Augustinian rules.[162] It is likely that this is what occurred in later medieval Ireland, the vast majority of the nunneries being of Augustinian Arroasian observance. The requirement for strict segregation according to gender, the requirement for enclosure, and the onerous burden on the male brethren – as many saw it – to sustain the nuns were among the reasons for the ultimate demise of most of the double houses established by Gilbert of Sempringham (the Gilbertines) and Norbert at Prémontré (Premonstratensians).[163]

The Order of Fontevraud established by Robert Arbrissel was different, in that the male element was integrated into a structure specifically designed for women. He believed his statute was a 'unique solution to the problem of the *cura monialium* by integrating into the structure of the women's order a group of men whose role was not to supervise but to serve'.[164] It too was not without its difficulties, however, as aristocratic nuns complained of not being treated properly according to their rank, while the death of Robert was followed by the infamous lay brothers' revolt.[165]

Of these double-house orders, only the Premonstratensians established in Ireland. The General Chapter of the Premonstratensians officially dissolved double houses in 1138 but accepted separate houses where the nuns moved to a new monastery.[166] Subsequently, it completely disengaged from nunneries in 1197–8, which 'condemned the female branch of the order to gradual extinction'.[167] The earliest Premonstratensian house in Ireland was established at Carrickfergus, County Antrim, in 1183 but was relatively short-lived and dissolved in 1212. The majority were founded in the thirteenth century. No Premonstratensian nunnery was founded in Ireland[168] and their absence has been explained due to their prohibition of the 1190s.[169] However, the order did continue to found nunneries after their official renunciation elsewhere, particularly in northern Europe.[170] In fact no double houses were established in later medieval Ireland,[171] but a number of religious houses with male and female religious in proximity did exist (see Chapter 4).

The early decision of the Premonstratensians to abandon the *cura monialium* must have put pressure on other male orders, such as the Cistercians, to accommodate nunneries, which it formally did in 1213 by enacting statutes of observance for nuns.[172] By 1228 the Cistercians had also officially dispensed with female communities,[173] though nunneries were welcome to imitate Cistercian statutes but the order would no longer officially recognise them – and so nunneries continued to be established, in some cases outnumbering male houses.[174] Many individual nunneries and patrons made their own arrangements with local bishops and followed the Cistercian or other religious rule.[175] Towards the end of the thirteenth century the Cistercian chapter was still officially calling for the stricter enclosure of nuns, many of whom were reported to the chapter of 1298 as roaming freely outside their cloisters and electing their own abbess without male supervision.[176]

The mendicant orders of the Franciscans and the Dominicans were only recognised by the church hierarchy when they dispensed with their female aspects, leaving St Clare and Diana d'Andalo to fight for recognition separately. Saints Francis and Dominic had syneisactisic tendencies – celibate men and women living together in a holy vocation as in the early church – which they dispensed with in order to get official recognition from the church. The male mendicant orders were also successful in that they had an urban focus which could supplement the over-stretched parish system at that time.[177] Despite the view that the Franciscans and the Dominicans severed all ties with women religious at their foundation, both orders maintained close alliances with female houses and opened the way for the Third Order.[178] When the Poor Clares and Dominican nuns were finally recognised by the church hierarchy, they too had to accept strict enclosure, unlike their mendicant brethren.[179]

MONASTIC RULES AND THE DIVINE OFFICE

All medieval religious, male and female, took three substantial vows of poverty, chastity and obedience, along with stability. These were at the core of monastic life and by definition it was governed by a rule.[180] However, despite the fact that all orders had a routine of the divine office,[181] with masses and a liturgy of prayers, readings and hymns for the canonical hours, a variety of distinct monastic cultures did develop.[182] It is clear that monastic rules first developed in the early medieval period, such as those of Augustine of Hippo and Benedict of Nursia, strongly influenced those in the later medieval period. The Benedictine rule stressed enclosure and separation from the world, though was not gender specific,[183] and became the most widespread and influential rule. Many later orders based their own rule upon it, for example Cistercian, Gilbertine, Cluniac, Carthusian, and the Order of Fontevraud.[184] The Cistercian order has been considered the first true religious order due to its administration and uniformity of practices throughout its houses.[185] Berman, however, has controversially suggested that this administrative uniformity occurred much later in the history of the order, and as such is a product of revisionism.[186]

The Augustinian rule was also not gender specific. It did not stress enclosure and embodied a more pastoral ethos of service to the wider lay community.[187] The mendicant orders did take a gender-specific view of their rule, and it has been noted that the male mendicant rule was 'strikingly different' from the female. The main difference between the two was that the female rule made claustration a vow. The Poor Clares were officially recognised as a distinct order in 1263, though Pope Urban IV modified Clare's original rule and did not grant the privilege of poverty, becoming known as the Urbanist rule.[188] In England and France, St Clare's rule was modified by Blessed Isabella, sister of Louis IX of France, for minoresses. Isabella's rule did not include the vow of poverty that Clare had originally fought so hard to achieve during her lifetime.[189]

Nunneries in medieval Ireland, whether Cistercian, Augustinian or Franciscan, followed rules, as nunneries elsewhere. Indeed, every nunnery must have had at least one copy of their rule for reference and education, but unfortunately none has survived.[190] There is also no known contemporary evidence of the routine of life in a nunnery in later medieval Ireland and its day-to-day management,[191] as there is for some male religious houses.[192] Therefore, in an attempt to elucidate the Irish archaeological evidence, British and continental historical parallels have been employed out of necessity, though with obvious caution.[193] Despite the lack of written evidence, the routine that the nuns would have celebrated through the daily divine office can be estimated, because though it may have varied in detail between religious houses, it was a fairly standardised monastic practice.[194] In a rare record of a visitation, to the nunnery of Grace Dieu, County Dublin in 1468, the assessor noted that 'the divine offices are duly celebrated'.[195]

The purpose of following the divine office was to mark the hours of each day and sanctify it with prayer. It was central to the spiritual lives of the nuns, in addition to the celebration of mass which would have been the highlight of each day. The divine office comprised a maximum of eight offices throughout the day,[196] each composed of psalms and supplemented by hymns, readings and other prayers. It was performed together by the religious community, who were called by the sacristan by the ringing of bells. In some religious houses, sundials were used to keep relative time, particularly for sext, and examples have been found on the northern cloister arcades of the friaries at Askeaton, County Limerick and Muckross, County Kerry.[197] Furthermore, in the celebration of the divine office at friaries it has been noted that the rhythm of the day and the schedule differed between summer and winter, and it is likely that this also occurred in nunneries.[198]

During the course of the middle ages elaborate books were produced for the celebration of the divine office, such as psalters for psalms, lectionaries for scripture readings, Bibles for proclaiming the reading, hymnals for singing and music. Breviaries were also produced, which were at first lists of tasks in the celebration of the divine office, but by the fourteenth century contained the entirety of the divine office text. The laity also celebrated an amended version of the divine office by following books of hours which frequently invoked the Virgin Mary, and several were clearly associated with women.[199] An appreciation of the divine office becomes particularly important when the nuns' use of space is archaeologically considered later (Chapters 6 and 7).

DOCUMENTARY AND MATERIAL EVIDENCE

> Like the metaphor of the tomb to which women's monasticism was so often compared, the physical environment of the convent has been dead and buried.[200]

There are sixty-five later medieval nunneries in Ireland (Table 3.1; Figure 3.2). This number covers the entire spectrum of preservation: from nunneries only known from a documentary reference, such as the nunnery in Wicklow town, to those with extensive archaeological remains such as Killone. In some cases, the nunneries have little or no historical evidence, and so local information and folk memory, coupled with extant archaeological evidence, forms the only record. Of the remainder, some information on their foundations and use can be found in various contemporary documents. Ten nunneries were either re-used early medieval female religious establishments, or may have actually continued in use from the early medieval period (Chapter 2). There are also several early medieval sites traditionally associated with males that have nunnery foundations in the later period.[201]

Currently, of the known nunneries, some thirty examples have little or no archaeological trace, having as little as a single graveslab extant, such as that from the nunnery at Clonfert,[202] or the Romanesque head from St Peter's Cell, Limerick. Other nunnery complexes have not survived as extant monuments, such as Addrigoole, Aghade, Buttevant, Carrick-on-Suir, Cork, Derry, Fooran, Galway, Kellystown, Kilbride, Killaraght, Kilculliheen, Killeenmulrooney, Lismullin, Lusk, Plary, Skreen, Youghal, St Brigit's Armagh, St Mary de Hogges, Temple-na-Ferta, Timolin, and Wicklow.[203] In some cases, this high level of attrition of nunneries was due to their fabric being re-used. For example, in the case of Grace Dieu, stone was removed for the building of Turvey House, while stone from St Mary de Hogges was used in the repair of Dublin Castle.[204] Although not recorded, it is likely that the once large and important nunnery of Lismullin may have also been dismantled for the construction of Lismullin House, which lies to the northwest of the nunnery's location. The remainder have a variety of archaeological remains, extant churches, domestic accommodation and claustral ranges.

In addition to the definitively identified nunneries, there are several sites which were possibly nunneries in the past, or have been considered by some to be nunneries, though their history and archaeology remains uncertain.[205] This illustrates the importance of the archaeology of these sites, which has hitherto been largely overlooked. A number of errors have emerged in the previous

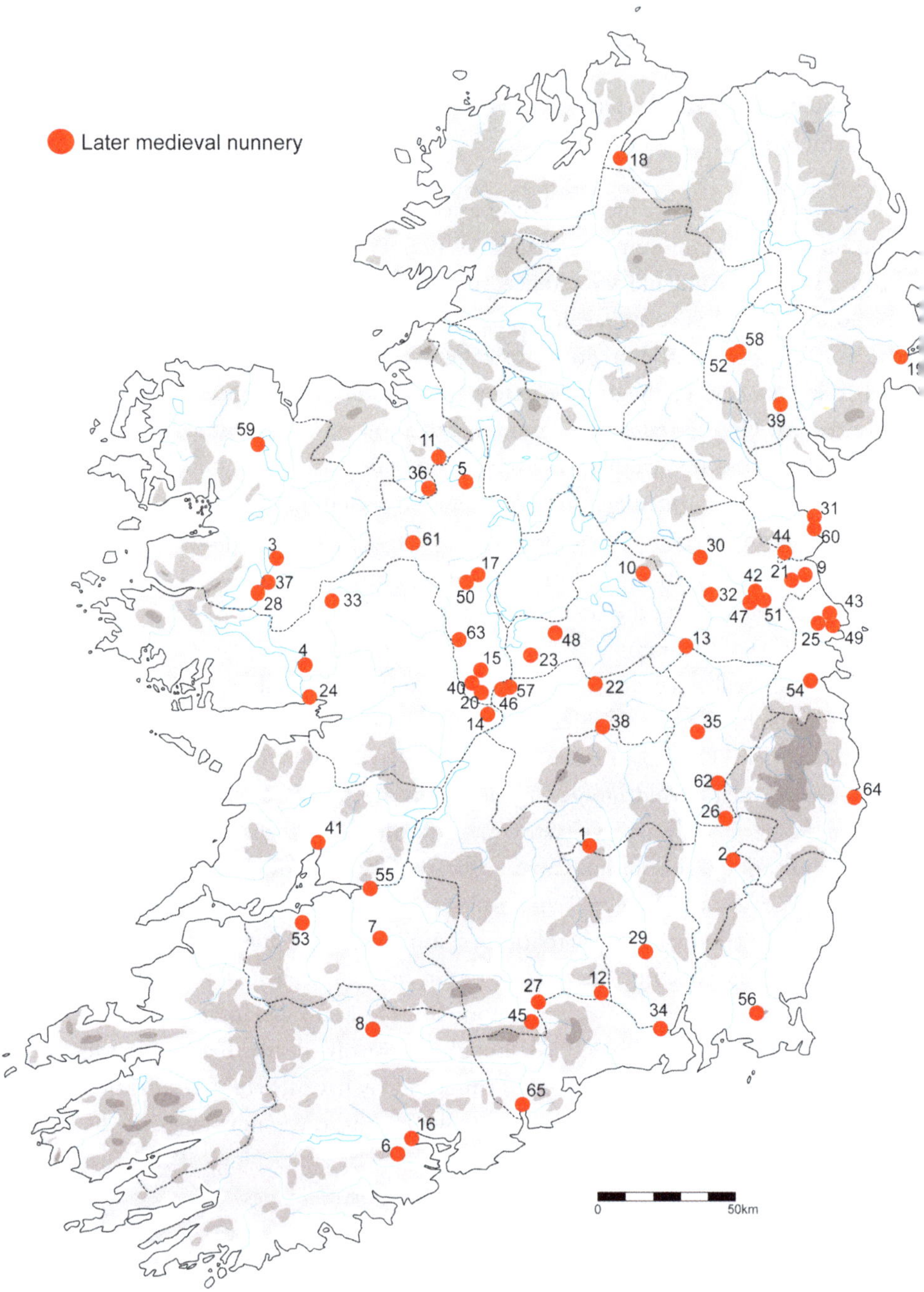

3.2 Distribution of later medieval nunneries in Ireland. Image: Tracy Collins and Frank Coyne

Table 3.1. List of later medieval nunneries in Ireland (modern boundaries used throughout). AA: Augustinian of Arroasian Observance; A: Augustinian; B: Benedictine; C: Cistercian; F: Franciscan; PF: Prominent Family; RH: Religious House; RP: Religious Person

Map Number	*Name*	*County*	*Order*	*Foundation Date*	*Founder Type*	*Dedication*
1	Addrigoole	Laois	AA?	Unknown	PF	Unknown
2	Aghade	Carlow	AA	1151	King	Unknown
3	Annagh	Mayo	AA	-1440	PF	Unknown
4	Annaghdown	Galway	AA	+1144 or -1223	King	Mary
5	Ardcarn	Roscommon	AA	+1144 or -1223	RP?	Mary
6	Ballymacdane	Cork	A	1450?	King	Unknown
7	Ballynagallagh	Limerick	A	1283	PF	Unknown
8	Buttevant	Cork	Unknown	Unknown	Unknown	John the Baptist (Owen)
9	Calliaghstown	Meath	AA	+1195	Unknown	Unknown
10	Caltragh	Westmeath	AA	+1144	Unknown	Mary
11	Carricknahorna	Sligo	Unknown	Unknown	Unknown	Unknown
12	Carrick-on-Suir	Tipperary	F	-1385	Unknown	Unknown
13	Clonard	Meath	AA	1144	King	Mary
14	Clonfert	Galway	AA	+1144 or -1223	RP	Mary
15	Cloonoghil	Roscommon	AA	-1223	Unknown	Mary
16	Cork	Cork	A?	1297	Religious	John the Baptist
17	Derrane	Roscommon	AA	+1144	King	Mary
18	Derry	Derry	C	1218	King	Mary
19	Downpatrick	Down	C	12th century	PF	Mary
20	Drumalgagh	Roscommon	AA	-1195	RH	Mary
21	Duleek	Meath	AA	+1144	Unknown	Mary
22	Durrow	Offaly	AA	+1144	Unknown	Mary
23	Fooran	Westmeath	F	-1385	Unknown	Unknown
24	Galway	Galway	F	1511	PF	Unknown
25	Grace Dieu	Dublin	AA	+1195	Episcopal	Mary
26	Graney	Kildare	AA	1200	PF	Mary
27	Inishlounaght	Tipperary	C?	Unknown	Unknown	Mary
28	Inishmaine	Mayo	AA	1223	King	Unknown
29	Jerpoint	Kilkenny	C?	Unknown	Unknown	Mary
30	Kells	Meath	AA	+1144	Unknown	Mary

Table 3.1. *(continued)*

Map Number	Name	County	Order	Foundation Date	Founder Type	Dedication
31	Kellystown	Louth	AA	+1507	Unknown	Unknown
32	Kilbride	Meath	AA	+1144	Unknown	Brigit
33	Kilcreevanty	Galway	AA	1200 or -1223	King	Mary
34	Kilculliheen	Waterford	AA	1151	King	Mary, Cailchín (Kilkin)
35	Kildare	Kildare	AA	+1171	King	Brigit?
36	Killaraght	Sligo	AA	1223?	Unknown	Unknown
37	Killeenatrava	Mayo	AA	+1223	RH	Unknown
38	Killeigh	Offaly	AA	+1195	PF	Unknown
39	Killevy	Armagh	AA?	1144 or 1148	Unknown	Unknown
40	Killinmulrooney	Roscommon	AA	-1223	Unknown	Mary
41	Killone	Clare	A	1189	King	John the Baptist
42	Lismullin	Meath	A	1240	Episcopal	Holy Trinity
43	Lusk	Dublin	AA	+1144	Episcopal	Mary
44	Mellifont	Louth	C?	Unknown	Unknown	Mary
45	Molough	Tipperary	A	14th century	PF	Brigit
46	Nuns' Church	Offaly	AA	1144 or -1195	King	Mary
47	Odder	Meath	AA	1144?	PF	Brigit
48	Plary	Westmeath	C	1218	PF	Mary
49	Portrane	Dublin	AA	1539	RH	Catherine
50	Roscommon	Roscommon	AA	+1144	King	Mary
51	Skreen	Meath	AA	+1144	Unknown	Mary
52	St Brigid's	Armagh	AA	1144?	RP	Brigit
53	St Catherine's (de O'Conyl)	Limerick	A	-1261	PF	Catherine
54	St Mary de Hogges	Dublin	AA	1146	King	Mary
55	St Peter's Cell	Limerick	A	1171 or 1189	King	Peter
56	Taghmon	Wexford	AA	-1171	Unknown	Unknown
57	Temple Finghin	Offaly	AA	1144 or -1195	King	Mary
58	Temple na Ferta	Armagh	AA	1144?	RP	Unknown
59	Templenagalliaghdoo	Mayo	Unknown	Unknown	Unknown	Unknown
60	Termonfeckin	Louth	AA	+1144	King	Mary
61	Termonkeelin	Roscommon	AA	+1223	RH	Unknown
62	Timolin	Kildare	AA	1199	PF	Mary
63	Tisrara	Roscommon	Unknown	Unknown	Unknown	Unknown
64	Wicklow	Wicklow	B	1448	Unknown	Unknown
65	Youghal	Cork	F	-1385?	Unknown	Anne

literature of individual nunneries in Ireland and these have usually originated in early misidentifications which are then repeated.[206] For instance, the identification of hospitals and other similar institutions as possible nunneries is due to the likely presence of women there, some of whom may have been nuns.[207] In later medieval Ireland there were other foundations in operation that may have been jointly staffed by female religious, nuns or lay sisters, for instance *Fratres Cruciferi* foundations or Third Order Franciscan and Dominican foundations.[208] These foundations are not easily classified archaeologically and form part of what Gilchrist has insightfully termed 'The Other Monasticism', along with quasi-double houses and double preceptories.[209] In this book, these foundations have been deliberately omitted, as they are not considered to be specifically nunneries – though they certainly merit archaeological research in their own right, very little of which has been conducted to date.

Religious orders and affiliation

Nunneries in later medieval Ireland were affiliated to five religious orders: Benedictine, Franciscan, Cistercian, Augustinian, and Augustinian of Arroasian observance (Figures 3.3 and 3.4). There are four nunnery sites for which the order remains unknown. The majority of foundations were Augustinian or Augustinian of Arroasian observance following the rule of St Augustine of Hippo.[210] Augustinianism was not fully recognised by Rome as an order until the 1050s, and first officially recorded at St Denis, Rheims, France in 1067. The order had been particularly successful in restoring religious discipline and reforming the church on the continent. It is thought that the order was functioning in Ireland by 1137, and is likely to have been introduced some ten years prior to that.[211] The relative autonomy of the Augustinian order in comparison to the Cistercian which was ruled centrally through the General Chapter may have made it the more attractive choice of patrons in Ireland.[212] Also, St Malachy's influence perhaps can be perceived in the relatively large numbers of Arroasian observance houses established, which followed the Augustinian rule tempered with some stricter Cistercian provisions, formulated at Arrouaise, and seen first-hand by Malachy.

Visitation records of Stephen of Lexington in 1228 are the only references to Cistercian nuns at the male houses of Jerpoint, Inishlounaght and Mellifont,[213] with other Cistercian nunneries recorded at Downpatrick, Derry and Ballymore (Plary). There are very few references to Benedictine nunneries in medieval Ireland; at Wicklow, and possibly Kilcreevanty at its foundation, and a possible house at Cork.[214] In Ireland there were also relatively few male houses of that order founded, with just sixteen known. It has been noted that

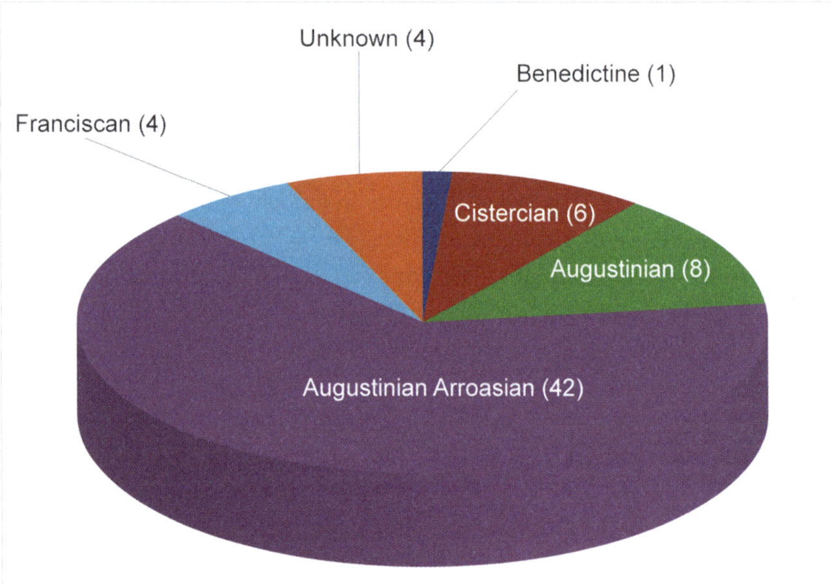

3.3 Numbers of orders of nunneries in later medieval Ireland. Image: Tracy Collins and Frank Coyne.

some early medieval ecclesiastical communities may have adopted or been influenced by the Benedictine rule just before or in the early stages of church reform in Ireland, perhaps being influenced by earlier continental and English church reform.[215] Furthermore, it has been noted that several foundations may have been at first Benedictine, only later to change affiliation, usually to the Cistercian order, and the male monasteries of Holycross and Kilcooly, County Tipperary, Jerpoint, County Kilkenny and Monasterevin, County Kildare are cases in point.

The Franciscan order was the latest introduction to medieval Ireland and it is thought that their first friary was established in Cork in 1214.[216] The Franciscan Second Order refers to specifically female houses, being established by St Clare in 1211 or 1212 on Palm Sunday.[217] The Irish houses are known from a record from the chapter of Naples in 1316 when six houses were recorded. In 1325 no Irish Poor Clare house was recorded, and in a list drawn up in 1384–5 by a Dalmatian Franciscan, there were three Poor Clare houses mentioned in Ireland.[218] Irish records have a single reference to Walter Lynch's foundation in 1511 in Galway for his daughter. It has been suggested elsewhere that all Poor Clare foundations in Ireland were post-reformation in date, or were actually Third Order houses.[219] It may first appear unusual that there is no medieval Dominican foundation in Ireland, but England only had a single house at

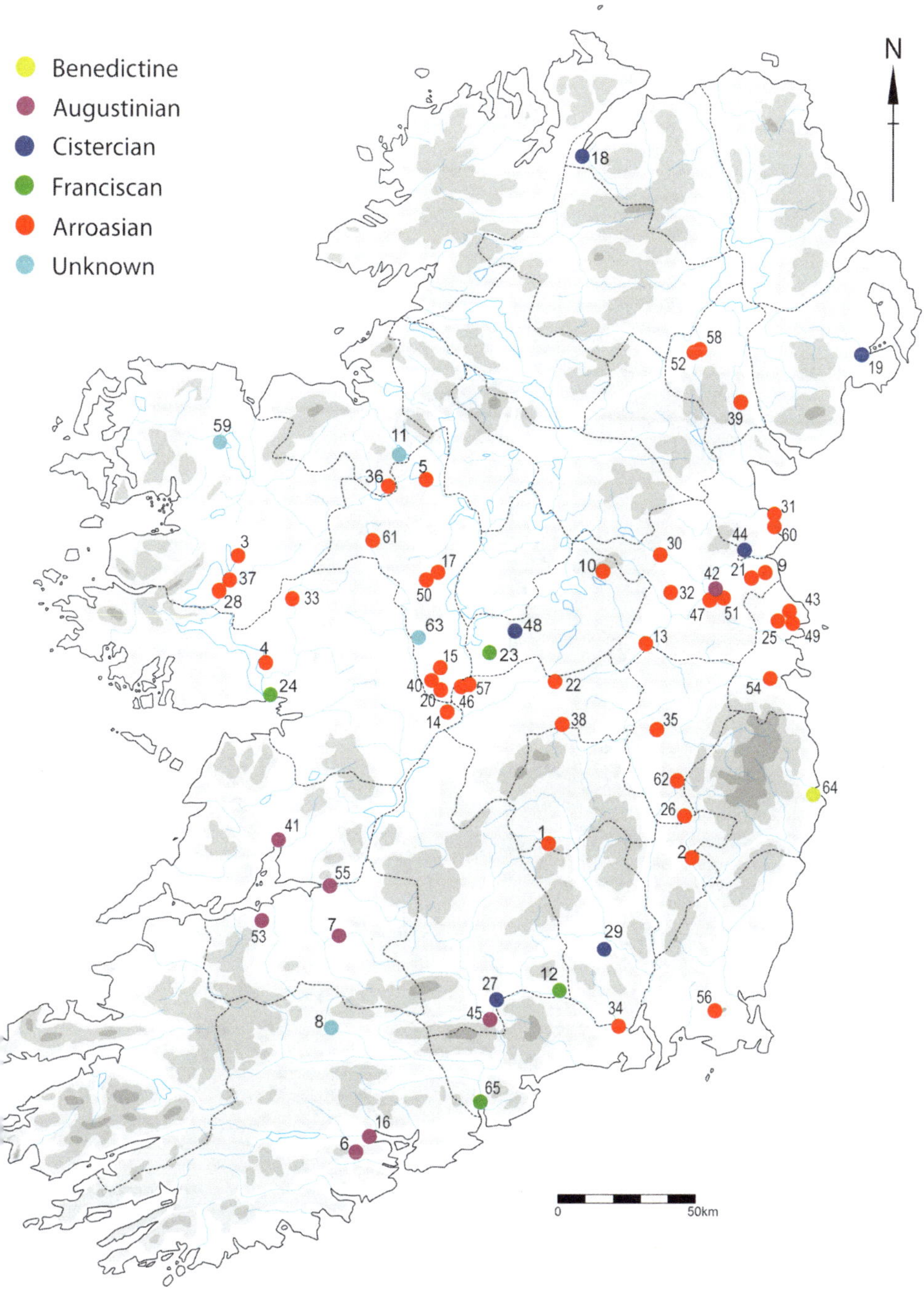

3.4 Distribution of later medieval nunneries according to order. Image: Tracy Collins and Frank Coyne.

3.5 Distribution of later medieval nunneries in Britain. Image: Frank Coyne.

Dartford, Kent.[220] Interestingly, however, later medieval and post-medieval Dominican nunneries in Spain record their origin to a medieval Dominican nunnery at Galway; this putative house has left no trace in the medieval historical records of Ireland.[221]

The pattern of affiliation of nunneries in Ireland that has emerged is interesting as it contrasts sharply with that of Britain (Figure 3.5). The monastic identity of English nunneries[222] was Benedictine for the most part, while in Scotland[223] and Wales[224] this identity was predominately Cistercian.[225] Power did not categorise her nunneries by order, though she used the Benedictine rule as a template for her investigation of the workings of a nunnery in medieval England.[226] Continental evidence shows that nunneries there were predominantly Cistercian,[227] though other orders such as the Poor Clares were also popular.[228] The figures for later medieval Ireland show that the monastic identity of female monasticism was overwhelmingly Augustinian of Arroasian observance. To what extent this female identification with St Augustine was based on the nuns' admiration of the saint, or to the vigorous reforms of the Irish church promoted by St Malachy, is perhaps a moot point. The contrast between the Augustinian nunneries of Ireland and Benedictine nunneries in England is rooted in both time and function, as church reform in England occurred at least one hundred years before Ireland, and nunneries in Ireland may have performed more pastoral functions than those in England.[229] The concept of Augustinian/Arroasian identity is further explored later (Chapter 7).

Studies of male religious houses in Ireland usually use the order of a house as a primary criterion for research and analysis. This is a common methodology and fruitful results have emerged.[230] In contrast, an architectural and archaeological analysis of later medieval nunneries through their affiliation produces no clear pattern. This is unsurprising considering that only nunneries affiliated to the Augustinian and Arroasian observance have upstanding remains in Ireland.[231] This is similar to other regions, where it has emerged that considering nunneries according to order does not yield meaningful results. Burton, for example, has not categorised nunneries by order, although the double-house orders of Fontevraud and Sempringham are considered separately.[232] Difficulties in tracking nunnery affiliations, which on occasion were insecure, have been highlighted,[233] and it has been suggested that it is more appropriate to treat houses of religious women separately, '... rather than discussing them like men according to order or congregation. To do this would be to squeeze women into categories which may better describe male rather than female congregations'.[234] Gilchrist listed religious houses represented in medieval England: Augustinian, Benedictine, Cistercian, Franciscan and Dominican, in addition to the double houses of the Gilbertines, Birgittines, and Fontevraud.[235] Nunnery foundations of the Premonstratensians, Dominicans and Carmelites are notable in medieval Ireland by their absence.[236] The military orders of the Knights Templars and Knights Hospitallers do not seem to have been associated with the provision of nunneries in Ireland either.[237] There is no evidence that the double houses of the Gilbertines, Fontevraud, or the Birgittines were founded in medieval Ireland.[238]

Foundation dates

The known foundation dates of later medieval Irish nunneries span a period from the mid-twelfth century to the sixteenth century, and this period was broadly bracketed by the important events of church reform and the dissolution of the monasteries (Figures 3.6 and 3.7).[239] In many cases, the precise date of establishment is unknown, and for others their foundation is relative, being recorded as after or before a certain date or dates. In these cases, the earlier of the dates has been used in this comparison. Eight nunneries have no known foundation date and their general later medieval period date has been allocated on the basis of association with other religious houses, a documentary reference, or upstanding remains.[240] In the case of the male Cistercian houses of Jerpoint, Mellifont and Inishlounaght, the foundation dates of the male

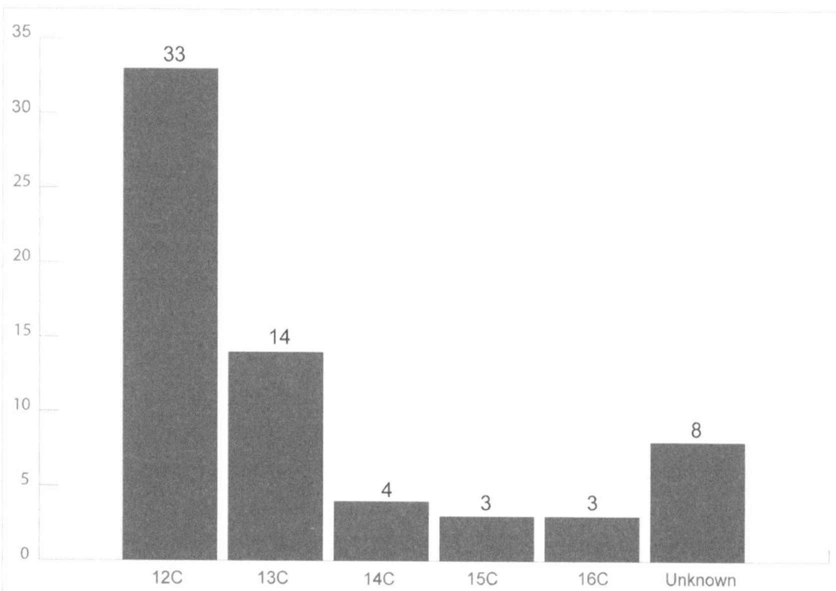

3.6 Breakdown of later medieval nunneries in Ireland by date of foundation. Image: Tracy Collins and Frank Coyne.

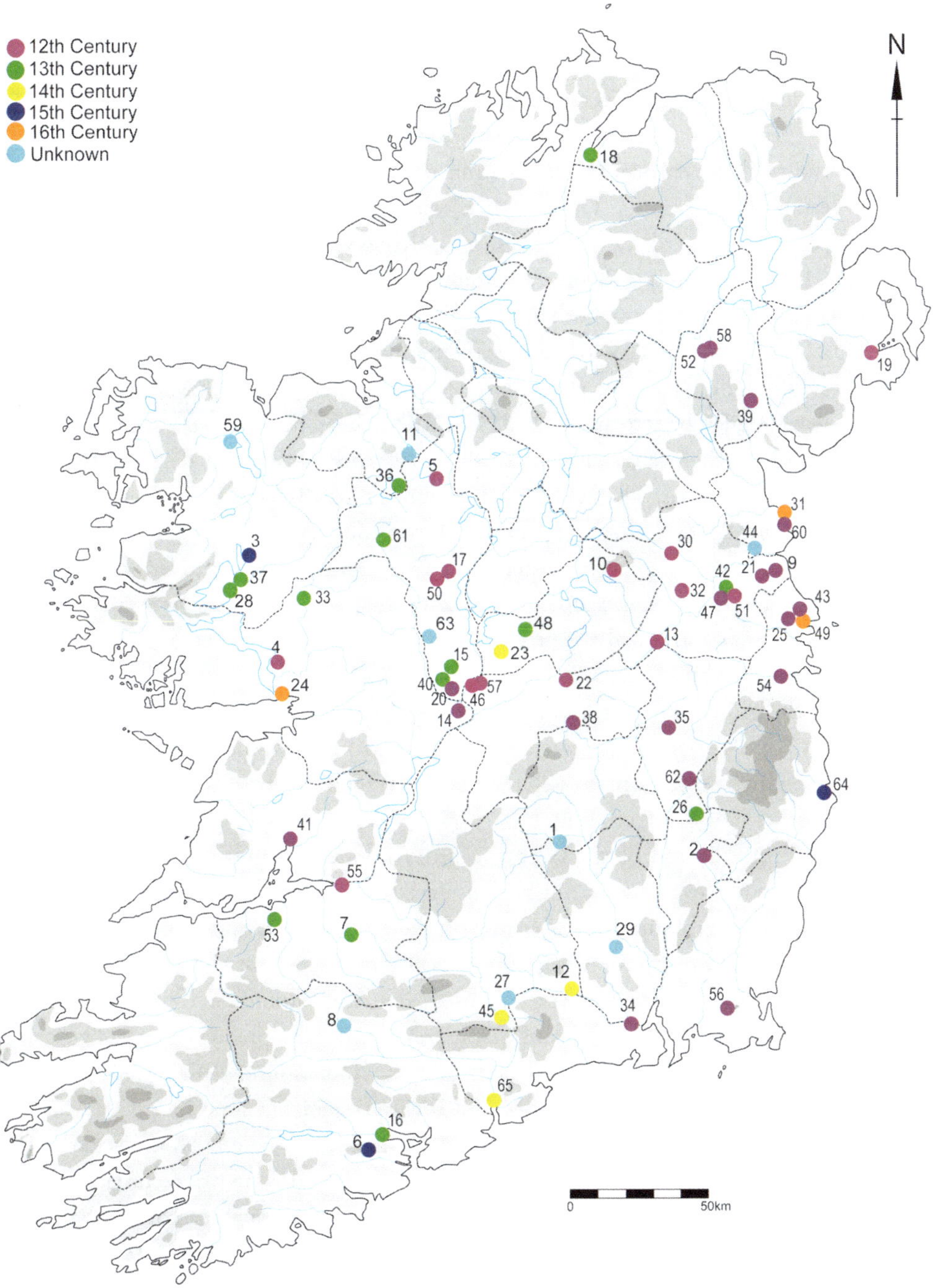

3.7 Distribution of later medieval nunneries according to date of foundation. Image: Tracy Collins and Frank Coyne.

monasteries are known: 1160–2, 1142 and 1148, respectively.[241] However, the dates of establishment of the communities of nuns at those locations, which were noted by Stephen of Lexington in 1228, may have been different to the male communities and remain unknown.[242]

Over half of all the nunneries were founded throughout the course of the twelfth century, though within this group, few nunneries have precise establishment dates. Downpatrick was founded sometime in the twelfth century, Clonard was founded in 1144, Killevy in 1144 or 1148, and the Nuns' Church and Temple Finghin at Clonmacnoise in 1144 or 1195. Odder, St Brigit's and Temple-na-Ferta, both in Armagh, were all probably founded in 1144, with a further ten nunnery foundations sometime after this date.[243] Three nunneries are thought to have been founded after 1144 but before 1223. St Mary de Hogges was founded in 1146 and Aghade and Kilculliheen both in 1151. Taghmon was established before 1171 and St Peter's Cell was probably founded in 1171, though 1189 is also cited. The later medieval nunnery at Kildare was re-founded after 1171 and Killone in 1189. Drumalgagh was founded before 1195 and a further three nunneries sometime after this date.[244] Timolin was founded at the very end of the century in 1199. The date of 1144 is important as it was the date traditionally assigned to the Augustinian of Arroasian observance nunneries established by Malachy, as listed in the *Vision of Tnugdal*, with Clonard named as the group's mother house. In 1195 possessions of Clonard were confirmed by Pope Celestine III. Later, in 1223, a papal bull would transfer several of Clonard's possessions to Kilcreevanty, the then newly established Arroasian mother house in Connacht.[245]

From the end of the twelfth century nunnery foundation declined. This decline however should not be considered as indicating a fall-off in patronage or support for nunneries. Many of the nunneries founded in the twelfth century continued to fill requirements in subsequent centuries and, as a result, fewer new foundations were required. Fourteen nunneries were founded in the thirteenth century and, of that number, nine have precise dates.[246] Two are recorded as being established before 1223: Cloonoghil and Killinmulrooney, and two after 1223: Killeenatrava and Termonkeelin. St Catherine's, Old Abbey was recorded as founded by 1261, and its architecture suggests a foundation date sometime in the 1240s.[247] Only four nunnery foundations are recorded in the fourteenth century. All but one is affiliated with the Franciscan Second Order or the Poor Clares.[248] Their foundation date is believed to be sometime before 1385. Molough was founded sometime in the fourteenth century, possibly on the site of an early medieval foundation. The fifteenth and sixteenth centuries record three establishments each. Annagh was founded before 1440, Wicklow

Table 3.2. List of nunneries established in a locality before any male religious house.

Date of Nunnery Foundation	*Nunnery Name (Affiliation)*	*Townland*	*County (modern)*
1123	Ardcarn (AA)	Ardcarn	Roscommon
1144	Addrigoole (AA)	Addergoole	Laois
1144	Caltragh (AA)	Collinstown	Westmeath
1144	Killevy (AA)	Ballintemple	Armagh
1151	Aghade (AA)	Aghade	Carlow
1151	Kilculliheen (AA)	Abbeylands	Waterford
1171	Kildare (AA?)	Kildare	Kildare
1171	Taghmon (AA)	Taghmon	Wexford
1171	St Peter's Cell (A)	Limerick historic town	Limerick
1195	Grace Dieu (AA)	Grace Dieu	Dublin
1218	Derry (C)	Derry historic town	Derry
1223	Termonkeelin (AA)	Moor	Roscommon
1240s	St Catherine's (A)	Old Abbey	Limerick
1450	Ballymacdane (A)	Old Abbey	Cork

in 1448 and Ballymacdane in 1450. The only later medieval nunnery in the city of Galway was founded in 1511, Kellystown was established sometime after 1507, while Portrane was founded towards the very end of the period in 1539 by nuns vacating Grace Dieu.

It has been suggested that the fashion of establishing nunneries in later medieval England was about a generation behind their male counterparts, and it has been demonstrated that male religious house building in medieval England peaked in the middle of the twelfth century, with nunneries peaking towards the end of that century.[249] Furthermore, male religious houses have long been associated with the first phase of colonisation, with nunneries associated with later consolidation of holdings.[250] While this may have generally been the case, when foundation dates and locations of later medieval female houses in Ireland are considered, fourteen – a significant number – were actually established as the first religious house in a locality, prior to the foundation of any male religious house (Table 3.2).[251] In a further two cases, nunneries were founded at an early date in the overall monastic development of their localities. For example, Killone was founded in 1189 at the same time as the Augustinian male house of Clare Abbey.[252] St Mary de Hogges at Dublin was founded in 1146 and was only predated there by the male Cistercian house of St Mary's founded in 1139.[253] This suggests that for at least fourteen locations in later medieval

Ireland the first monastic presence in the locality was female. This is particularly interesting when it is considered that the historic towns of Dublin, Waterford and Limerick (based on dates of foundation) had established nunneries very early in their monastic development, sometimes even before any male religious house. Significantly, this reveals that the need for a female religious house in a particular locality was more immediate than for a male house.

Founders and patronage

In many cases the name of the founder of a nunnery is now lost,[254] and seventeen nunneries were founded by royal kings or ruling families (Figures 3.8 and 3.9).[255] For example, the Ó Conchobhair (O'Conor) family in Connacht founded nunneries at Annaghdown and Kilcreevanty, by Cathal Crobderg Ó Conchobhair; Inishmaine and Derrane by Toirrdelbach Ó Conchobhair (Turlogh O'Conor); and probably also the houses of canons and nuns at Roscommon town.[256] Diarmait Mac Murchada (Dermot Mac Murrough), king of Leinster,[257] founded nunneries at Mary de Hogges, Kilculliheen and Aghade. It is also likely that he re-founded the nunnery at Kildare, possibly with the co-operation of Dublin's Archbishop Laurence O'Toole, to whom he was related by marriage. The nunnery at Termonfeckin, co-located with canons in its earlier stages, was founded by the king of Oriel (Airgialla) Donnchad O'Carroll,[258]

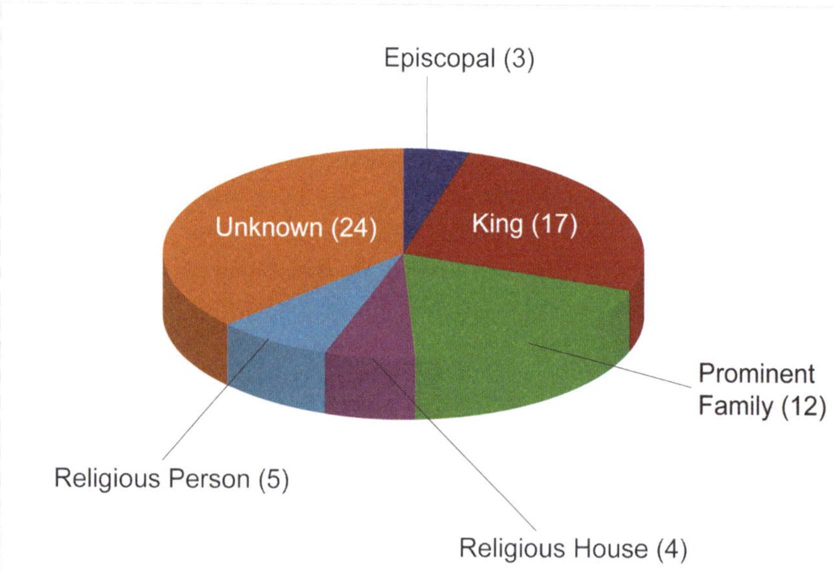

3.8 Numbers and type of nunnery founder in later medieval Ireland. Image: Tracy Collins and Frank Coyne.

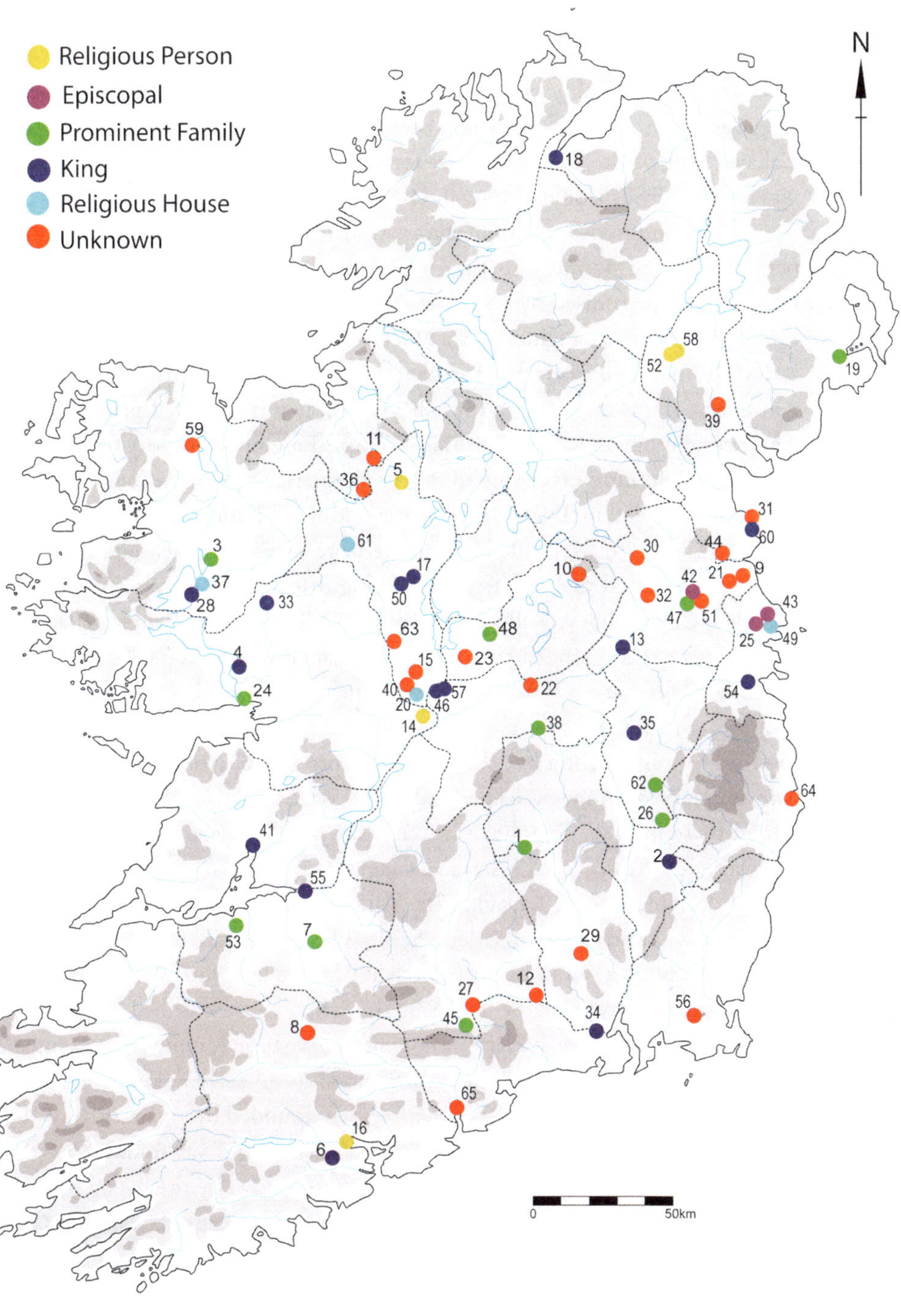

3.9 Distribution of later medieval nunneries according to foundation type. Image: Tracy Collins and Frank Coyne.

supposedly with St Malachy's encouragement. Clonard was re-founded on an early medieval ecclesiastical site by Murchad O'Melaghlin,[259] ruler of Meath, who was also probably encouraged by St Malachy. It is thought that the religious house at Duleek may have been founded by Muirtertach O'Kelly (Ua Cellaig), king of Bréga, but evidence for this is sparse.[260] The nunnery at Derry was founded by Turlough Luineach O'Neill of Strabane Castle.

The two nunneries at Clonmacnoise were also founded by important royal personages. The nunnery to the east of the monastic complex, the Nuns' Church, was patronised by Derbforgaill,[261] the wife of Tigernán Ua Ruairc, king of Bréifne and daughter of Ua Máel Sechlainn, king of Mide, in 1167. It is known from both historical and archaeological evidence that there was already a nunnery at this location, and it is likely that it was occupied prior to 1167. The second nunnery at Clonmacnoise, Temple Finghin, was likely founded by MacCarthaigh, king of Desmond.[262] The nunneries of Killone and St Peter's Cell were founded by Donal Mór O'Brien, king of Thomond.[263] Some of the abbesses known to have ruled at Killone were of the O'Brien family and it has been suggested that a federation of Augustinian houses was created that included Clare Abbey, Killone, St Peter's Cell and later Ballynagallagh.[264] Ballymacdane was founded by Cormac MacCarthy of Muskerry.[265]

After kings and royal patronage, prominent families form the next largest group of patrons for later medieval nunneries. The nunnery at Galway was founded for his daughter by Walter Lynch, a prominent citizen of the town.[266] The nunnery at Annagh was founded by Walter de Burgo[267] and he was buried there in 1440. Timolin was founded by Robert, son of Richard Lord of Norragh,[268] who placed his grand-daughter there. Graney was founded by Walter de Riddlesford.[269] David Fitz Milo,[270] baron of Overke, granted the nunnery of Addrigoole to Kilculliheen. The Barnewall family[271] founded Odder, to which the community of nuns at Clonard later moved. The nunnery at Killeigh was founded by the Warens, who were described as 'English settlers'.[272] The nunnery at Plary is thought to have been founded by a member of the de Lacy family.[273] Molough, re-founded on an early medieval site, was established by the Butlers.[274] St Catherine's was founded by an ancestor of the earls of Desmond, John FitzThomas.[275] Ballynagallagh was founded by the Fitzgibbons. The nunnery at Downpatrick was founded by the Bagnalls.

Foundations made by a named saint or religious person are relatively few. Saint Malachy is traditionally thought to have directly founded nunneries at Clonfert and Ardcarn, and the two nunneries at Armagh. Furthermore, Malachy appears to have had great influence over kings in Ireland and this influence brought about many further nunnery foundations. It is likely that he also co-operated with local ruling families or church authorities in the establishments at Clonfert, Ardcarn and Armagh.[276] The establishment of the nunnery at Cork in 1297 has been attributed to a female recluse, Agnes de Hareford, after a need in the city for a nunnery was identified by jurors working on behalf of the justiciar John Wogan: 'for there is no other house of nuns where knights and other freemen in those parts may have their daughters brought up or maintained'.[277] She was assisted by the Barry family in her foundation.[278] Of similar scale, just four nunneries were established by existing religious houses. Killeenatrava was founded by the male religious house at Cong, Termonkeelin was founded by the nunnery of Kilcreevanty, by then the Arroasian mother house in Connacht. Drumalgagh was likely founded for the nunnery community of Temple Finghin at Clonmacnoise and Portrane was founded just before the dissolution by nuns from Grace Dieu. Only three nunneries have been recorded as being founded by bishops or archbishops. Grace Dieu and Lusk were both founded by the archbishop of Dublin John Cummin, and Lismullin was founded by the bishop of Meath on behalf of his sister Avicia de la Corner. As previously mentioned, the nunnery re-founded at Kildare may have been influenced by the then archbishop of Dublin Laurence O'Toole, in association with the king of Leinster.

Patronage of monasteries had, by the medieval period, become part of the fabric of society. It was regulated by canon law, based on the respect and interdependency of all parties: the founder and their family, and the religious community.[279] Notwithstanding the twenty-four nunneries in Ireland for which founders are unknown, patterns do emerge when the data are analysed. Thompson listed at least eighteen nunneries in England that had an unknown or uncertain founder. She suggested that it may be misleading to search for a single founder of a nunnery, and it may actually distort the reality of patronage as they may have been corporate foundations which included a number of families. As most of the founders appear to be from middle-ranking families in England, they may have needed to pool their resources in order to fund such a venture. This may also be a reason why many nunnery founders are not recorded.[280]

Only three women are identified as being founders of nunneries in Ireland.[281] Derbforgaill, wife of the king of Bréifne and daughter of the king of Mide, re-founded the eastern nunnery at Clonmacnoise. Derbforgaill is an interesting historical figure and was clearly very influential in her social sphere. She was related to Agnes the abbess of Clonard. She also patronised several male religious houses in her lifetime and was permitted to retire to the male monastic house at Mellifont and was buried there after her death in 1193.[282] It is not known how this arrangement would have operated or where she was accommodated at Mellifont. Indeed, this situation may have been considered unusual at the time, although there is other evidence for the burial of women at male religious houses.[283]

The second woman associated with a nunnery foundation was Agnes de Hareford, a female recluse at Cork. Very little is known of her life, though it is likely that she was very well regarded and had influence. The justiciar took it upon himself to enquire if lands could be donated to her, so she must have been influential in her social sphere. It is also clear that the establishment of a nunnery at Cork, at her instigation, fulfilled a necessary social need for the town and its hinterland. Ó Clabaigh notes that the social and educational requirements of the social elite appear to have out-weighed Agnes' personal desire for solitude. It is a unique example in medieval Ireland of a former recluse fulfilling such a social role, though in England and the continent this was common.[284] There are few female recluses or anchorites recorded from medieval Ireland, though some are associated with nunneries (see Chapter 6). The third woman associated with a nunnery foundation was Avicia da la Corner, who founded Lismullin with the bishop of Meath, who was her brother Richard. It has been described as a 'joint venture'.[285] It is highly likely that she used her brother's influence to obtain permission to make such a foundation. He also endowed it with the manors of Dunsink and Ballugodman.

Therefore, relatively few women have been recorded as founders or patrons of female foundations in an Irish context.[286] While more women certainly did patronise nunneries in England, the statistics also show that women were by no means the sole founders.[287] Welsh women did not appear to be in a position to offer land for founding nunneries – and only three were founded in any case – though they did seem to find ways to procure land for other purposes.[288] Members of the social elite who were wealthy enough to be able to establish, or subsequently patronise, a religious house were open to diverse interpretations of religious life. They were pleased to fund a wide range of religious houses for the betterment and salvation of their souls, the souls of their ancestors, and others that were named in the foundation charter.[289]

This situation might be best described as preventing an 'all eggs in one basket' approach, where funding was spread over a wide spectrum of religious establishments for the good of the patron's eternal soul. Having said that, monks' and priests' prayers for the donor's salvation were generally regarded as being more effective than those of female religious, such as nuns.[290] This infers that the establishment of a nunnery may have had other motivations, such as accommodation of female family members who had a spiritual vocation, or who did not wish to marry. Political and social considerations were also important in the establishment of such a permanent feature as a nunnery on the physical and cultural landscape of the founder.[291] Other rights too were bestowed on the founder, such as the right to burial at the nunnery, the right to place members of their family there, and influence in the choice of abbess. For example, it was implicit in a charter that the founder exercised considerable control over the nunnery at Foukeholme in Yorkshire, England.[292]

Stöber has considered the patronage of late medieval monasteries in England and Wales in great detail: at their foundation, at 1300, and again at their dissolution *c.*1540.[293] She concluded that nunneries were founded by royals, ecclesiastics or the laity, with the remainder having an unknown founder. The largest group of founders were the laity. In 1300, the largest group were unknown patrons, but this was closely followed by lay patronage. By the time of the dissolution, after unknown patrons, patronage from the laity and royalty was almost equal. Stöber suggested that the nunneries that were once patronised by the laity could end up in royal hands for a variety of reasons. Indeed, many monasteries were neglected after this time and passed into the patronage of the king because of this.[294]

The common perception that the relationships between monastery and founder changed significantly from the twelfth to fourteenth centuries was also interrogated, and Stöber suggested reasons as to why this change may have taken place.[295] In particular, she noted that from *c.*1300 the patronage of a religious house in England and Wales was increasingly considered to be an outdated expression of piety. Other more fashionable forms of patronage took over, such as chantry chapels, secular colleges and houses of friars. These new forms failed, however, to completely replace the older practice of patronage of religious houses. Convenience, dynastic tradition, prestige and status, and ancestral burial places were important factors for older families in the continuation of patronage of monastic houses and the reasons why they did not change their patronage patterns. For the newer gentry families that emerged after 1300, they chose the patronage of a religious house as their form of piety for a different reason – it was a symbol of their status in later medieval society and a buy-in to a prestigious tradition.[296]

Stöber's analysis, in addition to Gilchrist's and Thompson's earlier studies on nunneries, has concluded that in England and Wales the majority of nunnery founders were from the laity and, specifically, local gentry.[297] If Ireland's local kings are considered comparable in social class to the English gentry, then over half of nunnery founders in Ireland come from this social class. The remainder of the founders have a religious background. However, they too would have originated in the prominent elite classes of later medieval

Ireland. Unfortunately, a large percentage of founders of nunneries in later medieval Ireland still remain unknown. This is also true for England and Wales, where 'reading between the lines of the evidence for active lay patronage, the indication is that in reality there was much more patronal activity than was ever recorded or is now evident'.[298] The same might be concluded of the Irish evidence. Despite this lacuna, much can be learned when this data is coupled with the extant evidence of the female religious communities.

A crucial point has been made that while few elite women have been recorded in the actual establishment of a nunnery, 'it was common for women to participate in … the foundation of monasteries' and they may have been the driving force behind their male founders.[299] Indeed, charters and founder records may obscure female agency of foundation by only recording males, such as husbands' names, as it has been realised in several cases in England that a nunnery was usually positioned on land which formed part of the wife's dowry, interpreted as her influential role in the establishment of the house.[300] Additionally, it was fairly common practice that female relations of the founder would become active members of the community, usually rising to a position of authority. For example, Timolin nunnery was founded by Richard of Norragh, a relation of its first prioress, Lecelina. Walter Lynch founded a house in Galway in 1511 for his daughter. Killcreevanty was founded by the Ó Conchobhair (O'Conor) kings and staffed by family members. Killone – and probably St Peter's Cell also – was founded by the O'Briens and staffed by family members. Clonard was re-founded by Ua Mael Sechlainn – Agnes, the first abbess was his granddaughter.[301] The entrance of family members related to the nunneries' founder would have undoubtedly deepened the relationship between founder and nunnery.[302]

The overall pattern that emerges from an analysis of the founders of nunneries in later medieval Ireland is that the majority were founded by local kings, followed by prominent members of elite families. There was then a significant drop in other types of founders, for instance a saint or recluse, other religious houses, or episcopal. In just three documented cases women were associated with foundation: Cork, Lismullin and the Nuns' Church, Clonmacnoise. It is likely that many of the recorded male founders were encouraged and guided by influential women who remained in the historical background of such nunnery foundations, their agency masked by fathers, husbands or brothers. In several instances they may themselves have become prominent members of the female religious community.

Founders were motivated to found nunneries for their own spiritual well-being and, on a more practical level, to facilitate family members becoming nuns, for family burial, and in the management of family land given in the form of donations. It is not known how a site may have been assessed for suitability for the foundation of a nunnery, though there is a single instance, dated to 1171–5, where the process was recorded for a Cistercian male house in Ireland.[303] The episode illustrated how a suitably qualified member of the religious community first assessed a location for a foundation, obtained through donation or request. In the case of nunneries, however, the establishment process may have been different, perhaps being more informal and organic. It has been suggested that the location, uncertain affiliation and variable layout of many continental nunneries was due to the fact that patrons may have first provided existing structures for the re-use of new communities of female religious, only to be later formalised by a religious order and its architecture. This crucial difference in establishment between male and female religious houses provided a nunnery with a specific ethos and spiritual identity which was quite different from male monasteries from the outset (see Chapter 7).[304]

Dedications

It was usual for a monastery or nunnery to have been dedicated to a saint or a compound dedication to a number of saints. In over a third of nunneries in Ireland their dedication is now forgotten (Figure 3.10). This practice of religious house dedication began in the early medieval period when many of the founding saints were used as dedications and the practice has continued to the present day.[305] It has been shown that the dedication of a later medieval religious building was central to its iconography.[306] Gilchrist has analysed nunnery dedications in relation to cloister orientation, which could be to the north or south of the nunnery church, and realised a correlation between northern cloisters and dedication to a female saint.[307] Unfortunately for nunneries in Ireland, this type of analysis is impossible as the evidence currently does not exist and there are only three examples where the cloister orientation can be positively determined (see Chapter 5). In many instances, the dedication had an influence on the figure sculpture and interior decoration of the nunnery buildings and ultimately its dedication became part of the nunnery's identity (see Chapter 7).[308]

Mary is the most popular dedication of nunneries in Ireland, with thirty nunneries dedicated to her. All Cistercian houses, whether male or female religious, were dedicated to Mary, considered queen of heaven and earth,[309] as this was the dedication of the churches at Molesme and Cîteaux where the order originated.[310] Sometimes an additional dedication to St Benedict may have been added.[311] Most of the Augustinian of Arroasian observance houses in Ireland

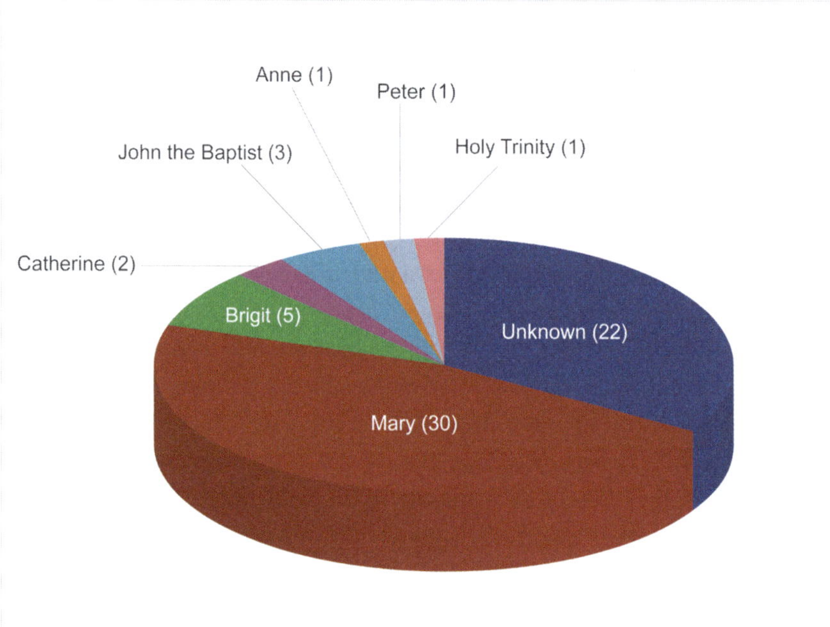

3.10 Dedications of later medieval nunneries in Ireland. Image: Tracy Collins and Frank Coyne.

were also dedicated to Mary 'to whom all Arroasian houses were dedicated'.[312] The Virgin Mary was an obvious choice in a dedication of a nunnery, and was very popular in the later middle ages throughout Europe,[313] and the choice likely mirrored the shifts in female piety and devotion previously mentioned.

Unsurprisingly, dedications to St Brigit,[314] a native female saint, were also popular, with five nunneries being dedicated to her. A dedication to St Brigit may indicate an early medieval origin for the nunnery, and while this is true in the cases of Kildare, Molough and Armagh, it is less clear for Kilbride and Odder.[315] Dedications to St Catherine[316] occur only twice, and St John the Baptist three times.[317] The remainder of the saintly dedications are used only once: St Anne[318] at Youghal and St Peter[319] at Limerick. The Augustinian house of Lismullin was dedicated to the Holy Trinity and is the only nunnery that had a non-saintly dedication.[320]

Saints Mary and Peter were considered universal saints of the church in the later medieval period and so were very common dedications at that time.[321] The numerous dedications to St Mary both at nunneries and monasteries of this period highlights the particular devotion that monastics and other religious had to Christ's mother. The cult of St Mary particularly suited the religious life as Mary personified duty, servitude and humility. She was also described as 'full of Grace', so in their devotion to her she could intercede directly with God. Moreover, as a human, chosen by God, she had a particular closeness with humankind which ensured a special fondness for her amongst Christians.[322]

The dedication to St Anne at Youghal could be considered to be an extension of the universal Marian devotion, as Anne was the mother of Mary. Saint Peter, although only having one dedication at Limerick, is considered in Christian doctrine to be a founder of the church. Saint John the Baptist might first be considered an unusual choice for a dedication of a nunnery.[323] However, in the Bible he was a pre-figure to Jesus and was the child of Elizabeth, cousin to Mary. Like Mary, he is considered an intercessor for Christians. Therefore, St John the Baptist is strongly associated with the cult of Mary and perhaps this is the reason he was chosen as a suitable dedication for a female religious community.

Notwithstanding the evidence for the use of St Brigit, the use of native saints in nunnery dedications was rare. St Mary *de Bello Portu* was the dedication of Kilculliheen but its name also maintained the name of the native St Cailchín.[324] While the patron and community may have had some influence in a nunnery's dedication, in particular cases, such as houses of Cistercian or Arroasian affiliation, it was the order's rule that took precedence, with both favouring the universal dedication of St Mary. This overview of the historical evidence for women, religious women, and the nunneries themselves now creates a firm basis for exploring the archaeology of nunneries. I will now consider the location of nunneries, presenting the siting and topography of female religious houses in Ireland and their associations with other forms of contemporary medieval settlement.

CHAPTER 4

Situating Nunneries in Later Medieval Ireland

DISTRIBUTION

Later medieval nunneries in Ireland are fairly evenly distributed throughout the country, although there are some areas which have none – mainly as a result of patronage patterns (Figure 4.1).[1] Nine modern counties had a single nunnery foundation.[2] County Sligo had two foundations, with six further counties each having three nunneries.[3] Cork, Dublin, Galway, Mayo and Offaly each had four nunneries. Counties Meath and Roscommon had the largest number of nunnery foundations throughout the later medieval period, each having eight nunneries. It is suggested that not all of these nunneries were in use contemporaneously, and it is estimated that a maximum of between twenty to thirty were operating at any one time. There are notable gaps. The counties of Antrim, Cavan, Donegal, Fermanagh, Kerry, Leitrim, Monaghan and Tyrone do not have any nunnery foundation within their modern borders.

It has been postulated that 'topographically difficult areas ... did not support many Celtic monasteries, nor were there monasteries attracted there after the twelfth-century church reform'.[4] This is perhaps an over-simplification, as peninsular Kerry, for example, is particularly rich in early ecclesiastical and monastic remains,[5] and Donegal,[6] Fermanagh,[7] Leitrim[8] and Monaghan[9] are also rich in various forms of ecclesiastical heritage. Rather, as has been already suggested, the wide distribution of female religious houses in later medieval Ireland was influenced by patronage, ruling elites, their lordships and boundaries. It is likely that links and networks developed between nunneries – and indeed between nunneries and monasteries – of the same patron and perhaps affiliation. This clustering effect has been noted in religious houses elsewhere, being formed through the motivations and social links which joined the founders.[10] Nunneries in Ireland have been grouped into clusters: Clonard, Killone, Kilcreevanty and Gaelic houses, and Anglo-Irish foundations based on historical sources such as the 1195 papal confirmation of possessions of Clonard.[11] This method is of some use in assessing nunneries and their

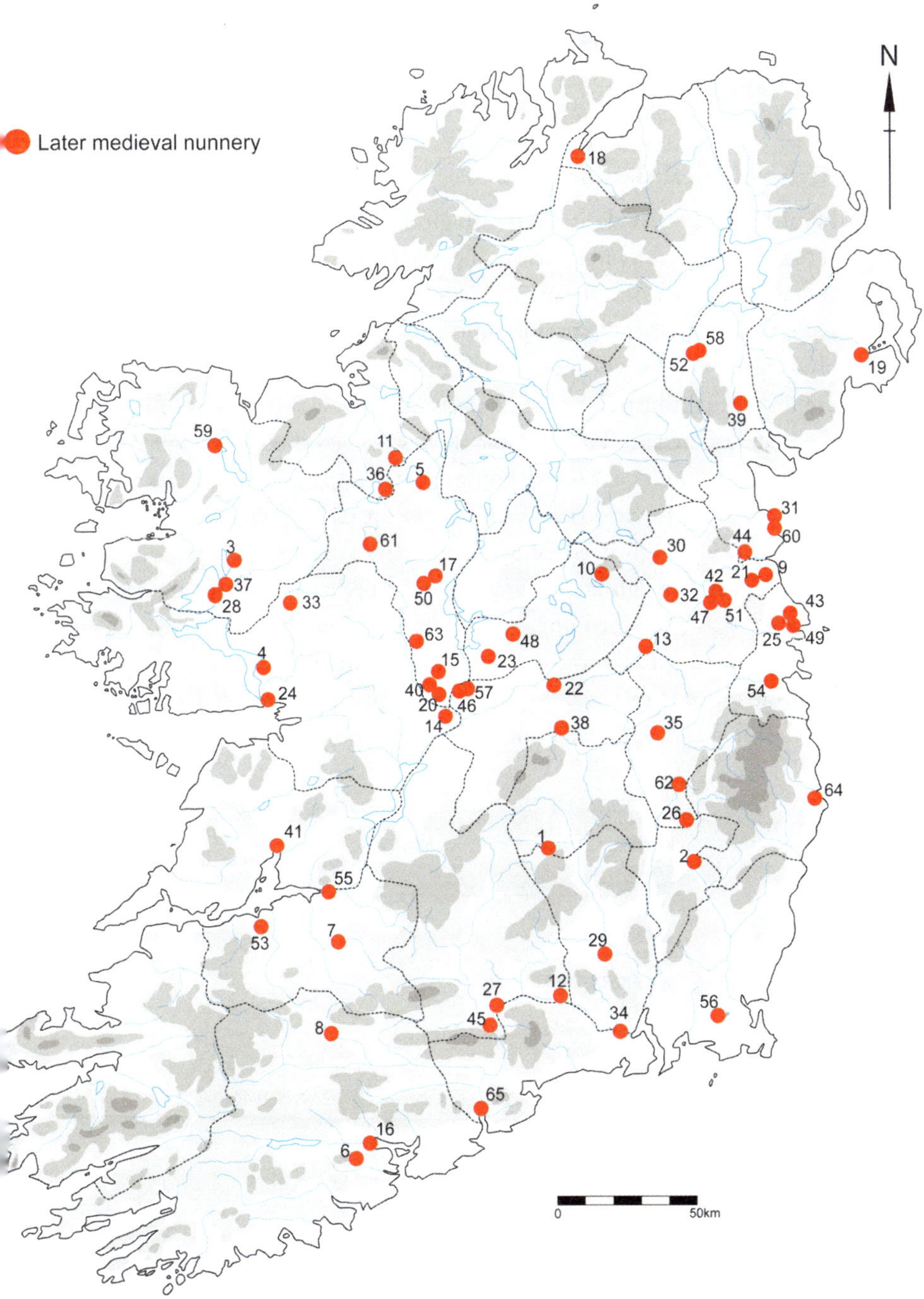

4.1 Distribution of nunneries in Ireland. Image: Tracy Collins and Frank Coyne.

possible connections in a fluid way, but these groups have nothing distinctive archaeologically. Furthermore, some nunneries appear in more than one group due to changing circumstances over time, so that there are significant overlaps within this type of grouping.

Archaeological classifications

Nunneries are listed as archaeological monuments,[12] but many are not actually classified as nunneries; and they can be found in nineteen separate archaeological classifications.[13] This is understandable, as the identification of a site with an archaeological monument type is usually based on the standing physical remains at the site, which may vary considerably from its original use. Figure 4.2 illustrates current archaeological classifications of nunneries on the island of Ireland. For example, Killevy is classified as a single Augustinian nunnery and Odder as a tower house (Figure 4.3). Seven nunneries are classified as churches.[14] Downpatrick is classified as a Cistercian nunnery, and Derry, a convent. Caltragh is classified as an ecclesiastical enclosure, while the two nunneries at Armagh and Fooran are classified as ecclesiastical sites. Kilbride is classified as a fortified house, while three nunneries at Galway, Duleek and Kells are classified as elements of the historic towns.

Nine separate categories of religious house are recorded. Three nunneries are classified as Augustinian canons: Roscommon, Termonfeckin and Durrow,

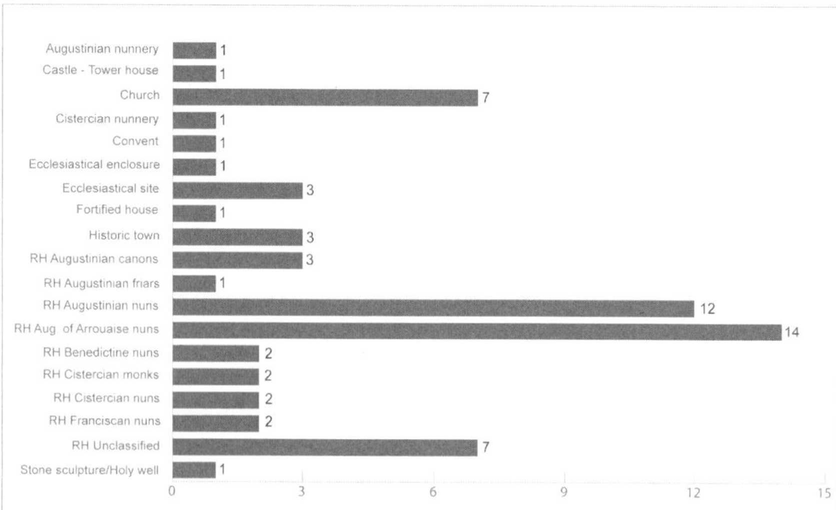

4.2 Classifications of nunneries in Ireland (RH: religious house; after data from Archaeological Survey of Ireland and Northern Ireland Sites and Monuments Record). Image: Tracy Collins and Frank Coyne.

4.3 Odder, Co. Meath is classified as a fortified house or a tower house. Its rear façade shows early fabric has been incorporated into the later structures. Image: Frank Coyne.

4.4 Nunneries exhibit a variety of archaeological classifications, as at Youghal, Co. Cork (*left*) and Carrick-on-Suir, Co. Tipperary. Image: Tracy Collins and Frank Coyne.

while the nunnery at Cork is supposed to be near the Augustinian friary of Red Abbey. Twelve sites are classified as Augustinian nuns,[15] and a further fourteen are Arroasian nuns.[16] Just two sites are classified as Benedictine: Kilcreevanty and Wicklow. Two sites related to Cistercian nuns are only classified under monks – Jerpoint and Mellifont – though Inishlounaght and Plary are classified as Cistercian nuns. There are two religious houses for Franciscan nuns recorded at Youghal and Carrick-on-Suir (Figure 4.4). Seven sites identified as nunneries have been categorised as unclassified religious houses,[17] and Calliaghstown is classified as a stone sculpture at a holy well (Figure 7.36). In this book I have taken the broadest approach possible regarding classification. I am deliberately less concerned with the order of the nunnery, as this has been shown to be a problematic distinction in other regions.[18] I have considered all the sites as nunneries first and foremost, and have analysed them as a diverse group on that primary basis.

Co-located religious houses

True double houses as they occurred in medieval England and France are not thought to have been founded in Ireland.[19] However, the classifications outlined highlight an interesting phenomenon: that nuns were recorded at several male religious houses, and both groups may have shared facilities. Most of these relate to the Augustinian of Arroasian observance. Flanagan coined the term 'co-located' for these houses of nuns and canons living adjacent to each other and perhaps sharing a church.[20] This is a useful term, as it first distinguishes them from 'double houses' or mixed communities of the early period in Ireland and, second, differentiates the Irish sites from the double houses of the later medieval period in England, some of which had a distinctive arrangement such as twin cloisters, as at the Gilbertine house at Watton, Yorkshire (Figure 4.5).[21]

4.5 Ground plan of the Gilbertine house at Watton, Yorkshire. After Gilyard Beer, 1959. Reproduced with permission of the Historic England Archive.

4.6 Annaghdown, Co. Galway ecclesiastical complex, possibly a co-located house for a time. Possible location of nunnery indicated. Re-drawn from first-edition six-inch Ordnance Survey map. Image: Frank Coyne.

Co-location was pragmatic, as a nunnery required at least one priest to celebrate the sacraments. They may have been experimental and a time-limited phenomenon, as several co-locations seem to have become single-sexed after a time, most becoming so by the end of the twelfth century. For example, Termonfeckin became a female house, while Annaghdown, exclusively male (Figure 4.6). It has been postulated that the Annaghdown nuns moved to Inishmaine. The nuns from Durrow moved to the nunnery at Killeigh, although there was also an Augustinian (and later Franciscan) male house there. Co-location occurred elsewhere, as at Swine in Yorkshire, England, where a mixed female and male Cistercian community lived for a time.[22] Another example is the Benedictine abbey at Bec in Normandy, France, which is of particular interest as Bec's original foundation at Bonneville was located on the dower lands of Heloise, the founder's mother, who herself later retired to the monastery.[23]

Eleven Augustinian male religious houses have recorded nuns nearby.[24] These co-located sites, considering their number, have left remarkably little

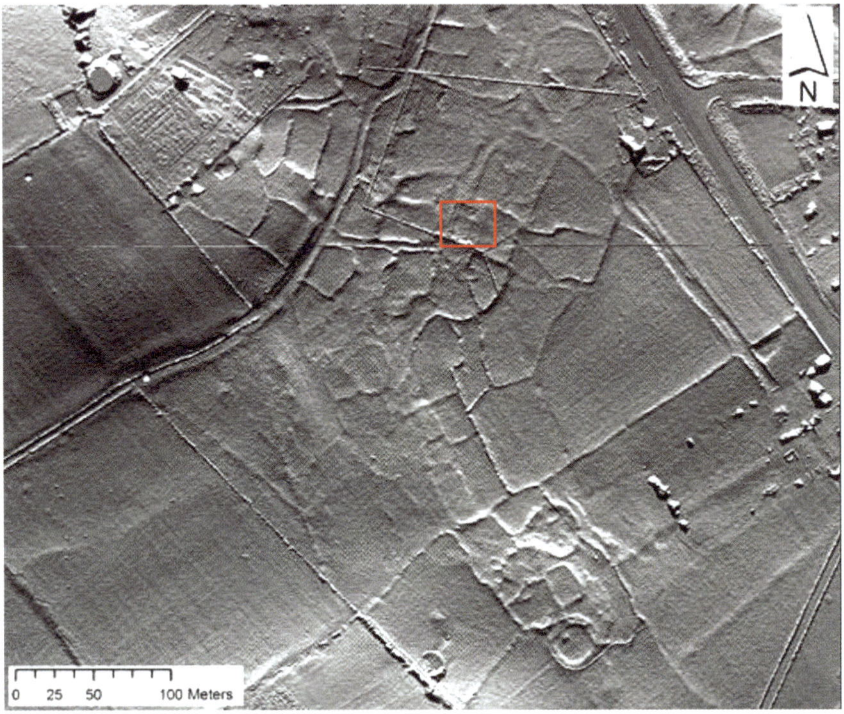

4.7 Ardcarn, Co. Roscommon, LiDAR image. Nunnery location indicated. Courtesy of Dr S. Davis, School of Archaeology, UCD.

trace in the Irish archaeological record.[25] For example, at Termonfeckin and Clonfert the nunnery locations are known, and are thought to have been adjacent to but separate from the male religious houses. At other Augustinian male religious houses, nunnery churches are known, as at Clonmacnoise[26] (the Nuns' Church and Temple Finghin) and Annaghdown. At Ardcarn, the location of the nunnery can be estimated, but the precise location of the male religious house remains unclear (Figure 4.7). It was described in the sixteenth century as a church with two houses of stone, perhaps one each for canons and nuns.[27] The remainder – Clonard, Derrane, Duleek, Durrow, Kells and Roscommon – have no extant trace of the nunneries. Geophysical surveys at Clonard have revealed anomalies which are very suggestive of later medieval monastic buildings (Figure 4.8).[28]

Other connections with nunneries and Augustinian male religious houses are more tentative. For example, the nunneries at Armagh were physically close to Augustinian canons, as was the nunnery at Killeigh. Kilcreevanty, even though at some distance from the Augustinian abbey at Cong, had several historical connections to it.[29] Nuns are recorded at Skreen which also had a

4.8 Clonard, Co. Meath. Aerial view after Google Earth. © Maxar Technologies 17/1/2020.

house of Augustinian friars.[30] The nunnery at Cork is thought to have been close to the Augustinian friary of Red Abbey,[31] and Templenagalliaghdoo church is situated on a peninsula in close proximity to Errew. The Cistercian nunnery known as Plary apparently used the services of Augustinian canons, though this as yet cannot be confirmed.[32]

Three further sites are considered co-located communities of monks and nuns: Inishlounaght, Jerpoint and Mellifont (Figure 4.9). Nuns are only known at these sites through Stephen of Lexington, who made a visitation to those monasteries in 1228 and objected strenuously to the proximity of female religious.[33] Suggestions have been made as to where the nuns were located.[34] Gilchrist thought that a separate nunnery church should be expected and the *capella ante portas* at Jerpoint was suggested as a suitable location for the nuns. There is also a substantial deserted medieval settlement or manorial village with a parish church dedicated to St Nicholas, to the northwest of the abbey (Figure 4.10).[35] Although there is no conclusive evidence, it is possible that nuns

4.9 Jerpoint, Co. Kilkenny, Mellifont, Co. Louth, and Inishlounaght, Co. Tipperary (*from left to* where nuns are known to have lived, through the letters of Stephen of Lexington in 1228.

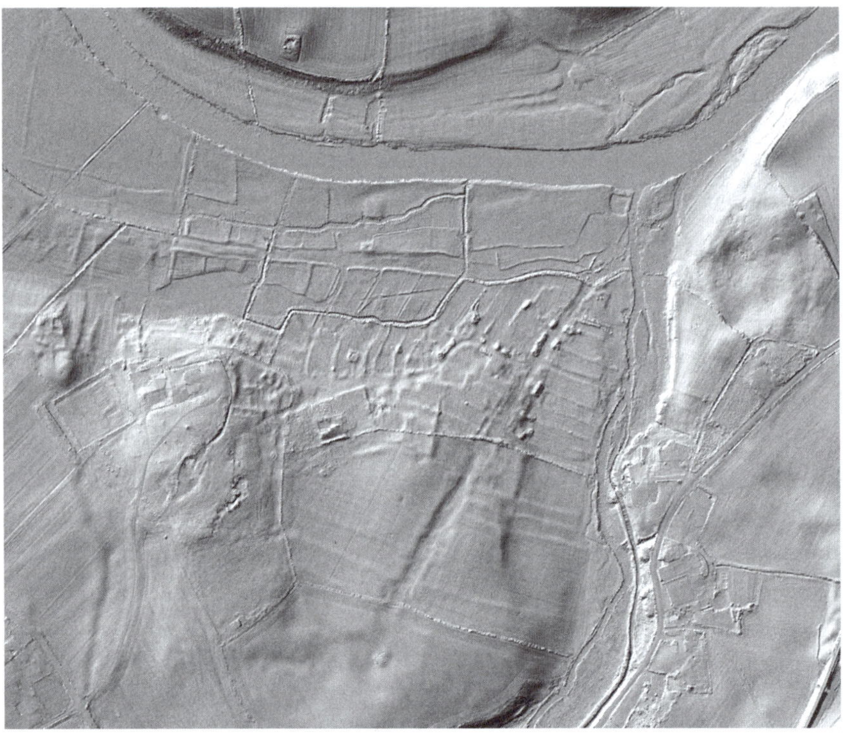

4.10 LiDAR image of Newtown, Jerpoint, Co. Kilkenny; a manorial village settlement adjacent to Jerpoint Abbey and a tentative possible location for the nuns recorded there. Reproduced with permission of the Heritage Council of Ireland/the Discovery Programme.

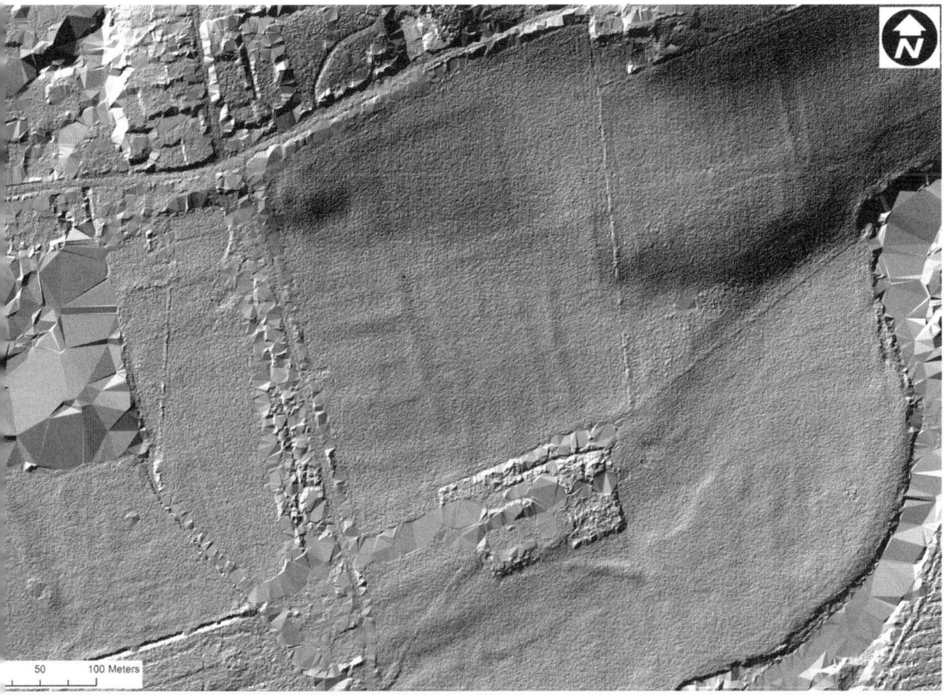

4.11 Inishlounaght, Co. Tipperary, LiDAR image. Courtesy of Dr S. Davis, School of Archaeology, UCD.

were attached to the parish church in this settlement, as occurred at several parish churches in England, for example the Cistercian nunnery at Swine, which functioned as a parish church from its foundation.[36]

It has been speculated that at Mellifont, the *curtis* of nuns within which was located the abbot's quarters recorded by Stephen of Lexington corresponded to a courtyard of Augustinian nuns.[37] Excavations at Mellifont did not yield any evidence of nuns, but it is tempting to suggest Mellifont's gatehouse as a possible location.[38] Mellifont, like Jerpoint, has an adjacent deserted settlement, across the river Mattock in the townland of Hurcle, and this settlement may have housed a small community of nuns, although there are no remains of a church known at this location.[39]

No one has speculated on where the nunnery at Inishlounaght was located, despite the fact that indiscretions of the monks there were immortalised in the poem *The Land of Cokaygne*.[40] There is now no extant trace of either of the religious houses at Inishlounaght, apart from a doorway and two medieval graveslabs incorporated into the Church of Ireland church and graveyard at Marlfield (Figure 4.11). It is suggested that at these co-located sites the church was likely shared, with the religious communities being segregated from each other and the laity.[41] Little is yet known archaeologically about these co-located sites in Ireland or how segregation would have been achieved. Similarly, nothing is yet known of the domestic lives and accommodation utilised by the female religious communities which were in close proximity to their male counterparts.[42]

SITING AND TOPOGRAPHY

In Britain, there have been several studies on the siting of medieval religious houses generally.[43] There has been detailed landscape-type studies on specific orders, such as the Augustinians,[44] on Yorkshire nunneries,[45] and specific sites such as Bordesley Abbey,[46] Stanley Abbey[47] and Strata Florida.[48] In contrast, there have been fewer published studies in Ireland, and those concentrate on Cistercian houses.[49] The location of nunneries in the medieval landscape of England may have been influenced by concepts of strict enclosure and segregation of religious women, which encouraged isolation.[50] There, deliberate isolation may have been sought out by nunneries as a pre-condition. The Cistercian General Chapter in 1216 set down that a nunnery had to be at least six leagues[51] (29.4km) from a male abbey and ten (49km) from another nunnery,[52] though from archaeological evidence this was rarely achieved in practice.[53] The double houses of the Premonstratensians were separated by an

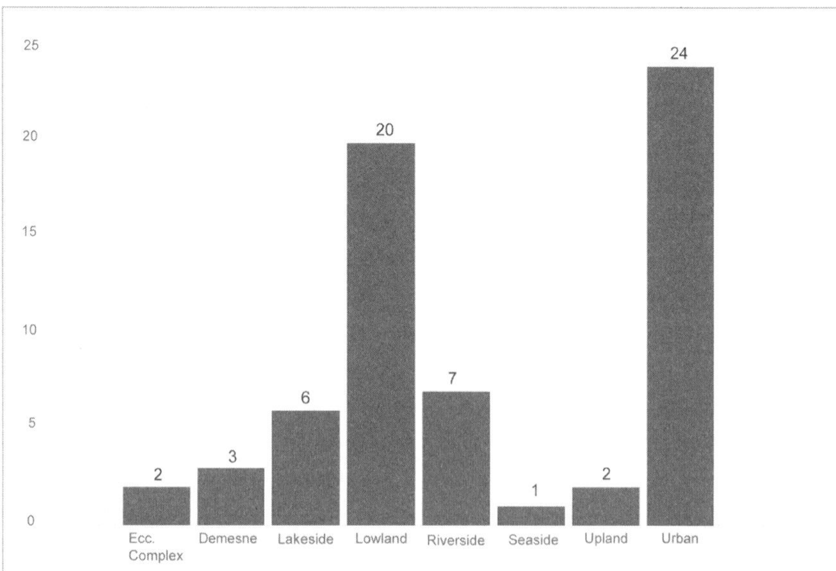

4.12 Siting and topography of later medieval nunneries in Ireland. Image: Tracy Collins and Frank Coyne.

4.13 Killevy, Co. Armagh, on the slopes of Slieve Gullion, is the highest nunnery in Ireland. Aerial view after Google Earth. © CNES/Airbus 25/4/20.

order in 1137 that nuns should be at least a league away from canons, although it has been noted that many of the unofficial double houses had already been disbanded in England by this time.[54]

Nunneries achieved isolation in medieval England by being situated on islands or peninsulas, such as the Poor Clares of Denny Abbey in the Cambridgeshire fens.[55] There are no definite later medieval nunneries on islands in Ireland, though Inishmaine (which may have once been a large island) and Templenagalliaghdoo are now located on lakeshore peninsulas. Rules on distance are not specifically recorded for nunneries in Ireland,[56] and an analysis of distance between nunneries and other religious houses has suggested that orders' rules on distance were rarely achieved in practice. When the location of a monastery was chosen, siting and topography were key practical criteria and it is likely that it also had some ideological aspect. Suitable ground conditions for construction and proximity to water were essential requirements.[57]

It is clear that nunneries in Ireland were situated in a variety of locations (Figure 4.12; Table 4.1). The height above sea level of later medieval nunneries averaged 55m, but this masks a significant variation from 10m to 230m above sea level. The highest nunnery is Killevy on the southeastern slopes of Slieve Gullion (Figure 4.13).[58] The majority of nunneries are well below the 60m

Table 4.1 Nunneries' heights above sea level and distinctive topography.

Height Above Sea Level	*Nunnery*	*Topography**
010m	Carrick-on-Suir	Urban (sub)
010m	Grace Dieu	Lowland pasture
010m	Portrane	Seaside
010m	St Catherine's	Lowland pasture
010m	Templenagalliaghdoo	Lakeside (Conn)
015m	Cork	Urban
015m	Termonfeckin	Urban
018m	Annaghdown	Lakeside (Corrib)
020m	Buttevant	Urban
020m	Downpatrick	Urban
020m	Inishlounaght	Riverside (Suir)
020m	Killone	Lakeside (Killone)
020m	Lusk	Urban
020m	St Mary de Hogges	Urban (sub)
022m	Inishmaine	Lakeside (Lough Mask)
025m	Annagh	Lakeside (Carra)
025m	Calliaghstown	Lowland pasture
025m	Duleek	Urban
025m	Galway	Urban
025m	Killeenatrava	Urban (sub)
030m	Jerpoint	Riverside (Little Arrigle)
030m	St Peter's Cell	Urban
035m	Kellystown	Lowland pasture
035m	Lismullin	Demesne
040m	Derry	Urban
040m	Kilcreevanty	Riverside (Clare)
040m	Kilculliheen	Urban (sub)
040m	Molough	Riverside (Suir, suburban)
040m	Youghal	Urban (sub)
045m	Clonfert	Lowland
045m	St Brigit's	Urban

* Urban and suburban relates to medieval towns, both walled and unwalled. Land descriptions have been based on the Ordnance Survey first-edition six-inch maps (dated to 1830s to the late 1840s) to avoid modern interventions such as drainage in addition to site inspections. In many cases, the location may include a number of criteria, such as near a river and in or near a town, such as Kilculliheen. In these instances, for the purpose of analysis only one type has been chosen.

Table 4.1. *(continued)*

Height Above Sea Level	*Nunnery*	*Topography*
045m	Temple na Ferta	Urban
050m	Caltragh	Lakeside (Lene)
050m	Nuns' Church	Ecclesiastical complex (riverside, Shannon)
050m	Temple Finghin	Ecclesiastical complex (riverside, Shannon)
050m	Timolin	Urban
055m	Derrane	Lowland pasture
060m	Cloonoghil	Lowland (lake floodplain)
060m	Roscommon	Urban
060m	Wicklow	Urban
065m	Durrow	Demesne
065m	Killinmulrooney	Lowland (rough pasture)
070m	Aghade	Lowland pasture
070m	Ardcarn	Lowland (ecclesiastical complex?)
070m	Clonard	Riverside (Kilwarden)
070m	Drumalgagh	Lowland pasture
070m	Taghmon	Urban
075m	Plary	Lowland pasture
075m	Tisrara	Lowland pasture
080m	Ballynagallagh	Lowland (Red Bog)
080m	Kells	Urban
080m	Mellifont	Riverside (Mattock)
083m	Kilbride	Demesne
085m	Fooran	Lowland pasture
090m	Killeigh	Urban
090m	Termonkeelin	Lowland pasture (next to bog)
095m	Killaraght	Lowland pasture
095m	Odder	Lowland pasture
100m	Addrigoole	Lowland pasture
100m	Graney	Riverside (Graney)
100m	Kildare	Urban
110m	Ballymacdane	Lowland pasture
120m	Skreen	Urban
150m	Carricknahorna	Upland lower mountain slopes (Bricklieves)
230m	Killevy	Upland lower mountain slopes (Slieve Gullion 1798m)

contour in lowlands, river valleys, lake shores or towns. It is thus concluded that – excepting perhaps two nunneries above the 150m contour – site elevation was not a contributing factor in the site choice and other topographic factors were relevant. Land quality does not appear to have been a significant factor either in siting, and the majority of nunneries were located in an urban or suburban environment or on more rural lowland pasture of varying quality.

Nunneries are found in modern rural locations, adjacent to major rivers, beside lakes, and three are associated with later demesne landscapes.[59] Portrane is the only nunnery in a rural location by the sea. The distinctive topographic feature of some twenty-six nunneries is that they are located in what is considered a medieval urban/suburban environment or a large ecclesiastical complex.[60] This is in stark contrast to the English evidence, where urban locations were avoided. One reason for this marked difference is that in turbulent later medieval Ireland, protection and security were important considerations for the location of a nunnery.[61]

Land capability and self-sufficiency

It remains a common perception that nunneries were located on poorer land and were generally 'less fortunate' than their male counterparts.[62] In some specific instances in England this was certainly true, where problems such as fires and flooding were commonplace.[63] It has been demonstrated elsewhere, however, that nunneries were not particularly disadvantaged in land terms in comparison to many houses of Augustinian canons or friars.[64] The association of poorer land with certain religious orders perhaps reflects a bias in earlier scholarship in favour of the Cistercians, who specialised in an agricultural economy as an important part of their religious ethos. As a result, Cistercian houses tended to favour better land away from centres of habitation.[65] Cistercian male houses in Ireland are found in a variety of environments, but distinctly favoured the freely drained soils of the south and east of the country, though there are notable exceptions. For example, Corcomroe, County Clare and Abbeyknockmoy, County Galway were situated on poorer soils in the west, though were on the better-quality land in both these areas.[66]

The vast majority of nunneries are located on land that has a wide land use capability, in the south, east and midland regions (Figure 4.14).[67] The remainder are situated on land that is considered to have limited land use capability. However, even this land is suitable mainly for grazing and probably smaller units of tillage. No nunnery is situated where land use capability has been designated 'very limited' or 'extremely limited'.[68] When nunnery location is considered in conjunction with agricultural regions of Ireland, the majority

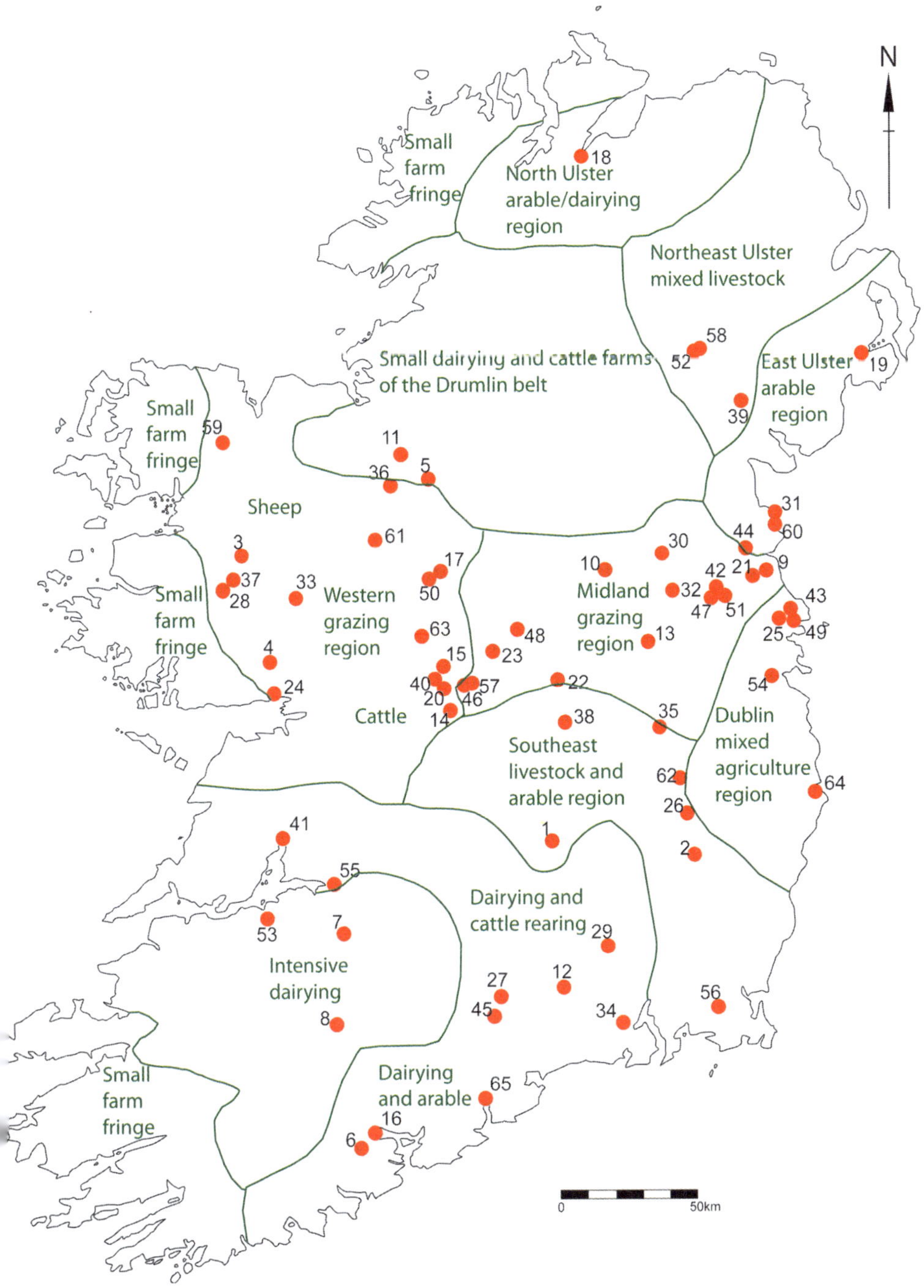

4.14 Distribution of nunneries in relation to modern agricultural regions in Ireland. Image: Tracy Collins and Frank Coyne.

correspond to the grazing and arable regions which stretch across the central portion of the country. A number of nunneries are located within the intensive dairying and cattle-rearing regions of counties Limerick, Cork, Tipperary and Waterford. Therefore, for later medieval nunneries in Ireland it is concluded that they were not positioned in liminal or marginal positions on poorer land. All are located on land that has a limited to wide land use capability which is suitable for grazing of sheep, cattle, some tillage and in some cases intensive dairying. It is likely that the land was used seasonally and in rotation for both animal husbandry and some arable farming.

The differences in the land fertility of a religious house site, then, may have originated in the spiritual ethos of the particular order. The Augustinians were canons – ordained priests who followed a regular life[69] – with friars being introduced slightly later.[70] As such, their spiritual ethos differed from monks, and they concentrated on pastoral work within a community. Thus, the Augustinians preferred sites from which they could follow this ethos, and they located their houses closer to habitation centres and were less concerned with good soils and isolation.[71] Therefore, the perception that nunneries and male religious orders, such as the friars, were disadvantaged, as they may have been situated on poorer land, is false. Even in the case of some Cistercian houses, such as the important foundation of Mellifont, remedial construction works had to be undertaken due to the soft ground on which the church had been built,[72] indicating that other factors, not least of all patronage, were also important considerations in the siting of a religious house.[73]

The siting and land acquisition of male religious houses was particularly important as they were expected to be self-sufficient and produce a surplus.[74] The traditional view of nunneries is that they too were expected to be self-sufficient.[75] However, other scholarship has suggested that there is no strong evidence to confirm that self-sufficiency was expected of nunneries in the same way as male houses. Rather, records show that nunneries were mainly consumers, rather than producers. Moreover, means were not provided at foundation for self-sufficiency, suggesting that patrons never expected nunneries to be self-supporting.[76] Self-sufficiency, however, was a major tenet of medieval monasticism and so it was unusual that such a tenet was not adhered to, at least in certain larger nunneries. This has led to the conclusion that self-sufficiency was not as important a consideration for female religious houses as for male houses.[77]

For instance, nuns did not generally undertake manual work as lay brothers or *conversi* in male houses were expected to do,[78] and so had no requirement to be close to their farmland, which instead could be farmed by labourers, leased or rented. Nunneries employed bailiffs, stewards, attorneys and labourers to manage much of this work, as well as servants.[79] The hiring of officials was a wider monastic strategy rather than a purely female one for managing property, in medieval France at least.[80] As nunneries were not expected to produce all of the community's food requirements, much of this would have to be purchased and so proximity to markets was also important.[81] These differing priorities of nunneries in relation to male religious houses had a bearing on their siting and this is reflected in the evidence from Ireland.

Water sources

Easy access to a water supply was a primary requirement for the foundation and continuation of any religious house.[82] It has been noted that most Cistercian houses in Ireland were located along major rivers, particularly at their confluence with smaller tributaries.[83] Water was required for the functioning of the religious house, and larger water bodies would also have been used as routeways. Most of the nunneries in Ireland are also located on or near an obvious water source, with several located near major rivers such as the Shannon and the Suir (Figure 4.15).[84] It is reasonable to suggest that the rivers supplied water to the adjacent nunneries. Water was obviously used for drinking, cooking and washing, but was also required for domestic sanitation, agriculture, fishponds, and hydraulic power creation for mills. In many friaries,

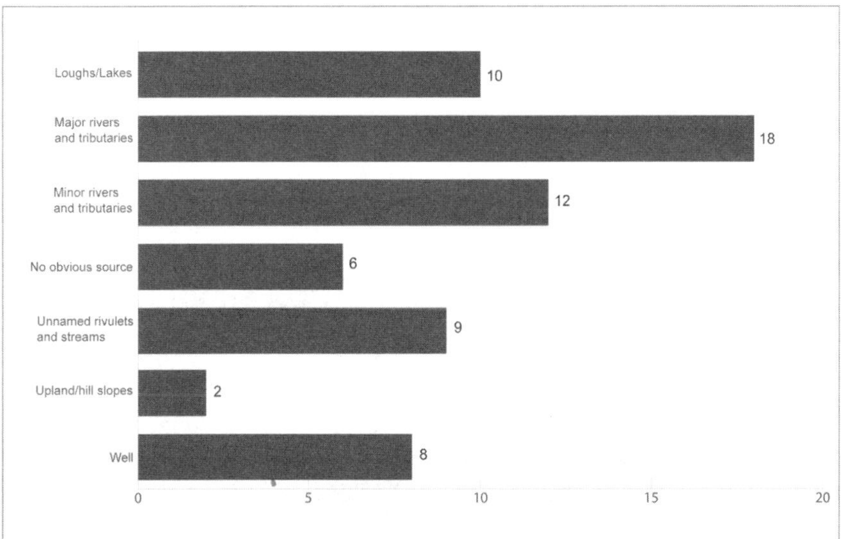

4.15 Siting of nunneries in relation to water sources in Ireland. Image: Tracy Collins and Frank Coyne.

4.16 One of two extant footbridges at St Catherine's, Co. Limerick. Although it shows evidence of repair, it is likely to be of medieval date and contemporary with the nunnery. Image: Tracy Collins.

4.17 Killone, Co. Clare, situated adjacent to Killone and Ballybeg Loughs, from southwest. Image: Frank Coyne.

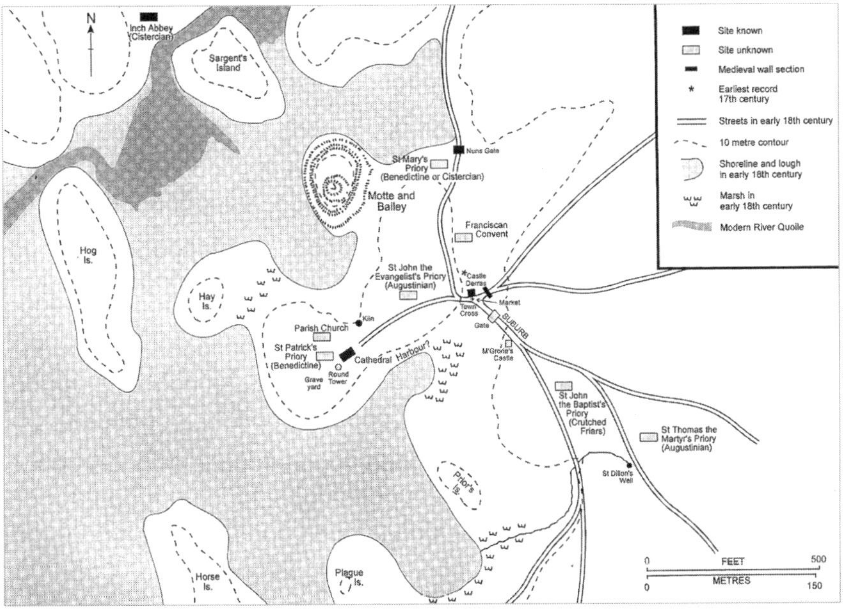

4.18 Medieval Downpatrick, Co. Down. Nunnery labelled as St Mary's Priory. Reproduced with permission of the IHTA.

a single water source was put to several uses within a complex, such as at Moyne, County Mayo.

Waterways also functioned as routeways for travel, communication and commerce. In addition, they were a food source for the religious house, providing fish and other foodstuffs such as greens and herbs. There are records of friaries owning boats for fishing, for example Holy Trinity Priory, County Sligo, or for use as a ferry, as at the male Franciscan house at Youghal.[85] There are no extant records for the use of boats by nunneries. However, the inferred economic strength of Kilculliheen in historical evidence suggests that it may have utilised boats on the river Suir and that a ferry may have been in operation across the river from the nunnery to the town.[86]

Grace Dieu and St Catherine's are interesting as they have retained evidence for water management in the form of directed streams and bridges, and both are situated just 4km from large estuaries that have access to the sea (Figure 4.16).[87] Killone is one of ten nunneries that are on lakeshores, and it stands picturesquely at a narrowing between two loughs (Figure 4.17).

Several nunneries appear to have used wells as a water source and some are venerated now as holy wells, as at Calliaghstown.[88] The nunnery at Downpatrick may have used a well, as some are noted in the town. However, the river Quoile in the medieval period was much wider than today and formed a lake known as Lough Cuan to the west of Downpatrick and so it is possible that water from this lake was also utilised (Figure 4.18).[89] Wells have been found through excavation from religious houses, for example the well at the Augustinian Victorine house at Bridgetown, County Cork, that was located in the cloister ambulatory outside the processional doorway into the nave of the church.[90] A well was discovered near the north range of the Franciscan friary at Ennis, County Clare,[91] and wells are associated with several other mendicant houses.[92]

Routeways

Roads and waterways are a common location of nunneries and the majority are found either in urban or suburban environments and/or along important rivers. The same is true of English nunneries, which 'were often on the rivers and roads which formed main routes of communication into towns'.[93] Excepting those nunneries that are already located in or adjacent to medieval towns and settlements, and those on navigable rivers and lakes, there is a small but significant number that were associated with early routes, many of which are indicated on early mapping but which are now no longer extant (Table 4.2).

4.19 Termonkeelin, Co. Roscommon, and its associated routeway 'ancient road', connecting it to a church site in Termonmore townland to the south. Re-drawn from first-edition six-inch Ordnance Survey map. Image: Frank Coyne.

Table 4.2 Nunneries associated with older routeways.*

Nunnery	*Evidence of Route and Source*	*Description*
Ardcarn	Line of track labelled 'ancient road' marked on first and second edition of the six-inch OS map.	Traverses in southwest direction from nunnery site and terminates at a small circular enclosure. Midway along the track is a second large circular enclosure classified as a ringfort in the townland of Rusheen (RO006-149).
Cloonoghil	Track marked within nunnery complex.	Difficult to identify on the ground though would seem to provide access to church.
Termonkeelin	Line of track labelled 'ancient road' marked on first and second edition of the six-inch OS map.	Traverses in a southeast direction from nunnery site and terminates at a church site in the adjoining townland of Termonmore (RO026-034). This church site has been associated with an early female saint.
Tisrara	Line of track not marked on any six-inch OS map though is visible on the ground.	A section of a sunken roadway runs east from the graveyard for about 100m and would appear to now form part of the access road to the west of the complex. The destination for the route is no longer known.
Killaraght	Indicated on the 1914 (second-edition) six-inch OS map.	Linear feature running from nunnery complex in a northeast direction towards border with Co. Roscommon towards Boyle. It runs for some 750m and is 10m width flanked by field boundaries. Southwestern end now has no above-ground register.
Grace Dieu	An ancient road leading to Swords was still extant in the eighteenth century, 'paved with a reddish stone whereon are several small bridges'.	Roadway no longer visible. Remnants of one of the bridges does remain.
Nuns' Church and Temple Finghin Clonmacnoise	First-edition six-inch OS map and later showing 'pilgrim's road' passing Nuns' Church at eastern side of monastic complex. Annalistic references and archaeological investigations revealed a bridge in river Shannon crossing to Co. Roscommon. Roadway in Co. Roscommon leading to bridge site.	Pilgrim's road runs across the 'patron green' in the old and new cemeteries paved with large flat stones. Continues to the Nuns' Church which has a tarred surface between the church and 'the carn of the three crosses'. This section mentioned in the annals as being laid down by abbot Breasal Conailleach in 1026. Road used to run much further east than Nuns' Church and sections can also be identified in the townlands of Ballyduff and Clonascra. Annalistic reference in the *Annals of Clonmacnoise* for the year 1158 refer to a bridge, which was proven to exist in its early medieval form – remains were dated to the ninth century – during archaeological investigations in 1994. Road in Co. Roscommon leads through boggy terrain to river directly opposite the complex of Clonmacnoise.

Table 4.2 *(continued)*

Nunnery	*Evidence of Route and Source*	*Description*
Ballynagallagh	'*Cladh na Leac*' noted on early maps.	This routeway to the northwest of the nunnery is traditionally thought to have connected Ballynagallagh and another nunnery, now the location of the RC church at Grange. Tradition notes that the nuns from both communities regularly met at Holy Cross crossroads via *Cladh na leac*
St Catherine's	Modern road leading to church site historically connected to Old Abbey.	There are no routeways associated with this site that are recorded archaeologically. However, when cartographic evidence is used it is postulated that the very straight road leading northward from Old Abbey to Robertstown church (once in the ownership of the nunnery) is the likely remains of the medieval routeway to that church. This road forms the townland boundaries of Robertstown on its north and east sides. It is also possible that the stream course to the south of the nunnery may also have been used as a routeway though this is much more tentative. This route provides fairly direct access to the church site of Kilmoylan (though this church is not recorded as being in the possession of the nunnery; it possessed Dunmoylan further south).

* Further routeways can be identified in the hinterland of the nunneries of Caltragh, Clonard, Plary, Killone, Lismullin, and Odder. In all these cases the routeways have been considered and then discounted. In all cases it can be estimated that the routes either pre-date the nunneries and do not appear to be associated with the nunnery site itself. For example, the tracks identified near Lismullin and Odder are situated on the Hill of Tara which lies to the east of both locations.

For example, Termonkeelin nunnery was connected to another church to the south, in the townland of Termonmore, which itself has an association with a female saint (Figure 4.19).[94] Ballynagallagh is connected to a possible second nunnery, now marked by Grange church, by the *Cladh na Leac* (Figure 4.20). Clonmacnoise might be considered to be the destination rather than a point along a route. The 'Pilgrim's Road' runs in an easterly direction from the main complex to the Nuns' Church. The route follows a natural esker and can be identified in the townlands of Ballyduff and Clonascra to the east. This feature has an archaeological register and is referred to in historical records. Indeed, it is known that many other toghers and roadways, many of which were surfaced with gravel, exist in the bog lands surrounding Clonmacnoise.[95]

It would appear that these roads led pilgrims to Clonmacnoise and, in the case of the Pilgrim's Road, passed by one of the nunneries there. A second

4.20 Ballynagallagh, Co. Limerick, and the Cladh na Leac to the north and west. Re-drawn from historic mapping. Image: Frank Coyne.

routeway associated with Clonmacnoise is located in the adjoining county of Roscommon in Coolumber townland, which runs from higher ground in the east, across low-lying boggy terrain to the right (west) bank of the river Shannon. It is likely that this route provided access to both the river and the ecclesiastical complex beyond via a bridge in the medieval period. This bridge was confirmed archaeologically (Figure 4.21).[96] Temple Finghin is close to the location of this bridge, being situated on the northern side of the ecclesiastical complex. The ecclesiastical complex at Clonmacnoise is important in regard to routeway connections, and in being a destination. It became a strategic hub situated at the junction of the river Shannon and the east–west route facilitated by the bridge, which has been demonstrated to have connected many religious houses, and 'meant that it had relatively easy access to the outside world throughout the medieval period'.[97] The nunneries at Clonmacnoise may not

4.21 Clonmacnoise, Co. Offaly. Aerial view with Pilgrims' Road and Nuns' Church in trees bey Below, further medieval routeways in vicinity, including location of the medieval bridge a the river Shannon. Nunneries indicated with stars. Upper image © National Monuments Ser Department of Housing, Local Government and Heritage. Lower image after Shee Twohig, © Royal Society of Antiquaries of Ireland.

have been the prime motivation for such communication networks, but they were an intrinsic part of the religious fabric at Clonmacnoise throughout the medieval period.

Furthermore, communications in the form of waterways, routeways and rights-of-way were also important in the functioning of monastic estates (Chapter 9). Dimensions of these routes are recorded in contemporary accounts in England, where some rights-of-way were described variously as wide as 20 feet, two loaded wagons wide, or four perches.[98] Monastic routeways were the backbone of that country's infrastructure until the advent of the turnpike road system and in some cases monastic houses planned for this network, where they first secured rights-of-way which connected lands that only later became important.[99] Monastic effort in England also improved transport through ferries, bridges, causeways, canals, ports and harbours.[100]

RELATIONSHIP TO CONTEMPORARY SETTLEMENT

We have already discussed that the patron would have been a key motivator in the foundation of a nunnery and also likely determined its location 'according to an accepted social norm'.[101] Unfortunately for medieval Ireland, this accepted 'social norm' is no longer known. The majority of nunneries in Ireland had a male patron, who may have had different motivations to those of the female religious community he was endowing. English and Welsh evidence has shown that less than 17 per cent of nunnery foundations could be considered in any way urban,[102] and on the rare occasions they were placed in towns, for example at Chester or Ilchester, the primary motivation seems to have been protection.[103]

Occasionally a nunnery was the catalyst to village establishment, as occurred at Chatteris, Cambridgeshire. But what is currently understood as a medieval town or village differs between England and Ireland, and a wider consideration of historic settlement is required, coupled with a re-evaluation of what is meant by urban and rural.[104] In an English context, smaller towns and larger unenclosed later medieval clustered settlements are termed villages. In Ireland, however, the term 'village' has not gained archaeological currency in a medieval context. Where these have been abandoned, they are 'deserted settlements'.[105] In instances where occupation has continued or evolved, they may be termed 'historic town', or by their individual elements, such as motte and bailey, church, castle or enclosure.[106]

Indeed, it is likely that what is considered a medieval town in Ireland, with a few notable exceptions, may actually have more in common with a medieval English village, some of which were quite extensive. In that case, the trend of nunneries being located near villages in England may correspond more readily with nunneries in medieval towns and settlements in Ireland. Having said this, medieval Dublin, for instance, was large enough to have been considered a proper town in England. Armagh, Cork, Limerick and Waterford, all of which had later medieval nunneries, are also comparable with English medieval towns.[107]

Nunneries in a suburban context in England were more common, where they 'maintained a further sense of separation'.[108] In reality, however, most were just situated in the fields beyond the town and the suffix *de la pré* – literally 'beyond the town' – recalls this location, such as Northampton de la Pré and St Mary de Pré at St Albans. A symbiotic relationship between nunnery and urban settlement could develop as the village provided a workforce, tenants and other industrial activities, while the nunnery provided prayer, some pastoral care, education and employment.[109] In these cases, their siting might be considered suburban.[110]

Of eleven nunneries in the medieval diocese of Norwich in England, four were urban, which is similar to the pattern in medieval Ireland. However, isolation was deemed important as the nunneries of Norwich were 'in places that were considered to be outside of or removed from society' and so the majority of sites tended to be in geographically marginal areas.[111] In England, nunneries are considered in the main isolated, and 'in certain cases nuns actively sought marginality and isolation like earlier monastics who had emulated the desert fathers',[112] for example the Yorkshire nunneries.[113] A study of 114 nunneries in France showed that fifty-two lay some 16–35kms from the nearest town, while just ten were situated within 5kms.[114] A more specific study of nunneries in Normandy concluded that the majority were situated in a predominantly rural environment.[115]

The locations of medieval nunneries in Ireland have been considered in relation to other contemporary settlement forms such as walled towns, unenclosed towns and larger settlements, smaller nucleated settlements, various castle types and other religious houses. For the purposes of this discussion, a settlement is defined as a town, village or settlement cluster, such as a stone or earthen/timber castle such as a motte or ringwork, sometimes with a church. The nunnery may be quite central to this arrangement or be within a radius of less than 2km of the settlement. A settlement has only been considered where it can be demonstrated to be contemporary or slightly earlier than the nunnery it is associated with.

As a caveat, the dating of medieval settlements in Ireland cannot be exact, and the majority have not been extensively archaeologically investigated. The date of settlements adjacent to nunneries is estimated by using currently accepted chronologies for archaeological monument types, accepted dating for the founding of towns, and the construction of town walls, where employed. In many instances only a broad timeframe can be estimated, especially without the benefit of archaeological investigation and precise dating. It is possible that in some instances, nunneries may pre-date surrounding medieval monuments and settlements by some years, and may have been the catalyst for establishment of a settlement. Forty-one nunneries were located close – that is less than 6kms – to some form of contemporary urban settlement, which is at odds with the English and French evidence.

Walled towns

Nunneries enclosed within English towns are rare, and only Chester and Ilchester nunneries were situated within walled towns.[116] This is a very small percentage out of the 153 or so nunneries there. In contrast, the Irish evidence shows thirteen nunneries were located within or adjacent to walled towns (Figure 4.22, Table 4.3).[117] Nunneries were placed in more populous locations in medieval Ireland perhaps for protection in the event of war or conflict, though more secluded locations were still preferred, even in urban environments, where for example 'the convents in the towns of Dublin, Derry, Limerick, Armagh, Cork, Youghal, Waterford and Galway were all close to the walls or within them, but usually in a quieter part of the settlement'.[118]

Protection is certainly one explanation for the urban location of many nunneries, though it remains difficult to prove that their locations were in the quieter parts of towns, and in many cases in fact there is evidence to suggest otherwise. For example, in the case of St Peter's Cell at Limerick, it was first situated outside the defences of the Englishtown only to be later incorporated within.[119] It was situated less than 300m from the medieval main street and very close to St Mary's Cathedral, and both were likely intervisible.[120] This would have been a busy place in medieval Limerick.[121] St Peter's Cell is interesting as it was the first later medieval religious house to be established in Limerick.[122] St Mary de Hogges was situated outside the walls and immediately to the east of Dublin's medieval core, but was situated near the original thing motte, Hoggen Green, the river Liffey and its medieval quayside, which would have been a prominent location outside the walls of the town. The Augustinian canons' house of All Hallows Priory stood just further east of the nunnery in the same district.[123]

While Kilculliheen was situated on the left bank of the river Suir and separated from Waterford, it is still likely to have been a busy place as it sat opposite the medieval quays.[124] Indeed, this must have been a very successful

Table 4.3 Nunneries associated with contemporary walled towns[1]

Foundation Date	*Town*	*Date of Walling*	*Outside Wall*	*Inside Wall*
Unknown	Buttevant	Medieval[2]	-	Thought to be within central core of town, to south of Franciscan abbey.
Before 1385?	Carrick-on-Suir	E14C[3]	The circuit of the town wall at its southeast angle where the castle now stands is unclear. It may be on the line of the town wall. However, the street pattern of the town, which does not extend this far east, suggests that this location was outside the walled town.	-
1297	Cork	Before end of 12C[4]	Precise location unknown but possibly near Augustinian friary to southeast of walled town.[5]	-
1200s?	Downpatrick	L13C[6]	Unlocated. Could be outside at Cathedral to southwest of town, or outside Nun's gate to north.	Could be located inside circuit at Nun's Gate in northern stretch of town wall.
1511	Galway	1250–70[7]	-	Unlocated but it is suggested that it lay within the walled town.
After 1144	Kells	By end of 14C[8]	Unlocated. Possibly to west or east of town in vicinity of either male religious house.[9]	Or inside town wall at parish church in town centre.
1151	Waterford	13C and later[10]	On northern (left) bank of River Suir, directly to north of town in suburb called 'Ferry bank'.	-
After 1171	Kildare	1515 grant for murage[11]	-	Enclosed by wall and located in northern quadrant of enclosure.
After 1144	Roscommon	L13/E14th C (possible)[12]	To south of town.	-
1146	Dublin	12C with extensions and upgrades[13]	To east of town.	-
1171	Limerick	12C English-town 1175–1237–1310/11 rebuilding 14/15C[14]	Outside Hiberno-Norse earthen enclosure.	Later enclosed by third phase of walling dated to 1175–1310.

Table 4.3 (*continued*)

Foundation Date	*Town*	*Date of Walling*	*Outside Wall*	*Inside Wall*
*c.*1199	Timolin	Doubtful evidence of walling[15]	Line of wall unknown (not shown on Figure 4.22).	Nunnery location presumed in centre of town.
Before 1385?	Youghal	E to mid 13C, probably 1275[16]	To south of town.	-

NOTES TO TABLE 4.3

1 Armagh and Derry are considered to be medieval walled towns but evidence for walling at Armagh is poor and very late, about 1536; Thomas, *The Walled Towns*, vol. 2, p. 222. Derry's walls are post-medieval in date; see Thomas, *Irish Historic Towns Atlas: Derry-Londonderry*; so for the purposes of this research they have been excluded from this table. **2** There is no specific date that can be allocated to the walling of medieval Buttevant. It is thought to probably have been walled although there are several possibilities for its circuit; Thomas, *The Walled Towns*, vol. 2, pp. 28–9; E. Cotter, 'Archaeological and Environmental Heritage at Buttevant, County Cork' (unpublished report for Buttevant Heritage Group Cork, 2010). **3** Thomas, *The Walled Towns*, vol. 2, p. 45. **4** See Thomas, *The Walled Towns*, vol. 2, p. 62; D. Power, *Archaeological Inventory of County Cork. Volume 2: East and South Cork* (Dublin: The Stationery Office, 1994), p. 275. **5** See Bradley et al., *Urban Archaeology Cork*, pp. 46–52, 92. **6** Date and discussion by Thomas, *The Walled Towns*, vol. 2, pp. 70–2. **7** Dates and discussion of walling of Galway from Thomas, *The Walled Towns*, vol. 2, p. 112; Prunty and Walsh, *Irish Historic Towns Atlas: Galway*, with references. **8** Dates and discussion by Thomas, *The Walled Towns*, vol. 2, p. 121; A. Simms, *Irish Historic Towns Atlas No. 4: Kells* (Dublin: Royal Irish Academy, 1990). **9** The precise location of the nunnery at Kells is not known and there are several possibilities. It is possible that it was one of the co-located Augustinian establishments with male canons. There seems to have been two Augustinian foundations at Kells, one to the west of the town and the other to the east. They are not contemporary with each other. The nunnery might be located at either of these sites; Thomas, *The Walled Towns*, vol. 2, p. 121 for location of male houses, although the one to the west of 'canon's gate' might be preferred, due to the name. **10** See Thomas, *The Walled Towns*, vol. 2, pp. 200–10. **11** Dates and discussion in Thomas, *The Walled Towns*, vol. 2, pp. 123–5. This date is quite late in the walling of medieval towns in Ireland generally. Andrews suggests a circuit for the town wall which places the supposed site of the nunnery at Kildare within the circuit and in the northern quadrant of the enclosure. He notes that the later medieval nunnery at Kildare may not necessarily have been on the site of the earlier foundation marked by the round tower and high cross; Andrews, *Historic Towns Atlas: Kildare*, pp. 3–4. **12** Dates and discussion by Thomas, *The Walled Towns*, vol. 2, pp. 188–9. **13** See Thomas, *The Walled Towns*, vol. 2, p. 89. **14** Dates and discussion of the walling of Limerick; Thomas, *The Walled Towns*, vol. 2, p. 146; Collins et al., 'Limerick City Walls'; O'Flaherty, *Historic Towns Atlas: Limerick*, p. 2. **15** Discussion by Thomas, *The Walled Towns*, vol. 2, p. 239. Thomas suggests that the walling of Timolin, if it occurred at all, occurred late, perhaps in the 1530s. Thomas suggests that by 1223 the town was already a borough settlement. The foundation date for the nunnery at Timolin is *c.*1199 and so this nunnery may be one of the few examples in Ireland where a settlement grew up around a nunnery. She notes the town as an important point along the routeway from Kilcullen in the north and Castledermot to the south along the road from Dublin, Carlow and Waterford. Hall suggested that the founder of the nunnery at Timolin, Lord of Norragh, did so near his own castle; Hall, *Women and the Church*, p. 95. If the town of Timolin did grow up around the nunnery there, it would be rare in an Irish context. However, many villages were planned around nunneries in England, such as Orford Priory, Lincolnshire; Gilchrist, *Gender and Material Culture*, p. 70. **16** Dates in Thomas, *The Walled Towns*, vol. 2, p. 217; Power, *Archaeological Inventory of County Cork*, vol. 2.

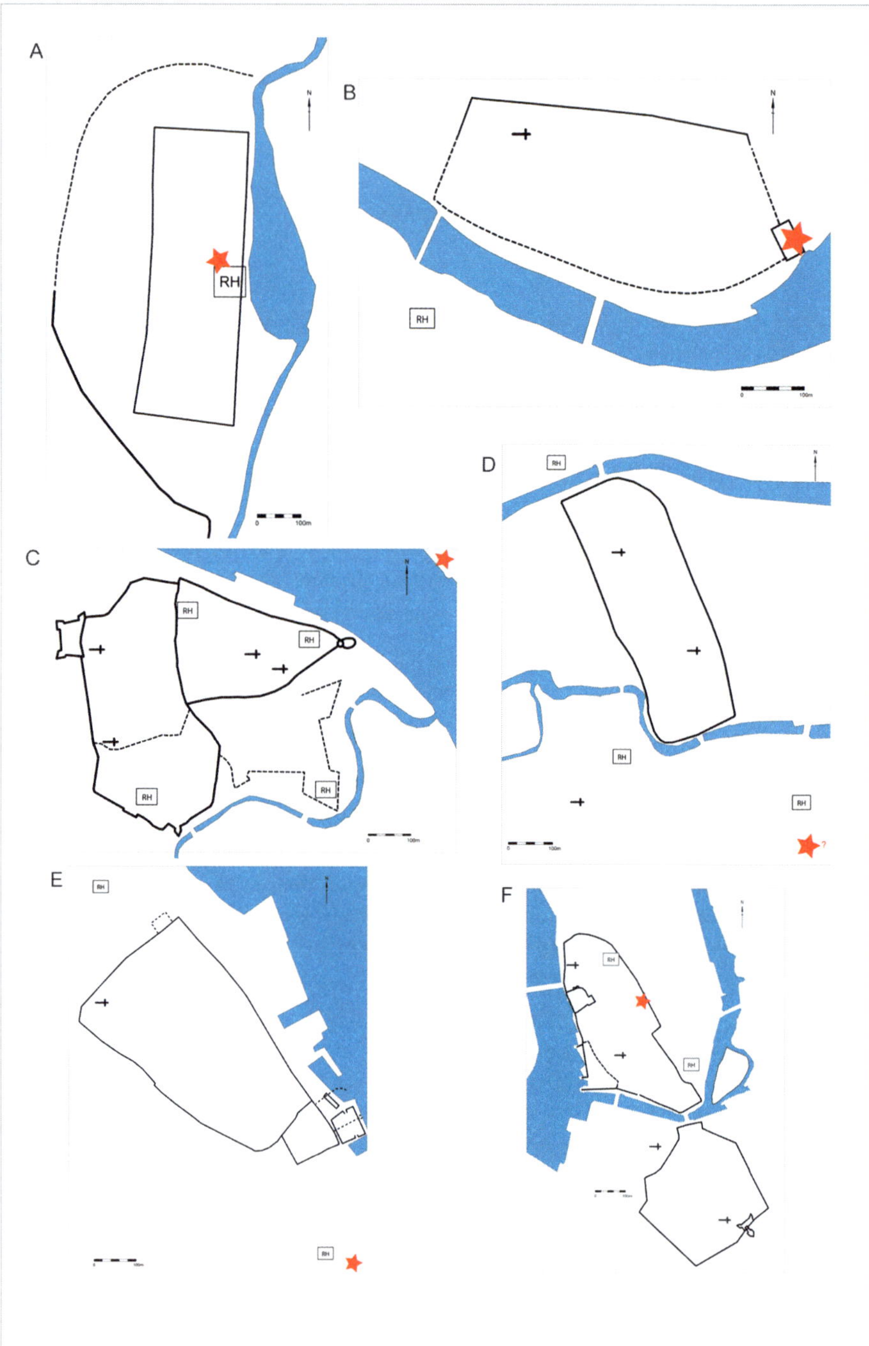

4.22a Nunneries associated with walled towns. A. Buttevant; B. Carrick-on-Suir; C. Kilculliheen at Waterford; D. Cork; E. Youghal; F. Limerick. Image: Frank Coyne.

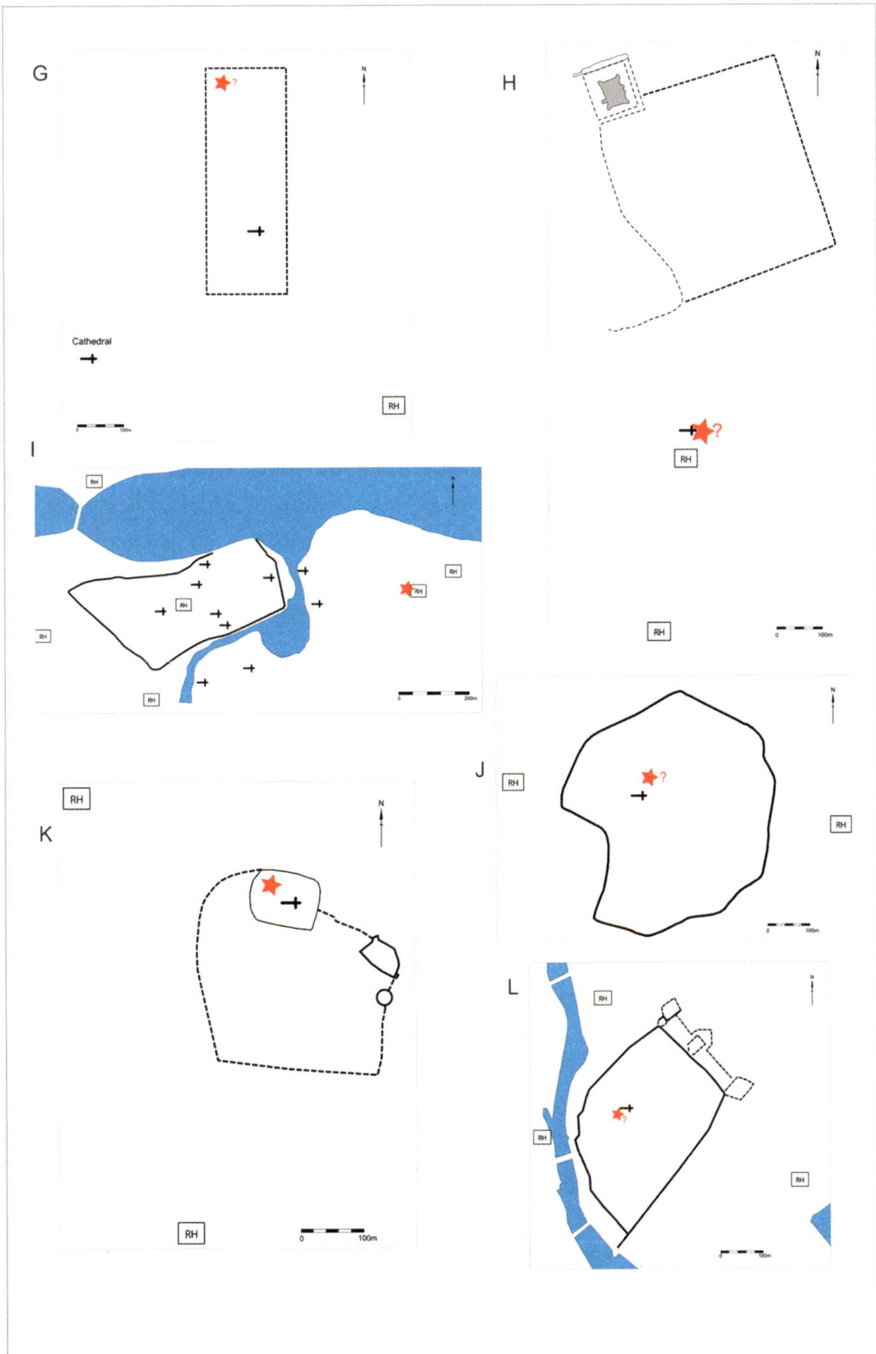

4.22b Nunneries associated with walled towns, continued. G. Downpatrick; H. Roscommon; I. Dublin; J. Kells; K. Kildare; L. Galway. Image: Frank Coyne.

location for Kilculliheen as the townspeople of Waterford complained of its competition economically, and at its dissolution it was granted to the city's corporation.[125] Downpatrick was the principal medieval urban centre of the strategic Lecale peninsula.[126] The location of the nunnery there remains unclear. It has been suggested that it was located within the town wall or just outside it, due to the presence of a north gate called 'Nun's Gate'; or alternatively, that the cathedral marks its site, the nunnery buildings being incorporated into the cathedral structure (see Figure 4.18).[127] There is no known location for the nunnery founded in 1511 in Galway, a prosperous walled town with a number of religious houses.[128]

The nunneries associated with walled towns, whether located within the confines of the enclosure itself or immediately outside it, are described in an Irish context as being urban. Their location appears to share similarities in urban contexts with foundations of the mendicant orders and also more secular dwellings and castles.[129] Perhaps they all maintained a particular urban character, interacting with the other urban institutions, enjoying the patronage of the town's wealthier citizens and perhaps providing alms for the poorer members of the urban population.

Non-walled towns and larger settlements

Eleven nunneries were located within or close to unenclosed towns and larger settlements (Table 4.4). These are characterised as smaller urban centres, such as boroughs or manors, and could be termed villages.[130] These settlements were urban in character but remained unenclosed by a defensive wall. Derry is included in this group as the town was not enclosed until much later in its history.[131] It is interesting that nine of these locations were originally established in the early medieval period, so there may have been some remnants of the early enclosing elements extant in the later period. At Killeigh, for example, it has been suggested that its substantial early medieval earthen enclosure was re-used in the later medieval period (Figure 4.23).[132]

At Killeigh, Armagh, Taghmon and Termonfeckin, the nunnery locations are thought to have been on the periphery of the settlements. The two nunneries at Armagh were located at the base of the central highpoint of the settlement (Figure 4.24), while at Taghmon the nunnery was to the southwest of the settlement and at Termonfeckin to the south. At Derry the nunnery is thought to have been placed at the settlement's centre, now occupied by St Columb's Cathedral (Figure 4.25).[133] The precise locations of the nunneries associated with Duleek, Lusk and Wicklow remain unknown, despite several suggestions.

ble 4.4 Nunneries associated with contemporary non-walled towns and larger settlements.

Nunnery	*Foundation Date*	*Town*	*Foundation Date of Settlement and Comment*	*Nunnery Location in Relation to Settlement*
rry Mary's	1218	Derry	Derry is considered a walled town but was not so until the seventeenth century. It was an important ecclesiastical centre with St Columba establishing a monastery there in 546, which was given cathedral status in the Anglo-Norman period.	Suggested to have been on the island of Derry at the site of the current St Columb's Cathedral.
leek Mary's	After 1144	Duleek	Early medieval foundation with an Augustinian priory established at centre of early medieval monastic enclosure in twelfth century. Was also site of grange for the English Augustinian abbey of Llanthony.	As a probably co-located Augustinian foundation, nunnery likely to be close to male Augustinian house the remains of which are incorporated into modern church. No known extant remains of nunnery.
leenatrava	After 1223	Ballinrobe	Ballinrobe is not a walled town and it is likely that the settlement built up around its Augustinian Friary, founded about 1313.	Nunnery is situated to the west of Ballinrobe less that 1km from the site of the friary.
leigh	After 1195	Killeigh	An early medieval monastic site established in the sixth century, it became an important centre in the medieval diocese of Kildare.	Location of nunnery confused, though it has been suggested that it was located on the site of the post office on the northern side of the village. A stone head of a female was found at this spot. The Archaeological Survey of Ireland marks site in eastern portion of village to east of location of Augustinian and later Franciscan friary.
sk St Mary's	After 1144	Lusk	Early medieval monastic centre, after Anglo-Norman invasion possessions granted to St Mary's Abbey, Dublin. The nunnery at Lusk was in the possession of Grace Dieu.	Unlocated within settlement.

Table 4.4 (*continued*)

Nunnery	Foundation Date	Town	Foundation Date of Settlement and Comment	Nunnery Location in Relation to Settlement
Molough	14C	Newcastle	Newcastle never appears to have been walled and is described as a manor. The townland immediately to the west of the nunnery is Moloughnewtown, which is suggestive of an adjacent medieval settlement. There are no extant archaeological monuments recorded in Moloughnewtown to show if it was indeed a settlement.	Nunnery 1km northeast of the settlement and on the opposite (northern) bank of the river Suir.
Taghmon, St Mary's	Before 1171	Taghmon	An important early medieval church site reputedly founded by St Munna.	Location of nunnery on recorded on first edition of the OS six-inch map. It is located on the edges of the settlement to the southeast. The Urban Archaeology Survey not that there is no evidence for the nunnery indicate on the maps though ver low-level earthworks th may mark its site.
Temple na Ferta and St Brigit's	1144?	Armagh	Early medieval foundation when a number of enclosures employed. No evidence for later medieval walling.	At base of hill where cathedral sited, to the southeast and south respectively.
Termonfeckin St Mary's	After 1144	Termonfeckin	Early medieval foundation with twelfth-century co-located foundation of Augustinian canons and canonesses. Likely to have been a smaller medieval settlement around the religious houses, medieval occupational remains found during excavations and two tower houses recorded. Historic town of Drogheda within 7km of this nunnery.	Nothing now extant.
Wicklow St Mary's	1148	Wicklow	Settlement with Viking origins in the ninth century but unlikely to have ever been walled. Settlement presumed to have been centred on Franciscan friary and parish church rather than castle.	Unlocated, though local tradition suggests nunne was located near friary which is now occupied by the parish priest's residence.

4.23 Killeigh, Co. Offaly. Location of nunnery indicated. © National Monuments Service, Department of Housing, Local Government and Heritage.

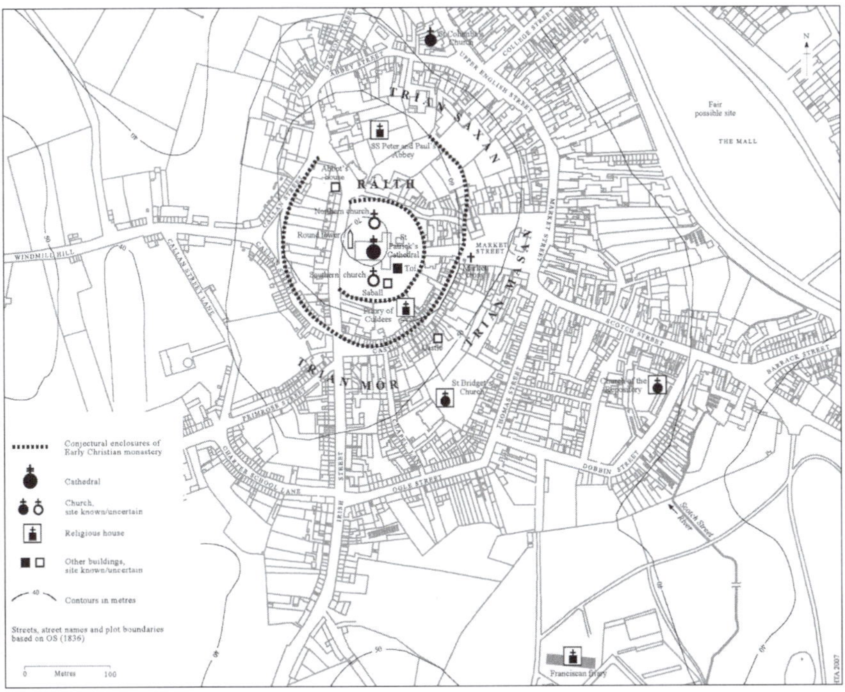

4.24 Medieval Armagh, showing locations of two nunneries there, St Brigit's and the Church of the Repository (Temple na Ferta). Reproduced with permission of the IHTA.

4.25 Medieval Derry showing location of nunnery. Reproduced with permission of the IH

Smaller nucleated settlement clusters

Ten nunneries are located in or close to less urban, though nevertheless nucleated, settlements, or deserted medieval villages (DMVs) (Table 4.5).[134] The nunnery at Ardcarn is situated within a settlement which includes two church sites, a graveyard, house platforms, multiple field boundaries, several ringforts,

Table 4.5 Nunneries associated with smaller settlement clusters within 2km of nunnery location.

Nunnery	*Foundation Date**	*Adjacent Settlement Forms*	*Nunnery Location & Comment*
Ardcarn	1123–44	Settlement deserted, medieval.	Within settlement.
Ballynagallagh	1283	Settlement deserted, medieval.	Within 2km of nunnery.
Clonard	1144	Results of geophysical survey, Castle motte (Clonard Old), castle ringwork Mulphedder moated site (Kilrathmurray).	Not classified as a deserted medieval settlement, though has many of the elements of such, including a field system. Clonard is situated on the left (northern) bank of the Clonard river close to a crossing point at Clonard bridge.
Fooran	1385	Settlement cluster.	Within 2km of nunnery.
Jerpoint	?1180	Settlement deserted, medieval.	There are two deserted medieval settlements recorded in the townland of Jerpoint church, adjacent to the Cistercian house. Limited excavations and survey were undertaken at the more distant of the two, 'Newtown Jerpoint'.
Mellifont	?1142	Settlement deserted, medieval.	There is a deserted medieval settlement recorded in the townland of Hurcle which lies to the northwest of the Cistercian abbey and is located on the opposite bank of the river.
Nuns' Church	1144–1223	Ecclesiastical centre.	Two nunneries at Clonmacnoise were in use in the later medieval period. The siting of the Anglo-Norman castle there highlights the continued importance of the complex in the late medieval period.
Plary	1218	Castle motte and bailey (Ballymore), tower house (Clare) and two castles unclassified (Ballymore and Mullaghcloe).	Nunnery located about 2km to the south of the De Lacy motte.
Skreen	1144	Settlement deserted, medieval.	Skreen itself is recorded as a deserted settlement, within which the nunnery is thought to have been situated. There are a further two deserted settlements within 5km of Skreen, one at Macestown and the other at Clowanstown.
Temple Finghin	1144–1223	Ecclesiastical centre.	Two nunneries at Clonmacnoise were in use in the later medieval period. The siting of the Anglo-Norman castle there highlights the continued importance of the complex in the late medieval period. It seems this nunnery community moved to Drumalgagh in about 1195.

* Dates taken from Gywnn and Hadcock, *Medieval Religious Houses*; Hall, *Women and the Church*.

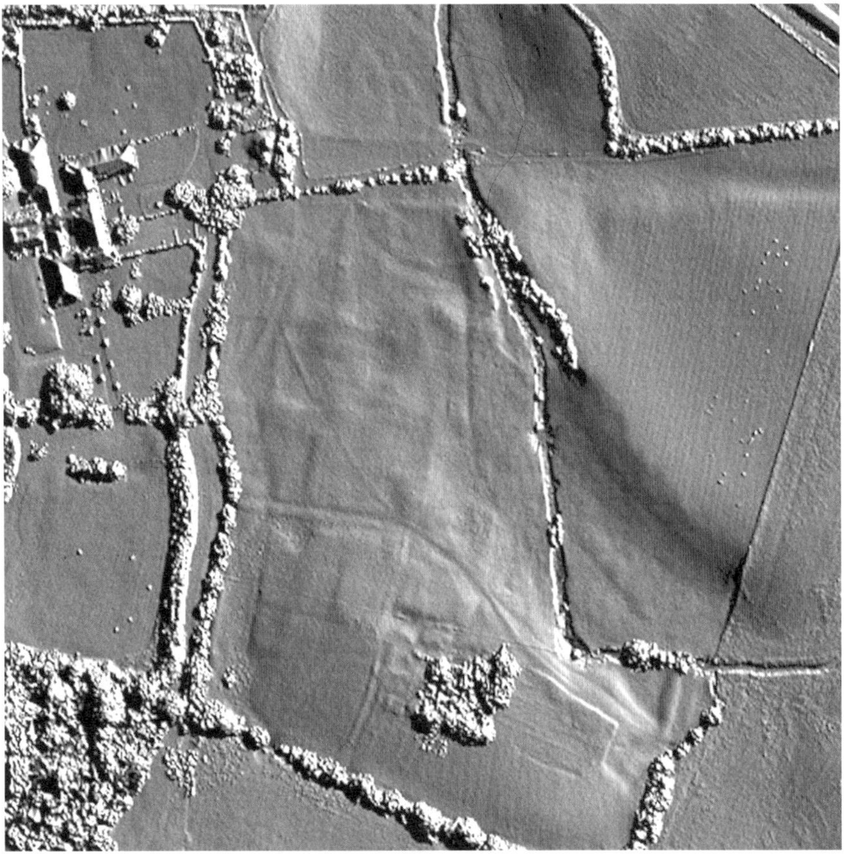

4.26 Lismullin, Co. Meath, LiDAR image. Courtesy of Dr S. Davis, School of Archaeology, UCD.

and cashels. The extant archaeological remains, although of very low register, are suggestive of an important centre with intensive occupational activity (see Figure 4.7).

As already discussed, Jerpoint and Mellifont are both better known as male Cistercian foundations, and it is possible that nuns were located in the now deserted settlements at Newtown Jerpoint[135] and Hurcle, near Mellifont.[136] The precise location of the nunnery at the deserted medieval settlement of Skreen is not known. It was short-lived and dissolved in the 1240s, when the community probably moved to Lismullin (Figure 4.26). Plary nunnery is less than 2km from an Augustinian canons' house, a motte and bailey castle of the De Lacys, two unclassified castle sites, and a tower house in the adjacent townland of Clare (Figure 4.27).[137] The precise location of the nunnery at Clonard remains unknown, but it is likely that it was in or around the church site there.[138] A

4.27 Plary, Co. Westmeath, showing location of nunnery and other monuments. Image: Frank Coyne.

motte, ringwork and moated site close to Clonard represent further adjacent settlement in the later medieval period (Figure 4.28).

The Nuns' Church and Temple Finghin are situated adjacent to the religious complex at Clonmacnoise (Figure 4.29). While most of its settlement archaeology relates to its early medieval period,[139] it has much to interest scholars of the later medieval period.[140] Many structures on the site were modified and continued in use from the earlier period, such as the cathedral,[141] and additions were also made to the site. The most obvious was the castle constructed in the early thirteenth century, which has both earthwork and masonry remains. It has been suggested that the castle, built in 1214 by the crown, was commissioned to subdue the local Irish septs and to control Clonmacnoise as an important ecclesiastical and population centre in the late

4.28 Clonard, Co. Meath, extant motte adjacent to site of nunnery. Image: Tracy Collins.

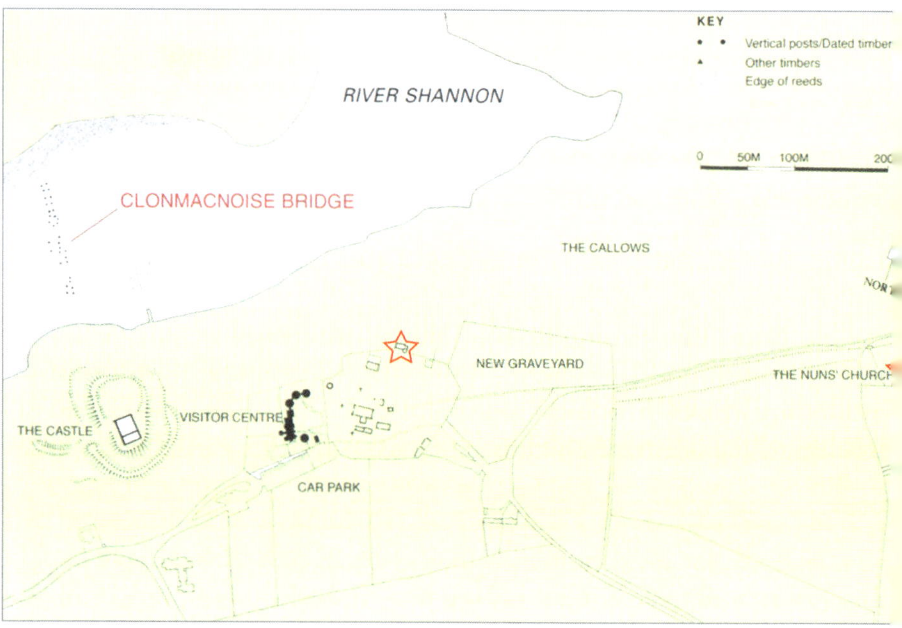

4.29 Clonmacnoise, Co. Offaly, showing bridge location. After O'Sullivan and Boland 2000. Reproduced with permission of A. O'Sullivan.

medieval period.[142] Geophysical survey at Clonmacnoise has also highlighted its intensive past activity (see Figure 2.7).[143] While it is impossible to verify if this activity relates to either the early medieval or late medieval period, without targeted archaeological excavation, it is interesting to note that one of the areas of densest activity surveyed was around Temple Finghin and northward towards the river's edge. Further significant evidence of activity was found westwards towards the castle.[144]

The previous nunnery groups were those that were either placed within a medieval settlement itself or situated within just 1km radius of it. This range would easily have allowed daily communication. To these groups can be added the seven nunneries that were within 6km of a larger urban settlement or historic town – a distance that could easily be travelled in a day (Table 4.6). For example, St Catherine's is located in sheltered, low-lying though generally good land, only 3km east of the medieval town of Shanagolden (Figure 4.30). In addition, there is the record of a deserted medieval settlement immediately adjacent to St Catherine's, which may suggest that a settlement pre-dated or grew up around the nunnery itself (see Figure 9.17).[145] The purpose of this detailed analysis is to assess how isolated or not nunneries may have been in their

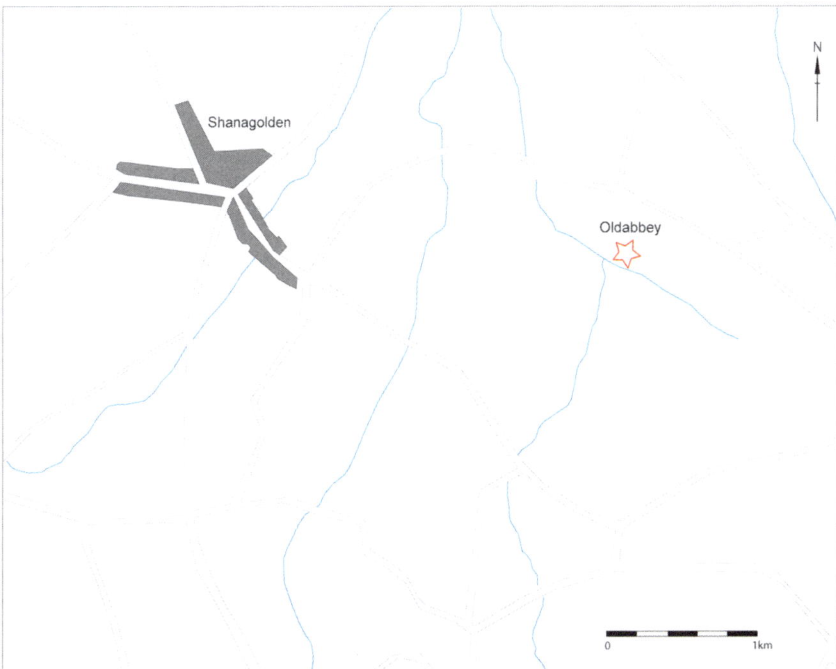

4.30 The location of St Catherine's, Old Abbey, Co. Limerick, east of the medieval town of Shanagolden, Co. Limerick. Image: Frank Coyne.

Table 4.6 Later medieval nunneries in Ireland associated with towns within 6km of nunnery location.

Nunnery	*Foundation Date*	*Adjacent Settlement Form*	*Distance of Nunnery Location from Settlement*
St Catherine's	*c.*1240s	Historic town Shanagolden	3km
Annagh	1440	Historic town at Castlecarra	4km
Graney	1200	Historic town of Castledermot	4km
Killone	1189 or 1240	Historic town of Ennis	4.5km
Calliaghstown	1195	Historic town of Drogheda	5km
Caltragh	1144	Historic town of Fore	5km
Kilbride	1144	Historic town of Trim	6km

contemporary landscape. It is clear that the examples discussed show that they were in relatively close proximity to their secular neighbours. Other medieval rural settlement types were also coeval with nunneries, such as various castle forms and moated sites.

Other rural settlement: castles and moated sites

In later medieval Ireland the social elite would have occupied a variety of castle types, both earthen and stone, as well as a variety of earthen enclosures,[146] and wealthier middle-ranking families occupied moated sites and other earthen enclosures.[147] Previous scholarship suggested that different types of castle and earthwork were used by the native Gaelic population and the incoming Anglo-Normans.[148] It was thought that the location and distribution of the two distinctive ethnic groups could then be revealed in the landscape based on archaeological field survey and morphology.[149] This may be true of the first generation of earthen and timber castles, as well as early masonry castles constructed by the Anglo-Normans; however, the construction and use of other enclosures throughout the period is now considered much more complicated.[150] It has been suggested that a micro-scalar landscape approach, considering lordships, may represent a more productive and nuanced study of this period.[151]

Archaeological investigations also suggest that the perceived ethnic divide between Gaelic and Anglo-Irish is not as clearcut as was first thought, when the totality of the archaeological evidence is considered. For example, an enclosure interpreted as a ringwork at Ballysimon, County Limerick had a later medieval artefact assemblage, yet its central structure was clearly circular in plan rather than rectangular, as might be expected in a classic ringwork. The excavator suggested that this site may represent a fusion of native and incomer traditions.[152]

ole 4.7 Nunneries within 2km of castles and moated sites.

Nunnery	Castle					Tower House	Moated Site Enclosure
	Unclassified	*Motte*	*Motte & Bailey*	*Ringwork*	*Anglo-Norman masonry*		
drigoole	Aghmacart					Aghmacart	
hade	Castlegrace	Castle-grace					
nagh	Lough Carra					Castleisland	
naghdown						Ballylee	
lymacdane							Rigsdale*
ly-gallagh	Knock-fennell Grange				Lough Gur	Lough Gur	Ardanreagh
liaghs-vn						Dardistown	
nard		Anneville/ Clonard Old		Mulphedder			Kilrath-murray
rane	Roxborough						Roxborough
malgagh	Tonvey						
rrow	Ballybought Durrow Demesne	Durrow Demesne					
ran	Mountemple		Labaun			Creeve Carnpark	
ce Dieu							Newtown-corduff
ney	Graney West						Oldtown Ballyraggan
h-naght				Patrickswell Marlfield/ Patrickswell			
hmaine	Inishmaine					Knock-namucklagh	
lystown		Mayne				Glapistol	
ride						Moymet	
reevanty						Fartamore	
araght							Killaraght
in-rooney	Cuilleen						
one	Edenvale						
nullin							Skreen Clowans-town

* P.D. Sweetman, 'Excavations of a Moated Site at Rigsdale, County Cork, 1977–8', *Proceedings of the Royal Irish Academy*, vol. 81C, 1981, pp. 103–205.

Table 4.7 (*continued*)

Nunnery	**Castle**					**Tower House**	**Moated Enclos**
	Unclassified	***Motte***	***Motte & Bailey***	***Ringwork***	***Anglo-Norman masonry***		
Odder						Riverstown	
Portrane						Portrane	
Skreen		Skreen				Skreen	Skreen
St Catherine's	Kilcosgrave Craggard						Old Abb
Temple Finghin					Clon-macnoise		
Termon-keelin	Demesne						
Tisrara						Cloghan	

Excavation of a rectangular enclosure at Ballintotty, County Tipperary showed that it was very similar in morphology to a moated site. This enclosure had been re-used on several occasions, and it was in proximity to the remains of a hall house (chamber tower) within its own rectangular enclosure, and a tower house. Based on morphology, these sites would be considered typically 'Anglo-Norman' but the historical evidence quite strongly suggested that Ballintotty remained in the hands of a native Irish family – the O'Kennedys – well into the seventeenth century. It would appear in this case that the Butlers (the Anglo-Norman lords of this region) held the nearby walled town of Nenagh and the Gaelic family of the O'Kennedys maintained their nearby settlement at Ballintotty, and constructed enclosures and structures similar to those of the Anglo-Normans. In this instance, it would appear that fashion rather than ethnic grouping can be identified in the archaeological record.[153]

It has already been mentioned that in medieval England nunneries tended to avoid castles.[154] But in medieval Ireland nunneries were sometimes located in the vicinity of these structures; for example, Graney, Timolin and St Catherine's were situated close to the castles of their founders, Walter de Riddlesford, Richard Lord of Norragh and John Fitzthomas, respectively.[155] The archaeological record of all castles and moated sites within a chosen radius of 2km of all of the nunneries was considered (Table 4.7). In this analysis only monuments classified as castles or moated sites were listed, as these monument types are fairly closely datable and overlap with the occupation of nunneries.[156] The analysis excluded those nunneries in close proximity to towns and other medieval settlements, which already included castles. The result of this analysis shows that thirty-one nunneries are within 2km of a castle or moated site. Earthwork castles, including mottes, motte-and-baileys and ringworks,[157]

4.31 Moated site at Killaraght, Co. Sligo, adjacent to the nunnery. © National Monuments Service, Department of Housing, Local Government and Heritage.

feature within 2km of seven nunnery locations. For example, the nunnery of Clonard is situated close to a motte and a separate ringwork castle (see Figure 4.28). Fourteen nunneries are close to tower houses.[158]

Ten nunneries are close to moated sites and the one near Killaraght is a particularly good example (Figure 4.31). It is acknowledged that not all of these nunneries may have been used at the same time as all of the castles and moated sites discussed. However, it is highly likely that in most cases some contemporary use did occur in particular periods, and it is postulated that some interaction may have taken place between the religious community and the social elites that used the castles and enclosures. While moated sites have only been considered in this analysis – as they are considered to be of firm later medieval date and their morphology makes them distinctive – there is growing archaeological evidence to suggest that some ringforts, cashels and crannógs may have also been re-occupied in the later medieval period.[159] Ringforts and unclassified enclosures are ubiquitous in the Irish landscape and so it is unsurprising that most nunneries are in the vicinity of at least one ringfort-type enclosure, and in many cases, several (see Chapter 9 for a case study discussion of St Catherine's).

RELATIONSHIP TO MALE RELIGIOUS HOUSES

An important settlement element in the landscape of later medieval Ireland is the religious house itself,[160] yet many publications on medieval rural settlement do not consider them, creating a false dichotomy.[161] These were obviously places of religious practice, but were also places of domestic accommodation and work. It has already been noted that various medieval monastic statutes decreed that great distances should be maintained between male and female religious houses, and between nunneries. Many have taken these rules at face value; here it is now investigated whether they were adhered to in practice.

The relationship between male and female religious houses in the landscape has not been widely explored in Ireland.[162] For England and Wales, a correlation has been identified between the location of female and male Cistercian houses, and indeed the proximity of a male Cistercian house may have been a dynamic in the adoption of the Cistercian rule at many female houses.[163] From the meagre historical evidence available for medieval Ireland, it is known that on occasion male religious houses and clerics both helped and hindered nunneries in Ireland, for example the nuns of Clonard and Kilbride, and the canons at Trim.[164] It also has to be remembered that the nunneries were always dependent on at least one male priest for the celebration of the mass and sacraments, and so male interaction was unavoidable.[165] It is likely that in some cases male religious houses – and perhaps other non-monastic churches – would have provided priests for services and sacraments at nunneries, as has been suggested for the Cistercian nunnery at Plary, although this cannot be historically verified.[166]

Table 4.8 details the period of use of each nunnery in Ireland, and its distance from its closest male religious house (of any order). This is in an effort to consider the distances of male houses from nunneries, to investigate if the distance rules noted by some historians were actually adhered to in practice, and to ascertain if it is feasible that male religious orders could have provided the sacraments and mass. Secular priests also undertook the role of nunnery priest. This is known from historical references, for instance the priest appointed by the prioress at St Catherine's in the fifteenth century.[167] These priests might be identified in the archaeological record by later medieval parish churches and other smaller churches. These churches are very numerous and in many cases

Table 4.8 Spatial and historical relationships between nunneries and male religious houses.

Nunnery	*Period of Later Medieval Use*	*Male Houses in Vicinity*	*Order*	*Period of Use of Male House*	*Distance from Nunnery in km*[1]	*Historical Connection to Male House/or Other*	*Cathedral Location of Medieval Diocese*
Addrigoole	1144?–1240	Aghmacart Fertagh Abbeyleix	Aug. Canons Aug. Canons Cistercian	1168?–1540 1251–1540 1184–1541/1552?	1 6 14		-
Aghade	1151–1500?	Tullow Down Leighlinbridge	Aug. Friars Aug. Canons Carmelite friars	1314–1541? 1170–1567 1265/72–1541	5 10 16		-
Annagh	1440–1543?	Burriscarra Ballintober Mayo Ballinrobe	Carmelite/Aug. Friars Aug. Canons Aug. Canons Aug. Friars	1298/1407–1605? 1216–1585 1370–1569? 1312–1584?	4.2 7.5 9.4 8	Franciscan?	-
Annaghdown	1144–1223?	Annaghdown	Aug. Canons Premonstratensian	1140–1578 1224–1542	Co-located		1189 (1327 united with Tuam)
Ardcarn	1123/1144 or 1223–1590?	Ardcarn Loughkey Boyle	Aug. Canons Premonstratensian Cistercian	1144–1593 1217–1600? 1148–1589?	Co-located 4 6		1111 (although not an episcopal, see Gwynn and Hadcock)
Ballymacdane	1450–1539?	Kilcrea	Franciscan	1465–1542	10.3	Kilcrea Friary	-
Ballynagallagh	1283–1548	Monasteranenagh Hospital Milltown (a Ballynagally Td adjacent) Rochestown (Friarstown Td near L Gur)	Cistercian Knights Hospitallers Carmelite Friars Dominican Friars	1148–1580 1215–1540 1459/60–1544 ?–1544	9 7.5 10 4		-
Buttevant	?	Buttevant Ballybeg	Franciscan Aug. Canons	1276/9–1540 1229/37–1541	0.5 1.5		-

1 These distances have been calculated 'as the crow flies' from the location of the nunnery to the male religious house.

Table 4.8 (*continued*)

Nunnery	*Period of Later Medieval Use*	*Male Houses in Vicinity*	*Order*	*Period of Use of Male House*	*Distance from Nunnery in km*[1]	*Historical Connection to Male House/or Other*	*Cathedral Location of Medieval Diocese*
Calliaghstown	1195–1500	Drogheda	As above	As above	5		-
		Duleek	Aug. Canons (2)	1140–1537/1180–1538	6		
		Beybeg	Cistercian	1216–1332	2.5		
		Colp	Aug. Canons	1183–1540?	4.5		
Caltragh	1144–1195?	Fore	Benedictine monks	1185–1539	3		-
		Multyfarnham	Franciscan	1236/1268–1460	12		
Carricknahorna	?	Inchmacnerin	Aug. Canons	1140/70–1596	7.5		-
		Loughkey	Premonstratensian	1217–1600?	8		
		Boyle	Cistercian	1148–1589?	7		
Carrick-on-Suir	1385–1542?	Carrick-on-Suir	Order of Acon	1236–1536?	>1?		-
		Carrickbeg	Franciscan	1336–1540	0.6		
Clonard	1144–1535?	Clonard	Aug. Canons (2)	1146?–1540	Co-located	Envoy from Trim to act for Kilbride & Clonard	1111 (1202 to Trim)
		Ballyboggan	Aug. Canons	1200?–1537	5		
		Trim	Aug. Canons	1140/1186–1539	17		
			Dominican Friars	1263–1540	17		
			Franciscan	1282–1506/1525?	17		
			Fratres Cruciferi	1206?–1539	17		
			Carmelite Friars	?	17		
Clonfert	1144–1540	Clonfert	Aug. Canons	1140–1571	Co-located		1111
Cloonoghil	1223–1543?	Bellaneeny	Carmelite Friars	1437–1567	11		-
		Eglish	Carmelite Friars	1393/8–1540s?	12		
		Athlone	Benedictine (Cluniac)	1150–1567?	11		
Cork	1297–1540?	Red Abbey	Aug. Friars	1229?–1500	Co-located?		1111 (united with Cloyne 1429)
Derrane	1144–1223?	Derrane	Aug. Canons	1156–1578?	Co-located.		-
		Roscommon	Aug. Canons	1140–1578	5		
			Dominican Friars	1253–1573	5		
		Cloontuskert	Aug. Canons	1140–1463?	9.8		
Derry	1218?–1512	Derry	Aug. Canons	1233?–1576	Within town		1254 (from Maghera)

Nunnery	Period of Later Medieval Use	Male Houses in Vicinity	Order	Period of Use of Male House	Distance from Nunnery in km[1]	Historical Connection to Male House/or Other	Cathedral Location of Medieval Diocese
Downpatrick	1200–1513?	Downpatrick	Benedictine (Cd Pr) Aug. Canons (2) Fratres Cruciferi Franciscan	1183–1541 1138–1541/1183–1541 1200–1541 1240/3–1569	Within town		1111 (1453 with Connor; Benedictine 1183–1541)
Drumalgagh	1195–1543?	Clonmacnoise Clonfert Clontuskert	Aug. Canons Aug. Canons Aug. Canons	1140–1268? 1140–1571 1140–1562	8 8.7 8	Clonmacnoise	-
Duleek	1144–1195?	Duleek	Aug. Canons (2)	1140–1537/1180–1538	Co-located		1111 (merged after 1152)
Durrow	1144–1195?	Durrow	Aug. Canons	1144–1569?	Co-located		-
Fooran	1385–1540s?	Ballymore Athlone	Aug. Canons Benedictine Franciscan	1250–1540 1150–1542/1567 1239–1587	9.3 11 11		-
Galway	1511–1540s?	Galway	Aug. Friars Carmelite Friars Dominican F Franciscan F Premonstratensian	1500–1578 1332?–1648 1488–1651 1247–1460[2] 1235–1451	Within town		-
Grace Dieu	1195–1539	Dublin St Patrick's Is. Holmpatrick	Various Aug. Canons Aug. Canons	Various 1140–1220 1220–1537	18 13 10	Archbishop of Dublin, John Cumin (Comyn) & 1468 visitation[3]	-
Graney	1200–1539	Castledermot Castledermot Baltinglass Tullow	Fratres Cruciferi Franciscan Cistercian Aug. Friars	1216–1540 1247–1540 1148–1536 1314–1541?	3.5 3.5 7 11.5	Bishop of Leighlin 1318	-
Inishlounaght	1150–1228?	Inishlounaght	Cistercian monks	1147/8–1540	Co-located		-

2 Alterative dates of 1296–1520/33 also cited; Gywnn and Hadcock, *Medieval Religious Houses*, p. 240. **3** A visitation by the archbishop in 1468 recorded that at that time there were five nuns and one prioress at Grace Dieu; Hall, *Women and the Church*, p. 130.

Table 4.8 *(continued)*

Nunnery	*Period of Later Medieval Use*	*Male Houses in Vicinity*	*Order*	*Period of Use of Male House*	*Distance from Nunnery in km*[1]	*Historical Connection to Male House/or Other*	*Cathedral Location of Medieval Diocese*
Inishmaine	1223–1546/ 1587?	Cong Ballinrobe	Aug. Canons Aug. Friars	1134–1568? 1312–1584?	6.2 5.8	Cong Annaghdown	-
Jerpoint	1180–1228?	Jerpoint	Cistercian	1180–1540	Co-located		-
Kells	1144–1400?	Kells	Aug. Canons Fratres Cruciferi	1140–1539 1199–1539	Co-located		1152 (*c.* 1211 merged)
Kellystown	?	Termonfeckin Drumshallon Drogheda	Aug. canons Aug. canons As above	1144–1195 1202–1262 As above	5 1 8		-
Kilbride	1144–1400?	Trim Athboy	Aug. canons Dominican Friars Franciscan Fratres Cruciferi Carmelite Friars Carmelite Friars	1140/1186–1539 1263–1540 1282–1506/1525? 1206?–1539 ? 1317–1539	6 6 6 6 6 6	Envoy from Trim to act for Kilbride & Clonard	-
Kilcreevanty	1200–1543	Tuam	Aug. Canons[4] Premonstratensian	1140–1574 1203/04/17–1574	6	Cong (Aug. Canons) Archbishop of Tuam, 1308–21	-
Kilculliheen	1151–1540	Waterford Dunbrody	Aug. Canons Benedictines Dominican Friars Franciscan Cistercian	1207–1539 1190/1204–1536 1226–1540 1240/5–1540 1182–1536	1.5 1.7 1.5 1.5 9.2		1111 (united to Lismore 1363)
Kildare	1171?–1460/1540	Grey Abbey Kildare Kildare	Franciscan Carmelite Friars Aug. Canons?	1254/60–1520 1290–1539 ?	Within town		1111
Killaraght	1223–1591?	Cloonshanville Boyle Ardcarn	Dominican Friars Cistercian Aug. Canons	1385–1596 1148–1589? 1144–1593	7.5 6 10.5		-

4 It is also recorded in some sources that a house of the Fratres Cruciferi was also established in Tuam, as well as an unclassified house known as the abbey of Scrin; Augustinian friars are recorded as succeeding the canons at Tuam; Gywnn and Hadcock, *Medieval Religious Houses*, pp. 216, 305.

Nunnery	Period of Later Medieval Use	Male Houses in Vicinity	Order	Period of Use of Male House	Distance from Nunnery in km[1]	Historical Connection to Male House/or Other	Cathedral Location of Medieval Diocese
Killeenatrava	1223–1560?	Ballinrobe Cong	Aug. Friars Aug. Canons	1312–1584? 1134–1568?	1.2 10.5		-
Killeigh	1195–1569?	Killeigh	Aug. Canons Franciscan	1144?–1569 1293/1303–1598[5]	Co-located	Durrow	-
Killevy	1144/8–1542	Dundalk Carlingford Newry	Fratres Cruciferi Franciscan Dominican Friars Cistercian	1189–1539 1246–1540 1305/07–1541 1148–1550	14 14 17 5		-
Killinmulrooney	1223–1543?	Ballaneeny Eglish Aughrim Clontuskert	Carmelite Friars Carmelite Friars Aug. Canons Aug. Canons	1437–1567 1393/8–1540s? 1170–1562? 1140–1562	6 10.2 12 8.7		-
Killone	1189–1584 or 1240–1540	Clare Abbey Ennis Friary	Aug. canons Franciscans	1189–1543 1240/7–1536/40	3.6 4.7	Clare Abbey	-
Lismullin	1240–1539	Skreen Navan Bective Trim	Aug. Friars Aug. canons Cistercian As above	1341–1539 1170?–1539 1147–1536 As above	3.5 10 7 13.5	Bishop of Meath, 1322, 1409	-
Lusk	1144–1195?	Dublin St Patrick's Is. Holmpatrick	Various Aug. Canons Aug. Canons	Various 1140–1220 1220–1537	20 9 6	Archbishop of Dublin, John Cumin (Comyn)	-
Mellifont	1142?–1228?	Mellifont	Cistercian	1142–1539	Co-located		-
Molough	14C–1540	Lady's Abbey Inishlounaght	Carmelite Friars Cistercian	1314–1541? 1147/8–1540	6.8 8.4		-
Nuns' Church	1144 or 1223–1500?	Clonmacnoise	Aug. Canons	1140?–1268?	Co-located		1111

5 This Franciscan house was re-established and continued in use into the post-medieval period; Gywnn and Hadcock, *Medieval Religious Houses*, p. 241; FitzPatrick and O'Brien, *Medieval Churches of County Offaly*, pp. 88–89.

Table 4.8 (*continued*)

Nunnery	Period of Later Medieval Use	Male Houses in Vicinity	Order	Period of Use of Male House	Distance from Nunnery in km[1]	Historical Connection to Male House/or Other	Cathedral Location of Medieval Diocese
Odder	1144–1539	Skreen	Aug. Friars	1341–1539	4.5		-
		Navan	Aug. Canons	1170?–1539	10.5		
		Bective	Cistercian	1147–1536	5.5		
		Trim	As above	As above	11		
Plary	1218–1470?	Ballymore Plary	Aug. Canons	1250–1540	0?		-
		Tristernagh	Aug. Canons	c.1200–1539	18		
		Abbeyshrule	Cistercian	1200–1569/1592	10.5		
		Kilkenny West	Fratres Cruciferi	1200–1541?	10.4		
		Ardcranny	Carmelite Friars	1291/1329–1540	8		
Portrane	1539–1577?	Dublin	Various	Various	18	Archbishop of Dublin, John Cumin (Comyn)	-
		St Patrick's Is.	Aug. Canons	1140–1220	10		
		Holmpatrick	Aug. Canons	1220–1537	8		
Roscommon	1144–1223?	Roscommon	Aug. Canons	1140–1578	Co-located		1152 (move to Elphin c.1168)
		Roscommon	Dominican Friars	1253–1573			
Skreen	1144–1240?	Skreen	Aug. Friars	1341–1539	0		-
		Navan	Aug. Canons	1170?–1539	11.5		
		Bective	Cistercian	1147–1536	10		
		Trim	As above	As above	15.5		
St Brigit's	1144–1562?	Armagh	Aug. Canons	1126–1562	Within town		1111
			Franciscan	1263/4–1566			
St Catherine's	c. 1240s–1428 or 1567?	Rathkeale	Aug. Canons	1210–1542	10.6	Bishop of Limerick	-
		Canon's Island	Aug. Canons	1180–1577	12.3		
		Askeaton	Franciscan	1400–1513	7		
		Adare	Trinitarian	1226–1559	20.5		
			Franciscan	1464–1539/40	21.4		
			Aug. Friars	1316–1539/40	21		

Table 4.8 *(continued)*

Nunnery	*Period of Later Medieval Use*	*Male Houses in Vicinity*	*Order*	*Period of Use of Male House*	*Distance from Nunnery in km*[1]	*Historical Connection to Male House/or Other*	*Cathedral Location of Medieval Diocese*
St Mary de Hogges	1146/95–1536	Dublin: All Saints St Mary's Holy Trinity St Thomas St John the Baptist Dublin Dublin Dublin Dublin Dublin	Aug. Canons Cistercian Aug. Canons Aug. Canons Fratres Cruciferi Aug. Friars Carmelite friars Dominican Friars Franciscans Friars of the Sack	1166–1539 1139-/1147–1539 1163–1541 1177–1539 1185/8–1539 1282–1540 1274–1539 1224–1539 1233–1521 1268–1309/10	Within town	Archbishop Visitation, 1468[6]	Holy Trinity 1152 (Archbishopric, Aug. Canons) St Patrick 1213 (secular)
St Peter's Cell	1171?–1541	Limerick	Dominican Friars Franciscan Fratres Cruciferi	1227–1543 1267–1534 1216–1537	All within town	Clare Abbey Aug. Canons	1111
Taghmon	1171–1330	Wexford Horetown Clonmines	Aug. Canons Franciscan Carmelite Friars Aug. Friars	1190/1216–1540 1268–1540 1350/87–1541? 1317–1539	13 13 6 10.5		-
Temple Finghin	1144 or 1223–1500?	Clonmacnoise	Aug. Canons	1140?–1268?	Co-located		1111
Temple na Ferta	1144–1562?	Armagh	Aug. Canons Franciscan	1126–1562 1263/4–1566	Within town		1111
Templenagalliaghdoo	?	Errew	Aug. Canons	1413–1585?	Co-located		-

6 This visitation recorded that there were just three nuns and the prioress/abbess at St Mary's at this time; Hall, *Women and the Church*, p. 130.

Table 4.8 (*continued*)

Nunnery	*Period of Later Medieval Use*	*Male Houses in Vicinity*	*Order*	*Period of Use of Male House*	*Distance from Nunnery in km*[1]	*Historical Connection to Male House/or Other*	*Cathedral Location of Medieval Diocese*
Termonfeckin	1144–1539	Termonfeckin Drumshallon Drogheda	Aug. Canons Aug. Canons Fratres Cruciferi (3) Aug. Friars Carmelite Friars Dominican Friars Franciscan Benedictine	1144–1195 1202–62 1202–1540 1300–1539/43 1272–1539 1224–1540 1240/5–1506-21 1171–1238	Co-located 6 8 8 8 8 8 8	Archbishop of Armagh, 1440	-
Termonkeelin	1223–1543?	Cloonshanville Tulsk Elphin	Dominican Friars Dominican Friars Aug. Canons Franciscan	1385–1596 1448–1591 1140–1442 1453–1632	9.7 14 19		-
Timolin	1199–1530s	Athy Athy Baltinglass Castledermot Castledermot	Fratres Cruciferi Dominican Friars Cistercian Fratres Cruciferi Franciscan	1199/1253–1540 1253/7–1539 1148–1536 1216–1540 1247–1540	11 11 8 8.7 8.7	Archbishop of Dublin, John Cumin (Comyn), 1291 (Hall 2003, 44)	-
Tisrara	?	Rindown Rindown Inchcleraun Athleague	Fratres Cruciferi Knights Hospitallers Aug. Canons Aug. Canons	1216–1569? ? 1140–1541 1266–1466?	14.5 14.5 15 6		-
Wicklow	1448–70	Wicklow	Franciscan	1268–1551	Within town		-
Youghal	1385–1542?	Youghal	Dominican Friars Franciscan	1268–1583? 1229–1541/2	2 0.5		-

their establishment and period of use is far from clear. Due to this ambiguity, these were excluded and only male religious houses have been considered.

Male religious houses which pre-date and post-date the nunneries' foundations have been included in each case to analyse if the presence of a nunnery may also have affected the choice of location of a male house. Historical connections have been noted in the table to show that in some cases the nunnery was at some remove from the male house with which it was associated, such as Kilcreevanty and Cong. Some nunneries, such as Grace Dieu and Kilcreevanty, are historically associated with archbishops and bishops, and so cathedral locations were included. Co-located houses, where a house of Augustinian canons and nuns are thought to have been in close proximity and may have shared facilities, are included in the table and have already been discussed.

From an analysis of these data several interesting trends have emerged. For example, a small but significant number of nunneries – fourteen – were established in places that at the time of their foundation had no male house in proximity and so were the first later medieval religious houses in those areas (see Table 3.2). In time, male religious houses were established in the vicinity of these nunneries at an average distance of 8.3km. It could be suggested that communities of nuns would not have had influence over the siting of a neighbouring male religious house. However, if both houses shared a patron, s/he might be petitioned by the nuns and their views may have been considered. Even in these cases, it may have been favourable for the patron to have religious establishments in close proximity, and patrons' requirements may have been considered over and above the community of nuns. This distance of 8.3km highlights that the male foundations were accepting of the fact that the nunneries would be much closer than prescribed. The mean distance masks a wide variation, as in several cases the minimum distance between the existing nunnery and new male religious house is less than 1km, while the maximum distance is some 17km.

Of particular interest are the nunneries of St Peter's Cell and Kilculliheen, as both were situated either in and near important medieval walled towns. St Peter's Cell was established in 1171. The earliest male religious house in Limerick was the *Fratres Cruciferi* founded forty-five years later in 1216, followed by the Dominican Friary at St Saviour's in 1227.[168] However, while St Peter's Cell appears to have been the first later medieval religious house in Limerick, it was pre-dated by St Mary's Cathedral, with which it shared its patron, Donal O'Brien. The location of St Peter's Cell is close to the cathedral and it can be suggested, although not historically proven, that the patron of both foundations located them together deliberately.

Kilculliheen is the second example of a nunnery being the first religious house in an area. It was founded in 1151 on the left (northern) bank of the river Suir opposite the medieval town of Waterford. The first male religious house in the town was that of the Benedictines in 1190, thirty-nine years after the nuns' community had been established. Like Limerick, Waterford was already a cathedral town when the nunnery was founded.[169]

Interaction between nunneries and male religious houses and senior clerics is recorded in historical evidence. However, it is not easily revealed in the archaeological evidence of those religious houses. Associations might be tentatively tracked in architectural details and decoration, but only in a very few instances in Ireland. This is because most of the nunneries have little decorative fabric remaining.[170] For example, connections on the basis of ornamentation and architecture could be suggested between the Nuns' Church and Temple Finghin and their similar Romanesque style.[171] The 'School of the West' architecture at the nunneries of Inishmaine and Killone is similar in style and execution to that used at the Cistercian male house at Boyle, the Augustinian male house at Cong and the cathedral at Annaghdown.[172] The fine limestone west doorway and piscina at St Catherine's shows a peculiar fashion of using non-matching capitals and bases in later medieval architectural detailing. St Catherine's east window, as reconstructed by Westropp, is similar in style to – though smaller than – the windows in the Augustinian friary of Adare and the priory of Rathkeale (see Figure 9.18).

Furthermore, it has emerged that sixteen nunneries were situated in places that were at one time the seat of a bishop or archbishop, although in just three cases were they founded by a bishop. In the case of St Catherine's, the bishop of Limerick appears to have had some role in the foundation of the nunnery although is not recorded as founder. He was to be paid 8*s* yearly by the patrons of the nuns for land that was granted to the nuns by the patron, and a further 26*s* 8*d* in order to acquit the demesne land which is described as 'belonging to the Bishop'.[173] This suggests that the bishop of Limerick, upon a yearly payment, would provide land for rent on which the nuns' estate could be established and perhaps spiritually oversee the community of nuns on behalf of the patron.

Archbishops and bishops had the right of visitation at religious houses including nunneries.[174] Visitations and procuration – the maintenance of the bishop and his retinue engaged in the visit – were regularly abused and protests were recorded. For instance, in *The Black Book of Limerick*, a manuscript detailing medieval archives from the see of Limerick, abuses such as too many visitations or demands for procuration when no visitation subsequently took place were recorded by the chapter.[175] This right was sometimes abused at nunneries, as at Kilcreevanty, for instance.[176] The nuns there had difficulties with the archbishop of Tuam in the fourteenth century and had to appeal first to the abbot of Cong and then the pope for release from onerous visitations.[177]

Senior clerics such as bishops and the pope could be called upon by abbesses to mediate in disagreements with their patrons. For example, the bishop of Limerick was instructed by the pope to investigate an accusation of dissolute living against the nuns of St Catherine's by their benefactor the earl of Desmond in the fifteenth century.[178] Remnants of this interaction between senior clerics and nuns may be visible in the archaeological record in the proximity of some of the nunneries to cathedrals, for example St Peter's Cell, and in the cases of Kildare and Downpatrick, where the cathedrals are thought to actually mark the nunneries' locations.[179]

Following all this 'number-crunching' on the location of nunneries in Ireland, how can this data now inform a more interpretive discussion of the siting of those nunneries? A starting point is a comparison with the English evidence. There, 'relative isolation is a marked characteristic of the orders including Benedictine, Augustinian and Franciscan … choices of relatively inhospitable sites are too common to be merely a product of incompetence, ignorance or bad luck'.[180] Gilchrist has suggested that most nunneries in England and Wales must have deliberately chosen these sites in order to pursue a long-established ascetic eremitic monastic tradition: '… other nunneries were established in remote and isolated situations far from worldly distractions. These nunneries appear to have catered for women with a more penitential vocation'.[181] Of the nunneries in England and Wales, 125 of them are considered remote rural locations, with the remaining twenty-five described as suburban rather than being truly urban.[182]

In contrast, nunneries in Ireland have been sited much closer to contemporary settlement. Hall noted this pattern and suggested that it provided protection to female religious communities.[183] This hypothesis may indeed help to explain the contrast between nunnery siting in medieval Ireland and the relatively less turbulent landscapes of medieval England. However, it is not entirely satisfactory as an explanation. A similar pattern is noted in male mendicant houses in Ireland, many of which were located in proximity to castles and tower houses of their patrons and sometimes re-used secular dwellings and fortifications.[184] These locations were mutually beneficial to both parties: the patron providing protection and material support, while the proximity of the religious house enhanced the reputation of the patron as benefactor with a serious commitment to the church. Furthermore, this proximity juxtaposed the art and architecture of the aristocratic residences with more austere religious foundations.[185]

It is possible that monastic/religious consciousness in medieval Ireland differed from its English counterpart in that it did not fully share a strictly isolated eremitical tradition in the later period. For example, it has been demonstrated that religious women in early medieval Ireland travelled, some extensively, and probably lived in a variety of situations such as at smaller family ecclesiastical sites, mixed communities, and proprietary churches (see Chapter 3). Therefore, the enduring tradition in medieval Ireland may have been for female religious communities to be closer to contemporary settlements than has been previously realised. This ethos might lead to a secluded rather than isolated location – which could be symbolic rather than actual, but no less powerful – for the religious house within the community. Evidence for this perspective might be found in Gerald of Wales' disapproving descriptions of nunneries that did not have permanent boundaries, that were regularly breached and that were located close to their male counterparts, as illustrated at Kildare in his history and topography of Ireland (Figure 4.32).[186]

Several nunneries in England were delimited by a water-filled moat. It has been suggested that this was a metaphor for the medieval understanding of medical humours, which identified the female body as watery by nature. It may also highlight the aspirations, and indeed origins, of the nunnery community aligning itself with the gentry classes, who were associated with moat construction.[187] Unlike England, there is now little indication of how nunnery precincts in Ireland were delimited (see Chapter 5); they may have been surrounded by moats, but none are now visible.[188] Several nunnery sites in Ireland are adjacent to moated sites. From the family ties of patronage and the physical proximity of many nunneries to their local contemporary communities in medieval Ireland, it can now be suggested that their primary function was one of service and interaction with that surrounding community. This is a conclusion only reached for a minority of English nunneries: 'the situations of some nunneries indicate that they were intended by their founders to interact closely with the local community'.[189]

Therefore, the interactions of the majority of nunneries in medieval Ireland appear to differ slightly from those in England. In Ireland, the vast majority can be considered to have had regular interaction with the local community in which they were situated. In England, this was a characteristic of only a minority of nunneries. There, the majority were isolated, and devoted to a more eremitical vocation mirroring that of early desert monasticism. No clear reason for this regional difference has yet emerged, though religious ethos may offer an explanation. English nunneries tended to be Benedictine, while the majority of Irish nunneries were Augustinian of Arroasian observance. This

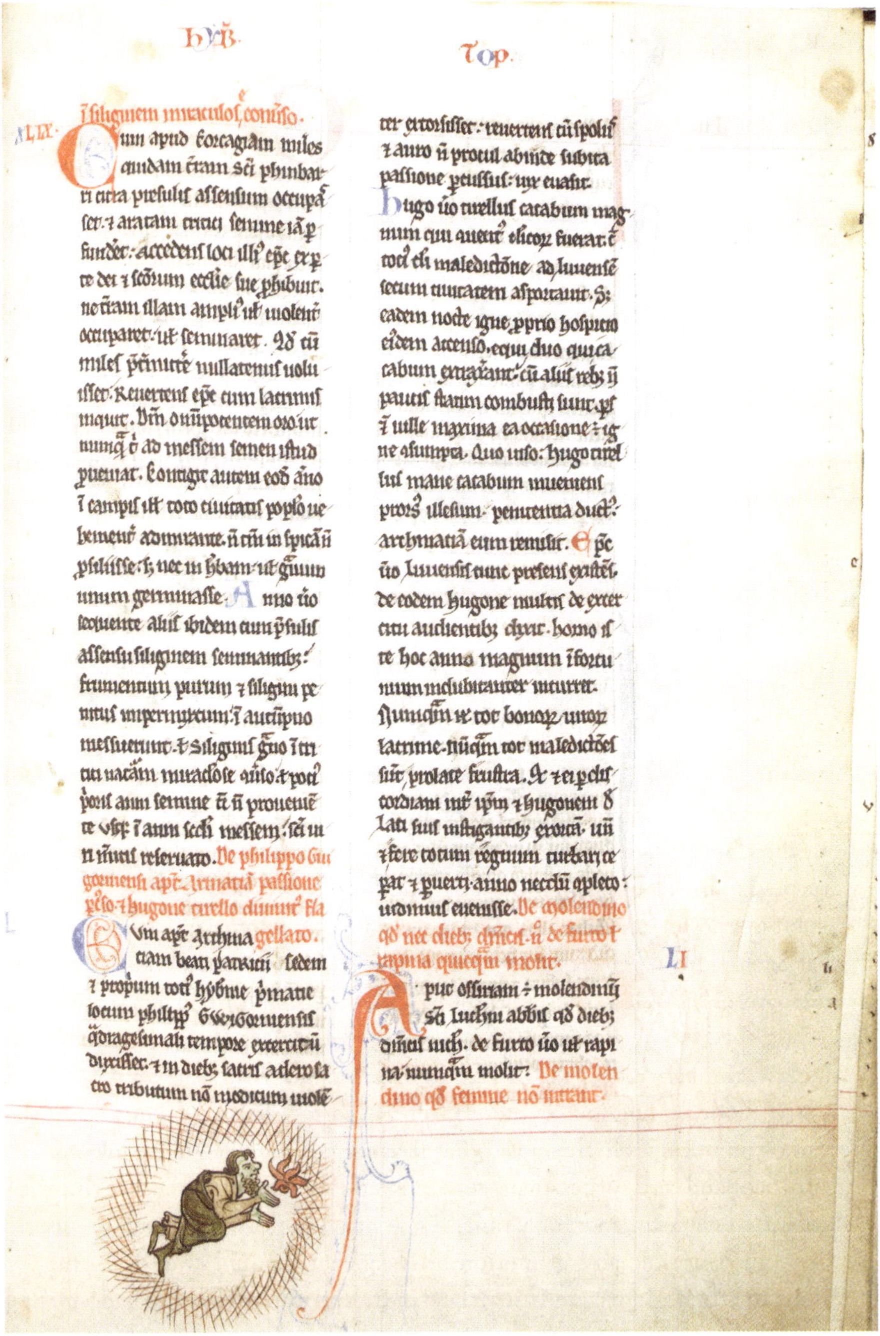

4.32 The thicket boundary around Kildare as illustrated in MS 700 F[31]R from Giraldus Cambrensis' *Topographica Hibernica Expugnatio Hibernia*. Courtesy of the National Library of Ireland.

difference has been noted elsewhere but not extensively discussed.[190] Perhaps it was differences in ethos and the religious identity of the medieval female orders in the two regions that resulted in different relationships with their situations in respective medieval landscapes (see Chapter 9).

Interactions between male and female religious houses and between nunneries themselves are very difficult if not impossible to perceive in the archaeological record. However, the historical record can supplement the narrative.[191] Monks and priests are known to have acted on behalf of nunneries. There are accounts and some inferences of abbesses creating discrete nunnery networks, such as those houses affiliated to Clonard as the mother house of the Arroasian observance in Ireland,[192] or Killone.[193] Sometime later a nunnery network, which sprang up around Kilcreevanty, as the Arroasian mother house in Connacht, saw nuns interacting with each other and with male authority, most notably the archbishop of Tuam.[194]

DENSITY OF NUNNERIES ELSEWHERE

Female religious houses in Britain and mainland Europe operated in parallel with male monasticism in the later middle ages. Many accounts of medieval monasticism in England have been accused of omitting or marginalising the role of women,[195] though several important publications have certainly improved this position.[196] Current estimates of numbers of nunneries in England vary but there are at least 153 examples, plus eighteen double houses, six nuns' cells attached to male houses and four quasi-double houses (see Figure 3.5).[197]

Nunneries in Scotland and Wales are much less numerous. It is estimated that Scotland had thirteen to fifteen female religious houses,[198] and just three foundations in Wales. This apparent lack of provision for female monasticism in later medieval Wales 'is quite astonishing', and it has been suggested that the low numbers represent 'private devotion rather than claustration … [as] … the mode of religious expression preferred for Welsh women'.[199] On the basis of numbers it would appear that Ireland may have had more in common with Scotland and Wales than with England in regard to the provision of monastic establishments for women. The provision of new monastic houses for women was already in motion in Ireland in the mid twelfth century.[200] When the Anglo-Normans first arrived in Ireland in 1169 they too had a mental template of what a nunnery ought to be, and had influence over the character of female monasticism within their ambit. It is sometimes forgotten, but many of these first settlers to Ireland were actually of Cambro-Norman origin rather than English, and perhaps this origin may go some way to explaining possible similarities between Ireland and Wales, in contrast to the larger neighbour England.[201]

Hundreds of nunneries were operating in continental Europe throughout the later medieval period, particularly in what is now modern Germany.[202] Many of these establishments were a continuation of early medieval foundations, many under royal patronage.[203] In stark contrast to Britain and Ireland, in many regions of Europe numbers of Cistercian houses of nuns actually exceeded those of male houses.[204] Nunneries were particularly plentiful in the low countries of modern Holland and Belgium.[205] Therefore, the nunneries of later medieval Ireland were part of a much wider medieval European phenomenon, but with their own regional distinctiveness in their distribution and siting. We now turn our attention to the detail of the nunnery complexes and their buildings.

CHAPTER 5

Nunnery Enclosure and Layout

NEGOTIATING SPACE AND PLACE

The spaces utilised by people and their transformations into places is a complex issue. Although 'place' is becoming the favoured term in much of the literature and is identified by many as a better guide to medieval thinking, in the discipline of archaeology the term 'space' is considered more objective than 'place', which has implications of interpretation and is thus more subjective. Put succinctly, space is practised place.[1] A monastic setting is a particularly good place to consider the concept of space, as a monastery or nunnery was a place where individuals lived under a monastic rule.[2] These rules provide normative views of the ideal monastic structure of space, while also embodying the codified behaviour of the later medieval period.[3]

As already outlined, there are no extant rules for later medieval nunneries in Ireland (Chapter 3).[4] The Benedictine rule has been described as being 'obsessed with space',[5] and in the context of thirteenth-century England space had very specific meanings for Cistercian monks.[6] Attitudes towards use of space in monastic settings were formed by a shared knowledge of ancient monastic rules and mores, sermons and written tradition,[7] and 'once a nunnery space had been constructed (both textually and physically) it in turn defined and constrained the individuals it encompassed: that is, the space defined the people'.[8]

Real observation of the monastic rules and how they informed space can be made for Britain and the continent through the available historical documentation, such as monastic accounts, wills, correspondence and visitations,[9] which are lacking for medieval Ireland.[10] The Rich Clares' rule of Ghent, Belgium, dated to 1263, is a good example, where prescribed behavioural standards are set out according to architectural spaces in the nunnery, especially the parlour and dormitory. Punishments were issued when these codes were breached, which included excommunication or isolation from the community as a form of public humiliation for the wrongdoer.[11] The Rich Clares' rule was found to be very similar to those of others, such as Francis, Benedict or Augustine.[12]

Space in a monastic context itself was used as a form of punishment, through distancing and isolation from the community. Some religious houses were equipped with a house prison specifically for this purpose.[13] It has been suggested that this monastic correction method later informed other secular punishment forms, such as perpetrators being sent away on pilgrimage, isolated from their own community and the scene and victims of their crimes. Thus 'the psychological power of space was clearly recognised in the monastic communities' from an early period.[14] Furthermore, drawing on the work of Foucault[15] and his ideas of space as a tool of discipline, correction and power, Cassidy-Welch has suggested that structures – articulations of space – can be used to express and maintain institutional interests, especially in the monastic strategy of enclosure.[16]

Female monastic space and its uses has also been explored in ethno-archaeological studies of modern religious communities, such as that undertaken by Gilchrist at Burnham Abbey in Buckinghamshire, England – a medieval foundation in modern use.[17] She found that the space structure in the medieval nunnery was likely to have been very similar to its modern use as an Anglican contemplative convent that continued to follow the Augustinian rule.[18] Gilchrist concluded that space within the nunnery was influenced by four related internal stratifications: seniority; male and female liturgical roles; division of secular (both worker and guest) and religious; and recognition of difference between the nun as a part of the community and the nun as an individual.[19] Turk, in his archaeological analysis of modern Cistercian houses of both men and women in Ireland, found a careful arrangement of public and private lives in actions, architecture and landscape. Private space is lacking and an individual is rarely free from observation, though monks and nuns now utilise individual cells. Modern monastic life is structured through egalitarianism, with the sharing of humble tasks along with sleeping, eating and working.[20]

Monastic space was hierarchically ordered, mirroring the series of office-holders below the abbess.[21] Seniority within the community underpinned its social hierarchy and was the primary factor in the spatial arrangements and ordering of the nunnery. Seniority was based on time of entry (and merit) rather than age, and on occasion this must have caused tension between members of the community. The seating arrangements in the church were based on seniority, and this arrangement was carried through all aspects of life: from processions, to dining in the refectory, to sleeping arrangements in the dormitory. Postulants and novices (new entrants) were discretely separated from the rest of the nuns and they ate and slept together in their own quarters.[22]

The Burnham Abbey study showed that although at the bottom of the authority structure, those in this nunnery group were cocooned in the deepest space of the monastery. This spatial buffer zone meant that they were doubly protected during the course of their novitiate. The abbess was in charge within the nunnery, though the priest had a place of authority in his liturgical role as intermediary between Christ and the nuns.[23] Others within the remit of a medieval nunnery may have included oblates (a person who has offered themselves, or a child who has been offered to a monastery, to serve God as a nun), pupils, servants, workers, tenants and visitors.[24] In later nunnery phases, tenements are even known to have existed within nunnery precincts, as at St Mary Clerkenwell, London.[25]

The medieval social hierarchy played out in the physical arrangement of monastic space around the cloister,[26] though alternative models with less formal spatial arrangements are also known for both religious men and women.[27] Indeed, from the archaeological evidence for nunneries in later medieval Ireland, it appears that claustral arrangements were the exception rather than the rule. Boundaries and divisions within the monastic space could be either physical – walls, screens, grilles – or conceptual and expressed through the liturgy, sermons or rules.[28] There is very little extant archaeological evidence of boundaries at nunneries and it is likely that many divisions of space were also created more ephemerally through the performance and celebration of daily ritual and liturgy. The division of space between outer court and inner cloister divided more everyday chores from more spiritual work while also helping to regulate encounters between the laity (servants and workers of both sexes) and the religious of the nunnery. The more discrete divisions of space in the church and domestic quarters would have further segregated guests, as well as the different grades of nuns within the community, while also facilitating the trend towards private spaces.

The qualities of spaces within a nunnery would appear to be of particular importance. I am not suggesting the existence of a qualitative scale of spaces from 'poor' to 'excellent'; rather we should seek to identify and consider the particular qualities of different places within the nunnery complex. Architecture and time are manipulated to create spaces in different places in the nunnery that had these particular qualities, perhaps only at specific times. As previously stated, binary oppositions are sometimes unhelpful, and therefore merely identifying public/communal versus private/individual spaces in a nunnery, such as a communal dormitory, refectory or church, versus more private spaces of individual cells within a dormitory, private accommodation or the cloister garth, is to miss the point. When time is added to this binary equation, understandings of space and its use become much more complex. Indeed, almost every space in a nunnery could be considered in this way. Dormitories[29] may have been for communal sleeping, but added timber cubicles provided some privacy for the individual nun to pray and perhaps meditate at her own private altar, with a devotional book or a Christ figure, returning to a more eremitical way of living.[30] Indeed, in a nunnery items which were not considered communal or public were described as 'worldly' – personal private items of the nuns, many of which were also spiritual, such as private prayer books and devotional imagery.[31]

In the same way, refectories were a place for communal dining and perhaps for daily chapter, as in the early years of the Cistercian house at Clairvaux.[32] Listening to a reader during mealtimes still allowed for private understanding of, and meditation on, the text being read. The church, a place for communal gathering, in turn allowed for the individual to contemplate devotional images and pray. Just one method of how this private quality of space was achieved was through the use of silence, which all monastic rules included to a greater or lesser extent.[33] For example, the rule of St Benedict makes provisions for personal silent time and space in Chapters 6, 7 and 42. Solemn silence was usually observed through the night from vespers until after mass next day. There were also spaces within the monastery where silence was observed at all times, such as the church, refectory or dormitory. By respecting silence, it was thought the nuns could concentrate more fully on their relationship with God, while maintaining harmony in the community.[34] Cluniac reform brought in absolute silence in the cloister as a special place for prayer and reflection.[35]

The cloisters were also multi-functional spaces. Cloister ambulatories (walkways) were used generally for circulation but also for communal procession, burial and communal reading (for example, the collation bay, abbot's seat and lectern base excavated at Tintern, County Wexford).[36] Total silence within the cloister, or periods thereof, aided individual contemplation, prayer and even pilgrimage. In some nunneries of the Low Countries, their cloisters became the set for virtual pilgrimages to Jerusalem. A nun would walk three times around the cloister to replicate the distance Christ walked when presented to Pilate; to the cloister fountain to signify Christ before Herod; and three more times around the cloister representing Christ's return to Pilate after meeting Caiaphas and Annas.[37]

Cloister arcading further added to this individual space in the ambulatories by limiting visibility across the garth, in addition to its practical function of supporting a roof. It also provided a canvas for carved or painted images that could be contemplated during individual prayer.[38] Those at the Cistercian male monastery of Jerpoint, County Kilkenny include religious imagery such as St Catherine, and more secular motifs such as women and knights (Figure 5.1).[39] These images carved on cloister arcading are thought to have served a didactic function for the community, who contemplated their messages as they walked

5.1 An image of St Catherine on the cloister arcading of the male Cistercian monastery at Jerpoint, Co. Kilkenny. Image: Frank Coyne.

through the ambulatories or meditated on the enclosed garth space. There are now no upstanding cloister arcades at nunneries in Ireland, though this would be less surprising if the number of claustral nunneries was not great, perhaps fewer than ten or eleven. Extant medieval arcades of male religious houses in Ireland suggest that in most cases the garth itself was not entered, as most do not have entrances.[40] Other evidence proves that at least some garths were used and contained plants or wells, and on occasion were used for burial.

Monastic rules which were followed also had subtle effects on space. In theory the Benedictine rule as followed by Cistercians, for instance, stressed enclosure and separation from the world, and stated that a minimum of twelve persons was required for a religious community. The Augustine rule, on the other hand, had a more pastoral ethos which allowed for more interactions and local community service. It did not prescribe minimum numbers for a religious community. Therefore, the negotiation of space and place in the context of a religious house is complex. The extant archaeological evidence shows what spaces were created at nunneries over time and archaeologists can theorise over possible multiple uses. Furthermore, the archaeological evidence from Ireland suggests that the enclosure of nunneries was more conceptual than physical. Let us now consider that evidence.

ENCLOSURE: SYMBOLISM AND MATERIAL EXPRESSION

The basis of the profession of a nun was the acceptance of the universal monastic values of chastity, obedience and poverty, along with stability and behaviour appropriate to the religious life. Enclosure can be added to this list, and in theory enclosure was a universal precept for all medieval monastics. However, it was unequally enforced and was strictly imposed on women religious, even Third Order Tertiaries, so much so that some scholars refer to it as a fourth vow.[41] 'Nunnery space as constructed by the nunnery rules was both physical and notional space', as it not only defined the nuns who were confined, but also those who lived outside the space, who 'constituted a threat to the chastity and well-being of the sisters'.[42]

Nunnery enclosure is therefore an important manifestation of the concept of 'space as practised place' as it has both symbolic and material expression. An important aspect of the nature of enclosure is the subtle shift in its meaning over time from a passive enclosure of protection,[43] to an active enclosure likened to imprisonment.[44] Implicitly, the attempts to strictly enclose nuns highlighted the distrust felt for female religious and the misogynistic tendencies of some of the church's male hierarchy. Consequently, enclosure is usually viewed negatively as a controlling tactic of the church hierarchy over religious women through time, and is considered by many as misogyny and suppression. While the church did not issue a papal decree on universal enclosure until 1298, it was preceded by a long tradition of cloistering female religious (Chapter 3). This tradition was perpetuated for the ultimate benefit of male religious, as 'it was safer for monks to have nuns enclosed in nunnery space'.[45]

However, enclosure continued to be accepted by every woman who entered religious life as a professed nun, and in the case of the Rich Clares at Ghent it was 'never contested'.[46] Enclosure thus may be considered a positive part of religious life;[47] the cloister was a paradise for the inner self and a glimpse of Heaven while on earth. For nuns, it was the world itself that was a prison. They were escaping it within the confines of the nunnery.[48] Because enclosure was so ingrained in the mental template of female monasticism and probably of the nuns themselves, it seems to have been taken for granted. Contemporary records of the nature and practice of female monastic enclosure are extremely rare, and so it is difficult to make generalisations and universal statements; 'only through incidental evidence are we able to catch a glimpse … [which has] … plagued modern scholars in their studies on the existence and significance of female enclosure in the medieval world'.[49]

Therefore, paradoxes are inherent in the concept of female monastic enclosure. Strict enclosure for a nunnery, as a corporate structure, may have been a negative force, as it did not permit nunneries to flourish in society in the same way as male monasteries, and could devastate a nunnery community.[50] For the individual nun, however, and her life course within the nunnery, enclosure could be a positive experience, providing separation and protection from the trials and tribulations of life outside, while providing a place of calm contemplation in their efforts to get closer to God. Enclosure in this capacity also nurtured the community's positive awareness of its own identity.[51] Furthermore, discrepancies between the written norm of enclosure, its acceptance, and its practice have been revealed.[52] The fact that the lack of strict enclosure emerges so regularly in the historical documentation of nunneries abroad, and at nunneries in Ireland – for example, Lismullin – suggests that its enforcement was never completely successful. Lismullin was probably not alone in its flouting of enclosure. Later medieval Irish nunneries of every affiliation have accounts which illustrate how permeable their cloisters could become,[53] and particular cases have become legendary, such as Elicia Butler, abbess of Kilculliheen,[54] or Renalda O'Brien.[55] In the case of co-located houses (Chapter 4), a certain degree of contact between religious men and women was probably tolerated, though both groups were likely segregated. Therefore, the somewhat ephemeral and illusive nature of enclosure in the historical evidence has led some to suggest that segregation of nuns has been overestimated,[56] and that 'the cloister was more a state of mind than physical imprisonment'.[57]

But the picture of female religious in a European context was certainly not monolithic in regard to enclosure,[58] and it should be remembered that ordered enclosed nuns were not the only religious women of the later middle ages. The unenclosed way of life of vowesses[59] and secular canonesses on the continent was safeguarded by their long tradition, and certain tertiaries had obtained papal approval for their *modus vivendi*.[60] Other quasi-religious groups, however, who lived in uncloistered communities and led a *vita apostolica*, such as the Beguines, were continually condemned by the church hierarchy for their lack of enclosure and male supervision.[61] It seems that it was the lack of male supervision at these communities, and the disregard of active enclosure by those religious women, that made them targets for clerical derision.

Enclosure suggests limits and boundaries. A strong emphasis on physical boundaries in Ireland is clearly evident in early medieval monastic practice, which was likely indicative of status rather than confinement (see Chapter 2).[62] The precinct or outer court of a religious house was a legal and idealised boundary as well as a physical one.[63] Moreover, Everson and Stocker have suggested from their study of a male Cistercian house at Kirkstead, Lincolnshire that monastic precinct boundaries should be considered a zone 'permeable in different circumstances and to different degrees rather than as a hard line in the landscape traditionally conceived in archaeological thinking'.[64] A brief overview of precinct boundaries of male religious houses and nunneries in Britain now follows, in order to set the scene for a consideration of precinct boundaries at nunneries in Ireland.

An overview of enclosure elsewhere

The precinct of a monastery, its enclosure and its varying number of courts was primarily dictated by the affluence of the monastic house, and then by the rules of the order, the religious significance of the house and the geographical features of the site.[65] In the late 1980s it was noted that the plans of outer precincts of both male and female religious houses in England and Wales were 'imperfectly known' and very little archaeological investigation had taken place.[66] More recent work there has shown that male religious houses had a variety of precinct enclosures, including stone walls, earthen banks, ditches and hedges,[67] as at Thornholme Priory (Augustinian), Lincolnshire,[68] and the Cistercian houses of Buildwas, Shropshire; Tintern, Gwent; Dore, Herefordshire; and Stanley, Wiltshire.[69] In some cases, different forms of enclosure, such as walling and hedging, were used in a single precinct circuit, as identified at the Cistercian house of Hailes Abbey, Gloucestershire.[70] In Scotland, excavations at Arbroath, Tayside (Tironensian) revealed a stone wall interpreted as the precinct boundary.[71]

Nunneries in England show a variety of precinct enclosures, where they can be seen to exist. The dissolution surveys provide most information known about precincts, as at Romsey, Wherwell, and St Mary's Winchester, all in Hampshire, and Amesbury, Wiltshire.[72] Sixteenth-century descriptions of six Cistercian nunneries in Yorkshire (Kirklees, Baysdale, Wykeham, Esholt, Handale and Swine) in the survey *Valor Ecclesiasticus* has enabled the reconstruction of 'virtual' final-phase plans. The survey description of Esholt was the best, which enabled a complete reconstruction of the nunnery cloister and outer court. The precinct enclosure was detailed as 'a dry walle of stone', while the nunnery orchard was 'well pailed about'.[73] In each case, the precinct was enclosed (although the method of enclosure was not always specified as at Esholt), with restricted access to the cloisters, and usually had its entrance controlled by a gate.[74] Larger urban nunneries, such as Holywell,[75] Clerkenwell,[76] and St Helen's Bishopsgate, all in London,[77] or Chester,[78] do appear to have had stone precinct walls. In each case their layout influenced the surrounding urban street pattern. The only Dominican nunnery in England – Dartford, Kent – had remains of its precinct wall extant.[79] The more rural Lacock Abbey, Wiltshire had a precinct boundary formed by the outer court attached to the claustral complex without enclosing a large area.[80]

Many nunnery precincts in England were moated,[81] as at Burnham, Buckinghamshire.[82] Typical nunnery precincts were smaller, with less elaborate water systems and slighter earthworks than their male counterparts.[83] Field survey has revealed precincts defined by earthworks at Stainfield and Orford, both in Lincolnshire.[84] Orford's precinct was planned in conjunction with a single-sided village.[85] Godstow's Oxfordshire precinct was bounded by ditches and the river Thames.[86] Excavations at Elstow, Bedfordshire clearly identified two sides of its precinct, the south and east, which were formed by outbuildings rather than a wall and there was no evidence of a gatehouse.[87] On occasion, enclosing earthworks may have been re-used and it has been suggested that the extensive earthworks noted at Denny Abbey, Cambridgeshire originated in a Romano-British settlement.[88]

Turning to male religious houses in Ireland, there is some precinct enclosure evidence at Cistercian houses, as for example at Fore, County Westmeath,[89] Baltinglass, County Wicklow,[90] Mellifont, County Louth,[91] Corcomroe, County Clare,[92] and Tintern, County Wexford;[93] and the dearth of information regarding precincts is due to the lack of large-scale archaeological excavation at these sites.[94] Excavations at Abbeyknockmoy, County Galway did not reveal an enclosing element.[95] A preliminary survey of Duiske Abbey, County Kilkenny suggested that the precinct of the monastery had an effect on the adjacent village's street pattern but no physical evidence of a precinct wall was found.[96] It has been noted that at many Cistercian male houses by the sixteenth century, 'the formal barrier between the enclosed world of the monks and the local population outside had long since disintegrated'.[97]

Male Augustinian houses in Ireland are noted for their architectural variety, and many were smaller foundations.[98] The precinct and features of the Augustinian priory of St John's, Kilkenny has been reconstructed through rental archives.[99] Excavations at St Thomas', Dublin revealed a deep enclosing ditch, which was later replaced with a stone wall on a plinth foundation, with an external ditch, interpreted as the precinct boundary, which has been shown to have had a profound effect on the layout of Dublin in its immediate surroundings.[100] The precinct boundary of Christ Church Cathedral in Dublin

5.2 Kells Priory, Co. Kilkenny. © National Monuments Service, Department of Housing, Local Government and Heritage.

5.3 Athassel Priory, Co. Tipperary. © National Monuments Service, Department of Housing, Local Government and Heritage.

5.4 St Peter's Cell, Limerick, possibly the nunnery precinct wall, later incorporated into the city wall. Image: Tracy Collins.

(Holy Trinity) is known from nineteenth-century antiquarian drawings.[101] Investigations at Trinity College Dublin, the site of the Augustinian priory of All Hallows, have revealed some aspects of the monastery, but the precinct and its enclosure are still only known from documentary sources.[102] At some Augustinian houses, precinct boundaries remain unclear, as at Bridgetown Priory, County Cork[103] or Clontuskert, County Galway.[104] However, the best-preserved examples of precinct walls in later medieval Ireland are at two Augustinian male houses, Kells, County Kilkenny,[105] and Athassel, County Tipperary (Figures 5.2 and 5.3).[106] Kells is unusual in that it retains an attached *villa prioris* to the south, which is a large castellated enclosure 1.08 hectares in extent, which functioned as a monastic bawn within which tenants and stock could seek refuge in times of danger.[107]

For the mendicant orders, strict enclosure was not entirely compatible with their ethos, which included preaching and the quest of begging for alms.[108] Yet despite this more open engagement with the local populace they maintained a cloister-centred model.[109] Precinct walls and gates are known from several Franciscan and Third Order houses, for example Adare, County Limerick, Lislaughtin, County Kerry, Killeenbrenan and Moyne, County Mayo. Excavations at the Dominican priory of St Mary's of the Isle, Cork did not reveal any precinct enclosing element, though the constraints of the site limited the excavation's extent.[110] The likely outline of the precinct at the Dominican

5.5 Kylemore, Co. Galway, the re-use of a big house for a modern enclosed nunnery and the surrounding mountains as its enclosure. Image: Frank Coyne.

priory at Drogheda, County Louth was established from historical evidence.[111] Excavations at Holy Trinity, an Augustinian friary at Dublin, revealed two portions of its stone precinct wall.[112]

The extant archaeological remains of nunneries in Ireland show that in most cases their enclosure was not a 'hard line in the landscape' and may not always have been given material expression. The concept may have been more symbolic. This is based on the fact that no extant later medieval nunnery in Ireland now possesses any trace of surrounding precinct walls. It is certainly possible that some nunneries in later medieval Ireland which are no longer extant, such as St Peter's Cell, Lismullin, St Mary de Hogges or Grace Dieu, had precinct walls. St Peter's Cell was originally outside the walled town of Limerick, which was later incorporated, and it is possible that the town wall circuit re-used some of the precinct wall of the nunnery, although there is now no indication of this in the visible fabric (Figure 5.4).[113]

Notwithstanding these, the absence of substantial stone enclosures is a pattern that cannot be easily dismissed.[114] One possibility is that less permanent or natural forms of enclosure, such as hedgerows, may have been employed. For example, Gerald of Wales described the nunnery at Termonfeckin as being enclosed by hedgerows with many gaps and, as has been mentioned, illustrated the nunnery at Kildare as being surrounded by a hedge rather than a wall (see Figure 4.32).[115] He wrote of Termonfeckin, 'Moreover, the monasteries were customarily enclosed, not with a wall or a ditch but only with hedges made of sharpened stakes and blackthorn, in which there are many openings not made by chance but deliberately … By this broken-down way and footpath an abbot has access to the abbess, by another a prior to the prioress, by a third a cellarer to the cellaress and so on, to the great scandal of the whole order and religion. Moreover, many people in the same way are received by the said persons of both sexes in their houses … and openly are luxuriously and extravagantly looked after beyond all measure.'[116]

So, while the ruins of nunnery churches, ranges and cloisters are available for archaeological debate, there is currently no evidence of the wider physical boundaries, such as precinct walls, which may have been placed around nunneries to achieve physical enclosure. Hedges and vegetation may have been used, as evidenced in the historical record, but what of other natural features? The archaeological potential of natural features has been considered in a prehistoric context,[117] but rarely in a medieval one. A modern example from a nunnery in Ireland serves to illustrate this potential. A Benedictine community of nuns from Ypres in Belgium with Irish connections purchased Kylemore, County Galway in 1920 to establish an enclosed community and boarding school (Figure 5.5). Enclosure of the community became an issue, as, after purchasing the house for a large sum, it was unfeasible to then construct an enclosing wall. With the advice of the archbishop of Tuam, it was agreed that the mountains surrounding the convent would act as a physical and metaphorical enclosure for the community.[118] It is interesting to postulate that this subtle and sophisticated use of the natural environment as a symbolic rather than a physical enclosing element for a nunnery may have also been used in the later medieval period in Ireland, at nunneries such as Carricknahorna and Killevy (see Figure 4.13).

Kilcreevanty and Termonkeelin are both close to large tracts of bog (with reclamation undertaken in modern times), which may have offered some sort of conceptual enclosure to the nunneries. If the bog was perceived as an enclosing element at Termonkeelin, mechanisms were used to negotiate it, as a trackway traversed the bog from the nunnery to a church at Termonmore (see Figure 4.19).

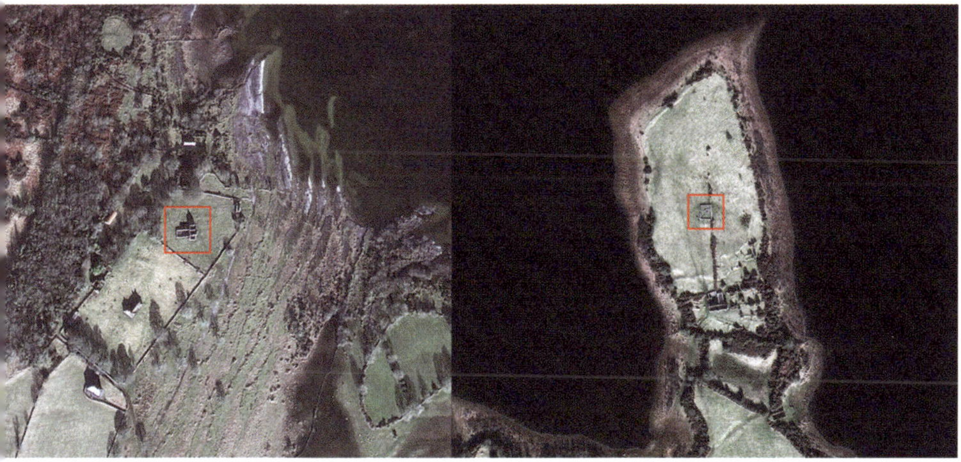

6 Inishmaine, Co. Mayo (*left*) and Templenagalliaghdoo, Co. Mayo, aerial view showing ıkeside peninsula locations. The male religious house of Errew is situated directly to the south ˙Templenagalliaghdoo. Google Earth © Maxar Technologies 17/1/2020. **5.7** (*below*) Temple nghin and the Nuns' Church, nunneries in red, at the ecclesiastical complex at Clonmacnoise, o. Offaly. After Ó Carragáin 2010, reproduced with permission of the author.

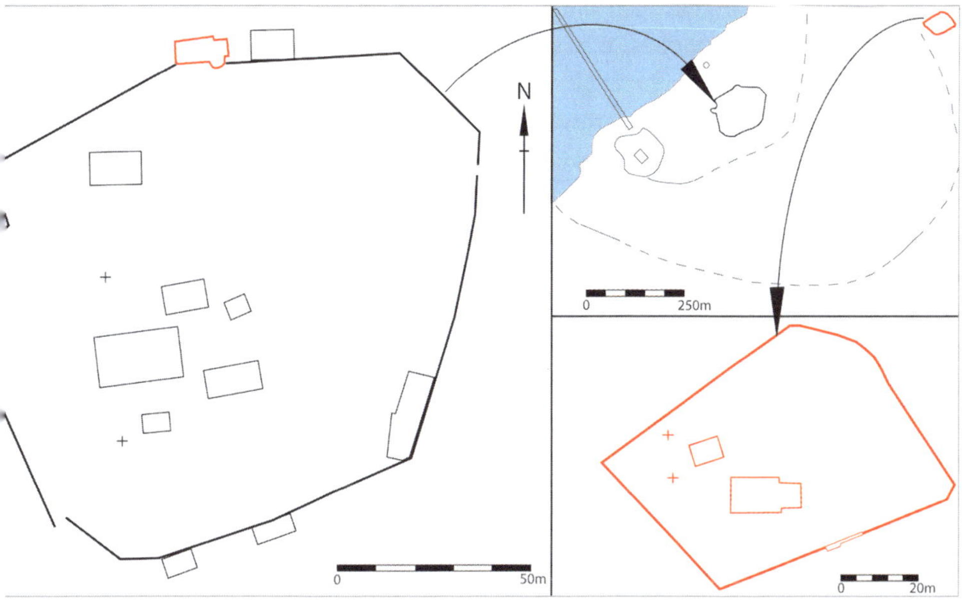

Templenagalliaghdoo and Inishmaine are now both located on lakeside peninsulas in County Mayo (Figure 5.6).[119] St Catherine's, despite being located in the generally flat land of west Limerick, is situated in a natural hollow or low-lying pocket, which makes the site surprisingly secluded (Chapter 9).[120] Therefore, while none of these nunnery sites have extant enclosing stone walls, it is possible that their situations in the landscape may have been considered by the communities of nuns to provide a symbolic enclosure.

Other nunneries might be considered in this way. Several nunneries are located within enclosures which once surrounded early medieval ecclesiastical sites. These nunneries are Annagh, Armagh, Cloonoghil, Duleek, Durrow, Kildare, Killeigh and Lusk. Several of these were important ecclesiastical centres in the early medieval period. While it has not yet been archaeologically established if these enclosures were still in use in the later medieval period, a strong case could be made that they were retained in some form at Armagh,[121] and possibly Killeigh (see Figure 4.23).[122] It is postulated that the nunneries at these locations may have also made symbolic use of earlier ecclesiastical enclosures.

It is interesting to add in this context that the Nuns' Church at Clonmacnoise was situated immediately outside the suggested line of the outer enclosure of the main ecclesiastical enclosure, in its own complex, though the second nunnery there, Temple Finghin, was positioned adjacent to what was likely the main inner enclosure (Figure 5.7).[123] Therefore, in later medieval Ireland, many nuns may not have been physically enclosed by any strong permanent boundary around their nunnery complexes, and banks and hedges may have been typical. Indeed, it has been stressed that in the often violent times of the medieval period, enclosure, whether of stone or otherwise, could never completely guarantee protection and security from potential marauders.[124]

Jäggi and Lobbedey have noted, specifically for Cistercian houses, that there was no guidance for the physical layout of a nunnery. Neither were there specific instructions for enclosure in extant nunnery statutes and these documents only ever recommended 'restraint' in matters architectural.[125] Rules for nunneries did contain behavioural conditions for different architectural components, such as the parlour, dormitory, church or refectory.[126] From this ambiguity, a variety of nunnery forms and layouts resulted, both between orders and within the same order,[127] and Coppack's reconstruction survey of several Yorkshire nunneries bears this out.[128] Many English nunneries achieved seclusion through isolated location rather than massive physical barriers.[129] Overall, then, it would seem that the precise form of enclosure at nunneries was open to interpretation. The archaeological evidence from Ireland suggests that enclosure could be expressed materially, but was mostly expressed conceptually. This symbolic rather than actual enclosure was dependent on the social relationships between those inside and those outside the nunnery, 'upon mutual respect between those who lived inside as well as outside the convent walls'.[130] This mutual respect was part of the codified behaviour and social order of the medieval period, notwithstanding the violent encounters of that age.[131]

For female, and indeed many male, medieval religious houses, permanent precinct enclosure has not yet been confirmed through archaeological investigation. The archaeological data to date indicates that permanent stone precinct walls may have been constructed infrequently. This phenomenon is certainly not unique to the Irish context; 'through textual and archaeological evidence it is clear that women's monastic communities did not always have protective physical walls; their walls were often notional and sprang from understandings of nunnery space'.[132] This shows that in some cases enclosure was considered conceptual rather than a physical protection or defence. In the case of the Rich Clares in thirteenth- and fourteenth-century Ghent it was their behavioural codes for observing enclosure within various architectural spaces inside the nunnery that gave enclosure its symbolic substance.[133] On special occasions, such as feast days (of which there were many), enclosure was often completely relaxed, when nuns could take part in celebrations and processions.[134] Thus, it can be tentatively suggested that women religious may have been symbolically 'ring-fenced' within their local community rather than being contained within permanent stone boundaries.

From the archaeological evidence of monastic precincts, a spectrum of enclosure emerges. It can be suggested that the more affluent and perhaps more urban religious houses, both male and female, had physical boundaries delimiting their precincts, for enclosing the community but also for prestige, protection of property and defence. For smaller houses and those which were situated in suburban or rural locations, a more symbolic concept of enclosure was enforced through the codified behaviour of medieval society. This situation seems to have been the norm in Ireland and abroad. Evidence that nuns indirectly provided pastoral services to their benefactors and the lay population at large when their churches functioned as parish churches further supports the notion of the more symbolic concept of enclosure and separation (Chapter 6). Nuns were then placed at the interface of local society and the universality of the church. More importantly, they were at the junction of their communities and God, where they represented the very humanity of Christ in a tangible way to both men and women.[135]

PRECINCTS AND THEIR FEATURES

The monastic precinct was an area of land immediately adjacent to the nunnery's cloister complex, which housed the church and domestic ranges.[136] The precinct would have contained subsidiary structures for agricultural activities – sometimes called the home farm – or subsidiary buildings for

5.8 Inishmaine, Co. Mayo, gatehouse, southern façade and plan. Image: Tracy Collins and Frank Coyne.

5.9 St Catherine's, Co. Limerick, remains of original gate entrance. Image: Tracy Collins.

visitors and servants.[137] The necessity for precincts seems to have originated in the Benedictine ideal that all buildings required for the running of the monastic house should be contained within the monastic enclosure, so that the community could avoid leaving its confines.[138] In English nunneries, the evidence shows that the nunnery itself and its home farm was a compact unit and, unlike many of its male counterparts, did not engage in industry or contain storage facilities.[139]

While there is little if any extant trace of precinct boundaries of nunneries, there is archaeological evidence of some of their features. In Britain precincts were usually entered through gatehouses, some of which were quite substantial free-standing structures, sometimes with guest accommodation and chapels. These gatehouses had a number of functions: regulatory, symbolic, defensive and for accommodation.[140] There are fifteenth-century examples at the Augustinian nunneries at Canonsleigh and Cornworthy, both in Devon.[141] There are just two extant gateways at nunneries in Ireland, at Inishmaine and St

5.10 An interpretive reconstruction of the Franciscan Third Order house and later friary of Bonmargy, Co. Antrim showing how a gatehouse may have functioned with other forms of enclosure, by P. Armstrong. © Crown DfC Historic Environment Division.

Catherine's.[142] The conserved gatehouse at Inishmaine is a substantial two-storey structure and dates to the fifteenth century (Figure 5.8). The St Catherine's gateway shows no evidence of having been a larger structure suitable for accommodation (Figure 5.9). This is situated some 200m to the south of the nunnery complex and would have been an original entrance to the nunnery precinct. At present it stands as an arched double gateway in the hedgerow, constructed of roughly coursed limestone masonry. The top is obscured with ivy, though the entrance can be seen to be a very slightly pointed arch. The jambs splay slightly inwards. Its width (*c.*3m) suggests it was for vehicles, such as carts, destined for the agricultural area of the nunnery. This is confirmed by the fact that this entrance is not in line with the original southern entrance to the nunnery itself. Rather, it appears to be focused towards a dovecote. To the

5.11 St Catherine's, Co. Limerick, dovecote. View of interior of blocked entrance and nesting holes (*right*). Image: Tracy Collins.

east of this gateway there is a sunken way, which leads to a causeway and the entrance to the nunnery (see Figure 7.17). This is not an unusual arrangement, and in Britain many gateways contained separate formal entrances for carts and pedestrians.[143] Neither Inishmaine's nor St Catherine's gates now show evidence of being connected to or abutted by a stone wall, which suggests that they were free-standing structures (perhaps along a hedge) which defined the entrance to the nunneries (Figure 5.10).

The gateway gave access to the working yards of the precinct, which in turn gave way to the cloister complex. The precinct would have contained the necessary features and structures for the home farm and any agricultural activities, such as barns, small enclosures used as haggards or paddocks, orchards, dovecotes, fishponds, brew and bake houses and mills. There is archaeological evidence for some of these features at later medieval Irish nunneries. The only extant remains of a columbarium/dovecote at a nunnery are at St Catherine's.[144] It is on the southern side of the nunnery complex,[145] near the double gateway. It is a circular structure, 4.6m in internal diameter, 3m in height (to top of wall plate), and has a corbelled roof with central ope. Its walls are almost a metre in thickness. Externally, it has two string courses, one at the junction of the wall plate and curving roof, and the second near the ope. While these are pleasing architectural details, they had a practical function of preventing vermin entering the structure. Internally, several of its nesting holes are visible. The small original door, now blocked, is located on the west side of the structure. Originally, the central roof ope was covered with a timber cupola or lantern to allow the movement of the birds but prevent rain from penetrating the structure.[146] This could be blocked when birds needed to be contained. Nesting holes would be reached by means of a ladder or potence – a ladder mounted on a centrally pivoting timber frame – which could be easily pushed around the perimeter of the structure (Figure 5.11).

The function of a dovecote was to husband pigeons in order to provide meat for the religious community. It would produce a steady food source throughout the year. Dung produced was used as a rich fertiliser and could also be used in tanning. Feather and down could be used for bedding.[147] There were rules governing the provision of dovecotes and it was particularly important that the owners of the pigeons maintained enough arable land under corn from which the birds could feed. They also had to be sited in the centre of the demesne land, so that pigeons would eat only the owner's grain, and not the neighbours'.[148]

Therefore, the presence of a dovecote at St Catherine's suggests that it was at the centre of a productive estate. A dovecote is also suggestive of grain being grown or received by nunneries. Tenants' rents on nunnery estates (Chapter 9) and church tithes were both likely to have been paid, at least in part, in grain. Therefore, watermills were also a common feature of precincts of monastic houses, so that grain might be processed, stored and used. The water, which was an essential requirement for a functioning cloister, could also be used for powering a mill. While there is no extant evidence for a mill at St Catherine's, it is highly likely that one existed along one of its fast-flowing streams.[149]

Dovecotes and other precinct features are known from written sources of other Irish nunneries.[150] For example, Grace Dieu had two dovecotes along with a bread house, two granaries, a barn, a kiln, two stables, a cow house, a sheep house, two pigsties and other buildings, two haggards, a garden, two orchards, and six acres of pasture.[151] In some cases, mill races were constructed to power the mill, as at Grace Dieu.[152] Timolin and Lismullin[153] also owned water mills,[154] and Grace Dieu also operated a horse-powered mill. From this meagre evidence it can be inferred that many nunneries probably once had mills of various types, though in most cases mill type or function is not specified (Chapter 9).

Shell, sea and fresh water fish were important components of the monastic diet.[155] The majority of fish consumed in monastic houses in Britain was dried; either salted, smoked or pickled.[156] Artificial fishponds allowed this food resource to be close at hand and therefore fresh, particularly in urban locations, where monastic fishponds are first thought to have developed, copying an aristocratic innovation.[157] The first pond recorded in England dated to 1069.[158] Again, water was a crucial element for such a resource and may have been channelled by stream or perhaps supplied from a nunnery well.

5.12 St Catherine's, Co. Limerick, the overgrown remains of the fishpond. Remains of stone culvert to east of pond, which diverted water from the adjacent stream to fill it (*right*). Image: Tracy Collins.

There is no historical evidence for fishponds at nunneries in medieval Ireland. However, the archaeological evidence shows that there was a fishpond at St Catherine's (Figure 5.12). It is shown on the first-edition six-inch Ordnance Survey map as an ornamental pond in the garden of Old Abbey House.[159] But as this pond is situated immediately to the southwest of the nunnery's claustral complex, it seems reasonable that it originated as a medieval fishpond. This long rectangular pond[160] is water-fed through a culvert at its east end from the stream, which runs past the nunnery's southern side and is emptied through a second culvert at its western end, which re-joins the stream. A fishpond in a religious house could be used as both a store for live fish and also a breeding place, where stocks could be increased.[161] At St Catherine's, therefore, the nuns maintained two obvious secure food sources: the pond and the dovecote.[162]

Other water-derived food sources can be deduced from the historical sources of nunneries and their locations. Weirs, for eels or salmon – although they had to be located on suitable rivers, which may have been away from the nunnery – were another food source. Molough nunnery had an eel weir, presumably on the adjacent river Suir.[163] It is likely that all four nunneries on the river Suir had such weirs. The dissolution records for the Cistercian house at Inishlounaght show that it had three eel weirs and a salmon weir.[164] The location of St Peter's Cell, in an urban location very near the Abbey and Shannon rivers, suggests that it too probably had weirs.[165] Those nunneries that were located near the sea – Portrane, Wicklow, Youghal, Derry and Downpatrick – likely had regular access to sea fish. The nunneries situated adjacent to lakes probably had no requirement for a fishpond, as the lakes maintained a wild supply, as at, for example, Killone.

At a few nunneries water management can be identified, most obviously at St Catherine's and Grace Dieu. At Grace Dieu a series of streams appear to have been utilised in the vicinity of the nunnery, and much later were used for powering a large mill near the nunnery in the nineteenth century. Along the eastern side of the entrance causeway at St Catherine's a channel was dug to connect two naturally occurring streams. This made the stream running immediately to the south of the nunnery much faster-flowing. A culvert from this stream allowed the fishpond to be fed. It then emptied through another culvert further along the watercourse. At these two nunneries bridges were used to facilitate access over the water courses near the precincts. At St Catherine's, there are now four low, narrow, small single-span stone bridges. Two of these have been replaced in modern times but two are extant (although they have been repaired). While it cannot be confirmed that they are medieval survivals, it is reasonable to suggest that at least some of the fabric may be medieval in date and that the bridges are in their original locations. The bridges at Grace Dieu were much more substantial than St Catherine's and at least one carried a roadway. It was dated to the fourteenth century.[166]

There is no extant evidence in the outer courts of nunneries in Ireland for gardens, barns, granaries or other outbuildings, as can be still seen in Britain at, for instance, Bradford-on-Avon, Wiltshire.[167] It is possible that these structures were of timber and consequently have not survived. The purpose of the precinct adjacent to the nunnery was to assist in the continued maintenance of the community of nuns.[168] The precinct court was likely to have also housed servants and visitors to the nunnery, although there are no extant structures at nunneries in Ireland that can be identified for this purpose. The precinct or outer court was adjacent to the main nunnery complex, which included the church and the nuns' accommodation. It is to this area we now turn.

CLAUSTRAL LAYOUTS

> Walls of the cloister marked out the nunnery buildings as a separate space, differentiated from the surrounding landscape by its standard design and meant to ensure that the women within remained separate from the world outside.[169]

The accepted ubiquitous male monastic template of a claustral plan has led to the perception that all nunneries were also of claustral layout and strictly enclosed. The archaeological evidence does not support this perception, however, and this book shows that a variety of flexible layouts were utilised. Indeed, when

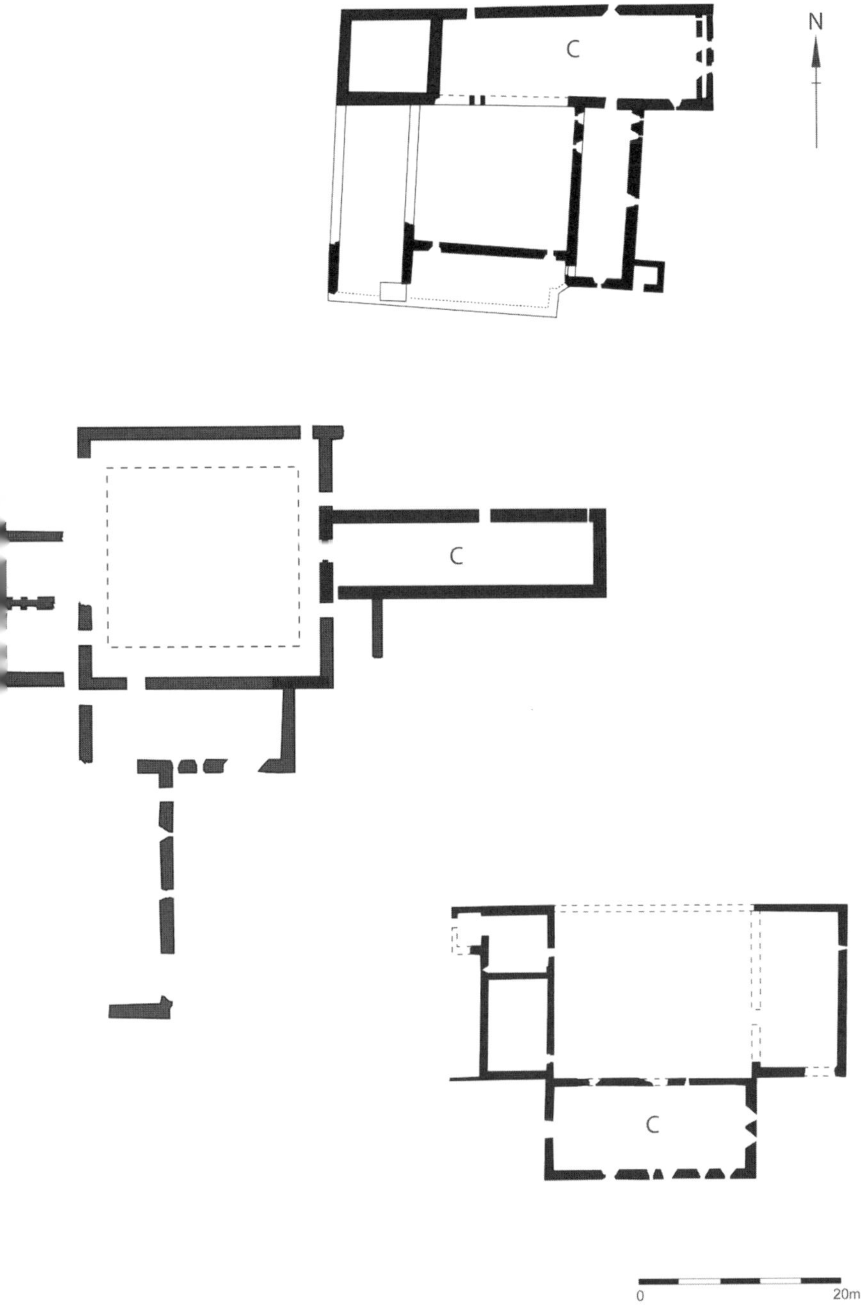

5.13 Claustral ground plans at nunneries: Killone, Co. Clare (upper), St Catherine's, Co. Limerick (middle) and Molough, Co. Tipperary (lower). C indicates the church. Image: Tracy Collins and Frank Coyne.

analysed, variation can also be identified in male religious houses and how they employed a claustral plan. This is particularly true of the Augustinian order, where for example at Inchicronan, County Clare and Kilmacduagh, County Galway a cloister was not employed.[170] As has been outlined, the impression of the universal use of a claustral plan originated in early scholarship, which tended to focus on larger sites with impressive and interesting architectural details in an Irish context,[171] and which set the tone and direction for future architectural and archaeological studies (Chapter 1).

The origin of the monastic cloister can be found in the courtyard and building architecture of the Mediterranean, which was employed as far as early medieval Syria in the fifth century. The monastic claustral tradition is thought to stem from the galleried courts of Roman *villae rusticae*. For example, St Martin used a villa and another was renovated at Lorsh to become a Benedictine monastery.[172] The U-shaped plan of buildings and church around a central court was thought to be an invention of the eighth and ninth centuries,[173] the best-known example being St Gall.[174] It became an enduring architectural tradition which perfectly symbolised and suited monastic life,[175] and it was adopted by all the major orders.[176] It is interesting to note that cloisters are also used in secular cathedrals and colleges in twelfth- and thirteenth-century England, as well as secular and episcopal palaces, with some particularly associated with queens as adjuncts to gardens and chambers.[177] Later medieval female monasticism also employed this claustral layout, but its use may have 'reflected men's own vision of women's religious life as often as women's own definition of their religious vocation'.[178]

There are now just three Irish nunneries which have upstanding cloisters: Killone, St Catherine's and Molough (Figure 5.13).[179] It is therefore possible, indeed likely, that a substantial proportion of nunneries did not employ a claustral plan, though this theory requires rigorous archaeological excavation. Furthermore, variation of plan may be a result of the materials used to construct the nunnery. It has been suggested that religious communities made use of free-standing timber structures before their stone monasteries were complete, as at the male Augustinian house of Norton Priory, Cheshire.[180]

Religious houses may have employed timber in their early or indeed latest phases, or used a combination of timber and stone throughout their use. Timber may have been used more frequently than the archaeological record now suggests, and future investigations at nunneries in Ireland will certainly discover evidence of the use of timber buildings. None of the extant nunnery remains in Ireland show explicit use of timber structures, excluding a putative garderobe at St Catherine's.[181] The early phase of the nunnery of Elstow

5.14 View of southern cloister at Killone, Co. Clare, viewed from church parapet, southeast corner, looking southwards. Image: Frank Coyne.

Abbey, Bedfordshire had a probable timber cloister walk, though ultimately it had a claustral plan in stone.[182] It has also been postulated that at Godstow, Oxfordshire a two-storey timber structure may have been attached to the stone church.[183] There are no historical references to timber construction at nunneries, as perhaps it was so commonplace to be unworthy of comment, but it is known from elsewhere. For example, the *Annals of Ulster* and the *Annals of the Four Masters* record the burial of Margaret O'Brien in 1512, in a timber church she had constructed for Franciscans at Dromahair, County Leitrim.[184]

The three upstanding examples are located in Munster and are all Augustinian foundations. Killone is the earliest foundation, having been established around 1189, St Catherine's is likely to date to the 1240s and Molough dates to sometime in the fourteenth century.[185] Not only is the claustral plan rarer than might be assumed, but the arrangement of the cloister in two of the three examples does not conform to the most common plan in male religious houses. At Killone the cloister is to the south of the church, while at Molough the cloister is to the north of the church. At St Catherine's, the cloister is located in a unique position for Ireland, being at the west end of the church.[186]

5.15 View of western range at Molough, Co. Tipperary, a single projecting corbel suggesting a pentice roof over an ambulatory. West wall of church with double bellcote visible to left. Image: Frank Coyne.

All three sites show architecture of various dates, along with evidence of different phases of construction and refurbishment.[187] Killone shows evidence of twelfth-century construction, with later fourteenth-century additions to the church. It has been suggested that the remains of the cloister ranges also date to the fourteenth century.[188] There are fifteenth-century additions. St Catherine's architecture shows an initial construction phase of the thirteenth century and alterations and additions undertaken in the fifteenth. Molough's initial construction dates to the fourteenth century (it is suggested perhaps *c.*1320–50) and has fifteenth-century additions.

Irish cloisters were usually built (although there are exceptions) as simple pentices with lean-to roofs on arcaded walls.[189] The Killone cloister is situated to the south of the church and is formed by a mostly extant east range, which has been conserved, while only the inner wall of the southern range is now visible (Figure 5.14). The west range is identifiable by the footings of its outer

5.16 The east cloister wall of St Catherine's, Co. Limerick. Image: Tracy Collins.

walls. The cloister is almost square in plan but slightly irregular. There is no above-ground indication of a cloister ambulatory or arcade (if one existed). There are no supporting corbels visible for a lean-to roof and neither are there any *ex situ* fragments of a cloister arcade.[190] The extant nunnery cloister at Molough is located to the north of the church and is now grass-covered with no indications of a cloister garth, ambulatory or cloister arcade wall.[191] It is almost square in plan. A stone wall, which seems later in date, forms the north side of the cloister. A single dressed corbel present on the upper portion of the east wall of the western range suggests a lean-to roof, at least along this side of the cloister (Figure 5.15).

St Catherine's nunnery is in the best state of preservation of the three examples still extant.[192] Its cloister is almost square in plan. It has a unique arrangement in that the church does not form one side of the cloister but rather projects from its eastern side. It is formed on its northern and eastern sides by high walls and on its western and eastern sides by ranges. Corbels of different mouldings and profiles are present on all sides of the cloister, indicating that it did have a lean-to roof over its cloister ambulatory (Figure 5.16).[193] There is no above-ground trace of any cloister arcade wall that may have supported a possible cloister arcade. This led some to believe that St Catherine's only ever

5.17 Inserted northern doorwa fifteenth century, providing direct access into the cloister at St Catherine's, Co. Limerick. Image: Frank Coyne.

had a timber post structure to support the ambulatory roof and never had a cloister arcade,[194] although this has been disproven through excavation.[195] Its original entrance was in the southeast corner, evidenced by a large blocked relieving arch, and the south range was made shorter to accommodate this doorway. There is a second doorway in the northeast corner of the cloister, which is clearly a later insert, dating to the fifteenth century, and is a limestone pointed-arched example (Figure 5.17). The lower western pivot stone for a door remains, as does a large bolt hole in the thickness of the wall, which secured the door from the inside. This doorway may have had an exterior porch, evidenced by projecting bond stones. It can be identified at St Catherine's that the west range was constructed first, then the exterior cloister walls, and then the south range and church, abutting those walls.[196] The cloister walls were constructed in sections, as a clear horizontal build-line (on average 2m above the current ground level) is visible in the cloister walls on the north, east and south sides (Figure 5.18).

Excavations were carried out at two locations in the cloister of St Catherine's, which revealed the foundations of a substantial limestone-faced rubble core wall, interpreted as the cloister arcade wall[197] (Figures 5.19 and 5.20), which formed an east ambulatory (walkway). It was surfaced with several layers

.18 St Catherine's, Co. Limerick south cloister wall. Note original build line which is also in vidence on north and east cloister walls. Image: Tracy Collins.

5.19 Excavated section of lower courses of cloister arcade wall on east side of cloister at St Catherine's, Co. Limerick. Note metalled floor surface of ambulatory. Image: Tracy Collins.

5.20 Excavated section of cloister arcade wall on north side of cloister at St Catherine's Co. Limerick. Image: Tracy Collins. **5.21** (*below*) Excavated section of cloister garth showing stony deposit and cloister arcade wall overlying it at St Catherine's, Co. Limerick Image: Tracy Collins.

5.22 Westropp's drawing of features at St Catherine's, Co. Limerick, including a possible *ex situ* fragment of cloister arcade, now lost (no. 5). Re-drawn by Frank Coyne after Westropp, 1904 © Royal Society of Antiquaries of Ireland.

of a stony metalling which sealed several burials (Chapter 8). Investigations along the northern side of the cloister revealed a similar cloister arcade wall foundation, that formed a narrower ambulatory which contained burials.

The garth (garden) area comprised a series of deposits of dark humic and loamy material. No human remains were found and so it appears that – in this area at least – the garth was never used for burial. Of particular interest were the earliest contexts of the garth. The builders of the nunnery deliberately removed the impervious boulder clay in the area of the garth and filled the void with fist-sized limestone pebbles. This was interpreted as an attempt to improve drainage, and it is suggested that plants were grown in this central area. The cloister arcade wall rested directly on this stony deposit, showing that the wall and the preparatory works for the garth were near contemporary activities (Figure 5.21).[198]

The ambulatory on the north side of the cloister was found to be wider than that on the east. A likely explanation for this is that the north ambulatory is south-facing and would have had the most natural light of all the sides of the cloister. It was likely used for other functions in addition to access, such as reading and writing. These functions are known to have been undertaken at male houses, such as Holy Cross, County Tipperary (Cistercian).[199] At

Tintern, County Wexford (Cistercian) the north ambulatory contained stone benches, the abbot's seat and collation bay.[200] The additional space supplied by the wider ambulatory at St Catherine's may also have supplemented work space as the nunnery did not have east or north ranges. The wall revealed has been interpreted as the original cloister arcade wall, though no cloister arcade fragments were discovered, and this remains puzzling (Figure 5.22). Westropp in the late nineteenth century identified just one fragment which might be considered part of an arcade – although he was dubious that such an arcade could be removed so completely.[201]

The presence of the substantial foundation of a cloister arcade wall would suggest that some form of arcading was present. However, the presence of a wall does not necessarily indicate a stone arcade. The superstructure may have been of rubble construction pierced with individual windows as at Adare Friary, County Limerick, Errew, County Mayo, or Athassel, County Tipperary. Leask has suggested that most of the stone arcades extant date to the fifteenth century. Many of the thirteenth-century monasteries may have used timber.[202] As the cloister wall found in the excavations in two places remained to a similar height, it is suggested that the entire structure was deliberately removed in one event from the site at some unknown time after the nunnery had been abandoned, perhaps for use in the later Old Abbey House. This would explain the lack of architectural fragments and rubble remaining on the site.

Using Westropp's sketch of the arcade fragment, some parallels can be identified. Fragments from the Augustinian Bridgetown Abbey, County Cork have similar spiral decoration, as do others from Ballintober Abbey, County Mayo and Buttevant Friary, County Cork.[203] The cloister arcade from Sligo Friary has a similar spiral or 'twist edge' design. In this case, it has been dated to the later fifteenth century.[204] From this, it can be suggested that St Catherine's did have a stone ambulatory wall perhaps from its foundation in the thirteenth century, though this may have first had a timber superstructure, until the fifteenth century when a cloister stone arcade – represented only by a single lost fragment – was fitted. It is not unknown for religious houses to alter or replace cloister arcading.[205] A timber pentice superstructure with low stone wall, which was later replaced by a stone arcade partially integrated into the ranges, was found through excavation at the Dominican house of St Mary's of the Isle, Cork.[206]

The location of the cloister in relation to the church was important. A cloister to the south of the church was more practical for light and heat purposes and was favoured in male religious houses. However, in several nunneries in Britain northern cloisters were used. Gilchrist has convincingly argued that this was a conscious decision of the planners of the nunnery, identifying it as being of symbolic significance, and she has linked the position of the cloister to the north of the church with gender.[207] This symbolism and association of female gender with northern locations is a well-established tradition in Christianity, which can be identified in several media.[208] Briefly, women are traditionally associated with cardinal north, an association that springs from the male/female duality intrinsic to medieval Christian philosophy in which male is associated with the soul and female the body. This duality can be noted earlier in pagan contexts of sun and moon, then personified by male and female respectively. North is related to night and cold, and south to light and warmth.

In medieval church architecture the north of the church embodied Old Testament symbolism while the south embodied the New Testament.[209] For example, St Augustine paralleled the Old Testament with the moon and the New Testament the sun. Moreover, in crucifixion scenes Mary is usually shown at the right-hand side of the cross – or the north as it is viewed, Christ representing the east, the location of the high altar. Lady chapels in medieval churches mirror this arrangement and tend to be located at the east end in the northern transept or northern side of churches, conforming to Mary's traditional position at the right hand of God, symbolised further by the cruciform plan of many churches as well as the altar. This association extended to female saints associated with the northern sides of churches, and women's seating in medieval parish churches.[210] Where medieval segregated burial occurs women tended to be associated with the northern and western areas of cemeteries.[211] In segregated congregations, such as medieval parish churches, women are usually placed on the northern side of the church. This engendered pattern originates quite early in medieval Christianity and is well illustrated as early as the seventh century in Ireland in Cogitosus' description of the nunnery church at Kildare, for example.[212]

At male religious houses in Ireland northern cloisters are much less frequent than southern cloisters, but are known, as at Hore Abbey (Cistercian), County Tipperary,[213] and the Augustinian houses of Inishfallen, County Kerry, Inchcleraun, County Longford, and Errew, County Mayo.[214] While it is not currently possible to undertake Gilchrist's level of analysis in cloister orientation in Ireland, the three nunnery cloisters there show a surprising variation in form, with a northern cloister at Molough, a southern cloister at Killone and a most unusual western cloister at St Catherine's.

Similarly, the ranges of buildings at these three nunneries vary greatly in preservation and detail. At Killone, two of the original three ranges are partially

5.23 The conserved interior of the east range at Killone, Co. Clare. Image: Tracy Collins

extant, though in a heavily modified form (Figure 5.23).[215] The east range is of two storeys and is directly connected to the east end of the church via a round-arched doorway in its north wall on its upper floor. On the ground floor of this range in the north wall is a small lintelled doorway, which provides access to an undercroft beneath the church via a set of steps in the thickness of the wall. A small loop provides light for the steps. The east range is lit by two rounded headed lights in its west wall which appear original. Shutter sockets are visible. In its east wall is an inserted fifteenth-century two-light ogee-headed window, the shaft of which is re-used. Two rectangular lights are in the upper floor of this east wall. There are three small lights in the southern gable of this range. All the ground-floor lights have evidence of pivots for shutters. Corbels in the upper portion of the east wall supported the roof of this range. Due to the re-building, there is no longer visible evidence of how the upper floor may have been supported. The upper floor of this range is interpreted as the

5.24 Upstanding remains at Molough, Co. Tipperary. Image: Tracy Collins.

dormitory, while the lower floor, with the double-light window, may have been the location of the chapter house, although there is no corresponding doorway.[216] The northern (inner) wall of the south range is extant at Killone. It has two doorways. The western example is round-arched (considered late by Westropp), while the single door has a pointed arch.[217] He described this range as the kitchen, likely because of its southern position relative to the church.

Molough also retains evidence of two ranges, west and east, and it is unknown if a northern range was ever constructed. Only the southern gable of the eastern range is extant. This abuts (and is not tied into) the northeast corner of the church. On the northern (inner) face of this gable is a ledge which supported the first floor. The remainder of this range can only be identified by grass-covered wall footings, or modern wall lines (Figure 5.24). The west range is a two-storey structure, though its northern gable shows that it had ample room for an attic space. This range abuts the church's southwest corner. The ground floor is subdivided into two units. The southernmost is rectangular in plan and entered through a doorway in its east wall from the cloister. This appears to have replaced an earlier doorway further to the south.

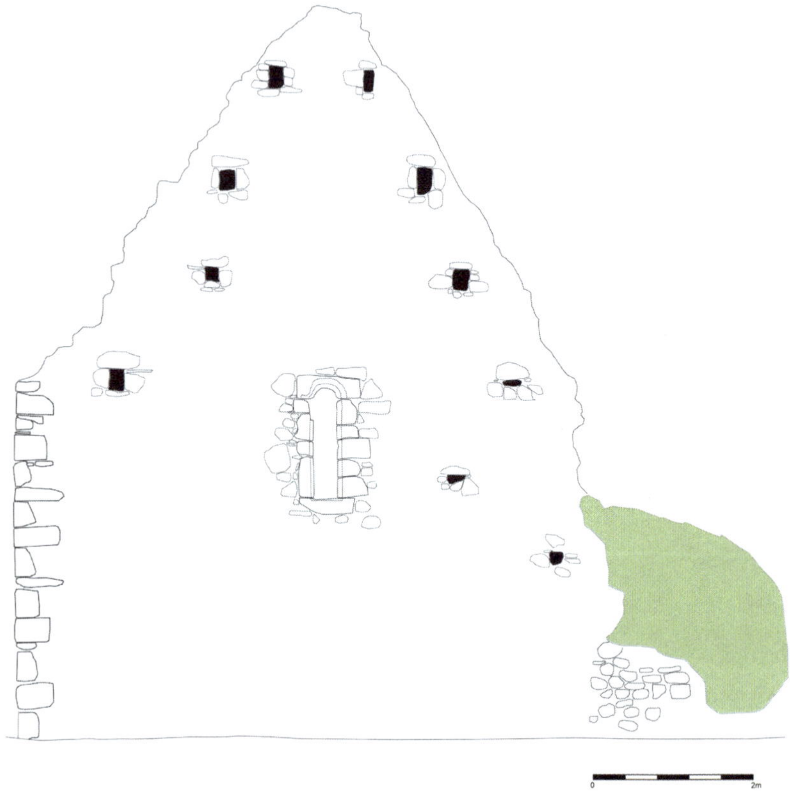

5.25 The north gable of the west range of Molough, Co. Tipperary. Image: Frank Coyne.

The southeast corner of this unit, on the interior, shows evidence of alteration and reconstruction. Corbels are situated in the west and east walls of this unit which supported the upper floor. Its north wall has been re-built. There is no access between the units. The northern unit of the west range is almost square. It has an east wall doorway which appears to be a later insertion. There is a niche in the southern end of the west wall which is lintelled and splayed. One corbel is present in the west wall. It is possible that there is a blocked doorway in the northwest corner of this unit. This corresponds to flashing stones on the exterior wall, suggesting that there was a structure attached at this point. This may have housed a stair to the upper floor. The upper floor has four windows, one ope in the west wall, possibly two on the east and one in the northern gable. This is a round-headed rebated light in sandstone that is an original feature (Figure 5.25).

5.26 Western face (interior to cloister) of east cloister wall of St Catherine's, Co. Limerick showing evidence of blocked doorways, perhaps indicative of an originally planned east range. Central doorway is the west doorway into the projecting church. Note string course indicating the line of a pentice roof and supporting corbels. Image: Frank Coyne.

The west and south ranges at St Catherine's are the most complete of the three nunneries. There was never a range along the northern side of the cloister and the church projects from the eastern side of the cloister and there are no range buildings along this side. However, an analysis of the fabric of the eastern wall of the cloister, coupled with excavation evidence, suggests that it may have been an original intention to have an east range. First, the architectural evidence: the interior and exterior faces of the east cloister wall show evidence of three distinct large openings for doors (Figure 5.26). The most northerly is visible by a blocked relieving arch. The blocking fabric is very similar in style to that of the fabric of the wall itself, which suggests it was blocked very early in construction.[218] The second opening is the west doorway into the church. This is a fine doorway in Gothic style, though is clearly off-centre with the projecting church (Chapter 6). The third opening is of similar dimension to the first, though has its original sandstone flat-arch and jamb-stones *in situ*. This was subsequently blocked by the fifteenth-century addition of the 'sacristy' feature.

Second, the archaeological evidence: a trench was excavated outside the cloister at the junction of the west end of the church and the cloister wall immediately outside the northerly blocked doorway, to investigate it and the external northeast corner of the cloister wall which seemed to be a very ruinous buttress. It was quickly discovered that this was a continuation of the

5.27 Excavated trench outside the cloister at St Catherine's, Co. Limerick showing that the north wall of the cloister originally continued eastwards, perhaps as part of an east range. Image: Tr… Collins.

northern wall of the cloister, orientated west–east. However, it was not found to make a return (Figure 5.27).

To the south of this wall a mortar spread was found. This was interpreted as the bedding for a floor and therefore an interior space. This space could be accessed from the cloister through the blocked doorway to the west. Furthermore, the mortar spread was later cut by burials and the foundations for the church's northern wall – indicating that the church was later in the sequence of building. This archaeological evidence indicates that there was a change of plan in the building arrangements at St Catherine's – which is rarely demonstrated through analysis of standing fabric alone. Originally, it seemed it may have been planned to build a range or, more probably, the church, along the north side of the cloister. This is shown by the continuation of the north wall of the cloister beyond the cloister line to the east. Perhaps an eastern range was also planned. This is evidenced by the three large door opes in the eastern cloister wall. It is further suggested by the mortar spread found in the excavation trench (outside the cloister but within the footprint of

5.28 Western face (exterior to cloister) of west range at St Catherine's, Co. Limerick. Note clasping pilaster on right of image. Image: Frank Coyne.

a range), which implies an interior space such as a floor.[219] It is suggested that this change of plan occurred early in the building programme at St Catherine's as the blocking of the northerly ope is similar in style to the actual fabric of the wall around it.[220]

The church was then placed in a unique position (in Ireland), projecting from the cloister, while maintaining its essential east–west orientation (Chapter 6).[221] One explanation for this arrangement can be found in the church's west doorway. The cloister wall was constructed first and contained this elaborate doorway. If an east range was originally intended along this side of the cloister then this elaborate doorway would be fitting for an important room in a typical east range, such as a chapter house. However, when the layout change occurred (for reasons unknown but perhaps financial) a new use had to be found for the elaborate doorway, and in this case it was re-deployed as the church's west doorway without having to modify it. This change of thought can be seen in the fact that the doorway is placed centrally in the east wall of the cloister (its western face) but when viewed from the interior of the church (i.e. its eastern face) it is clearly off-centre with the church structure. While this interpretation explains the possible re-purposing of the doorway, it still does not explain adequately the radical divergence from a claustral plan and the projecting church – the northern side of the cloister could have been used as a more traditional location and there is no clear reason why it was not. Indeed, this location would also have been more convenient to the nuns' dormitory situated in the west range.

The most substantial range at St Catherine's is the west range. It was the earliest stage of construction on the site and was probably a re-purposed structure. The architectural sequence of the above-ground remains confirms this. It is of two storeys, with unusual pilasters at both corners of its southern end (Figure 5.28). The ground floor comprises three vaulted chambers. The most northerly one is destroyed save its west wall, which has a door. The middle chamber has a small slit light in its west wall and niches in its south wall. Its east wall is all but destroyed, but a door and window were previously recorded.[222] The southernmost chamber has an external door in its west wall, splayed in order to provide light to the adjacent niches, and a window was previously recorded.[223] There are a further two blocked opes in the southern wall of the southernmost vault. These are considered later (Chapter 7).

The vaulting appears not to have been bonded to any of the exterior walls of the range. This suggests that the ground-floor vaulting of the west range is a fifteenth-century alteration.[224] The cross walls sub-dividing the west range were also added later and the middle and southernmost chambers both have two large niches in their cross walls and the dressing suggests a later fifteenth- or sixteenth-century date. It appears that the chambers were interconnected, although this can no longer be confirmed. Of particular note is the chambers' access; two can be accessed from outside the cloister, suggesting they may have been used for guest or corrodian accommodation.[225]

The upper floor of the west range is now very ruinous and only its west wall and south gable survive. The west wall had a series of small rectangular chamfered lights with internal splays, though now only a base and jamb of one of the lights are extant. One blocked window ope is evident in the south wall. There is a blocked doorway in the upper portion of the south gable and Westropp recorded a fireplace, but this is no longer visible. It is suggested that this first-floor doorway led to a timber structure at the external junction of the west and south ranges, evidenced by large joist holes and undressed corbels in their external walls, which is interpreted as a possible garderobe constructed in timber (Figure 5.29). This location is close to the stream mentioned earlier, though there is no evidence that it was diverted to flush a latrine drain and it is more likely it was serviced by a cess pit arrangement. The original access route to the upper-floor dormitory is no longer obvious. It is most likely that a stair was located at the northern end of the west range,[226] which fits well with how the complex may have been used by the nuns (Chapter 7).

The range at the south side of the cloister at St Catherine's has been identified as the refectory. It is a single space which appears to have been of

5.29 Although very overgrown with ivy, joist holes and corbels are visible on the exterior gables of the west and south ranges of St Catherine's, Co. Limerick which may indicate the presence of a timber structure at this location, perhaps a garderobe. South range wall shown. Image: Tracy Collins.

one storey.[227] Although large opes in the east and west gables were said to contain doorways, there is little evidence to support this and they are more likely modern. The refectory is accessed from the cloister ambulatory via a large flat-arched sandstone doorway at the western end of its north wall. There is a large breach to the west of this doorway, which I suggest is the location of the lavabo or laver (a place for handwashing prior to entry to the refectory; Figure 5.30).[228] The refectory is lit by a series of lancet windows in its southern wall. There was originally probably five such windows, two of which are extant (Figure 5.31).[229] At the east end of this south wall is the remains of a reader's recess. The wall accommodated this feature beneath the windows in a shallow return which slightly projected from the refectory.[230]

5.30 Remains of the doorway into the south range refectory from the cloister, St Catherine's, Co. Limerick. Breach to the right of the doorway is the likely location of a lavabo. Image: Tracy Collins.

5.31 Remaining lancet windows (interior view) in refectory of St Catherine's, Co. Limerick. Reader's recess was situated in breach to the left of these windows. Image: Tracy Collins.

5.32 Excavated trench at the reader's recess in the refectory at St Catherine's, Co. Limerick. Image: Tracy Collins.

Excavation of the reader's recess did not produce any evidence of a platform or steps and showed that the floor of the refectory had a stony metalled surface very similar to that found in the eastern cloister ambulatory. This rested directly on the natural parent material, a boulder clay (Figure 5.32).[231] An extension to the south range was added in the fifteenth century and this was interpreted as the kitchen by Westropp. It is clearly a later addition as it awkwardly abuts the south range by almost obscuring one of its windows.[232] This kitchen range is orientated north–south, where a managed stream flows past its southern end. Only the lowest courses of its east wall now remain, along with a portion of its now detached southern gable. There are the visible remains of a small rectangular window in the east wall.[233] A trench was excavated in the kitchen range to establish the location of its western wall and to assess the interior of the range. The foundation cut for the south wall was revealed, showing that the kitchen was about 7m in width. The earthen floor of the kitchen was created on exposed boulder clay, with depressions in the surface being filled with small lenses of imported clayey material to level the surface over time.[234]

Therefore, while the evidence of claustral living in later medieval nunneries in Ireland is limited to just three locations, much evidence can be gathered about how these complexes might have been used. What has also emerged, however, is that there seems to have been several alternatives to an enclosed cloister, where communities of nuns might live. These alternatives are now considered.

ALTERNATIVE LAYOUTS

When all nunneries with upstanding remains are considered, it becomes clear not all were organised to a strict claustral plan. It is acknowledged that due to poor preservation and lack of excavation it is likely that the larger, more important nunneries, about twelve in number[235] – in addition to the three just described – probably did employ some form of claustral layout.[236] However, of those for which dissolution surveys exist, only at Lismullin was a cloister specifically listed.[237] This does not definitively show, however, that cloisters were not employed. They may have been considered ubiquitous, so the surveyors may not have felt it necessary to describe them in detail. For example, Molough's upstanding cloister was not mentioned in its dissolution survey.[238] Others may never have employed a standard cloister. The important nunnery of Kilcreevanty, which became the mother house of the Augustinian houses of Arroasian observance in Connacht after 1223, had the extant remains of a large church, possibly with transepts, though little extant evidence of a cloister.[239] There are several low rectangular platforms to the west and southwest of the church which appear to be the footings of large free-standing structures associated with the nunnery, showing that it may have had a more fluid arrangement (Figure 5.33).

Barlett's seventeenth-century depiction of Armagh shows the nunnery of Temple na Ferta within a circular, possibly earthen, enclosure (see Figure 2.5). One explanation for this is that it originated in the early medieval period and so possibly this early morphology was maintained. At Caltragh the site is manifested as an irregular-shaped earthen enclosure on the edge of Lough Lene and there are no indications of a cloister complex there (Figure 5.34).

Annagh has the extant remains of a long, now featureless, stone wall, orientated east–west, possibly the remains of a church, within a large sub-circular enclosure formed of two concentric banks and wide central ditch. The wide causewayed entrance is clearly visible to the north (Figure 5.35). This enclosure has been considered early medieval and it is possible that an earlier enclosure was re-used, though it may also date to the later medieval period. The nunnery at Killeigh was enclosed by a large impressive earthwork of two

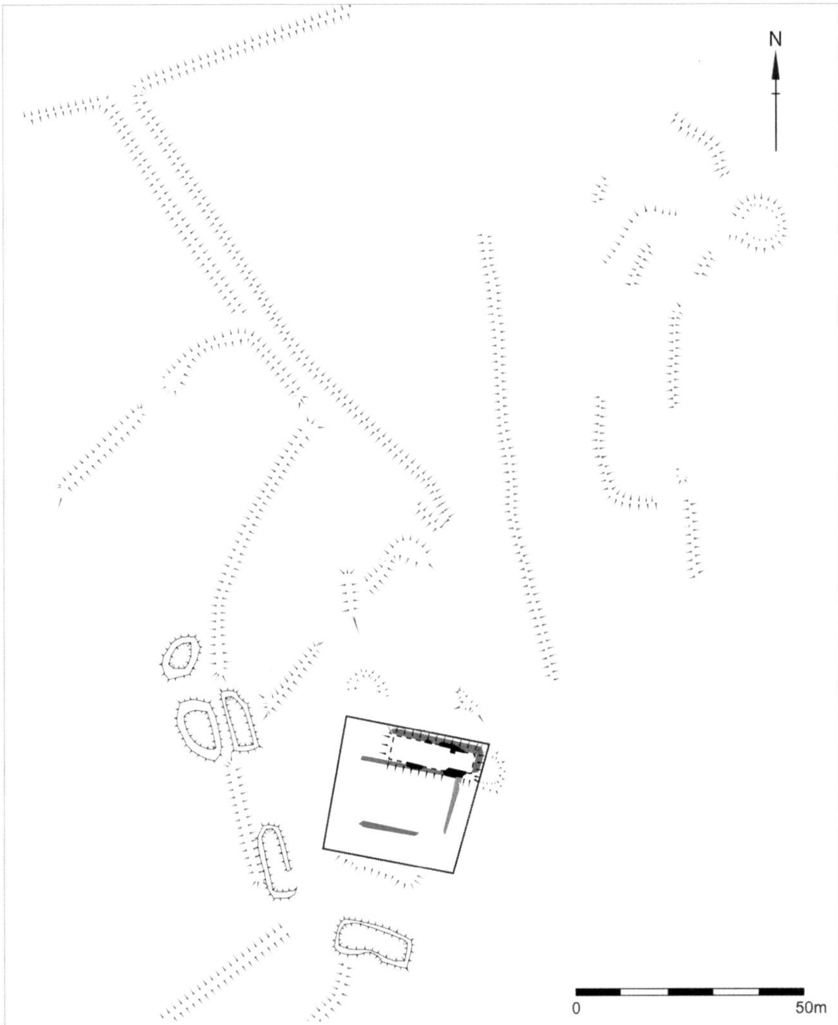

5.33 Kilcreevanty, Co. Galway, showing low register earthworks and platforms that may be free-standing structures associated with the nunnery, now enclosed by a modern graveyard wall. Image: Frank Coyne.

earthen banks which flanked a deep flat-bottomed fosse. This feature formed an annex to the early medieval enclosure at Killeigh, which appears to have been re-used in the later period (see Figure 4.23).[240] The nunnery sites of Ardcarn,[241] Cloonoghil, Drumalgagh and Killinmulrooney[242] all have evidence for extensive dispersed deserted settlements which include earthwork field systems and enclosures, roads, graveyards, architectural fragments and structures – such as houses, huts or other buildings – the precise function of which cannot be determined without excavation. The reputed site of the Franciscan nunnery

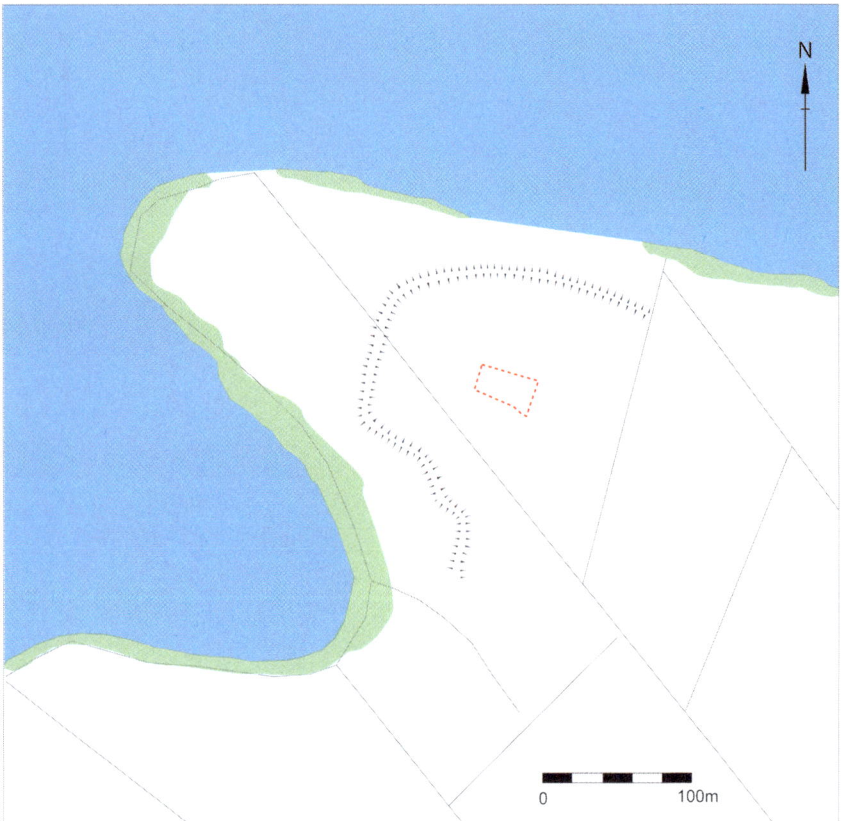

5.34 The earthen enclosure at Caltragh, Co. Westmeath, on a peninsula in Lough Lene. Red boundary indicates the location of a later children's burial ground. Image: Frank Coyne.

at Carrick-on-Suir, now occupied by a seventeenth-century manor house, has incorporated older castles.[243] While it cannot be archaeologically proven that the older castles are associated with the nunnery at this location, Carrick-on-Suir is one of a small corpus of nunneries directly associated with castles. The nunnery of Odder, which superseded Clonard, also has the remains of an earlier tower house incorporated into an early modern structure, called 'Odder Castle'. Some of the tower house fabric was once clearly visible in the walls of the house.[244] Kilbride has the remains of a fortified house incorporated into a later structure, which may, as is the case with many fortified and later houses, incorporate portions of yet earlier structures.[245]

Portrane, occupied by the nuns of Grace Dieu after its dissolution, has a church and, to the northwest, a castle, which from the contemporary historical description was quite a substantial settlement (Figure 5.36).[246] It is not known

5.35 Annagh, Co. Mayo. Now very overgrown with some upstanding remains (central structure in red). It is enclosed by a large double-banked enclosure with large causeway at north. The structure to west is a second medieval church. Image: Frank Coyne.

what accommodation the late medieval nuns at Kildare used and there is no suggestion of a cloister there. From the historical evidence it had a castle or 'fortilage' within its precincts, while Timolin nunnery was described as 'a castle and other houses, dwelling-places of the nuns'.[247] It has been noted that castles were associated with Cistercian and Augustinian houses and their granges for both defence and protection,[248] and Mellifont's gatehouse has been described as a tower house.[249] If male religious houses were using castles in this fashion, it must be postulated that in some instances nunneries may also have used them.

Before specifically considering churches and liturgical space in nunneries (Chapter 6), a few nunnery churches are notable in that they show some

5.36 Portrane, Co. Dublin, view of interior and west tower. Image: Tracy Collins.

evidence for attached accommodation which is not in a claustral form. Inishmaine, for instance, has two chambers attached to its nave on its north and south sides. From an inspection of the fabric of the structure they are contemporary with the construction of the church. They are not church transepts for side chapels as they have dividing walls and small doors linking them to the church. The southern example had a first floor with a doorway

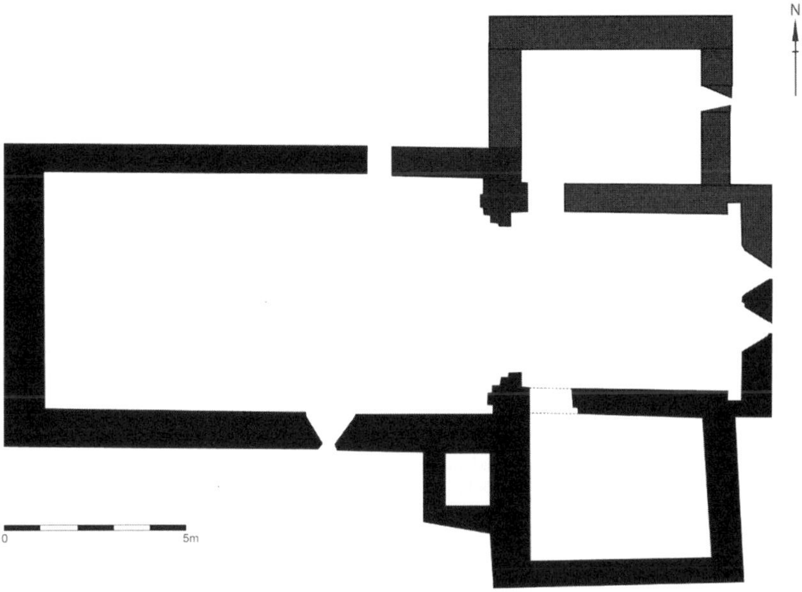

5.37 Ground plan of church at Inishmaine, Co. Mayo with likely attached accommodation to the south and perhaps also at the north. Image: Frank Coyne.

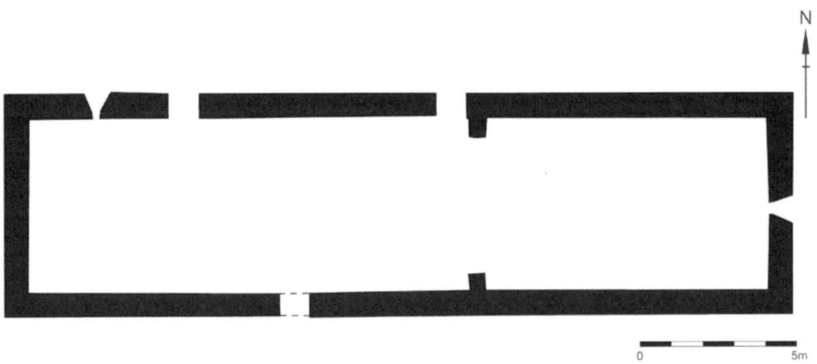

5.38 Ground plan of nunnery church at Annaghdown, Co. Galway with accommodation at its west end. Image: Frank Coyne.

into a small unit on its western side (possibly a garderobe) and so this was more likely for residential purposes. It is possible that a priest may have lived in these rooms but there is also the possibility that a small community of nuns did (Figure 5.37).[250] The church identified as the nunnery church at Annaghdown has a small chamber at its west end, lit by two small lights in its northern wall, one above the other, which has been interpreted as possible residential accommodation (Figure 5.38).[251] Portrane church, previously mentioned, has

5.39 Ground plan of church at Portrane, Co. Dublin. Image: Frank Coyne.

a tower which is large enough to have provided residential accommodation (Figure 5.39). The nunnery church at Termonkeelin is shown on historic mapping as a long narrow structure orientated north–south with a return to the east (Figure 5.40). It is probable that the eastern structure was the church, while the narrow structure was residential accommodation.

Tisrara is another nunnery church where domestic accommodation is attached in a block to the church, on its southern side.[252] The excavations at this site concluded that the church and residential block had been altered, with the church extended to the east and the residential block added, probably sometime in the fifteenth century. The southern residential block comprised two storeys (Figure 5.41). The ground floor was divided into two vaulted interconnected units, which could be accessed from the church and the exterior. Two substantial niches were located in the northeast corner of the eastern vault. It was suggested by the excavator that this may have been the sacristy. The upper floor was an undivided space, accessed via a stone stairway from the ground floor. The stone stair could be accessed via a doorway in the western vault and also through an exterior doorway with chamfered jambs and decorative chamfer stops. The upper floor was interpreted as a dormitory. Although very ruinous when conserved, *ex situ* window fragments suggested that the upper floor was lit by several small rectangular lights.[253] This residential block could have housed a community of nuns. The direct access to the outside via two possible doorways is puzzling in a nunnery context, though the local tradition of the church as a hostelry/hospital may offer some explanation.

The nunnery at Drumalgagh has not been excavated but bears some similarity to Tisrara (Figure 5.42). It is T-shaped and has north and south

5.40 Termonkeelin, Co. Roscommon re-drawn from the first-edition six-inch Ordnance Survey map and as it now appears. Image: Frank Coyne.

transepts, which like Inishmaine may have been used for accommodation rather than as part of the church. A wide window ope can be identified in the northern wall of the north transept. The southern transept is separated from the east end of the church by a wall. The southern transept space seems to have been lit by a window in its east wall, with evidence for a niche and

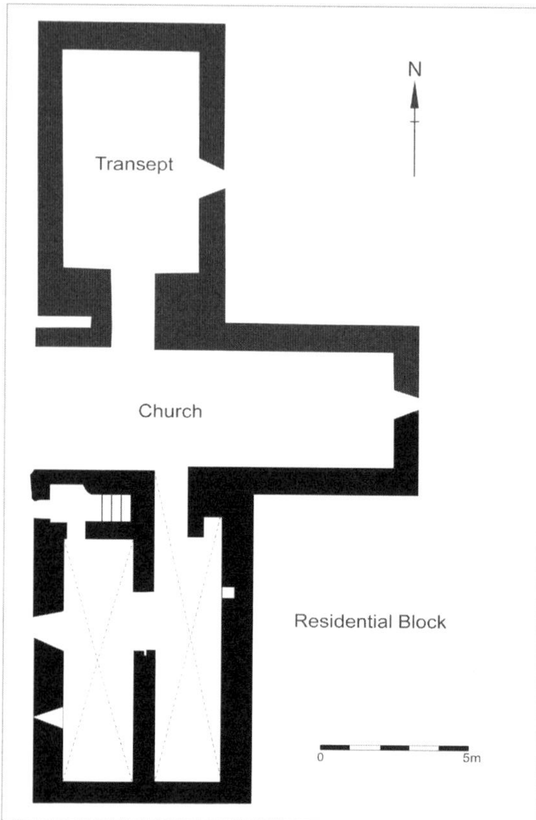

5.41 Ground plan of southern residential block and church at Tisrara, Co. Roscommon. After Higgins, 1995, reproduced with permission of the author.

5.42 Ground plan of church at Drumalgagh, Co. Roscommon, showing attached accommodation to south of church and possibly to north (in grey). Image: Frank Coyne.

a second window in its south wall. An external doorway is in its west wall, which leads to an enclosed rectangular area to the south of the church. The southern transept could be a large sacristy, or alternatively a residential space attached to the church. Alternative accommodation at Drumalgagh can also be identified in the many hut and house sites adjacent to this church.

DIVERSITY IN CONTEXT

From the archaeological evidence it appears that, throughout the later medieval period, only some nunneries utilised the claustral plan – which was similar but not the same as that of male religious houses – and in distinctly more flexible ways. This suggests that female religious were not constrained by a strict claustral layout because it was not deemed necessary for them in their fulfilment of their roles as brides of Christ. They also inhabited spaces that had more in common with secular living of the time, such as earthen enclosures, stone houses and huts and perhaps even castles. In some cases, they used relatively small domestic spaces which were directly attached to the church. This diversity and lack of uniformity noted in the Irish archaeological evidence for nunneries is not unique to Ireland and a similar fluidity has been identified in some British and continental nunneries.

Diversity was noted in nunnery plans in England as early as the 1920s,[254] and it has been argued that the diversity of nunnery complexes 'is itself their most distinctive characteristic'.[255] However, for the most part, this diversity in England is based on variations *within* a claustral plan, unlike Ireland. Burton has stated that the variety of arrangement of British nunneries, the majority of which were founded in the twelfth century, illustrates a period of monastic 'experiment and change'.[256] Thus, nunneries there may have developed a claustral plan slowly, as at Elstow Abbey[257] or Polsloe, Exeter.[258] Rarely, nunneries also used existing buildings from which a true claustral plan never developed, as at Grove Priory, Bedfordshire,[259] or indeed the male religious house at Cogges, Oxfordshire, when a manor house was donated to the community.[260] The structures at Kington St Michael, Wiltshire[261] were irregularly arranged around a central courtyard which has been suggested never possessed a fully developed claustral plan.[262]

Excavations at St Cross, Somerset did not reveal a typical claustral plan (Figure 5.43).[263] Indeed, despite historical and placename evidence attesting to the site as a nunnery, the excavators concluded that due to the lack of a claustral plan it was more likely a manorial farm. However, with further research on smaller nunneries elsewhere in Britain, St Cross is now accepted as a nunnery,

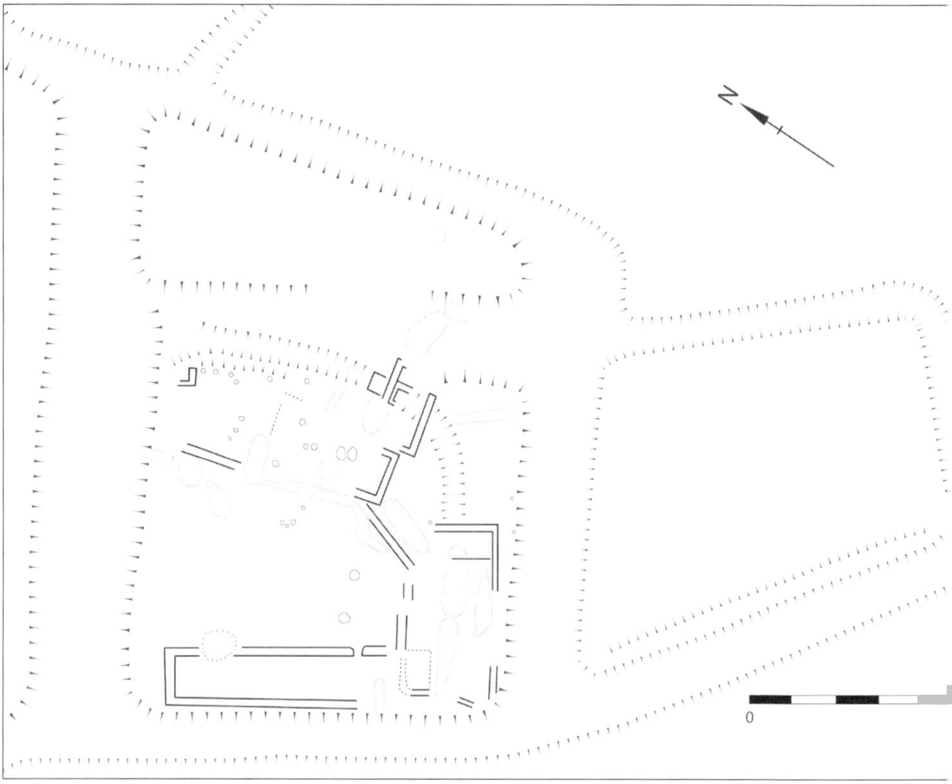

5.43 Plan of the nunnery of St Cross, Somerset, after Rahtz and Greenfield, 1977. Reproduced with permission of the Historic England Archive.

despite its form.[264] Godstow nunnery did not have a typical claustral plan – the church was located to the north of the nuns' enclosure and the nuns were accommodated in long halls.[265] Yorkshire nunneries have been shown to have varied in layout, both between each nunnery and at individual nunneries over time. It has been suggested that their architectural model – if indeed there was one – was Augustinian canons' religious houses rather than Cistercian monasteries, with which the nunneries had little in common (Figure 5.44).[266]

Some nunneries in England were established at existing parish churches, which may have affected their layout, and 'resemble secular manor houses and monasteries not dedicated to a regular conventual life, in particular preceptories and alien priories',[267] for example St Helen's Bishopsgate, London[268] or Davington, Kent.[269] It has also been suggested of nunneries in England that their use of non-standard claustral plans developed from the later trend of subdividing into *familiae* or households. The nunneries of Stixwould and Stainfield, Lincolnshire; Godstow, Oxfordshire; and Elstow, Bedfordshire

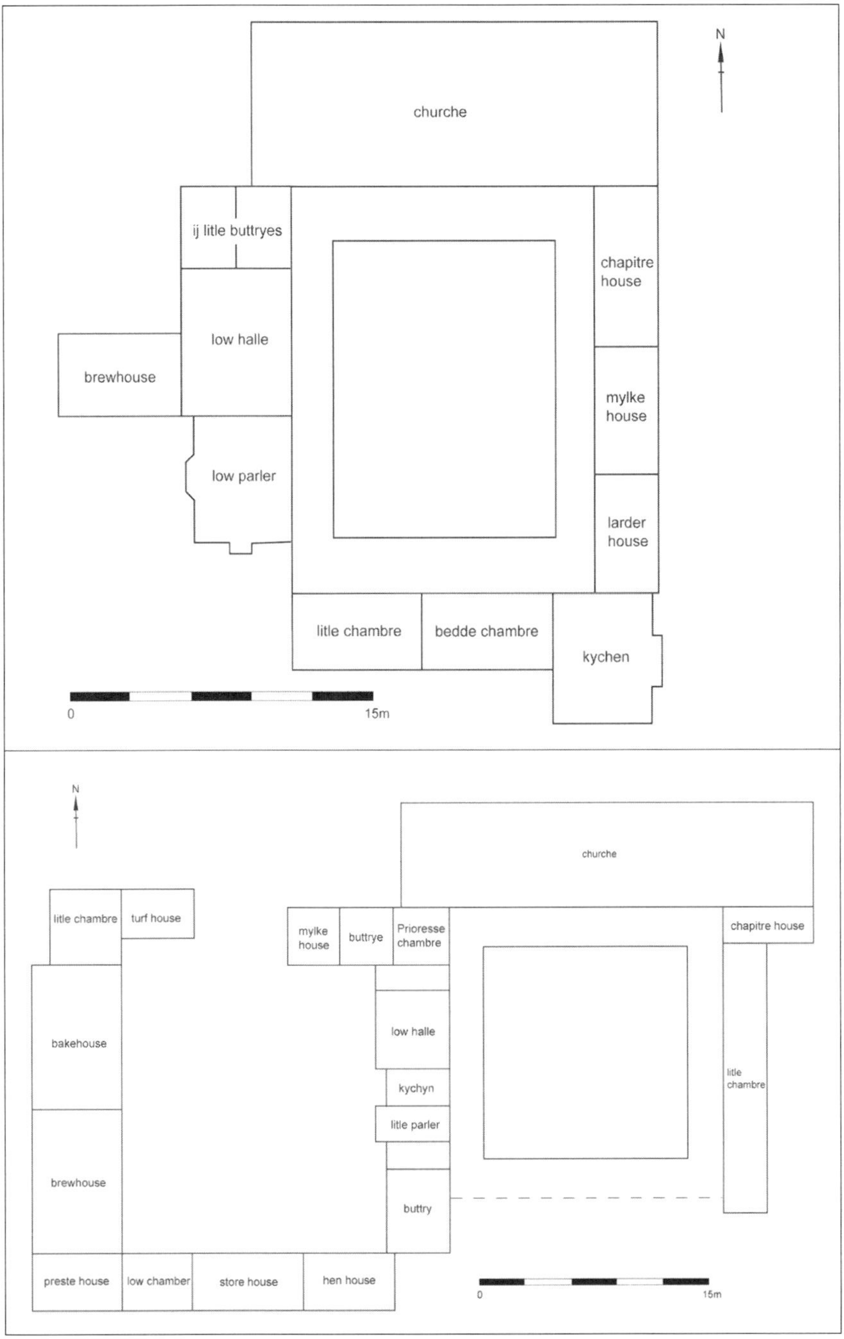

5.44 Ground plans of Baysdale and Wykeham in Yorkshire, Cistercian nunneries, reconstructed on the basis of contemporary survey evidence. After Coppack, 2006. Reproduced with permission of the author.

were recorded in visitation evidence as having separate households and this arrangement undoubtedly had an effect on the nunneries' spatial layout. Furthermore, additional functions at some nunneries such as schooling, caring for the sick, accommodation of guests or children, vowesses, recluses, and corrodians may have required modifications (though not always) to the usual layout of a monastic space.[270]

Nunneries on the continent show a similar diversity. For example, the Birgittines, originating in Sweden in the fifteenth century, rarely used a claustral layout despite the fact that they strictly observed enclosure.[271] In most continental examples a claustral plan was adopted eventually, which may now mask earlier, more diverse layouts, which without archaeological investigation cannot yet be confirmed. They too made use of pre-existing buildings and some were attached to established parish churches.[272] In France, a claustral plan was usual,[273] but a comprehensive study of French nunnery churches showed huge variety in their layout,[274] which certainly highlights openness to greater architectural variety in nunnery architecture. Both regular and highly irregular claustral plans are known from Germany, where there are examples of almost every conceivable arrangement of nunnery space.[275] Furthermore, the subdivision of religious communities into smaller households within the confines of nunneries, noted in England, also occurred on the continent. For example, in Germany in the fifteenth century the Poor Clares of Cologne replaced their communal dorm with individual cells.[276] It has been recently suggested that this change from dormitory to cell, which can be identified in both male and female religious houses, was not a straightforward development towards privacy, but rather an attempt by religious communities to return to a more eremitical spirituality.[277]

Fluid processes of foundation may have had a bearing on nunnery layouts. New foundations of male religious houses were usually instigated by monks/canons from an existing religious house, either being invited by a patron or actively seeking patronage themselves. However, at many nunneries the foundation process was more informal and somewhat organic. In these cases, a pious woman or man may have informally formed a group of religious women sometime prior to seeking affiliation with an established order.[278] For example, pressure exerted by a group of pious women and others led to the foundation of Tart near Cîteaux, France, the first female Cistercian house, in 1120.[279] For nuns at Fontaine-Guérard in Normandy their choice of secluded location was used to make a case for their later affiliation with the Cistercian order.[280]

Fluid processes of foundation are also thought to have initially occurred in both the Gilbertine and Fontevraud orders, where informal communities of

5.45 Various blocked opes in the west range at St Catherine's, Co. Limerick are suggestive of the repurposing of a structure for nunnery use, viewed from northeast. Image: Tracy Collins.

women were organised by the founders prior to formal affiliation to an order.[281] Indeed, many nunneries were considered non-ordered or unattached houses, in that they were not officially affiliated to any order but followed a rule under the authority of a local bishop sometimes in association with influential patrons.[282] Some of these patrons may have been women – several powerful queens were instrumental in establishing female communities, for example the large double house of Poor Clares and Franciscan Friars at Santa Chiara, Naples; Pedralbes, Barcelona; or Longchamp near Paris.[283]

There is just a single example of this organic method of nunnery foundation known in Ireland, at Cork, but it is likely that it was not unique.[284] These more informal groups of nuns living in re-purposed non-claustrally arranged buildings may not have been uncommon. Their probable existence is supported by a comment in Archbishop Alen's register (dated to *c.*1172–1534) regarding the nuns of Timolin and Grace Dieu, in an entry dated 14 March 1326, that they were 'originally cloistral without a cloister and regulars without a rule'.[285]

Inextricably linked with the fluid nature of some nunnery foundations is the re-use of sites (Chapter 2) and particularly the re-use of secular structures, examples of which have been noted in Britain and on the continent. It can be postulated that secular structures may have been donated for use or earlier ecclesiastical structures continued to be used, which then became the later medieval nunnery and were never intended to possess a standard claustral plan. Unfortunately, thirty-four of known later medieval nunneries in Ireland do not have any above-ground register so currently nothing is known of their original layout. Of the remainder, St Catherine's is a single possible example of the re-use of a secular structure at a nunnery, where its west range was likely to have been a chamber-tower or hall house (Figure 5.45).[286] It is tentatively suggested, based on the presence of the blocked opes, similar dimensions and unusual clasping pilasters, that the west range of St Catherine's was the re-purposing of a secular structure hall-house.[287]

Furthermore, there is a particular concentration of five hall houses in this part of County Limerick, in the townlands of Tomdeely North, Ballycahane Upper, Castletown (Connello Barony), Clonshire More and Kilfinny (Figure 5.46). Tomdeely is closest to St Catherine's, being less than 5km (Figure 5.47). It was a manor of the bishop of Limerick in the thirteenth century, later passing to the Desmonds (patrons of St Catherine's) in the early fourteenth century.[288]

It is also tempting to suggest that nunnery affiliation to the Augustinian order may be a factor in the diversity of nunneries in Ireland. All nunneries with extant remains are Augustinian (or of Arroasian observance).[289] The popularity of Augustinianism was perhaps due to the relative flexibility of the rule in that it did not specify minimum numbers for a community,[290] could be used in a variety of contexts, such as pastoral care in parish churches, cathedral chapters and hospitals, while also accommodating the cloistered life.[291] It could be adopted by existing ecclesiastical communities, including nuns, and could

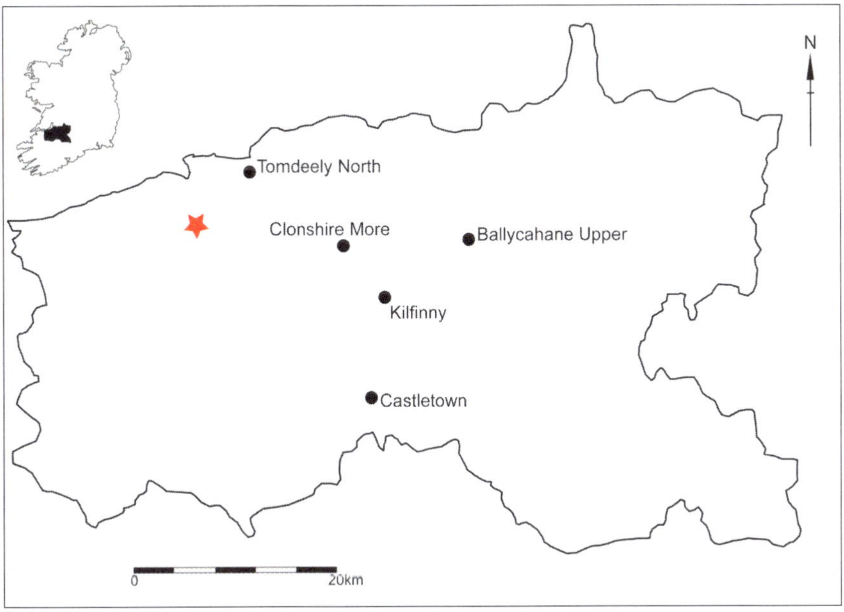

5.46 Recorded hall houses or rectangular chamber towers in Co. Limerick. St Catherine's is indicated by the red star. Image: Frank Coyne.

5.47 The rectangular chamber tower or hall house of Tomdeely, Co. Limerick. Image: Frank Coyne.

accommodate both men and women in co-located houses.[292] Authority over Augustinian religious houses was maintained by the local bishop, usually in co-operation with the patron, which gave autonomy in comparison to other orders, and this particularly suited local lay politics.[293] The congregation of Augustinian of Arroasian observance in Ireland was thought to have been stricter and more contemplative than Augustinian houses. Following Cistercian organisation, Arroasian houses were also dependent on a mother house, although bishops maintained an important role, sometimes interfering, as recorded at Kilcreevanty.[294] Unfortunately, information, either historical or archaeological, on specific institutional arrangements of Arroasian female communities in medieval Ireland remains sparse and so it is difficult to reach any firm conclusions as to how their spaces were used.[295]

At the time of church reform in Ireland in the twelfth century many early religious communities, male and female, adopted the Augustinian rule but may not have physically changed their settlements and continued to use existing structural arrangements that were not claustral.[296] In these cases, the communities may have had a sense of longevity in their community identity and a tangible connection to their place and so may not have wished to physically change their architectural surroundings. New female communities also re-used older ecclesiastical sites which may have been abandoned, not wishing to structurally change these sacred and revered locations.[297]

Augustinian architecture, whether male or female, has always been considered fluid.[298] As a result it has been somewhat neglected and no modern comprehensive study of Augustinian architecture – male and female – has yet been published. This is on account of a number of factors, which have been summarised by Robinson.[299] Male religious houses of the Augustinian order in Ireland do not conform to a rigid standard plan and a claustral plan was 'not an essential part of the Augustinian package',[300] and 'there is then no such thing as a typical Augustinian monastery, within Ireland or without, and so a study of Augustinian monastic architecture in Ireland would thus be nothing less than a study of the entire spectrum of architectural forms and sculptural motifs used in the ecclesiastical environment of medieval Ireland'.[301] The same is true of Augustinian nunneries in medieval Ireland.[302]

Furthermore, it has been pointed out that Augustinianism is important as it cuts across perceived boundaries in archaeological discourses: chronologically, Augustinian houses were established prior to and after the Anglo-Norman conquest; geographically they were founded by both Gaelic Irish and Anglo-Norman. Augustinian houses then can form a lens through which these divisions might be critiqued, and represent 'a complex exchange that diluted the cultural integrity of both populations'.[303]

The flexibility of the Augustinian rule, however, while appearing to explain why nunnery layouts in later medieval Ireland were so diverse, is inherently problematic. This rule cannot be considered to be the primary reason for nunnery diversity in Ireland, as nunneries of other orders in different regions also show diversity in plan, perhaps most especially Cistercian nunneries in Germany, but also the nunneries of England, which were predominantly Benedictine;[304] yet diversity there is also a primary characteristic.[305] This clearly brings into question the idea that order affiliation was a primary factor in the diversity of layout. The re-use or continuity of use at some earlier sites in the twelfth century by Gaelic patrons may have led to non-claustral forms being perpetuated, especially at co-located religious houses. So, it can be concluded that variation and diversity in nunnery plans, rather than a consistent layout, both between orders and within the same order, is not unusual in a female monastic context in any part of the medieval monastic world.

It is precisely because of this variation that it is difficult to generalise about monastic architecture for women religious across Europe. Female monastic architecture was influenced more by domestic rather than ecclesiastical architecture, which has also contributed to such diversity,[306] and it can be concluded from the current evidence that the typical monastic 'standard' claustral plan was not considered appropriate or necessary for all female religious communities.

CHAPTER 6

Church Form and Ritual Practice

FORM AND FUNCTION

The church was the central building in any nunnery complex and usually the largest and most important.[1] The church as a structure was considered different in that it was the centre of the elaborate rite of consecration,[2] being marked by nine or twelve crosses throughout its interior during the ceremony.[3] We now consider the shape, proportions, features and internal differentiation of nunnery churches in Ireland. An exploration of the uses of the sacred space within the church is made, first by the nuns and second when the space may have been shared with other groups. St Catherine's church is used as a case study to highlight some of the conclusions that can be drawn from the archaeological evidence. Twenty nunnery churches in Ireland have some structural evidence upstanding, with several more showing tentative evidence of a church structure (Table 6.1).[4] Of these twenty, the majority are in a quite ruinous condition although meaningful ground plans of the church structure can be identified in seventeen cases.

Shape

The size and plan of nunnery churches in Ireland vary (Figure 6.1). Most of the churches associated with nunneries appear to have been parallelograms, without aisles or transepts. Many are no longer extant, like that of Grace Dieu, or are only partially visible, as at Annagh, Ballynagallagh or Killeenatrava. A small number of nunnery churches have a distinct partial base batter (an external thickening of the wall at the base), as at St Catherine's, Killone or the east church at Killevy. Six churches are thought to have been sub-divided into distinct nave and chancel areas, including Annaghdown, Inishmaine (Figure 6.2), the Nuns' Church, and Temple Finghin. Ballymacdane church could be considered to be divided, as its crossing tower separated the chancel from the nave. The tower may be a later addition in which case the church was originally undifferentiated.[5] Kilcreevanty church was recorded in 1988 as a long nave with a slightly narrower chancel, though this cannot now be confirmed in the field.[6] It is likely that all nunnery churches were subdivided in some fashion; those that lacked stone arches probably used textiles or timber screens.

Table 6.1 Internal dimensions of extant nunnery churches.[1]

Nunnery	*Date*	*Length (m) East–West*	*Width (m) North–South*	*Proportion*[2]
Annagh	-1440	13.5	6.2	1:2.77
Annaghdown[3]	+1144 -1223	15.2 (n) 9.8 (c)	6.1 (n) 5.5 (c)	1:4.09
Ballymacdane	1450	26.5	6.0	1:4.42
Ballynagallagh[4]	1289	-	2.7 (portion)	-
Cloonoghil	-1223	10.0	5.4	1:1.85
Drumalgagh	-1195 or -1223	15.0	5.7	1:2.63
Grace Dieu[5]	+1195	24.7	6.4	1:3.85
Inishmaine	1223	12.6 (n) 5.9 (c)	6.5 (n) 4.6 (c)	1:2.84
Kilcreevanty	1200	15.4 (n) 5.3 (c)	7 (n) 5.8 (c)	1:2.95
Killeenatrava	+1223	2.4 (portion)	3.2	-
Killevy (West Church)[6]	1144-8	12.5	6.5	1:1.92
Killevy (East Church)	1144-8	20.2	6.7	1:3.01
Killone	1189	39.4	10.3	1:3.82
Molough	+1300	21.4	9.5	1:2.25
Nuns' Church[7] Clonmacnoise	+1144 -1223	12.9 (n) 5.3 (c)	7.8 (n) 5.2 (c)	1:2.33
Portrane	1539	15.3	5.4	1:2.84
St Catherine's	1240s	25.0	5.5	1:4.54
Temple Finghin Clonmacnoise	+1144 -1223	8.8 (n) 2.6 (c)	3.8 (n) 2.6 (c)	1:3
Templenagalliaghdoo	-	6.9	4.2	1:1.64
Tisrara	-	14.0	5.4	1:2.59

1 This table includes twenty churches. Measurements are from field survey, excepting Grace Dieu and Kilcreevanty that can no longer be accurately measured. 2 Proportions have been calculated on extant remains (width: length). In some cases, proportions cannot be estimated. 3 There is some confusion in the identification of the nunnery church at Annaghdown. The first edition Ordnance Survey six-inch map identifies a structure in the northwest corner of the claustral priory as the nunnery. The Archaeological Survey of Ireland identifies the nunnery as the most northerly structure in the complex, which was later re-used or replaced by the Premonstratensians. 4 A very small portion remains. It has been previously interpreted as a church by Westropp. 5 This church is no longer extant. Dimensions taken and converted to metres from Berry, *Register of Wills and Inventories*, p. 211. 6 The churches at Killevy were conjoined by walls some time in the post-medieval period and the west wall of the east church removed. They have been considered as two separate churches here. 7 In some contexts, the Nuns' Church and Temple Finghin are considered early medieval structures. These churches are considered to date to after the reform of the church in the twelfth century and so are better placed with post-reform nunneries in the context of this book.

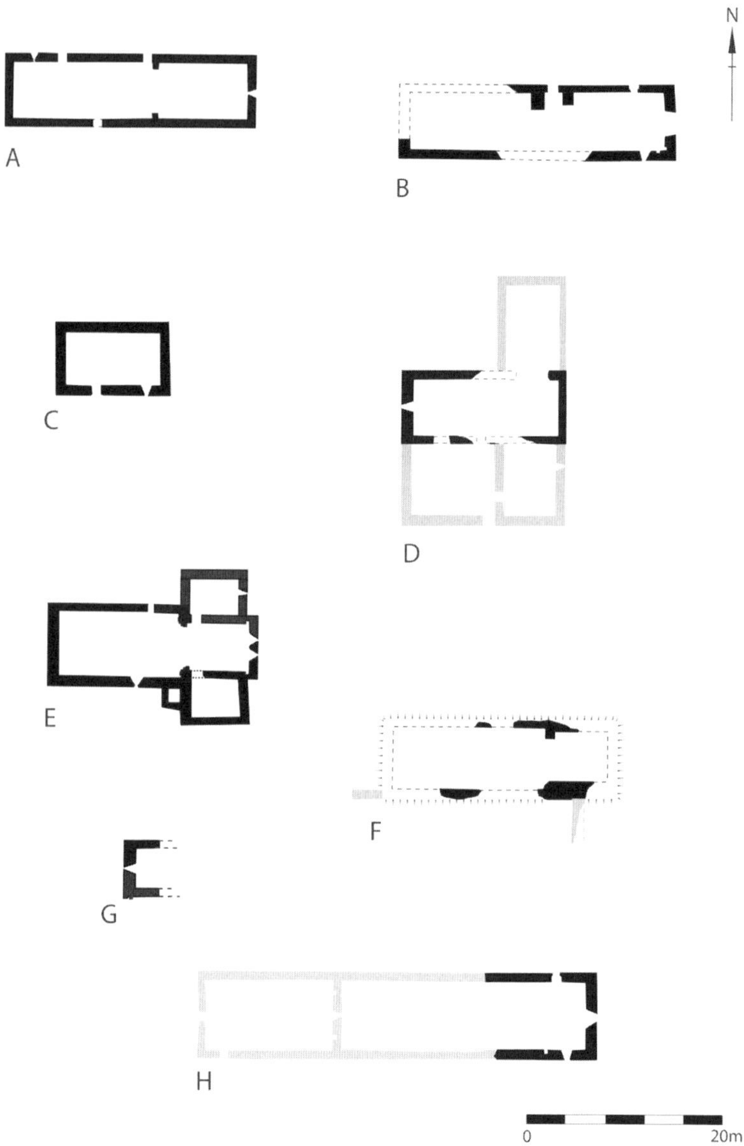

6.1a Extant nunnery church plans (in black): A. Annaghdown; B. Ballymacdane; C. Cloonoghil; D. Drumalgagh; E. Inishmaine; F. Kilcreevanty; G. Killeenatrava; H. Killevy.

The majority of extant nunnery churches are of simple rectangular plan. The average length of a nunnery church is 17.03m and 6.01m in width, though this mean disguises some variation. The largest church recorded is Killone – though it was shortened by almost 10m at some time in the fifteenth century. Most churches are much smaller, the smallest complete church being

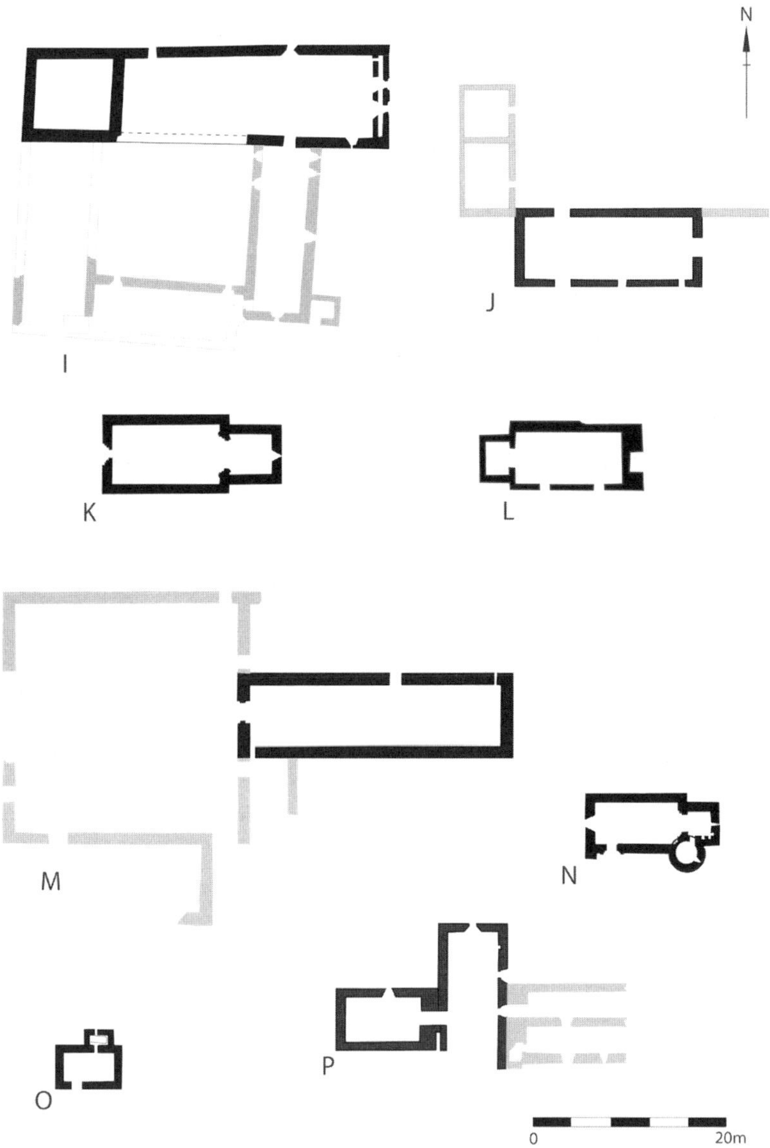

6.1b Extant nunnery church plans (in black, continued): I. Killone; J. Molough; K. Nuns' Church; L. Portrane; M. St Catherine's; N. Temple Finghin; O. Templenagalliaghdoo; P. Tisrara. Image: Frank Coyne.

Templenagalliaghdoo measuring 6.9m in length and 4.2m in width. The church at Killeenatrava is incomplete, though its full width is 3.2m, suggesting that it too was a small structure. Only the churches of Killone, St Catherine's and Molough are clearly part of a claustral plan. Ballymacdane may have had

6.2 Late Romanesque chancel arch and east window at Inishmaine, Co. Mayo. Image: Frank Coyne.

a northern cloister, and Kilcreevanty a southern cloister, but clear evidence in either case is lacking.

The church identified as the nunnery church at Annaghdown is rectangular in plan and is free-standing, with residential accommodation at its western end (Chapter 5). This church is the most northerly structure of the monastic complex, comprising a cathedral, an oratory, an abbey of Augustinian canons, and an unlocated bishop's house.[7] There is no evidence to suggest that the Killevy churches were connected to any ranges or other structures. Hamlin has suggested that the door in the north wall of the eastern (later) church may have exited to a cloister or suchlike, but this interpretation was considered to explain the door's unusual position, rather than on any structural evidence extant at the site.[8] There is no evidence at Killevy of domestic accommodation and it could be suggested that the accommodation was of timber and free-standing, in which case it would not have survived above ground. Portrane is the latest of the nunnery churches, becoming one in the sixteenth century

6.3 Portrane church, Co. Dublin. Image: Frank Coyne.

when the nuns of Grace Dieu moved there. This church itself is rectangular in plan with a tower at its west end. It is undivided and, apart from narrow window lights and a doorway in its south wall, and a window in its west and east walls, there is little architectural detail remaining.

A small number of nunnery churches are associated with towers. Kilcreevanty is described in the historical records as having a belfry,[9] though no trace now survives. Ballymacdane has the footings of a tower, which appears to be a later addition to the church structure. The foundations of two large piers were exposed during excavations at Tisrara at the junction of the north transept and chancel/nave. The excavator thought these piers too massive for an arch and suggested they supported a narrow tower.[10] Portrane's tower is positioned at the western end of the church (Figure 6.3). Temple Finghin has an unusual engaged round tower at the junction of its nave and chancel in its south wall and the tower is clearly contemporary with the church structure (Figure 6.4). Other nunnery churches, such as Killone, Molough and possibly St Catherine's, have bellcotes at the apex of their western gables, instead of

6.4 3-D scan of Temple Finghin, Clonmacnoise, Co. Offaly. © Discovery Programme.

6.5 Bellcotes at Killone, Co. Clare and Molough, Co. Tipperary. Image: Frank Coyne.

towers (Figure 6.5).[11] Molough's is a double example, which suggests two bells. This is interesting as there may have been a bell for the nuns and a second for the parishioners, as at the Augustinian male religious house of Corneville in Normandy.[12]

Proportions

Significant ratios were used in the setting out of the ground plan, and also vertically, in door dimensions and wall heights of medieval churches and religious houses.[13] Proportions can be difficult to pinpoint, however, as in relatively smaller structures centimetre differences will affect the outcome of the ratio. In addition, it is unknown if the medieval mason who laid out the church was using internal or external measurements to embody the significant ratio.[14] Despite these limitations, it has been demonstrated at several later medieval male religious foundations that significant ratios were applied, such as at the Augustinian house at Kells, County Kilkenny[15] (see Figure 5.2), and the Cistercian houses of Corcomroe, County Clare, Jerpoint, County Kilkenny, Mellifont, County Louth, Tintern, County Wexford and Graiguenamanagh, County Kilkenny.[16] Indeed, in some cases significant ratios were used to lay out the entire monastic claustral complex, sometimes using multiples of a ratio unit.[17]

Eighteen nunnery churches were assessed for these significant proportions (see Table 6.1). None conformed to known important medieval ratios, such as the Golden Section (1:√2 or 1:1.414), or the other of 1:1.618. In fact, all the proportions – excepting Temple Finghin which has a proportion of 1:3 – are irregular and average 1:2.97, indicating that nunnery churches in Ireland tend to be long. This has implications for how the churches might have been used.

Significant proportions were used at churches at important ecclesiastical sites in the early and later medieval periods.[18] On a practical level, ratios were convenient to use for master masons as they produced pleasing architectural results. It is likely they were also used to imbue a structure with symbolic harmony, providing the structure with divine or mystical connotations.[19] In relation to the eighteen nunnery churches it emerges that proportional ratios did not conform to any of the ratios known to have been symbolically significant – excepting perhaps Temple Finghin. This may be an expression of the modesty and purpose of the churches in question – as these nunnery churches were modest, without aisles or transepts. The lack of significant ratios could be interpreted as an ascetic statement by the nunnery community that ostentation and grandly proportioned interiors were not required in a humble female religious house. Alternatively, the distinct lack of significant ratios may

6.6 Killone, Co. Clare. Reconstructed doorway at the western end of the south wall of the church, providing access to the cloister. Image on right shows detail of floriate decoration (? dog rose) in the cavetto of the arch. Image: Frank Coyne.

suggest that master masons were not usually employed at nunneries and that local craftspersons and local building crafts were preferred.

Features

Fourteen of the extant nunnery churches have some archaeological remains of their doorways, windows, and interior fittings such as altars, piscinas (stone basins), daises (low platforms), and tomb niches for example, and some are well preserved.[20] They also contain some unusual features in medieval church architecture in Ireland, for example the undercroft, intramural stairs and parapet wall walk at Killone. The main structural features are considered here, and smaller internal features and fittings are considered later in this chapter. Several nunnery churches exhibit more than one doorway. Many of these are due to alterations over time and changes in function and were unlikely to be contemporary. For example, Killone had an original doorway

6.7 St Catherine's, Co. Limerick, west doorway into church from cloister. Image: Tracy Collins.

6.8 Molough, Co. Tipperary, church doorway in south wall. Image: Tracy Collins.

in its west wall and an inserted second doorway at the western end of its north wall. These doors provided access to the church directly from outside the claustral complex. Another door at the church's eastern end of the south wall provided access to the first floor of the eastern range: the location of the nuns' dormitory. A fourth door which is now reconstructed at the western end of the south wall of the church provided access from the cloister to the church (Figure 6.6).[21] St Catherine's church had three doorways (Figure 6.7). Its original doorway in its west wall is an elaborate moulded and filleted pointed-arched doorway, dated on architectural grounds to *circa* the 1240s. Each of its four capitals is of different design. Its exterior face (cloister side) originally had two elaborate label stops on its hood moulding, the northern example being a female head of an 'old hag',[22] now lost.[23] The second doorway is clearly a fifteenth-century insertion midway along the north wall.[24] The third doorway is also a fifteenth-century insertion in the southwest corner of the church. This led to an extension described as a sacristy (see Figures 5.13 and 6.29).[25] The large west doorway at St Catherine's was made smaller in the fifteenth century when a pointed-arched doorway was inserted.[26]

Molough church has one extant doorway and evidence for a further three. A breach in its north wall marks the likely location of a doorway into the cloister. A blocked doorway is evident in its west wall by a relieving arch noted on the interior.[27] There was a third blocked doorway towards the eastern end of its north wall. Its only extant doorway is an insertion,[28] having a fine circular mason's mark on its eastern jamb[29] (Figure 6.8). A third possible doorway is noted by a relieving arch near the eastern end of the south wall. This ope corresponds to a possible structure, now only indicated by a line of flashing stones, on the exterior of the wall. It is possible that this door provided access to a sacristy, as it is situated close to the east end of the church.

Ballymacdane has two doors, both in the church's north wall (Figure 6.9). The first is located at the eastern end. The outer face of this pointed-arched doorway faces into the church. The door would have been secured from outside the church structure by a large timber beam, evidenced by the remaining bolt holes. The fact that this door faces *into the* chancel suggests that it provided access from a building or range. This door allowed the nuns to move directly into the chancel of the church for the divine office.

However, apart from the positioning of the doorway, the only other clue to a possible range is a single projecting corbel at the northeast external corner of the church. The second and the larger of the two doors is located in the western portion of the north wall of the church and would have accessed the church under the crossing tower. This door faces out of the church and

6.9 Ballymacdane, Co. Cork, doorway into east end of church. This door was clearly secured from outside the church and a hanging eye is in situ. This doorway likely led from the nuns' quarters and could be locked from that side. It is not known if a claustral plan was used at Ballymacdane. Image: Frank Coyne.

is also a pointed-arch example in limestone, though its jambs are now lost. Immediately inside the door to the west, within the pier of the crossing tower, is a small niche suitable for a stoup.

Inishmaine church has a single re-used trabeate doorway in its north wall (see Figure 2.14). The west church at Killevy also has a re-used early door, with a second lintelled example in its south wall (see Figure 2.15). The east church (later church) has a single doorway with large lintel at the eastern end of its northern wall. Hamlin noted that this was an odd siting.[30] As a nunnery church, however, it is not unusual as the nuns could enter the east end, perhaps from their lodgings situated somewhere to the north. At Clonmacnoise the Nuns' Church has an impressive Romanesque west doorway (Figure 6.10), while the location of Temple Finghin's single doorway was at the western end of its south wall.

There are eight nunnery churches with some remains of an east window. The most elaborate of these is at Killone, an example of the 'School of the

6.10 The Nuns' Church, Co. Offaly, west doorway. Image: Tracy Collins.

West' or Late Romanesque style.[31] It is a double-light window with two semi-circular heads. The inner heads have plain hood mouldings and an inner band of lozenges in high relief. The arches rest on foliate capitals (or crockets), positioned immediately below a stringcourse, on plain detached shafts supported by ornate corbels. The outer face of the east window has a recess and chamfer. Glazing bar holes are in evidence (Figure 6.11).[32]

The east window at Inishmaine is of similar style and includes human and animal motifs on its exterior face (Figure 6.12). This church has a second window in its south wall. The east window at Killone is particularly interesting as it incorporates an elaborate intramural passage. The passage is accessed through a rectangular doorway in the northern end of the east wall. The intramural passage traverses through two trefoil-headed opes in the embrasures of the lights, along the sills to an intramural stair in the southeast angle of the church, which leads to the roof's parapet (Figure 6.13). The point where the

6.11 Killone, Co. Clare. East window of church, exterior and interior elevations. Note unusual intramural walkway. Image: Tracy Collins.

6.12 Inishmaine, Co. Mayo. East window of church exterior and interior elevations. Image: Tracy Collins.

6.13 Killone, Co. Clare. Intramural passage through east window to roof parapet, viewed along the sill of east window. Image: Tracy Collins.

stair emerges on the parapet is marked by a figure-sculpted corbel of a woman's head and arms which appears to support the roof (though only visible from the ground outside the nunnery). This parapet location provides excellent views of Killone Lake immediately to the southeast, and is unusual and unique for a nunnery church (see Figure 7.40).

St Catherine's east window is now ruined, though it can be reconstructed from its remaining limestone frame which indicates tracery mullions and glazing bar holes. Westropp suggested that this was a later insertion into a larger window. His reconstruction shows the later window as a three-light example with simple switch line tracery (Figure 6.14).[33] This is very similar to extant windows at the nearby Augustinian priory, Rathkeale and the Augustinian friary, Adare. Molough's east window is original to the structure and comprises twin lancets with sandstone jambs. The rear arches have pronounced pointed heads, set in widely splayed embrasures with sandstone surrounds. Externally, the windows are rebated with glazing bar holes, and some original iron is in evidence (Figure 6.15).

6.14 St Catherine's, Co. Limerick, remains of the east window of the church (see Figure 5.22, no. 1 for reconstruction drawing). Image: Tracy Collins.

6.15 Molough, Co. Tipperary. East window of the church, exterior and interior elevations shown. Note plaster fragments adhering to interior (right). These once showed evidence of wall painting. Image: Tracy Collins.

6.16 Killevy, Co. Armagh. East window of east church, exterior view. Insert shows label stop. Image: Frank Coyne.

The east window in Temple Finghin is a small round-headed example in contrast to its more elaborate west window, and the east window in the west church at Killevy is also a plain round-headed example. The east church retains only portions of its fifteenth-century window, complete with external label stop of a veiled woman (Figure 6.16). This church has a smaller splayed light at the eastern end of its south wall. The east window at Ballymacdane is poorly preserved and little can be said of its original form. Tisrara's east window was recovered and reconstructed after excavation and is of two lights with a traceried head.[34]

6.17 Killone, Co. Clare. Internal division of the church by a raised dais forming the chancel. Image: Tracy Collins.

Evidence of internal differentiation

Internal differentiation in churches can be considered on two levels. First is the division of degrees of sacred space, sanctuary/chancel and nave, relative to each other;[35] and second is the segregation of people – clergy, female religious, and laity – using those spaces. Most nunnery churches do not show any structural indication of internal differentiation, apart from those already listed as being of distinct nave-and-chancel type. At Killone, the chancel is differentiated from the nave by steps and a dais, so that the floor level of the chancel is some 1.1m above that of the nave (Figure 6.17).[36] This height accommodates a vaulted undercroft, now a crypt, incorporated under the church at its east end. The undercroft is now accessed externally through a doorway in its east wall – this is a later insertion. Originally, the undercroft was accessed via a narrow intramural stair from the east range, which makes the interpretation of its function as a burial place problematic, due to the narrowness of the passage.

There is no extant evidence in any nunnery church on their internal walls of screens of stone or timber that must have subdivided chancels from naves.[37] At St Catherine's there are a number of putlog holes, which have been plastered around and internally, suggesting they had a function when the church was in use. These are present on both the north and south walls of the church, but do not correspond to each other. It is possible that they supported some form of timber division such as a rood screen. Several nunnery churches were known to have functioned as parish churches. This meant that in addition to the division of the church into chancel and nave, the nuns also had to be separated from the parishioners. The uses of the sacred space within the church, and how those uses might have been accommodated, is now considered.

RITUAL USES

Rather than being passive onlookers in the liturgy celebrated in the church, nuns were active participants in the performance of devotion, which had daily mass and communion at its core, included the celebration of holy feasts, processions, the office of the dead, and was regulated daily by the divine office.[38] Archaeological study of monastic churches through time can illustrate the movement, expansion and contraction of the community associated with it.[39] The use of space in nunnery churches is more difficult to assess in Ireland due to the absence of archaeological excavation and dearth of portable artefacts. The archaeological excavations carried out at St Catherine's have attempted to partially fill this lacuna.[40] Nunnery churches in Ireland do not manifest themselves as being architecturally distinct from smaller male religious house churches or indeed other medieval churches more generally. They are usually smaller than their male counterparts but have features, such as windows, in the same locations as male monastic and religious house churches. An east window and usually a smaller one in the south wall would have lit the area of the high altar located at the east end of the church, while the remainder of the church would have been lit with a few windows in the north or south walls.

Of the twenty nunnery churches which have extant remains in Ireland, most are in such a ruinous condition that without archaeological investigation little specific can be said about how their interior space was used (see Table 6.1). However, they are all aisleless parallelograms, without transepts or side chapels, like most of the nunnery churches in later medieval England. This type of nunnery church is also found in France,[41] and in Germany where they are known as single nave churches, *einschiffige kirchen*.[42] It has been suggested that most nunnery churches did not possess extra chapels as the presence

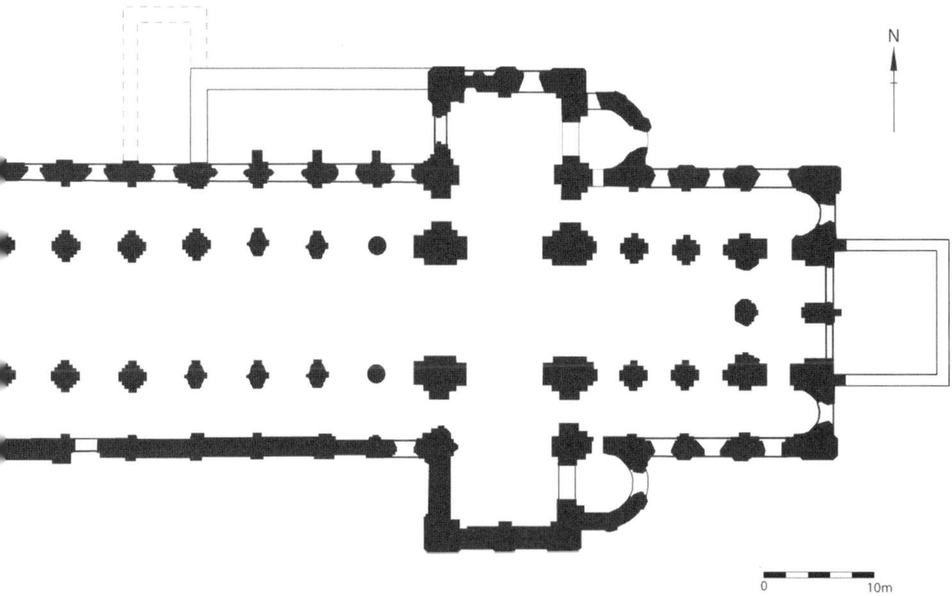

6.18 Larger nunneries abroad did possess chapels, as the fifteenth-century ground plan of Romsey, Hampshire illustrates. Image: Frank Coyne.

of a priest to say mass at each one would have been an extra expense to the nunnery;[43] although this reason is now rejected in more recent scholarship.[44] Larger nunneries elsewhere did possess places for such chapels, for example the important Benedictine nunnery at Romsey, Hampshire (Figure 6.18).[45]

Use of church space by nuns

There is nothing recognisable in the extant architecture of nunnery churches in Ireland that makes them distinctly 'female' spaces. However, already knowing from the historical sources that these churches were used by nuns, a more gendered archaeological approach can be adopted in assessing their use of space, such as asking new questions of the evidence. For instance, it can be considered how these female religious communities may have used the space themselves and also how other groups were accommodated, such as male priests, corrodians and guests, and, in some cases, parishioners. Any nunnery church had to be shared with at least one priest. Despite clearly having a religious standing in society, nuns could still not perform all the sacraments, could never be ordained, and thus required a priest.[46] This has been considered a distinct 'sacramental disability' that placed nunneries at an economic disadvantage in comparison to male religious houses. Male clerics had to be paid and so this was an expense to any nunnery. Furthermore, nunneries could not generate the same amount of income as male houses in the provision of masses and other sacramental services.[47] Nunnery disadvantage in comparison to their male counterparts has been, up until recently, the traditional narrative. Scholars like Berman are challenging this view and have concluded that this narrative is incorrect and nunneries were not disadvantaged to any great extent.[48]

There is one key difference between churches of male and female monastic and religious houses. In male churches the high altar, situated at the east end of the church, was the primary focus for the monks or canons whose choir was usually immediately to the west of the location of the high altar. The high altar in nuns' churches remained the principal focus of the liturgy of the Eucharist, though the nuns' choir was strictly segregated and physically separated from this male space by a screen. In some cases, this separation was so strict that nuns could only hear the mass at the high altar and could not actually see the proceedings.[49] For nuns then it was *their choir* that was the most important space, where they could actively participate in the celebration of mass and the divine office through prayer and chant.[50] As will be demonstrated, the nuns' choir can be in the same location as a male monastic choir but can also be placed in different spaces within the church, particularly when the nunnery church is parochial. An archaeological assessment of the location of nuns' choirs is made presently, but first the performance of the daily divine office for nuns in their churches is considered.

The routine of the divine office in a nunnery would have been similar across female religious orders, so it is possible to say something about how nuns in later medieval Ireland may have structured their rituals within their church. Canonical hours did not all require the services of a priest and so some of the time nuns could have used their churches without a male presence. The divine office was celebrated daily in the church over the course of the day at set times, when specific prayers and psalms were said, and hymns were sung. Mass was performed by a priest at least daily, and feast days would have had two masses.[51] It was not part of the divine office but a mass was the highlight of the nuns' liturgical observance each day. Therefore, using a priest in the nunnery was at least a daily occurrence and certainly not a case of weekly visits. Indeed, nunneries that possessed churches on their estates also had the expense of priests at those locations.[52]

The nuns were called to the church by the ringing of a bell. A large bell was used for major hours and a smaller one for minor hours.[53] In the fifteenth century, especially if the church also functioned as a parish church, a bellcote may have been used. At this time bell ringing became an important part of the ritual of the mass,[54] and bellcotes were added to facilitate these changes in liturgy and ritual. Three nunnery churches, Killone, St Catherine's and Molough, have bellcotes as likely later fifteenth-century additions to the west ends of their churches (see Figure 6.5). No later medieval parish churches in Ireland – whether at nunneries or otherwise – are known to have employed detached bell towers. In England, two nunneries that functioned as parish churches had detached bell towers: Romsey, Hampshire and Elstow, Bedfordshire.[55] Some nunnery churches in Ireland did have attached towers. The small rectangular tower at the west end of the church at Portrane would have been a suitable location from which to ring a bell – it has windows at its four cardinal points (see Figure 6.3). The remains of putative crossing towers at Ballymacdane and possibly Tisrara, the unusual engaged tower at Temple Finghin, and the belfry recorded at Kilcreevanty were likely used for this purpose.

Hand bells, of course, would not require any architectural feature to facilitate use. In a place where silence reigned for most of the time, a peal of a bell would be noticed and the significance of the aural sensation from bells, singing, praying and chanting should not be overlooked. The nunneries' audial environment is difficult to rescue from the past but can be reconstructed from known liturgical manuscripts such as psalters, antiphonaries, processionals and books of hours.[56] It is also likely that people in the hinterland of the nunnery would be able to hear bells and perhaps singing. The peal of bells would be a constant reminder of the presence of the nunnery, both in the locality and in the minds of the inhabitants. Graves has suggested that churches identified by their bells were the centre of sensory landscapes which created a sense of 'rootedness, of belonging and social cohesion within an area that could be easily walked'. Bell ringing was a signal across a wider landscape to a far larger 'congregation of listeners'. Moreover, a bell could signal the passing of members of the religious community, 'accurate as to the gender and age of the deceased'.[57]

Ó Carragáin has also suggested in an early medieval church context that the act of bell ringing from a round tower, or *cloicteach*, made the site 'the centre of an auditory landscape'.[58] Bells must have been an important object in the nunnery as they were worthy of record in several of the extent surveys at the dissolution. Grace Dieu, Kilculliheen and Odder are recorded as being parish churches and that the 'church bell belongs to the parishioners'.[59] Despite Molough being described a parish,[60] a bell is not recorded there, though it has a double bellcote, which implies a nunnery bell and a separate parochial one. Bells are noted at non-parish nunnery churches also. For example, at Termonfeckin, a single small bell is recorded in the nunnery's dissolution survey as remaining unsold, and at Lismullin there were no fewer than four bells.[61]

It has been mentioned that nuns required at least one priest to undertake various sacraments on their behalf. How would such a clerical male presence have been accommodated within the nunnery and the church? It is not known if priests lived at nunneries, or visited from adjacent churches or religious houses.[62] For example, the shortening of the nave at Killone, probably undertaken in the fifteenth century, may have been to provide accommodation for a priest or, less likely (due to the position of the doorway), separate lodgings for the abbess. It is likely that arrangements varied and links with adjacent male religious houses might have been commonplace. For example, the nunnery of Clonard was represented on several occasions by canons of Trim, suggesting a link between the two religious houses, though it is not recorded if the canons celebrated mass for the nuns.[63] Gilchrist has clearly demonstrated that the sacristy in English nunneries, along with the east end and high altar of the church, can be considered distinct male domains within the female space of the nunnery.[64]

The remains of nunnery sacristies are very slight. St Catherine's has a possible sacristy,[65] and flashing stones evident on the exterior of the south wall of the church at Molough may indicate the location of the sacristy, but nothing remains of the structure itself. The church at Templenagalliaghdoo has a very small annex attached, the function of which is unclear, but it is far too small to be considered a sacristy. I suggest that it is an anchorhold (see below). The proximity of the male religious house at Errew suggests that priests may have visited from there and so perhaps a dedicated space for them within the church was unnecessary. Some of the rooms attached to the churches at Inishmaine, Drumalgagh and Tisrara churches may have functioned as sacristies. The possible sacristy at Tisrara has two large wall niches suitable for the storage of ecclesiastical objects. A floor in the towers of Portrane and Ballymacdane churches could also have fulfilled this function.

So, while the archaeological evidence is sparse, priests must have been accommodated at nunnery churches in order for them to fulfil their liturgical role. Storage of liturgical items and consumables for the mass and other sacraments also had to be achieved, but currently it is difficult to identify unequivocal archaeological evidence for either. Interestingly, in the thirteenth-century phases of use at the claustrally planned nunneries of Killone and St Catherine's there was no direct external access to the churches' interiors, and so the priest must have entered via the nuns' cloisters. This thus required a male presence, even for a short time but on a regular basis, in areas traditionally thought of as exclusively for nuns. The church at Molough had a door in its west gable, which was later blocked. Churches in a more open system would

6.19 St Catherine's, Co. Limerick. Slots in the east end of the church under the window are evidence of a possible reredos. Image: Tracy Collins.

6.20 Remains of aumbries and piscinas at Ballymacdane, Co. Cork and St Catherine's, Co. Limerick, both located at eastern end of south walls of church. Image: Tracy Collins.

have been more easily accessible to the priest as he could access from the non-enclosed area outside.

Within the church itself, division of the internal space by a screen between the priest at the east end (in the sanctuary or chancel) and the nave was the norm. The nuns would be separated from the sacred space of the high altar and the location of the priest by a chancel screen of stone, timber or textile. As already remarked, some later medieval nuns were so screened from the high altar that they may not have actually seen the celebration of the mass, and only heard it, with the ringing of a sacring bell to mark important junctures like the Consecration and Elevation of the Host.[66] Indeed, other senses may also have become more important than sight, such as smell – of candles burning and being extinguished or incense being used in some of the rituals.[67] The high altar may have been further separated from the rest of the church through the use of a dais and nuns would have been seated in timber stalls, or misericords, like those at St Mary's Cathedral, Limerick, which are unique survivals in an Irish context.[68]

The interiors of nunnery churches in Ireland are all in a very ruinous condition and exhibit little architectural detail for fixtures. It is likely that many fixtures were of timber and textile and may not have left an archaeological imprint on the structure. For example, none indicate the possible location of stalls in the nuns' choir. Slots are visible at the east end of the church at St Catherine's, which are suggestive of timber panelling around and behind the altar, such as a reredos, but there is little evidence for any dividing chancel screen (Figure 6.19). Based on the British extant evidence of timber screens it is possible that many of the screens were supported on a timber frame or a series of corbels.[69] It is also very possible that many screens were of textile.

No medieval nunnery high altar survives *in situ* and there was no evidence of an altar found at the east end of the church during the investigations at St Catherine's.[70] An *ex situ* fragment of a mensa (stone altar) was recovered from Tisrara.[71] The east end of Killone church has a substantial dais but no remaining evidence of the high altar. There is some evidence for the liturgy of the mass extant, however. There are the remains of stone aumbries (cupboard) and piscinas (shallow stone basin with a drain hole) at Ballymacdane and St Catherine's (Figure 6.20). Two piscinas were recorded in a farmhouse in the townland of Clonamanagh, now identified as the location of Plary nunnery.[72] Possible aumbries are located at the east end of the churches at Inishmaine and Tisrara. These spaces would have contained liturgical vessels used in the mass and the piscina was used for the disposal of water used in the washing of the sacred vessels.

6.21 St Catherine's, Co. Limerick. Niche in south wall of church possibly for a devotional image. Image: Tracy Collins.

Nuns using the church space several times daily would have required easy access to the church from their dormitory during the late and early hours, and from other spaces during the course of the day. In the case of nunneries that have an extant claustral plan, access routes to and from the church can be considered (Chapter 7), and the nuns usually processed to the church in an orderly fashion according to seniority within the nunnery. In the more open-system arrangements where the nuns' accommodation was non-claustral and free-standing, knowing how the churches might have been accessed from those buildings is much more difficult, though particular processional routes were likely followed.

The maintenance of the divine office, and indeed private prayer, would have required spiritual and devotional material. It is reasonable to suggest that prayer and hymn books, Bibles, sheet music, stoups (small holy water fonts), altar furnishings such as book stands, candlesticks, crosses and church plate, and priest's vestments, along with other fittings such as statues, were all required and used in nunnery churches. The dissolution survey of Kilculliheen nunnery records that 'a chalice and old vestments [of the nunnery] were given by the commissioner to the parish church of the place'.[73] This is the only case where objects from a nunnery church are listed, excepting the bells discussed earlier. A niche located in the south wall of the church at St Catherine's probably held such a statue or a devotional image on which the nuns and parishioners could meditate (Figure 6.21). The only other item of this nature known from a medieval nunnery church is the fragment of a candlestick from the excavations at St Catherine's, at the east end of the church in the location of the high altar (see Figure 7.56). This candlestick is similar to fifteenth- and sixteenth-century examples from domestic rather than ecclesiastical contexts. Due to nunneries' similarities with contemporary secular architecture it is not surprising that their material culture would also be similar.

Sharing space: nunnery churches as parish churches

A parish church was the epicentre of a medieval community's pastoral care.[74] In Britain from the eleventh century onwards, the possession of a font was the measure of parochial status.[75] In Ireland there is an implication of association between parish status and baptism in Gille's writings in the twelfth century,[76] though fonts at this time were still likely to be mostly of timber.[77] Gille stated that baptism should take place inside the church and that the font should be consecrated by a bishop.[78] Primary archaeological indicators of parish status in Ireland are a baptismal font – with the proviso that timber examples do not survive in the archaeological record – a fenced graveyard and a parish church. Other features that may suggest parish status are defined spaces indicating a chancel and nave, stone chancel or beam-holes indicating the former position of a rood screen to separate laity from celebrant, a sacristy, a bellcote or similar feature, a chantry chapel, priest's quarters, graveslabs, a graveyard cross, a piscina, a stoup, an aumbry, furnishings such as stone altars, timber rood screens, rood crosses in timber or stone, church plate, statuary and statue niches.[79]

A key indicator for parish operation was the payment of tithes, which according to Gerald of Wales were not being paid in Ireland in 1185, which may suggest that even by this date some parishes were not fully operational.[80] Indeed, the parish system was still evolving in Ireland in the fifteenth century,[81] and the extant architecture of some parish churches records this *longue durée*.[82] Functioning as a parish church would have given a nunnery an extra income stream in providing services to the parishioners. It would have entitled the nunnery to tithes, some land, baptismal and burial rights, and surplice fees and dues for baptism, last unction, and burial.[83]

FitzPatrick has made the point, in a Gaelic Irish context, that pastoral ministry was quite often provided at religious houses, especially in the later medieval period.[84] Indeed, the Augustinian ethos was particularly suited to pastoral care, and there is no reason why nunneries could not provide those services with the assistance of their priest. Several nunneries in England were established at pre-existing parish churches,[85] including Romsey Abbey, Hampshire;[86] Godstow[87] and Goring,[88] Oxfordshire; and Clerkenwell, London.[89] Double houses such as Watton, Yorkshire also functioned as parish churches though separate churches were employed there: a chapel for the canons, a larger church for the nuns and a free-standing third church, for the parishioners, which lay to the south of the religious complexes. The canons shared the nuns' church on feast days when they were separated by a median wall in the church (see Figure 4.5).[90] At Barking, Essex the nunnery cloister and its parish church, dedicated to St Margaret's of Antioch, were completely separate structures.[91] The use of pre-existing parish churches as nunneries is also recorded in Germany.[92]

In some cases, in England, even non-parochial nunnery churches maintained connections to local people through lay confraternities and guilds. Occasionally the nuns shared their churches with these groups, as at the Dominican nunnery of Dartford Priory near London,[93] the Benedictine nunnery of Romsey Abbey, Hampshire or the Cluniac nunnery, Delapré Abbey.[94] In Ireland, several nunnery churches became parochial sometime *after* foundation, reversing the trend recorded in England for the establishment of nunneries at pre-existing parish centres. This difference in region is likely due to the slower processes of parish formation in Ireland, or changes in parish structure and division over time.[95]

The use of nunnery churches as parish churches is likely to have had a significant effect on how the space was used. This may sometimes have resulted in a re-positioning of the nuns' choir – their liturgical space within the church building – as nuns in this situation not only had to be separated from the priest on the high altar, they also had to be segregated from lay parishioners. Architectural responses to a parochial function varied considerably. It has been demonstrated elsewhere that location of nuns' choirs in their churches is diverse and changed over time, as the nunnery's circumstances changed.[96] The criteria for the location of a nuns' choir were not universal, and factors influencing location included the different spiritualities of different religious orders and the extent to which their enclosure was enforced.[97] This is most perfectly demonstrated by Mohn, who has recorded nuns' choirs in almost every location possible within the church space.[98] Untermann has also concluded that the use of various – if not all – locations in a nunnery church was indeed common in the later medieval period.[99] Several reasons for such

6.22 Extant medieval timber rood screen with squints as an internal division at the church of Ss Peter and Paul, Lavenham, England. After Raguin and Stanbury, 2005. Reproduced with permission of Virginia Raguin.

variety at nunnery churches in Germany have been suggested, including siting, patronage, and the acquisition of existing churches.[100]

Space in secular parish churches was segregated between clergy and laity (Figure 6.22), and men and women, and so segregation was not a phenomenon exclusive to nunnery churches.[101] In many parish churches in England women were seated on the northern side of the church and men on the southern side. In others, women were seated at the west end of the church, with men positioned closer to the east end.[102] It has been suggested in England that parishioners were seated in nunnery churches as in contemporary manorial chapels, either in galleries or high pews to separate them from the nuns.[103] Elsewhere in England segregation was achieved by accommodating the nuns' choir in a gallery, as at Burnham, Buckinghamshire where an eastern gallery was used.[104] At others, a specific space was allocated to parishioners, such as the aisle at St Mary Clerkenwell, London (Figure 6.23).[105] The later medieval nunnery on Iona, where it is believed that some of the first nuns may have been Irish, has clear evidence of a west end gallery.[106] Galleries in various locations

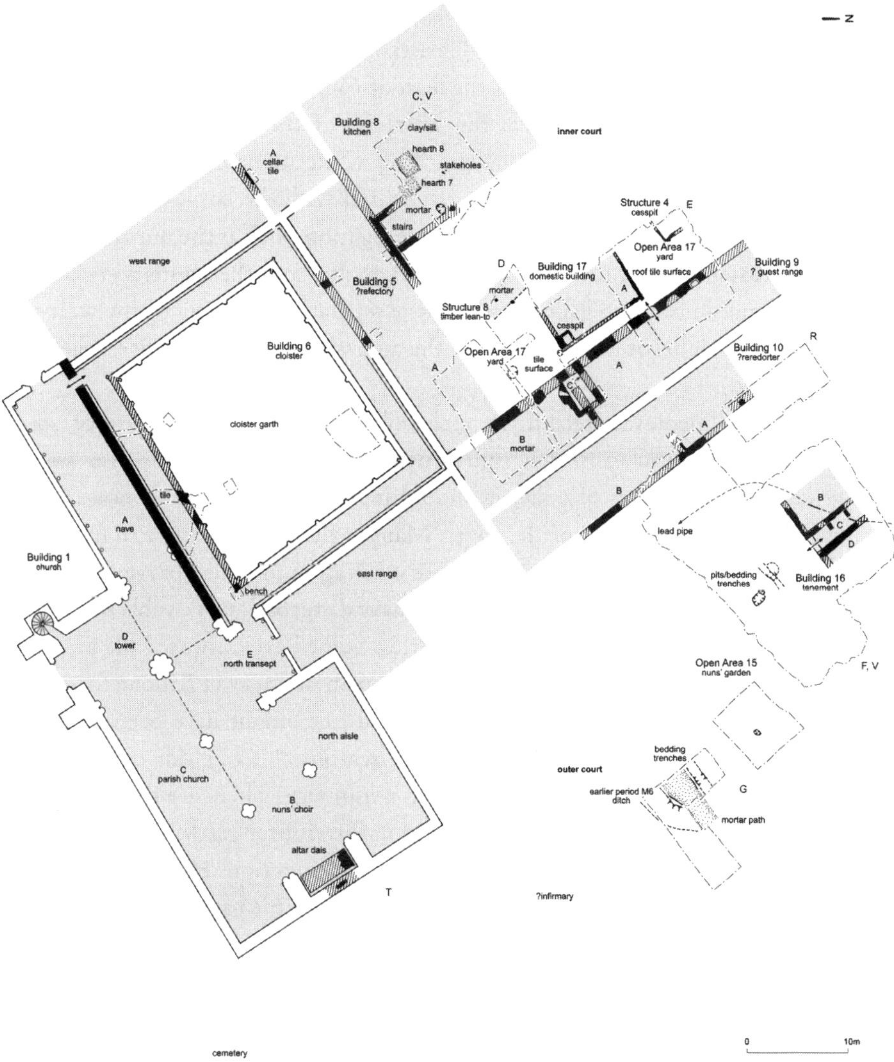

6.23 St Mary Clerkenwell, London, showing location of parish church in south aisle of nunnery church. After Sloane, 2012, reproduced with permission © MOLA.

or in multiple locations and ground-floor locations at the west end of churches were also employed for nuns on the continent and in northern Europe.[107]

In these various arrangements of nunnery church space, each group was provided with their own altar or altars: a high altar at the east end of the church, an altar at the eastern end of the nave for the laity and possible other side altars. The nuns' choir, wherever it was located within the church, also had an altar. In continental nunneries the nuns' altar was particularly used for a monstrance displaying the consecrated Host. Devotion to the Eucharist, channelled through the contemplation of the Body of Christ, became popular from the thirteenth century onwards, culminating in the feast of *Corpus Christi*.[108] Even where nuns were positioned in a gallery at the west end of the church, a separate altar was situated for them in the gallery.[109] So while monastics usually used the eastern end of the church when it was shared with the laity, some nunneries did employ more novel innovations of segregation, such as the use of transepts, aisles, eastern choirs to the east of the high altar and the western end of the nave, sometimes using galleries to achieve separation. The use of the west end of the church becomes important in the analysis of space use at St Catherine's (see below).

In later medieval Ireland the archaeological record for the use of space in nunnery churches which functioned as parish churches is also sparse. Archaeological traces of galleries should include corbels or joist holes in the walls at the western end of the naves. Many walls do not survive to first-floor height at this location, however. Future excavation may also prove fruitless in this regard as later burial would certainly have disturbed any possible subsurface traces of timber structures such as galleries. Some have dismissed the idea that nunneries could be parochial – 'the Augustinian nunnery at Killone for which parochial duties can most certainly be ruled out, might have been built as a simple rectangular church for functional reasons'[110] – but this conclusion is solely based on the fact that Killone was a nunnery. There are the remains of a baptismal font at Killone, now situated in the cloister garth, which is one of the key archaeological indicators of a parochial function. Historical evidence records that seven nunnery churches were at some time parochial: Grace Dieu, Portrane, Kilculliheen, Killone, Molough, Odder, and St Catherine's. There are a further seven where nunnery churches may have been parochial: Killaraght, Kilcreevanty, Tisrara, Graney, Aghade, Termonfeckin, and Ardcarn.

The architecture and use of space at nunnery churches may have had more in common with the architecture of medieval parish churches than those used exclusively by a male monastic or religious community.[111] Nunnery observances of the liturgy, particularly those of the Augustinians, may also have been more similar to parish churches than to male monastic houses.[112] Usually, parish churches possessed differentiated spaces: an east end sanctuary (or chancel) and west end nave, which indicated the division of the clergy and laity. Undifferentiated parish churches, which probably utilised screens, are also known.[113] Most nunnery churches with parochial functions are undifferentiated structurally, with the possible exception of Kilcreevanty. The cathedral church at Kildare is differentiated, though the extant structure

6.24 Evidence of wall plate changes at St Catherine's, Co. Limerick and Killone, Co. Clare, likely both dating to the fifteenth century, indicative of roof replacement. Image: Tracy Collins.

is unlikely to reflect the ground plan of the later medieval nunnery church there. O'Keeffe has commented on the variety in the division of space in parish churches, concluding that, 'we do not yet know why some … parish churches had their naves and chancels as separate structures while others did not'.[114] Furthermore, it has been noted that many parish churches in Ireland lacked aisles, and O'Keeffe suggests that this absence is significant. Aisles in medieval parish churches did not function as additional congregational space. In a British context, aisles were used as places of liturgy associated with baptism, matrimony and chantry, for instance. In Irish medieval parish churches these rituals all had to compete for space within the nave.

The majority of nunnery churches in Ireland are also aisleless parallelograms. It has been suggested in the context of parish church architecture that this arrangement stems from an earlier Gaelic-Irish building tradition, coming from native builders and masons, who influenced the imported template of the Anglo-Norman parish church. Moreover, it has been postulated that parish churches did not lack aisles due to a lack of money; it was rather due to function. They were centres of piety and administration – the aisleless nave mirrored the secular lord's hall of the manor[115] – and were ambiguous spaces hosting a variety of liturgical and non-liturgical activities.[116] In the present context, this interpretation again echoes Gilchrist's view that later medieval nunneries in England were influenced by the domestic architecture of the gentry.[117]

The re-building of many parish churches in Ireland in the fifteenth century has been commonly attributed to the fact that churches were dilapidated after their initial construction in the twelfth and thirteenth centuries, and that they had been ravaged by war in the fourteenth. But O'Keeffe considers re-building as a symbolic effort at social power rather than a pragmatic one, as it 'carried symbolic weight for those whose endowments financed the work'.[118] Many of the extant nunnery churches that are known or considered to have been parochial also show evidence of modifications in the fifteenth century, most notably St Catherine's. In the case of all nunnery churches that became parochial, it is likely that they had to be renovated in some way to accommodate parishioners. For example, doors had to be inserted into the church to allow direct entry to the laity. Doors were inserted into the north walls of the churches at Killone and St Catherine's. Molough's church had a doorway inserted into the western end of its south wall. In the cases of Molough and St Catherine's, the inserted doors were of high quality. At this time, St Catherine's church had its wall plate heightened, as did Killone, which suggests that new roofs were constructed (Figure 6.24). This is an interesting point, as Graves has highlighted the importance of decorative roofs as an alternative focus of lay piety which united the entire congregation within the parish churches of Norfolk, England.[119]

These fifteenth-century renovations to the nunnery churches could be considered as 'symbolic acts of social power', as the benefactors who funded this work were able to showcase their generosity to both the nunnery and the parishioners in a highly visible way. The nunneries, through the alteration of their churches, were also showing symbolically their embracing and welcoming of the wider community by making their churches accessible to the general population and expressing an ethos of sharing. In particular, at St Catherine's, further symbolism in group association might be explored. A new doorway with possible porch was inserted in the northern wall of its cloister in the fifteenth century (dated on architectural detail), which provided direct access into the cloister. This doorway could be locked from the ambulatory – inside the nunnery – evidenced by the draw bar holes extant in the fabric of the wall. This new doorway was at the opposite side of the cloister to the original access point, which was subsequently blocked. This original entrance was orientated southwards towards the founder's castle at Shanid, while the new entrance looked northwards towards the nearby contemporary medieval village of Shanagolden. This changing orientation of entrance may be symbolic of the nunnery's subtle shift of focus from patron to parishioner (Figure 6.25).

The modest nunnery churches of later medieval Ireland do not reveal precisely how they were divided to accommodate the three groups of nuns, priest and laity. Having said this, there is also currently little archaeological evidence as to how parish churches were divided, and this is an area that would

6.25 St Catherine's, Co. Limerick. Ground plan showing its thirteenth- and fifteenth-century phases and excavated trenches. Image: Tracy Collins and Frank Coyne.

greatly benefit from a research programme of archaeological investigation. By considering comparable evidence from Britain and the continent, it is possible in a few cases to suggest how church space might have been used in later medieval Ireland. While direct transposition from large continental nunnery churches to the smaller nunnery churches of later medieval Ireland is clearly problematic, some of the arrangements used are applicable. For example, in addition to the east end of the nave, the western end of the church may have been used by nuns, particularly when the church was parochial. It is also highly likely that screens of timber or textile were employed in Ireland, as structural walls of stone were not used for internal divisions. Also largely absent from the archaeological evidence in Ireland are the fittings, art and decoration that once adorned the interior of these churches, which is thought to have been similar to the imagery used in contemporary English medieval parish churches.[120]

St Catherine's: a case study of nunnery church space

The shared use of space in a later medieval nunnery church can be archaeologically explored at St Catherine's. First, an exploration of its use by the nuns and a priest can be considered from its thirteenth-century phase. Second, its use by the nuns, priest and the laity can be explored in its fifteenth-century phase in its use as a parish church. Due to the unusual position of the church at St Catherine's, a brief consideration of its location within the nunnery is required. There is no known topographical reason why the church at St Catherine's projects from the cloister. The church could have been positioned along the northern side of the cloister, making use of the north wall and producing a more conventional claustral plan. In fact, this arrangement would have located the church closer to the nuns' dormitory and so would have been more convenient for the divine office. Projecting churches are rare in monastic plans but are found at some other nunneries, for example the Dominican nunnery at Dartford, England and a Franciscan nunnery at Provins near Paris,[121] and several nunneries in Germany.[122]

The construction changes at St Catherine's, taken in conjunction with the unusual projecting church, might initially suggest that local craftsmen and not master masons were employed, a fact noted at several continental nunneries.[123] The positioning of the projecting church could show that inexperienced builders were employed who knew little of church-building – and this may well have been the case – but medieval society's experience of religion was actually quite sophisticated, being full of symbolism and pararituals,[124] and so it is likely that the builders of St Catherine's were very familiar with ecclesiastical structures and arrangements. Therefore, it is possible to suggest that the unusual layout of St Catherine's was chosen for more subtle and symbolic reasons (see Figure 6.25).

The thirteenth-century church at St Catherine's was accessed through a single door in the west end. Thus, the nuns and the priest and any other people using the church, such as guests or corrodians, had to enter from the eastern cloister ambulatory of the nuns. This suggests that at least at times when the church was in use people other than nuns were permitted into the cloister. The interior of the church was lit by several windows. Five windows lit the eastern end of the church in this phase, and it was probably quite bright and airy. This was the location of the high altar and the priest, with the nuns positioned

6.26 St Catherine's, Co. Limerick. Fragment of a tapering graveslab (on bottom right of image) within niche or possible sedilia at the east end of the church. Image: Tracy Collins.

slightly to the west. The single large window in the western gable of the church was the only one to light its western end. Westropp suggested that another window was located midway in the south wall but this is no longer in evidence. (This is now a large niche with aumbry, discussed below.)

Fixtures and fittings of the church in this phase included a piscina and a tomb niche in its south wall at the eastern end. Slots in the east wall suggest panelling or a reredos behind the high altar (see Figure 6.19). The height of these features in the wall suggests that perhaps there was originally a dais at this end of the church, although there is now no clear evidence for this. Two aumbries under the east window were previously recorded.[125] This east end of the church could be characterised as 'male' space used primarily by the priest, although there is now nothing, such as architectural decoration, to show this. In this phase there is nowhere that could be considered a sacristy, and it has already been mentioned that the priest had to access the church via the nuns' cloister. The tomb niche may have originally housed a painting or suchlike due to the large

6.27 St Catherine's, Co. Limerick. Exterior view of a low window in the eastern end of north wall of church. This window provided a view of the high altar. Image: Tracy Collins.

flat space it encloses. It may have also doubled as a sedilia (a set of stone seats for officiating priest and assistants at mass). This tomb niche interpretation is based on the remains of a small fragment of stone which tapers and is filleted, appearing to be the remains of a graveslab (Figure 6.26). There is no record of a patron being buried at St Catherine's, but this is an appropriate location for such a tomb. Other burials were undertaken within the church, and a single tapering and chamfered graveslab recorded by Westropp attests to this fact (see Figure 7.43).[126] It is not known if this slab was for a nun's burial. These slabs, and the burials identified during the excavations, show that burial and associated rituals were undertaken within the church.[127] The nuns celebrated the office of the dead upon their passing, remembered these individuals in their daily prayers, and celebrated an annual anniversary mass. Perhaps they were even related (Chapter 8).

In this phase of the church's use, a small rectangular window would have been visible in the interior at a low level at the eastern end of its north wall. (This window is now only visible from the exterior, Figure 6.27.) This window

6.28 St Catherine's, Co. Limerick. Remains of the doorway in the north wall of the church inserted sometime in the fifteenth century. Image: Tracy Collins.

would have given a clear view of the high altar and it may have functioned as a squint or hagioscope for an anchorite (see below). Based on survivals at other contemporary churches, it is suggested that St Catherine's probably had timber stalls in the nuns' choir where the nuns would have carried out their office. There is no indication as to how the interior space of the church in the thirteenth century may have been subdivided, because of the fifteenth-century alterations. The size of the religious community at St Catherine's is not known; it is likely that it was relatively small, and varied over time, probably not exceeding fifteen, though this is conjecture.

Sometime in the fifteenth century, St Catherine's church became parochial and the space arrangements in the church changed accordingly. The largest change was that parishioners had to be accommodated within the space. Parishioners accessed the church through an inserted door midway along the north wall. This insertion obscured one of the thirteenth-century windows and it is not at all clear why the window ope itself was not converted into a doorway (Figure 6.28). A niche and aumbry, which re-used a window (see Figure 6.21), was constructed opposite this doorway. This niche may have contained a devotional object such as an image or statue, which would have reinforced the devotion of the parishioners to a particular saint such as its patron Catherine, or perhaps Mary. The nuns could still enter the church's nave via their elaborate west doorway directly from their cloister, passing the door's label stop – shaped like the head of the old woman – as they entered. The doorway's large ope was substantially reduced and a smaller pointed-arched doorway inserted. The narrowing of the doorway into the heart of the cloister can be interpreted as an attempt at controlling access to this space from the then more accessible church. In further alterations, windows were blocked or reduced in size. The piscina and tomb niche appear to have been re-configured, resulting in a deformation of their arches. The large east window was replaced by a smaller switchline tracery example exhibiting evidence for glass in the form of glazing bar holes (see Figure 6.14).[128]

Fragments of plaster on the walls shows that the entire interior of the church was plastered. Several layers of plaster in an area at the eastern end of the northern wall shows evidence of incised lines – although no motifs can be identified – which may be the remains of wall decoration or painting. Further substantial alterations at this time included the raising of the wall plates on the north and south walls of the church, showing that the structure was re-roofed.[129] A single bellcote was added to the western gable of the church, indicating that a bell was likely used in calling parishioners to church and reminding them to pray at certain times of the day.[130] A structure first interpreted by Westropp as a sacristy was added to the southwest corner of the church and a small pointed-arched door was inserted at the western end of the south wall of the church for access (Figure 6.29).[131] The interpretation of this space as a sacristy is problematic and there are other possible interpretations (see below).

From the upstanding remains at St Catherine's and nunnery comparisons from abroad, it is postulated that nuns used the west end of the nave of the parochial church; the parishioners the eastern end of the nave; while the priest administered the sacraments in the sanctuary or chancel at the east end. The space was probably subdivided with screens of timber or textile. As the nuns of St Catherine's were located at ground level at the west end of the church – there is no evidence of a gallery – they were unlikely to clearly see the high altar at mass, and so senses such as hearing may have been particularly important. How much could be seen of the high altar by either the parishioners or the nuns at the west end of the church is open to debate. In England, evidence of extant timber screens from Norfolk and Devon show that some were open, formed by

6.29 St Catherine's, Co. Limerick. Doorway inserted at the western end of the south wall of the church, providing access to the 'sacristy' or possible anchorhold. Image: Tracy Collins.

a series of wide mullions and transoms, which could easily be passed through, while others were clearly very restrictive and included doors that could be locked. This has led to the conclusion that 'we must abandon the assumption that in all churches and all conditions … people encountered their religion in the same way'.[132]

6.30 St Cathe Co. Limerick. Location of th incised ship in church indicat (upper); and d of the ship in plaster (lower) Image: Tracy Collins.

Further consideration can be given to the nuns' space at the west end of the fifteenth-century parochial church. There were no windows on the walls in this part of the church. The single large rectangular window in the west gable would have allowed ample light to illuminate the nuns' space. By utilising a single large window high in the gable, it would have provided light from above, while it also allowed the expanse of walls to be used for other functions, such as a canvas for religious imagery and scenes. One interesting aspect of this possible function is the presence of an incised ship in the uppermost layer of plaster on the church's south wall (Figure 6.30; Chapter 7).[133]

The location of the ship at St Catherine's is at first puzzling, but if the use of west ends of shared churches at other nunneries is taken into account, an explanation is forthcoming. It is likely that the ship marks the location of an altar for the nuns in their choir at the western end of the church.[134] There is ample evidence for multiple altars in later medieval religious houses in Ireland.[135] Few are now extant and are usually identified through ancillary features like piscinas or aumbries.[136] Alternatively, the ship may mark the location of the baptismal font.[137] The watery associations of ships and fonts is self-evident, and a ship would be a particularly pertinent religious image to have beside such a feature. Fonts tend to be located towards the western end of medieval parish churches, like the location of the ship at St Catherine's. While no baptismal font is extant at St Catherine's, it must have possessed one when it became parochial. While there is now no evidence of painting in the interior of St Catherine's, paint may have been used on the ship and in parts of the interior of the church, as at, for example, the Augustinian nunnery church at Molough and the Cistercian house at Coyroux, France where in both cases ashlar and other motifs were painted onto the plaster.[138]

MAKING SPACE FOR OTHER RELIGIOUS WOMEN

The small low rectangular window of the thirteenth-century phase of use at the church of St Catherine's requires further exploration (see Figure 6.27). This feature is situated at the eastern end of the north wall of the church and would have originally provided a clear view of the high altar from outside. In England, external low side windows have been interpreted as providing a space for the sacring bell to be heard outside at the canon of the mass, Sanctus and the Consecration.[139] This is a possible function for the window at St Catherine's. It may have been blocked when the church became parochial, being no longer required as members of the wider community were then present within the church. Elsewhere, however, these low window features are associated with recluses or anchorites, used as a squint or hagioscope. Several anchorites are known from later medieval Ireland and, while an anchorite might follow an eremitical life in a desert or cave, many lived enclosed lives beside churches.[140] The presence of this low window at the east end of the church may suggest that an anchorite once lived at St Catherine's. A structure, cell or anchorhold – either in stone or timber – would be expected to be associated with such a window, but neither the building survey nor the geophysical survey showed any remains of such a feature.

Although there is no historical evidence for an anchorite at St Catherine's, many anchorites are known from the continent, England and Wales,[141] and anchorites in England from the thirteenth to fifteenth centuries were predominantly female.[142] There are instances in the historical records of nunneries and male religious houses in Ireland supporting female anchorites. For example, an anchorite named Felicia lived at Ballymadun church, where the nunnery of Grace Dieu held a rectory.[143] The nunnery of St Mary de Hogges used the courts to remove a female anchorite named Maria from its property at either Aghade or Kilselli.[144] A third case records a woman at Fore on lands owned by the nunnery at Clonard. Although the precise location is not named, it is likely identified as Caltragh (see Figure 5.34).[145] In 1447, an Augustinian nun from Kildare requested enclosure as an anchorite at St Leonard's, Exeter, in England to escape the violence of the Irish, which was accepted by the bishop there.[146] Earlier, in 1397 there was another anchorite at St Leonard's, named Alice, who lived in a house in the graveyard.[147] Despite the extreme form of enclosure under which an anchorite lived, they drew people to them and became conspicuous religious foci, for example the female anchorite at the Martini church in Groningen in the thirteenth century, who became an important focus of lay devotion for the entire town.[148]

It is reasonable then to suggest that some nunnery churches may have incorporated spaces for anchorites, as did male religious houses. The support of an anchorite was considered an important act of charity by a religious house.[149] Peculiarly, the gender of the anchorite did not appear to be of concern. For example, the Premonstratensian canons housed a female anchorite at Holy Trinity Island in a cell attached to their church in 1436. Excavations carried out there revealed a structure interpreted as a sacristy (Figure 6.31),[150] although an alternative interpretation has been suggested as a fifteenth-century anchorhold.[151] Therefore, if there was an unrecorded anchorite resident at St Catherine's in the thirteenth century, who resided in a building attached to the church at its east end and who used the low window in the north wall, it could have been either a woman or a man. Furthermore, anchorites' cells were sometimes located in graveyards or cemeteries. Nunneries' cemeteries are traditionally on the northern side of the church, and archaeological excavation on this side of the church at St Catherine's has proven that burial did occur here[152] (see Chapter 8).

There are about twenty-five anchorholds recorded in England, of which about five are associated with females.[153] They exhibit a wide variety of forms, with two directly associated with nunneries – Kilburn and Tarrant – though in both cases the cell predated the nunnery and was thought to be the impetus for

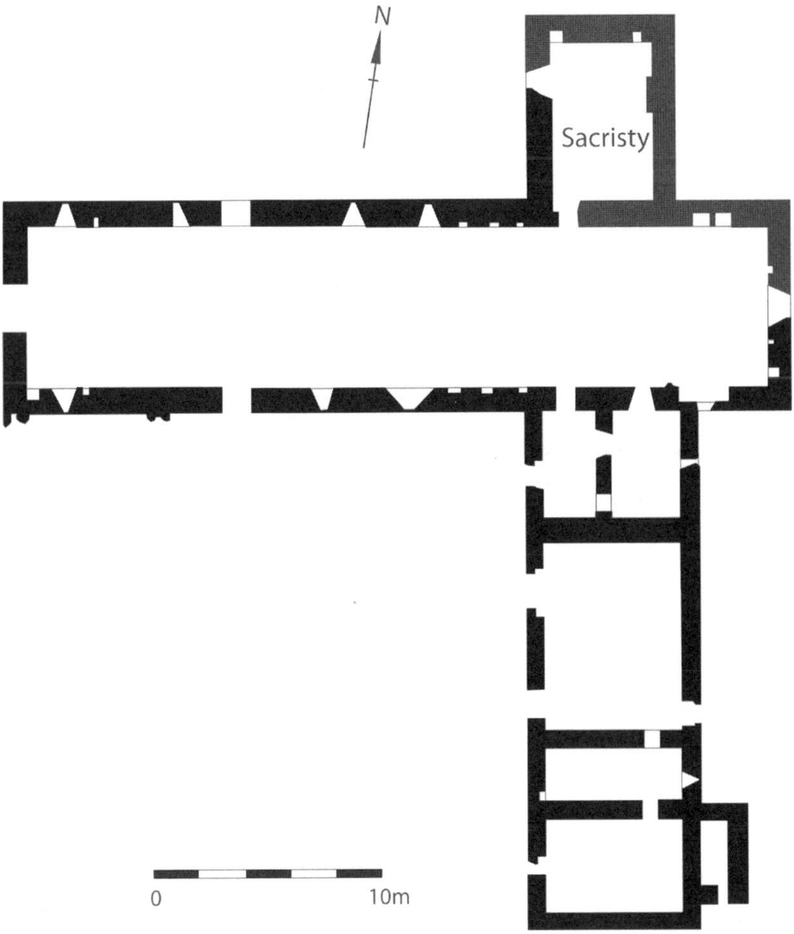

6.31 Ground plan of Holy Trinity Abbey, Co. Roscommon (Premonstratensian), noting the sacristy which may mark the location of the documented anchorhold there. After M. Clyne, 'Archaeological excavations at Holy Trinity Abbey, Lough Key, Co. Roscommon', *Proceedings of the Royal Irish Academy*, vol. 105C, 2005, pp. 23–98, at p. 32, figure 3. Reproduced with permission.

the nunnery foundation.[154] Evidence for an anchorhold of any date has yet to be identified at any nunnery in Ireland.[155] While the usual position for a recluses' cell is to the north of, and at the east end of, the church, which is the position indicated by the thirteenth-century rectangular hagioscope at St Catherine's, there are notable exceptions. For example, St Marwenne's, Marhamchurch, Cornwall had a female anchorite in the fifteenth century whose cell was at the west end of the church. All Saints, North Street, York also had a female anchorite situated in a two-storey cell at the western end of the north aisle

6.32 St Catherine's, Co. Limerick. Extant remains in the east wall of the 'sacristy'; a rectangular niche with two upper projecting corbels. Image: Tracy Collins.

of the church.[156] The medieval parish church at Compton in Surrey has the remains of two anchorholds, one to the south of the chancel and an earlier one at the eastern end of the south aisle.[157]

There is a large corpus of medieval written material on the anchoritic tradition and ritual, not least the *Ancrene Wisse*, which was in effect an instruction manual for female anchorites.[158] There have been several commentaries on the significance of the *Ancrene Wisse*, particularly in relation to the juxtapositioning of the sacred and the domestic spheres of the anchorite's life in her anchorhold.[159] It has been suggested that the location of the anchorite's cell in respect of the church may reflect the anchorite's enclosure ceremony itself. Immediately prior to enclosure in the cell a postulant underwent an enclosure ritual in the church. For clerics this occurred in the choir and for unordained men at the choir's entrance. For women, the ritual took place at the west end of the church.[160] If the west end of the church is thus an unusual, but not unknown, location for female anchorites' cells, this draws attention to the second possible location of an anchorite at St Catherine's.

6.33 Templenagalliaghdoo, Co. Mayo. A possible second anchorhold at a nunnery church. Location of anchorhold attached to the northern wall of the church and detail of grave feature in interior. Image: Frank Coyne.

The fifteenth-century addition to the church at St Catherine's at its west end and to the south has been identified as a sacristy and is known locally as the 'Black Hag's Cell'. It is located in the angle of the east wall of the cloister and the south wall of the church. It is clear from the remains that it was not very large and was a single storey, with a lean-to roof supported by a slot and a corbel on the exterior face of the cloister wall. The line of its roof can be traced on the exterior of the south wall of the church. The interpretation of the structure as a sacristy is problematic, first given its location at the western end of the church and, second, its very small doorway accessing the church (see Figure 6.29). The cell is in a very ruinous condition, with only the extant remains of an aumbry with supporting corbels directly above, at the northern end of its east wall (Figure 6.32). Most of its east and south walls are now missing.[161]

A plausible alternative interpretation of this space is that it is an anchorhold, dating to some time in the fifteenth century. Anchorites were often visited for advice and spoke through a veiled window,[162] and the window described by Westropp would have been a convenient ope through which to conduct such conversations. This interpretation is slightly problematic, however, in that this anchorhold could not have had any view of the high altar – though several confirmed anchorholds, mentioned above, did not have this view either. But it would have been adjacent to the putative altar in the nuns' space at the west end of the church, perhaps indicated by the incised ship. This juxtaposition is interesting, as the *Ancrene Wisse* specifically associates ships and anchorites, 'anchored under the church as an anchor under a ship, to hold the ship so that neither the waves nor storms may overwhelm it'.[163]

Furthermore, the anchorhold may have become the tomb of its anchorite, which served as a 'solemn reminder of the end'.[164] The anchoritic life was a social practice, holding death and life in the same space. The enclosing ceremony for an anchorite paralleled a burial ceremony, and in some cases the anchorite was to dig in the floor of her cell daily and prepare her own grave;[165] 'such morbid practices were integral to the denigrating qualities of the anchoress' life'.[166] The possible nunnery church of Templenagalliaghdoo has a very small annex containing a curious rectangular pit (Figure 6.33). It is possible that the annex, on the north side of the church, is an anchorhold, and the rectilinear pit an open grave. This function has not been suggested previously, but the shape, orientation and dimensions of this feature clearly support this interpretation, and its name, 'church of the black nun(s)', underlines a female religious association.

VARIETY IN FORM AND RITUAL

The majority of nunnery churches in medieval Ireland were undifferentiated parallelograms in plan, though it is likely that interior variety was introduced through the use of screens of timber or textile. A key difference between male religious house churches and those of nuns is that nuns must always have shared the sacred space of their church with at least one individual of the opposite sex, due to their necessary reliance on a male priest to deliver certain sacraments and mass. Therefore, space segregation by gender was always an issue at nunnery churches. This segregation might be considered in two ways: on one hand the necessary division of male and female and, on the other, the separation of the sacred space of the sanctuary/chancel and female persons – as even though they were female religious they were not ordained – in the same way as the laity were separated from sacred space in secular churches.

An essential point is that the use of space in nunnery churches is more varied than the popular preconception of monastic church space. Nunnery churches appear to have more in common with parish churches of the period, and a diversity of layout and use can be concluded. The similarity with parish churches may show the agency of the nunneries' benefactors and the ecclesiastical architecture with which they were familiar. It also again underlines the nunneries' links and close connections to their local communities.

These links were further strengthened when some nunnery churches achieved parochial status. At some churches this transition was facilitated through minor changes such as door insertion, while at others, such as St Catherine's, the changes were more substantial, with windows, doors, interior fittings and even the roof being renovated. The use of space and changes over time in these mostly aisleless parallelograms can be difficult to assess, but it is possible to do so in a few nunnery churches such as St Catherine's. The addition of a separate group of people – the parishioners – and their accommodation in a shared parochial church has led to a variety of architectural responses outside Ireland – for example, median and lateral walls or screens, the exclusive use of aisles or transepts by certain groups, or the utilisation of upper-floor galleries. Within Ireland, it can be concluded that lateral or median division of the church was most likely, as no evidence has been found for aisle, transept or gallery use. These divisions were not of stone, as no evidence was found for this and it is thus likely that lightweight timber or textile screens were employed.

The archaeological evidence has been interpreted thus. At some churches the nuns' space was located at the eastern part of the nave while at others it was positioned at the west end of the church. The use of screens would have meant that senses such as hearing – and smell when incense was used – may have been more important than seeing during the community celebration of the mass. In these arrangements, lines of vision to the high altar for both nuns and parishioners would have been obscured or in some cases even blocked. While the different sections of the congregation were also obscured from view from each other, each would have been well aware of the others' presence. This would have created further links with the local community. The nuns may have had family in the parochial section of the church, may have been tasked with praying for the deceased relatives of members of the parish, or been asked to intercede to the Virgin Mary or other saints on behalf of penitents in the parish. Despite segregation, all sections of the parish were within the parochial church and under the same roof, which in part would have been visible to all. This fact would not have escaped members of the congregation, and parish church roofs were alternative foci for lay piety within the church. The renovation of St Catherine's roof in the fifteenth century suggests that it may have been an important devotional feature of the parochial church and was probably decorated.

Furthermore, parochial status for a nunnery church would have drawn it ever closer to the local community through the provision of pastoral services. For example, a church that had a right to baptism could also perform a proper Easter liturgy as the baptismal liturgy was an integral part of it.[167] Parish status may have also allowed the nuns to be part of processions on particular feast days, such as the great processions of *Corpus Christi*, where canons, monks and nuns came together to share food and then jointly distribute it to the local communities.[168] Some nunneries, such as St Catherine's and Templenagalliaghdoo, may have supported anchorites. The presence of an anchorite would have further encouraged people to visit the nunnery church and interact with the religious community, seeking intercession and divine guidance. Having now considered the most sacred and important structure of the nunnery, the church itself, we move on to the rest of the nunnery complex and how it may have been used in the daily lives of the nuns.

CHAPTER 7

Daily Life and Identity Formation

We have just considered the nunnery church, a most important space, which gave the nuns' lives a rhythm through the performance and celebration of the divine office. The entire nunnery complex gave meaning to their lives in different ways, however. This chapter is an exploration of the social archaeological context of later medieval nunneries, the nuns themselves, and their communities. Some of the questions first raised in Chapter 1 are returned to now, including: how did the nuns use the sacred architecture of their nunneries in the context of a wider secular world? What were the various identities of the nuns themselves and of their communities, and how did these identities co-exist with, enhance, or perhaps contradict each other? How can the archaeology of these nunneries elucidate the routine of the nuns and the performance of their roles on an everyday basis? Can the life course of a nunnery community be considered in tandem with the personhood of its individual nuns, such as the abbess, nuns, vowesses, corrodians and servants? In essence, what can now be learned from the archaeological data through the lens of an engendered archaeological approach? I explore what might be concluded, from the archaeological evidence, about what life was like within the confines of a nunnery in later medieval Ireland. Uses of the monastic space within the nunnery are considered through an analysis of access where possible, and the routine and performance of everyday life is imagined.[1]

FEMALE RELIGIOUS IDENTITIES

Life in a nunnery offered a woman an alternative to marriage and childbearing,[2] but the intentions or agencies of the women entering a nunnery are usually far from clear. On one hand, she may have decided freely to join a religious community or, on the other, her family may have chosen that life course on her behalf with or without her agreement. Perhaps she did not wish to marry or re-marry, or her opportunity to do so may have passed, or no suitable men presented themselves as husbands. She may have joined a religious community for an education, a career with potential for advancement, or to follow a genuine religious vocation and dedication to God (see Chapter 3).[3]

It is likely that becoming a professed nun was much more complex than just being a wholly positive or wholly negative experience for those who embarked upon it. A key aspect in the consideration of the identity of women religious is that they ultimately saw themselves as a 'religious person rather than woman'.[4] A medieval woman who became a nun in later medieval Ireland went through a transforming process. She dedicated her life to God as a bride of Christ through her profession, and joined a community of like-minded women in this regard. These nuns held various identities, some simultaneously. For example, the nunnery community had a corporate identity manifested in their seal, the iconography of which may have changed over time. Individual nuns maintained individual identities as office-holders and remained connected to their families through visits, letters, gifts and maintenance of family names. They had all dedicated themselves for various reasons as brides of Christ[5] (or lesser non-professed roles such as vowesses or corrodians), to follow a life of contemplation in order to get closer to God and pray for their patrons' salvation. They did this through the use of devotional imagery such as statuary depicting Mary and the Christ Child, and probably used a rich range of material culture which is now lost for later medieval Ireland, but still extant in many continental nunneries.

In addition to the intentions of the woman becoming a nun, there is the agency of the patron and, later, benefactors to consider. In cases where an individual may have been forced by her family to join a nunnery, the agency of her family was clearly all-powerful. There is little documentary evidence for this occurring in medieval Ireland, though it may have happened occasionally. Certainly, though, the agency of the patron and, later, benefactors, whether that be an immediate family member or leader of a kin group, had impacts on the nunnery architecture and its community of nuns. None of these relationships between patron, benefactor and nun is fully recorded for later medieval Ireland, so a definitive narrative cannot be known. What can be concluded from the evidence is that these relationships between individual nun, nunnery community, and patron/benefactor were usually symbiotic. Each brought their own power to bear and relationships were reciprocal.[6] For example, an obituary document from the Dominican nunnery of Unterlinden, France records deceased benefactors along with their donations, such as rent, estates, houses, grain and wine, along with the day on which mass was to be celebrated on the donor's behalf.[7]

De Paermentier has suggested that entry into a nunnery had an impact on the personal identity of a nun, through depersonalisation.[8] Becoming a professed nun, by taking monastic vows – chastity, obedience and poverty (along with

7.1 A nun's finger ring from the post-medieval nunnery at Bethlehem, Co. Roscommon, inscribed 'to obey is better then [sic] sacrifice EL'. © National Museum of Ireland.

stability)[9] – meant a renunciation of her former social status, private property and sexuality. It was 'a denial of the nun's previous secular individuality in favour of a wish to assimilate into an alternative collective identity that represented the ideal virtues of a nun as a bride [of Christ]'.[10] However, notwithstanding the perceived depersonalisation process of becoming a professed nun, the historical evidence that is available suggests that many of these nuns still managed to maintain strong links with their families, through visits, letters, gift exchange, management of family land and assets and guardians of family history. In these cases, their lives within the nunnery may not have been very different to that in their homes – with the exception that they were now under the authority of the abbess rather than their male kin.[11] Moreover, in theory, on the basis of merit, career progression was open to a nun in a nunnery, in a way that was not so readily achievable for a secular lady.[12]

A priest or bishop carried out the profession ceremony after the woman had spent a set period of time dependent on the rule of order, first as a postulant and then as a novice.[13] The ceremony was considered a rite of passage.[14] The initiatory rite of profession for a nun involved the adornment in bridal clothes, cutting of hair, changing of clothing to a habit, a veil as a sign of admission and betrothal and a finger ring[15] indicating their marriage to Christ (Figure 7.1). These changes were an outward sign of the nun's renunciation of self, class and sexuality. Her habit, in particular – as she was completely covered with wimple and veil – was an extension of monastic space.[16] Later rites included the wearing of a fabric crown decorated with gold thread and red crosses, to continue the symbolism of a bride of Christ, and also to symbolise His crown of thorns. These rites were framed within a structure of psalms and prayers, incense, candles and singing, performed in the nunnery's church.[17] The medieval nun committed her celibacy to the church, as a union with Christ, and her body became their shared private space.[18] By experiencing the ritual of the profession, the woman's individual identity was transformed into a community identity.

Being part of any community, religious or otherwise, has many implications. Taken at face value, a community can suggest an artificial utopia of cohesion, harmony and belonging, which in reality may not have existed. The concept of community is multifaceted and laden with aspirations and contests of interpretive power.[19] Therefore, a community identity in a nunnery was certainly not stagnant or fixed, and shared identity could change over time.[20] It has been suggested that religious women formed a community of outsiders or 'other', in that they were perceived as marginal to the mainstream religious male community.[21] A most important factor affecting nunnery community identity was patronage. Families or individuals who supplied the funding for monastic enterprises had their own agendas and so their agency cannot be discounted or underestimated. Moreover, founders' agendas were various. In summary, they may have supported a nunnery for status and prestige; for close family members (wives, sisters, daughters and granddaughters are all recorded); or to be prayed for and remembered to ensure the safe passage of their souls to heaven. It has also been suggested that land colonisation may have been a motivating factor in the establishment of nunneries in certain areas.[22]

It has already been demonstrated for England, Wales, Scotland and Ireland that nuns were sometimes related to their patrons, who for the most part came from the gentry of society.[23] In light of this, the nunnery's community identity was inextricably linked to its patron, as they were close relatives of members of that community. Therefore, a complex interaction between individual and community identity must have been forged, rather than a single notion of identity replacing another. Moreover, Curran has noted that medieval women who became nuns retained their original surnames, so this also helped to maintain links with their families and their local communities of which they were part before profession. It also makes them more recognisable in the historical records. The names of 232 nuns have been identified for later medieval Scotland.[24] Some 189 names of religious women are known from the records of later medieval Ireland and some have recorded histories.[25] These numbers must represent a mere fraction of all the professed nuns in these regions.[26]

Upon joining a nunnery community, the choice of order affiliation must have had some impact on ethos and identity. Nunnery affiliation of houses in medieval Ireland has already been set out (Chapter 3; see Figures 3.3 and 3.4). It is broadly thought that the categorisation of nunneries through order is unhelpful as it squeezes female monasticism into a male template.[27] This is particularly true where nunneries did not have a specific order in mind at foundation and only officially affiliated at a later date. This may also explain why there is sometimes confusion over the order of a particular nunnery. This is the case with some nunneries in Ireland, for example Kilcreevanty, which has been described as Benedictine, Cistercian and Augustinian.

It may be that affiliation was unimportant and a woman joined the familial nunnery whatever its affiliation. However, a conscious choice may have been made, where the chosen ethos of the order would greatly add to its community identity. For example, the Cistercian rule was considered much more austere than the Benedictine rule – even though both were based on the rule of St Benedict – while St Clare's rule placed a particular emphasis on poverty and enclosure.[28] The choice of one rule over another may have held particular significance for the woman becoming a nun, and in later medieval Ireland that choice was overwhelmingly Augustinian. Furthermore, location may have been a factor in a woman's choice of nunnery, choosing a nunnery that was linked to her family through patronage or benefaction and perhaps close to her home place. It has been shown that nunneries in Ireland were in secluded but not isolated locations and many were close to walled towns, unenclosed settlements and settlement clusters (Chapter 4).[29] These locations may have been preferred for nunneries as they offered an element of protection – protection that was perhaps not deemed so necessary in English nunneries, which for the most part were situated in isolated locations. This protection factor may have facilitated more interactions between nuns and the local population in medieval Ireland, as nuns may have been a more common sight and part of the everyday experience of local lay society. This proximity over time perhaps contributed to a slightly different sense of what female religious represented in wider society in later medieval Ireland.

DAILY LIFE IN THE CLOISTER

This section explores, through the archaeological evidence, how female religious may have lived as brides of Christ and used the enclosed space of the nunnery. First, though, it is necessary to briefly consider how their spaces and time were structured. The imposition of strict enclosure on female religious, first by social norm and tradition and later formalised by papal decree (Chapter 3), stripped abbesses of their public roles – which was considered important – and left them with a much lesser private role within the confines of their nunneries.[30] The question then arises: how private was a nunnery for its community and for its nuns as individuals? Schulenburg has considered nunneries as 'private spaces', while Kleinschmidt has described them as 'spaces of daily experience', beyond the gaze of the world.[31]

In contrast, Smith has argued that through monastic rules one was expected to entirely lose one's individuality and worldly identity and become part of the spiritual whole of the community. A nun created a spiritual space around herself through the observance of the rule, to concentrate on her relationship with God. But this space was not considered personal or private because it was shared with God.[32] De Paermentier has also argued that nunneries were in fact public spaces, albeit with their specific monastic codified behaviour in the form of a rule.[33] Ideally, the professed nun was depersonalised, and sacrificed her individual identity for the common public identity of the community. Private space and the individual did exist for nuns but only on a spiritual level, through their meditation and communication with God. The ways which these nuns experienced space was restrained both physically and symbolically, publicly and privately.[34]

These views suggest that personhood was re-defined for those who entered a nunnery as they eschewed privacy and other privileges. But there are opposing views in relation to the extent of loss of individuality. Hall and others have suggested that while nuns were part of a religious community, they did not shed their individual and family connections entirely;[35] for example, in Scotland they retained their family names[36] and, on occasion, the nuns used their worldly connections for the benefit of their nunneries.[37]

While later medieval society generally considered public space to be more prestigious than private space, when it came to living accommodation privacy was becoming increasingly desirable from the thirteenth century onwards.[38] This desire for private individual space is manifested in the archaeological record of nunneries in various ways. For instance, communities of nuns in England were known to have sub-divided into smaller *familia* or households, possibly along family lines.[39] In many cases, dormitories were divided into individual cells and large refectories were no longer used for communal dining, the household taking meals in smaller rooms instead.[40] The Rich Clares of Ghent had partitioned cells in their dormitory to which they could retreat for private space, though all were overseen by the abbess who also slept in the dormitory.[41] By the sixteenth century in many nunneries, such as Burnham Abbey, the abbess had her own lodgings,[42] and it is possible that the shortening of the church of Killone was undertaken to create more private residential accommodation. These subtle changes in the use of space by nunnery communities likely reflected the privatisation of space within the domestic sphere at this time and the proliferation of individual rooms in wealthier later medieval houses.[43] Moreover, it may mirror changes in later medieval women's piety more generally, which was shifting to a more personalised approach to prayer, and these changes in turn may have become more acceptable for members of religious communities.[44] Alternatively, this shift in spatial arrangement from dormitory to cell has been interpreted as a return to the eremitical tradition of early monasticism.[45]

By viewing space within a nunnery in this public versus private way a contradiction does emerge. Binary oppositions can sometimes be unhelpful and it is perhaps more useful to consider a negotiation between the two positions. It is too simplistic to consider nunnery spaces as entirely public or private, as while part of the ethos of the nunnery community was one of separation from secular society, the individuals of that community remained enmeshed in the world through various networks. Indeed, as will be demonstrated, these networks and connections between nunnery, patron and tenant were essential for the continuance of the nunnery community, which has led it to be described as a 'permeable cloister'.[46]

Time was as structured as space in a medieval monastery through the universal ritual of the divine office, a framework which structured all activities (Chapter 3),[47] in addition to the particular rule. As the medieval period wore on, a more individualistic approach to prayer and meditation in the eremitical tradition began to re-emerge in tandem with the privatisation of space already discussed. This private quality of the space was dependent on the individual reflection and prayer which were built into the daily routine of the community.[48] As such, the duality of individual space and time and community ritual time is an important consideration when exploring monastic space. This subtle shift in monastic ideals reached its zenith in the architecture of the Carthusians, who in effect led a coenobitic life but were striving for eremitic meaning.[49]

While a primary function of a nunnery was to pray for the eternal salvation of its patrons and benefactors, daily tasks of living were also required. An important spatial consideration for nunneries is that while they are popularly thought of as purely sacred places, in reality they were 'machines for living in', to borrow Le Corbusier's phrase, or 'spaces of daily experience'.[50] The abbess had ultimate authority in the nunnery. She guided her community through both spiritual tasks and more mundane daily tasks of life in a nunnery.[51] The daily schedule of a nunnery, according to the rule of St Benedict, was threefold. There was liturgical time which comprised the divine office. The daily celebration of mass was the highlight of liturgical observance. The rest of the time was dedicated to *lecto divina* or reading and contemplation, and the more mundane tasks of eating, sleeping and working.

Reading for instruction and contemplation was important at nunneries and this would have required them to have a library or at least a collection of reading material. Reading could be a communal activity, such as at chapter, in church or in the refectory, or for private meditation. Very little is known about what nuns read in Ireland and indeed whether the majority could read or write,[52] but more is known for nunneries in other countries.[53] It is thought that English nuns were expected to be literate, though by the end of the thirteenth century this literacy was mostly in the vernacular (French and English) and very little if any Latin was written or understood by English nuns.[54] But Latin was the language of the liturgy and there must have been sufficient 'practical literacy' or understanding for nuns' participation, although this understanding may not have extended to proficient reading and writing.[55] It has been suggested that access to Latin meant that the nuns had a degree of social power as it was the language of power throughout the middle ages.[56]

Nunnery libraries generally included three types of books: service books, books of biblical material, and texts of contemplative literature. Service books would have included missals, antiphons and psalters, used in the divine office: examples are two from Campsey Ash and three from Carrow, both in England, one of which is highly illuminated. A French copy of the Old Testament is known from Flixton Priory, and Thetford nunnery possessed an English version of the New Testament. Contemplative literature included saints' lives, for example *The Revelations of St Bridget* owned by the nuns of Thetford.[57] It is thought that the twelfth-century *Martyrology of Turin* may have been composed for use by the nuns at Lismullin.[58] There are also a small number of images, maps and texts, either in books, paintings or dioramas, that represented virtual pilgrimages that nuns enclosed in their nunneries could undertake in spirit (Figure 7.2).[59]

7.2 A copy of a medieval world map *c.*1300 from Ebstorf, thought to have been used in virtual pilgrimages within the cloister. Reproduced with permission of the abbess, Ebstorf nunnery, Lower Saxony, Germany.

Monastic cloisters, despite observed silence, would not have been quiet places, as bells, music, singing, the noise of daily business and work, possibly animals and workers, would be audible on a daily basis. In Ireland, a claustral arrangement appears to have been the exception, though it is likely that a rhythm and routine of monastic life was also followed even in more flexible layouts. Silence was observed, as a symbol of God's eternal silence and to allow meditation and contemplation. There were specific times and spaces where conversation was permitted, such as the chapter house, parlour and sometimes the cloister. Acceptable topics of conversation would be the monastic life, theological issues, elections and perhaps their life before entering the nunnery.[60] Some nuns and monks developed sanctioned sign languages within their houses, in order to preserve silence while facilitating necessary conversation, and created methods of sophisticated communication that were not always verbal.[61]

As will be further considered in Chapter 9, nunneries interacted on a number of levels with their hinterland and locality; 'the space of regular communication'.[62] Within that space, the nunnery provided places where encounters between various groups occurred regularly. These encounters might be framed by ritual, in the church, for instance, where priests, nuns and a lay congregation, if a parish church, might interface, or in the cemetery for burial (Chapter 8). Many daily encounters were mundane, such as those between nuns and their lay servants, either within the cloister or the outer court, interactions with builders or masons for repair work, interactions with tenants arriving with rent, tithes or produce, and with patrons for hospitality or family visits.

Other benefactors might arrive on short visits, perhaps to venerate a relic, as a stopping point on a journey, or longer term, as a corrodian. Annual or more intermittent encounters included those with a bishop or abbot and his retinue on visitation or for the celebration of feast days, such as that of the patron saint of the nunnery. The historical evidence shows clearly that in many cases nuns were related to their patrons and benefactors – some closely, being siblings or children – and may have also been related to their appointed confessors and priests. It is easy to imagine many of these encounters between patrons to be for the most part friendly, warm, and not unusual occurrences. The various historical accounts of nuns,[63] albeit meagre, departing their nunneries for various reasons and being active in secular society, such as at court, or being witnesses to marriages and on occasion sharing accommodation with priests, go some way towards showing a more realistic and broader picture of how these female religious followed their everyday lives.

These daily interactions would have often taken place within the confines of the nunnery complex or its outer court. Can the archaeology and architecture of later medieval nunneries indicate where these interactions might have occurred within the monastic space? While accepting earlier considerations of nunnery enclosure,[64] it has been suggested that 'a much more subtle categorisation of cloister space can be reconstructed through which individual and group identities were forged'.[65] This more subtle categorisation of the use of monastic space in nunneries in medieval England was realised through an analysis of the location and form of religious imagery extant in many medieval nunnery buildings in England. Particular meanings of the imagery are best read in their original spatial context, so Gilchrist concentrated on those images that appeared *in situ*.[66] Through this analysis she demonstrated that more male-oriented imagery was used in parts of nunneries where males might be regularly permitted, particularly the sacristy, thus showing how architecture could reflect usage.

This type of analysis is not possible with the Irish evidence but is worth bearing in mind when considering the upstanding remains. Without exception, the church was the most important structure in any monastery. Other monastic spaces were sacralised also, for example the cloister, refectory, dormitory and smaller cells, via the performance of ritual through sound, silence, chanting and the Word, and through the use of devotional objects such as statues, sepulchres, altars and portable altarpieces.[67] Therefore a nun was surrounded by sacred space in her daily life. First, daily life in those nunneries that have claustral arrangements is explored, followed by a shorter discussion on life in nunneries that employed other arrangements.

Spaces and places were negotiated by the people who created and used them. One method of archaeologically analysing such use is through access analysis.[68] Successful spatial and access analysis of monastic space has been demonstrated,[69] in order to critically evaluate negotiations of space there.[70] The permeability of the monastic space was dependent on various access points and lines of accessibility, throughout the various doors and gates used.[71] Gilchrist's novel use of this technique opened up new avenues of archaeological inquiry into how monastic space was used in a nunnery. She concluded that space there was subtly used and generally interpreted differently, when compared to spatial uses within male religious houses. Her study proved that it was more difficult to enter a nunnery cloister from its precinct (outer court) than it was in a male religious house. This was interpreted as indicating a greater enclosure of female religious than male. Thus, the extant architecture and archaeology of nunneries in later medieval England concurred with religious history and papal decree.

The three nunneries in Ireland that still possess partially extant cloisters have been considered using access analysis to investigate how they were used in the daily lives of the nuns.[72] All were Augustinian houses, which is arguably the most varied of all religious house architecture in Ireland. Killone was founded in 1190 and dissolved in the 1580s, St Catherine's was founded about 1240–60 and was dissolved perhaps as late as the 1560s. Molough was founded sometime in the fourteenth century and was suppressed in 1540. Following Gilchrist's approach, the final phase layout for each of the three nunneries was used. The results can only be considered partial in two of the three cases, as at Killone and Molough significant portions of the ground plan are no longer extant. In these nunneries, the variety of layout and form used is a most striking feature. Gilchrist's access analysis results were 'deeper' than those of the Irish examples, due to the fact that the remains she used were more extensive and larger than the Irish examples. Many were archaeologically investigated, which provided more data regarding access.[73]

Killone, County Clare

At Killone, the earliest of the three foundations, only the footprint of the west range is known. Little of its internal layout can be seen from the remains. Therefore, it is unknown if the central cloister could be accessed directly from the exterior of the nunnery (for example, through a slype or passage in this range), or if it was accessed through external doors in the ranges (Figures 7.3 and 7.4). Interestingly, the levels of permeability at the nunnery at Killone are quite shallow, in that only two levels separate the outside of the nunnery (the

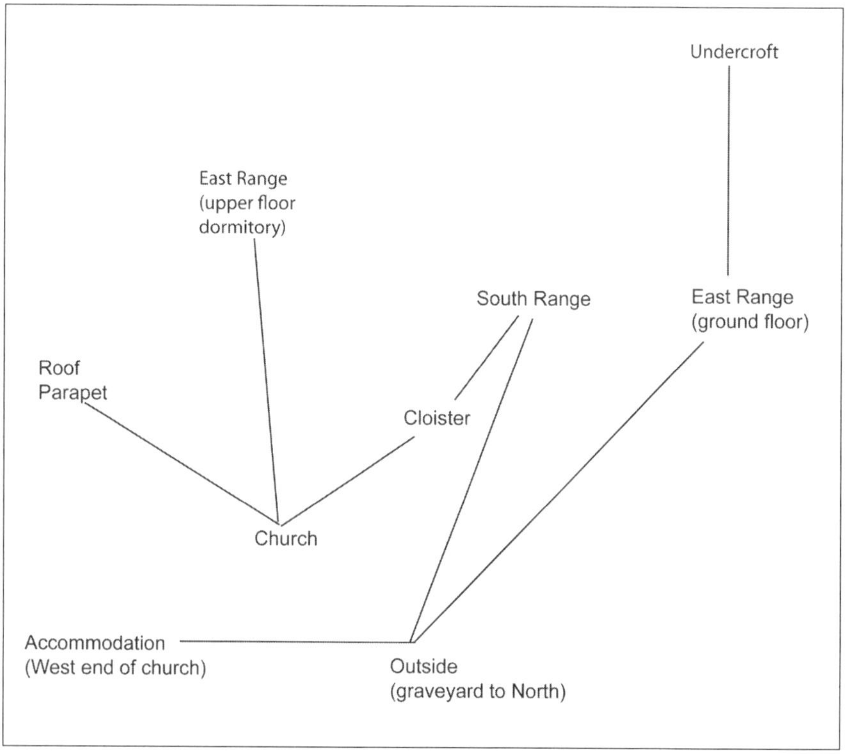

7.3 An access analysis diagram of Killone, Co. Clare. Image: Tracy Collins.

7.4 Annotated ground plan and section of Killone, Co. Clare. A. cloister garth; B. east range; C. church; D. west range; E. south range; F. undercroft (crypt); G. shortening of nave by the insertion of a wall indicated in blue. Image: Tracy Collins and Frank Coyne.

7.5 Killone, Co. Clare, doorway. The nuns' access to the chancel of the church from their dormitory. Image: Tracy Collins.

precise location of its precinct is not known, though likely lay to the south of the cloister), from its deepest interior. For example, the cloister can be accessed through the north wall doorway in the nave of the church and through an opposite south wall doorway. The cloister can also be accessed from the south through an external door in the east wall of the south range and two internal doorways in the north wall of the south range. In addition, the east range has an external doorway in its eastern wall, providing access to the ground floor of the east range (this doorway was inserted and may have made use of an earlier window location).

Gilchrist has shown in her access analysis that the nuns' dormitory is usually the 'deepest' space in a female monastery, in that it is the most difficult space to access. At Killone, however, this is not the case. It is assumed that the first floor of the east range was the dormitory (small windows suggest that it was). A door from the upper floor of the east range exits directly into the chancel, which gave the nuns direct access to the east end of the church for the divine office (Figure 7.5). In turn, this space is easily accessible from the church, which has a doorway to the outside of the nunnery in the north wall of the nave. Therefore, the nuns' dormitory at Killone is just two doorways from the outside of the nunnery, if they were all in use contemporaneously. For the

7.6 Killone, Co. Clare. The original access route to the undercroft was via an intramural stairway from ground floor of east range, to the lower right of the image. Note the nuns' door accessing the church on the first floor. Image: Tracy Collins.

7.7 (*below*) Killone, Co. Clare. The undercroft under the church is accommodated by the natural slope of the site. The undercroft can now be accessed from outside the cloister through an inserted doorway in its east wall. Image: Frank Coyne.

majority of nunneries in Gilchrist's study the dormitories were significantly 'deeper' in the monastic complex than Killone. This can be explained as the nunneries in her sample were much larger and had many more rooms. The arrangement at Killone is in common with many male religious houses where the night stairs directly accessed the church, which in turn could be accessed by the laity by a nave doorway. (Although at Killone there is not a stair – the natural slope of the site has been managed with the undercroft to allow direct access from the first floor of the east range to the chancel.) So, the nuns accessed the church's chancel directly, which is now separated from the nave by a dais (a low platform) but is likely to have originally been fitted with a rood screen of timber for further separation. Therefore, the space in the church would have been restricted and defined by the screen and would not have been as open as now appears.

The undercroft, located under the east end of the church, commonly referred to as the 'crypt', is the deepest space at Killone. The undercroft was originally accessible from the ground floor of the east range via a narrow intramural stair lit by a single light accommodated within the external base batter of the wall (Figure 7.6). The undercroft is now also accessible from the outside via a doorway in its north wall. This door is a later insertion. It made use of an original single splayed light and may have been inserted *after* the nunnery went out of use. Because of this, this doorway has been discounted in the access analysis (Figure 7.7).

Molough, County Tipperary

The precise foundation date of Molough is unknown but it is thought to have been established by the Butlers sometime in the fourteenth century, on the possible site of an early medieval ecclesiastical enclosure.[74] Portions of its west and east ranges and church are upstanding. There is no extant evidence of a northern range and it is unclear if one was ever constructed in stone. In Molough's case, the cloister lies to the north of the church. The access analysis shows that the nunnery at Molough was more enclosed in its last phases of use than Killone (Figures 7.8 and 7.9).

The extant remains show that the cloister was only accessed through the church. It is probable, however, that there were other entrances into the cloister which are now not visible. Access to the complex was through an elaborate door at the western end of the south wall of the church (Figure 7.10). This doorway is an insertion, and the earlier access to the church was through a door in its west wall. A second door at the western end of the north wall

.8 An access analysis diagram of Molough, Co. Tipperary. (Dotted line shows a possible access route that now cannot be confirmed.) Image: Tracy Collins and Frank Coyne.

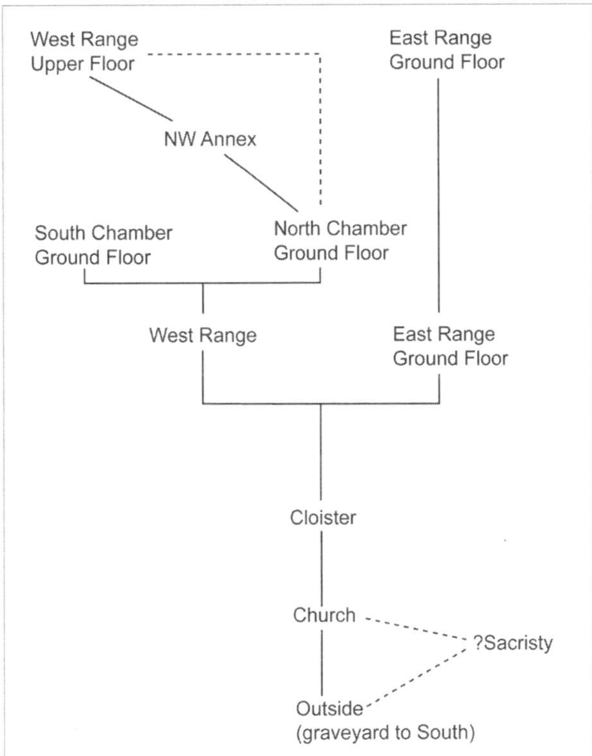

.9 Annotated ground plan f Molough, Co. Tipperary. .. cloister garth; B. east range; :. church; D. west range.

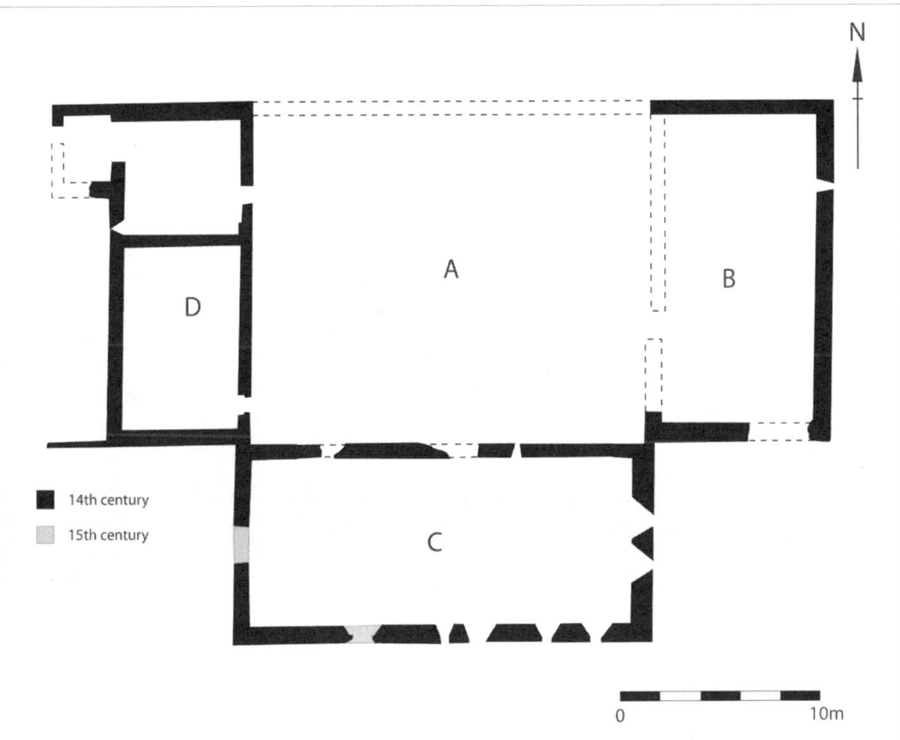

7.10 Molough, Co. Tipperary. Doorway in the south wall of the church, exterior and interior faces. Middle image of elaborate mason's mark on the external eastern door jamb. Image: Tracy Collins.

7.11 Molough, Co. Tipperary. A view of the location of the east range, with its southern gable still extant. Image: Frank Coyne.

7.12 Molough, Co. Tipperary. The west range. The west gable of the church to left of image. Image: Frank Coyne.

of the church provided access to the cloister ambulatory. This doorway from the church allowed access to both the east and west ranges of the cloister. The footprint of the east range is extant and visible as an earthwork but there is no indication of how this range was sub-divided and how it might have been used. Its southern gable suggests the range was a two-storey structure. A break in the earthworks shows the likely location of a doorway into the ground floor (Figure 7.11). It is not known which range was used as the nuns' dormitory.

The west range is the best preserved and was subdivided into two chambers on the ground floor (Figure 7.12). They were both accessed from the cloister via narrow doorways in their east walls, both of which have been reconstructed. The southern chamber is the larger and no longer has any features extant, excepting a supporting corbel on its east wall exterior, which likely supported a pentice roof over an ambulatory on this western side of the cloister (Figure 7.13). The northern chamber has a blocked window in its west wall and a single corbel. The upper floor of the west range appears to have been a single space, lit by two windows in its west wall, at least one in its east

7.13 Molough, Co. Tipperary. Detail of the southern end of the west range with a later rebuilt doorway. Note the single corbel for a pentice roof of cloister ambulatory, indicated. Image: Tracy Collins.

7.14 Molough, Co. Tipperary. The upstanding gable of the west range. Note putlog holes. Image: Tracy Collins.

wall (and probably two) and a single light in its northern gable (Figure 7.14). A ledge or offset above this window suggests that there was an attic space above. There is now no indication as to how the first floor of the west range was accessed. It may have been via an internal ladder or timber stair. There is a small two-storey unit at the external northwestern corner of the west range, now completely overgrown, which was accessed from the ground floor and first floor of the range. It has been suggested that it was a stairwell.[75] This is possible, though it could also have functioned as a garderobe, especially if the west range was the location of the nuns' dormitory. Therefore, in the case of Molough, the supposed location of the dormitory – that is on the upper floor of either the west or east ranges – shows that it was at the 'deepest' space within the cloister, being some four levels from outside the cloister complex. In this case, unlike Killone, the nuns at Molough had no direct access into their church and had to pass through the cloister to gain access.

St Catherine's, County Limerick

The best-preserved and therefore most easily studied of the three claustral nunneries is St Catherine's (Figures 7.15 and 7.16). This nunnery was established sometime in the thirteenth century, with significant changes, in particular to its church, in the fifteenth century (Chapter 6). Like the others, its latest plan was used in the access analysis of the nunnery, although in this case a discussion of its earlier access is warranted.

In its earliest phase of construction, St Catherine's had a gate into its outer court to the south of the cloisters. A sunken way (track) and causeway led from the gate's location to the nunnery's entrance, which led directly into the cloister in its southeastern corner (Figure 7.17). This entrance was subsequently blocked, possibly in the fifteenth century (Figure 7.18), when a new entrance was inserted directly into the cloister, with a possible external porch. This later entrance is situated opposite the original, in the northeastern corner of the cloister (Figure 7.19). The refectory was accessed from the cloister through a doorway at the western end of its north wall (Figure 7.20). While there are now two opes in the refectory's west wall and one in its east wall, these are interpreted as late post-nunnery features and have not been considered in this analysis.[76] Although the evidence is now gone, it is presumed that access to the kitchen range to the south of the refectory would have been through the refectory. It is also likely that the kitchen range had its own doorway to the outer court to the south.

The upper floor of the west range at St Catherine's is the likely location of the dormitory of the nuns (Figure 7.21). Its lower floor is particularly

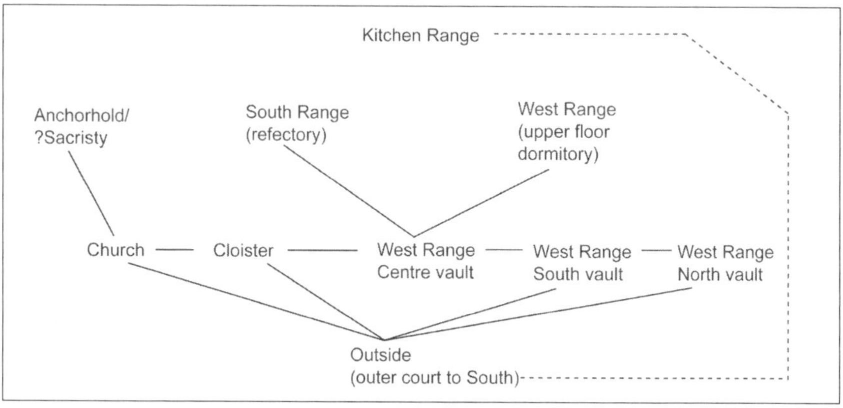

7.15 An access analysis diagram of St Catherine's, Co. Limerick. (Dotted line indicates possible access routes now no longer demonstrable in the field.) Image: Tracy Collins and Frank Coyne.

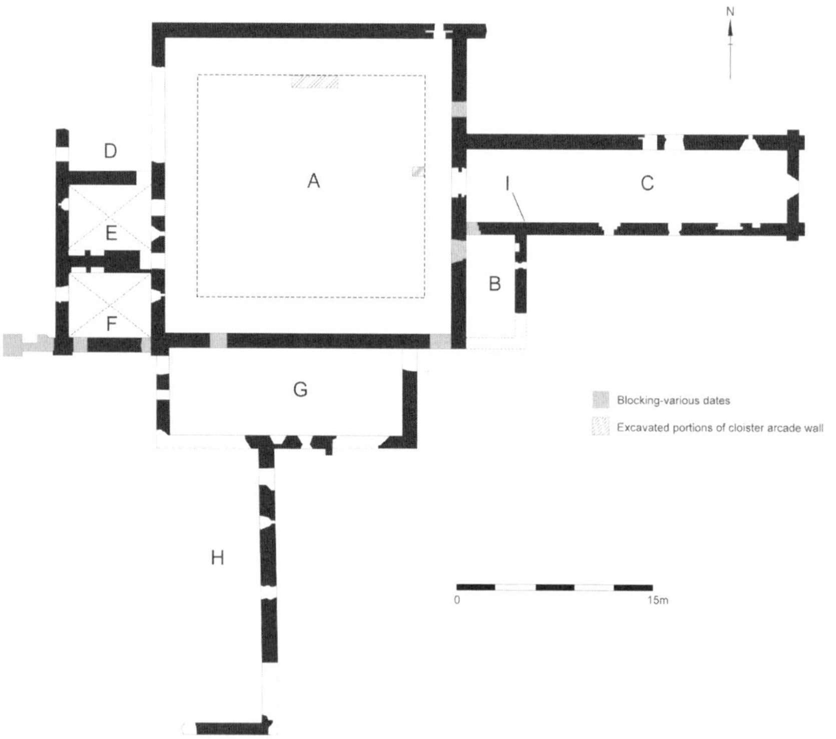

7.16 Annotated ground plan of St Catherine's, Co. Limerick. A. cloister garth; B. 'sacristy' or possible anchorhold; C. church; D. west range north vault; E. west range middle vault; F. west range south vault; G. south range refectory; H. extension to south range kitchen; I. location of incised ship. Image: Tracy Collins and Frank Coyne.

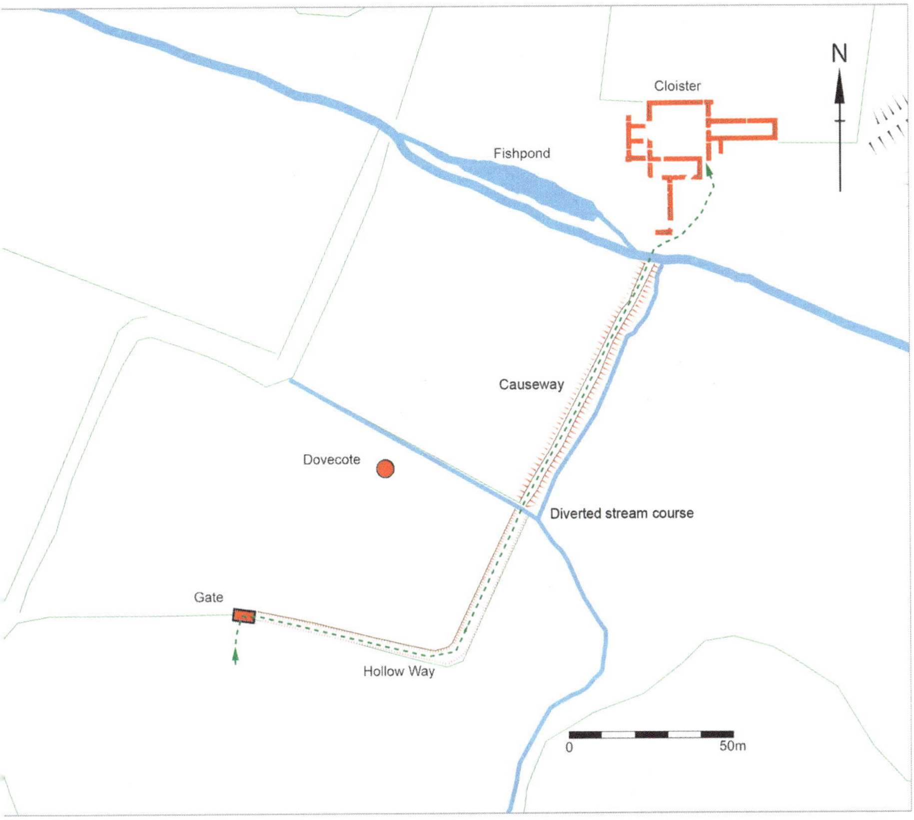

7.17 St Catherine's, Co. Limerick and its associated features. Image: Frank Coyne.

7.18 St Catherine's, Co. Limerick. The blocked location of the original thirteenth-century entrance into nunnery cloister in its southeast corner. Image: Tracy Collins.

7.19 St Catherine's, Co. Limerick. The fifteenth-century inserted northern doorway into cloister, exterior and interior faces. Image: Tracy Collins.

7.20 St Catherine's, Co. Limerick. Doorway into south range refectory from cloister. Image: Tracy Collins.

7.21 St Catherine's, Co. Limerick. View of its west range. Image: Tracy Collins.

7.22 St Catherine's, Co. Limerick A view of the interior of the central vaulted chamber in west range. Note the wall niches. Image: Tracy Collins.

7.23 St Catherine's, Co. Limerick. The joist holes and corbels on exterior face of west wall of south range, evidence for a timber structure possibly housing the garderobe. The larger ope is interpreted as a post-nunnery access route around the ruins. Image: Tracy Collins.

interesting. From the upstanding remains and earlier descriptions, only the middle of the three vaulted rooms was accessed from the cloister, having a doorway in its east wall. The other two – the north and south vaulted chambers – had external doorways in their west walls. They could not be accessed from the cloister. The southern vault also had a single light which would have given a view into the cloister ambulatory. It is not known if the northern vault would have had a similar window. There is also a suggestion of interconnecting doorways linking the chambers. Two further blocked opes in the south wall of the southern vault might be earlier doorways.[77] It is possible that these chambers functioned as guest or corrodian accommodation (Figure 7.22). The vaulting was an insertion, perhaps as a safety measure against fire or to provide more privacy for the nuns' dormitory overhead on the first floor. If the external west entrances in the west range are contemporary with the vaulting – their relationship is unclear from the ruins – this would suggest a change in the relationships between the nuns and the outside world. This could

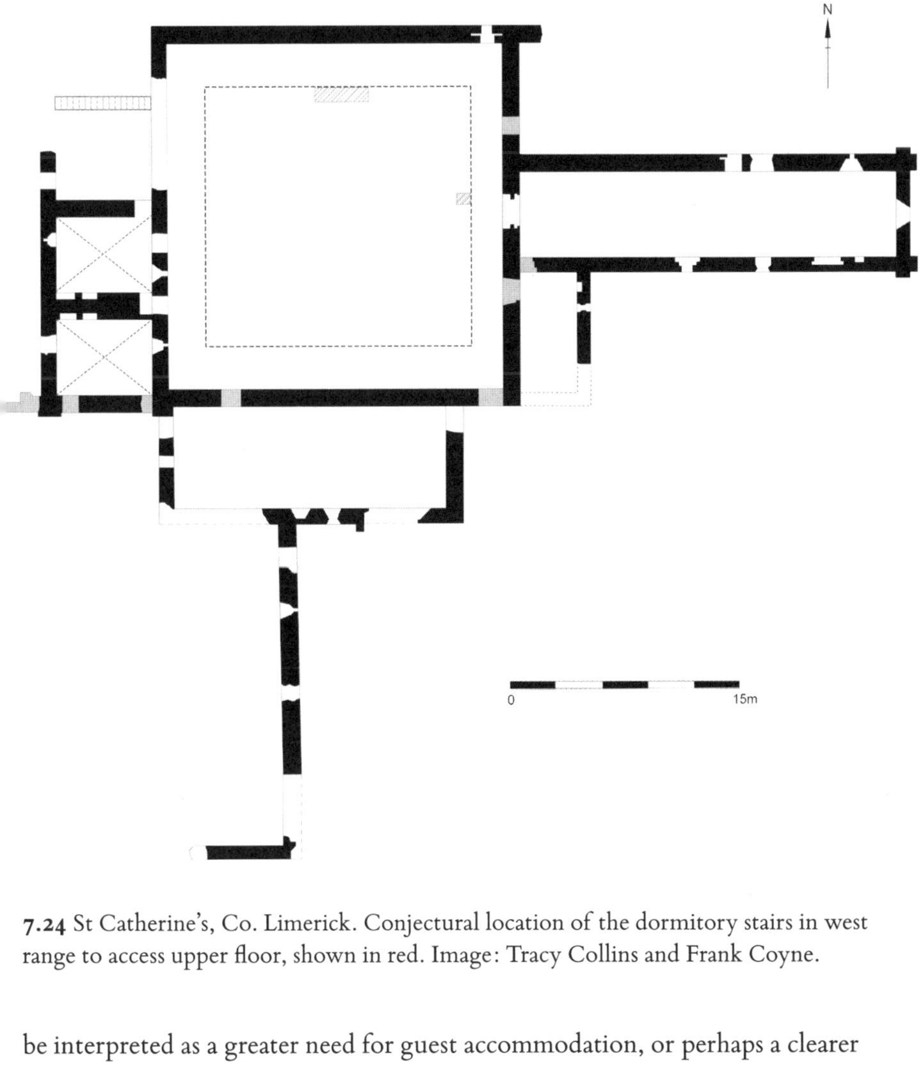

7.24 St Catherine's, Co. Limerick. Conjectural location of the dormitory stairs in west range to access upper floor, shown in red. Image: Tracy Collins and Frank Coyne.

be interpreted as a greater need for guest accommodation, or perhaps a clearer division between nuns and guests. It is also possible that these vaulted rooms were used for storage.

Interpretation of access to the nuns' dormitory was problematic at St Catherine's, due to the lack of extant fabric. Westropp described the west range in detail but did not suggest how access was gained to the upper floor.[78] It has been suggested that access was gained to the nuns' dormitory from outside the complex, in the angle space between the west of the refectory and the west range.[79] I suggest that this location might be better suited as a garderobe for the nuns' dormitory, and based on the visible joist holes, it was constructed in timber (Figure 7.23). Access to the nuns' dormitory on the upper floor of the west range may have been via a stair, now no longer extant, located immediately to the north of the northern chamber of the west range. This theory is supported by the dimensions of the range. Both the southern and central chambers are about 5m in length. If the northern vault (now destroyed) is estimated as being 5m in length also, this allows ample space – in excess of 2m even allowing for the extant return of cloister wall at its northwest corner – for an internal stairwell to gain access to the upper-floor dormitory (Figure 7.24).[80]

There is now little evidence as to the internal layout of the dormitory at St Catherine's. There are the remains of two rectangular and internally splayed windows at the southern end of its east wall, suggestive of locations of bed spaces. Based on this arrangement it can be postulated that the dormitory was lit by twelve such windows, six each in the east and west walls, and perhaps twelve nuns was the intended size of the religious community.[81] It has been noted in a male monastic context that each monk would have a window in order to read, which suggests that the dormitory could also function as a study and reading place,[82] and it is possible that the nuns' dormitory was used similarly. There is no evidence for the privatisation of the dormitory space at St Catherine's, though if this was undertaken it is probable that timber cell partitions were used.[83]

Discussion

Gilchrist found in her study of English nunneries that the dormitory was the most protected space. In the male religious houses she chose for analysis, she concluded it was the chapter house that was the most secure space. The access analysis of the three extant claustrally planned later medieval nunneries in Ireland has revealed variety in both layout and permeability of space.[84] At Killone the nuns' dormitory was not found to be the most secure space in the nunnery. The most secure space was its undercroft. At Molough, the location of the nuns' dormitory was more secure than at Killone, being the deepest space in the nunnery. At St Catherine's, the dormitory of the nuns was in a secure location. Most interesting here was the fact that the cloister continued to have direct access from outside the complex. In its earliest phase, this entrance was on the south, though access to this entrance may have been somewhat curtailed by the south gateway of the nunnery. This cloister entrance was then blocked and replaced by a doorway situated in the north wall of the cloister. The indication of a possible porch outside this doorway suggests that access may have been limited by a porter located here.

The nuns' day was governed by the divine office, which was celebrated in the nunnery's church, which would have been visited eight times a day at a

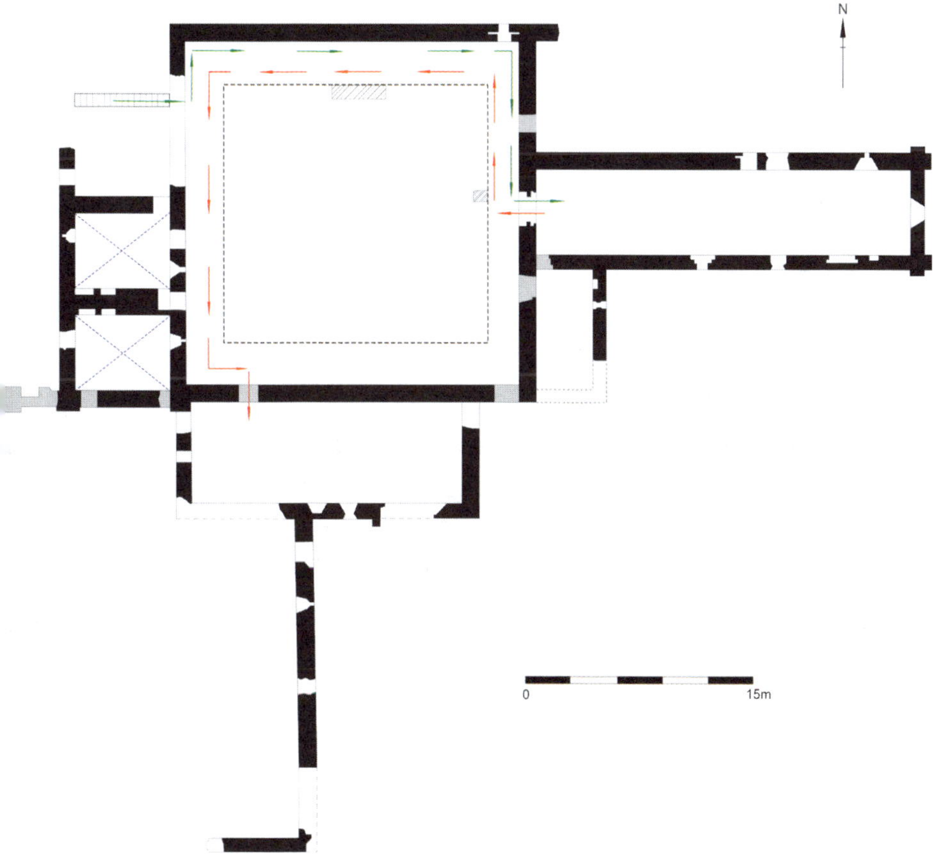

7.25 St Catherine's, Co. Limerick. Suggested processional route of nuns for the divine office through the cloister from the dormitory to the church (green) and then the church to the refectory (red). Image: Tracy Collins and Frank Coyne.

minimum (Chapter 3).[85] In the morning and evening the nuns would process from their dormitory to the church and this route was different at each nunnery. At Killone it was a short distance, as nuns accessed the church directly from the upper floor of the east range where their dormitory was located. At Molough, the nuns must have walked through the cloister ambulatory, although it is unclear if their dormitory was located in the east or west range. At St Catherine's the nuns' route to the church was even more circuitous. From the suggested stair in the northwest corner of the cloister in the west range, the nuns likely processed along the northern cloister ambulatory around to the west doorway of the church, passing the stone head of the old woman on the northern label stop of the church's west doorway (Figure 7.25).

7.26 An example of an east range chapter house doorway and flanking windows at Cong, Co. Mayo (Augustinian male religious house). Image: Frank Coyne.

The daily business of a monastery is traditionally thought to have been set out in the chapter house, which is usually situated in the east range of the complex.[86] In time the chapter house came to be considered a sacred room, only second in importance to the church. Chapter houses in male religious houses commonly have more elaborate doorways than other rooms, sometimes flanked by a window. They are usually positioned in the east range, having the same orientation as the church, as at the Augustinian monastery of Cong Abbey, County Mayo, for example (Figure 7.26).[87] It is expected that a monastery would have a chapter house. Some were quite elaborate, as the investigation of the chapter house at Jesus College Cambridge – site of the Benedictine nunnery of St Radegund – showed. This room was entered from the cloister through an elaborate doorway flanked by a large double-light window. A column base revealed at the centre of the room indicated that it was vaulted.[88] Several nunneries in central Germany also had chapter houses, some of which were quite elaborate, though certainly not all German nunneries included one.[89]

The chapter house was a place where 'the community was created daily [...] whether through disciplinary action or through forms of community

7.27 Killone, Co. Clare. The twin-light ogee-headed window which may be a chapter house window. Image: Tracy Collins.

shared *memoria*, making the chapter house a sort of generator for the collective memory'.[90] It took some time in male Benedictine houses for a chapter house to be adopted, however. In the oldest Cistercian statutes dating to 1123–4, which lists the necessary buildings for a monastery, a chapter house is not mentioned. Even at the important Cistercian house of Clairvaux founded in 1114, a chapter house was not initially used and the community gathered to conduct its business in the refectory.[91] At the Cistercian nunnery of Coyroux, France it has been suggested on the basis of layout that the nave of the church probably functioned as the chapter house.[92]

No upstanding nunnery chapter house is known from medieval Ireland,[93] and it is likely that chapter houses were not used at all nunneries in Ireland.[94] St Catherine's did not have an east range, so a chapter house could not be located there. However, following Müller's theory, St Catherine's refectory might have been used to carry out the functions of a chapter house, where the community could be symbolically recreated daily. Like the church, the refectory was orientated east–west with possibly five large lancet windows along its southern wall and would have been a large, bright space suitable for gatherings of the chapter. Indeed, at nunneries, refectories are considered particularly important female spaces (see below) and therefore it seems quite plausible that they were used for other important functions in addition to eating. It is possible that a chapter house was originally intended for St Catherine's, as its church's west doorway – the typical position for such a chapter house – has unusually fine detail and may have been originally planned as a chapter house. If nunneries in medieval Ireland did have dedicated chapter houses, they were not made architecturally distinct, for example with an eastern projection, vaulting, or with an elaborate doorway and window into the cloister, and so they cannot be definitively identified in the remains. The twin ogee-headed window, set in a deep embrasure on the ground floor of the east range at Killone, may mark the location of its chapter house, though it is unclear if this window is in its original location (Figure 7.27).

At mealtimes the nuns would gather together in the refectory – although in later times meals were taken in small groups in smaller rooms in the nunnery. It has been suggested that the refectory was an important space in nunneries for sacred reading and communal meals, particularly those refectories that were situated on an upper floor. They were reminders of the cenacle (*coenaculum*), the upper room in which the Last Supper was held and also the room that was used by the apostles, Mary, Mary Magdalene and other holy women after the crucifixion.[95] The use of first-floor refectories symbolised the *coenaculum* in male Augustinian houses in England and Wales, and may be a particular architectural trait of that order.[96] The phenomenon has also been noted at Premonstratensian and Gilbertine male houses in England, for example Easby Abbey, Yorkshire.[97] First-floor refectories are rare in an Irish context,[98] though not unknown, for example the Cistercian house at Boyle, County Roscommon and the Augustinian friary at Adare, County Limerick, and none has been identified at a medieval female religious house in Ireland.[99]

Therefore, the refectory may have had additional significance at St Catherine's as a venue for its daily chapter. The door to the refectory was located at the western end of its north wall and would have provided access directly into the cloister's southern ambulatory. There is a large breach to the west of the doorway where the laver (lavabo) was located in the cloister, as it was part of the rule that hands would be washed prior to entering the refectory.[100] The laver was composed of a basin and water source.[101] In the case of St Catherine's this was probably an aquamanile (a water container typically in the form of a mammal or bird), though in larger religious houses a piped water supply was used.[102] Water pipes and stone channels were discovered during excavations at the male Cistercian house at Mellifont, County Louth,

St Catherine's, Co. Limerick. The remains of e reader's recess n the refectory. Image: Tracy Collins.

which were interpreted as remnants of a water system there; these are very rare in an Irish context.[103] The fact that the laver was located to the west, or right-hand side, of the refectory doorway at St Catherine's suggests the direction of the processing nuns around the cloister. It was usual to go to the refectory *after* being in the church. Therefore, it is suggested that the nuns processed from the church's west door, around the northern cloister ambulatory, passing the stair to the dormitory, then southwards along the western ambulatory, to use the laver and enter the refectory (see Figure 7.25).

The refectory at St Catherine's was single storey and rectangular in plan. It would have been furnished with a top table at its east end, perhaps on a dais (low platform), and tables down each long side. Although now destroyed, it is likely that there was access to the kitchen to the south, made through the refectory's western end of its south wall. From excavation, it is known

7.29 St Catherine's, Co. Limerick. A single corbel in the north wall of the refectory may have been used as a support for a devotional image. Image: Tracy Collins.

that the floor covering of the refectory at its eastern end was a stony metalled surface. Ceramic floor tiles are known from elsewhere, like those discovered at the refectory of the Franciscan nunnery at Denny, Cambridgeshire, England.[104] Silence was to be maintained when eating, when 'edificatory reading' would take place. The mouth would be nourished with food and the ears would be nourished with the Word.[105] This occurred at St Catherine's, as a reader's recess was accommodated in the thickness of the south wall, beneath the lancet windows. It appears to have projected slightly externally. Excavation of this feature did not reveal any associated steps, though the reader may have been elevated in the space on a timber structure (Figure 7.28). This feature is important as it also proves that at least some of the nuns at St Catherine's were literate.

A large single corbel projects from the north wall of the refectory which has no obvious structural function. This probably supported a devotional

7.30 St Catherine's, Co. Limerick. Excavation in progress of northern and eastern cloister ambulatories. Image: Tracy Collins.

image, such as a statue, that the nuns could meditate on while eating and listening to the reading (Figure 7.29). The excavation of the refectory at the male Dominican house of St Mary's of the Isle, Cork identified posts which may have been to support the roof or to support dining tables. Stones benches were revealed along its long walls. The refectory's pulpit (or reader's recess) was found to project slightly from the eastern end of the northern wall of the refectory. This was accessed by a series of intramural stone steps.[106] There was no indication of a dais at Cork, though one was found in the excavations of the nunnery at Denny.[107]

Archaeological evidence for other activities at later medieval nunneries in Ireland is sparse, mainly due to the lack of excavation. It is known from historical sources that hospitality of guests took place. The various spaces in the ranges of claustral nunneries provided accommodation, such as the vaulted west range at St Catherine's. The cloister ambulatories may also have been used for a variety of purposes. First, they were used to access parts of the nunnery and likely used in sacred processions. The northern and eastern ambulatories at St Catherine's have been excavated (Figure 7.30).[108] The northern cloister ambulatory was found to be wider (almost 3m) than that on the eastern side of the cloister (2.25m). Both had a metalled stony surface. The northern cloister, being south-facing, had the best light and it is suggested that it was deliberately made wider than the other ambulatory so that it could be used for other functions (study, reading, writing) and perhaps to accommodate seating. Both ambulatories were used for burial (see Chapter 8).

At Tintern, County Wexford (Cistercian) the northern ambulatory has a bay and seating incorporated into its fabric to facilitate the monks' collation ceremony. In this case, the ambulatory is 6m wide and the northern wall along the ambulatory may have been painted.[109] At Kells, County Kilkenny (Augustinian male house) stone benches were constructed along both the north and west ambulatories.[110] At the Augustinian Clerkenwell nunnery, London an eighteenth-century watercolour shows an internal view of the cloister's southern ambulatory complete with rib vaulting, stone benches on both sides and stepped access into the garth. Excavations discovered that in the sixteenth century the ambulatory had been tiled with tiles from the Low Countries.[111]

The cloister garth itself was imbued with symbolic meaning for nuns and monks as a model for the garden of Paradise and was an important part of any monastic complex.[112] Indeed, enclosed gardens were important in medieval elite society, for contemplation, pleasure and cures.[113] The ground within the garth at St Catherine's was deliberately improved for drainage, over which were found several layers of garden soils. Unfortunately, no macro-plant remains were retrieved to ascertain what may have grown there.[114] Environmental remains from Romsey Abbey, Hampshire showed that box and plants from the *Allium* genus were grown there.[115] In addition to growing plants, the garth was sometimes used for burial, although at St Catherine's this was found not to be the case, at least in the portion that was excavated (see Figure 7.30). Very few nunnery garths have been archaeologically excavated. For example, excavations at Holywell Augustinian nunnery, London did not extend into the cloister garth area, which lay to the north of the church,[116] and neither did the Clerkenwell nunnery excavations, also in London, reveal any features dating to the nunnery phase in the area of the garth.[117] One excavation trench at the Benedictine nunnery at Chester extended into the garth and a stone-lined drain was found which ran at a slight angle to the ambulatory.[118]

DAILY LIFE IN OTHER ARRANGEMENTS

The use of the many nunneries that did not employ a claustral plan is difficult to assess. The majority have no above-ground register and so little can be said currently without the benefit of excavation. However, some manifest themselves as churches with or without attached accommodation, or as amorphous earthworks and walls. It is likely that nunneries that used

7.31 Annaghdown, Co. Galway (*left*) and Tisrara, Co. Roscommon showing evidence for attached accommodation to the church structure. Image: Frank Coyne.

earlier sites or those that continued in use after church reform in the twelfth century may have been predisposed to more open systems of living.[119] The co-located houses of Augustinian canons and nuns, for example at Roscommon, were probably arranged in such a way, rather than the double houses of the Gilbertines and the Order of Fontevraud.[120] In the cases of co-location at Cistercian sites at Inishlounaght, Jerpoint and Mellifont it is likely that nuns had their own accommodation close to the monks' cloister, but which may have been non-claustral.

The reasons why cloisters may not have been used were diverse. Urban nunneries may have had to fit into tight plots or into existing parish buildings. It may not have been financially viable for many smaller nunneries with numbers not exceeding twelve nuns to have constructed cloisters at all. The nuns may have used existing buildings that were never developed into a claustral form, or a nunnery complex may have remained unfinished.[121] It can only be speculated how nuns may have carried out their day-to-day activities and rituals in non-claustral nunneries, as the structure of the cloister is not present to inform routes of access and egress. A church was essential to nunnery living, but the lack of a cloister may not have really affected the nuns' quality of life. The lack of a cloister highlights the importance of performance and ritual in religious daily life. The nuns could still perform their divine office through visiting the church multiple times daily and experience the solitude of prayer and contemplation. Through performance and repetition, they were sacralising their environment,[122] regardless, it could be argued, of whether they were contained within an angular cloister.

7.32 Tisrara, Co. Roscommon. The stairway providing access to upper-floor accommodation. Image: Frank Coyne.

Nunneries that employed non-claustral layouts probably had a variety of domestic accommodation. Free-standing structures of stone, earth or timber, or a combination of fabric, may have been used. Where a church can be positively identified at a nunnery location, five have attached structures, which can be interpreted as possible accommodation: Annaghdown, Drumalgagh, Termonkeelin, Inishmaine and Tisrara (Figure 7.31). Tisrara and Inishmaine have the best-preserved evidence for attached accommodation at nunnery churches. At Tisrara, a residential southern block was attached to the original parallelogram church sometime in the fifteenth or sixteenth century. The east end of the church was also extended at this time. This block was of two storeys and comprised two vaulted units on the ground floor and a single space on the first floor. The east vault could be accessed from the church and both vaulted rooms were interconnected. The east vault contained two large wall niches and this space was interpreted by the excavator as a sacristy. The west vault had two exterior doorways and a small single-light window low in its western wall. The upper floor was accessed via a stone stairway through a doorway in the western vault. A second doorway at the bottom of the stairs provided access outside (Figure 7.32).

7.33 Inishmaine, Co. Mayo. The transepts attached to the church may have been used for accommodation or a sacristy. Image: Tracy Collins.

The upper floor of the block was interpreted as a dormitory by the excavator due to the presence of architectural fragments and a number of small single- and twin-light windows in its western wall.[123] This residential block could have comfortably housed a small community of nuns, while facilitating easy access to the east end of the church. The presence of two external doorways on the ground floor of the residential block is a little problematic, especially the one at the bottom of the stairs leading to the dormitory. Perhaps an exterior structure may have provided security or they may have been locked. Tisrara has a complicated building history and other possible uses, such as a male Carmelite house and a hostel for pilgrims, have been postulated. It is possible that the nuns used a different configuration than that now visible.

The accommodation at Inishmaine is situated in two rectangular transepts, one to the north and the other to the south, accessed via the church's chancel through doorways, so are clearly not part of the church's space (Figure 7.33).

Both are lit with small windows in their east walls. The north transept possibly had a second storey or attic space, indicated by two joist or corbel holes in its west wall. The south transept also had a second storey and, although now no longer visible, a small doorway in its west wall provided access into a small annex to the west. This is little over a metre squared in area and its function is not known, though it may have been a stairwell. It has already been suggested that the south transept functioned as a residence,[124] while the northern one may have been a sacristy. It would have been secure accommodation for a small group of nuns at Inishmaine.

It is likely that many other nunnery churches used free-standing accommodation. It is more difficult to locate such accommodation, which may have been constructed of stone or timber, or a combination of both. None of these structures is now extant, though some are noted from documentary evidence. For example, the nuns at Portrane, having moved from Grace Dieu, shared a small dwelling with a chaplain and celebrated the divine office in the parish church.[125] The location of their dwelling in relation to the church is not known. There is no obvious accommodation space at the Nuns' Church, Clonmacnoise. Wall fabric in a boundary wall there has been interpreted as an earlier church and probably the one burned in 1082 in the 'Cemetery of the Nuns'.[126] A geophysical survey around the Nuns' Church failed to identify any structures or enclosing element. Fragments of walling visible through the turf north of the Nuns' Church may indicate a stone building for the accommodation of nuns or guests.[127]

At the important site of Kilcreevanty, large platforms to the south of the church's location are perhaps suggestive of free-standing structures, in addition to the claustral plan as described by the Archaeological Survey of Ireland (see Figure 5.33).[128] In this case, it is likely that both a cloister and free-standing structures were employed, perhaps in its precinct area. Cloonoghil, Ardcarn and Killaraght have field systems and enclosures in close proximity and this is where the nunnery communities may have lived. Killaraght has an excellent example of a moated site adjacent to the site of the nunnery and it is possible that such an enclosure was utilised by the nuns (see Figure 4.31).

A dissolution survey of the nunnery of Timolin described it as a castle and other houses, 'dwelling places of the nuns', while Termonfeckin was described as a site with houses, gardens, and yards.[129] An inquisition of the nunnery at Ardcarn in 1590 recorded that it contained within its precincts a church and two houses of stone.[130] These descriptions all suggest free-standing structures rather than a cloister. Indeed, of the eleven nunneries surveyed at the dissolution, only one – Lismullin – lists a cloister in its extent.[131] As has been previously mentioned, cloisters may not have warranted a record, however; Molough's description does not mention its cloister.[132]

Without the benefit of archaeological excavation, it is difficult to ascertain precisely how the nuns would have used these more variable open system spaces, but some observations can be made. First, the sheer variety of extant remains in the archaeological record suggests that physical enclosure at these sites was probably not strictly enforced. This highlights again the contradiction between the popular perception of strictly enclosed nuns in later medieval Ireland and the material remains. Even a nunnery such as Inishmaine, which appears to have been quite secluded, lies within 2km of a castle site and a tower house at Knocknamucklagh. It also has a gate house which may have housed protectors. Termonkeelin is also located near a castle site at Demesne.

A critical assessment of the available historical evidence for nuns in later medieval Ireland (Chapter 3), and indeed elsewhere, such as Scotland[133] or Wales,[134] when taken in tandem with the archaeological evidence, strongly suggests that strict physical enclosure may not have been of primary concern. Instead, a social concept of female religious enclosure may have applied which was reinforced through codified behaviour. Female religious enclosure may have been maintained through societal respect and mores for the religious women, as they contributed to medieval society – whatever their physical living arrangements may have been. Indeed, a nunnery community would have contributed much to its local benefactors and the wider community. The greatest contributions, such as prayer, are intangible, though there was material culture and a body of works known from nunneries which enhanced medieval society as a whole. These works are now considered.

MATERIAL CULTURE

Material culture and devotional art can shed light on the identities of a particular nunnery and its nuns. Material culture from English nunneries such as architectural carving, statuary, stained glass and ceramic tiles can be used to highlight aspects of identity. A ceramic tile from St Katherine's nunnery (Benedictine) at Polsloe near Exeter was decorated with a wheel, the instrument of the saint's martyrdom, and another tile from Dartford Dominican nunnery illustrated the Sacred Heart, an important motif in the iconography of the Dominicans.[135] More recent excavations, such as Holywell Priory[136] and St Mary Clerkenwell,[137] both in London, did not produce any such finds. There are two nunnery tiles known from Ireland, one from Timolin and the other

7.34 Medieval tiles from nunneries: Timolin, Co. Kildare (*left*) and St Mary de Hogges, Dublin. After E. Eames and T. Fanning, *Irish Medieval Tiles* (Dublin: Royal Irish Academy, 1988), pp. 122, 124, L46, L69, reproduced with permission.

from part of a tile pavement uncovered in the nineteenth century from St Mary de Hogges. Both are line-impressed of differing four-foil design (Figure 7.34).[138]

Some nunneries in continental Europe have impressive assemblages of medieval material culture, including furniture, devotional objects, books and manuscripts.[139] Devotional art such as manuscript production and illumination, panel paintings and sculpture were intended as devotional foci for many categories of people and were used also in private prayer, as they provided an atmosphere conducive to worship as well as instruction.[140] Hamburger has suggested that many meditative and devotional images of this period were created for and by nuns, which played a critical role in their spiritual care.[141] These devotional images used by nuns became highly influential among the laity.[142] It is known from the historical evidence from Ireland that elaborate furnishings, shrines, reliquaries and statuary were given to nunneries by benefactors and patrons. Unfortunately, none of these items now exist,[143] but there is currently a small but significant assemblage of material culture from nunneries in Ireland.

A number of statues may provide a glimpse into devotional practices at nunneries. The wooden statues thought to be associated with nunneries are those from Clonfert; the post-medieval nunnery of Bethlehem, County Roscommon, also known as 'The Athlone Madonna'; and Ballyvourney (Figure 7.35).[144] Two illustrate the image of the Seat or Throne of Wisdom

7.35 (*left*) An example of a wooden statue from Clonfert, Co Galway, possibly associated with the nunnery there. Image courtesy of Dr Christy Cunniffe. **7.36** Calliaghstown, Co. Meath. The nunnery is marked by a medieval statue located at a holy well. Image: Frank Coyne.

(commonly called Madonna and Child), which was a popular devotional image throughout Europe.[145] The Ballyvourney example is thought to represent St Gobnait.[146] Devotion to the Madonna and Child was a particularly popular form of piety in later medieval Ireland. Some sixty-three images from pre-1600 Ireland have been identified and the original number was probably much greater.[147] A similar fervour of devotion to Mary has been noted in England and the continent from about the twelfth century onwards and by the early thirteenth century most modest parishes had at least one devotional image of Mary, usually in statue form.[148] Nunnery communities would have particularly identified with Mary as she was at once understood as human and divine, was privileged with purity and virtue, with powers to act miraculously in the world and to intercede on behalf of humankind.[149] This image must have been a strong unifying force in the collective identity of a nunnery, while also being a focus for devotion and contemplation for individual nuns.

There is but one other fragment of statuary associated with a later medieval nunnery in Ireland. This is now located at a holy well dedicated to St Colmcille, at Calliaghstown, County Meath, though originally from the nunnery. It is dated to the early fourteenth century and interpreted as part of a larger sculpture, most likely the Adoration of the Magi, as the single statue appears to represent a king (Figure 7.36). It is of imported oolitic limestone and possibly from an altar piece.[150] The Magi would have been an appropriate devotional image for the nuns at Calliaghstown to have contemplated, as it represents pilgrimage and is thematically linked to the birth of Christ (the Nativity) and worship of the Christ Child. It would have provided a prompt to meditate on other devotional topics such as the humanity of Christ, His birth and ultimately His death and resurrection.[151]

The collective identity of particular nunneries was expressed in their seals, which also used devotional imagery. A nunnery would have had several seals and matrices over its lifetime and seals reflected current fashions in religious imagery. They were symbols of the corporate and community identity of the individual nunneries, and to show authenticity would have been attached to various official documents. Gilchrist's study of 136 English nunnery seals dating from the twelfth to the sixteenth centuries shows that both religious and secular imagery was used. A pre-existing vocabulary of imagery was employed and nunneries did not use new or novel representations. Iconographic themes were used, such as the imagery of Christ (as the *Agnus Dei* – Lamb of God – or crucified), a patron saint, or the Virgin. The Throne of Wisdom, already discussed, was the most common theme on English nunnery seals.[152] Regional variation was noted, for example Yorkshire nunneries preferred round-shaped seals and it was concluded that the degree of complexity on the nunnery seal directly reflected the importance of the nunnery to which it belonged.[153] This suggests that wealthier nunneries could afford the production of more complex seal matrices.

Medieval Welsh seals show a similar iconography, though there is just one known from any Welsh nunnery, at Usk, Gwent, which shows the Virgin and Child.[154] Only a single nunnery seal is known from Ireland (Figure 7.37).[155] It is from St Mary de Hogges and is attached to MS 1207/165 in Trinity College Dublin, and is the seal of Juliana, abbess of Hogges, attached to an indenture dated to 1462. It is of red wax with the letters LIVSCCM visible. The scene is the Throne of Wisdom, the figures being the Virgin seated under the remains of a canopy with the Infant Jesus sitting on her lap. The Virgin is turned to face the Child, whose hand may be raised in benediction. To the Virgin's left is a kneeling figure interpreted as an abbess, with covered head and crosier

7.37 The single extant example of a medieval nunnery seal from Ireland is from St Mary de Hogges, Dublin, dated to the fifteenth century. Image courtesy of Dr Dianne Hall. Reproduced with permission of the Board of Trinity College Dublin.

of her office, with arms raised towards the Infant.[156] It is a particularly apt image for the seal of St Mary de Hogges given the dedication of that house to the Virgin Mary. Hall noted that the use of this motif on a nunnery seal in Ireland suggests that nunneries in Ireland were aware of imagery used on nunnery seals elsewhere.[157] It is perhaps indicative of a wider corporate identity of nunneries across orders and regions. Furthermore, the use of this specific image in statuary and seals shows that nunneries in Ireland were aware of and responded to trends in monastic devotional imagery elsewhere.

The precise function of the carved stone heads associated with several nunneries is more difficult to realise. In most cases the heads are now lost, *ex situ*, or too worn to identify the gender. For example, a stone head depicting a nun was found at Killeigh.[158] A very weathered *ex situ* head is known from St Catherine's and located in a nearby farmhouse.[159] A stone head is also recorded from Grace Dieu, which was subsequently moved to Turvey House, as Grace Dieu was reputedly demolished to provide building materials for the big house.[160] A second stone head from Grace Dieu is in the National Museum of Ireland.[161] A Romanesque grotesque head was found at St Peter's Cell, Limerick[162] (Figure 7.38).

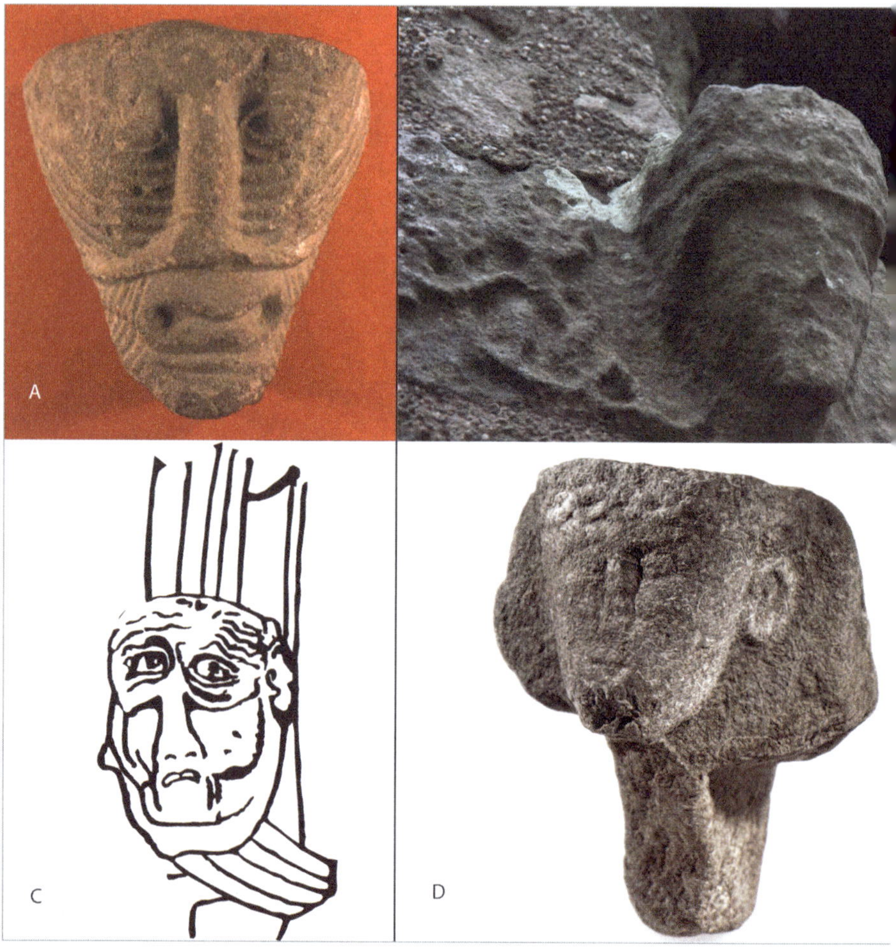

7.38 Examples of carved stone heads from nunneries: A. St Peter's Cell, Limerick, courtesy of Dr Matthew Potter, Curator Limerick Museum; B. Killevy, Co. Armagh, image: Frank Coyne; C. St Catherine's, Co. Limerick, now lost, re-drawn after Westropp, 1904 © Royal Society of Antiquaries of Ireland; D. Grace Dieu, Co. Dublin © National Museum of Ireland.

St Catherine's second carved head once formed a label stop on the northern side of the church's west doorway. It clearly represented an old woman or hag,[163] and it is interesting to consider what collective identity this may have imparted to the nuns who would have passed it each time they entered or exited their church, or walked the eastern ambulatory of the cloister. Perhaps its location, on the northern side of the church door, may imbue some of the symbolism Gilchrist realised in her study of northern cloisters in English nunneries. This carving may have symbolised the *Cailleach* or the old wise woman, which is

7.39 Examples of later Romanesque decoration at nunneries. Killone, Co. Clare (*left*); Temple Finghin, Co. Offaly, after Petrie 1845; the Nuns' Church, Co. Offaly (*lower right*); Inishmaine, Co. Mayo (*upper right*).

a prominent motif in Irish folklore.[164] It is also represented, most famously, in a natural rock known as the Hag of Beara, which still stands adjacent to Kilcatherine church in County Cork, itself a reputed nunnery.[165]

Two small carved human heads were recorded on the wall at either side of the aumbry and piscina at Ballymacadane church, but these are now lost.[166] The later church at Killevy has a sculpted head on the exterior of its east window. The Nuns' Church,[167] Temple Finghin, and the late Romanesque window at Inishmaine[168] all show animal and human figures. The east window at Killone might be added to this group, which forms an important corpus of later twelfth-century decorative architectural sculpture at medieval nunneries (Figure 7.39).

Killone also has an impressive *in situ* female head which forms the external southeast corner corbel of its church (Figure 7.40). The corbel depicts a woman with her hair in plaits and her arms upraised at either side of her head, in an act of supporting the church's roof.[169] This would not have been visible to the nuns when they were within the cloister. It was clearly intended primarily for the world outside the cloister, perhaps representing the community of nuns or

7.40 Carved human head corbel at Killone, Co. Clare; detail and location of corbel at the southeast corner of the church. Image: Tracy Collins.

an individual patron, and showing them supporting their local church, and by extension supporting the wider population. The church's wall walk and parapet could be reached by the nuns via an intramural stair in its east wall, although the corbel itself cannot be viewed from the wall walk. This position provides a panoramic view of the lake adjacent to the nunnery and the landscape beyond to the east and south (Figure 7.41).

It is possible that this unusual space facilitated contemplation and individual prayer for the nuns, allowing them to look outwards on the world (and into the cloister from above) towards the adjacent lake, though very much from within the confines of the nunnery. Therefore, this space in the nunnery may have provided a dual expression of identity. It possibly expressed the corporate identity of the nunnery or a nunnery patron as assisting in supporting the church, symbolised by the corbel, while perhaps also marking a place of private

7.41 View from parapet immediately above the carved corbel at Killone, Co. Clare, view southwards. Image: Frank Coyne.

contemplation by individual nuns who used the parapet walk. This unusual location for individual devotion at Killone might be considered similar to the liminal location of a cell dedicated to St Michael at the nunnery of Pedralbes, Catalonia, which was positioned between two of the church's buttresses.[170]

Carved stone heads which are clearly of early medieval date may have been re-used at two later medieval nunnery sites (Figure 7.42).[171] The church now extant at Clonard is modern, but incorporates an early medieval head in the south façade of its tower. Clonard was an important religious centre both in early and later medieval times. In its later medieval phase, it was for a time the mother house of Arroasian nunneries in Ireland.[172] It is thus worth considering that the stone head continued to be used or was re-used at the religious site, and quite possibly the nunnery, as a link to identify with the nuns' long religious past at Clonard.

The stone heads re-used at Portrane are also located in the north and south walls of the church's west tower.[173] This church was in the ownership of the nuns at Grace Dieu and the community moved there in 1499. Perhaps the re-use of these heads in the tower façades identified the nuns with a long religious past

7.42 Examples of re-used stone heads associated with nunneries: A. Clonard, Co. Meath; B. an
C. Portrane, Co. Dublin; D. The 'Gadai Dubh' from the later medieval parish church at Ballyvo
Co. Cork; E. Kilcatherine, Co. Cork (tentative nunnery). Image: Tracy Collins and Frank Coyn

7.43 Examples of graveslabs from nunneries (from left): St Catherine's, re-drawn after Westropp, 1904 © Royal Society of Antiquaries of Ireland; Grace Dieu, Co. Dublin; Graney, Co. Kildare, courtesy of Dr Peter Harbison; Clonfert, Co. Galway.

7.44 A fragment of an abbess' graveslab from Romsey Abbey, Hampshire. Image: Tracy Collins.

7.45 Effigy of Robert FitzRichard, thirteenth century, Church of Ireland, parish church, Timolin, Co. Kildare © Edwin Rae Collection, reproduced courtesy of TRIARC (Trinity Irish Art Research Centre). **7.46** (*below*) The possible tomb of Elicia Butler, abbess of Kilculliheen, in St Canice's Cathedral, Kilkenny. Image: Tracy Collins.

in the region. It is possible that the carved stone heads at nunneries may have represented various saints, whose identities cannot now be determined due to erosion and damage, or that some represent patrons or benefactors.[174]

Medieval graveslabs are known from many religious houses in Ireland,[175] though relatively few nunneries retain medieval graveslabs (Figure 7.43).[176] These graveslabs are mostly rectangular in shape, tapering from top to bottom. It is unknown if any of them formed the lid of stone coffins, or if they marked the locations of graves of more important people. None can be linked to a particular individual, nor is any in its original location. For example, those at Killone are set out in neat rows in the floor of the east end of the church, after conservation, two of which appear to be medieval in date. The single example from Clonfert is now housed in Clonfert Cathedral.[177] While many medieval graveslabs have very elaborate motifs and inscriptions,[178] those from the nunneries have the remains of simple crosses, and only occasionally are shown with expanded bases. None retain motifs that would be consistent with a nun or abbess, such as the abbot's graveslab from Boyle, County Roscommon, which illustrates a hand and crosier, a symbol of the abbacy used extensively by the Cistercians.[179] In England, an abbess' graveslab at Romsey Abbey, Hampshire shows the same design of hand and crosier, although only nunneries of the highest status shared such symbols of monastic power (Figure 7.44).[180]

Two effigies may be related to nunneries. The first is at Timolin. It is of Robert FitzRichard de Valle, lord of Norragh, portrayed as a knight, and dates to the first half of the thirteenth century (Figure 7.45).[181] The second is an effigy of a vowess or nun (Figure 7.46).[182] It is located in St Canice's Cathedral, Kilkenny, the traditional burial place of the Butler family.[183] The sixteenth-century tomb was likely made by an Ormond group of sculptors working in the region, rather than the better-known O'Tunney workshop. Both groups have several works in St Canice's.[184] The limestone tomb, later Gothic in style, was in pieces by the seventeenth century and was reconstructed in its current form and location in the eighteenth century.[185] The tomb abuts the west end of the south wall of the cathedral's southern aisle and is directly under a large window. It is formed of an effigy of a woman (orientated west–east with head to the west), with one long side and two short ends. Based on the physical remains and the iconography, it has been argued that the current tomb represents portions of two separate tombs that have been combined.

The long panel has six figures (see Figure 7.46 and described from left to right), the first two from one panel and the remaining four from a second.[186] There is a neat but still visible bonding joint between the second and third figures, clearly indicating reconstruction, and the style of the first two is more

7.47 St Catherine's, Co. Limerick. A possible tomb niche in the church (see Figure 6.26
Image: Tracy Collins.

archaic. The figures have been identified as a blessing bishop or abbot, possibly St Patrick; an unidentified female saint in a gesture of sorrow; a woman in a Virgin Mary pose, but likely another of the biblical Marys; St Catherine with her wheel and sword; a braided woman identified as the Magdalen;[187] and the last of the group – and a place of distinction – is a crowned female saint holding a book in her right hand. Rae suggested that this is the Virgin Mary,[188] her items indicating her intellectual and saintly qualities.[189] The east end panel of the tomb has the image of a bishop, which has been identified as belonging to another monument in the cathedral, while the west end panel has a second image of the Magdalen. The repetition of this saintly woman on the tomb suggests that this panel is also from another monument.[190]

The effigy is that of a woman, and based on her dress has been identified variously as 'the unknown lady'; a vowess; a widow; or Elicia Butler, abbess of Kilculliheen nunnery.[191] When the sum of the evidence is considered – notwithstanding the tomb's reconstruction – this was clearly a wealthy person's tomb in the traditional burial place of the Butler family,[192] the effigy is dressed as a religious woman, and the date of the tomb based on stylistic detail is the

7.48 Examples of water stoups and fonts from nunneries. A. Clonard, Co. Meath, which may have come from the nunnery; B. and C. Killone, Co. Clare, stoup and font; D. Aghade, Co. Carlow. This is a bullaun stone previously described as a font. Image: Tracy Collins.

sixteenth century[193] – so it is wholly consistent and reasonable to conclude that this is indeed the tomb of Elicia Butler, abbess of Kilculliheen.

This corpus represents the sum total of stone burial monuments relating to nunneries. St Catherine's has the only possible tomb niche extant at a nunnery church. This feature is quite shallow, however, and there is no evidence of a stone canopy. Instead the niche is fully plastered, perhaps for a picture or

7.49 Example of a depiction of St Catherine on a tomb at St Canice's Cathedral, Co. Kilkenny. Image: Tracy Collins.

painting. It is flanked at either side by columns with moulded capitals and bases with plain shafts. The capitals are of slightly different design.[194] The base of the niche has been robbed, apart from a single fragment on the western side. This shows the basal sill to have been slightly tapered and filleted along its outer edge, and is suggestive of graveslab set within the niche (Figure 7.47).

Additional stone features such as stoups and fonts are relatively rare but are recorded at a number of nunnery churches (Figure 7.48).[195] Portrane has a stoup in the interior of its tower and the stoup at Killone has been inserted into the north wall of its church.[196] A stone trough feature is situated in the graveyard at Clonard. There are the remains of a free-standing font at Killone dating to the fifteenth century, and there is an extant font at Clonard, though this has not been previously associated with the nunnery there.[197] There is the

7.50 Molough, Co. Tipperary. Some remaining evidence of paintwork on a window in the church. Image: Tracy Collins.

fragmentary base of a stoup or font near the north doorway of the nunnery church at Molough.

The survival rate of internal furnishing and decoration of religious houses in Ireland is much less than elsewhere, and internal furnishings and decoration of nunneries in Ireland is almost unknown. This is in stark contrast to England and the continent, where there is a wealth of written records and survival of medieval church and cloister timber furnishings and artefacts.[198] Painted scenes and incised motifs are known from a number of male religious houses in Ireland.[199] It is interesting to consider that nunneries in Ireland once contained wall paintings as devotional material that nuns could meditate upon. For example, St Catherine and her iconic wheel may have been illustrated in some form at the nunneries dedicated to her, as found in other religious contexts in Ireland, such as the cloister arcading at the male house at Jerpoint (Cistercian) or the tomb of abbess Elicia Butler in St Canice's Cathedral, Kilkenny (Figure 7.49). Painting on the church wall at Molough was identified by Sheila Ronan as an 'orange pigmented paint depicting continuous quoining [ashlar]

7.51 St Catherine's, Co. Limerick. A highlighted image of the incised ship discovered in the church (see Figure 6.30). Image: Tracy Collins.

outlined in black against a white background' along with evidence of possible foliage.[200] She recorded the presence of this decoration around the east window embrasures, the east gable and the eastern end of the south wall. Unfortunately, most of this painting is now quite fragmentary and very difficult to see in the field (Figure 7.50).

During the archaeological survey at St Catherine's the remains of an incised ship was discovered in the church.[201] The lines are located on the interior of its south wall, some 6m from its western end and 2m above the current ground surface (see Figure 6.30). The lines are incised on the final layer of a small section of wall plaster. The ship is faint and is formed of twelve vertical and nine horizontal incised lines. The image illustrates a vessel of the keel tradition of ship-building in use throughout the later medieval period (Figure 7.51). A ship is a fitting image to be used at St Catherine's as it has a particular religious significance.[202] Its location within the nave has symbolic connotations, the nave deriving from *navum*, God's people in the ship of the church, heading

7.52 The Domnach Airgid reliquary book shrine, associated with St Lasair of Aghavea, Co. Fermanagh. © National Museum of Ireland.

to the Promised Land. This association perhaps helped identify this particular location as a symbolically appropriate one for the nunnery community. This ship was likely painted and may have been part of a broader scene, used by the nuns as a focus for devotion and meditation, while also signifying a patron's maritime connections or wealth.

Nine recorded locations of incised ships in Ireland are from ecclesiastical contexts, such as monasteries, parish churches or chapels.[203] The ships range in date from the thirteenth to the eighteenth centuries. Some earlier commentators discounted the ships as mere graffiti, though it is now accepted that they are important motifs of medieval religious significance. Ships have long been considered a Christian symbol and are associated with Christ symbolised as a fish; and the apostles as 'fishers of men'; a motif of pilgrimage; salvation of the soul; and sanctuary,[204] as well as being associated with anchorites (Chapter 6). These ships are usually found in important areas of the church and represent a variety of ship-building traditions and forms.[205] The incised ship at St Catherine's is the first Irish example to be found at a nunnery.

7.53 St Dympna's Crosier, associated with Tedavnet, Co. Monaghan. © National Museum of Ireland.

Other artefacts that are reputed to have been associated with nunneries include St Dympna's crosier; St Attracta's relics – a cup and crosier (although this has also been described as a cross); St Brigit's shoe[206] and mantle;[207] and the reliquary the Domnach Airgid associated with St Lasair of Aghavea (Figure 7.52).[208] Some of these artefacts appear to date from the early medieval period, although have later medieval additions. St Dympna's crosier, from Tedavnet, County Monaghan, was a family heirloom of the O'Luans (Figure 7.53).[209] It dates from the tenth century though appears to have both earlier additions (ninth-century) and later additions, such as the figure on the drop, which has been dated to the fourteenth century.[210] Although not as elaborate, this crosier is likely to have been from the same workshop as the Kells crosier.[211] Dympna's crosier belongs to the early medieval corpus of

7.54 The Clonard Crosier.
© National Museum of Ireland.

insular-type crosiers (crooked), of which there are at least thirty-one in total.[212] Of these, five have inscriptions; unfortunately, the inscription on St Dympna's crosier is now too worn to read.[213]

Bishops and abbots used crosiers as a symbol of their position. Ó Floinn has commented that it is almost impossible to distinguish between crosiers of bishops and abbots – and, by extension, abbesses. Due to the fact that they have not been found in burials, he has suggested that they were not regarded as the property of an individual,[214] and so it can be inferred that they were a symbol of the office which was passed on. Leading on from this, it can be postulated that the Clonard crosier, dating to the twelfth century, was associated with the abbess and nunnery at Clonard, rather than the male religious house there (Figure 7.54).[215]

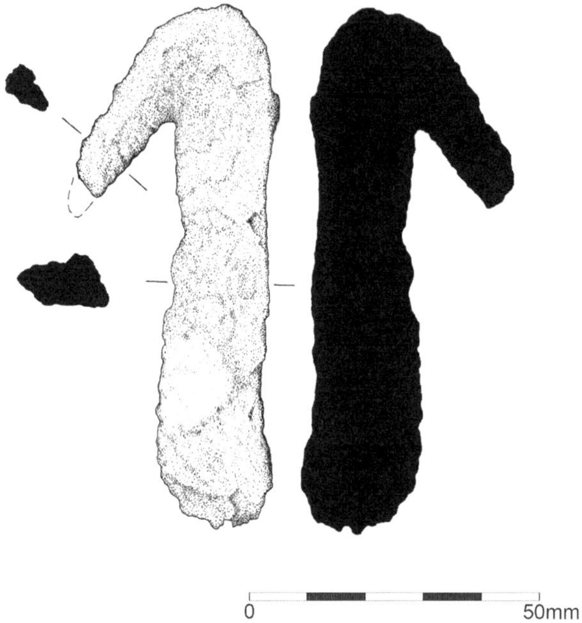

7.55 One of two pruning hooks found at St Catherine's, Co. Limerick. Image: Andrzej Wójtowicz and Frank Coyne.

The early medieval saint Attracta is associated with the nunnery of Killaraght. However, her relics – cup and crosier/cross – were not explicitly connected to the early or later medieval nunnery, though the dedication does at least suggest some connection. By the fifteenth century her relics were in lay hands.[216] Neither now survives but it has been suggested that St Attracta's cross may have resembled the Cross of Clogher.[217]

The small number of excavations that have taken place at or near nunneries have produced more day-to-day items. The excavations at Tisrara produced a quantity of finds, some relating to the medieval occupation of the site, including quern fragments, some with incised cross decoration, rubbing and smoothing stones, a honestone, pottery and several ferrous and non-ferrous objects and iron slag.[218] Excavations carried out about 60m from Grace Dieu recovered a bronze pin, waste metal, iron nails and staples, slates, clear window glass and a fragment of a vessel.[219] The excavations carried out at St Catherine's recovered artefacts relating to the nunnery's use.[220] A range of medieval local and imported pottery wares was found dating to the thirteenth to fourteenth centuries (Chapter 8).[221] Two iron pruning hooks, one from the east cloister ambulatory, were found (Figure 7.55), as well as a fragment of a fifteenth- to

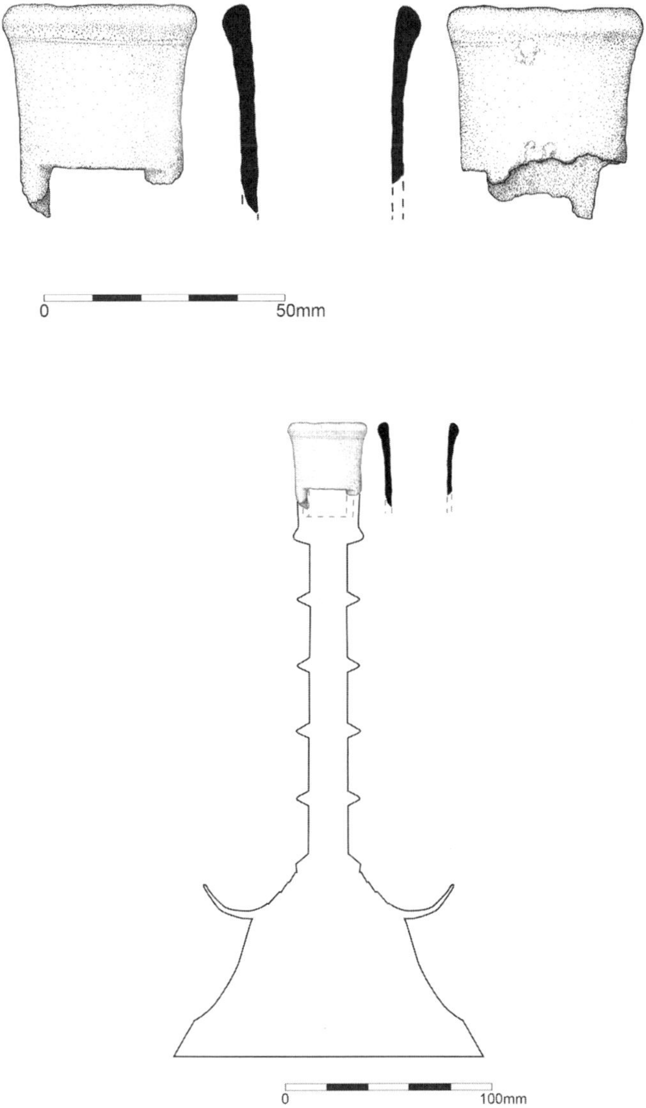

7.56 Fragment of a socketed candlestick and reconstruction, found at St Catherine's, Co. Limerick. Image: Andrzej Wójtowicz and Frank Coyne.

sixteenth-century candlestick of domestic type from the east end of the church. This was probably part of the furnishings of the high altar (Figure 7.56).

A number of nunnery locations have *ex situ* architectural fragments relating to their structures. In particular those at Kilcreevanty and Buttevant give an idea of the decorative stone that was once part of the nunnery structures, most likely the church. A number of *ex situ* architectural fragments were found during the investigations at St Catherine's, which dated to both its thirteenth- and fifteenth-century building phases; one retains a simple mason's mark.[222]

CONTRIBUTION TO INTELLECTUAL AND SPIRITUAL LIFE

In the daily life of a nun there was time allocated to study, reading, or activities such as needlework, manuscript illumination and copying, and many other artistic endeavours.[223] Unfortunately, evidence for these activities in nunneries in later medieval Ireland is completely lacking, but nevertheless it is important to acknowledge that the nunneries did contribute to the intellectual and spiritual life of the nuns themselves and others.

Nunneries dating to the post-medieval and early modern periods in Ireland produced a variety of material, including clerical vestments and altarpieces, such as the finely embroidered antependium (altar façade) and chasuble made by the Poor Clares (Franciscan) in 1712, while they took refuge in Market Street, Galway.[224] There is a collection of post-medieval Dominican textiles including three antependia (panel for use on an altar façade), made by the nuns at Galway.[225] At this time also, many nunneries, for example the Poor Clares at Kenmare, County Kerry, began teaching and producing lace for sale, which became sought after internationally. A tabernacle veil produced by the nuns at Kenmare is in the National Museum of Ireland collections (Figure 7.57).[226] It is reasonable to suggest that nuns in later medieval Ireland also created textiles for both ecclesiastical and secular use.

Notwithstanding the lack of material culture produced by medieval nuns in Ireland, there is a wealth of comparative evidence from nunneries abroad to give an indication of what these contributions may have been. Female religious played a particularly important role in the development and progression of mysticism and writings on female spirituality,[227] and indeed female religious produced the vast majority of writing by medieval women.[228] Perhaps mysticism and spiritual writing were particularly favoured by women religious as other avenues of spiritual performance, such as the administering of many of the sacraments, remained closed to them.

Previously, work produced by nuns was considered in somewhat derogatory terms, as *Nonnenarbeiten/nonnenwerk* ('nuns' work'), *Nonnenarbeit* ('handiwork of nuns') or *Nonnenmalerei* ('nuns' painting'), which was characterised as naive, childlike or unskilled, and primarily created to overcome idleness.[229] Their art

7.57 A lace tabernacle veil produced by the Poor Clares (Franciscan), Kenmare, Co. Kerry. © National Museum of Ireland.

is now considered part of a fluid and long meditative tradition and the product of sophisticated ways of looking at the self in relation to the divine, which had mystical and Eucharistic interpretations.[230] Nuns also manufactured and curated various text and music books. The Poor Clares of Cologne are noted for having a very active scriptorium in the mid fourteenth-century, which produced liturgical books for their own use and for patrons.[231] The Augustinian nunnery of Jericho in Brussels had an extensive literary network that included religious houses of Beguines, Benedictine and Cistercian nunneries, and male religious houses.[232] Many nuns were scribes and illuminators and some of these female monasteries produced books since the eleventh century, and in some cases nuns signed their own work.[233] Nuns created and donated textiles and embroideries for ecclesiastical garments, for decorative and didactic purposes, and for memorialisation of their own community.[234]

While medieval Ireland currently lacks the creative evidence that continental nuns created, it is likely that a similar contribution, though smaller in scale, was made to medieval society in Ireland by nuns. A very significant though intangible contribution by nuns was their prayer, which could be considered their *raison d'être*. They prayed for their benefactors, founders, supporters and each other, through the generations of the nunnery community, in perpetuity. We have explored the formation of identities for nuns through what is known historically and through their material culture. Due to the current dearth of information available for medieval Ireland, I have made use of comparative British and continental medieval evidence, and post-medieval evidence from Ireland.

A complex picture of identities has emerged. Nuns were, first, brides of Christ but had other identities which linked them to the outer world, as mothers, daughters, widows and land managers. These more individual identities were in the shadow of the more corporate identities of the nunnery itself as religious institution and lord of a lordship (Chapter 9). This multiplicity of identities should not be considered unusual, as all people at this time had a range of identities, formed through their interactions with other individuals and groups over time in very fluid ways.[235]

CHAPTER 8

Living and Dying

It is recognised that food and diet were of particular symbolic and religious significance in women's piety in the later medieval period.[1] Food and diet can also be considered as material culture, as they link the life course to social structure, religion, and landscape change.[2] This chapter explores the wider aspects of diet, health, life, and their effects on the bodies of medieval female religious. Nutrition and diet clearly have some bearing on the skeleton through time and are apparent in osteological evidence. However, contrary to popular belief, we are not completely what we eat, and other factors such as family genetics also play an important role.[3] There is a dearth of archaeological and historical syntheses available specifically relating to the medieval Irish lay or religious diet;[4] so the English evidence, which is particularly good, has been relied upon.[5]

There are certain limitations to the study of diet. First, theories about foodstuffs are driven by what is recorded in the written evidence, which is generally only a partial record which favours the upper classes of society. Second, the archaeological record is dominated by cereals, as they are generally better preserved and more easily retrieved than other foodstuffs. Having said this, the medieval diet consisted mainly of grain in various forms: bread, ale, and pottage (a type of soup made of grain), vegetables and herbs. Grains grown included wheat, winter and spring barley, rye, oats, or a mix of these (dredge, maslin, mixtil). Legumes (peas and beans) were additional field crops for food and nitrogen fixing in the soil.[6] This diet was supplemented with smaller quantities of fruit and vegetables, fish, meat and dairy produce.[7] Vegetables and fruit were grown and consumed for personal use, in gardens rather than large-scale production, and so much has escaped the documentation. Despite fruit and vegetables being commonplace and relatively cheap, some items were highly regarded, for instance fruits were given as gifts, though they were not a major component of the medieval diet.[8] Fish was consumed, with dried or salted marine fish being predominant,[9] though freshwater species were also eaten and given as gifts, particularly by the aristocracy, who constructed fishponds to maintain supply (Chapter 5).[10] Animals such as cattle, pigs, sheep and/or goats were kept for both dairy products and meat supply,[11] and birds along with their eggs were consumed in large quantities.[12] Wild animals, including wild birds, were consumed, but were considered part of the aristocratic hunting tradition, rather than being regularly caught and eaten for survival.[13]

The study of diet and consumption in medieval England has led to the identification of 'group diets'. This means that those of a similar social class shared a similar diet, such as armies, harvest workers or the aristocracy, which in some cases differed greatly.[14] However, there are no simple associations between medieval diet and demography, and it is currently estimated that perhaps 20 per cent of the medieval population in England were vulnerable to shifting patterns of food production and consumption.[15] Obviously, seasonality of food supply influenced what medieval people ate at particular periods, and the poorer groups were more strongly influenced by seasonality, as preserved forms of food were expensive, and in many cases considered luxury items. As a result, May and June were known as 'the hungry time' before the coming harvests. Poor harvests affected supply and thus diet and, again, these occurrences affected the lower classes of society more than the aristocracy.[16] Medieval religious communities are generally considered to be of the elite classes in the study of diet and consumption, and it is specifically to this group we now turn.

HEALTH AND DIET

Strict regulations in relation to diet were imposed by the church on everyone, lay and religious alike. This included compulsory abstinence from meat, leading many to the consumption of fish on Fridays, and abstaining at other times of fasting, which could include Wednesdays and Saturdays.[17] Dairy produce, including eggs, was forbidden to all during Lent;[18] however, there were exceptions to this rule.[19] These regulations were even more extreme in nunneries and monasteries,[20] where meat was entirely forbidden in the thirteenth century, though this rule was later relaxed. Abbots, abbesses and church representatives, however, could feast on gifts received and partake in visitor hospitality.[21]

There are very few extant medieval internal religious community records on diet in Ireland for males or females, unlike England.[22] One rare survival in an Irish context is the kitchen account of Brother Walter from the Augustinian male house of Kells Priory, County Kilkenny, dated to 1382.[23] Harvey has highlighted the higher standard of monastic living in the documentary sources of the Benedictine abbey of Westminster relating to diet. The monks' calorific intake was about twice what was actually required, which has led her to suggest that the monks at Westminster must have been severely overweight.[24]

A synthesis of the provisioning of Norwich Cathedral Priory, from 1260 to 1536 from detailed priory accounts, has led to some very interesting discoveries on the production and consumption of a religious community. Grain was a very important product for the community and it possessed several mills for processing.[25] Three different types of bread were produced at Norwich, based on contents, fineness and weight: the finest quality, monks' bread *panis monachorum* or *panis ponderis maioris*;[26] a lower-quality bread, for the *famuli* and guests, *panis ponderis minoris* (lighter than monks' bread); and the lowest quality, *panis militum* or knights' bread, for labourers and alms to paupers, prisoners and anchorites.[27] Grain was also used in the production of two types of ale at Norwich: *cervisia bona* for monks, aristocratic guests and master masons; and *cervisia aule/secunda* for the remainder, though up to four types of ale are known from other places, for example the Cistercian male house of Beaulieu.[28] There are unfortunately no comparable written records for nunneries in Ireland, though historical evidence for Kilculliheen does provide a glimpse. Its dissolution extent lists a granary,[29] for grain storage, and a fiant dated to 1568–9 lists rooms there for corn processing, brewing and baking.[30] This suggests that the nunnery at Kilculliheen was producing bread and ale, but the details of which we know nothing.

There are limitations in any region when assessing the health and diet of monastics in particular. It is known that a broad range of secular outsiders were accepted for burial in religious houses and so only in exceptional cases, where it can be confirmed that excavations are limited to the monks' or nuns' cemeteries, that assessments of monastic health and diet can be made.[31] The lifestyle of male religious communities is considered to have been of a relatively higher standard than the peasant laity and similar to that of the gentry, and their sanitary provisions were higher than at any other form of settlement.[32] It has been noted that general provision for sanitation at nunneries was of a lower standard than at male houses in England, however. This has been interpreted as a deliberate short-coming pivotal to a penitential and denigrating life specifically for female religious.[33] Another limitation is that currently there are no archaeological syntheses on the diet or health and well-being of nuns in medieval Ireland, or male religious for that matter, on which we might draw,[34] so out of necessity research from other regions, mostly Britain, has been considered.

Documentary evidence relating to the foundation of the Augustinian nunnery of St Mary Clerkenwell, London, 1144–85, in a confirmation document, shows that it was granted an existing fishpond, ten pigs, four trunks of wood for the nuns' fire and that it held a mill powered by water from the adjacent river Fleet. The excavator of St Mary's thus concluded that pork, fish and bread were eaten by the community of nuns, at least in its earlier generations. Excavated archaeological evidence[35] relating to diet, derived from the nunnery's kitchen area and associated rubbish pit, included beef, pork, mutton, venison, lamb, brown hare, chicken, goose, fish (eight types including eel), cockles, oysters and whelks. Plant remains included wheat, rye, oats and barley, figs and possibly elderberries. An earlier phase of kitchen activity also included roker (a type of sea fish) and eggs, while from later contexts, dated to the fourteenth–fifteenth century, blackbird and sprat appeared in the faunal assemblage.

The sixteenth-century use of the nunnery provided the widest range of foodstuffs and added mallard, swan, woodcock and thrush to the fowl assemblage. The range of fish increased to twenty-six species. The archaeological evidence dating to the latest period was supplemented by the documentary sources, which listed Malmsey wine, theriac (for medicinal purposes), almonds, rice, raisins, fish and pheasant.[36] The good historical evidence for St Mary's Clerkenwell shows that the nunnery was a crowded place filled with boarders, corrodians, tenants and male conventual members in addition to the community of nuns. The excavator thus makes the point that these 'surprising numbers … makes it impossible to accurately match dietary evidence to the intake of the nuns themselves. It remains highly likely, however, that the majority of foodstuffs recognised were utilised by the [nunnery]'.[37]

Archaeological excavations at Holywell Priory, an Augustinian nunnery in London founded in the twelfth century, also produced some evidence of the diet and consumption of the nuns who lived there. It was suggested by the excavators that cereals – wheat, barley, oat and one instance of cereal bran – were eaten and that the diet was supplemented by fruit and nuts. These included local sloe, blackberry/raspberry, wild strawberries and hazelnuts. Evidence for more exotic foodstuffs was also recovered, including grape, fig, plum, raisins, currants, dried figs and prunes. The animal bone assemblage recovered included sheep, sheep/goat, fish (cod, haddock, plaice/flounder and conger), poultry (chicken/goose) and cattle. The excavators suggested that this evidence, which could be considered to be a rich diet, was consistent with the wealthy status of Holywell Priory. This conclusion was further supported by the level of caries (decay) found in the dentition of the burials excavated. At Holywell Priory some 12 per cent of the excavated remains showed dental caries, much higher than the national rate from late medieval British cemeteries of just under 6 per cent. This high rate suggested starchy and sugary foods were being consumed; however, it was pointed out that there was no significant variation in dental caries by biological sex.[38]

The published evidence of human remains analyses from modern excavations of British nunneries, despite being a relatively small sample, does elucidate the health and diet of medieval nuns.[39] Excavations at nunneries in Britain have provided human remains, interpreted as nuns, from: Chester, Cheshire (Benedictine), Elstow, Bedfordshire (Benedictine), Gorefields, Buckinghamshire (?Cluniac), Nunnaminster, Winchester, Hampshire (Benedictine) and Clementhorpe, York, Yorkshire (Benedictine),[40] and more recently Holywell Priory, London (Augustinian),[41] Syon Abbey (Birgittine)[42] and Littlemore Priory, Oxford (Benedictine).[43] The first season of excavations were carried out in 2014 at the Cistercian nunnery of Llanllŷr in Wales.[44] A single fragment of a human skull (initially thought to be male) was recovered and features interpreted as grave cuts were also revealed.[45]

Rescue excavations at the nunnery at Chester in 1939 and later in 1964 revealed female human remains interpreted by the excavators as nuns of the community there.[46] Four female individuals from the 1939 investigation were described as elderly or old.[47] The remains showed evidence of osteoarthritic changes, dental overcrowding, caries and a tendency for the non-eruption of the third molar – which suggests that the individuals were related – though the sample was very small. The 1964 assemblage comprised eighteen individuals and all appeared to be female.[48] There was a high incidence of metopic sutures in five individuals, which again highlighted that individuals might be related. In one individual there was a variation in the lamboid suture or 'Inca bone'. Over forty-five individuals showed evidence for Paget's disease.[49] There were no obvious signs of dental hypoplasia, which suggested to the specialist that there was not any substantial malnutrition or childhood disease episodes in the group and that health was generally good.

Osteoarchaeological analysis of a recently excavated assemblage of ninety-one individuals from the priory of Littlemore, Oxford showed that there were seventy-five adults, three adolescents, and thirteen children. Of the seventy-five adults, thirty-five females and twenty-eight males could be positively identified, and the majority were over the age of forty-five years. Dental disease was normal for a medieval population and pathological conditions of the female group included healed blunt force trauma and various congenital defects. The most frequent condition was degenerative joint disease due to the unusually older age of the population.[50]

Keeping undertook a biocultural study of women's health through the use of human remains assemblages from British nunneries in the later medieval period 1066–1540 and was able to make several meaningful comparisons with male monastic assemblages. Her sample was taken from the nunneries of Clementhorpe and Elstow. Her nunnery assemblages of female human remains showed lower death rates in the 20–49.9 years category than the 50+ years category, when compared to male human remains from monasteries. Women buried at nunneries were shown to have lived longer than men buried in male monasteries. While the male monastic population was found to have higher dental caries, both male and female populations showed similar levels of endocrine problems, osteoarthritis, spondylosis deformans, dental calculus (tartar) and periodontal disease. This suggested that both communities had a similar diet, oral hygiene, and similar types of physical activity. From her comparison of males and females Keeping concluded that DISH (diffuse idiopathic skeletal hyperostosis) was an occupational disease of men and not of women – rather than just nuns.

Childhood diseases were more prevalent in the male monastic population than in the nunneries' populations. This indicated that the men were more disadvantaged in childhood, suggesting that they came from a lower socio-economic class than the nuns. Men buried in male monasteries showed more stress and physical hardship than females buried in nunneries. This may have been down to environmental factors – urban and rural locations may have had an effect – but overall she concluded that life in the nunneries in her sample was more conducive to good health than in her monastery sample.[51] Within the female population of her study she noted regional differences between the nuns from the northern nunnery at Clementhorpe and the southern nunnery at Elstow, which highlighted to her the better quality and health at the southern nunnery – trends which continue in modern-day studies of health between northern and southern England.[52] She also noted differences between females buried at nunneries, male monasteries, and parish churches. Women buried at male monastic houses had more chronic infections, while those from the parish graveyard showed more congenital defects. This suggested to Keeping that the women were not all sharing the same quality of life and each group had a different socio-economic status.

In the case of those females buried at nunneries, celibacy may have reduced the mortality rates of that group in the 20–29.9 years category, as they would have avoided the risks and complications of childbirth. Even if some of the nuns were not avoiding pregnancy, their upper-class origins would have made them better prepared and better nourished to withstand the stress of childbirth.[53] High incidences of hypertostosis frontalis interna (HFI) were noted in the nunnery populations (15 per cent at Elstow and 5 per cent at Clementhorpe), which is a condition particularly associated with post-menopausal women and results from prolonged oestrogen stimulus, in cases such as breast cancer.[54]

The condition manifests itself as a benign bone formation on the endocranial surface of the frontal bone of the skull.[55] This condition is very rare at other monastic sites and the relatively high instances of the disease in females buried at nunneries may also be linked to the celibate lifestyle of nuns.

Overall, Keeping concluded that those females buried in nunneries had a better quality of life than their female contemporaries who were buried in male monastic houses and parish churches. They were also healthier and had a better quality of life than their male counterparts and so were not *less* successful than monks in monasteries. Indeed, based on the osteological evidence, Keeping legitimately suggested that nunneries in her sample were actually *more* successful than the male houses in her study.[56] She also drew attention to a key limitation in her study, and one which is pertinent to this discussion. The nunnery cemeteries used in her study did not have any areas reserved exclusively for adult female burials and none of the female burials had grave goods or markers, such as a chalice, rosary or crosier that indicated the females were nuns, so 'it is difficult, if not impossible, to make definitive statements about the health of nuns because there is no effective means of locating them in the cemetery'.[57]

Evidence from Ireland: Graney, County Kildare and St Catherine's, County Limerick

The opportunity to osteologically analyse female human remains, which might be interpreted as nuns, has only occurred at two sites in Ireland to date: Graney and St Catherine's.[58] Two females were excavated and analysed at Graney, and five were analysed at St Catherine's (discussed further below). Quarrying adjacent to the nunnery at Graney necessitated archaeological testing and monitoring (Figure 8.1).[59] To the northeast of the supposed location of the nunnery, a small cemetery was discovered, measuring 11.8m north–south by 9.6m, on the highest point of ground. It appeared to the excavator that the human remains were stratified and all were orientated east–west with the heads in the west, following medieval Christian tradition.[60] The stratification of the burials indicated that the cemetery was used over a period of time. Due to the number of burials encountered they were preserved *in situ*,[61] but two outlying skeletons were excavated.[62]

Burial 1[63] was of indeterminate sex, though possibly female,[64] and was the remains of a young adult, aged to the late teens or early 20s. If the burial was a female, the stature was estimated at 172.02 +/– 3.66cm, which makes this individual slightly taller than average for the medieval period, though still within a normal height range.[65] This burial showed evidence of pathology

8.1 Graney, Co. Kildare. Extant earthworks and possible church outlined in red. Burials were found in a circular area to east of nunnery during archaeological works associated with modern quarrying. After Byrne, 2001. Image: Frank Coyne.

including joint fracture.[66] Moderate arthritic changes to the backbone, such as Schmorl's nodes, were also present, despite the relatively young age of the individual at death. This was interpreted as early development of degenerative joint disease indicative of a lifestyle involving considerable physical stress, particularly of the weight-bearing kind.[67] Burial 2[68] at Graney was probably female, and the remains of a middle-aged adult, aged between 35 and 50. The stature was estimated at 159.26 +/– 3.66cm, which corresponds closely with medieval stature for females.[69] The individual manifested diffuse degenerative joint changes, including an arthritic left knee, right hip, right elbow and wrist, left wrist and left collar bone. The backbone also showed mild evidence of arthritis.[70] In addition the left collar bone had some evidence of an old, well-healed fracture.[71]

It is important to note that these two individuals were not buried within the small cemetery found at Graney. Both were outliers, situated to the southwest of the burial ground and some distance from each other. Neither had associated grave goods or had evidence for a coffin or shroud. Radiocarbon dating was not undertaken on either individual but they were both interpreted as being medieval in date. If these individuals can be considered to be contemporary with the nunnery at Graney it is possible that they represent professed nuns. However, their positions as outliers may mitigate against this, as if nuns they would likely have been buried within the cloister or church or adjacent graveyard.

No patterns or trends can yet be realised in the Irish archaeological evidence for specific health or dietary issues relating to a nunnery community population, due to the small numbers excavated. Comparisons between female and male religious communities are also not yet possible in regard to health and diet.[72] Some initial conclusions might be drawn, however, in regard to overall general health and lifestyle of nuns. The female individuals excavated at both nunnery sites showed evidence of Schmorl's nodes,[73] degenerative joint changes, arthritis, invertebral osteochondritis,[74] spondylolysis,[75] and in one instance a healed joint fracture. While the fracture may have been the result of an accident, the other conditions are indicative of a lifestyle characterised by physical labour. Moreover, the osteological analysis of the females at St Catherine's concluded that the population represented in the assemblage carried a high pathogen load that resulted in elevated levels of physiological stress, perhaps resulting from periods of poor diet, represented in bone lesions such as periostitis and porotic hyperostosis, and in the dentition in the form of dental enamel hypoplasia. The complete absence of dental caries and abscesses is suggestive of a non-sugary diet.

Notwithstanding the fact that the human remains sample under discussion is small, these conclusions of physical labour and physiological stress are at odds with the common perception that nuns came from the elite strata of society, such as the nobility and knightly families, where physical work would not be expected of these women.[76] This view has been challenged – though rarely so, and even Keeping's detailed bioarchaeological study suggested that female burials from nunneries, some of which were presumably nuns, and those female burials from male monasteries 'came from a similar privileged social class'.[77]

Harris' study of wives and daughters of noblemen and knights of *c.*1450–1540, through genealogical information, wills, and pension lists in England, concluded that actually very few aristocratic women entered nunneries. In fact, nunneries played a rather peripheral role in their spiritual and philanthropic lives.[78] Oliva's study of nuns in the diocese of Norwich also concluded that only a small minority of the nuns were from the aristocracy. The majority were

8.2 A selection of the medieval pottery assemblage found during excavations at St Catherine's, Co. Limerick. A. Limerick-type ware; B. Saintonge green glazed ware; C. Adare-type ware. Image: Tracy Collins and Frank Coyne.

Table 8.1 Medieval pottery identification from St Catherine's*

Fabric Type	*Sherd Count*	*MVR (minimum vessels represented)*	*Form*	*Date*
Limerick-type ware	3	1	Jug	Thirteenth to mid-fourteenth century
Adare-type ware	13	1	Jug	Mid-thirteenth to early fourteenth century
Saintonge green glazed	4	2	Jugs	Thirteenth to mid-fourteenth century
Total medieval	**20**	**4**		

* After McCutcheon, 'Medieval Pottery'.

8.3 St Catherine's, Co. Limerick. The distribution of the medieval pottery found during excavations. Image: Tracy Collins and Frank Coyne.

from what she termed the parish gentry or 'middling ranks'.[79] It has already been discussed that patrons of nunneries in Ireland are more comparable with the gentry classes of medieval England than with its aristocracy (Chapter 3).

The archaeological human remains evidence, although admittedly slight, shows that female religious in medieval Ireland had lifestyles characterised by physical labour and, at times, hardship. This lifestyle might be explained if perhaps life in later medieval Ireland for all social strata was harder than is currently thought, or if women became nuns at a young age and undertook physical work as part of their tasks in the nunnery. This type of work would usually be expected to be carried out by lay sisters or servants, and not professed nuns, but perhaps this perception is incorrect. Of course, another explanation

Table 8.2 Medieval pottery locations at St Catherine's*

Trench Location	*Excavated Context No.*	*Pottery Type and Sherd Amount*
East ambulatory	1	Limerick-type x2
East ambulatory	3	Limerick-type x1
East ambulatory	18	Saintonge green glazed x1
Reader's recess refectory	15	Adare-type ware x1
North ambulatory and garth	900	Adare-type ware x1
North ambulatory and garth	905	Adare-type ware x1
North ambulatory and garth	910	Saintonge green glazed x1
North of church	100	Adare-type ware x1
North of church	103	Adare-type ware x3
North of church	104	Adare-type ware x1
North of church	109	Saintonge green glazed x1; Adare-type ware x1
North of church	112	Limerick-type ware x1
North of church	141	Adare-type ware x1
North of church	705	Adare-type ware x1
Kitchen area	604	Saintonge green glazed x1; Adare-type ware x1

* After McCutcheon, 'Medieval Pottery'.

is that the females under consideration, despite being buried at nunneries, were not nuns, and are rather representative of women from the lower strata of society who, for a variety of reasons, ended up being buried in a nunnery.

The excavations at St Catherine's were the first archaeological research investigation of a later medieval nunnery in Ireland.[80] Soil samples taken for environmental analysis did not yield any data relating to diet or consumption in the nunnery, and so as yet there has been no opportunity for environmental evidence to shed light on diet, consumption and health. Medieval pottery, dating to the thirteenth–fourteenth centuries, were all identified as jug forms, with local type wares, from Limerick and Adare, and imported green-glazed Saintonge from France being represented (Figure 8.2; Table 8.1).[81] While it cannot be determined what liquid was contained in the locally made jugs, the Saintonge pottery is a consequence of the wine trade with Bordeaux, France, which suggests that at least some wine was consumed by the nuns.[82] It is likely that these jugs were re-used on a regular basis. The spread of the pottery sherds throughout the nunnery complex was somewhat unusual (Figure 8.3; Table 8.2).[83] Though the majority were from secure contexts, only two sherds were associated with the area interpreted as the kitchen and a single sherd was recovered in the refectory. The remainder came from the ambulatories, garth, and the area to the north of the church, and suggests that the sherds were deliberately discarded in these locations.

The excavation at Graney also found medieval pottery dating from the twelfth–fourteenth centuries and included pottery from southeast Wiltshire, Leinster cooking ware and a possible French sherd, and eight sherds of a local ware of possible Castledermot type.[84]

DEATH AND BURIAL

Death in the medieval period was a particularly important event, where one passed from this world into the next. These people were not considered completely departed, however, and they 'did not cease to be members of the human community'.[85] Religion in the medieval period was not merely 'believed' in a rigid and set way, but rather 'danced',[86] and medieval Christians were pre-occupied with their death. The act of passing on was described as a 'good' or a 'bad' death, involving rites of separation and reinstalling.[87] They thus consciously made preparations to die 'well' in the tradition of *Ars moriendi* or 'the art of dying'.[88] A good death involved one that could be consciously prepared for. A bad death was usually sudden, when there was no time for preparation or to administer last rites; for example, deaths of victims of crimes or accidents, criminals, or death caused by catastrophes such as disease or war.[89] People who had died a 'bad death' were thought to refuse to settle in the grave and the living feared 'these dangerous and disruptive dead'.[90] It was imperative in order to have a good death that the office of the dead and mass was followed in order to allow the individual to rest in peace until Judgement Day.[91]

The rituals immediately following death were elaborate – depending on the wealth and status of the individual – including the preparation of the body, and the rituals within the church and at the graveside. Memorials of the deceased were undertaken when the funeral liturgy was repeated, a week, a month and a year after the initial burial. Death in the medieval period 'was surrounded by enormous anxiety, evidenced in memorial practices, macabre imagery and the widespread belief in ghosts, ghouls and the dancing dead'.[92] In this context of death in the medieval period, it is highly likely that nuns were not only mindful of their own 'good death' but also of their community of nuns and their benefactors. Death must have been a constant in monastic psyches given that the funeral liturgy was commonplace, as the recently deceased were buried and the longer-dead were commemorated.[93]

The process of dying in a religious house was a communal affair and the community would have rallied around the dying nun, to offer support, comfort and solace in her final hours. There are no records of how the process of a nun's death would have been managed, so evidence from a male monastic house must be used.[94] For example, the entire household of a Cistercian monastery would witness the last rites to a dying monk – unction, confession, absolution – and the *Credo* (Creed) would be recited three times. They then withdrew for the monk to die alone, as death was thought to be ultimately a private matter. After death, bells were rung and the corpse was stripped, washed and clothed while the community recited the office of the dead and the psalter. The corpse's head, hands and feet were covered and it was moved to the church in the company of the brethren. A constant vigil was kept over the dead monk's body and psalms were sung. No one was allowed to leave the monastery until after the funeral, and this rule extended to visitors and guests. Complete silence was observed in the cloister until after the burial.

The death of a community member must have had an impact on the remainder. Companionship and special friendships are likely to have developed over time. For a community of nuns – which in Ireland was likely to be relatively small – to lose one of their number must have left some if not all of the community grieving, with feelings of absence, loss and loneliness.[95]

Evidence for burial at religious houses

The rite of burial is a deliberate act and burial at a religious house and the location within that space would have been carefully chosen by those who were burying the body. Burial was permitted in a religious house in all places that had been consecrated, which might include the church, cloisters, and dedicated graveyards.[96] Archaeological evidence allows specific research questions to be posed regarding the status, position and identity of the buried individuals and the possible motivations of the people undertaking the burial rite. From archaeological evidence a spatial hierarchy appears to be emerging in relation to preferential location for burial. There is a preference for the church, particularly near the high altar, other altars, and locations of specific sacred foci. A preference is also emerging for specific places in the cloister such as the chapter house, cloister ambulatories and, to a lesser extent, the cloister garth, and in a British context differences in how various religious orders used these spaces for burial can be perceived.[97] There is a great deal of evidence available in Ireland for burial at male religious houses, as these are the more frequently excavated. Varying numbers of men, women and children have been identified,[98] though understandably some of the earlier excavations did not record burial to modern archaeological standards.[99]

History tends to have a more rigid view of burial practices at monastic locations, based on contemporary normative rules, and expects to find different strata of society in segregated areas,[100] although it is acknowledged that these rules changed over time, reflecting the changing concerns of the living.[101] Archaeology often finds that the theory of medieval burial and the perceived rules that governed it may not have been always adhered to in practice and over longer periods of time.[102] Burial regulation, rites and practices are particularly difficult to ascertain in the absence of targeted archaeological excavation and comparative syntheses of burial assemblages. Religious houses were often burial places for its religious community, and others, so it is sometimes difficult to ascertain from the archaeological evidence alone which individuals might be of the religious community and which are other burials, such as priests, benefactors or other members of medieval society.[103] This, coupled with the extensive use of some graveyards over a long period of time – sometimes to the present day – makes it increasingly difficult to clearly archaeologically identify the burials of particular groups, such as female religious.

Burial of women at religious houses

The popular notion that high-status women only chose to be buried at nunneries is not currently supported by the evidence. Elite medieval women, both in Ireland and England, did on occasion request burial at male religious houses, sometimes with their fathers or husbands – even when a nunnery was available to them.[104] For instance, in 1252, Mór, granddaughter of Turlough O'Brien and wife of Cormac MacCarthy, was buried at Killone nunnery, though her relics were soon taken to *les na mBráthar*, translated as 'the enclosure of the brothers', considered to be the nearby Clare Abbey.[105]

Archaeological evidence from Britain also shows that females were buried in male religious houses.[106] For example, the male houses of St Saviour's, Bermondsey (Cluniac),[107] the southern cemetery of St Mary Merton (Augustinian),[108] and Fountains Abbey (Cistercian)[109] all contained female burials. Moreover, the choice of a male religious house for burial was sometimes made even when the woman was a nun. Renalda, after an eventful life in the world,[110] became abbess of Killone. In her will of 1510, she requested that, rather than being buried in Killone, she wished to be interred with her ancestors at Ennis Friary (Franciscan).[111] Abbess Elicia Butler was buried with her ancestors at St Canice's Cathedral, County Kilkenny, rather than her nunnery of Kilculliheen (Chapter 7).[112]

It is generally thought that both male and female segregation and lay and religious segregation was undertaken at burial, although archaeological evidence is not clear on this point in a later medieval context.[113] The rite of formal separate burial of women and men has been generally accepted, at least in certain locations, in the early medieval period (Chapter 2).[114] The historical sources for the later medieval period do not appear to show evidence for this practice, though 'while the sources provide no evidence that separate burial of the sexes or children was normal in Ireland from 900–1500, there is a good deal of evidence to show that there were cemeteries in Ireland devoted exclusively to the burial of men or women or children'.[115] The further segregation of burial of the laity from monks, canons, and nuns at religious houses is even more difficult to archaeologically demonstrate at present.

Burial at nunneries and burial of nuns

The historical evidence for burial at later medieval nunneries in Ireland comes from a number of limited sources,[116] and the archaeological evidence currently comprises two sites: Graney and St Catherine's.[117] Before discussing human remains at nunneries, we will first consider the other archaeological evidence for burial. Tomb niches, graveslabs and various grave markers are indicative of burial,[118] and we have seen how few are now extant at nunneries (Chapter 7). These burial monuments were *aides-memoire*, for the living to pray for the dead. They also express social identity. Monuments such as effigies may have served as proxies for the dead, either depicting the dead person as in life or at their resurrection.[119] The lack of tomb niches might be explained in part by the poorer preservation of nunnery churches in comparison to male religious houses, though the very small number of nunneries with medieval graveslabs is more difficult to explain. The lack of such funerary monuments might be attributed to the ascetic poverty of nunneries and a lack of ostentation. One may expect, though, that some benefactors buried at nunneries – if not the nuns themselves – would illustrate their status in their choice of lavish burial monuments. For example, Elicia Butler's fine tomb befitted her status as a lady of the Butler household and her dress indicated her position as a religious woman (Figures 7.46 and 8.4).[120]

Another possible reason for the dearth of funerary monuments at nunneries might be considered. One of the nuns' important tasks was the praying for benefactors and remembrance of the dead. They would be remembered in their intercessory prayers in the church and at the office for the commemoration of the dead at the daily chapter – as male religious orders like the Cistercians did.[121] Although none survives, *tabula*, lists and other documentation must have been

8.4 The tomb of the unknown lady at St Canice's Cathedral, Kilkenny, thought to be Elicia Butler, abbess of Kilculliheen, Co. Waterford. Image: Tracy Collins.

used in nunneries, in order to remember all those community members and benefactors that had passed on, particularly those from previous generations. Perhaps at nunneries, these lists may have been the primary *aide-memoire*, rather than an ostentatious burial monument in the church or graveyard.

Despite the paucity of burial monuments, undoubtedly burial of nuns and others did take place. The undercroft at Killone may have originally functioned

8.5 The undercroft at Killone, Co. Clare. Original entrance on left via a narrow intramural stair from the ground floor of the east range; and the later-inserted entrance in the east wall, which seems to have re-used one of the two original lights. Image: Tracy Collins.

as a crypt, though due to the narrowness of its original access route it may have had another function (Figure 8.5). This undercroft is best paralleled at Buttevant Friary, County Cork (Franciscan). It is a vaulted undercroft of two storeys, which has been variously interpreted as a structural element to account for the site's slope, a parlour or chapter house, an anchorhold, a burial vault or reliquary, or possibly an earlier castle.[122] Killone's undercroft may also have functioned as a chapter house, anchorhold or reliquary.

Any place within the religious house that had been consecrated could be used for burial, which for some included the church, entire complex and central garth. Many cloister arcade walls in Ireland do not allow access to the garth. However, at several religious houses, such as Franciscan houses at Adare, County Limerick and Muckross, County Kerry, the cloister arcades were altered to permit access to the garth for burial.[123] At Ennis Friary, County Clare (Franciscan), burials were revealed in the cloister garth, though these were dated to the post-medieval and early modern phases of use. Medieval burials there were exclusively confined to the ambulatory.[124] From this archaeological evidence it is suggested that a cloister garth may have been used for burial at religious houses when other privileged space was at a premium. In an English context, burial was undertaken in cloister garths, but this was not a common practice.[125] Excavations at St Catherine's showed that burial did not occur in the excavated portion of the garth, so pressure for burial space in other privileged locations seems not to have occurred there.

Indeed, the cloister as a whole – where it was utilised – was considered an important space, a symbol of monastic identity, and was a metaphor for Paradise. The four-sided nature of the cloister was reminiscent of the four elements of creation: air, fire, earth and water; the four rivers in Paradise: Pishon, Gihon, Euphrates, Tigris; the four winds; the four seasons; the four gospels; the four cardinal virtues; and the four walls of heavenly Jerusalem. Cistercian thought saw the cloister as both a prison and a place of purification and salvation.[126] The cloister was also a liminal space, as monks and nuns left the outside world to enter the liminal state of the monastery on their way to perfection.[127]

Space is practised place, so the continual use of the cloister in the daily routine of the nunnery would have added significantly to its special qualities as a place for burial (Chapter 7).[128] The actions of the community of nuns, using the space with the rhythm of hourly prayer and recurring rites over the liturgical year, would have transformed the cloister into a space of meditation, peace and tranquillity. It has been suggested that the circular movement around the cloister – despite its angular plan – of monastics in their liturgical processions also imbued the space with sacred significance, as the monks or nuns preformed 'eternity' and 'endlessness' within the confined space of their monastery. 'In this sense the cloister might be identified as a central space where the liminal mode of monastic existence found expression in regularly performed circular movements.'[129]

If the cloister, including the ambulatories and garth, are considered in this way, this location may have been a particularly privileged area in the monastic enclosure in which to be buried. Thus, those buried in the cloister ambulatories at St Catherine's may have been close to the community there and would be particularly remembered in the nuns' daily rituals. The presence of burials in the cloister would have been known to the nuns at St Catherine's (indeed, due to the shallowness of the grave cuts excavated there was undoubtedly an odour from the more recent burials) and this may have affected their choice of prayers and meditation when using the cloisters on a daily basis.

The burial of nuns in the cloister ambulatories was particularly important at Syon Abbey, England (Birgittine). Burial locations in pairs were assigned below each window in the cloister and thirty such locations were identified. Records show that burials began in 1485 and plots were already required for re-use by 1502, just seventeen years later. It has been noted that this practice was unique among English monasteries.[130] At the double house at Königsfelden, Switzerland (Franciscan), sixty-two nuns were buried in their northern cloister ambulatory in vaults against the exterior of the south wall of the nunnery church.[131]

Most archaeological investigations on or near nunneries in Ireland have been carried out either for conservation purposes or to facilitate development.[132] During conservation works at Tisrara the excavation of burials – which were mostly modern – was avoided.[133] No medieval funerary monuments were found during the excavations, though it is highly likely they did once exist.[134] In 2004, testing was carried out at Portrane to facilitate new lighting. Several trenches were excavated inside the northern and western walls of the graveyard. Disarticulated human bone and artefacts dating to 'at least the medieval period' were revealed. The testing and subsequent monitoring also revealed that the graveyard had been reduced in size and was actually much more extensive than the modern boundary walls suggested.[135] There are further reports of human remains being found intermittently on or near nunnery sites, such as Clonfert,[136] and the putative nunneries at Nurney, County Kildare[137] and Coolmine, Saggart, County Dublin.[138] In several cases only legends and local folklore retain any memory of burial.[139]

In common with Ireland, the evidence for burial at nunneries in Britain is limited due to the dearth of cemetery excavation at nunneries generally.[140] Single-sexed communities tend to show a bias, so some nunneries do show a bias in favour of women, sometimes between two to three times more women than men, as at Clementhorpe and Elstow.[141] It has been concluded that nunneries tend to show more mixed burials than contemporary male monastic houses, and they do not show clustering or segregation according to biological sex.[142] It is presumed that contemplative religious were buried separately from the laity, at least in their earlier years after foundation.[143] Generally, the cemeteries of monastics were placed to the east or north of the church and away from lay cemeteries.[144] At nunneries certain areas may have been designated specifically for the nuns.[145] However, later and modern burials often mask the original distribution of burial around a religious house, making it sometimes difficult to ascertain the precise layout of the contemporary medieval burials. As previously stated, church interiors, cloisters, chapter houses and sometimes other spaces in monastic ranges were consecrated in order to be used for burial – first for monastics and possibly later for important benefactors.[146]

It is supposed that contemplative religious persons, monks, canons and nuns were buried in their habits, though there is little archaeological evidence to date to prove this fact for nuns. Gilchrist and Sloane cite a report of 1908 by Benton of a burial exposed at St George's nunnery, Thetford (Benedictine), which wore the remains of a cloth and a pair of leather shoes. Head-dresses may also have been used in burial. Evidence of green staining on female skulls excavated at Clementhorpe, Syon Abbey[147] and Holywell Priory[148] was interpreted in each case as staining from copper-alloy (bronze) pins and frames that would have held a head-dress in place and that these females were likely nuns. No such evidence has been yet found in Ireland.

EXCAVATED BURIAL EVIDENCE FROM ST CATHERINE'S

Saint Catherine's was particularly suited to excavation as there was no tradition of early modern or modern burial there (Figure 8.6).[149] No grave markers were visible and there was no area that could be positively identified as a graveyard. Wardell in his historical account of the nunnery recorded that human remains had been found on at least two occasions there in the nineteenth century. The first, in the 1840s, records that a flexed inhumation accompanied with a clay pot in a stone cist was found. Based on the description, this was probably a

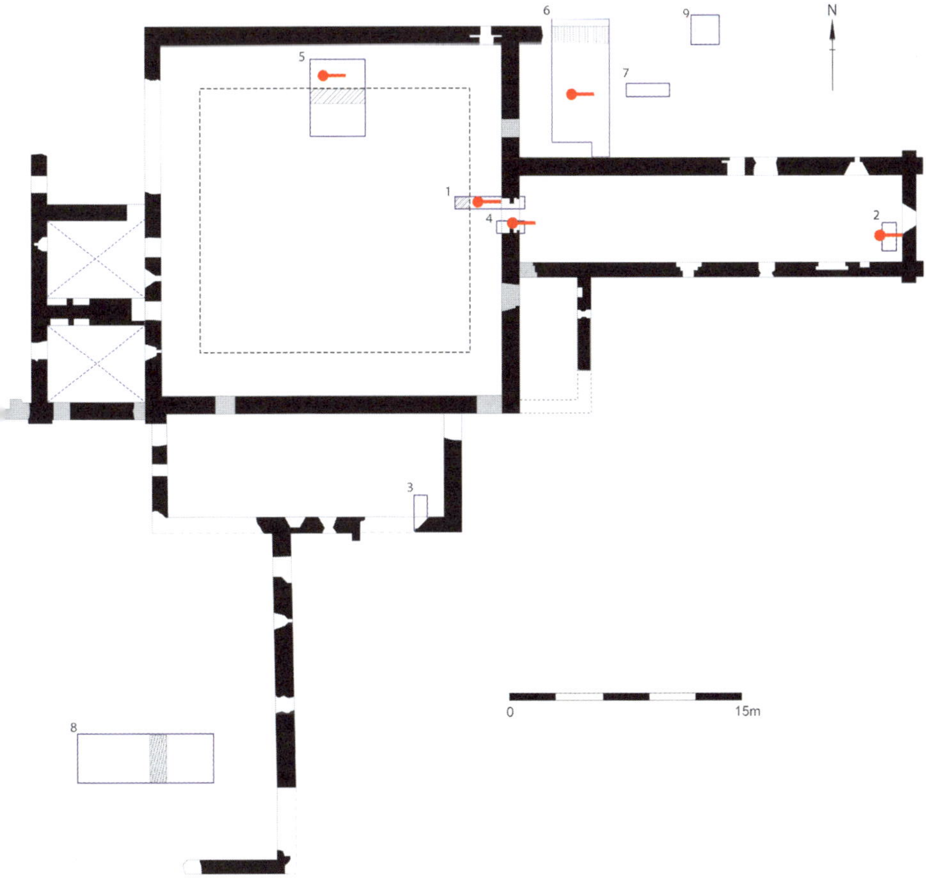

8.6 St Catherine's, Co. Limerick. The location of excavated burials. Image: Tracy Collins and Frank Coyne.

Table 8.3 Summary of human remains analyses from St Catherine's**

Skeleton (context no.)	*Burial Location*	*Biological Sex*	*Age*	*Stature*	*Dental Defects*	*Pathologies*	*Calibra Radiocar Date (C sigma*
22*	Church west end	M	Adult	-	-	None	Undated
23*	Church west end	F	Adult	-	-	None	Undated
26*	East ambulatory	-	6–9 yrs	-	-	None	Undated
27*	East ambulatory	M	Adult	173.8 ± 2.99cm	-	None	Undated
28*	East ambulatory	-	1.5–2.5 yrs	-	-	None	Undated
29*	East ambulatory	-	4–5 yrs	-	-	None	Undated
112	North of church	F	Middle or Older Adult	162.2 ± 3.72cm	-	Vertebral osteophytosis Schmorl's nodes Intervertebral osteochondritis	AD1500 AD1510–1 AD1620–
114	North of church	-	5–6 yrs	-	Occlusal and buccal pits Hypoplastic defects Enamel fenestration	Cribra orbitalia in right orbit (left not recovered)	AD1470–
128	North of church	F	18–21 yrs	151.1 ± 3.72cm	Hypodontia Calculus Mild attrition Enamel hypoplasia	Porotic hyperostosis Spondylolysis	AD1440– AD1590–
160	North of church	F	Middle or Older Adult	156.0 ± 3.72cm	Hypodontia Calculus Mild attrition Enamel hypoplasia	Metopic suture Inca bone 2 button osteomata Mild osteophytic lipping on several bones	AD1280–
163*	North of church	-	Adult	-	-	-	AD1280– AD1340–

* The extents of these human remains were recorded and preserved *in situ*.
** O'Donnabhain, 'Human Remains'. Radiocarbon dates were funded by Aegis Archaeology Limited.

ble 8.3 *(continued)*

eleton ontext no.)	*Burial Location*	*Biological Sex*	*Age*	*Stature*	*Dental Defects*	*Pathologies*	*Calibrated Radiocarbon Date (Cal sigma 2)*
908	North ambulatory	F	Middle Adult 25–39 yrs	-	Calculus Moderate attrition Enamel hypoplasia	Mild osteophytosis	AD1300–60 AD1380–1420
909	North ambulatory	-	3–4 yrs	-	Hypoplasia Mild attrition	Cribia orbitalia	AD1170–1270
914	North ambulatory	M	Older Adult	-	-	Degenerative changes in hip joints and vertebral centrum (osteoarthritis)	AD1290–1410
917	North ambulatory	F	18–21 yrs	153.8 ± 3.72cm	Hypodontia Calculus Wear suggestive of tooth grinding Enamel hypoplasia	Metopic suture Multiple Schmorl's nodes Severe periostitis	AD1440–1640

prehistoric Bronze Age burial. In 1901, fifteen burials were exposed, one of which was a male and was orientated north–south in line with the earlier cist. Most of the other burials seemed to be children. These burials were located to the northwest of the nunnery complex, in the area of Old Abbey House, and would appear, based on Wardell's description, to have pre-dated the nunnery.[150]

Despite the lack of extant funerary monuments at St Catherine's, five of nine excavation trenches opened revealed burials and a total of fifteen individuals was revealed. Of these, eight individuals were fully excavated and radiocarbon dating has suggested that all were buried at the nunnery when it was in use (Table 8.3). All burials were extended, supine (lying on the back) and orientated east–west with the head at the west, in typical Christian tradition. None had any associated grave goods.[151] There was no evidence for the use of coffins, either of timber or lead. One adult female,[152] whose knees and feet were very close together, suggested the use of a shroud or winding sheet. No shroud pins were found with any burial. Two of the five females were in the 'modest man' position, with the hands crossing on the pelvis.

Men, women and children were represented from the earliest phases of burial at the nunnery and these results are similar to nunnery excavations in England. No clustering or segregation of the burials by biological sex or age was noted. It was initially presumed that the children and men may be representative of fifteenth-century parishioners, when it is recorded that the nunnery church became parochial. The radiocarbon dates, however, confirmed that many of these burials pre-dated the fifteenth century and so burial of the laity (or perhaps clergy in the case of the men) in the nunnery must have been permitted prior to its church ever becoming parochial. Evidence for burial was found within the church, at its east and west ends, the north and east cloister ambulatories and immediately outside the church on its northern side.

Within the church, the skulls of an adult male and an adult female, along with a disarticulated juvenile jaw, were revealed immediately inside the church's west doorway. At the east end of the church, immediately under the east window, large quantities of disarticulated human bone were exposed, along with two distinct grave cuts, which lacked burials, indicating disturbance of this area probably through continued grave-digging. Most of the excavated burial evidence from St Catherine's came from the cloister ambulatories, though no burial evidence – not even disarticulated human remains – was found within the excavated portion of the garth. Both the northern and eastern ambulatories were found to have burials. Some of these were dated to the thirteenth-century phase of the nunnery's use, which suggests these areas were used not out of necessity due to lack of space elsewhere, but because it was an appropriate location in which to be buried. These were all buried in shallow grave cuts, which is not unusual in a medieval context,[153] and there must have been a malodour as a result of this. The use of deeper graves is a development of the Enlightenment period with scientific advances in public sanitation and hygiene.[154]

Four burials – three children and one adult male – were exposed in the east ambulatory of the cloister, immediately outside the church's west door. A disarticulated jaw of a fourth child, 1.5–2 years old, was also present. The burials did not have any distinct grave cuts and overlay and intercut each other, suggestive of burial over time. They were sealed by a stony metalled surface – the ambulatory's ground surface. Four burials were fully excavated in the northern ambulatory: two adult females, one adult male, and a child. Again, these burials were relatively shallow, with some intercutting and none had distinct grave cuts. No evidence was found of any ambulatory surface along this side.

Five burials were found outside the nunnery complex to the north of the church: three adult females, a child, and an unsexed individual. Two of the females and the child did not have any distinct grave cuts. The third female and the unsexed individual were contained within well-defined grave cuts, the latter also being contained within the foundation cut for the north wall of the church. The burial of children is at first suggestive of a domestic environment,

Table 8.4 Comparison of medieval female stature averages*

Human Remains Assemblage	*Number of Individuals*	*Date*	*Mean Female Stature (cm)*
Dublin, Fishamble St	2	10th/11th century	162.5
Dublin, Wood Quay	8	12th century	159.8
Dublin, Temple Lane	2	10th/11th century	159.0
Kilshane, Co. Dublin	-	Early Medieval	160.0
St Catherine's, Old Abbey, Co. Limerick	4	Late Medieval	155.8
Dublin, Temple Lane	19	13th–16th century	159.2
St Thomas, Dublin	14	13th–14th century	156.0
Tintern, Co. Wexford	54	14th–16th century	159.8
Pooled British sample	1,747	5th–11th century	161.0
Pooled British sample	16,423	11th–16th century	159.0

* O'Donnabhain, 'Human Remains', with references.

or a parish population. When radiocarbon dating is considered (see Table 8.3), some of the children could belong to the parish populations, as one child was dated to the fifteenth or sixteenth century, the time when St Catherine's was parochial. One of the children, however – and the earliest dated burial excavated – belonged to the early years of use of the nunnery, long before it became parochial, and so cannot be part of its parish population. This is an unusual occurrence in a religious house and is further discussed below.

Of the eight burials fully excavated, six were adults, and two were non-adults aged 3–4 years and 5–6 years.[155] Of the adults, five were female[156] and one was male.[157] While the results of the excavation could not definitively prove that all five females were in fact nuns, they are interpreted as such for the purposes of this discussion.[158] One male was fully excavated, and based on his burial location within the northern cloister ambulatory and within the nunnery complex, it can be postulated that he may have been a higher-status individual and of importance to the nunnery community, such as a benefactor, priest or agent. The group of females included two in their late teens or early twenties,[159] one middle adult,[160] and two women who were either middle or older adults.[161] Stature could be determined in four of the group, which showed the women to be slightly smaller than the recorded later medieval average, with a mean of 155.8cm and a range of 151.1–162.2cm (Table 8.4).

An analysis of the dentition of four female individuals showed that the rate of hypodontia (the congenital absence of one or several teeth) was high at 9.9 per cent of the assemblage, which may reflect consanguinity, or relatedness, between individuals. This is a relatively high incidence as, for example, the human remains dated from the fourteenth to the sixteenth century from the Cistercian abbey at Tintern, County Wexford showed a rate of hypodontia of just 1.1 per cent,[162] while the condition was not noted at all in the human remains from the Augustinian priory at Kells, County Kilkenny.[163] Hypodontia was not noted in the children's dentition, which suggests that they were not directly related to the female population excavated. Small to moderate deposits of calculus (tartar) were noted in all adult dentitions, and this is expected in a sample of this date. Apart from the congenital absence of teeth, the female dentitions had very low levels of dental pathology with no evidence for antemortem tooth loss, caries or abscesses. However, all six adult individuals excavated had evidence for DEH (dental enamel hypoplasia). This is a non-specific reflection of systemic stress on the body when the tooth enamel was being formed in childhood. The defects recorded in the St Catherine's enamel sample are considered mild, but can still be interpreted as poor levels of nutrition or the presence of a high pathogen load in the individuals' youth. This is interesting as the females interpreted as nuns – who are generally supposed to come from the elite families of local society – still showed some stresses in their youth, such as low nutrition levels related to a poor or restricted diet, which would have occurred when they were growing up with their families.

Two of the female burials had retained metopic sutures (these were the only two where the frontal survived) and one had an Inca bone. These features are normal variations in the architecture of a skeleton but may have some genetic expression. For example, a metopic suture typically occurs in less than 10 per cent of adults in an Irish human remains assemblage.[164] Having two examples from St Catherine's may be interpreted as a chance occurrence in a small sample, but coupled with the congenital absence of teeth, it may be a further indication of a high degree of relatedness between at least some of the individuals buried at the site.

Men

The burials of three adult males were excavated at St Catherine's, two in the eastern ambulatory (immediately outside the west door of the church and undated) and one in the northern ambulatory. The radiocarbon date returned for the male in the northern ambulatory was AD 1290–1410 and he was an older adult, probably fifty years of age or older (Figure 8.7). This places the burial well within the lifetime of the nunnery and likely to sometime in the thirteenth century and thus before the church was parochial. What are the possibilities for the status and identity of this older man? His presence suggests that he may

8.7 St Catherine's, Co. Limerick. A burial of a male in the northern ambulatory of the cloister (C914). Image: Tracy Collins.

have been a man of importance such as a patron, benefactor or priest that was allowed by the abbess to be buried in the sacred space of the cloister. It could be argued that the presence of male burials in the cloister compromised the quality of space for the nuns, by diluting its enclosed and segregated nature. However, it is unlikely that this was the case as the resting place of all the men buried was a deliberate choice by those undertaking the burial. Had the nuns not wished men to be buried there, they would surely have been buried elsewhere, for instance outside the cloister.

Children

The earliest burial excavated, dated to AD 1170–1270, was that of a 3–4-year-old child (Figure 8.8). This child was buried in the northern ambulatory of the cloister, at a period before the nunnery church became parochial, which did not happen until the fifteenth century. From the osteoarchaeological analysis, this child did not exhibit any traits to suggest that it might be related to one of the other burials. In England, the burial of infants or small children within or adjacent to monastic complexes is rare.[165] However, a relatively large number of young children under ten years (twenty-one individuals) were excavated at Elcho nunnery in Scotland, and this was considered noteworthy. None of the remains was dated, however, and these remains could span a long period of time.[166]

The four other children recorded in the human remains from St Catherine's ranged in age from 1.5–2.5 years to 6–9 years old. One of this group was radiocarbon dated to AD 1470–1650, a period when the nunnery church was parochial in the fifteenth and sixteenth centuries, or had been recently abandoned by the end of the sixteenth century. This suggests that at least certain groups of children were connected to the nunnery over its entire use. Three were buried in the eastern ambulatory of the cloister, immediately outside the west doorway of the church, and the fourth was buried outside to the northwest of the church (Figure 8.9).

What possibilities can be explored about the identities of these young individuals? Who was this child who was likely buried at St Catherine's in the early thirteenth century and what of the later children's burials? Most obviously, if the salacious scandals which surrounded some nunneries are to be believed, then it is possible that some may have been children of the nuns.[167] However, it is equally possible that the children were members of the local community, perhaps an important benefactor's child, or were some relation of a member of the religious nunnery community. Less likely, due to the young age of some of the individuals (one was an infant), though still plausible, is that the children were being educated at the nunnery. While there is no historical evidence that St Catherine's functioned as a school, there are other nunneries that did offer this service,[168] so it is reasonable to postulate that the children at St Catherine's may have been pupils there.

The sacred significance of being buried in the cloister has been discussed, but of particular significance within the cloister is the location of three children outside the west doorway of the church in the eastern ambulatory (which were

8.8 (*above*) St Catherine's, Co. Limerick. A burial of a child in the northern ambulatory of the cloister (C909). Image: Tracy Collins.

8.9 St Catherine's, Co. Limerick. A burial of a child to the north of the church (C114), which truncated an earlier adult female burial (C112). Image: Tracy Collins.

8.10 St Catherine's, Co. Limerick. Burials were located in trenches located immediately outside west doorway of church and immediately inside the church. Image: Tracy Collins.

not radiocarbon dated; Figure 8.10). It has been discussed that the nuns used the west end of the church when the church became parochial, and that the nuns may have had an altar there, indicated by the incised ship in the plaster, or that this place was used for the sacrament of baptism as it was commonly the location of the water font (Chapter 6). It might be postulated then that these young children were buried near the location of their baptism at the west end of the church. The latest dated child, who returned a date of AD 1470–1650, was buried outside, to the north of the church and in an area where several female burials were found.

Women ... nuns?

The majority of burials excavated at St Catherine's were female. This is not surprising as bias in favour of the gender of the community at religious houses

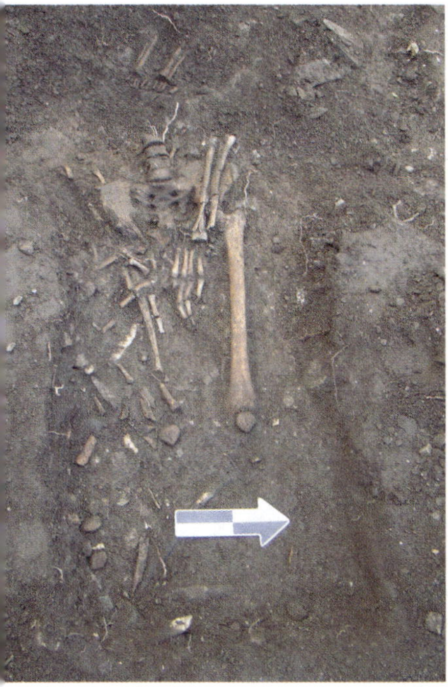

8.11 (*above left*) St Catherine's, Co. Limerick. A burial of a female to north of the church (C112). Image: Tracy Collins. **8.12** St Catherine's, Co. Limerick. A burial of an adult female to north of the church (C160). Image: Tracy Collins

is usual, even in small assemblages. Six female burials were excavated. While it is probable that most of these women were nuns, some of them may not have been, but for the purposes of this discussion they are interpreted as nuns (see Tables 8.3 and 8.4). Having said this, none had coffins, grave markers with symbols (see Figure 7.44),[169] grave goods, clothing or other accessories that would provide positive evidence to support the assumption that they were nuns. Three females were buried outside and to the northwest of the church at the angle between it and the cloister. Two were middle or older adults, aged either 35–49 years or over 50 (Figures 8.11 and 8.12) and the third was aged 18–21 years at death (Figure 8.13). Two female burials, one aged 18–21 years (Figure 8.14) and a middle adult aged 25–39 years at death (Figure 8.15), were buried in the cloister's northern ambulatory in the vicinity of the child and man already discussed. The sixth female was buried in the west end of the church.[170] The females buried in the ambulatory dated to the thirteenth–fourteenth centuries and the fifteenth century, which suggests a continuity of burial there throughout the use of St Catherine's (AD 1300–60 or AD 1380–1420 and AD 1440–1640). They were probably buried at this ambulatory location for similar reasons already suggested for the child and man.

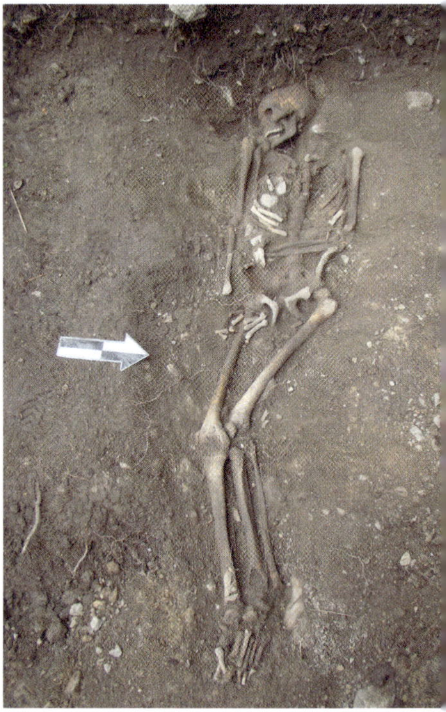

8.13 (*top left*) St Catherine's, Co. Limerick. A burial of a female to north of the church (C128), from south.
Image: Tracy Collins.

8.14 (*top right*) St Catherine's, Co. Limerick. A burial of a female in the northern ambulatory of the cloister (C917).
Image: Tracy Collins.

8.15 The burial of a female in the northern ambulatory of the cloister (C908).
Image: Tracy Collins.

8.16 St Catherine's, Co. Limerick. The excavation of Trench 6 to the north of the church and main features mentioned in text. Image: Tracy Collins.

While there was no clustering evident in the burials of the ambulatories of the cloister, it is possible to interpret the other three female burials – acknowledging the small sample size – to the north of the church as being in an area possibly reserved for special burials, such as nuns (though a single burial of a child dating to AD 1470–1650 was also excavated at this location and was the last burial in the stratigraphic sequence). This area could not be considered a proper 'cemetery', due to the small numbers of burials found in the excavated trench.[171] The female burials here ranged in date from AD 1280–1400, AD 1440–1520 and AD 1590–1620, to AD 1500, AD 1510–1600 or 1620, and AD 1620–60. These again show burial in the thirteenth and fifteenth centuries at this location. What might be the significance of this specific location as a place for burial? The earliest burial was that of a middle or older adult female. She was positioned in the angle formed by the north wall of the church and the east wall of the cloister. Her grave truncated a layer of bedding mortar, interpreted as a base layer for a floor of a putative east range that was never constructed (Figure 8.16).[172] The other two females buried in this location were buried a generation or so later, in very shallow grave cuts. The location of this discrete burial area in the early generations of the nunnery could be considered to be secluded from the nunnery complex. It was located to the north of the church, which was a usual place for a monastic cemetery, although other locations have been recorded.[173]

During this phase of St Catherine's use (thirteenth century) there would have been no direct access to this burial plot from the church or the cloister itself. The original southern entrance from the nunnery would have to have been used, and if the plot was to be visited, the projecting church would have to have been negotiated into order to reach the burial ground (see Figure 7.16). Despite the invisibility and seclusion of this burial location from the church and cloister, it does remain in close proximity to the west doorway of the church, which would have been used by the nuns to access their church during all phases of the nunnery's use. Therefore, for the nuns of St Catherine's, actually seeing or regularly visiting the graves of colleagues may not have been as important as being aware of their proximity and closeness. Indeed, it has been suggested that the line between the living and the dead members of religious houses was blurred,[174] and that the closeness of the cloister to its cemeteries encouraged the dead's continued 'physical engagement with the living'.[175]

In the fifteenth-century use of St Catherine's, the orientation of the cloister's access was altered (Chapter 7), and both the nunnery church and cloister could be directly accessed from the north. This would then have made this burial location very visible. First, visible to those who visited the nunnery, to its new entrance in the north wall of the cloister; and, second, to the parishioners who shared the church with the nuns and accessed the church through a doorway in its north wall, immediately beside this burial place. While there was no evidence for any burial marker at any of the burials excavated at St Catherine's, it is interesting to postulate that memorials may have been present, perhaps timber crosses, which would have acted as a reminder of those burials to those entering the church.[176]

From the human remains analysis it is possible to conclude that some of the females buried at St Catherine's were related. This supports the historical evidence that members of the same family – mothers, daughters, granddaughters and sisters – perhaps over generations, often entered the same nunneries. The burial evidence from St Catherine's also supports the conclusion that nunneries have a mixed burial assemblage and do not tend to show strict segregation. The children's burials are rare in a nunnery context and are suggestive of a community of nuns integrated with its wider local community – possibly providing education.

The ritual of burial was celebrated through the office of the dead and would have been undertaken several times – the burial itself, then a week, a month and a year after burial – for each of the burials excavated. The office would have been carried out by the nuns' priest, and probably attended by at least some of the nuns and perhaps the wider community too. As the nuns carried out their daily routine and celebrated the rituals of the divine office and mass, throughout the nunnery complex, these burials represent some of the individuals they would have prayed for and remembered, as a crucial part of the nunnery's *raison d'être*. The archaeological evidence shows that the cloister was not exclusively a female space – at least after death – and men and children were accepted for burial in this special place. Indeed, the location of the burials in the cloister may have had a direct effect on the type of contemplation practised by the nuns and the prayers they would have said when using the space in their daily processional ritual around the cloister space. The archaeological evidence and the radiocarbon dates show that there was not one specific place for burial in a particular period, as the ambulatories of the cloister and outside to the north of the church were used for burial concurrently.

To modern eyes, the proximity to the dead in the medieval period might be somewhat unnerving. However, the juxtaposition of the living and the dead in a medieval context was the norm: '[the] perennial presence of the supposedly absent dead meant that the living were in constant and very tangible communication with the other world'.[177] The nuns at St Catherine's would have encountered the dead in all corners of their world, as they prayed and knelt on the burials in their church, walked over the graves in the ambulatories, or remembered or visited the burials to the north of the church. Similarly, the parishioners of St Catherine's would also have been acutely aware of the people buried in their parish church and those graves they would pass as they entered and exited by the doorway in the church's north wall. Undoubtedly, they would remember some of these people first hand and others perhaps would just be known by family name. In many cases they may have been related.

The preceding chapters have explored the diverse nature of nunnery layouts and the fluid architectural arrangements of their churches. The lives led by nuns have been explored through the archaeological evidence and the nature of space as practised place. This chapter has discussed the current archaeological evidence of nuns' health and diet, death and burial, in Ireland and elsewhere, in an attempt to produce a more rounded picture of nuns in the later medieval period. This discussion has deliberately focused on the nunnery and its nunnery community. In the next chapter we will broaden the scope of the narrative by outlining nunneries' estates and their various interactions within their wider landscapes.

CHAPTER 9

Estates: Nunneries in a wider landscape context

The broad study of medieval settlement in Ireland still remains largely unproblematised, despite several important publications on various aspects.[1] Themes such as secular[2] and religious settlement,[3] military fortifications,[4] parish structure,[5] manors,[6] Gaelic regions[7] and agriculture[8] still tend to be studied in isolation of each other.[9] In Ireland, there has been some exploration of interfaces and interactions of these and other themes,[10] but in Britain more progress has been made in these areas of research.[11] For instance, there is no clear definition of a medieval village or town in Ireland, and how they might compare – if indeed they should compare – to medieval villages and towns in Britain and the continent. Should a 'typical' English lowland nucleated village be expected in the archaeology of a Gaelic or Anglo-Irish settlement? It has been suggested that it should not.[12] So despite the innovative work thus far, many archaeological studies and syntheses remain to be undertaken.[13] For example, to create a research strategy and widen the agenda to investigate medieval settlement and landscape as cultural identity, concepts of continuity and change through landscapes of Gaelic, Anglo-Norman and later Anglo-Irish lordships, and comparative studies, through space and time.[14]

Bearing all this in mind, in order to reach some understanding of how nunneries may have functioned, generated incomes, and were sustained over time in their wider medieval world, it is necessary to look beyond their complexes, into the hinterland of their wider estates and their relationships with other settlements in the medieval landscape. It must not be forgotten that the nuns themselves came from this wider medieval world and family connections bound them to it.[15] Through the archaeological record and historical accounts of nunneries in Ireland interactions between nunnery and the wider world might be highlighted and explored. We now discuss the information available on the estates that nunneries once held, and what their archaeological signature and pattern in the landscape might be.[16]

It has been previously discussed that women who became professed nuns generally came from the gentry classes in both Ireland and England,[17] although the current archaeological evidence for Ireland presented here is somewhat at odds with this general conclusion (Chapter 8). In any case, had these women married, they would have been expected to run their husbands' estates in their absence. As such, it is supposed they would have been educated to some level and capable of managing people, lands and money. Therefore, it is reasonable to suggest that an abbess or prioress would be able to undertake a similar role on behalf of her religious community. Moreover, historical evidence has shown in other regions, such as England and Scotland, that prioresses forged and maintained important relationships with the outside world, balancing the needs of their religious and local communities.[18] Earlier historical accounts have characterised nunnery communities as being incompetent in their role as estate managers, due to poor management and extravagance,[19] and this is but one of the reasons traditionally used to explain the relative poverty of nunneries.[20] More nuanced discussions of the economic status of nunneries have emerged.[21] Nunneries received modest endowments from patrons and benefactors from the outset in comparison to their male counterparts, and it is inferred that those patrons and benefactors had different expectations of male and female religious houses,[22] and that nunneries were not actually required to be self-sufficient (see Chapter 3). Moreover, it cannot be discounted that poverty may have been an ascetic choice for nunnery communities as a method of living out their spiritual ethos and monastic vows.[23]

Furthermore, an analysis of the location of medieval nunneries in Ireland within their landscape (Chapter 4), and their associations with other contemporary medieval sites such as castles, churches and towns, proves that they are not as isolated as has been popularly thought and certainly not as isolated as those in medieval England.[24] The Irish siting of nunneries has more in common with places on the continent, where suburban fringes emerged in the thirteenth century as spaces of religious house renewal, particularly for female religious.[25] In the case of female monasticism in the Irish medieval landscape – as there are fewer upstanding remains to study relative to England, and also a general paucity of documentary records – it is necessary to analyse these remains in the widest possible sense. Nunneries are now considered in an archaeological landscape to include their hinterland and their neighbours, such as contemporary secular settlements and male monasteries. Therefore, by following Gilchrist's and others' theoretical perspectives (see Chapter 1), it should be possible to explore and theorise the inter-relationships between these elements of medieval society. It is likely they were connected on several levels, such as kinship, patronage and economy; similar studies have been undertaken for other site types in Ireland, such as early medieval crannógs.[26]

NUNNERY HOLDINGS

> The medieval countryside was not, however, a series of obvious 'sites' but a fully integrated landscape which provided a wide range of facilities for [monastic] landlord and peasant alike.[27]

Nunneries, like male religious houses, had parcels of land in their possession and various legal rights to certain privileges and incomes. A religious house may have acquired land and rights in various ways, for example as a gift, purchase or bequeath.[28] These donations required prudent and effective management for the benefit of the religious community.[29] Nunneries' estates are generally considered to have been smaller than their male counterparts, though they could all vary in size. Some were very large, for example the male Cistercian house of Strata Florida in Wales was almost 50,000 acres in extent.[30] The nuns either managed their holdings directly, or employed officials, labourers, servants or agents to act on behalf of the nunnery in the temporal world.[31] These holdings, both actual (real estate) and benefices and rights, are collectively referred to as the monastic estate.[32]

Nunnery estates have been considered here in their broadest sense – their spiritual (church) and temporal (worldly) incomes, rights, and holdings of real land.[33] This has been done in an attempt to elucidate all the possible interactions that a nunnery community may have had with its hinterland in later medieval Ireland. In the religious houses of England, prior to the thirteenth century, estate income was usually derived from the direct management – perhaps through a bailiff – of monastic lands rented to tenants. After this time, leasing of land for cash became common practice.[34] This shift also occurred in medieval Ireland. This was particularly the case from the fourteenth century onwards, when the medieval economy changed, due to pressures such as disease and war, leading to a smaller workforce and subsequently a more cash-based economy.[35]

On occasion, donations and bequests, particularly after the Statute of Mortmain legislation in 1279, which tried to limit the unauthorised donation of land to religious houses, may have actually cost the nunneries through hospitality, expenses and various licences.[36] Occasionally nunneries purchased land for the community directly. Grace Dieu, Termonfeckin and Lismullin purchased additional parcels of land to improve their estates. On at least one occasion, parcels of lands were swapped through negotiation by an abbess, for instance in the defence of the estate of Odder in 1456, when the abbess petitioned parliament to exchange lands at Calliaghstown for twenty acres in Dexterstown and Jordanstown, which were closer to the home nunnery and so easier to collect rents from.[37]

These interactions cast the nunnery in very different roles from its primary religious one. The nunnery was employer, landlord, legal supporter or opponent, rectory and advowson holder and tithe collector. The nunnery communities were in effect feudal lords, in charge of maintaining, extending and defending their landholdings.[38] Indeed, for prioresses in Scotland they were explicitly considered lords over a lordship, in the same way as any secular lord, and some in the late thirteenth century had to swear fealty to Edward I.[39] The nunneries of Kilculliheen, Clonard and St Mary de Hogges were subject to the crown in their election of abbesses,[40] and through the function of landowner and lord, some nunnery communities in Ireland had to interact with the crown, leading to expense and, on occasion, conflict.[41] Income and interaction were generated through the provision of church services – especially if the nunnery church functioned as a parish church (Chapter 6) – such as pastoral care, almsgiving, education, healing, land rental, agricultural and other production, and employment. For the most part these interactions were mutually beneficial. On occasion, however, the nunnery itself or its estates were the subject of violence, through conflict, local unrest or theft.[42]

Differences have emerged in how religious orders, both male and female, established and managed their estates over time,[43] and some in medieval England were extensive.[44] Interactions between the nunneries and their estates are found in contemporary documentation and records. These are extant in England but currently for Ireland there are no known contemporary documents relating to the running of a nunnery estate.[45] These records elucidate various – usually seasonal – interactions between the nunneries and their hinterlands in a variety of ways and this comparative information has been used in this consideration. In the case of daily or weekly interactions between nunnery and locality and neighbours, which are of particular interest to the discipline of archaeology, it is highly unlikely that these were ever documented, even by the largest nunneries. Furthermore, nunnery estate income was gained through benefices related to churches, such as vicarages, rectories and tithes.[46] Benefices do not leave an archaeological signature and so historical evidence must also be relied upon when they are considered.[47]

A balance of upland and lowland would be the ideal for any monastic estate, which would ensure a variety of land types for exploitation.[48] Nunnery estates have been negatively described as constricted and over-specialised. They were usually constructed of small dispersed parcels of land, which caused them to be less productive and yield lower returns than their male counterparts – which by contrast, consolidated their lands to yield surpluses. The non-consolidation of nunnery estates, however, may have been a deliberate policy, in effect releasing the nuns from the responsibilities and distractions of running a large home estate. Even the wealthiest English nunneries had insignificant holdings when compared to the larger male monasteries.[49] On a practical level, the consolidation of estate lands was also dependent on what the land was used for. For example, Cistercians in England were large wool producers and needed large tracts of land to maintain flocks. But other forms of agriculture may not have required such consolidation of land, particularly if land was rented to tenants. The traditional narrative has been that male religious houses engaged with their landscapes in active ways, physically changing the landscape within which they were situated through land and estate improvement, and in so doing re-negotiated their economic, political and religious identities.[50] In contrast, nunneries with the same problems did not improve their locations and either abandoned sites or used them seasonally, as at Crabhouse, Norfolk, England. The lack of financial resources is a possible reason why improvements were not carried out by the nuns,[51] or it may be interpreted as an effort to maintain their seclusion.[52] But there is evidence that nunneries could also be proactive, such as the nunnery of Coyroux in France,[53] and large-scale land reclamation by Cistercian nuns in Flanders.[54]

Land was farmed directly by labour employed by the nunnery, or through rental and leasing for cash. Parts of the estate were managed and exploited for the resources they possessed, such as woodland for timber, fuel, the animals that lived there and the plants that grew.[55] There are historical accounts that nunneries leased or rented their lands, for example Timolin rented out lands in Dublin, St Mary de Hogges rented out lands at Skinner's Street in the town, while the nunnery itself leased this land from the archbishop of Dublin. Grace Dieu re-negotiated rent of its holdings at Swords several times and leased its church, rectory and manor at Portrane for either a cash sum of eight pounds per year, or forty measures of corn and forty of malt, at the discretion of the abbess. The nunnery of Lismullin sub-let land, as it rented 137 acres of arable land at Betagheston, County Louth from the grange at Colp and placed its own tenants on the land, presumably at a profit.[56] This is a particularly interesting arrangement as Colp was an Augustinian cell of Llanthony Prima in Monmouthshire and functioned primarily as a grange.[57] This is a rare historical example of interactions between a nunnery and a male religious counterpart. Nunnery estates in Ireland also possessed manors. For example, Kilculliheen held the manors of Dysertmoon and Seneboth (probably Shanbogh), County Kilkenny, while Lismullin held the manor of Belgree in counties Meath and Dublin.[58]

All nunneries likely had some form of income from spiritualities, for example Lismullin had the rectory at Kilpatrick, County Meath at its

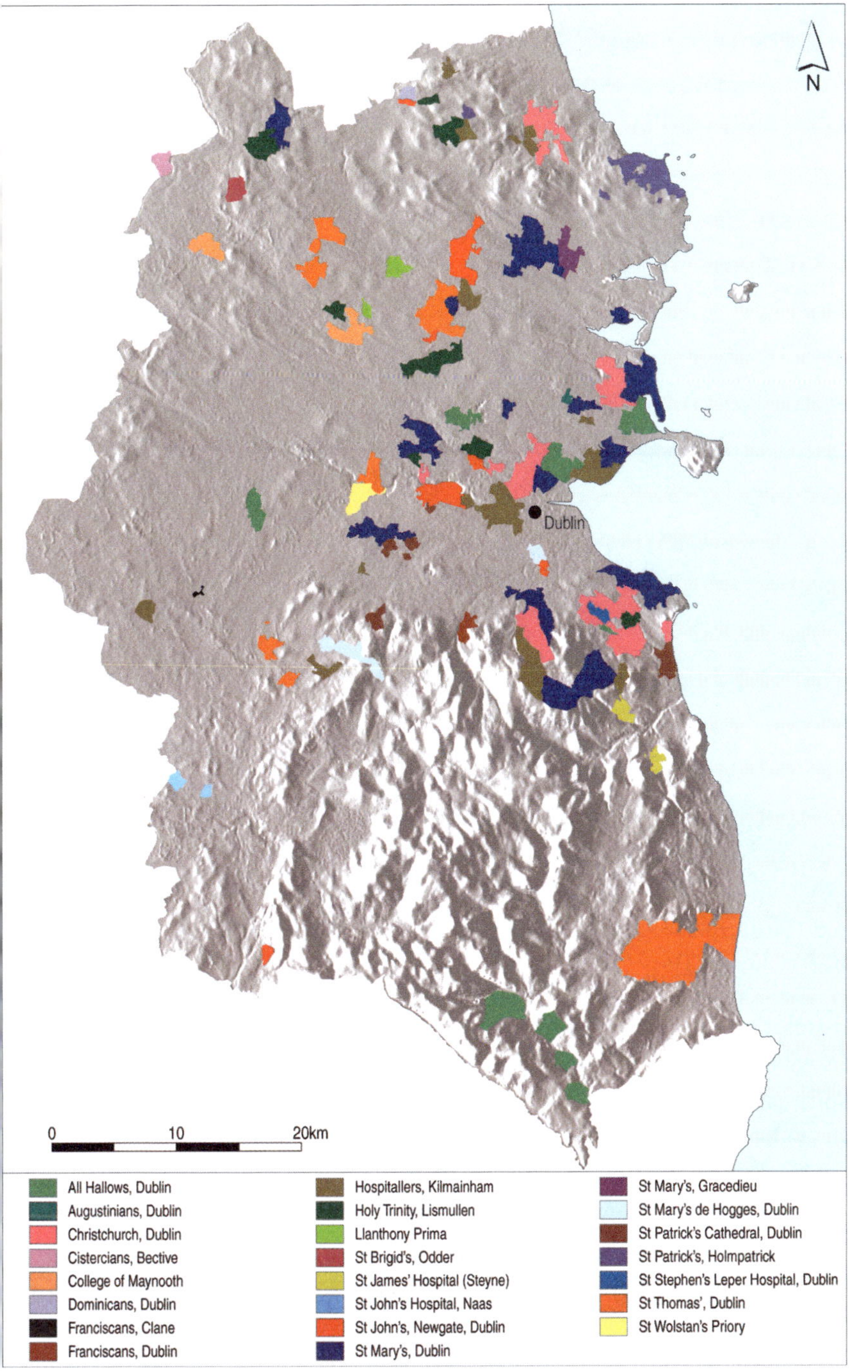

9.1 Religious houses' documented land holdings in the Dublin region, including the nunneries of Grace Dieu, Lismullin, Odder, and St Mary de Hogges. After Murphy and Potterton, 2010. Reproduced with permission of the authors.

9.2 The distribution of known holdings of Plary, Co. Westmeath. Nunnery indicated by star. Image: Tracy Collins and Frank Coyne.

dissolution, while Graney was given all the churches in the barony of Bray, by its founder.[59] The Gaelic nunneries of Kilcreevanty and Killone also had spiritual income from tithes and rectories.[60] However, all the religious houses in medieval Ireland, along with some lay people, were entitled to a portion of spiritualities and so, on occasion, there was stiff competition in their division. In some instances, nunneries had to fight to maintain their rights to tithes and advowsons with archbishops, bishops and even the laity.[61]

Studies of nunnery estates have been made, usually as part of wider monastic analyses,[62] in England,[63] Scotland[64] and France.[65] The holdings of the nunnery of Llanllŷr in Wales have been recently analysed as part of an archaeological landscape study.[66] Bezant has argued that the nunnery's estate was overwhelmed by its larger neighbour of Strata Florida at an early date,[67] but through various

9.3 The distribution of known holdings of Graney, Co. Kildare. Nunnery indicated by star. Image: Tracy Collins and Frank Coyne.

analyses she has untangled the nunnery's possessions, re-creating and mapping its twelfth-century holdings. Interestingly, she discovered that Llanllŷr's estate corresponded to holdings of the early medieval St David's ecclesiastical estate, which also had female associations.[68] The patron of Llanllŷr was able to gift this entire holding 'to maintain a link to its former identity by granting it to the women's house at Llanllŷr'.[69]

There have been few studies of nunnery estates in Ireland. The holdings of the nunneries of St Mary de Hogges, Lismullin and Grace Dieu were discussed

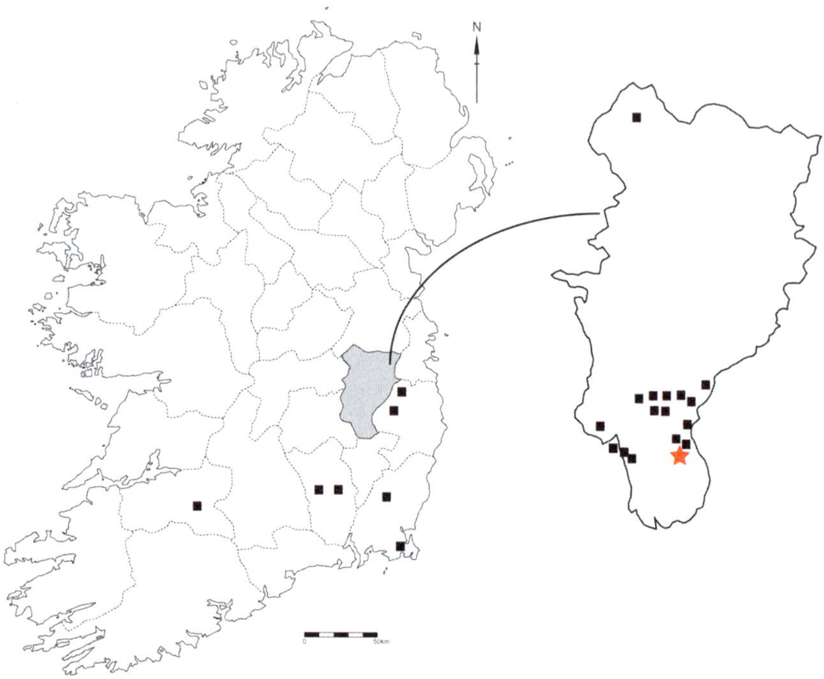

9.4 The known holdings of the nunnery of Timolin Co. Kildare. After Collins, 2014. Nunnery indicated by star. Image: Frank Coyne.

in the wider context of all medieval church lands in County Dublin.[70] This study showed the nunnery holdings to be substantially less than those of the other contemporary male religious orders and the archbishop (Figure 9.1). The study of the Cistercian nunnery of Plary (Ballymore) and its nearest Cistercian male house, Abbey Shrule, concluded that the nunnery's estate holdings were far more dispersed than those of the male house. In fact, none of the nunnery's holdings was adjacent to the nunnery, in stark contrast to Abbey Shrule, where the monastery was placed centrally within its consolidated wider estate (Figure 9.2).[71] In the case of Graney nunnery its landholdings were consolidated around the nunnery complex, though its churches were not (Figure 9.3).[72]

A desk-based archaeological study of the holdings of Timolin nunnery showed that for the most part Timolin's holdings were consolidated in three fairly large groups to the north, northwest and southwest of the nunnery itself and were situated 10km or less from Timolin (Figure 9.4).[73] These holdings encapsulated a wide variety of resources; the land quality varied from good to poor, upland and lowland was represented and there were several rivers. The more distant holdings of Timolin at Wicklow, Kilkenny and especially Limerick are suggestive of distant benefactors most of whom are not recorded.

Its dissolution survey sheds some light on its interactions in its wider community and how its landholdings were used. In 1538 Timolin possessed, amongst other land, ten messuages[74] occupied by tenants.

Customs included that tenants worked on the demesne land, in addition to each tenant and cottager owing two days' weeding, two days' reaping and two days' digging turf. Each tenant gave the nunnery a hen at Christmas, and those that sold beer donated one gallon of beer from each brewing.[75] The analysis of the Timolin holdings highlighted immediate limitations in the study of nunnery estates in Ireland. Most obviously, the documentary evidence is incomplete and it is likely that the total holdings of the nunnery were not recorded or are now lost,[76] and so placename evidence was used to supplement the record. Later, we will consider the holdings of St Catherine's using the historical record, mapping and archaeological fieldwork. However, before discussing this case study, it is first necessary to outline the archaeological indicators of a monastic estate.

ARCHAEOLOGICAL INDICATORS OF ESTATES

How precisely would a monastic estate expect to be manifested in the landscape? Moorhouse has considered monastic estates from both a male and female religious house perspective in Britain. He created a practical model of several features that together might constitute a monastic estate. In the first instance, however, most of the information pertaining to monastic estates comes from the documentary evidence, such as charters, rights, accounts, cartularies, registers and maps.[77] The archaeological evidence then clarifies and expands these historical sources.[78] The study of monastic estates in Ireland, therefore, is at a distinct disadvantage as much of its documentary evidence is no longer available, making the archaeological evidence even more important. The main features of a monastic estate are now summarised.

Granges

The Cistercian order has been credited with the introduction of granges or model farms to medieval Ireland. They are considered as a medieval farming system rather than purely a site type. A grange could refer to either the farm, inclusive of land and buildings, or just the farmyard where plough teams and grain were stored. The purpose of a grange was to sustain the mother house with agricultural produce, which were then processed on the home grange or farm.[79] In Wales, a number of farmsteads together are considered a single

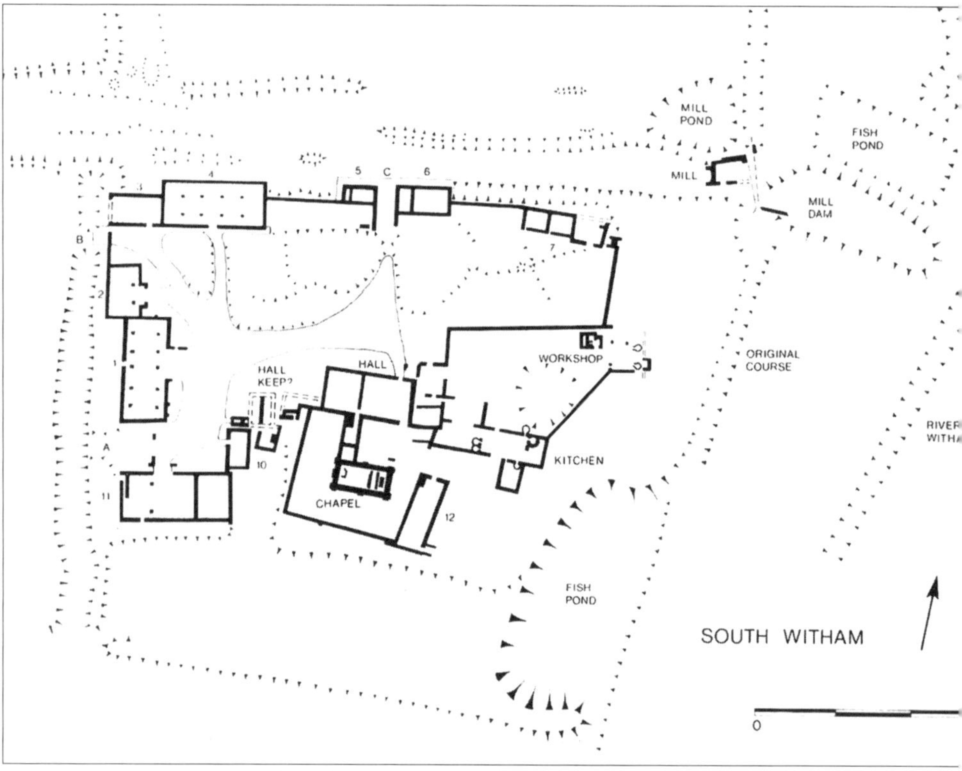

9.5 Excavation plan of a grange and preceptory at South Witham, Lincolnshire. After Coppack, 2006. Reproduced with permission of the author.

grange.[80] While the Cistercians may have developed the grange system, other religious orders adopted it, such as the Augustinian canons at Grangegorman or Hartwell Upper, both in County Dublin.[81] Many granges had specific functions, such as agrarian (arable), vaccaria (cattle), bercaria (sheep) and equicium (horses),[82] and these functions can be reflected in placenames, as at Strata Florida, Wales.[83] Furthermore, the grange system was first thought to have been imposed on lands which had not been systematically managed previously. But recent research in Wales has suggested that the Strata Florida estate did make use of earlier administrative systems and that a typical classic grange system was not utilised fully, suggesting that the Cistercians in this region imposed a 'regional gloss' on their administrative practices there.[84]

The archaeology of granges bears striking similarities to that of lay manor houses,[85] and this creates difficulties in field identification. Furthermore, the function of granges changed over time. They may have grown to become monasteries in their own right, or may have re-used abandoned monastic sites, or themselves been abandoned over time. Many, particularly in England, still

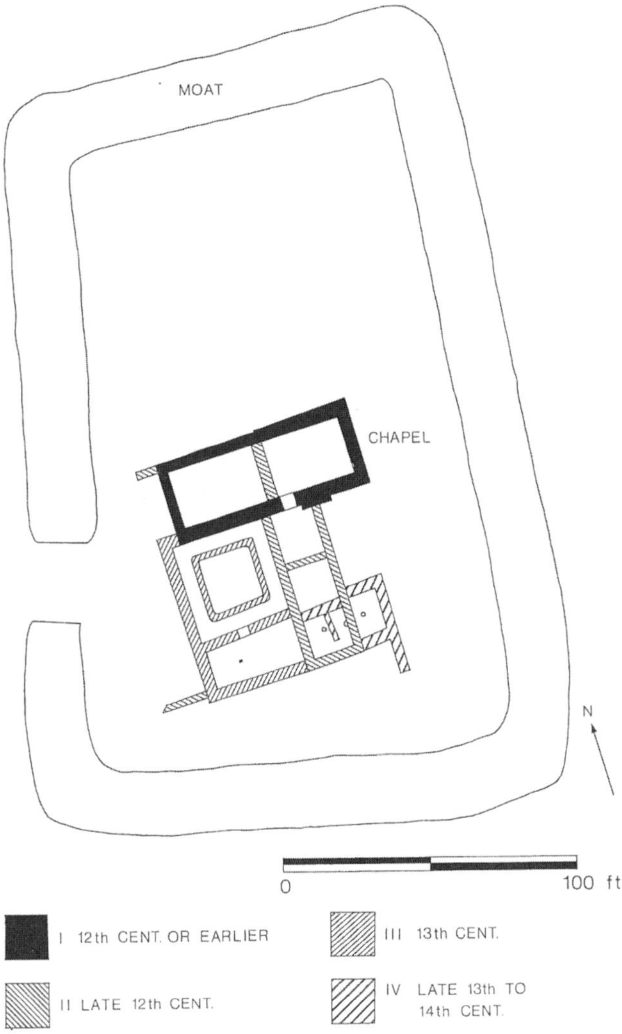

9.6 Plan of grange at Gorefields, Bedfordshire. After Coppack, 2006. Reproduced with permission of the author.

function as farms. Detailed study, field survey and recording have taken place at several granges, for example those of Stanley Abbey.[86] Relatively few granges in Britain have been extensively excavated,[87] though there are exceptions, for example South Witham, Lincolnshire, which was a grange and preceptory of the Knights Templar (Figure 9.5).[88]

Gorefields, Bedfordshire is particularly pertinent as it was a grange of Cluniac nuns of Delapré, Northampton. There, a twelfth-century chapel was augmented in the thirteenth century with building ranges and a central courtyard in the manner of a cloister (Figure 9.6).[89] Archaeological remains of granges have been identified in Ireland, for example Haggard, County

9.7 Aerial view of Jerpoint, Co. Kilkenny. Male Cistercian house of Jerpoint Abbey indicated in white. Parish church at Newtown, Jerpoint in red. Image Google Earth. © Maxar Technology 13/4/2020.

Wexford,[90] Ballinlig, County Sligo,[91] Knowth, County Meath[92] and Primrose Grange, County Sligo.[93] Granges have also been identified as crop marks at Monktown Skreen and Monktown Trim, County Meath, and Grangerosnolvan, County Kildare.[94]

There has been some excavation of monastic granges in Ireland. A gatehouse and drawbridge pit with a ditched enclosure was found at Stalleen, County Meath,[95] which was in the possession of the Cistercian house at Mellifont from at least 1185, forming part of its extensive estate in the region.[96] Excavations at Jerpointchurch, County Kilkenny revealed a complex described as an outlier of the medieval settlement of Jerpoint, interpreted as a possible manor house, manorial village, or perhaps a grange (Figure 9.7).[97] Geophysical survey and excavations at Kilbeggan Abbey, County Westmeath revealed both

9.8 The castle at Killogeenaghan, Co. Westmeath shown on a seventeenth-century map, was associated with the Nuns' Church, Co. Offaly, and may have been the site of a grange. Ms 723-4 Parish maps with terriers showing forfeited lands in County Westmeath, commonly known as the 'Down Survey'. Courtesy of the National Library of Ireland.

the abbey itself and its home grange, including enclosures, pits, roads and a grain-drying kiln.[98] Excavations on top of the main Neolithic passage tomb mound at Knowth, County Meath discovered a rectangular bawn with interior buildings, interpreted as the grange held by Mellifont there since the 1150s.[99] The Bective Abbey Project, based on excavations of its home farm, has yielded important new data on the agricultural economy of a male monastic house in medieval Ireland.[100]

There is archaeological evidence for granges in Wales, particularly of the Cistercian order,[101] and especially of Strata Florida which dominated the medieval Welsh landscape.[102] Its grange of Hafodwen is interesting as it was thought originally to have belonged to the nunnery of Llanllŷr.[103] The granges of Whitland Abbey at Manorforion and Maerdref granted to Talley Abbey have also been archaeologically assessed.[104] Monastic granges in Wales functioned differently to the classic grange farms of English monasteries – as tools of lordship, as well as a means of agricultural production.[105] Of the thirteen or so medieval nunneries in Scotland, six are recorded as possessing granges.[106] Larger monastic granges, as documented in England, would have possessed their own ranges of domestic and farm buildings, including animal sheds, stables, barns, granaries, woolhouses, dovecotes, orchards and vineyards, chapels, gatehouses, water supply and sometimes a moat. Granges were vulnerable to attack and in many cases may have contained a castle or used crenellations (battlements) on some of the structures.[107] At both Timolin and St Catherine's there are recorded castles in the same townland as a number of their holdings.[108] Killogeenaghan, County Westmeath is associated with the Nuns' Church at Clonmacnoise as a likely grange, and a castle was recorded there in the seventeenth century (Figure 9.8).[109]

Upland evidence of monastic granges is particularly rich due to the better preservation of archaeological remains there. In some cases, they have been found to have re-used prehistoric field systems and the medieval systems themselves may be multi-phased, with enclosed areas, pens and hut sites.[110] The value of farming, in particular of sheep, to male religious houses is well-attested in England, though it is less well-known that several nunneries also traded in sheep and wool, and exported it to the continent. In the fourteenth century, Stixwould, Lincolnshire was the largest nunnery-producer of wool in England, producing fifteen sacks per year,[111] and Llanllŷr nunnery in Wales was associated with the development of pedigree dairy herds.[112]

Mills

Mills were already used in early medieval Ireland and in the later medieval period their use continued throughout the country. The Anglo-Normans and religious houses increased capacity particularly in grain milling through improved construction and water management practices.[113] Rights to build mills and their associated water rights were part of the 'manorial monopoly' enjoyed by both lay and monastic estates.[114] They provided a convenient block grant of income to a religious house, as mills could have been directly used by the monastery while also providing an income when others paid to use it.[115] In addition to water mills, medieval horse mills, tide and wind mills are known, which were used for a variety of purposes. Tuck and fulling mills used in the preparation of cloth are also known. Water-powered corn mills were the most common form of mill in England associated with monastic houses, and may have been held many miles from the monastery itself.[116] More unusual mill-types are also known, such as those used in the manufacture of iron, and the processing of bark for the tanning process.[117] The excavations of mills at the Cistercian abbey of Bordesley, England showed that they had a variety of purposes, including metalworking and repair of metal items.[118]

There are now no upstanding mills at nunneries in Ireland. But mills are known from the dissolution extents: Timolin had a single water mill, Kilculliheen had two water mills, and Lismullin possessed three. Grace Dieu possessed a water mill and a horse mill.[119] In no case is the precise function of these mills provided, though it is likely that in the majority of cases they were for grain milling. It is likely that the mills used by nuns were similar to those at male religious houses, such as that recorded at Ennis Friary (Franciscan), County Clare and the upstanding example at Lorrha (Dominican), County Tipperary.[120]

Dovecotes, fishponds, rabbit warrens, parks, gardens and woodland

The presence of dovecotes, fishponds, rabbit warrens, parks, gardens and woodland may also indicate other aspects of monastic estates. Other indicators, though more difficult to detect in the archaeological record, include unenclosed features like barns, kilns, bread ovens, bird and animal traps and archery butts, or animal pound enclosures such as horse corrals, haystacks – which in England were protected by shallow ditches or fosses – peat stores, sheep folds and washes, and hut sites related to the use of upland pastures. These were 'the ordinary things of the countryside that were familiar to medieval people'.[121] Unfortunately, many of these ordinary features are now difficult to detect and interpret through fieldwork alone.

The only extant nunnery dovecote is located in the precinct of St Catherine's (see Figure 5.11). It is similar in morphology to the round dovecote at the Cistercian monastic house of Kilcooly, County Tipperary,[122] and the example at Fore, County Westmeath (Benedictine), of which only the lower courses of the nesting holes and central potence support remain.[123] The Ballybeg, County Cork (Augustinian) example, in contrast to those just mentioned, has perhaps more in common with English types, being circular in plan but much taller, its outer wall projecting well over its corbelled roof, in order to protect the birds' access and egress, and having an upper doorway in addition to the more usual ground-floor entrance.[124] In addition, the Ballybeg dovecote appears to have been partially engaged with the precinct wall, whereas all the other examples are free-standing structures.

Fish was an important part of the monastic diet, and ponds, rivers and coastal supplies of fish were all exploited (Chapter 5). As such, fishing rights and rights to weirs were jealously protected.[125] Records of monastic houses in England provide details of the numbers and types of fish consumed. For instance, Bicester Priory (Augustinian) purchased 200 herring in 1296 along with other fish types, and in 1302 10,000 herring were delivered to its kitchen.[126] The

9.9 A possible unrecorded fishpond near the nunnery at Kellystown, Co. Louth re-drawn from the first-edition six-inch Ordnance Survey map. Image: Frank Coyne.

documents in Britain show that not only the weirs were important. Rights of access, rights of processing, and building of plant on adjacent banks, and pack animal enclosure were all part of the wider exploitation of fish resources.[127]

The fishpond at St Catherine's is likely an original medieval pond relating to the nunnery (see Figure 5.12). A long rectangular pond marked on the first-edition Ordnance Survey six-inch map immediately to the south of Kellystown, County Louth appears to be a fishpond, though there is now no evidence to substantiate this (Figure 9.9). Weirs also provided fish and eels. For example, Molough had an eel weir close to the nunnery and Kilculliheen had no less than six salmon weirs listed in its possessions at its dissolution. Kilcreevanty held an eel weir at Cong, County Mayo. In Limerick, St Peter's Cell's dissolution record does not specifically list a weir, but the adjacent St Saviour's Dominican male house had weirs in its possession and with the proximity of the Shannon and Abbey rivers it is not unreasonable to suggest that the nunnery also possessed at least one.

Rabbits were introduced in the twelfth century into Britain, and later Ireland, and were exploited for meat and fur.[128] It is difficult to imagine now, but in the medieval period they were a rare and luxurious commodity. Most monastic houses would have had a warren, and a warrener to maintain

9.10 An accurate copy of the Great Charter Roll of Waterford, 1373, depicting a rabbit warren. Drawn by Jonathan Millar and Sarah Nylund, Rubicon Heritage Services. Reproduced by permission of Transport Infrastructure Ireland.

it. Warrens may manifest themselves in the landscape as long, low, narrow constructed mounds, known as 'pillow mounds', which encouraged the rabbits to burrow.[129] Nine rabbit warrens are archaeologically recorded in Ireland currently, and at least two are likely associated with medieval monastic estates.[130]

A drawing of a warren was included at the end of the Great Charter Roll of Waterford dated to 1373 (Figure 9.10). It is shown opposite the town on the other side of the river Suir, where the nunnery of Kilculliheen was situated.[131] It is also possible that the unusual quartering of the interior of a large early medieval ringfort enclosure adjacent to Shanid Castle, one of the residences of the patrons of the nunnery of St Catherine's, shows its re-use as a rabbit warren.[132] Many more warrens have been identified in Britain and they vary in size considerably. For instance, the warren at Lakenheath, Suffolk is 2,226 acres in extent with a ten-mile perimeter.[133]

Parks were part of the manorial landscape of England and extensive monastic deer parks are known from there.[134] Enclosed parks were also a feature of medieval Ireland – at least forty-six parks were used in Ireland up to *c.* 1400. They were particularly associated with the Anglo-Norman settled areas, providing timber, seasonal foodstuffs, and on occasion contained deer, for recreational and food purposes.[135] There are no known medieval deer parks associated with religious houses in Ireland.[136] Deer Island is located in the Shannon estuary near the village of Ballynacally, County Clare. The nunnery of Killone had landholdings in this locality, and on the basis of placename evidence it can be tentatively associated with the nunnery.[137] A fiant dated to 1547 noted six 'closes' or parks, owned by the nunnery of Lismullin – Le High Parke, Le Lowe Parke, Le Hors Parke, Le Moote Parke, Le Kill Parke and Le Broode Parke – suggesting that this nunnery held parklands with specific functions.[138] Other land might also be considered in this context. The association of marshy land with nunneries has been interpreted as a protective measure, 'a higher value upon the seclusion of the unreclaimed waste', though alternatively this waste ground may have also been of economic value, particularly for summer pasture, fishing, turbary (turf cutting), and even wheat-growing.[139]

Other ancillary features

Wayside crosses, which were associated with monastic lands in the contemporary documents to delimit lands, are considered another indicator of monastic estates. Others, perhaps more unusual in an Irish context, are tanneries for the production of leather, which would have been located near cattle production, but also near mills, due to their common requirement of water. Both industries needed access to water, a mill pond, and a dam. The documentary record in

England shows that rights were in place to prevent tanneries being located too close to mills, where they might adversely affect the run of water and also cause pollution.[140] In larger monastic estates, extractive industries such as stone and millstone quarrying, and coal and lead mining, took place.[141] Other industrial activities such as ceramic tile and brick production, glass-making, iron manufacture and working, bell production, and salt-panning are also known to have been undertaken on monastic estates.[142] There is currently little archaeological evidence for these activities being undertaken by religious houses in Ireland, but the placenames of Saltgrange and Irongrange, Saltmills,[143] and the Saltee Islands[144] certainly suggest that these activities took place. Further historical evidence of nunnery estates in Britain shows that their holdings additionally included woodland and its management, clay pits, salt pans, mines, quarries, urban property, markets and fairs, along with various rights.[145]

Property

Many monasteries and nunneries held urban and rural properties as part of their estates. The urban property may have been used as monastic lodgings when on business, and also as a source of rental income. Some also had gardens. In monastic life, gardens were particularly important, both for physical work and plant production but also for contemplation and reflection. The cloister garth, as we have already discussed, could be considered such a garden (see Chapter 8), but outlying monastic estates would also have maintained kitchen and flower gardens, which may have been tended in conjunction with bee-keeping.[146]

Excavation of monastic urban property in Britain has yielded wide-ranging ceramic assemblages, which has been interpreted in this context as evidence for pottery discarded while on journeys.[147] Nunneries in medieval Ireland similarly held urban property. For example, the nuns at Timolin held several messuages, one in the medieval town of Gowran, County Kilkenny.[148] Grace Dieu held a messuage and seven cottages in the town of Lusk, County Dublin; Kilcreevanty held a house, garden and eel weir in Cong, County Mayo and a tenement in Tuam, County Galway;[149] and Molough held one messuage in Clonmel, County Tipperary. St Mary de Hogges had a large portfolio of urban property in Dublin.[150]

This consideration of monastic estates is largely informed by data from Cistercian houses. However, religious house estates might be a better term, as brethren from religious houses who were not monks also managed estates. Augustinian canons have been briefly mentioned in relation to granges, and friars are also worthy of mention. Due to their ethos as mendicants, friaries had relatively smaller landholdings than their monk counterparts, but also have some remains which highlight their holdings and rights. For example, a dairy herd is known to have been kept by the Dominicans at Athenry, County Galway, a fish weir at Meelick, County Galway is likely to have been used by the Franciscans, and dovecotes at Adare, County Limerick (Trinitarian) and Drogheda, County Louth (Dominican) along with many recorded orchards, gardens and woodland show that at least some mendicant houses had landholdings which were probably not dissimilar to smaller monasteries and nunneries.[151]

An important aspect of religious house estates is that they were an intrinsic part of the wider settlement landscape, particularly in those regions under Anglo-Irish influence. These regions are described as 'manorialised' landscapes in which features associated with lordship and symbols of seigneurial power have been identified, such as dovecotes, rabbit warrens, fishponds and deerparks, which together form elite 'landscapes of lordship'.[152] The settlement pattern in the Anglo-Irish-controlled parts of Ireland was in many ways similar to that of England, although a diversity and complexity particular to medieval settlement in Ireland can be identified.[153] Manors were created around masonry and earthwork castles which were employed for defence and administration. Farming was carried out at many of them.[154] Other archaeologically identified settlement types include walled towns, unenclosed villages (settlement clusters, DMVs), rural boroughs, dispersed defended farmsteads such as moated sites, and unenclosed house clusters. In addition, field systems have also been identified in the settlement pattern.[155] All of these features have at one time or another been associated with later medieval nunneries in Ireland. Furthermore, the dissolution surveys of eleven nunneries list various customs due from tenants, which included, for example, days of weeding, gallons of beer from each brewing, hens at Christmas, and days of ploughing – this information is invaluable as these customs are difficult if not impossible to gather from the archaeological evidence alone.[156]

PLACENAMES

Placename evidence is useful in identifying some monastic estate features in Britain, especially when there is a dearth of historical records. For example, rabbit warrens are associated with placenames such as burg, burrow, buries, coning-erth or conygarth.[157] This also proves useful in an Irish context, such as in the case of Snugburrow townland situated near the holdings of the nunnery of Timolin,[158] while the worth of placename evidence in a monastic context in Ireland – which is sometimes discounted – has been recently highlighted.[159]

Other specifically Irish placenames may indicate female religious activity in an area. The word *Calliagh* or *Cailleach* and its many derivatives, originating in the Irish for 'veiled one', has long been accepted as relating to females and particularly nuns or old/wise women.[160] Placenames incorporating these derivatives are commonly – though not exclusively – associated with nunneries, such as Templenagalliaghdoo, Ballynagallagh, Callystown or Calliaghstown. Sometimes this association is obscured through translation, such as Collinstown (Caltragh) or Kellystown. An alternative name for St Catherine's, and one that is still used locally, is *Monasternagalliaghdubh*, or the monastery of the black nuns, remembering the black habit of the Augustinians.[161]

In several instances, townlands or placenames also contain this derivative form, which may not be necessarily close to the nunnery itself. It is suggested that these townland names may embody a memory of being held by a nunnery as part of its wider estate. For example, the village of Ballynacally, which locally is thought of as 'town of the nuns' in County Clare, has no documented historical connection to the nunnery of Killone, but on the basis of its name it might be suggested that such a connection once existed.[162] Similarly, the townland of Ballycally, County Mayo is located to the northwest of Annagh nunnery.[163] There is no recorded historical connection between these places, though Ballycally contains the remains of a dovecote. Without excavation, the precise date of the dovecote cannot be known, but an association with the nunnery can be tentatively suggested. Other examples include Farrangalliagh (land of the nuns)[164] near Ardcarn; Monagalliagh (bog of the nuns)[165] near Clonard; Ballynagalliagh (townland of the nuns) and Rossnagalliagh (wood of the nuns) near Derry;[166] Ballynagalliagh (townland of the nuns) near Armagh;[167] Calliaghstown in County Dublin[168] (town of the nuns, possibly relating to holdings of St Mary de Hogges there); and perhaps even Collierstown, County Meath, the Irish of which is *Baile na gCailleach*.[169] In all these cases, there is little or no documented historical evidence to link the nunneries to these locations.

ST CATHERINE'S ESTATE: A CASE STUDY

St Catherine's in the townland of Old Abbey, County Limerick, arguably the best-preserved nunnery in Ireland, has been used as a case study throughout this book and results of the excavations there have been used to illustrate points in the previous chapters.[170] I now undertake an archaeological consideration of its historically recorded holdings – both temporal and spiritual – along with local placenames, in order to draw in as much evidence as possible. Unfortunately, many of the archaeological monuments in the townlands where land was

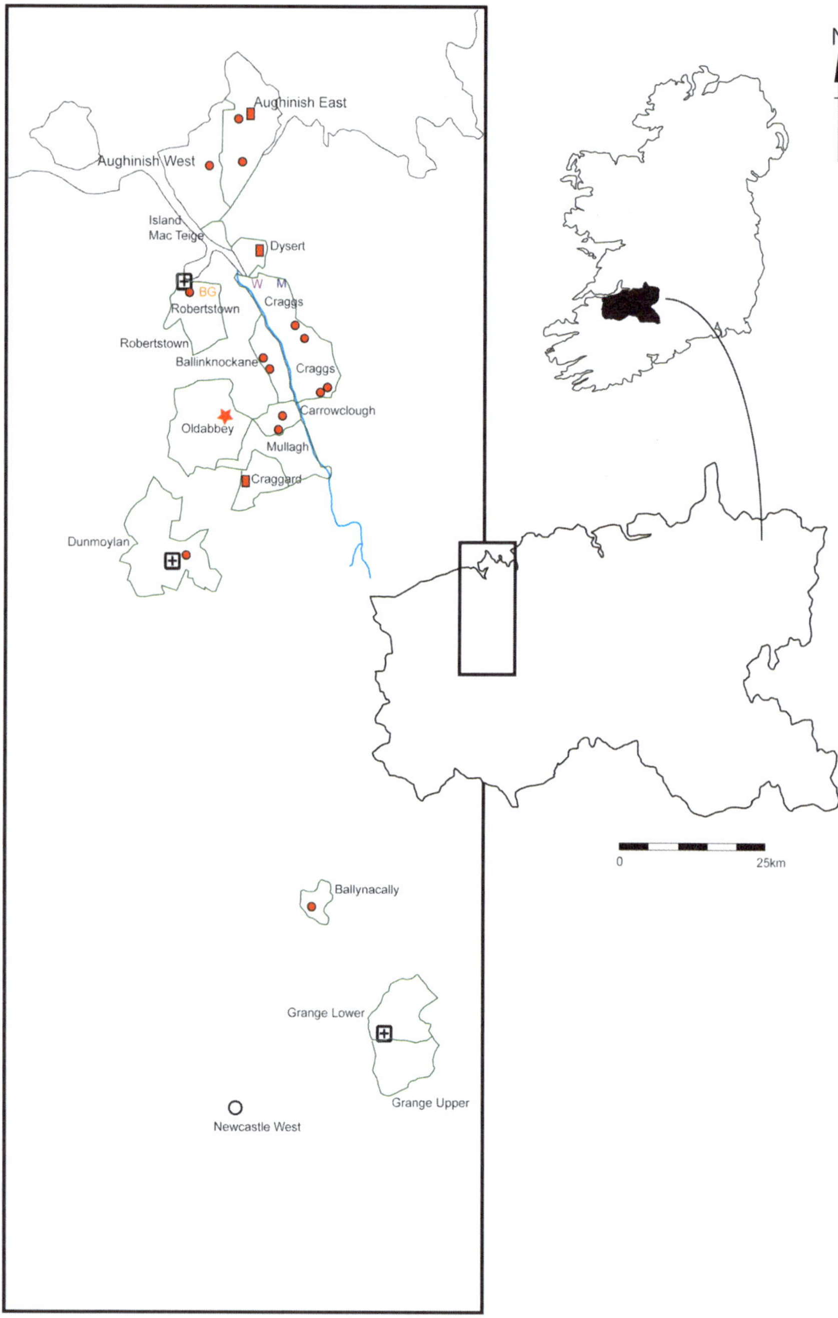

9.11 Locations of the known land holdings of St Catherine's, Co. Limerick. Its known estate holdings cover 12 modern townlands, and contemporary archaeological monuments are indicated: red dot: enclosure (non-ringforts); red rectangle: castle; black cross: church; BG: burial ground; M: metal working site (from excavation); W: well; star: St Catherine's nunnery. Image: Tracy Collins and Frank Coyne.

once held by the nunnery are now no longer upstanding, and only excavation would elucidate their precise nature, extent, and periods of use. Fortunately, Westropp undertook an intensive survey of enclosures in the townlands of west Limerick, which included those associated with St Catherine's, and this information has been relied upon.[171]

The known holdings of St Catherine's have been listed by Wardell,[172] Hall,[173] and most recently by MacCotter.[174] They cover twelve modern townlands, within a 12km radius of the nunnery itself (Figure 9.11). Table 9.1 provides the known details of each holding, its location to townland and the archaeological medieval monuments known from that townland. This list represents what is *now known* of the holdings of St Catherine's, and it is highly probable that it represents just a fraction of its holdings through time.[175]

The nunnery held a quarter of land in each of the townlands of Ballinknockane and Mullagh, one plowland at Carrowclogh and an unspecified amount of land in the townland of Craggard and possibly also in Craggs and Dysert. Some of this land may have been worked by the nunnery directly with employed labourers. It is known from a recorded legal dispute between the nuns and Maurice FitzPhilip of 1306 that the nuns had tenants on their estate lands at that time.[176] St Catherine's was entitled to rent from Aughinish (Island), which infers that St Catherine's may have held lands there, as MacCotter has suggested,[177] or that a benefactor bestowed a rental fee to the nunnery. All these townlands have contemporary archaeological remains, which may have been used either by the nunnery's tenants and labourers or by the gentry who patronised it.

Saint Catherine's also held spiritualities in the form of benefices of the rectories of Dunmoylan, Grange and Robertstown. All three townlands retain archaeological evidence of these churches (Figure 9.12). It is likely that the nuns of St Catherine's had a reciprocal arrangement with these churches and, in return for the benefice, may have supplied priests, textiles or devotional items to the church, as has been recorded at nunneries elsewhere.[178] MacCotter has shown that St Catherine's possessed all the tithes from the parish of Robertstown, which would have increased the nunnery's revenues.[179] In addition, in 1586, St Catherine's is recorded as having possessed a parcel of land containing one quarter called 'Downesahell' situated in the parish of Monasternegellagh, and another parcel of one quarter at Carrowemonasternegelly, 'these two parcels belonging to the said monastery are parcels of the earl's [of Desmond] chargeable land … said quarters are manured and inhabited'.[180] The precise location of Downesahell is unknown. It is possible that Carrowemonasternegelly equates to the townland of Carrowclogh, though this cannot be yet proven.[181]

Table 9.1 Holding and type of holding of St Catherine's, related to townland and contemporary monument

Townland Identification (modern)	*Name as Identified by D. Hall*	*Historical Record of Type of Holding; (T) Temporal Income (S) Spiritual Income*	*Distance from St Catherine's*	*Near Contemporary Archaeological Monuments within Townland. SMR Number and Classification.*	
Aughinish East Aughinish West	Aughinish	Rent 20s (T)	6km	LI010-018	Enclosure (no longer extant)[1]
				LI010-020	Castle – tower house[2]
				LI010-108	Enclosure[3] (no longer extant)
				LI010-114	Church (no longer extant)
				LI010-014	Enclosure (no longer extant)[4]
				LI010-015	Ringfort – rath (no longer extant)
				LI010-016	Ringfort – rath (no longer extant)
Ballin-knockane	Ballin-knockane[5]	Land 1 quarter (T)	2km	LI019-033	Enclosure (site levelled)[6]
				LI019-036	Ringfort – rath (site levelled)[7]
Ballynacally	-	-	9.5km	LI028-139	Designed landscape feature, ?tree ring
Carrow-clogh	Carrow	Land 1 plowland (T)	1km	LI019-035	Enclosure (no longer extant)
				LI019-038	Ringfort – cashel
				LI019-234	Enclosure
Craggard	Crag McTiege Craggard	Land (T) Church 'church toghe of Cragmacteig' including townlands of Craggs and Dysert	1km	LI019-119	Ringfort – rath
				LI019-120	Castle – poss. tower house marked on 1750 map[9] (no longer extant)
				LI019-121	Ringfort – rath
				LI019-122	Ringfort – rath
				LI019-123	Ringfort – rath
				LI019-124	Ringfort – rath
				LI019-128	Ringfort – rath
				LI019-240	Ringfort – rath
Craggs	-	?Land (T)	2km	LI010-078	Ritual site – holy well
				LI010-079	Ringfort – rath
				LI010-080	Ringfort – cashel
				LI010-081	Ringfort – rath
				LI010-082	Ringfort – cashel
				LI010-084	Ringfort – rath
				LI010-087	Enclosure (rectangular, stone)
				LI019-040	Ringfort – rath
				LI019-041	Ringfort – rath
				LI019-042	Ringfort – rath
				LI019-043	Ringfort – rath
				LI019-045	Ringfort – rath
				LI019-046	Enclosure (rectangular, stone)[10]
				LI019-047	Ringfort – rath
				LI019-048	Ringfort – rath
				LI019-049	Enclosure (ovoid, earth and stone)
				LI019-238	Enclosure (sub-circular)
				LI010-145	Metalworking site (early med.)
				LI019-241	Castle – unclassified

1 This enclosure was excavated; see H. Hickey, 'Excavation of an Enclosure on Aughinish Island, Co. Limerick', *North M… Antiquarian Journal*, vol.16, 1973–4, pp. 15–28. 2 The bawn of this castle was excavated by Dr Ann Lynch in 1974. v… excavations.ie/Pages/Details.php?Year=1974&County=Limerick&id=5563. Accessed 15 September 2020. 3 This was o…

le 9.1 *(continued)*

ownland entification modern)	*Name as Identified by D. Hall*	*Historical Record of Type of Holding; (T) Temporal Income (S) Spiritual Income*	*Distance from St Catherine's*	*Near Contemporary Archaeological Monuments within Townland. SMR Number and Classification.*	
nmoylan	Dunmoylan	Rectory (S)	2.5km	LI019-098 LI019-101 LI019-102001 LI019-102002 LI019-103 LI019-108 LI019-243	Ringfort – rath Ringfort – rath Church Enclosure (associated with church) Ringfort – rath Ringfort – rath Castle – unlocated within td
sert	-	?Land? (T)	3.5km	LI010-075 LI010-076 LI010-077	Ringfort – rath Ringfort – rath (not extant) Castle – tower house
ange per and wer	Grange	Rectory (S)	12km	LI036-042 LI036-037 LI036-038 LI036-040001 LI036-040002 LI036-041 LI036-043 LI036-189	Ringfort – rath Bridge Ringfort – rath Church Graveyard Ringfort – rath Ringfort – rath Castle – unlocated within td (lwr)
illagh	Mullagh	Land 1 quarter (T)	1km	LI019-030 LI019-031 LI019-037001	Ringfort – rath Ringfort – rath Ringfort – rath
dabbey	-	Nunnery location	-	LI019-026001 LI019-026003 LI019-026005 LI019-026007 LI019-026009 LI019-026002 LI019-026004 LI019-026006 LI019-026008 LI019-026010 LI019-026011	Settlement deserted – medieval Gateway Structure Burial ground R. h. – Augustinian nuns Enclosure Dovecote Fishpond Cist Anomalous stone group Megalithic structure
berts-vn	Robertstown	Rectory (S) Tithes of parish (S)	3km	LI010-068 LI010-069001 LI010-069002 LI010-070 LI010-071 LI010-144	Ringfort – rath Church Graveyard Ringfort – rath Burial ground Enclosure (not extant)

enclosures excavated by E. Kelly in 1974. www.excavations.ie/Pages/Details.php?Year=1974&County=Limerick&id=5560. essed 15 September 2020. **4** This site was excavated by M. Byrnes www.excavations.ie/Pages/Details.pho?Year= ounty=Limerick&id=2057. Accessed 15 September 2020. **5** Hall identified this as Ballyknockane in the parish of Kilmoylane Croom, Co. Limerick. I suggest it is the townland of Ballinknockane, which lies much closer to St Catherine's. **6** This was levelled during land reclamation in 1993 according to the landowner. www.archaeology.ie. Accessed 15 September . **7** As above. **8** This research suggests that this was likely a medieval enclosure. **9** Westropp, 'On Certain Typical hworks', p. 245. **10** Described as 'nearly levelled late cattle pen' Westropp, 'On Certain Typical Earthworks', p. 32.

9.12 Churches associated with St Catherine's and its holdings of benefices in the form of rectories in Co. Limerick: Grange (top); Dunmoylan (left); Robertstown (right). Image: Frank Coyne.

Unlike the known larger estate of Timolin nunnery, which likely had an out farm or grange,[182] no location associated with St Catherine's presented itself as a suitable candidate for the location of a grange. However, the holdings of St Catherine's are consolidated and all within about 12km of the nunnery itself. In this case, it is likely that its home farm, which was situated to the south of the nunnery complex, and identified by the dovecote and enclosed fields, met all its agricultural needs (see Figure 7.17). Neither are there any clear indications in its wider known holdings that could be considered typical features of a monastic estate as discussed above, such as wayside crosses, barns, animal pounds and folds, mills, fisheries, industrial workings, rabbit warrens or parks.[183] From fieldwork, it is clear that rabbits are now plentiful in the fields around the nunnery and so it is not unreasonable to suggest that rabbits were exploited in the past by the nuns. However, no evidence – archaeological or placename – was identified which would suggest a formal warren, as there was at Timolin (Snugburrow). Similarly, limestone has been quarried in several locations near St Catherine's in the recent past, and several limekilns – including one each in Old Abbey and Mullagh townlands – indicate exploitation of that resource for lime in the early modern period. Limestone was exploited as construction stone in the medieval period and it is reasonable to postulate that it was exploited for lime for various purposes, as smaller industrial operations.

It is important to remember that the holdings discussed are only those that have been recorded in various historical documents. It is likely that the nuns had other entitlements and land that have remained unrecorded. Indeed, it is likely that the nunnery's entitlements may have changed over time, as generations of benefactors and bishops changed.[184] There is one instance in the locality of St Catherine's of a townland name that may recall its use by the nuns. The townland of Ballynacally is located 3km to the northwest of St Catherine's known holding at Grange Lower, and 9.5km south of the nunnery itself and contains one archaeological monument.[185] Based on this placename evidence it is likely that this townland represents just one of the additional holdings of St Catherine's that escaped the notice of the historical record.

The main function of a nunnery estate was to sustain and support the nunnery community, if not to produce a surplus. Could this have been achieved with the holdings listed for St Catherine's? It is now impossible to answer this question, for a number of reasons. First, it is not known if these places represent the entirety of the landholding of the nunnery, and they probably do not. Second, it is not known if they were all held at the same time. Third, sustenance cannot be measured without detailed internal records – such as those examined by Power for English nunneries – of the production values of lands, or of pastoral or arable farming being pursued.[186] Yet despite these limitations, something can be concluded. On at least one occasion in the documents the nuns at St Catherine's were described as impoverished,[187] and their church became parochial sometime in the fifteenth century.[188] This change of status may have been permitted in order to generate some additional income for the nunnery. It seems though that St Catherine's did ultimately succeed as it was still in operation in the 1500s.[189] The over-arching consideration of the sustainability of any religious house was the prudent management over time of all its resources. Even the wealthiest house could become impoverished if not properly managed.[190] Therefore, as St Catherine's sustained itself into the sixteenth century, probably through a variety of means, it must be deemed to have been a successful religious foundation.

Medieval perceptions of St Catherine's: an exploration

In order to try to understand the significance of a nunnery in a wider medieval community it is important to try to perceive it, not in a modern way, but rather through an understanding of the medieval mentalities that founded, sustained and peopled these female monasteries. The medieval world's bounds of reality

9.13 The remains of Shanid Castle, Co. Limerick. Image: Frank Coyne.

included the unseen – a concept that is now all but alien to modern thought.[191] St Catherine's is used as a case study for an exploration of these perceptions.

It was located in the medieval county of Limerick, in the diocese of Limerick within the manor of Loghill (modern Loughill) – the entirety of which was cross (church) land and included the nearby borough of Shanagolden. It has been estimated that at a minimum the nunnery was endowed with Aughinish Island, Old Abbey and the tithes for the parish of Robertstown.[192] St Catherine's also lay within the lordship of Cork/Desmond, and the cantred of Shennede (Shanid), which was one of four that made up the region known as Uí Chonaill (O'Conyl). Shanid is a high point in this landscape, which provides panoramic views of west Limerick, the river Shannon, and beyond into County Clare. Shanid was recorded as early as the 830s when the Vikings were defeated there. It is also likely to have been an óenaig (fair) or assembly site, certainly of Seanad and probably of all Uí Chonaill.[193] The stone castle at Shanid is first referred to in 1298, though is clearly of earlier date and is built on an earlier motte (Figure 9.13). A large ringfort showing evidence of later re-use shares this high ground.[194] It is known that the founder of the nunnery, John FitzThomas,[195] originated at Shanid and he was killed along with his son Maurice at the Battle

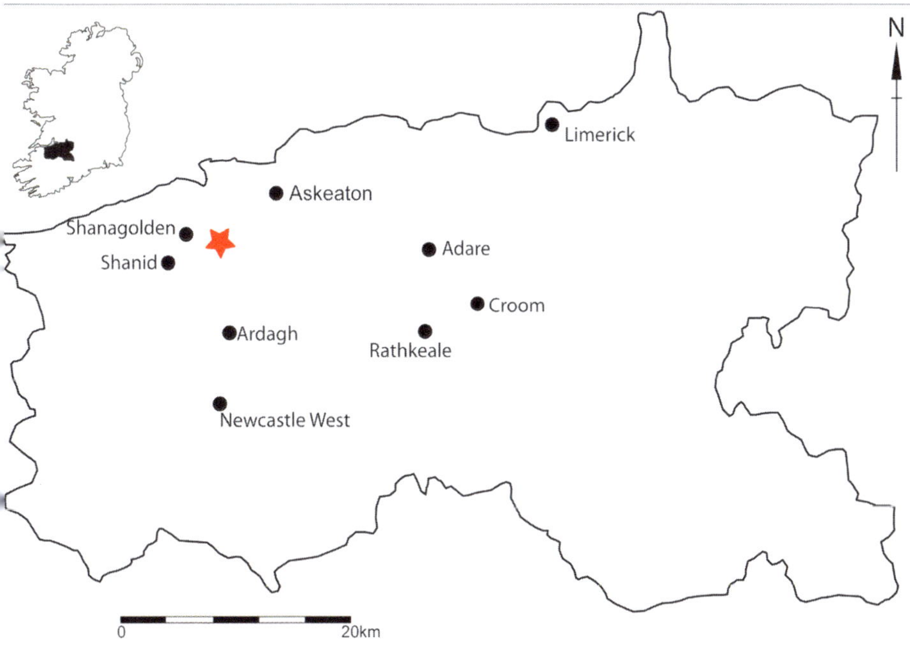

9.14 Map of County Limerick showing St Catherine's (star) in the heartland of its patrons, in relation to contemporary settlements mentioned. Image: Frank Coyne.

of Callan in 1261 by the Gaelic McCarthys. On the basis of this date, the nunnery was in existence prior to this and is thought to have been founded sometime in the 1240s, though its precise foundation date is not recorded.[196] Therefore, St Catherine's nunnery was located in the heartland of its founders, the immediate ancestors of the earls of Desmond, who later continued to be benefactors (Figure 9.14).[197]

St Catherine's location in its medieval landscape

The Anglo-Norman settlement of Limerick occurred in three broad stages; the first, 1175–94, the granting of lands, though with little actual colonisation; the second, 1195–1215, new and re-grants made by King John to about ten recipients; and the final stage, 1216–1321, which saw the consolidation of a manorial system including the granting of fairs.[198] The founder's immediate ancestors were present in Munster from the initial Anglo-Norman invasion and were part of the new order.[199] As the nunnery was founded sometime in the 1240s, it coincided with the final stages of the consolidation of Anglo-Norman settlement in the region.[200] Having said this, it was also the first religious house in the locality,[201] being only predated by the Augustinian canons at Rathkeale founded in 1210 by Gilbert Harvey.[202] Furthermore, as the first religious house in the locality, it could be suggested that the medieval monastic landscape of the region around the nunnery was distinctly female for a time, when female religious represented the monastic way of life to the wider community (see Chapter 7). This particular female monasticism would have been perceived by the ordinary people of the locality, who probably rarely left the vicinity of this part of west Limerick.

The nunnery is situated just 4.5km northeast of the stronghold at Shanid. Now in the townland of Old Abbey, the nunnery is not located on a major river though is serviced by two conjoined fast-flowing streams, which flow from east to west. It is within 1.5km of the larger river Ahacronane, which flows northward into the river Shannon's estuary just 3km away. This river may well have provided food and access to a wider transport network beyond the nunnery.

There are no ancient routeways associated with the nunnery at Old Abbey, and at first it is easy to think that it is in an isolated position.[203] The nunnery's original focus in the thirteenth century, when it was founded, was the founder's castle at Shanid to the southwest. While there are now no direct routes between them, the nunnery's original entrance/gateway was on its southern side, which would have welcomed visitors to the nunnery from this approach. There is now a network of modern small roads and tracks in the vicinity of the nunnery. One in particular traverses northward almost directly to the nunnery's church in Robertstown and the river Shannon. It is suggested that this road may mark the medieval route taken by the nuns when visiting their associated church there and perhaps their possible rental lands further north on Aughinish Island. It would also have facilitated visitors to the nunnery coming from that direction.

The choice of location for the nunnery at Old Abbey within the patron's lands is particularly interesting. St Catherine's is located in the very visible lowlands beneath its founder's castle at Shanid. This is a location which is encircled by its patrons' and episcopal settlements at Rathkeale, Askeaton, Newcastle West, Shanid and Shanagolden (see Figure 9.14).[204] St Catherine's might be considered to be at the very centre of this area and its location was probably well known to the inhabitants of the locality. Indeed, 'all medieval people must have been aware of the presence of houses of religious women and men scattered about the countryside and it would have been almost impossible not to have had feelings about these ubiquitous monastics'.[205] It is likely that St Catherine's was situated in this location as a safe and secure environment for the nuns.

9.15 View of the landscape north eastwards from Shanid Castle over the lowlands of west Limerick to the river Shannon, the locality where St Catherine's is situated. Image: Frank Coyne.

Of greater significance is that the nunnery cannot be seen from the castle at Shanid, in contrast to the much more distant town of Rathkeale and the Shannon estuary which are clearly visible from there (Figure 9.15). Due to the siting of the nunnery in a natural, gently undulating landscape of less than 20m above sea level, it is not visible from the top of the motte on which Shanid Castle sits. Considering the uninterrupted vistas from the castle across this part of Limerick, it can be suggested that the restricted view of the nunnery may have been a conscious decision. This would suggest that St Catherine's was deliberately located in a secluded place in its patron's hinterland. Indeed, it should be noted that despite the impressive remains of the nunnery, it is situated in a natural hollow and, because of this, cannot be seen from any direction until one is within about 100m of the ruins. This physical invisibility, which is quite striking when it is realised, places St Catherine's into other less tangible landscapes, such as those of the mind and of memory.

Why might it be hidden from view? On a most basic level, it can be considered coincidence, but this is not a wholly satisfactory explanation. One of the key tenets of the monastic ideal since its inception is that of withdrawal from society as a method of getting closer to God.[206] This withdrawal from society was further underscored in the later thirteenth century when strict enclosure was enforced by papal decree (see Chapter 3).[207] The physical invisibility of St Catherine's from its patron's castle may be a manifestation of the physical withdrawal of the nunnery and its female community from the secular world, which was literally all around it. Therefore, the location of the nunnery within its patron's lordship could be considered as a symbol of its entire community's sacrifice to God. The transformation of an elite woman into a professed nun made her 'dead to the world'.[208] The nunnery then, as a symbol of the nuns withdrawing from the outside world, might be considered a type of ritual death. In this case, the nunnery would become a memorial – one that was hidden from gaze but was a society-wide mental reminder of the religious community's transition from one world to the other.

It has been suggested that this ritual death embodied negative connotations for female religious. Medieval society also incarcerated the anti-social, criminals, and corpses, that were thought to damage and infect society. In a similar way, it has been contended that medieval society imprisoned religious women, separating them from wider society.[209] Within the church, female religious were considered dangerous to male clerical celibacy: 'canons inhabited a psychological space in which they defined female reality only by a woman's biology, so that they could only see other aspects of femaleness if that bodiliness were negated by virginity'.[210]

Following on from this, viewed with more modern eyes, being invisible has further negative connotations of silencing, ignorance, forgetting and control.[211] Could it be that the patrons of the nunnery realised a social and spiritual requirement for such a foundation, in order to accommodate their female kin, but did not wish to openly acknowledge its existence and thus 'shut them away' as a necessary evil? Furthermore, could the duality of physical invisibility of the nunnery from the patron on the one hand, but his acknowledgement of its existence through benefaction and funding on the other, be a strategic method of control? Admittedly, this standpoint is particularly negative and has its origins in biased contemporary negative criticism, such as visitations and scandals.[212]

This view creates a perception of St Catherine's as obscured from its hinterland of the world 'outside' – a world that was dominated by men, where male agency was active and female agency passive. The religious women of St Catherine's were once part of the wider world as symbolised by the castle at Shanid, an elite existence in a very structured society. The invisibility of the nunnery from that worldly symbol may highlight this withdrawing, placing it in sharp contrast with the more spiritual religious sphere represented by the nunnery itself. Alternatively, the invisibility of the nunnery from the patron's castle may in part have expressed concern about the protection of the female religious community from attack, nestled as it was in the heart of the lordship in west Limerick. The elite social position of the nuns – if indeed they were from the elite (see Chapter 8) – may have added to this perception of separation and seclusion.

Visibility and mobility of later medieval elite women in England was strictly controlled.[213] For such women spatial segregation was the norm in ceremonial settings such as church, feasting, tournaments, pageants and funerals. Furthermore, they were segregated to the more domestic spheres of castle living. They were further protected in places like enclosed medieval gardens through the ideology of enclosure. What is of crucial importance to the understanding of place and space in this discussion is that medieval domestic spaces were not considered inferior to more public spaces. Rather than being considered negatively, seclusion and segregation of elite women was considered in the medieval mentality as a positive, as measures to protect chastity and fidelity, which were essential elements of the patrimony. For example, the king himself, who was considered a sacred body, was also secluded.[214]

This more positive outlook opens up the discussion surrounding public and private spaces. In the medieval period, those distinctions were very different to modern times. For example, the king was considered the government, so wherever *he was* became the political administrative sphere, whether that was a great hall or a bed chamber. Therefore, this lack of distinction between public and private spheres – in modern perceptions – could lead to opportunities for elite women, in that, for example, a queen would have direct access and influence over the king, and thus government.[215]

In a later medieval Irish context, McAuliffe has considered the social and political roles of elite women in tower houses.[216] They used the upper chambers of the castles, and the contemporary historical evidence provides tantalising glimpses of lavish furnishings. On occasion, when husbands were away or indisposed, women constructed their own tower houses, in order to protect family land.[217] While McAuliffe did not explicitly state that these elite women were secluded, it is inferred from many of the descriptions that they were separated, in a similar way to elite English women, as discussed by Gilchrist and others.[218]

Therefore, in medieval English feudal elite society, and from the more limited evidence from Ireland, separation and seclusion was a mark of high prestige. Furthermore, 'seclusion was used in addition to denote the special status of monks and nuns, the elect, whose prayers were closer to God'.[219] Thus the view that seclusion was an entirely negative connotation, illustrating female religious suppression by a male elite, cannot be totally sustained. The seclusion of St Catherine's can be viewed in a positive sense, adding to its prestige in the locality. These women, who took religious vows, were thus accommodated in a secluded, protective environment with impressive buildings, at the expense of their patron and benefactors – just as their secular female counterparts were. As such, perhaps like any institution, a nunnery may have had both negative and positive connotations for its religious community and the wider community of its hinterland. Indeed, these perceptions likely varied between individuals and changed over time.

Moreover, it can be suggested that religious houses were considered a further elite, the 'spiritual athletes' of a wider community.[220] Nuns were not considered second-class monastics but equivalent to a monk. Nunneries were the wider community's source of charity, prayers and comfort, insurance policies to the next life, as well as being landlords, landholders, patrons, clients, protectors and on occasion judges. Johnson suggested, in her study of nunneries of northern France at least, that medieval people explicitly trusted the intercession of religious women. She has illustrated this respect and trust through naming customs of various regions, where the names of important abbesses such as Heloise and Agnes were used and were very common in the wider community.[221]

A landscape palimpsest

St Catherine's was not established in an 'empty' landscape and the archaeological monuments show that this part of west Limerick was in use in the prehistoric and early medieval periods.[222] There is a Neolithic megalithic structure immediately to the southeast of St Catherine's and a possible Bronze Age standing stone to the north. Finds of prehistoric burials and objects were made in the nineteenth century immediately to the northwest of the nunnery.[223] It is interesting to postulate whether the community of nuns were cognisant of this earlier use of the landscape. The discovery of earlier artefacts and monuments on or near later medieval sites is usually deemed coincidental, as due to the preponderance of prehistoric monuments it is common to find a religious house within some range of a prehistoric monument in Ireland. However, at many later prehistoric and early medieval ecclesiastical and secular sites it has been suggested that the deposition or use of earlier monuments and artefacts was a deliberate act of social memory and ownership.[224]

There are early medieval examples of this in Ireland. For example, at Armagh there was a distinct kink in the outermost enclosure where it avoided

– so as not to destroy or enclose – a prehistoric stone circle.[225] The large enclosing element around Faughart has been interpreted as a prehistoric hilltop enclosure or smaller hillfort, which suggests continuity and an appropriation of an important prehistoric place for female religious use in the early medieval period.[226] The re-use of religious places in continental Europe is well-attested throughout the early and later medieval period in re-purposing, and also the deliberate incorporation of earlier fabric as spolia in ecclesiastical structures.[227] The use of spolia for practical and more symbolic uses in church construction is a phenomenon also identified in early medieval Ireland, which has been interpreted as an act of creating legacy and memory.[228] Prehistoric finds at early medieval crannógs 'seem to mark out and create a long-term commitment to the landscape'.[229]

In a later medieval context, both Augustinian canons and Cistercian monks purposefully re-used earlier sites for their foundations, as did several nunneries (see Chapter 2). This is interpreted as a deliberate act for the religious houses to gain historical currency and rootedness in a particular area.[230] The choice of location for St Catherine's near several prehistoric monuments and adjacent to probable prehistoric burials – revealed in the nineteenth century – suggests that it was a deliberate act of social memory. Again, this re-use can be perceived in negative or positive ways. The re-use of pagan monuments by Christians could be viewed as a source of kudos, a method of controlling the power of the monuments, and could be harnessed to protect a Christian site. Alternatively, pagan monuments in the past have also been considered dangerous and to be avoided,[231] and the stone circle avoided by the enclosures around Armagh could also be perceived in this way.[232] However, the proximity of pagan monuments to Christian settlements of any period might also reflect the ascetic nature of some of those foundations – putting themselves in danger and open to temptation in order to test their faith, as Christ did in the desert. The past is important as it defines the self in the present.[233] Moreover, the past is frequently represented by things, objects or monuments: 'objects anchor time'.[234] Perhaps it was in this sense that older monuments around the nunnery of St Catherine's might have been perceived by its community.

Multiple uses, and use through time of the landscape around St Catherine's, are still in evidence. Within a 2km radius of the nunnery itself there are no fewer than forty-four recorded enclosures, highlighting the dispersed settlement of the locality: thirty-six ringforts, three cashels, one moated site and four amorphous enclosures (Figure 9.16). The sites of two castles – now no longer visible – are within 2km of the nunnery. Six of the enclosures, including the moated site, are located within the townland of Oldabbey. While these

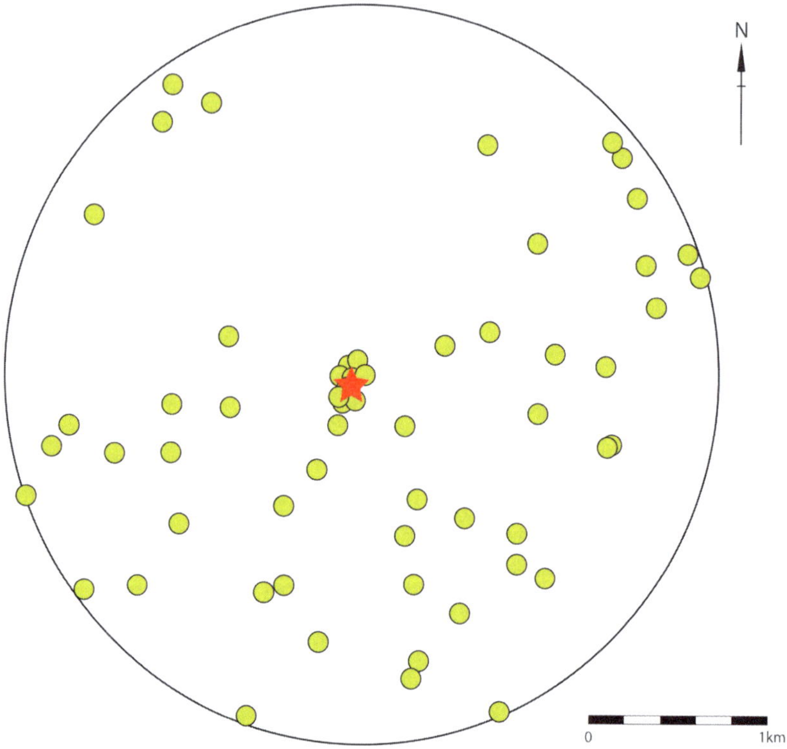

9.16 Distribution of recorded archaeological monuments within a 2km radius of St Catherine's, Co. Limerick, generated from Archaeological Survey of Ireland data. Image: Frank Coyne.

monuments were certainly not all contemporary with each other, or with the nunnery, it is reasonable to suggest that at least some, such as the moated site, or the castles, were in use at the same time.

Furthermore, while the period of primary occupation for ringforts/cashels is clearly the early medieval period, the later re-use of some cannot be ruled out as later medieval native enclosed settlement,[235] and so it is possible that some of these monuments were used in some form by the tenants of the nunnery. Westropp recorded a deserted settlement to the northwest of St Catherine's which now has a very low register, though is visible on aerial photography. It comprised two stone forts, an old road, along with several stretches of curving earthworks and enclosures, which he described as 'a really curious set of enclosures … strange curved enclosures of doubtful age and at least twice modified' (Figure 9.17).[236] If one accepts the later medieval use/re-use of some cashels, then it is possible that tenants or servants of St Catherine's may have lived in this settlement adjacent to the nunnery.

9.17 The topography of St Catherine's, Co. Limerick (nunnery complex in red), showing low register earthworks in the vicinity of the nunnery likely to represent contemporary settlement. Image: Frank Coyne.

Attachment to 'homeland'

While St Catherine's could not be seen from Shanid, it is reasonable to suggest that its community remained in the minds of the patrons and inhabitants of the locality as part of its social landscape. It is supposed that some of the patrons' female family members were nuns of the religious community. The nunnery would perform social functions, such as almsgiving, caring for the sick, and education within its own local community. The nuns, while enclosed in the nunnery, would also probably still know the region quite well, having perhaps grown up locally. They maintained a mental map of their locality. Their landscape would be learned from an early age, through processes of way-finding, and as adults they would be familiar with the routes, waterways and the resources within the immediate territory.[237] It is thus reasonable to suggest that the nuns would have held an attachment to their homeland and a rootedness which is based on being a native of a locality: 'attachment to homeland is a common human emotion … the more ties there are, the stronger the emotional bond'.[238]

Therefore, it is likely that the nuns would be familiar with landmarks, both natural and artificial, such as earlier archaeological monuments. Although they may not have recognised them for what they are, they may well have had their own society's interpretations of their original function, such as mythological associations and folklore. Natural landscape signage might include large boulders, bends in rivers, or large trees. Familiarity with the landmarks of a homeland enhanced a person's sense of identity, encouraging awareness, loyalty, familiarity and ease. It also provided a memory of sounds, smells, communal activities and homely pleasures that accumulated over time.[239] These together produced the mental map which could be retained by the women upon entering the nunnery and perhaps used, in the same way as other enclosed religious undertook mental virtual pilgrimages within the confines of their monasteries through the use of maps, texts and drawings.[240]

It can be further postulated that this experience would be a very different one from other female members of a nun's family, in that, if they married, they would be required to move to their husband's locality. Renalda O'Brien is one such example, who later returned to her own locality to become an abbess and be buried with her own kin at Ennis Friary, County Clare.[241] These marriages were usually strategic to form or strengthen family alliances, and in some circumstances might not be the wish of the woman concerned.[242] When perceived in this way a nun had an opportunity to remain within the circumscribed experience of her childhood, and, in some respects, freer from direct male control. Therefore, married siblings and lower-class women of the locality might have envied the secluded life within the nunnery, although there is little historical evidence to prove that this was the case. Some of the scandalous accounts of certain nunneries and their communities might be considered from this perspective – as expressions of envy and jealousy – and were meant to cause rancour and grief to the secluded and privileged women within the nunnery walls.[243]

Other social aspects of the medieval world around the nunnery would be learned and participated in, prior to entering the community of nuns. Relationships between families, individuals, men and women would be known over time and through generations. Information and stories would be passed through families and down the generations to form a social landscape. For example, Elicia Butler, abbess of Kilculliheen, was called in 1501 to give evidence at a hearing to Oliver Cantwell, bishop of Ossory. She testified that she had been present at the wedding of Sir James Butler and Sadhbh Kavanagh some thirty-three years earlier and that their son Piers Butler had been born subsequent to this marriage.[244] Indeed, St Catherine's itself must also have formed part of this social landscape for women in the locality after the first few generations of its existence. It is also in this sense that the landscape in which St Catherine's was set was not empty – its nuns would be entwined in the wider social landscape beyond the nunnery walls.

Neighbours in the locality

What was the relationship (if any) between St Catherine's and the other contemporary settlement forms in its locality? The medieval town of Shanagolden lay just 2.5km to the west. This town was never walled but was a thriving unenclosed settlement, described as an episcopal manor in the later medieval period.[245] Like the relationships noted between villages and nunneries in England,[246] it is likely that Shanagolden interacted with the nunnery, having a symbiotic relationship on a number of levels, through trade, employment, and some pastoral services.

The analysis of nunneries in relation to towns, settlement clusters and other contemporary settlement features such as castles, moated sites and other enclosures suggests that physical isolation from others was not of primary concern to most nunneries in medieval Ireland (see Chapter 4).[247] However, their seclusion and perceived separation may have been an important symbolic consideration. It is concluded that nunneries were embedded in both the physical landscape and the social landscapes of later medieval Ireland. They were an intrinsic part of the diversity of religious life.[248] Indeed, it has been suggested that nuns were due a greater honour than their monk counterparts for entering religious life as 'nuns inspired an inflated esteem because they were believed to be overcoming greater natural odds than were their male counterparts'.[249]

St Catherine's was situated within an area flanked by important medieval urban settlements, and each, at different points in time, were strongholds for its patrons, the earls of Desmond (see Figure 9.14).[250] Askeaton, which may have been walled and has a large castle, lay 6km to the northeast.[251] Rathkeale, which may also have been walled, lay 9km to the southeast.[252] Newcastle West, which was unlikely to have been walled, has a large impressive castle, 13km to the south.[253] The smaller medieval unenclosed settlement of Ardagh lay between St Catherine's and Newcastle West and is 8.5km distant. It is also interesting that St Catherine's known holdings are all situated within the area delimited by these settlements. The most important walled town in the wider region, excepting Limerick some 30km to the northeast, was Adare, situated 12km to the east.[254] Although there is no historical evidence extant, on the basis of proximity and the fact that the urban centres and the nunnery were protected by the same patrons, it is reasonable to think that some interaction, even if not daily, occurred between them. It could also be suggested that the nuns were familiar with these places, especially if they themselves had grown up in the area and were members of the extended gentry families of the region, which they were likely to be, on the basis of historical evidence from other nunneries in medieval Ireland.[255]

Monastic landscapes

St Catherine's is the only known later medieval nunnery in the region, the closest nunnery being St Peter's Cell in the medieval town of Limerick. There is no historical evidence of any interactions between St Catherine's and other nunneries. The fact that it was of the Augustinian Order – and not of Arroasian observance – suggests it was an independent religious house since its foundation, and was never subject to a mother house. There is no historical evidence for the interaction of the female religious community of St Catherine's with any of the male religious houses in the region either. The bishop of Limerick appears to have had authority over the nunnery since its foundation, though his influence is rarely noted in the historical evidence. The see of Limerick owned the land on which St Catherine's was built, and was paid a yearly rent by the patron. The prioress – as she was termed in the historical account – appointed her own priest in the fifteenth century, though arrangements for the celebration of the sacraments and mass are unknown before this date.[256]

There were just three male religious houses in the wider region at the time of the foundation of St Catherine's: Canon Island, County Clare, established in 1180; Rathkeale, founded in 1210, which were both Augustinian foundations; and the Trinitarian monastery established at Adare in 1226. Canon Island is situated in the Shannon estuary, 12km north of the nunnery.[257] The Augustinian house at Rathkeale is just outside the medieval town, some 10km distant of St Catherine's (Figure 9.18).[258] The monastery at Canon Island was founded by the O'Briens – the same patrons who had founded the nunneries of St Peter's Cell in 1171 and Killone in 1189 – and so it is unlikely but not impossible that it had formal contact with a female religious house of their Anglo-Irish neighbours. Therefore, Rathkeale Priory was the closest, and already established by Gilbert Harvey in 1210, when St Catherine's itself was founded in the 1240s. Rathkeale may have been colonised from the monastery at Rattoo, a place also in the Desmond lands of north Kerry.[259] The canons at Rathkeale may have had some interaction with the nunnery of St Catherine's,

9.18 Male religious houses in the locality of St Catherine's (clockwise from top left): Franciscan friary, Askeaton, founded 1400; Augustinian friary, Adare, 1316; Franciscan friary, Adare, 1464; Augustinian priory, Rathkeale, 1210. Image of Adare and Rathkeale, Frank Coyne; aerial views of Askeaton and Adare © National Monuments Service, Department of Culture, Heritage and the Gaeltacht.

though this must remain speculation, and both houses were granted together to Sir Henry Wallop at the dissolution.[260]

The remaining male religious houses of the region were established after St Catherine's: the Augustinian Friars at Adare in 1316; the Franciscans at Askeaton in 1400, and at Adare in 1464 (Figure 9.18).[261] The architecture of all these religious houses has been considered and evaluated for any possible associations and links with St Catherine's. No distinctive architectural traits emerged to show links between any of the monasteries, apart from the expected general trends and fashions in architecture during their use. However, despite the lack of distinctive traits, it can be speculated that interactions occurred between St Catherine's and other religious houses. Unfortunately, these types of everyday relationships and interactions are rarely manifested in the historical or archaeological records and it is likely that these mundane events were never recorded. For example, perhaps the same group of masons was used in the region, though a detailed study and comparison of the dressed stone would be needed to come to any firm conclusions.[262]

The monastic rules and ideas set down about the distance from male houses to female houses, which was about 30km, in the case of St Catherine's at least were not applied in practice (see Chapter 4). The contemporary male houses at Rathkeale, Canon Island, and the Trinitarians at Adare were situated 10.6km, 12.3km and 20.5km distant from the nunnery, respectively. The general proximity of an Augustinian male religious house at Rathkeale may have encouraged the nuns at St Catherine's to adopt the Augustinian rule.[263] It is interesting to note that St Catherine's was already up and running when the other religious houses in the locality were founded: Augustinian friars at Adare, Franciscan friars at Askeaton, and later at Adare. The Franciscans at Askeaton seem to be very close in proximity to the nunnery. Both shared a patron, and this common link may have overridden any relative 'proximity anxiety' issues.

In addition to the patronal bonds, the nunnery community would have developed important relationships with lay individuals and communities through their continued management of their holdings and estates. This created a social landscape that had to be negotiated through various obligations of the nuns to their benefactors, such as hospitality and prayer; to their tenants, in their roles as landlord and rent collector; and to their neighbours, through rights of way and various entitlements, almsgiving, education, some pastoral care and church services.[264] Indeed these obligations were reciprocated, with all these sections of society also having social responsibilities to the nunnery. It was through these negotiations and interactions that social networks and landscapes were created and transformed.

CHAPTER 10

Conclusions

FINDINGS

In this book I have taken a somewhat traditional approach in setting out the empirical archaeological evidence of female monasticism in a straightforward way. This approach is important for archaeological enquiry, especially when this information has not been archaeologically catalogued previously in Ireland. This methodology, however, was never intended as an end in itself, and it has provided the foundation for a more theoretical approach to the material. We can now return to the five questions posed at the outset.

The first question was related to the most pertinent theoretical approach for the archaeological study of medieval female monasticism. It has been demonstrated that an engendered theoretical approach is a particularly useful way of engaging with the archaeological evidence of female monasticism. This is due primarily to that approach's novel way of asking new questions of the evidence, and of posing existing questions in new ways. The basic premise of an engendered approach, as demonstrated most successfully by Roberta Gilchrist and applied here, is that female monasticism is not deviant to a monastic standard that is male. Archaeologists have previously misunderstood female monasticism by attempting to interpret it within the context of the wide spectrum of medieval male monasticism.[1] As has been explained, the study of male religious houses, and in particular male monastic houses of the Cistercian order, has become the template with which all other forms of monasticism has been compared.

When these other forms of monasticism (in its widest sense) such as friars, canons or female religious are compared to what is considered typical or mainstream medieval monasticism, it is frequently concluded that these other forms somehow deviate from this perceived standard and are therefore somehow inferior. This is not the case: they were different in ethos and purpose and this difference should be acknowledged and celebrated in both the archaeological and historical records. Indeed, female monasticism should be regarded as innovative in its fluid approaches to following that way of life. Researchers in these fields are now looking to these different forms of monasticism and teasing out sometimes key differences between, and indeed within, the various religious and monastic orders, so much so that the term 'medieval monasticisms' is gaining currency.[2] It is suggested that female religious, and indeed male religious orders such as the Augustinians – which should really be considered an umbrella term for several specific and nuanced medieval constitutions, such as Arroasian, Premonstratensian and Victorine[3] – have only been recently studied to date in Ireland precisely because they do not neatly fit into the conventions of older scholarship, formed over years of predominantly Cistercian studies.[4]

The second question posed related to the nature of the archaeological evidence. The dearth of excavated material in Ireland was partly tackled in the archaeological excavations carried out at the nunnery of St Catherine's, but much more archaeological excavation is needed.[5] It is especially true to say that the archaeological evidence of female monasticism in medieval Ireland does not fit neatly into the categories of contemporary male religious houses – but nor should it be expected to. There is no singular architecture or archaeology of female monasticism in Ireland, or indeed elsewhere. Rather, it has used the 'vocabulary' of early ecclesiastical and later religious house architecture and archaeology, which can be summed up in a single word: diversity. The archaeological evidence relating to female monasticism of the early medieval period is important and interesting, but is currently meagre, and so has been included primarily as a backdrop to the later medieval period. However, despite the current paucity of clear archaeological evidence, diversity is also seen in this earlier period, spanning a spectrum of sites. Unfortunately, very few of these sites have been archaeologically investigated and the sites have been categorised primarily on the basis of hagiographical and historical evidence rather than the archaeological record.

Three broad categories of sites relating to early medieval female religious have been identified, which is based on the currently known status of the sites in question: the major centres such as Ballyvourney, Clonbroney, Cloonburren, and Kildare; other lesser sites such as Aghavea, Cullen, and Kilkeary; and finally, those sites which clearly formed satellites to large ecclesiastical centres such as Armagh, Clonmacnoise, Glendalough, and Lemanaghan. It is acknowledged that many of the sites in the 'lesser' category may have held prominent positions regionally or locally, as recent studies of Faughart,[6] and Clenor,[7] for example, have shown. Therefore, the categories suggested here are out of necessity very broad, and it is envisaged that as more archaeological evidence becomes available, they will become more defined. But if a 'household virginity' was indeed the norm for female religious in much of this period –

that is, women living as vowesses singly at home or in small communities – it may prove difficult to ever clearly identify these in the archaeological record.

About one fifth of sites relating to early female religious subsequently became nunneries. Nunneries also re-used early male ecclesiastical sites. Whether this re-use represents a continuity of use over the period of church reform in the twelfth century, or re-occupation of sites previously abandoned, is perhaps a moot point, and it is likely that both scenarios occurred. Regardless of the mechanics of re-use, the fact that older sites were chosen as nunnery locations is important and not mere coincidence. It shows, as has been identified elsewhere, in Wales for example,[8] that continuity – or the impression of continuity – of religious use was of significance to the nunnery community and perhaps their patrons.

A total of sixty-five later medieval nunneries were considered, and it is estimated that a maximum of about twenty or so would have been in use at any one time. The majority of these were founded throughout the twelfth century, Ireland's period of church and monastic reform. Nunneries were founded in the subsequent centuries, from the thirteenth through to the sixteenth, but numbers were fewer. This perceived decline should not be considered as a fall off in nunnery patronage, rather that many of the earlier foundations continued to exist and filled demand in later times. Occasionally nunneries moved location, particularly when they were initially founded as co-located houses, described by some as 'monastic experiments'. Early nunnery patrons were first found among the Gaelic rulers of Irish kingdoms, and later by Anglo-Norman and Anglo-Irish settlers. In some cases, nunneries which had a Gaelic founder were subsequently supported by Anglo-Irish benefactors, due to a consequence of geography, and in the case of St Mary de Hogges in Dublin it was partially supported by the crown.

From the historical evidence it can be concluded that patrons rarely supported more than a single nunnery – the Ó Conchobhair (O'Conors) and Diarmait Mac Murchada (MacMurrough) were notable exceptions – but in addition may have patronised male religious houses and other religious institutions in their 'portfolios of patronage'. Female founders of nunneries were relatively rare in medieval Ireland, with only three clearly identified. It is possible that women's impetus and agency in the foundation of nunneries may have been masked in the record by those of their male relations: fathers, husbands, brothers or sons. The motives for nunnery foundation appear to have been out of family interest, and were of local or regional importance.

Diversity is key to understanding the archaeology and architecture of later female monasticism in medieval Ireland. Variation in nunnery plans in England is considered a defining feature of later female monasticism there;

however, this variation usually occurred within the context of the claustral plan, as eventually most nunneries there did develop a cloister. In medieval Ireland, notwithstanding the lack of above-ground remains, this study shows that typically claustrally arranged nunneries were not the norm and a range of layouts was adopted and persisted over the course of the period. No standardisation of plan was identified in nunneries in Ireland, either on a temporal or regional basis or along filial lines. This is similar to medieval England where it has been interpreted as indicating a lack of centralised nunnery planning.[9] On the basis of historical and archaeological evidence it is postulated that perhaps only ten or twelve nunneries ever exhibited a proper claustral plan in Ireland. Only three are now extant and all exhibit a variety of form: Killone, with a cloister to the south of its church; Molough, with a northern cloister; and, most unusually, St Catherine's, with a cloister at the west end of a projecting church. Therefore, only Molough's northern cloister indicates the symbolism of the cult of the Virgin Mary clearly identified by Gilchrist in English medieval nunneries.[10]

This variety of layout is similar to that found in Germany by Mohn, where a large proportion of nunneries there used what has been termed 'open systems'. The use of such open systems on the continent has been explained mainly through the use of existing churches, sometimes parochial, and on occasion secular structures for the nunnery community. In this study I have not found evidence for the use of earlier churches in later medieval Ireland, although earlier fabric has, on occasion, been incorporated into nunnery churches. There is one possible example of a secular structure being used at a nunnery – a chamber-tower (hall house) at St Catherine's.[11] As already stated, no correlation was found between nunnery layout and location in either Gaelic or Anglo-Irish regions; claustral planning and more fluid arrangements are known in both areas, over time. There may have been a purely practical reason for this – such as financial constraints – or it may have been a more cultural reason: that religious women in medieval Ireland were embedded in the community structure, perhaps slightly more so than elsewhere. In any case, the conclusion has been reached that a claustral plan was not considered essential for the majority of nunnery communities in later medieval Ireland.

Moreover, spaces which are considered important in other religious houses, such as chapter houses, do not seem to have been a necessary requirement for nunneries either, as only one – a very tentative example at Killone – is known from the archaeological evidence and only one, at St Mary de Hogges, is mentioned in the historical evidence.[12] Having said this, chapter houses have been identified at medieval English nunneries, though none projected beyond the eastern range and were rarely as elaborate as their male counterparts. Therefore, nunneries in medieval Ireland may have used chapter houses that were not architecturally distinctive and which have left no discernible archaeological traces. This is similar to what has been found in many nunneries in Germany.[13] Sacristies are similarly rare in an Irish nunnery context and only two possibilities can be noted in the archaeological evidence, at Molough and St Catherine's, though the interpretation in each case is problematic. In light of the poor material remains of nunnery sacristies in medieval Ireland, there is no evidence of any distinctive male symbolism – symbolism which has been clearly identified in the nunnery sacristies of medieval England.[14]

Despite the fluid arrangements of nunnery layout mentioned, the church was maintained as a constant in the nunnery complex. The archaeological evidence shows that nunnery churches in later medieval Ireland were aisle-less parallelograms, without transepts or structural internal divisions of stone, and this is very similar to the internal arrangements of the majority of medieval nunnery churches in England. There is little evidence for internal differentiation in nunnery churches in Ireland – such as stone walls – though it is suggested that it did occur through the use of textile and timber screens. The use of internal space within nunnery churches in Ireland closely follows arrangements found in England and the continent and evidence has been revealed to suggest that nuns used both the east and west ends of their churches in different periods, sharing the sacred space with clergy and, when parochial, also with the laity. The internal space was probably divided laterally with a north–south division in Irish nunneries whose churches were subdivided, as no evidence was found for the use of parallel aisles in any part of the church to separate the nuns from either canons or the laity, as occurred, for example, in churches of the double house order the Gilbertines in England (see Figure 4.5).[15]

The use of west end galleries in nunnery churches is a feature common in nunnery churches in Germany, but no such evidence was found in nunnery churches in Ireland. Rather, where the west end was utilised by the nuns, the ground floor seems to have been used, as seen in some nunnery churches in France. On the basis of the extant evidence of nunnery churches in medieval Ireland it can be concluded that they had more in common with the architectural traditions of medieval parish churches than of male monastic churches. This may be because nunneries were firmly embedded within their regional and local religious contexts, and further from the national and international male monastic sphere. Currently, the evidence for artefacts and material culture associated with female monasticism in Ireland is particularly sparse, and this is in the main due to the dearth of archaeological investigation. I have made use of the richer material culture from abroad and from the post-medieval period in Ireland to supplement the Irish medieval evidence and estimate what items nuns in medieval Ireland used in their nunneries, and indeed what they themselves had the capacity to create.

The identification of an architectural diversity and fluidity of form in the physical layout of nunneries has placed a greater emphasis on the nature of ritual and performance, 'space as practised place'. It can be supposed that nunnery communities usually followed the divine office as all religious houses did.[16] The celebration of the divine office, mass, feast days and the office of the dead punctuated the daily lives of nuns and created a daily and seasonal rhythm through regular performance. A claustral plan was clearly not essential in the creation of this rhythm. Any place where the divine office was celebrated could become, through repetition and performance, imbued with a sacred quality, which could accommodate and facilitate the nuns' vocations as brides of Christ.

Enclosure, which was expressed more symbolically than materially in later medieval Ireland, facilitated this quality of monastic space within the nunnery complex, and was crucial to the nuns' identities. While enclosure of medieval female religious is widely considered to have been a severe restriction imposed by a misogynistic male church hierarchy, contemporary medieval nuns seemed either never to have complained, or those complaints went undocumented. Therefore, it must be considered that, while it may have adversely affected the nunnery as an economic entity somewhat, religious enclosure may often have been perceived as a positive influence in the lives of individual nuns and the community itself, helping to forge their spiritual identities.

This follows onto the third question, which asked about the identity of female religious. It was quickly realised that the female religious of medieval Ireland did not have a monolithic static identity; rather they held multiple identities in medieval society.[17] My main focus in this book has been the later medieval period, but the conclusions reached in relation to identity could be broadly applied to the female religious of the early medieval period also. First, nuns were brides of Christ and were considered such in society, being set apart in their nunneries. As already highlighted, this seclusion should not be considered wholly negatively, as medieval seclusion manifested prestige: nuns formed a respected part of medieval life and their continued patronage and benefaction by wider society is testament to this. Second, and perhaps no less important, nuns were daughters, sisters, aunts, and in some cases mothers, who were thus interwoven into the fabric of medieval society itself.

Nuns could be office-holders within their respective nunneries,[18] and land owners, estate mangers and tenant lords through the more corporate identity of the nunnery and its temporal holdings. Where a nunnery was the location of the local parish church, it was enmeshed in parish pastoral care, providing church services, the sacraments of baptism and last rites, as well as a place for burial and remembrance. In several cases, these were in addition to services provided to the local population such as almsgiving and education. These relationships were reciprocal, the nunneries in return getting support from the local population through patronage and benefaction, tenants working on the land, trade, along with spiritual rights and benefices. The evidence shows that nunneries were an important part of the fabric of medieval society and particularly part of their local communities.

In one particular aspect of female monasticism, history and archaeology appear to diverge. It is generally accepted that it was elite females of the later medieval period who became nuns. For medieval England, this meant female members of the aristocracy and nobility, and for medieval Ireland female members of more local elites and kingdoms. This perception is based on valid evidence: for instance, nuns were commonly related to the nunnery's wealthy patrons and benefactors; or that a payment was required upon entry to a nunnery that only the upper strata of society would be able to afford.[19] Keeping concluded that the female human remains she studied from nunneries came from a privileged social class.[20] When the female human remains from St Catherine's and Graney in Ireland were considered, however, these were women whose lives were not luxurious, as their bones exhibited evidence of periods of physiological stress along with evidence that they engaged in physical labour in their youth. Due to the small sample size, it is possible that these women were not professed nuns and represent other non-elite medieval women. But this evidence does open the possibility that nuns may have also come from other strata in medieval society, a fact already highlighted by some important historical case study research in England.[21] In the case of medieval Ireland, archaeology is best placed to shed further light on this issue, which has yet to be satisfactorily answered.[22] More definitively, the archaeological evidence from St Catherine's did show that some of the females buried there were related.

A fourth research question set out to consider the wider situation of nunneries in the landscape of medieval Ireland and their possible impacts. Nunneries in medieval England were in the majority of cases deliberately isolated. In contrast, it has been demonstrated that nunneries in medieval Ireland were not isolated.[23] Indeed, most were closely associated with walled towns and larger unenclosed settlements. Even two that could be considered isolated – Inishmaine and Carricknahorna – have contemporary settlement within 5kms.

Therefore, I suggest that nunneries in later medieval Ireland were secluded by design, as an indication of prestige rather than seeking true isolation. While nunneries' situation in the landscape in medieval Ireland has been interpreted as a requirement for protection, which in part is probably true, it is equally valid to suggest that the location of nunneries is an indication that they were intertwined in the fabric of medieval society at a very local level.

A second important aspect of the medieval monastic landscape is that of nunnery estates. All nunneries held temporalities and spiritualities in the form of real estate, rights and benefices, as a means of continued support. In the past, it was thought that nunnery estates were dispersed and as a result uneconomic, as well as being mismanaged. When all of the evidence is considered, this view cannot be sustained. While nunneries generally did possess smaller estates than their male counterparts, their estates do compare favourably with smaller male religious houses and, in some cases, such as Timolin, were valued higher than most of the other religious houses in County Kildare at the dissolution.[24] Nunnery estates, rather than being non-consolidated, were either largely consolidated into a single block, such as St Catherine's, or consolidated into a number of blocks, as at Timolin. The consolidation of an estate was dependent on its uses. In many cases, for instance, if land was rented out to a number of tenants, consolidation was not an important consideration. This pattern of holdings shows that they were likely endowed by their local community, by the patron or benefactor, and it can be suggested that the occasional outlying holdings, which were usually spiritual benefices, represent a particular benefactor, who, for reasons that are now lost, chose to endow a nunnery.

FUTURE DIRECTIONS

An underlying principle of any scholarly endeavour is that it has the potential to be inherently limitless, as each question opens the possibility of many new ones. This has certainly been the case, and each of the themes considered has the potential to lead to new inquiries. Other published strategies also have an influence on future research directions.[25] With all of this in mind, there are several future avenues of inquiry that could yield important results. First, a particular limitation is the lack of archaeological investigation and evidence of female monasticism. There have been very few archaeological investigations of sites of either the early or later medieval periods. The results of those that have been undertaken, particularly of the early medieval period, have been disappointing, perhaps because the sites that were chosen, for example Faughart and Ballyvourney, had extensive use in later periods.

Several sites can be identified as very suitable candidates for geophysical survey followed by targeted archaeological investigation, notably Ardcarn, Ballymacdane, Cloonburren, Inishmaine, Kilcreevanty, Killevy, Lismullin, and Termonfeckin. Archaeological excavation would undoubtedly also add to the currently very small assemblages of material culture and human remains relating to female religious in Ireland. To date, human remains are only known from two sites: Graney and St Catherine's. The excavations at St Catherine's were undertaken in order to address this particular lacuna, and as outlined it yielded important results, and raised interesting questions.[26]

Patronage has emerged as a key factor in the archaeology of female monasticism. Patrons provided the finance and perhaps the spiritual motivation to found a house of female religious whether in the early of later periods. In many cases they were related in some way to the nunnery community, as many abbesses were related to the patron. My study has been, out of necessity, somewhat empirical as I have attempted to gather all archaeological evidence on female monasticism together. However, it has been brought to light that patrons in the later medieval period did not usually just endow a nunnery, they were part of larger portfolios of patronage, which in some cases covered a wide spectrum of religious institutions. As such, it would be very interesting to research, from an archaeological perspective, patronage of particular lordships through time, to ascertain if any distinct patterns in the archaeology of religious patronage emerge.[27] Future regional studies, such as those already undertaken for medieval Dublin and its hinterland,[28] and Normandy in France,[29] may also yield interesting results. Furthermore, an archaeological consideration of female religious houses and their possible relationships to the medieval diocese within which they were located could also be undertaken. Archaeology is well placed to make an important contribution to such a study, considering the fragmentary nature of the relevant historical records.

Further research is clearly required into the estate holdings of nunneries, as part of a wider inquiry into monastic estates in Ireland. While the totality of a particular nunnery's holdings over time is not known, there is enough evidence available, as has been demonstrated, to map other nunnery estates. This exercise may lead to new archaeological indicators or patterns for monastic estates being identified, particularly for Ireland, as currently there is a dependence on the English evidence for parallels, which is similar but not necessarily identical to the Irish archaeological evidence.[30]

Furthermore, there is also now the possibility that new light can be shed on the ecclesiastical estates of female religious of the early medieval period, first demonstrated by the study of Clenor in the medieval kingdom of Fir Maige in the county of Cork.[31] This type of study is, out of necessity, heavily reliant on the written historical evidence, and so is limited to where that evidence is currently available. However, the distinctive settlement pattern that has been identified at Clenor in relation to its early medieval female ecclesiastical estate might be archaeologically identified elsewhere, when the detail of the historical documentation of Fir Maige is lacking. One likely important candidate for such a study is Killeedy, which has been recently identified as being an important ecclesiastical centre of one of the Túatha of Uí Chonaill, which subsequently became a parish. Indeed, it has already been suggested that the pattern of parish formation noted in Fir Maige is repeated in Uí Chonaill, and perhaps similarly the early ecclesiastical estate pattern might also be repeated.[32]

In this book I have been primarily concerned with a consideration of female monasticism related to the religious orders. However, it is abundantly clear that there were other forms of female monasticism in both the early and later medieval periods. For the early medieval period, for example, single female religious or vowesses are in evidence from the historical sources.[33] This group merit archaeological consideration, although it may be particularly difficult to identify them in the archaeological record. Perhaps a starting point might be some of the hut sites and smaller enclosures located around larger early ecclesiastical sites, most visible in the southwest due to preservation conditions, such as those recently identified around the putative female religious site of Killabuonia, County Kerry.[34]

For the later medieval period, female recluses or anchorites, hospital sisters, and Franciscan Third Order tertiaries are all visible in the historical evidence and these female religious have the potential to have left traces in the archaeological evidence. Indeed, it has been suggested that some of the nunneries thought to have been Franciscan (Second Order of St Clare), may actually have been communities of tertiaries.[35] Moreover, in areas of Ireland where nunneries are peculiarly absent, such as Donegal, for example, Third Order houses may have fulfilled that role as communities accepting of religious women.[36]

The historical evidence for anchorites in medieval Ireland has been collated and a number of possible archaeological examples of anchorholds has been suggested.[37] Coupled with a contemporary guide for this way of life in the *Ancrene Wisse: Guide for anchoresses*,[38] it is feasible to identify some of these female anchorites in the archaeological record, and indeed those that have not been historically recorded. A starting point for such an archaeological study would be the investigation of the 'sacristy' at St Catherine's, or the annex feature at Templenagalliaghdoo.

10.1 One of the few images of Old Abbey House, showing the re-use of medieval architectural stonework from St Catherine's nunnery. Irish Tourist Association image, courtesy of Limerick Studies, Limerick City and County Library. http://www.limerickcity.ie/ Library/LocalStudies/IrishTouristAssociationSurvey/.

Archaeological study in Ireland to date has entirely neglected medieval hospitals,[39] and rigorous research in this area would certainly prove productive.[40] In some cases, such as Clonbroney and Killaraght, hospitals are directly associated with female religious communities. Furthermore, while there is currently no evidence to support the presence of female mystics in medieval Ireland – and again they are unlikely to manifest in the archaeological record alone – there remains the possibility that there were female mystics present, as there were several in medieval England and on the continent.[41]

The timeframe covered by this book is broadly the medieval period from *c.*450 to 1540, bracketed by the coming of Christianity and the dissolution. However, the dissolution of the monasteries did not mark the end of the use of nunneries in the post-dissolution period, and they were transformed for new uses – these later uses are worthy of some further research, as has been demonstrated elsewhere.[42] Indications in Ireland suggest that most nunneries were not altered to become secular living accommodation as many of the male religious houses were. This is interesting in its own right, as to why this variation of use between male and female religious houses may have been the case, and perhaps the nunneries' more diverse layouts did not lend themselves as well to post-dissolution spacious gentry living. In several cases, nunneries were demolished so that their valuable building stone might be re-used, as at Grace Dieu, demolished for the construction of the nearby Turvey House, or St Mary de Hogges, demolished for repairs at Dublin Castle. It is unrecorded, though likely, that Lismullin House was also partially built from the fabric of Lismullin nunnery. In the case of St Catherine's and Old Abbey House, County Limerick, some of the nunnery's decorative stone work was used in the new house and its garden while the nunnery structure became a yard and out-buildings (Figure 10.1).

Finally, a further natural progression from the study of the medieval period is an archaeological study of female monasticism in the post-medieval and early modern eras. Historians, predominantly but not exclusively female, are currently leading intensive and extensive global research in female religious and their foundations.[43] Many of these foundations were associated with Irish nuns and sisters, many of whom left after the dissolution, or in later waves of forced emigration.[44] They either joined existing foundations or established new convents abroad, the most famous example perhaps being the Abbey of Irish Dames, Ypres, in modern Belgium.[45] Convents which were later established or re-established in Ireland in the nineteenth century[46] also have much to offer an archaeological study, particularly in the study of material culture, for example in the lace they and their schools produced, which became internationally recognised and much sought after.[47]

FINAL REMARKS

I have purposefully entitled this book 'an archaeology' rather than 'the archaeology' of female monasticism in medieval Ireland, as considering the avenues open for further archaeological study, it is clearly the beginning rather than the final word. It is out of necessity a somewhat empirical work, in that all archaeological data currently available on female monasticism has been catalogued and considered, something that had not been done heretofore.

The consideration of that archaeological evidence, particularly that of the later medieval period, has been informed by archaeological theory. I have tried to employ an engendered multi-narrative approach to tease out possible archaeological interpretations of the evidence; though these interpretations have been evidentially-constrained throughout. I have concluded – to answer the final, fifth question posed in the Introduction – that female religious *were* an intrinsic part of the monastic landscape, their archaeology being in some ways similar to elsewhere in medieval Europe, though in other ways subtly different and peculiar to medieval Ireland. Their monasteries are representative of the regional 'micro-Christendoms' of the early medieval world, and – it could be argued – the later medieval world also, due to the sometimes incomplete standardisation of the church hierarchy across medieval Christendom.

Endnotes

CHAPTER 1. INTRODUCTION

1 D. Ó Corráin, 'Women in Early Irish Society', in M. Mac Curtain and D. Ó Corráin (eds), *Women in Irish Society: The historical dimension* (Dublin: Arlen House, 1978), pp. 1–14; L. Bitel, 'Women's Monastic Enclosures in Early Ireland: A study of female spirituality and male monastic mentalities', *Journal of Medieval History,* vol. 12, 1986, pp. 15–36; M. MacCurtain, M. O'Dowd and M. Luddy, 'An Agenda for Women's History in Ireland, 1500–1900', *Irish Historical Studies*, vol. 28, 1992, pp. 1–37; C. Harrington, *Women in a Celtic Church: Ireland 450–1150* (Oxford: Oxford University Press, 2002); D. Hall, *Women and the Church in Medieval Ireland* c.*1140–1540* (Dublin: Four Courts Press, 2003); G. Kenny, *Anglo-Irish and Gaelic Women in Ireland* c.*1170–1540* (Dublin: Four Courts Press, 2007); M.T. Flanagan, *The Transformation of the Irish Church in the Twelfth Century* (Woodbridge: Boydell, 2010).

2 N. Edwards, *The Archaeology of Early Medieval Ireland* (London: Batsford, 1990), p. 131; N. Edwards, 'Early Medieval Munster: Summary and prospect', in M.A. Monk and J. Sheehan (eds), *Early Medieval Munster: Archaeology, history and society* (Cork: Cork University Press, 1998), pp. 200–5, at p. 204; J. Burton and K. Stöber (eds), *Women in the Medieval Monastic World* (Turnhout: Brepols, 2015), pp. 1–4.

3 For example, T. Barry, *The Medieval Archaeology of Ireland* (London: Routledge, 1987); R. Stalley, *The Cistercian Monasteries of Ireland: An account of the history, art and architecture of the White Monks in Ireland from 1142 to 1540* (London: Yale University Press, 1987); A. Hogan, *Kilmallock Dominican Priory* (Kilmallock: Kilmallock Historical Society, 1991); B. Lalor, *The Irish Round Tower* (Cork: The Collins Press, 1999); T. O'Keeffe, *An Anglo-Norman Monastery: Bridgetown Priory and the architecture of the Augustinian canons regular in Ireland* (Cork: Cork County Council and Gandon Editions, 1999); T. O'Keeffe, *Romanesque Ireland: Architecture and ideology in the twelfth century* (Dublin: Four Courts Press, 2003); T. O'Keeffe, *Ireland's Round Towers* (Stroud: Tempus, 2004); T. Ó Carragáin, *Churches in Early Medieval Ireland: Architecture, ritual, and memory* (New Haven: Paul Mellon Centre for Studies in British Art by Yale University Press, 2010); B. Lynch, *A Monastic Landscape: The Cistercians in medieval Ireland* (Kilkenny: Xlibris, 2010); C. Doherty, L. Doran and M. Kelly (eds), *Glendalough: City of God* (Dublin: Four Courts Press, 2011); C. Ó Clabaigh, *The Friars in Ireland 1224–1540* (Dublin: Four Courts Press, 2012).

4 R. Gilchrist, *Gender and Material Culture: The archaeology of religious women* (London: Routledge, 1994); R. Gilchrist, *Contemplation and Action: The other monasticism* (London: Leicester University Press, 1995); R. Gilchrist, *Gender and Archaeology: Contesting the past* (London: Routledge, 1999).

5 For example, Barry, *Archaeology of Ireland*; Edwards, *Early Medieval Ireland*, pp. 99–131; T. O'Keeffe, *Medieval Ireland: An archaeology* (Stroud: Tempus, 2000); T. O'Keeffe, *Medieval Irish Buildings 1100–1600* (Dublin: Four Courts Press, 2015); A. O'Sullivan, F. McCormick, T. Kerr and L. Harney, *Early Medieval Ireland* AD*400–1100* (Dublin: RIA, 2014). Though see Ó Carragáin, *Churches in Early Medieval Ireland*, as an exception.

6 For example, P. Ó Riain, *A Dictionary of Irish Saints* (Dublin: Four Courts Press, 2011).

7 T.M. Charles-Edwards, *Early Christian Ireland* (Cambridge: Cambridge University Press, 2000).

8 B. Bradshaw, *The Dissolution of the Religious Orders in Ireland under Henry VIII* (Cambridge: Cambridge University Press, 1974).

9 For example, J. Eogan and E. Shee-Twohig (eds), *Cois tSiuire: Nine thousand years of human activity in the lower Suir Valley. Archaeological Excavations on the N25 Waterford City Bypass* (Dublin: The National Roads Authority, 2011), p. 9.

10 For example, A. Cosgrove (ed.), *A New History of Ireland. Volume II: Medieval Ireland 1169–1534* (Oxford: Oxford University Press, 1993); M. Murphy and M. Potterton, *The Dublin Region in the Middle Ages* (Dublin: Four Courts Press, 2010), pp. 37–8.

11 D.N. Dumville, *Councils and Synods of the Gaelic Early and Central Middle Ages* (Cambridge: Cambridge University Press, 1997).

12 Hall, *Women and the Church*, pp. 63–70.

13 Flanagan, *Transformation*. See also, D. Ó Corrâin, *The Irish Church, Its Reform and the English Invasion* (Dublin: Four Courts Press, 2017). For a broader perspective of the twelfth century in Ireland, see D. Bracken and D. Ó Riain-Raedel (eds), *Ireland and Europe in the Twelfth Century: Reform and renewal* (Dublin: Four Courts Press, 2006).

14 See Bradshaw, *Dissolution*; T.W. Moody, F.X. Martin and F.J. Byrne (eds), *A New History of Ireland. Volume III: Early Modern Ireland 1534–1691* (Oxford: Oxford University Press, 1976).

15 T. Collins, 'Unveiling Female Monasticism in Later Medieval Ireland: Survey and excavation at St Catherine's, Shanagolden, Co. Limerick', *Proceedings of the Royal Irish Academy*, vol. 119C, 2019, pp. 103–71.

16 Aspects have been published elsewhere: T. Collins, *The Other Monasticism, Killone Co. Clare. Heritage Guide No. 38* (Dublin: Wordwell, 2007); 'Nunneries in Ireland in the Middle Ages: An archaeological overview', *The Kerry Magazine*, vol. 23, 2013, pp. 11–12; T. Collins, 'Timolin: A case study of a nunnery estate in later medieval Ireland', *Anuario de Estudios Medievales*, vol. 44, 2014, pp. 51–80; T. Collins, 'An Archaeological Perspective on Female Monasticism in the Middle Ages in Ireland', in J. Burton and K. Stöber (eds), *Women in the Medieval Monastic World* (Turnhout: Brepols, 2015), pp. 229–51; T. Collins, 'Archaeologies of Female Monasticism in Ireland: Becoming and belonging *c.* 1200–1600', in E. Campbell, E. FitzPatrick and A. Horning (eds), *Becoming and Belonging in Ireland* AD c.*1200–1600: Essays in identity and cultural practice* (Cork: Cork University Press, 2018), pp. 69–87; T. Collins, 'Later Medieval Nunneries in Ireland: Form and function', in P. Barnwell (ed.), *Places of Worship in Britain and Ireland 1150–1350* (Donington: Shaun Tyas, 2018), pp. 168–87; T. Collins, 'Isolated in the Wilderness? An archaeological exploration of nunneries in the medieval landscape of Ireland', in J. Lyttleton and M. Stout (eds), *Church and Settlement in Ireland* (Dublin: Four Courts Press, 2018), pp. 142–56; T. Collins, 'Transforming Women Religious? Church reform and the archaeology of female monasticism In Ireland', in E. Bhreathnach, M. Kasnodębska-D'Aughton and K. Smith (eds), *Monastic Europe* (Turnhout: Brepols, 2019), pp. 277–301.

17 This catalogue is available online. It is subdivided into three sections: early medieval female religious communities; later medieval nunneries; possible early and later female religious communities. It can be accessed through DOI: http://doi.org/10.5281/zenodo.5035404.

18 Hall, *Women and the Church*; Kenny, *Anglo-Irish and Gaelic Women*.

19 A. O'Sullivan, F. McCormack, T. Kerr and L. Harney, *Early Medieval Ireland* AD *400–1100: The evidence from archaeological excavations* (Dublin: Royal Irish Academy, 2014), pp. 145–8. For a very accessible introduction to the archaeology of the early medieval period see Edwards, *Archaeology of Early Medieval Ireland*; and for ecclesiastical sites see K. Hughes and A. Hamlin, *The Modern Traveller to the Early Irish Church* (Dublin: Four Courts Press, 1997).

20 Ó Carragáin, *Churches in Early Medieval Ireland*, pp. 15–47.
21 For example, J. Sheehan, 'Caherlehillian, Co. Kerry: Ritual, domestic and economic aspects of a Corcu Duibne ecclesiastical site', in C. Corlett and M. Potterton (eds), *The Church in Early Medieval Ireland in the Light of Recent Archaeological Excavations* (Dublin: Wordwell, 2014), pp. 247–58.
22 See Ó Carragáin, *Churches in Early Medieval Ireland*, pp. 9–10 for summary.
23 For an introduction to the archaeology of the period, see Barry, *Archaeology of Medieval Ireland*; O'Keeffe, *Medieval Ireland*; O'Keeffe, *Medieval Irish Buildings*.
24 Stalley, *Cistercian Monasteries*, pp. 7–16.
25 E. FitzPatrick and R. Gillespie (eds), *The Parish in Medieval and Early Modern Ireland: Community, territory and building* (Dublin: Four Courts Press, 2006); R. Moss, 'Irish Parish Churches: 1350–1550', in P. Barnwell (ed.), *Places of Worship in the British Isles 1350–1550* (Donington, Shaun Tyas, 2019), pp. 174–90.
26 For an archaeological insight into medieval life, see R. Gilchrist, *Medieval Life: Archaeology and the life course* (Woodbridge: Boydell, 2012).
27 For extensive discussion on problems with terminology in an early medieval context, see S. Foot, *Veiled Women: The disappearance of nuns from Anglo-Saxon England*, 2 vols (Aldershot: Ashgate, 2000).
28 See M. Browne and C. Ó Clabaigh (eds), *Households of God: The regular canons and canonesses of Saint Augustine and of Prémontré in medieval Ireland* (Dublin: Four Courts Press, 2019).
29 J. McNamara, 'Monasticism and Nuns', in M. Schaus (ed.), *Women and Gender in Medieval Europe: An encyclopedia* (London: Routledge, 2006), pp. 579–85.
30 For a very useful list of such terms and explanations, see https://arts.st-andrews.ac.uk/monasticmatrix/vocabularium. Accessed 15 September 2020.
31 A. More, *Fictive Orders and Feminine Religious Identities 1200–1600* (Oxford: Oxford University Press, 2018).
32 For a recent review, see T. O'Keeffe, 'Theory and Medieval Archaeology in Ireland and Beyond: The narrative tradition and the archaeological imagination', *Journal of Irish Archaeology*, vol. XXVII, 2018, pp. 99–116.
33 M. Johnson, *Archaeological Theory: An introduction* (Chichester: Wiley-Blackwell, 2010). This book includes a glossary of terms, pp. 236–44.
34 Gilchrist, *Gender and Archaeology*, pp. xv, 1. This book also has a very useful glossary of theoretical terms, see pp. xiii–xviii.
35 For a full explanation of this concept and how it relates to archaeology, see Johnson, *Archaeological Theory*, pp. 188–90.
36 Bradshaw, *Dissolution*.
37 J. Lyttleton, *The Jacobean Plantations in Seventeenth-Century Offaly: An archaeology of a changing world* (Dublin: Four Courts Press, 2013), pp. 1–5.
38 P. Connolly, *Medieval Record Sources* (Dublin: Four Courts Press, 2002), pp. 45–9.
39 K. Simms, *Medieval Gaelic Sources* (Dublin: Four Courts Press, 2009).
40 For summary, see Hall, *Women and the Church*, pp. 15–20.
41 Flanagan, *Transformation*, p. 73.
42 For example, J. Ware, *De Hibernia et Antiqitatibus Ejus* (London: Crook & Thom, 1654); L. Alemand, *Historie Monastique D'Irlande* (Paris: Louis Lucas, 1690).
43 For example, J. Stevens (ed.), *Monasticon Hibernicum* (London: William Mears, 1722); W. Harris, *The Whole Works of Sir James Ware Concerning Ireland* (Dublin: S. Powell, 1745); M. Archdall, *Monasticon Hibernicum* (Dublin: Luke White, 1786); J. Morrin (ed.), *Calendar of the Patent and Close Rolls of Chancery in Ireland in the Reigns of Henry VIII,*

Edward VI, Mary and Elizabeth (Dublin: Alex Thom & Sons, 1861); Rev. P.F. Moran (ed.), *Monasticon Hibernicum or a History of the Abbeys, Priories and Other Religious Houses in Ireland, by Mervyn Archdall*, 2 vols (Dublin: W.B. Kelly, 1873, 1876).

44 E. Hogan, *Onomasticon Goedelicum* (Dublin: Royal Irish Academy, 1910).

45 N.B. White, *Extents of Irish Monastic Possession 1540–'41: Manuscripts held in the Public Record Office, London* (Dublin: Irish Manuscripts Commission, 1943).

46 A. Gwynn and R.N. Hadcock, *Medieval Religious Houses: Ireland* (Dublin: Irish Academic Press, 1970), pp. 20–46, 307–26.

47 Ibid., p. 307.

48 For example, F. Byrne, 'The Trembling Sod: Ireland in 1169', in A. Cosgrove (ed.), *A New History of Ireland. Volume II: Medieval Ireland 1169–1534* (Oxford: Oxford University Press, 1993), pp. 1–42; K. Nicholls, 'A List of Monasteries in Connacht, 1577', *Journal of the Galway Archaeological and Historical Society*, vol. 33, 1972, pp. 28–43; K. Nicholls, 'Towards a New *Monasticon Hibernicum*', *Peritia*, vol. 3, 1984, pp. 330–3.

49 For example, Monasticon, https://monasticon.celt.dias.ie/; Monastic Matrix, https://arts.st-andrews.ac.uk/monasticmatrix/home; CIRCLE, https://chancery.tcd.ie/content/welcome-circle. Accessed 15 September 2020.

50 J. Ryan, *Irish Monasticism: Origins and early development* (London: Longmans, Green & Co., 1931); K. Hughes, *The Church in Early Irish Society* (London: Cornell University Press, 1966); K. Hughes, *Early Christian Ireland: Introduction to the sources* (London: Sources for History, 1972); A. Cosgrove, 'The Emergence of the Pale 1399–1447', in A. Cosgrove (ed.), *A New History of Ireland. Volume II: Medieval Ireland 1169–1534* (Oxford: Oxford University Press, 1993), pp. 533–56; J.A. Watt, *The Church in Medieval Ireland*, 2nd edn (Dublin: UCD Press, 1998); C. Etchingham, *Church Organisation in Ireland AD 650 to 1000* (Maynooth: Laigin Publications, 1999). For a global perspective, see G. Melville, *The World of Medieval Monasticism: Its history and forms of life* (Minnesota: Cistercian Publications, 2016).

51 A. Harris, 'Saint Gobnet, Abbess', *Journal of the Royal Society of Antiquaries of Ireland*, vol. 68, 1938, pp. 272–7; D. Pochin Mould, *The Irish Saints* (Dublin: Clonmore & Reynolds, 1964); S. Connolly and J.-M. Picard, 'Cogitosus's *Life of St Brigit*: Content and value', *Journal of the Royal Society of Antiquaries of Ireland*, vol. 117, 1987, pp. 5–27; E. Johnston, 'Transforming Women in Irish Hagiography', *Peritia*, vol. 9, 1995, pp. 197–220; E. Johnston, 'Íte: Patron of her people?' *Peritia*, vol. 14, 2000, pp. 421–8; E. Johnston, 'Powerful Women or Patriarchal Weapons? Two medieval Irish saints', *Peritia*, vol. 15, 2001 pp. 302–10; I. Sperber, 'The Life of St Monenna or Darerca of Killevy', in A.J. Hughes and W. Nolan (eds), *Armagh: History and society* (Dublin: Geography Publications, 2001), pp. 63–97; T.M. Charles-Edwards, 'Early Irish Saints' Cults and Their Constituencies', *Ériu*, vol. 54, 2004, pp. 79–102; S. Haarländer, '*Innumerabiles populi de utroque sexu confuentes* … Klöster für männer und frauen im frühmittelalterlichen Irland', in G. Melville and A. Muller (eds), *Female* Vita Religiosa *between Late Antiquity and the High Middle Ages* (Berlin: LIT Verlag, 2011), pp. 137–50; Ó Riain, *A Dictionary*.

52 For an overview, see D.P. McCarthy, *The Irish Annals: Their genesis, evolution and history* (Dublin: Four Courts Press, 2008).

53 S. Leigh Fry, *Burial in Medieval Ireland 900–1500* (Dublin: Four Courts Press, 1999).

54 W. Reeves, 'The Ancient Churches of Armagh, Part 1', *Ulster Journal of Archaeology*, vol. 2, 1896, pp. 194–204; W. Reeves, 'The Ancient Churches of Armagh, Appendix', *Ulster Journal of Archaeology*, vol. 6, 1900, pp. 24–33.

55 For example, W.P. Burke, 'The Nunnery of Kilculliheen', *Journal of the Waterford and Southeast Ireland Archaeological Society*, vol. 8, 1902, pp. 9–17; J. Wardell, 'The History

and Antiquities of St Catherine's Old Abbey, County Limerick (with a description of the conventual buildings by T.J. Westropp)', *Journal of the Royal Society of Antiquaries of Ireland*, vol. 14, 1904, pp. 41–64; J. Brady, 'The Nunnery at Clonard', *Ríocht na Midhe: Records of the Meath Archaeological and Historical Society*, vol. 2, 1960, pp. 4–7; D. Hall, 'The Nuns of the Medieval Convent of Lismullin, County Meath and Their Secular Connections', *Ríocht na Midhe: Records of the Meath Archaeological and Historical Society*, vol. 10, 1999, pp. 58–70; G. Carville, 'St Mary's Abbey, Graney: To live an apostolic life', *Journal of the Kildare Archaeological Society*, vol. XX, part 2, 2010, pp. 33–56.

56 P.J. Dunning, 'The Arroasian Order in Medieval Ireland', *Irish Historical Studies*, vol. 4, 1945, pp. 297–315; N. Hadcock, 'The Origin of the Augustinian Order in Meath', *Ríocht na Midhe: Records of the Meath Archaeological and Historical Society*, vol. 3, 1964, pp. 124–31; Ó Clabaigh, *Friars in Ireland*.

57 D. Hall, 'Towards a Prosopography of Nuns in Medieval Ireland', *Archivium Hibernicum*, vol. 53, 1999, pp. 3–15.

58 G. Carville, *The Occupation of Celtic Sites in Medieval Ireland by the Canons Regular of St Augustine and the Cistercians* (Kalamazoo: Cistercian Publications, 1982); G. Carville, 'Cistercian Nuns in Medieval Ireland: Plary Abbey, Ballymore, Co. Westmeath', in J.A. Nicols and L. Thomas Shank (eds), *Hidden Springs: Cistercian monastic women. Medieval Religious Women*, vol. 3 (Kalamazoo: Cistercian Publications, 1995), pp. 62–84; G. Carville, *The Impact of the Cistercians on the Landscape of Ireland* (Wicklow: KB Publications, 2002).

59 A. Thomas, *The Walled Towns of Ireland*, 2 vols (Dublin: Irish Academic Press, 1992).

60 For example, J.H. Andrews, *Irish Historic Towns Atlas No. 1: Kildare* (Dublin: Royal Irish Academy, 1986); D. Kelly and T. O'Keeffe, *Irish Historic Towns Atlas No. 27: Youghal* (Dublin: Royal Irish Academy, 2015). See https://www.ria.ie/irish-historic-towns-atlas-online. Accessed 15 September 2020.

61 The Down Survey is an incomplete set of maps and accompanying terriers (lists) for Ireland dated to about 1665, and illustrates many antiquities of that time. See www.downsurvey.tcd.ie. Accessed 15 September 2020.

62 For example, C. Smith, *The Ancient and Present State of the County and City of Cork*, 2 vols (Cork: Guy & Company, 1750); P. Fitzgerald and J.J. McGregor, *History, Topography and Antiquities of the County and City of Limerick* (Dublin: McKern, 1826); S. Lewis, *A Topographical Dictionary of Ireland* (London: Lewis & Sons, 1837); J. Begley, *The Diocese of Limerick, Ancient and Medieval*, 3 vols (Dublin: Browne & Nolan, 1906); H.T. Knox, *The History of the County of Mayo to the Close of the Sixteenth Century* (Dublin: Hodges Figgis, 1908); R.C. Simington, *Books of Survey and Distribution, Being Abstracts and Various Surveys and Instruments of Title 1636–1703, County Clare*, vol. 4 (Dublin: The Stationery Office, 1967); L. Killanin and M.V. Duignan, *The Shell Guide to Ireland*, 2nd edn (London: Ebury Press, 1967).

63 M. MacCurtain and D. Ó Corráin (eds), *Women in Irish Society: The historical dimension* (Dublin: Arlen House, The Women's Press, 1978); M. MacCurtain and M. O'Dowd, *Women in Early Modern Ireland* (Dublin: Wolfhound Press, 1991); MacCurtain et al., 'An Agenda', pp. 1–37; Bitel, 'Monastic Enclosures', pp. 15–36; L. Bitel, *Isle of Saints: Monastic settlement and Christian community in early Ireland* (Ithaca: Cornell University Press, 1990); L. Bitel, *Land of Women* (Ithaca: Cornell University Press, 1996); L. Bitel, *Women in Early Medieval Europe 400–1100* (Cambridge: Cambridge University Press, 2002); L. Bitel, 'Ekphrasis at Kildare: The imaginative architecture of a seventh-century hagiographer', *Speculum*, vol. 79, 2004, pp. 605–27; L. Bitel, *Landscape with Two Saints* (Oxford: Oxford University Press, 2009); Kenny, *Women in Ireland*.

64 M. Ní Dhonnchadha, '*Caillech* and other Terms for Veiled Women in Medieval Irish Texts', *Éigse*, vol. 28, 1994, pp. 71–96; G. Ó Crualaoich, *The Book of the Cailleach: Stories of the wise-woman healer* (Cork: Cork University Press, 2003).
65 J. McNamara, *Sisters in Arms: Catholic nuns through two millennia* (Cambridge, MA: Harvard University Press, 1996).
66 MacCurtain et al., 'An Agenda', p. 5.
67 E. Bhreathnach, 'Review: Medieval Irish History at the End of the Twentieth Century: Unfinished work', *Irish Historical Studies*, vol. 32, 2000, pp. 260–71, at p. 266.
68 Ibid., p. 270.
69 For example, Harrington, *Women in a Celtic Church*; Hall, *Women and the Church*; M. MacCurtain, 'Late Medieval Nunneries of the Irish Pale', in H.B. Clarke, J. Prunty and M. Hennessy (eds), *Surveying Ireland's Past: Multidisciplinary essays in honour of Anngret Simms* (Dublin: Geography Publications, 2004), pp. 129–44; Kenny, *Women in Ireland*, pp. 169–84.
70 Hall, 'Towards a Prosopography'; Hall, *Women and the Church*, pp. 211–20.
71 Flanagan, *Transformation*, pp. 70–3, 149–54, 172, 200–2; Ó Corráin, *The Irish Church*.
72 For example, C. Meek and M. Simms (eds), *The Fragility of Her Sex? Medieval Irish women in their European context* (Dublin: Four Courts Press, 1996); C. Meek (ed.), *Women in Renaissance and Early Modern Europe* (Dublin: Four Courts Press, 2000); C. Meek and C. Lawless (eds), *Pawns or Players? Studies on medieval and early modern women* (Dublin: Four Courts Press, 2003); C. Meek and C. Lawless (eds), *Victims or Viragos? Studies on medieval and early modern women* (Dublin: Four Courts Press, 2005).
73 J. Hamburger and S. Marti (eds), *Crown and Veil: Female monasticism from the fifth to the fifteenth centuries* (New York: Columbia University Press, 2008); G. Melville and A. Müller (eds), *Female* Vita Religiosa *between Late Antiquity and the High Middle Ages: Structures, developments and spatial contexts* (Berlin: LIT Verlag, 2011); B. Garí (ed.), *Anuario de Estudios Medievales, Temas Monograficos: Espacios de spiritualidad femenina en la Europa medieval. Una Mirada interdisciplinar*, vol. 44, 2014; Burton and Stöber (eds), *Monastic World*.
74 J. Waddell, *Foundation Myths: The beginnings of Irish archaeology* (Dublin: Wordwell, 2005); J. Rockley, *Antiquarians and Archaeology in Nineteenth-Century Cork. BAR 454* (Oxford: Archaeopress, 2008).
75 T.J. Westropp, 'A Description of the Ancient Buildings and Crosses at Clonmacnois, King's County', *Journal of the Royal Society of Antiquaries of Ireland*, vol. 37, 1907, pp. 277–306.
76 T.J. Westropp, 'The Conventual Buildings', in J. Wardell, 'The History and Antiquities of St Catherine's Old Abbey, County Limerick', *Journal of the Royal Society of Antiquaries of Ireland*, vol. 14, 1904, pp. 53–64.
77 Rev. D. Healy, 'Two Royal Abbeys by the Western Lakes (Cong and Inishmaine)', *Journal of the Royal Society of Antiquaries of Ireland*, vol. 35, 1905, pp. 1–20.
78 T.J. Westropp, 'The Augustinian Houses of the County Clare: Clare, Killone and Inchicronan', *Journal of the Royal Society of Antiquaries of Ireland*, vol. 30, 1900, pp. 118–35.
79 K. Emerick, 'Whitby and Clonmacnoise', in H. King (ed.), *Clonmacnoise Studies*, vol. 2 (Dublin: The Stationery Office, 2003), pp. 209–21.
80 A. Champneys, *Irish Ecclesiastical Architecture* (London: G. Bell & Sons, 1910), pp. 116, 124.
81 H.G. Leask, *Irish Churches and Monastic Buildings*, 3 vols (Dundalk: Dundalgan Press, 1955–60). Nunneries at [1955], pp. 25, 52, 111, 112, 146, 147, 164–5; [1960], pp. 64, 66, 73–5, 92.

82 B. Kalkreuter, *Boyle Abbey and the School of the West* (Dublin: Wordwell, 2001), pp. 73, 197.

83 Edwards, *Archaeology of Early Medieval Ireland*, p. 131; Edwards, 'Early Medieval Munster', p. 204.

84 C. Manning, 'Finghin MacCarthaigh, King of Desmond, and the Mystery of the Second Nunnery at Clonmacnoise', in D. Edwards (ed.), *Regions and Rulers in Ireland 1100–1650* (Dublin: Four Courts Press, 2004), pp. 20–6; J. Ní Ghrádaigh, 'Temple Finghin and Two Unusual Voussoirs from Clonmacnoise', *Archaeology Ireland*, vol. 19, 2005, pp. 26–31.

85 J. Ní Ghrádaigh, '"But What Exactly Did She Give?" Derbforgaill and the Nuns' Church at Clonmacnoise', in H. King (ed.), *Clonmacnoise Studies*, vol. 2 (Dublin: The Stationery Office, 2003), pp. 175–207, at pp. 204–5; J. Ní Ghrádaigh, 'Mere Embroiderers? Women and art in early medieval Ireland', in T. Martin (ed.), *Reassessing the Roles of Women as Makers in Medieval Art and Architecture* (Leiden: Brill, 2012), pp. 93–128; J. Ní Ghrádaigh, 'Towards an Emotive Christ? Changing depictions of the Crucifixion on the Irish high cross', in J. Mullins, J. Ní Ghrádaigh and R. Hawtree (eds), *Envisioning Christ on the Cross: Ireland and the early medieval West* (Dublin: Four Courts Press, 2013), pp. 262–85.

86 A. Hamlin and C. Foley, 'A Women's Graveyard at Carrickmore, County Tyrone, and the Separate Burial of Women', *Ulster Journal of Archaeology*, vol. 46, 1983, pp. 41–6; J. O'Sullivan, 'Excavation of an Early Church and a Women's Cemetery at St Ronan's Medieval Parish Church, Iona', *Proceedings of the Society of Antiquaries of Scotland*, vol. 124, 1994, pp. 327–65; J. O'Sullivan and T. Ó Carragáin, *Inishmurray: Monks and pilgrims in an Atlantic landscape. Volume 1: Archaeological Survey and Excavations 1997–2000* (Cork: The Collins Press, 2008).

87 Ó Carragáin, *Churches in Early Medieval Ireland*, pp. 210–23; Ó Carragáin, 'The View from the Shore: Perceiving island monasteries in early medieval Ireland, *Hortus Artium Medievalium*, vol. 19, 2013, pp. 21–33; Ó Carragáin, 'The Archaeology of Ecclesiastical Estates in Early Medieval Ireland: A case study of the kingdom of Fir Maige', *Peritia*, vols 24–5, 2014, pp. 266–312; Ó Carragáin, 'Is There an Archaeology of Lay People at Early Irish Monasteries?' *Bulletin du centre d'études médiévales d'Auxerre BUCEMA*, vol. 8, 2015, pp. 2–17.

88 J. O'Sullivan, 'Nationalists, Archaeologists and the Myth of the Golden Age', in M.A. Monk and J. Sheehan (eds), *Early Medieval Munster: Archaeology, history and society* (Cork: Cork University Press, 1998), pp. 178–89; Waddell, *Foundation Myths*, pp. 125–7.

89 For example, T.J. Westropp, 'Killone Abbey, Co. Clare', *Journal of the Royal Society of Antiquaries of Ireland*, vol. 1, 1891, pp. 409–10; Westropp, 'Augustinian Houses'; Westropp, 'The Conventual Buildings'; Westropp, 'Clonmacnois'.

90 For instance, Barry, *Archaeology of Ireland*, p. 162; Stalley, *Cistercian Monasteries*; O'Keeffe, *Medieval Ireland*, p. 143; O'Keeffe, *Medieval Irish Buildings*; Kalkreuter, *Boyle Abbey*, p. 73.

91 See the Archaeological Survey of Ireland, www.archaeology.ie for the Republic of Ireland and https://apps.communities-ni.gov.uk/NISMR-PUBLIC/Default.aspx for Northern Ireland. Accessed 15 September 2020.

92 H. Mytum, 'Surface and Geophysical Survey at Clonmacnoise: Defining the extent of intensive monastic settlement', in H. King (ed.), *Clonmacnoise Studies*, vol. 2 (Dublin: The Stationery Office, 2003), pp. 35–58; P.J. Gibson, 'Geophysical Investigation Around the Sites of the Former Monastic Settlement, Killeigh, Co. Offaly'. Report No. EGU 01/05 (Maynooth: unpublished report, 2015); P.J. Gibson and D.M. George, 'Geophysical Investigation of the Site of the Former Monastic Settlement, Clonard, County Meath, Ireland', *Archaeological Prospection*, vol. 13, 2006, pp. 45–56; S. Greene, 'Killeen Cormac Colbinstown: An ecclesiastical site on the Kildare–Wicklow border', *County Kildare*

Online Electronic History Journal, 2011. Available at: http://www.kildare.ie/library/ehistory/2011/03/killeen_cormac_colbinstown_an.asp. Accessed 15 September 2020; S. Greene, 'Killeen Cormac: The archaeology and history of a significant early Christian foundation', *Journal of the Kildare Archaeological Society*, vol. XX, part 3, 2013, pp. 26–48.

93 M.J. O'Kelly, 'St Gobnet's House, Ballyvourney, Co. Cork', *Journal of the Cork Historical and Archaeological Society*, vol. 57, 1952, pp. 18–40; E.M. Fahy, 'Inishleena Abbey and Other Sites in the Lee Valley', *Journal of the Cork Historical and Archaeological Society*, vol. 62, 1957, pp. 65–76; L. O'Connor, 'Faughart Investigation 1966', *County Louth Archaeological Journal*, vol. 17, 1966, pp. 125–9; J.A. McDowell, 'Armagh 50–56 Scotch Street, Early Christian Cemetery and Medieval/Post-Medieval Settlement', www.excavations.ie/report/1985/Armagh/0000573/. Accessed 15 September 2020; M. Gowen, 'Excavations at Grace Dieu in Advance of a Gas Pipeline' (Dublin: unpublished draft text, Margaret Gowen & Company, 1988); M. Conway, 'Excavation at Gracedieu 99E0217', www.excavations.ie/report/1999/Dublin/0004132/. Accessed 15 September 2020; J. Higgins, *The Tisrara Medieval Church, Carrowntemple, Four Roads, Co. Roscommon: Its archaeology and history* (Ireland: Tisrara Heritage and Graveyard Restoration Committee, 1995); R. Ó Baoill, 'Excavations at Aghavea, Co. Fermanagh', in C. Corlett and M. Potterton (eds), *The Church in Early Medieval Ireland, in the Light of Recent Archaeological Excavations* (Dublin: Wordwell, 2014), pp. 159–72.

94 But as exceptions, see C.H. Berman, 'Medieval Agriculture, the Southern French Countryside and the Early Cistercians: A study of forty-three monasteries', *Transactions of the American Philosophical Society*, vol. 76, 1986, pp. 1–179; G. Stout, 'Settlement on Mellifont Abbey's Monastic Estate in Cos Meath and Louth (1540–1)', in J. Lyttleton and M. Stout (eds), *Church and Settlement in Ireland* (Dublin: Four Courts Press, 2018), pp. 157–81.

95 Ó Carragáin, 'The Archaeology of Ecclesiastical Estates in Early Medieval Ireland'.

96 For example, A. Hogan, *The Priory of Llanthony Prima and Secunda in Ireland 1172–1541* (Dublin: Four Courts Press, 2007); R. Masterson, *Medieval Fore, County Westmeath* (Dublin: Four Courts Press, 2014).

97 B. Colfer, *The Hook Peninsula, County Wexford* (Cork: Cork University Press, 2004); G. Stout, 'St Mary's Abbey, Dublin and Its Medieval Farm Suppliers', *Medieval Dublin*, vol. XIV, 2015, pp. 146–62; G. Stout, 'The Cistercian Grange: A medieval farming system', in M. Murphy and M. Stout (eds), *Agriculture and Settlement in Ireland* (Dublin: Four Courts Press, 2015), pp. 28–68; Stout, 'Settlement on Mellifont Abbey's Monastic Estate'.

98 J. Bradley, 'The Precinct of St John's Priory, Kilkenny at the Close of the Middle Ages', *Peritia*, vols 22–3, 2011–12, pp. 317–45.

99 Stout, 'St Mary's Abbey, Dublin'; Stout, 'The Cistercian Grange'.

100 G. Stout and M. Stout, *The Bective Abbey Project, Co. Meath: Excavations 2009–12* (Dublin: Wordwell, 2016).

101 Collins, 'Timolin'.

102 See the Monastic Ireland project at https://medieval.ie/. Accessed 15 September 2020.

103 D. Knowles, *The Religious Orders in England*, 3 vols (Cambridge: Cambridge University Press, 1948, 1955, 1959).

104 J.M. Bennett, 'Medievalism and Feminism', in N. Partner (ed.), *Studying Medieval Women* (Cambridge, MA: The Medieval Academy of America, 1993), pp. 7–29 at p. 23; Burton and Stöber, *Monastic World*, pp. 1–2.

105 E. Power, *Medieval English Nunneries* c.*1275 to 1535* (Cambridge: Cambridge University Press, 1922).

106 L. Eckenstein, *Women Under Monasticism 500–1500* (Cambridge: Cambridge University Press, 1896).

107 M. Bateson, 'The Origin and Early History of Early Double Monasteries', *Transactions of the Royal Historical Society*, vol. 13, 1899, pp. 137–98.

108 R.M. Clay, *The Medieval Hospitals of England* (London: Methuen & Company, 1909).

109 R.M. Clay, *The Hermits and Anchorites of England* (London: Methuen, 1914).

110 A. Bourdillon, *The Order of Minoresses in England* (Manchester: Manchester University Press, 1926).

111 J. Burton, *The Yorkshire Nunneries in the Twelfth and Thirteenth Centuries* (York: Borthwick Institute, University of York, 1979); J. Burton, *Monastic and Religious Orders in Britain 1000–1300* (Cambridge: Cambridge University Press, 1994); J. Burton, 'Looking for Medieval Nuns', in J. Burton and K. Stöber (eds), *Monasteries and Society in the British Isles in the Later Middle Ages* (Woodbridge: Boydell, 2008), pp. 113–23; J. Burton, '*Moniales* and *Ordo Cisterciensis* in Medieval England and Wales', in G. Melville and A. Müller (eds), *Female* Vita Religiosa *between Late Antiquity and the High Middle Ages: Structures, developments and spatial contexts* (Berlin: LIT Verlag, 2011), pp. 375–89; J. Burton, 'Medieval Nunneries and Male Authority: Female monasteries in England and Wales', in J. Burton and K. Stöber (eds), *Women in the Medieval Monastic World* (Turnhout: Brepols, 2015), pp. 123–43; C.V. Graves, 'English Cistercian Nuns in Lincolnshire', *Speculum*, vol. 54, no. 3, 1979, pp. 492–9; J. Nichols, 'The Internal Organisation of English Cistercian Nunneries', *Cîteaux: Commentaria Cistercienses*, vol. 30, 1982, pp. 23–40; J.A. Nichols and L. Thomas Shank (eds), *Distant Echoes: Medieval religious women*, vol. 1 (Kalamazoo: Cistercian Publications, 1984); J. Leclercq, 'Solitude and Solidarity: Medieval women recluses', in J. Nichols and L. Thomas Shank (eds), *Peace Weavers: Medieval religious women*, vol. 2 (Kalamazoo: Cistercian Publications, 1987), pp. 67–84; J. Luecke, 'The Unique Experience of Anglo-Saxon Nuns', in J. Nichols and L. Thomas Shank (eds), *Peace Weavers: Medieval religious women*, vol. 2 (Kalamazoo: Cistercian Publications, 1987), pp. 55–66; S.K. Elkins, *Holy Women of Twelfth-Century England* (Chapel Hill: University of North Carolina Press, 1988); D.K. Coldicott, *Hampshire Nunneries* (Chichester: Phillimore, 1989); M. Oliva, 'Aristocracy or Meritocracy? Office holding patterns in late medieval English nunneries', *Studies in Church History*, vol. 27, 1990, pp. 197–208; M. Oliva, 'The Convent and Community in the Diocese of Norwich from 1350–1540', unpublished PhD dissertation, Fordham University, 1991; M. Oliva, *The Convent and the Community in Late Medieval England: Female monasteries in the diocese of Norwich 1359–1540* (Woodbridge: Boydell, 1998); S. Thompson, 'The Problem of the Cistercian Nuns in the Twelfth and Early Thirteenth Centuries', in D. Baker (ed.), *Medieval Women* (Oxford: Blackwell, 1978), pp. 227–52; S. Thompson, 'Why English Nunneries Had No History: A study of the problems of the English nunneries founded after the Conquest', in J.A. Nichols and L. Thomas Shank (eds), *Distant Echoes: Medieval religious women*, vol. 1 (Kalamazoo: Cistercian Publications, 1984), pp. 131–49; S. Thompson, *Women Religious: The founding of English nunneries after the norman conquest* (Oxford: Clarendon Press, 1991); S. Hollis, *Anglo-Saxon Women and the Church* (Woodbridge: Boydell, 1992); B. Harris, 'A New Look at the Reformation: Aristocratic women and nunneries 1450–1540', *The Journal of British Studies*, vol. 32, 1993, pp. 89–113; B. Golding, *Gilbert of Sempringham and the Gilbertine Order* c.*1130–1300* (Oxford: Oxford University Press, 1995); B. Golding, 'Bishops and Nuns: Forms of the *cura monialium* in twelfth- and thirteenth-century England', in J. Burton and K. Stöber (eds), *Women in the Medieval Monastic World* (Turnhout: Brepols, 2015), pp. 97–122; J.A. Nichols and L. Thomas Shank (eds), *Hidden Springs: Cistercian monastic women. Medieval*

Religious Women, vol. 3 (Kalamazoo: Cistercian Publications, 1995); B. Kerr, *Religious Life for Women c.1100–c.1350: Fontevraud in England* (Oxford: Clarendon Press, 1999); R.A. McDonald, 'The Foundation and Patronage of Nunneries by Native Elites in Twelfth- and Early Thirteenth-Century Scotland', in E. Ewan and M. Meikle (eds), *Women in Scotland c.1100–c.1750* (East Linton: Tuckwell Press, 1999), pp. 3–15; Foot, *Veiled Women*; S. Foot, *Æthelstan: The first king of England* (New Haven: Yale University Press, 2011); P. Lee, *Nunneries, Learning and Spirituality in Late Medieval English Society: The Dominican Priory of Dartford* (York: York Medieval Press, 2001); J. Sorrentino, 'In Houses of Nuns, in Houses of Canons: A liturgical dimension to double monasteries', *Journal of Medieval History*, vol. 28, 2002, pp. 361–72; D. Wood (ed.), *Women and Religion in Medieval England* (Oxford: Oxbow, 2003); B. Yorke, *Nunneries and the Anglo-Saxon Royal Houses* (London: Continuum, 2003); K. Curran, 'Religious Women and Their Communities in Late Medieval Scotland', unpublished PhD thesis, University of Glasgow, 2005; V.G. Spear, *Leadership in Medieval English Nunneries* (Woodbridge: Boydell, 2005); D. Hall, *Scottish Monastic Landscapes* (Stroud: Tempus, 2006); K. Stöber, *Late Medieval Monasteries and Their Patrons: England and Wales c.1300–1540* (Woodbridge: Boydell, 2007); J. Cartwright, 'The Desire to Corrupt: Convent and community in medieval Wales', in D. Watt (ed.), *Medieval Women in Their Communities* (Cardiff: University of Wales Press, 1997), pp. 20–48; J. Cartwright, *Feminine Sanctity and Spirituality in Medieval Wales* (Cardiff: University of Wales Press, 2008); J. Cartwright, 'Abbess Agnes and the Ape', in J. Burton and K. Stöber (eds), *Monastic Wales: New approaches* (Cardiff: University of Wales Press, 2013), pp. 191–207; G. Coppack, 'How the Other Half Lived: Cistercian nuns in early sixteenth-century Yorkshire', *Citeaux: Commentarii Cistercienses*, vol. 59, 2008, pp. 253–98; K. Perkins-Curran, '"Quhat Say Ye Now, My Lady Priores? How Have Ye Usit Your Office, Can Ye Ges?" Politics, power and realities of the office of a prioress in her community in late medieval Scotland', in J. Burton and K. Stöber (eds), *Monasteries and Society in the British Isles in the Later Middle Ages* (Woodbridge: Boydell, 2008), pp. 124–41; J. Kerr, *Life in the Medieval Cloister* (London: Continuum, 2009); M. Carter, 'Silk Purse or Sow's Ear? The art and architecture of the Cistercian nunnery of Swine, Yorkshire', in J. Burton and K. Stöber (eds), *Women in the Medieval Monastic World* (Turnhout: Brepols, 2015), pp. 253–78.

112 L.V. Hicks, *Religious Life in Normandy 1050–1300: Space, gender and social pressure* (Woodbridge: Boydell, 2007).

113 See https://www.york.ac.uk/borthwick/publications/monastic-research-bulletin/. Accessed 15 September 2020.

114 R. Gilchrist, 'The Spatial Archaeology of Gender Domains: A case study of medieval English nunneries', *Archaeological Review from Cambridge*, vol. 7, no. 1, 1988, pp. 21–8; R. Gilchrist, 'Community and Self: Perceptions and use of space in medieval monasteries', *Scottish Archaeological Review*, vol. 6, 1989, pp. 55–64; R. Gilchrist, 'The Archaeology of Medieval English Nunneries: A research design', in R. Gilchrist and H. Mytum (eds), *The Archaeology of Rural Monasteries. BAR British Series 203* (Oxford: British Archaeological Reports, 1989), pp. 251–7; R. Gilchrist, 'Christian Bodies and Souls: The archaeology of life and death in later medieval hospitals', in S. Bassett (ed.), *Death in Towns: Urban responses to the dying and the dead 100–1600* (Leicester: Leicester University Press, 1992), pp. 101–18; R. Gilchrist, 'Blessed Art Thou Among Women: The archaeology of piety', in P.J.P. Goldberg (ed.), *Woman is a Worthy Wight: Women in medieval English society 1200–1500* (Stroud: Alan Sutton, 1992), pp. 212–26; Gilchrist, *Gender and Material Culture*; R. Gilchrist, 'Medieval Bodies in the Material World:

Gender, stigma and the body', in S. Kay and M. Rubin (eds), *Framing Medieval Bodies* (Manchester: Manchester University Press, 1994), pp. 43–61; Gilchrist, *Contemplation and Action*; R. Gilchrist, 'Ambivalent Bodies: Gender and medieval archaeology', in J. Moore and E. Scott (eds), *Invisible People* (London: Leicester University Press, 1997), pp. 42–58; R. Gilchrist, 'Women's Archaeology? Political feminism, gender theory and historical revision', in K. Hays-Gilpin and D.S. Whitley (eds), *Reader in Gender Archaeology* (London: Routledge, 1998), pp. 48–56; Gilchrist, *Gender and Archaeology*; R. Gilchrist, 'Landscapes of the Middle Ages', in J. Hunter and I. Ralston (eds), *The Archaeology of Britain* (London: Routledge, 1999), pp. 228–46; R. Gilchrist (ed.), 'Human Lifecycles', *World Archaeology*, vol. 31, 2000, pp. 325–8; R. Gilchrist, 'Unsexing the Body: The interior sexuality of medieval religious women', in R.A. Schmidt and B.L. Voss (eds), *Archaeologies of Sexuality* (London: Routledge, 2000), pp. 89–103; R. Gilchrist, *Norwich Cathedral Close: The evolution of the English cathedral landscape* (Woodbridge: Boydell, 2005); R. Gilchrist, 'Archaeology and the Life Course: A time and age for gender', in L. Meskell and R.W. Preucel (eds), *A Companion to Social Archaeology* (Oxford: Blackwell, 2007), pp. 142–60; R. Gilchrist, 'Magic for the Dead? The archaeology of magic in later medieval burials', *Medieval Archaeology*, vol. 52, 2008, pp. 119–59; R. Gilchrist, 'Medieval Archaeology and Theory: A disciplinary leap of faith', in R. Gilchrist and A. Reynolds (eds), *Reflections: 50 years of medieval archaeology 1957–2007* (Leeds: Maney, 2009), pp. 385–408; Gilchrist, *Medieval Life*; R. Gilchrist, 'Monastic and Church Archaeology', *Annual Review of Anthropology*, vol. 43, 2014, pp. 235–50; R. Gilchrist, *Sacred Heritage: Monastic archaeology, identities, beliefs* (Cambridge: Cambridge University Press, 2020); R. Gilchrist and H. Mytum (eds), *The Archaeology of Rural Monasteries. BAR British Series 203* (Oxford: British Archaeological Reports, 1989); R. Gilchrist and M. Oliva, *Religious Women in Medieval East Anglia: History and archaeology* c.*1100–1540* (Norwich: Centre of East Anglian Studies, 1993); H. Mytum and R. Gilchrist (eds), *Advances in Monastic Archaeology. BAR British Series 227* (Oxford: Tempvs Reparatvm, 1993); D. Gaimster and R. Gilchrist (eds), *The Archaeology of Reformation 1480–1580* (Leeds: Maney, 2003); R. Gilchrist and B. Sloane, *Requiem: The medieval monastic cemetery in Britain* (London: Museum of London Archaeology Service, 2005).

115 Gilchrist, *Gender and Material Culture*.

116 G. Thomas, 'Life Before the Minster: The social dynamics of monastic foundation at Anglo-Saxon Lyminge, Kent', *The Antiquaries Journal*, vol. 93, 2013, pp. 109–45.

117 S. Ward, *Excavations at Chester: The lesser medieval religious houses. Sites Investigated 1964–1983* (Chester: City Council Department of Leisure Services, 1990); I.R. Scott, 'Romsey Abbey: Benedictine nunnery and parish church', in G. Keevil, M. Aston and T. Hall (eds), *Monastic Archaeology* (Oxford: Oxbow, 2001), pp. 150–60; R. Bull et al., *Holywell Priory and the Development of Shoreditch to* c.*1600: Archaeology from the London Overground East London Line* (London: Museum of London Archaeology Service, 2011); B. Sloane, *The Augustinian Nunnery of St Mary Clerkenwell, London* (London: Museum of London Archaeology Service, 2012); E. Baker, *La Grava: The archaeology and history of a royal manor and alien priory of Fontevrault* (York: Council for British Archaeology, 2013).

118 J. Bezant, *Medieval Welsh Settlement and Territory: Archaeological evidence from a Teifi landscape. BAR British Series 487* (Oxford: Archaeopress, 2009), pp. 44–50.

119 P. Murray, 'Archaeological Excavations at Littlemore Priory Oxford' (unpublished report, 2015).

120 J.N. Brown and D. Alfano Bussell (eds), *Barking Abbey and Medieval Literary Culture: Authorship and authority in a female community* (Woodbridge: York Medieval Press, 2012).

121 For example, C. Platt, *The Monastic Grange in Medieval England* (London: Macmillan, 1969); S. Moorhouse, 'Monastic Estates: Their composition and development', in R. Gilchrist and H. Mytum (eds), *The Archaeology of Rural Monasteries. BAR British Series 203* (Oxford: British Archaeological Reports, 1989), pp. 29–81; M. Aston, *Monasteries in the Landscape* (Stroud: Tempus, 2000), pp. 125–57; D. Walsh, 'Bordesley Abbey Precinct: The definition and use of space in an English Cistercian abbey', in S. McNally (ed.), *Shaping Community: The art and archaeology of monasticism. BAR International Series 941* (Oxford: Archaeopress, 2001), pp. 91–9; J. Bond, 'Medieval Nunneries in England and Wales: Buildings, precincts and estates', in D. Wood (ed.), *Women and Religion in Medieval England* (Oxford: Oxbow, 2003), pp. 46–90, esp. pp. 70–86; J. Bond, *Monastic Landscapes* (Stroud: Tempus, 2004); P. Everson and D. Stocker, 'St Leonard's at Kirkstead, Lincolnshire: The landscape of the Cistercian monastic precinct', in M. Gardiner and S. Rippon (eds), *Medieval Landscapes* (Bollington: Windgather Press, 2007), pp. 215–30; Bezant, *Welsh Settlement*; J. Bezant, 'The Medieval Grants to Strata Florida Abbey: Mapping the agency of lordship', in J. Burton and K. Stöber (eds), *Monastic Wales: New Approaches* (Cardiff: University of Wales Press, 2013), pp. 73–87; J. Bezant, 'Revising the Monastic "Grange": Problems at the edge of the Cistercian world', *Journal of Medieval Monastic Studies*, vol. 3, 2014, pp. 51–70; G. Brown, *Stanley Abbey and Its Estates 1151–c.1640: A Cistercian monastery and its impact on the landscape. BAR British Series 566* (Oxford: Archaeopress, 2012).

122 Burton and Stöber, *Monastic World*, pp. 1–13; A.I. Beach and I. Cochelin (eds), *Medieval Monasticism in the Latin West*, 2 vols (Cambridge: Cambridge University Press, 2020); S. Vanderputten, *Medieval Monasticisms: Forms and experiences of the monastic life in the Latin West* (Oldenbourg: De Gruyter, 2020).

123 For example, J.T. Schulenburg, 'Female Sanctity: Public and private roles *ca* 500–1100', in M. Erler and M. Kowaleski (eds), *Women and Power in the Middle Ages* (Athens: University of Georgia Press, 1988), pp. 102–25; J.T. Schulenburg, 'Women's Monastic Communities 500–1100: Patterns of expansion and decline', *Signs*, vol. 14, no. 2, 1989, pp. 261–92; C.A. Bruzelius and C.H. Berman, 'Introduction', *Gesta*, vol. 31, no. 2, 1992, pp. 73–5; McNamara, *Sisters in Arms*; P. Ranft, *Women and the Religious Life in Premodern Europe* (New York: St Martin's Press, 1996); J.A. Smith, *Ordering Women's Lives: Penitentials and nunnery rules in the early medieval West* (Aldershot: Ashgate, 2001); M. Schaus (ed.), *Women and Gender in Medieval Europe: An encyclopaedia* (London: Routledge, 2006); M. Mersch, 'Programme, Pragmatism and Symbolism in Mendicant Architecture', in A. Müller and K. Stöber (eds), *Self-Representation of Medieval Religious Communities: The British Isles in context* (Berlin: LIT Verlag, 2009), pp. 143–66.

124 Nichols and Thomas Shank, *Distant Echoes*; J.A. Nichols and L. Thomas Shank (eds), *Peace Weavers: Medieval religious women*, vol. 2 (Kalamazoo: Cistercian Publications, 1987); Nichols and Thomas Shank, *Hidden Springs*; B. Degler-Spengler, 'The Incorporation of Cistercian Nuns into the Order in the Twelfth and Thirteenth Century', in J. Nichols and L.T. Shank (eds), *Hidden Springs: Cistercian monastic women. Medieval Religious Women*, vol. 3 (Kalamazoo: Cistercian Publications, 1995), pp. 85–134; C.H. Berman, 'Were There Twelfth-Century Cistercian Nuns?', *Church History*, vol. 68, 1999, pp. 824–64; C.H. Berman, 'How Much Space Did Medieval Nuns Have or Need?', in S. McNally (ed.), *Shaping Community: The art and archaeology of monasticism. BAR International Series 941* (Oxford: Archaeopress, 2001), pp. 100–16; C.H. Berman, *The Cistercian Evolution: The invention of a religious order in twelfth-century Europe* (Philadelphia: University of Pennsylvania Press, 2010); E. Jamroziak, *The Cistercian Order in Medieval Europe 1090–1500* (London: Routledge, 2013), pp. 124–55;

C.H. Berman, *The White Nuns: Cistercian abbeys for women in medieval France* (Philadelphia: University of Pennsylvania Press, 2018).

125 C.A. Bruzelius, 'Hearing is Believing: Clarissan architecture *ca* 1213–1340', *Gesta*, vol. 31, no. 2, 1992, pp. 83–91; C.A. Bruzelius, 'Nuns in Space: Strict enclosure and the architecture of Clarisses in the thirteenth century', in I. Peterson (ed.), *Clare of Assisi: A medieval and modern woman* (New York: The Franciscan Institute, 1996), pp. 53–74; C.A. Bruzelius, 'The Architecture of the Mendicant Orders in the Middles Ages: An overview of recent literature', *Travaux*, vol. 2, 2012, pp. 365–86; C.A. Bruzelius, *Preaching, Building and Burying: Friars in the medieval city* (New Haven: Yale University Press, 2014).

126 For example, E. Coester, *Die einschiffigen Cistercienserinnenkloster West- und Suddeutschlands von 1200–1350. Quellen und Abhandlungen zur mittelrheinischen Kirchengeschichte 46* (Mainz: Gesellschaft für Mittelrheinische Kirchenheschichte, 1984); C. Jäggi, *Fraunenkloster im Spatmittelalter. Die Kirchen der Klarissen und Dominikanerinnen im 13 und 14 Jahrundert* (Petersberg: Studien zur internationalen Architektur- und Kunstgeschichte 34, 2005); M. Untermann, *Architektur im Frühen Mittelalter* (Darmstadt: Wissenschaftliche Buchgesellschaft, 2006); M. Untermann, 'Das Nonnenhaus: traditionen eines klösterlichen bautyps', in R. Oldermann (ed.), *Gebaute Klausur: function und Architektur Mittelalterlicher Klosterräume* (Bielefeld: Verlag Regionalkultur, 2008), pp. 97–109; M. Untermann, 'The Place of the Choir in Churches of Female Convents in the Medieval German Kingdom', in J. Burton and K. Stöber (eds), *Women in the Medieval Monastic World* (Turnhout: Brepols, 2015), pp. 327–53; C. Mohn, *Mittelalterliche Klosteranlagen der Zisterzienserinnen: Architektur der Frauenkloster im mitteldeutschen Raum. Berliner Beitrage zu Bauforschung und Denkmalpflege 4* (Petersberg: Michael Imhof Verlag, 2006); C. Schleif and V. Schier, *Katerina's Windows: Donation and devotion, art and music, as heard and seen through the writings of a Birgittine nun* (Philadelphia: Penn State University Press, 2009); H. Röckelein, 'Frauen im Umkreis der Benediktinischen Reformen des 10 bis 12 Jahrhunderts. Gorze, Cluny, Hirsau, St. Blasien und Siegburg', in G. Melville and A. Müller (eds), *Female* Vita Religiosa *between Late Antiquity and the High Middle Ages: Structures, developments and spatial contexts* (Berlin: LIT Verlag, 2011), pp. 275–327; H. Röckelein, 'FemMoData: A database of medieval female monasteries in Europe', in J. Burton and K. Stöber (eds), *Women in the Medieval Monastic World* (Turnhout: Brepols, 2015), pp. 355–64.

127 Melville and Müller, *Female* Vita Religiosa.

128 J. Frings (ed.), *Krone und Schleier Kunst aus mittelalterlichen frauenklöstern [museum exhibition catalogue]. Herausgegben von der Kunst- und Ausstellungshalle der Bundesrepublik Deutschland, Bonn und dem Ruhrlandmuseum Essen* (Munich: Hirmer Verlag, 2005); Hamburger and Marti, *Crown and Veil*.

129 W. Scheepsma, *Medieval Religious Women in the Low Countries: The modern devotion, the canonesses of Windsheim and their writings*, trans. D.F. Johnson (Woodbridge: Boydell, 2004); E. Jordan, *Women, Power and Religious Patronage in the Middle Ages* (New York: Palgrave Macmillan, 2006); E. Jordan, 'Gender Concerns: Monks, nuns and patronage of the Cistercian order in thirteenth-century Flanders and Hainaut', *Speculum*, vol. 87, 2006, pp. 62–94; E. Jordan, '*Pro Remedio Anime Sue:* Cistercian nuns and space in the Low Countries', in J. Burton and K. Stöber (eds), *Women in the Medieval Monastic World* (Turnhout: Brepols, 2015), pp. 279–98; E. De Paermentier, 'Experiencing Space through Women's Convent Rules: The Rich Clares in medieval Ghent (thirteenth to fourteenth centuries)', *Medieval Feminist Forum*, vol. 44, no. 1, 2008, pp. 53–68; M. Van Hove, F. Chantinne and D. Willems, 'Dans La Clôture D'une Grande Abbaye:

Premiers résultats des recherches archéologiques menées sur la place de Nivelles (2009–2011)', *Medieval and Modern Matters*, vol. 3, 2012, pp. 165–210.

130 A. Dimier, *Recueil de Plans D'églises Cisterciennes. Supplément* (Paris: Aiguebelle, 1967); A. Dimier, 'L'architecture des Églises de Moniales Cisterciennes', *Cîteaux: Commentarii Cistercienses*, vol. 25, 1974, pp. 8–13; S.F. Wemple, *Women in Frankish Society: Marriage and the cloister 500–900* (Philadelphia: Penn, 1981); M. Desmarchelier, 'L'architecture des Églises de Moniales Cisterciennes, Essai de Classement des Différents Types de Plans (en guise de suite)', in B. Chauvin (ed.), *Mélanges á la Mémoire du Père Anselme Dimier, III Architecture Cistercienne, Volume 5 Ordre, Fouilles* (Arbois: Pupillin, 1982), pp. 79–121; P. Johnson, *Equal in Monastic Profession: Religious women in medieval France* (Chicago: University of Chicago Press, 1991); B. Barrière, 'The Cistercian Convent of Coyroux in the Twelfth and Thirteenth Centuries', *Gesta*, vol. 31, no. 2, 1992, pp. 76–82; B.L. Venarde, *Women's Monasticism and Medieval Society: Nunneries in France and England 890–1215* (Ithaca: Cornell University Press, 1997); B.L. Venarde, 'Robert of Arbrissel and Woman's *Vita Religiosa*: Looking back and ahead', in G. Melville and A. Müller (eds), *Female* Vita Religiosa *between Late Antiquity and the High Middle Ages: Structures, developments and spatial contexts* (Berlin: LIT Verlag, 2011), pp. 329–40; A. Helvetius, 'L'organisation des Monastères Féminins à L'époque Mérovingienne', in G. Melville and A. Müller (eds), *Female* Vita Religiosa *between Late Antiquity and the High Middle Ages: Structures, developments and spatial contexts* (Berlin: LIT Verlag, 2011), pp. 151–69; M. Gaillard, 'Female Monasteries of the Early Middle Ages (Seventh to Ninth Century) in Northern Gaul: Between monastic ideals and aristocratic powers', in J. Burton and K. Stöber (eds), *Women in the Medieval Monastic World* (Turnhout: Brepols, 2015), pp. 75–96.

131 J. Jarrett, 'Power Over Past and Future: Abbess Emma and the nunnery of Sant Joan de les Abadesses', *Early Medieval Europe*, vol. 12, 2003, pp. 229–58; J. Jarrett, *Rulers and Ruled in Frontier Catalonia 880–1010: Pathways of power* (Woodbridge: Boydell, 2010); B. Garí (ed.), *Redes Femenias de Promoción Spiritual en Los Reinos Peninsulares, s.xiii-xvi, Ircum-medieval cultures, 1* (Rome: Viella, 2013); Garí, *Anuario de Estudios Medievales*; N. Jornet-Benito, 'Female Mendicant Spirituality in Catalan Territory: The birth of the first communities of Poor Clares', in J. Burton and K. Stöber (eds), *Women in the Medieval Monastic World* (Turnhout: Brepols, 2015), pp. 185–210; G. Caverno-Dominguez, 'Spanish Female Monasticism: Family monasteries and their transformation, eleventh to twelfth centuries', in J. Burton and K. Stöber (eds), *Women in the Medieval Monastic World* (Turnhout: Brepols, 2015), pp. 15–52.

132 S. Evangelisti, *Nuns: A history of convent life* (Oxford: Oxford University Press, 2008); G. Cariboni, 'Cistercian Nuns in Northern Italy: Variety of foundations and construction of an identity', in J. Burton and K. Stöber (eds), *Women in the Medieval Monastic World* (Turnhout: Brepols, 2015), pp. 53–74; A. Rapetti, 'Women and Monasticism in Venice in the Tenth to Twelfth Centuries', in J. Burton and K. Stöber (eds), *Women in the Medieval Monastic World* (Turnhout: Brepols, 2015), pp. 145–66.

133 C. Jäggi, 'Eastern Choir or Western Gallery? The problem of the place of the nuns' choir in Koenigsfelden and other early mendicant nunneries', *Gesta*, vol. 40, no. 1, 2001, pp. 79–93; Jäggi, *Fraunenkloster im Spatmittelalter*.

134 T. Nyberg, 'On Female Monasticism and Scandinavia', *Medieval Scandinavia*, vol. 13, 2000, pp. 181–97; B.P. McGuire, 'Cistercian Nuns in Twelfth- and Thirteenth-Century Denmark and Sweden: Far from the madding crowd', in J. Burton and K. Stöber (eds), *Women in the Medieval Monastic World* (Turnhout: Brepols, 2015), pp. 167–84.

135 B. Lackner, 'Cistercian Nuns in Medieval Hungary', in J. Nichols and L. Thomas Shank (eds), *Hidden Springs: Cistercian monastic women. Medieval Religious Women*, vol. 3 (Kalamazoo: Cistercian Publications, 1995), pp. 159–70; C. Florea, '"For They Wanted Us to Serve Them": Female monasticism in medieval Transylvania', in J. Burton and K. Stöber (eds), *Women in the Medieval Monastic World* (Turnhout: Brepols, 2015), pp. 211–27.

136 For example, Berman, 'How Much Space Did Medieval Nuns Have or Need?'; V.C. Raguin and S. Stanbury (eds), *Women's Space: Patronage, place and gender in the medieval church* (New York: State University of New York Press, 2005); A. Müller, 'Presenting Identity in the Cloister: Remarks on Benedictine and Mendicant concepts of space', in A. Müller and K. Stöber (eds), *Self-Representation of Medieval Religious Communities: The British Isles in context* (Berlin: LIT Verlag, 2009), pp. 167–87; A. Müller, 'Symbolic Meanings of Space in Female Monastic Tradition', in J. Burton and K. Stöber (eds), *Women in the Medieval Monastic World* (Turnhout: Brepols, 2015), pp. 299–326; M. Cassidy-Welch, *Monastic Spaces and Their Meanings: Thirteenth-century English Cistercian monasteries* (Turnhout: Brepols, 2001); M. Cassidy-Welch, 'Space and Place in Medieval Contexts', *Parergon*, vol. 27, 2010, pp. 1–12; M. Cassidy-Welch, *Imprisonment in the Medieval Religious Imagination, c.1150–1400* (London: Palgrave Macmillan, 2011); J.A. Smith, '*Clausura Districta*: Conceiving space and community for Dominican nuns in the thirteenth century', *Parergon*, vol. 27, no. 2, 2010, pp. 13–36; G. Signori, 'Cell or Dormitory? Monastic visions of space amidst the conflict of ideas', *Journal of Medieval Monastic Studies*, vol. 3, 2014, pp. 21–49.

137 But see as exceptions: E. Jamroziak and J. Burton (eds), *Religious and Laity in Northern Europe 1000–1400: Interaction, negotiation and power* (Turnhout: Brepols, 2007); E. Jamroziak, *Survival and Success on Medieval Borders: Cistercian houses in medieval Scotland and Pomerania from the twelfth to late fourteenth century* (Turnhout: Brepols, 2011); E. Jamroziak and K. Stöber (eds), *Monasteries on the Borders of Medieval Europe: Conflict and cultural interaction* (Turnhout: Brepols, 2013); Beach and Cochelin, *Medieval Monasticism in the Latin West*.

138 https://arts.st-andrews.ac.uk/monasticmatrix/. Accessed 15 September 2020.

139 https://www.monasticwales.org/. Accessed 15 September 2020.

140 https://www.uni-goettingen.de/en/76297.html. Accessed 15 September 2020.

141 Röckelein, 'FemMoData', pp. 355–64.

142 http://historyofwomenreligious.org. Accessed 15 September 2020.

143 https://fmrsi.wordpress.com. Accessed 15 September 2020.

144 For example, K. Curran, 'Review article: *Feminine Sanctity and Spirituality in Medieval Wales* (J. Cartwright)', *Journal of Medieval Monastic Studies*, vol. 1, 2012, pp. 145–6; K. Curran, 'Review article: *Anchorites, Wombs and Tombs: Intersections of gender and enclosure in the middle ages* (ed. L. Herbert McEvoy and M. Hughes-Edwards)', *Journal of Medieval Monastic Studies*, vol. 1, 2012, pp. 155–6; A.L. Beach, 'Review article: *Inventing Sempringham: Gilbert of Sempringham and the origins of the role of master* (K. Sykes)', *Journal of Medieval Monastic Studies*, vol. 2, 2013, pp. 189–90; A.L. Beach, 'Review article: *Female* Vita Religiosa *between Late Antiquity and the High Middle Ages: Structures, developments and spatial contexts* (eds G. Meville and A. Müller), *Journal of Medieval Monastic Studies*, vol. 2, 2013, pp. 186–7; B. Garí, 'The Sacred Space of Meditation: Nunneries and devotional performance in the territories of the Crown of Aragón (fourteenth–fifteenth centuries)', *Journal of Medieval Monastic Studies*, vol. 3, 2014, pp. 71–95; K. Stöber, 'Review article: *Redes Femenias de Promoción Spiritual en Los Reinos Peninsulares, s.xiii–xvi* (ed. B. Garí)', *Journal of Medieval Monastic Studies*, vol. 3,

2014, pp. 133–5; P. Stoop, 'Review article: *Barking Abbey and Medieval Literary Culture: Authorship and authority in a female community* (eds J.N. Brown and D. Alfano Bussell), *Journal of Medieval Monastic Studies*, vol. 3, 2014, pp. 126–8.

145 For example, G. Cooney and E. Grogan, *Irish Prehistory: A social perspective* (Dublin: Wordwell, 1994).

146 For instance, T. O'Keeffe, *An Anglo-Norman Monastery*; O'Keeffe, *Romanesque Ireland*; O'Keeffe, *Round Towers*; C. Fredengren, *Crannógs* (Bray: Wordwell, 2002); Ó Carragáin, *Churches in Early Medieval Ireland*. For recent critiques see O'Keeffe, 'Theory and Medieval Archaeology in Ireland and Beyond'; K. Dempsey, 'Gender and Medieval Archaeology: Storming the castle', *Antiquity*, vol. 93, 2019, pp. 772–88; K. Dempsey, 'Planting New Ideas: A feminist gaze on medieval castles', *Château Gaillard*, vol. 29, 2020, pp. 85–98; K. Dempsey, 'Home is Where the Heart(h) is: Investigating medieval houses in Ireland 1100–1600 AD', *Archaeology Ireland*, vol. 34, no. 1, 2020, pp. 49–51; K. Dempsey, R. Gilchrist, J. Ashbee, S. Sagrott and S. Stones, 'Beyond the Martial Façade: Gender, heritage and medieval castles', *International Journal of Heritage Studies*, vol. 26, no. 4, 2020, pp. 352–69.

147 M. Tierney, 'Theory and Politics in Early Medieval Irish Archaeology', in M.A. Monk and J. Sheehan (eds), *Early Medieval Munster: Archaeology, history and society* (Cork: Cork University Press, 1998), pp. 190–9.

148 K. Hays-Gilpin and D.S. Whitley (eds), *Reader in Gender Archaeology* (London: Routledge, 1998), p. 4.

149 Gilchrist, 'Women's Archaeology?', p. 48; R.W. Preucel and I. Hodder (eds), *Contemporary Archaeology in Theory: A reader* (Oxford: Blackwell, 1996), p. 416; Bennett, 'Medievalism', p. 25; S.M. Nelson, *Gender in Archaeology: Analyzing power and prestige* (California: AltaMira Press, 2004), p. 158; M. Días-Andreu and M.L. Stig Sørensen, 'Excavating Women: Towards an engendered history of archaeology', in T. Murray and C. Evans (eds), *Histories of Archaeology: A reader in the history of archaeology* (Oxford: Oxford University Press, 2008), pp. 279–311; M.L. Stig Sørensen, *Gender Archaeology* (Oxford: Polity Press, 2000); M.L. Stig Sørensen, 'Gender Agenda? Review article', *Antiquity*, vol. 75, 2001, pp. 440–2.

150 L. Binford, *An Archaeological Perspective* (New York: Seminar Press, 1972); D. Clarke, *Analytical Archaeology* (London: Methuen, 1968); D. Clarke, 'Archaeology: The loss of innocence', *Antiquity*, vol. 47, 1973, pp. 6–18. For a critique of these early works see: B. Trigger, *A History of Archaeological Thought* (Cambridge: Cambridge University Press, 1989), pp. 289–328; Gilchrist, *Gender and Archaeology*, pp. 17–19; A. Wylie, *Thinking From Things: Essays in the philosophy of archaeology* (Berkeley: University of California Press, 2002), pp. 24–41; R.W. Preucel and L. Meskell, 'Knowledges', in L. Meskell and R.W. Preucel (eds), *A Companion to Social Archaeology* (Oxford: Blackwell, 2007), pp. 3–22, at pp. 4–5; A. Wylie, 'Gender Theory and the Archaeological Record: Why is there no archaeology of gender?', in J.M. Gero and M.W. Conkey (eds), *Engendering Archaeology* (Oxford: Blackwell, 1991), pp. 31–54, at pp. 31–2; A.J. Frantzen, 'When Women Aren't Enough', in N. Partner (ed.), *Studying Medieval Women* (Cambridge, MA: The Medieval Academy of America, 1993), pp. 143–69, at p. 146; Preucel and Hodder, *Contemporary Archaeology*, p. 415.

151 Gilchrist, *Gender and Material Culture*, pp. 2, 8; Gilchrist, *Gender and Archaeology*, p. 1; Preucel and Hodder, *Contemporary Archaeology*, p. 415; Stig Sørensen, *Gender Archaeology*, pp. 3–15; J. Murray, 'Femininity and Masculinity', in M. Schaus (ed.), *Women and Gender in Medieval Europe: An encyclopaedia* (London: Routledge, 2006), pp. 284–7, at p. 284.

152 S. de Beauvoir, *The Second Sex*, trans. H.M. Parshley (New York: Vintage Books, Random House, 1989); Bennett, 'Medievalism', p. 12; B. Friedan, *The Feminine Mystique* (London: Norton & Company, 2001), pp. 57–78; M.W. Conkey and J. Gero, 'From Programme to Practice: Gender and feminism in archaeology', *Annual Review of Anthropology*, vol. 26, 1997, pp. 411–37, at p. 430; Gilchrist, *Gender and Archaeology*, p. 20; Johnson, *Archaeological Theory*, pp. 126–7.

153 For example, Eckenstein, *Under Monasticism*; Bateson, 'Origin and Early History'; Clay, *Hermits and Anchorites*; Power, *English Nunneries*. For critique see C.R. Peyroux, 'Abbess and Cloister: Double monasteries in the early medieval West', unpublished dissertation, Princeton University, 1990; B.L. Voss, 'Feminisms, Queer Theories and the Archaeological Study of Past Sexualities', *World Archaeology*, vol. 32, 2000, pp. 180–92, at p. 181; S.M. Stuard, 'The Chase After Theory: Considering medieval women', in S.M. Stuard (ed.), *Considering Medieval Women and Gender* (Surrey: Ashgate, 2010), pp. 135–46, at p. 136; S.M. Stuard, 'The Three-Decade Transformation: Medieval women and the course of history', in S.M. Stuard (ed.), *Considering Medieval Women and Gender* (Surrey: Ashgate, 2010), pp. 1–21, at pp. 2–3; Bennett, 'Medievalism', p. 12; Gilchrist, *Gender and Archaeology*, p. 2.

154 For example, M. Gimbutas, *The Language of the Goddess* (London: Thames & Hudson, 1989). For critique see A.B. Knapp, 'Boys Will Be Boys: Masculinist approaches to a gendered archaeology', in K. Hays-Gilpin and D. Whitley (eds), *Reader in Gender Archaeology* (London: Routledge, 1998), pp. 365–71; M.W. Conkey and J. Spector, 'Archaeology and the Study of Gender', in K. Hays-Gilpin and D.S. Whitley (eds), *Reader in Gender Archaeology* (London: Routledge, 1998), pp. 12–45; M. Ehrenberg, *Women in Prehistory* (London: British Museum Publications, 1989); C. Roberts, 'A Critical Approach to Gender as a Category of Analysis in Archaeology', in H. du Cros and L. Smith (eds), *Women in Archaeology: A feminist critique* (Canberra: Dept of Prehistory, Occasional Papers in Prehistory 23, 1993), pp. 16–21; S.M. Stuard, 'The Annales School and Feminist History: Opening dialogue with the American stepchild', in S.M. Stuard (ed.), *Considering Medieval Women and Gender* (Surrey: Ashgate, 2010), pp. 135–43, at pp. 135, 139, 141; L. Meskell, 'Goddesses, Gimbutas and "New Age" Archaeology', *Antiquity*, vol. 69, 1995, pp. 74–86, at p. 83; R. Hutton, 'The Neolithic Great Goddess: A study in modern tradition', *Antiquity*, vol. 71, 1997, pp. 91–9; Gilchrist, *Gender and Archaeology*, p. 25.

155 I. Hodder (ed.), *Symbolic and Structural Archaeology* (Cambridge: Cambridge University Press, 1982); I. Hodder, *The Archaeology of Contextual Meanings* (Cambridge: Cambridge University Press, 1987); I. Hodder (ed.), *Archaeological Theory Today* (Cambridge: Polity Press, 2002); M. Shanks and C. Tilley, *Reconstructing Archaeology* (Cambridge: Cambridge University Press, 1987); M. Shanks and C. Tilley, *Social Theory and Archaeology* (Cambridge: Polity Press, 1987); M. Shanks and C. Tilley, *Studies in Archaeological Theory Practices* (Cambridge: Cambridge University Press, 1987); E. Engelstad, 'Images of Power and Contradiction: Feminist theory and post-processual archaeology', *Antiquity*, vol. 65, 1991, pp. 502–14; Gilchrist, *Gender and Archaeology*; Johnson, *Archaeological Theory*, p. 102; A. Giddens, *Central Problems in Social Theory* (London: Macmillan, 1979).

156 I. Hodder, 'Archaeology in 1984', *Antiquity*, vol. 58, 1984, pp. 25–32, at p. 27; Shanks and Tilley, *Social Theory*; M. Shanks, *Experiencing the Past* (London: Routledge, 1992).

157 Conkey and Spector, 'Study of Gender'. For critique see Preucel and Hodder, *Contemporary Archaeology*, p. 416; Gilchrist, *Gender and Archaeology*, p. 4; Johnson, *Archaeological Theory*, p. 135.

158 Gilchrist, *Gender and Archaeology*, p. 26; Stig Sørensen, *Gender Archaeology*, pp. 20–4.
159 Gilchrist, 'Women's Archaeology?', p. 47.
160 Gilchrist, *Gender and Material Culture*, p. 3; Gilchrist, *Gender and Archaeology*, p.26.
161 M. Foucault, *The History of Sexuality. Volume 1: An Introduction* (Harmonsworth: Penguin, 1981); J. Butler, *Gender Trouble: Feminism and the subversion of identity* (London: Routledge, 1990); R.A. Schmidt and B.L. Voss (eds), *Archaeologies of Sexuality* (London: Routledge, 2000); Voss, 'Feminisms, Queer Theories', pp. 183–6; I. Hodder, 'The "Social" in Archaeological Theory', in L. Meskell and R.W. Preucel (eds), *A Companion to Social Archaeology* (Oxford: Blackwell, 2007), pp. 23–42, at p. 36; M.A. McLaren, *Feminism, Foucault, and Embodied Subjectivity* (Albany, NY: SUNY Press, 2007); E.K. Feder, 'Review: *Feminism, Foucault, and Embodied Subjectivity*', *Foucault Studies*, vol. 6, 2009, pp. 131–5.
162 Gilchrist, *Gender and Archaeology*, p. 56.
163 Gilchrist, *Gender and Material Culture*.
164 For example, Eckenstein, *Under Monasticism*; Clay, *Medieval Hospitals*; Clay, *Hermits and Anchorites*; Bourdillon, *Minoresses*.
165 Waddell, *Foundation Myths*, pp. 225–31.
166 Power, *English Nunneries*.
167 Wylie, 'Gender Theory', pp. 31–2.
168 Preucel and Hodder, *Contemporary Archaeology*, p. 420.
169 J.D. Spector, 'What This Awl Means: Toward a feminist archaeology', in R.W. Preucel and I. Hodder (eds), *Contemporary Archaeology in Theory: A reader* (Oxford: Blackwell, 1996), pp. 485–500, at p. 485.
170 Gilchrist, *Gender and Material Culture*, p. 6.
171 For example, Leask, *Irish Churches and Monastic Buildings*; Stalley, *Cistercian Monasteries*; O'Keeffe, *An Anglo-Norman Monastery*; C. Ó Clabaigh, *The Franciscans in Ireland, 1400–1534: From reform to reformation* (Dublin: Four Courts Press, 2002); L. de Paor, 'Excavations at Mellifont Abbey, Co. Louth', *Proceedings of the Royal Irish Academy*, vol. 68C, 1969, pp. 109–64; T. Fanning, 'Excavations at Clontuskert Priory, County Galway', *Proceedings of the Royal Irish Academy*, vol. 76C, 1976, pp. 97–169; J. O'Sullivan, J. Roberts and S. Halliday, 'Archaeological Excavation of Medieval, Post-Medieval and Modern Burial at Ennis Friary, Co. Clare', *North Munster Antiquarian Journal*, vol. 43, 2003, pp. 21–42; M. Clyne, *Kells Priory, Co. Kilkenny: Archaeological excavations by T. Fanning and M. Clyne* (Dublin: Government of Ireland, 2007).
172 Gilchrist, *Gender and Material Culture*, p. 190.
173 Gilchrist, 'Women's Archaeology?', p. 53.
174 S. Frazer, 'The Public Forum and the Space Between: The materiality of social strategy in the Irish Neolithic', *Proceedings of the Prehistoric Society*, vol. 64, 1998, pp. 203–24, at p. 204.
175 J. Thomas, 'Archaeologies of Place and Landscape', in I. Hodder (ed.), *Archaeological Theory Today* (Cambridge: Polity Press, 2001), pp. 165–86, at p. 181.
176 M. Rubin, 'Presentism's Useful Anachronisms', *Past and Present*, vol. 234, 2017, pp. 236–44.
177 D. Ferriter, *The Transformation of Ireland 1900–2000* (London: Profile Books, 2012).
178 C.H. Berman, 'Medieval Monasticisms', in J. Arnold (ed.), *The Oxford Handbook of Medieval Christianity* (Oxford: Oxford University Press, 2014), pp. 337–95, at p. 337.
179 Thomas, 'Archaeologies of Place', p. 180; J. Thomas, *Archaeology and Modernity* (London: Routledge, 2004).
180 Thomas, *Archaeology and Modernity*, pp. 223–48.

181 A. Wylie, 'On "Heavily Decomposing Red Herrings": Scientific method in archaeology and the ladening of evidence with theory', in L. Embree (ed.), *Metaarchaeology* (Dordrecht: Kluwer, 1992), pp. 269–88, at pp. 269–75.
182 J. Brück, 'Experiencing the Past? The development of a phenomenological archaeology in British prehistory', *Archaeological Dialogues*, vol. 12, 2005, pp. 45–72, at pp. 57–8.
183 A. Wylie, 'The Interplay of Evidential Constraints and Political Interest: Recent archaeological research on gender', in K. Hays-Gilpin and D.S. Whitley (eds), *Reader in Gender Archaeology* (London: Routledge, 1998), pp. 57–84, at pp. 57, 65, 72–3.
184 I. Hodder, *Theory and Practice in Archaeology* (London: Routledge, 1995); Hodder, *Theory Today*; I. Hodder and S. Hutson, *Reading the Past: Current approaches to interpretation in archaeology* (Cambridge: Cambridge University Press, 2003).
185 Shanks and Tilley, *Reconstructing Archaeology*; Shanks and Tilley, *Social Theory*; Shanks and Tilley, *Studies in Archaeological Theory*.
186 Wylie, 'Interplay of Evidential Constraints', p. 60.
187 Gilchrist, *Gender and Archaeology*, p. 30.
188 M. Johnson, 'Conceptions of Agency in Archaeological Interpretation', in J. Thomas (ed.), *Interpretive Archaeology: A reader* (London: Leicester University Press, 2000), pp. 211–27; J.C. Barrett, 'Agency, the Duality of Structure and the Problem of the Archaeological Record', in I. Hodder (ed.), *Archaeological Theory Today* (Cambridge: Polity Press, 2001), pp. 140–64; Nelson, *Gender in Archaeology*, pp. 150–8.
189 Husserl cited by D. Moran, *Introduction to Phenomenology* (London: Routledge, 2000), p. 1.
190 Moran, *Phenomenology*, p. 21.
191 Thomas, 'Archaeologies of Place', p. 180.
192 Brück, 'Experiencing the Past?', p. 46.
193 Ibid., p. 51.
194 Ibid., pp. 55, 59.
195 Ibid., p. 56.
196 Thomas, 'Archaeologies of Place', p. 170.
197 Smith, *Ordering Women's Lives*.
198 Harrington, *Women in a Celtic Church*, pp. 86–9.
199 McNamara, *Sisters in Arms*, pp. 289–323; Hall, *Women and the Church*, pp. 169–76; Flanagan, *Transformation*, pp. 118–68.
200 Gilchrist, *Gender and Archaeology*, p. 81; Hicks, *Religious Life*, pp. 2–6.
201 Barrett, 'Agency, the Duality of Structure'.
202 Hodder, 'The "Social" in Archaeological Theory', p. 32.
203 Brück, 'Experiencing the Past?', p. 61.
204 E.M. Brumfiel, 'It's a Material World: History, artifacts and anthropology', *Annual Review of Anthropology*, vol. 32, 2003, pp. 205–23.
205 Butler, *Gender Trouble*; Gilchrist, *Gender and Archaeology*, p. 147.
206 Johnson, *Archaeological Theory*, p. 141.
207 J. Murray, 'One Flesh, Two Sexes, Three Genders?', in L.M. Bitel and F. Lifshitz (eds), *Gender and Christianity in Medieval Europe: New perspectives* (Philadelphia: Penn State University Press, 2008), pp. 34–51.
208 N.F. Partner, 'No Sex, No Gender', in N. Partner (ed.), *Studying Medieval Women* (Cambridge, MA: The Medieval Academy of America, 1993), pp. 117–41.
209 Hays-Gilpin and Whitley, *Reader in Gender Archaeology*, p. 7.
210 Gilchrist, 'Archaeology and the Life Course', p. 147.

211 Brück, 'Experiencing the Past?', p. 59.
212 P. Bourdieu, *Outline of a Theory of Practice* (Cambridge: Cambridge University Press, 1977); P. Bourdieu, *The Logic of Practice* (Cambridge: Polity Press, 1990).
213 Gilchrist, *Gender and Material Culture*; Gilchrist, *Contemplation and Action*.
214 Kenny, *Women in Ireland*, p. 170.
215 Gilchrist, *Gender and Archaeology*, pp. 81, 87.
216 Hodder, 'The "Social"', p. 33.
217 Nelson, *Gender in Archaeology*, p. 158; L. Meskell, 'Archaeologies of Identity', in I. Hodder (ed.), *Archaeological Theory Today* (Cambridge: Polity Press, 2001), pp. 187–213.
218 C. Tilley, 'Phenomenology', in A.C. Renfrew and P. Bahn (eds), *Archaeology: The key concepts* (London: Routledge, 2005), pp. 201–7, at p. 202; Johnson, *Archaeological Theory*, pp. 118–20.
219 R. Bradley, *An Archaeology of Natural Places* (London: Routledge, 2000); R. Bradley, *The Past in Prehistoric Societies* (London: Routledge, 2002).
220 For example, Spector, 'What this Awl Means?'
221 Gilchrist, *Gender and Archaeology*, pp. 83–7; Gilchrist, 'Archaeology and the Life Course', pp. 152–4.
222 Gilchrist, 'Archaeology and the Life Course', p. 154.
223 J.T. Schulenberg, 'Gender, Celibacy and Proscriptions of Sacred Space: Symbol and practice', in V.C. Raguin and S. Stanbury (eds), *Women's Space: Patronage, place and gender in the medieval church* (Albany: State University of New York Press, 2005), pp. 185–205, at p. 185.
224 For example, M. Foucault, *Discipline and Punish: The birth of the prison* (New York: Random House, 1977); P. Bourdieu, *Distinction: A social critique of the judgement of taste* (London: Routledge & Kegan Paul, 1979); B. Hillier and J. Hanson, *The Social Logic of Space* (Cambridge: Cambridge University Press, 1984); M. de Certeau, *The Practice of Everyday Life* (Berkeley: University of California Press, 1984); H. Lefebvre, *The Production of Space*, trans D. Nicholson-Smith (Oxford: Blackwell, 1991); D. Massey, *Space, Place and Gender* (Minnesota: University of Minnesota Press, 1994).
225 Y.F. Tuan, *Space and Place: The perspective of experience* (London: Edward Arnold, 1977); Hillier and Hanson, *Social Logic of Space*; Lefebvre, *Production of Space*; E.S. Casey, 'Place in Landscape Archaeology: A western philosophical prelude', in B. David and J. Thomas (eds), *Handbook of Landscape Archaeology* (California: Left Coast Press, 2008), pp. 44–50.
226 De Paermentier, 'Experiencing Space', p. 54.
227 K. Biddick, 'Decolonising the English Past: Readings in medieval archaeology', *Journal of British Studies*, vol. 32, 1993, pp. 1–23; B.A. Hanawalt and M. Kobialka (eds), *Medieval Practices of Space* (London: University of Minnesota Press, 2000), p. xii; Müller, 'Symbolic Meanings of Space'.
228 For example, Gilchrist, *Gender and Material Culture*; Cassidy-Welch, *Monastic Spaces and Their Meanings*, pp. 2–12; Hicks, *Religious Life in Normandy*; Smith, *Ordering Women's Lives*; H. Mytum, 'Functionalist and Non-Functionalist Approaches in Monastic Archaeology', in R. Gilchrist and H. Mytum (eds), *The Archaeology of Rural Monasteries. BAR British Series 203* (Oxford: BAR, 1989), pp. 339–57; O'Keeffe, *An Anglo-Norman Monastery*; T. O'Keeffe, 'The Built Environment of Local Community Worship between the Later Eleventh and Early Thirteenth Centuries', in E. FitzPatrick and R. Gillespie (eds), *The Parish in Medieval and Early Modern Ireland* (Dublin: Four Courts Press, 2006), pp. 124–46; T. O'Keeffe, 'Augustinian Regular Canons in Twelfth- and Thirteenth-Century Ireland: History, architecture and identity', in J. Burton and

K. Stöber (eds), *The Regular Canons in the Medieval British Isles* (Turnhout: Brepols, 2011), pp. 469–84; D.M. Hayes, *Body and Sacred Place in Medieval Europe 1100–1389* (London: Routledge, 2003); T. Ó Carragáin, 'From Family Cemeteries to Community Cemeteries in Viking Age Ireland?', in C. Corlett and M. Potterton (eds), *Death and Burial in Early Medieval Ireland in the Light of Recent Archaeological Excavations* (Dublin: Wordwell, 2010), pp. 217–26.

229 De Certeau, *Everyday Life*.

230 Müller, 'Presenting Identity', p. 169.

231 Bourdieu, *Theory of Practice*; Hanawalt and Kobialka, *Medieval Practices*; H. Kleinschmidt, *Understanding the Middle Ages: The transformation of ideas and attitudes in the medieval world* (London: Boydell, 2000), p. 33.

232 Gilchrist, 'Community and Self', p. 55; Cassidy-Welch, *Monastic Spaces and Their Meanings*, pp. 2–12; Kerr, *Life in the Medieval Cloister*, pp. 20–37.

233 For example, Mersch, 'Programme, Pragmatism and Symbolism'.

234 Müller, 'Symbolic Meanings of Space', p. 302.

235 Gilchrist, *Gender and Material Culture*, p. 152.

236 C.H. Lawrence, *Medieval Monasticism*, 3rd edn (Harlow: Longman, 2001), pp. 217–18; Hall, *Women and the Church*, p. 25; Kenny, *Anglo-Irish and Gaelic Women*, p. 170. For an alternative view, that nuns did not always come from the aristocratic classes in certain regions, see Chapter 8; Harris, 'A New Look at the Reformation'; Oliva, 'Aristocracy or Meritocracy?'

237 Gilchrist, *Gender and Archaeology*, pp. 113–18; Gilchrist, *Medieval Life*, pp. 68–113; R.H. Britnell, *Britain and Ireland 1050–1530: Economy and society* (Oxford: Oxford University Press, 2004), pp. 7–70.

238 De Paermentier, 'Experiencing Space', p. 53. It has been suggested that it is anachronistic to consider strict enclosure of female religious communities in early medieval Ireland: see Chapter 2.

239 Gilchrist, *Medieval Life*.

240 Gilchrist, 'Human Lifecycles', pp. 325–8; Gilchrist, 'Archaeology and the Life Course', p. 143.

241 N. Finlay, 'Outside of Life and Death: Traditions of infant burial in Ireland from cillín to cist', *World Archaeology*, vol. 31, 2000, pp. 407–22; J. Geber, *Victims of Ireland's Great Famine: The bioarchaeology of mass burials at Kilkenny Union workhouse* (Gainsville: University Press of Florida, 2015).

242 J.C. Barrett, 'Chronologies of Landscape', in P. Ucko and R. Layton (eds), *The Archaeology and Anthropology of Landscape* (London: Routledge, 1999), pp. 21–30, at p. 30.

243 W. Ashmore, 'Social Archaeologies of Landscape', in L. Meskell and R.W. Preucel (eds), *A Companion to Social Archaeology* (Oxford: Blackwell, 2007), pp. 255–71, at p. 255.

244 Ashmore, 'Social Archaeologies'; Johnson, *Archaeological Theory*, pp. 192–8.

245 But see O'Keeffe, *Romanesque Ireland*; O'Keeffe, *Round Towers*; Ó Carragáin, *Churches in Early Medieval Ireland*; O'Keeffe, 'Theory and Medieval Archaeology in Ireland'; Dempsey, 'Planting New Ideas'; Dempsey, 'Home is Where the Heart(h) is'.

246 Thomas, 'Archaeologies of Place', pp. 165, 181; M. Johnson, *Ideas of Landscape* (Oxford: Blackwell, 2007), pp. 193, 202.

247 Barrett, 'Chronologies of Landscape', p. 26; Thomas, 'Archaeologies of Place', p. 165.

248 Ashmore, 'Social Archaeologies', p. 266.

249 Wylie, 'Interplay of Evidential Constraints', p. 78.

CHAPTER 2. THE CHARACTER OF FEMALE RELIGIOUS IN EARLY MEDIEVAL IRELAND

1 For example, O'Keeffe, *Romanesque Ireland*, p. 64; Stupecki and Valor, 'Religions'; Ó Carragáin, *Churches in Early Medieval Ireland*; T. Ó Carragáin and J. Sheehan, 'Making Christian Landscapes: Settlement, society and regionality in early medieval Ireland, 2 parts' (unpublished report for the Heritage Council, 2010). Available at: https://www.yumpu.com/en/document/view/22251522/ar01049-christian-landscapes-summary-report-10pdf-the-. Accessed 15 September 2020; G. Thomas, 'The Prehistory of Medieval Farms and Villages: From Saxons to Scandinavians', in N. Christie and P. Stamper (eds), *Medieval Rural Settlement: Britain and Ireland AD 800–1600* (Oxford: Windgather Press, 2012), pp. 43–62; O'Sullivan et al., *Early Medieval Ireland*; L. Bitel, 'Monastic Identity in Early Medieval Ireland', in A.I. Beach and I. Cochelin (eds), *Medieval Monasticism in the Latin West*, 2 vols (Cambridge: Cambridge University Press, 2020), pp. 297–316; M. Callan, *Sacred Sisters: Gender, sanctity and power in medieval Ireland* (Amsterdam: Amsterdam University Press, 2020). For recent overviews of the history and archaeology of the early medieval period, see: E. Bhreathnach, *Ireland in the Medieval World AD 400–1000: Landscape, kingship and religion* (Dublin: Four Courts Press, 2014); M. Stout, *Early Medieval Ireland 431–1169* (Dublin: Wordwell, 2017); N. Edwards, R. Flechner and M. Ní Mhaonaigh (eds), *Transforming Landscapes of Belief in the Early Medieval Insular World and Beyond: Converting the isles II* (Turnhout: Brepols, 2017).

2 See, for example, Ó Riain, *A Dictionary*, which includes an extensive list of female saints. For a comprehensive list of ecclesiastical settlement in Ireland from the fifth to the twelfth century, see https://monasticon.celt.dias.ie/index.php. Accessed 15 September 2020. For a list of early medieval female religious sites and putative ones mentioned here, see the online catalogue at DOI: http://doi.org/10.5281/zenodo.5035404.

3 Harrington, *Women in a Celtic Church*, p. 185. Many religious women are mentioned in early texts such as various martyrologies and texts related to St Patrick. Most of these women are not associated with a specific location and little is known of them. Available at: https://confessio.ie/#. Accessed 15 September 2020. For context, see R. Bleier, 'Re-Examining the Function of St Patrick's Writings in the Early Medieval Tradition', *Proceedings of the Royal Irish Academy*, vol. 116C, 2016, pp. 95–117.

4 Bitel, *Land of Women*, p. 19; Ó Riain, *A Dictionary*.

5 C. Thomas, *The Early Christian Archaeology of North Britain* (London: Thames & Hudson, 1971); C. Thomas, *Christianity in Roman Britain to AD 500* (Berkeley: University of California Press, 1981); C. Thomas, *Christian Celts: Messages and images* (Stroud: Tempus, 1998); C. Swift, *Ogham Stones and the Earliest Irish Christians* (Maynooth: NUI Maynooth, 1997); E. Johnston, *Literacy and Identity in Early Medieval Ireland* (Suffolk: Boydell & Brewer, 2013). M. Callan, 'Líadain's *Lament*, Darerca's *Life*, and Íte's *Ísucán*: Evidence for nuns' literacies in early Ireland', in V. Blanton, V. O'Mara and P. Stoop (eds), *Nuns' Literacies in Medieval Europe* (Turnhout: Brepols, 2015), pp. 209–27.

6 E.R. Norman and J.K. St Joseph, *The Early Development of Irish Society: The evidence of aerial photography* (Cambridge: Cambridge University Press, 1969); Edwards, *Archaeology of Early Medieval Ireland*; N. Edwards, 'The Archaeology of Early Medieval Ireland, *c.*400–1169: Settlement and economy', in D. Ó Cróinín (ed.), *A New History of Ireland. Volume I: Prehistoric and Early Ireland* (Oxford: Oxford University Press, 2005), pp. 235–300; H. Mytum, *The Origins of Early Christian Ireland* (London: Routledge, 1992); M.A. Monk and J. Sheehan (eds), *Early Medieval Munster* (Cork: Cork University Press, 1998); Charles-Edwards, *Early Christian Ireland*; Bhreathnach, *Ireland in the Medieval World*; O'Sullivan et al., *Early Medieval Ireland*; M. Stout, *Early Medieval Ireland*.

7 Hughes, *Early Christian Ireland*, p. 17; Harrington, *Women in a Celtic Church*, pp. 16–19.

8 For example, Ó Carragáin, 'Is There an Archaeology of Lay People'.

9 Ó Corráin, 'Women in Early Irish Society'; A. Connon, 'The Banshenchas and the Uí Queens of Tara', in A.P. Smyth (ed.) *Seanchas: Studies in early and medieval Irish archaeology, history and literature, in honour of Francis J. Byrne* (Dublin: Four Courts Press, 2000), pp. 98–108; Harrington, *Women in a Celtic Church*, p. 19; Ó Carragáin, *Churches in Early Medieval Ireland*, pp. 12–13; H. Oxenham, *Perceptions of Femininity in Early Irish Society* (Woodbridge: Boydell, 2016).

10 T. Ó Carragáin, 'A Landscape Converted: Archaeology and early church organisation on Iveragh and Dingle, Ireland', in M. Carver (ed.), *The Cross Goes North: Processes of conversion in northern Europe AD 300–1300* (Woodbridge: York Medieval Press, 2003), pp. 127–52; T. Ó Carragáin, 'Church Buildings and Pastoral Care in Early Medieval Ireland', in E. FitzPatrick and R. Gillespie (eds), *The Parish in Medieval and Early Modern Ireland: Community, territory and building* (Dublin: Four Courts Press, 2006), pp. 91–123; T. Ó Carragáin, 'The Architectural Setting of the Mass in Early Medieval Ireland', *Medieval Archaeology*, vol. 53, 2009, pp. 119–54; Ó Carragáin, *Churches in Early Medieval Ireland*, pp. 225–8; Ó Carragáin, 'The Archaeology of Ecclesiastical Estates in Early Medieval Ireland'; Ó Carragáin and Sheehan, 'Making Christian Landscapes'; O'Sullivan et al., *Early Medieval Ireland*, pp. 139–78.

11 Charles-Edwards, *Early Christian Ireland*, pp. 71–80; T. Bolger, 'Status Inheritance and Land Tenure: Some thoughts on early medieval settlement in the light of recent archaeological excavations', in C. Corlett and M. Potterton (eds), *Settlement in Early Medieval Ireland in the Light of Recent Archaeological Excavations* (Dublin: Wordwell, 2011), pp. 1–10, at pp. 4–7; P. Gleeson, 'Constructing Kingship in Early Medieval Ireland: Power, place and ideology', *Medieval Archaeology*, vol. 56, 2012, pp. 1–33; Bhreathnach, *Ireland in the Medieval World*, pp. 40–129.

12 Bolger, 'Status Inheritance and Land Tenure', p. 4; F. Kelly, *Early Irish Farming* (Dublin: Institute for Advanced Studies, 1997), pp. 27–66, 399–420; Charles-Edwards, *Early Christian Ireland*, p. 134.

13 F. Kelly, *A Guide to Early Irish Law* (Dublin: Institute for Advanced Studies, 1988); D. Ó Cróinín, *Early Medieval Ireland* (London: Longman, 1995), pp. 125–34; T.M. Charles-Edwards, 'Early Irish Law', in D. Ó Cróinín (ed.), *A New History of Ireland. Volume I: Prehistoric and Early Ireland* (Oxford: Oxford University Press, 2005), pp. 331–70.

14 Harrington, *Women in a Celtic Church*, p. 132.

15 T.M. Charles-Edwards, *Early Irish and Welsh Kinship* (Oxford: Oxford University Press, 1993), p. 463; Charles-Edwards, *Early Christian Ireland*, p. 112; Harrington, *Women in a Celtic Church*, p. 133.

16 Bitel, 'Women's Monastic Enclosures', p. 21.

17 Foot, *Veiled Women*, p. 43.

18 Flanagan, *Transformation*, p. 201.

19 Bitel, 'Women's Monastic Enclosures', pp. 23, 27.

20 https://www.confessio.ie/etexts/confessio_english#01. Accessed 15 September 2020. Stout has provided a very accessible translation of the text; see Stout, *Early Medieval Ireland*, pp. 34–40, at p. 38.

21 Hughes, *Early Christian Ireland*, pp. 234–5; D. Ó Corráin, 'The Early Irish Churches: Some aspects of organisation', in D. Ó Corráin (ed.), *Irish Antiquity: Essays and studies presented to Professor M.J. O'Kelly* (Dublin: Four Courts Press, 1981), pp. 326–41; Ó Corráin, *The Irish Church*; Harrington, *Women in a Celtic Church*, pp. 112–22.

22 L. Bitel, 'Women's Donations to the Churches in Early Ireland', *Journal of the Royal Society of Antiquaries of Ireland*, vol. 114, 1984, pp. 5–23; L. de Paor, *Saint Patrick's World*

(Dublin: Four Courts Press, 1996), pp. 46–50; Charles-Edwards, *Early Christian Ireland*, p. 226; Ní Ghrádaigh, '"But what exactly did she give?"'

23 For example, Ryan, *Irish Monasticism*; D.A. Binchy, 'The Legal Capacity of Women in Regard to Contracts', in R. Thurneysen, N. Power, M. Dillon, K. Mulchrone, D.A. Binchy, A. Knoch and J.S. Ryan (eds), *Studies in Early Irish Law* (Dublin: Royal Irish Academy, 1936), pp. 207–34; Hughes, *The Church*; D. Ó Corráin, 'Women and the Law in Early Ireland', in M. O'Dowd and S. Wichert (eds), *Chattel, Servant or Citizen: Women's status in church, state and society* (Belfast: Institute of Irish Studies, Queen's University, 1995), pp. 45–57; C. Thom, *Early Irish Monasticism: An understanding of its cultural roots* (London: T. & T. Clark, 2007).

24 A. Firey, 'Cross Examining the Witness: Recent research in Celtic monastic history', *Monastic Studies*, vol. 14, 1983, pp. 17–30; R. Sharpe, 'Some Problems Concerning the Organisation of the Church in Early Medieval Ireland', *Peritia*, vol. 3, 1984, pp. 230–70; R. Sharpe, 'Churches and Communities in Early Ireland: Towards a pastoral model', in J. Blair and R. Sharpe (eds), *Pastoral Care Before the Parish* (Leicester: Leicester University Press, 1992), pp. 81–109; Etchingham, *Church Organisation in Ireland*; Charles-Edwards, *Early Christian Ireland*, pp. 586–99; Harrington, *Women in a Celtic Church*, pp. 112–18; P. MacCotter, *Medieval Ireland: Territorial, political and economic divisions* (Dublin: Four Courts Press, 2008), pp. 23, 82–5; Ó Carragáin, *Churches in Early Medieval Ireland*; Ó Carragáin, 'The View from the Shore', p. 21; Bhreathnach, *Ireland in the Medieval World*, pp. 152–213.

25 G. Boazman, 'Theme and Variations: Christianity and regional landscapes in early medieval Ireland', unpublished PhD thesis, University College Cork, 2013; G. Boazman, 'The Material Culture of Self-Promotion: The Conaille Muirthemne kings and the ecclesiastical site of Faughart, County Louth', *County Louth Archaeological and Historical Journal*, vol. XXVIII, 2015, pp. 327–50.

26 For example, the many churches associated with the female saint Rígnach; see T.M. Charles-Edwards, 'Early Irish Saints' Cults and Their Constituencies'; Ó Riain, *A Dictionary*, pp. 536–7.

27 Elsewhere these are termed twin or affiliated houses, or double houses in an English context. See Luecke, 'The Unique Experience of Anglo-Saxon Nuns', pp. 55–66.

28 Ballyvourney is thought to have been founded by St Abban and given to St Gobnait (Gobnaid) in the sixth century; Gwynn and Hadcock, *Medieval Religious Houses*, p. 313; Ó Riain, *A Dictionary*, pp. 368–9; Callan, *Sacred Sisters*, pp. 170–4.

29 Clonbroney was founded sometime in the later seventh or early eight century; although in the *Tripartite Life of St Patrick* it mentions that he left two sisters both called Emer here, which suggests a foundation in the late fifth century; see W. Stokes (ed.), *Vita Tripartita: The tripartite life of St Patrick and other documents relating to that saint*, 2 vols (London: Eyre & Spottiswoode, 1887). It is associated with St Samthann, d. 739; Gwynn and Hadcock, *Medieval Religious Houses*, p. 314; Ó Riain, *A Dictionary*, pp. 545–6; Callan, *Sacred Sisters*, pp. 135–55.

30 Cloonburren was founded sometime in the sixth century. Its founder Cairech Dergen (Caoireach Dheragáin) died 577–8; Gwynn and Hadcock, *Medieval Religious Houses*, p. 315; Ó Riain, *A Dictionary*, pp. 150–1.

31 Kildare was founded by St Brigid (Brigit, Brighid) possibly in the late fifth century, though its zenith (as with many early ecclesiastical foundations) was in the seventh century; Gwynn and Hadcock, *Medieval Religious Houses*, pp. 319–20; Ó Riain, *A Dictionary*, pp. 123–5; C. Swift, 'Brigid, Patrick and the Kings of Kildare AD 640–850', in W. Nolan and K. McGrath (eds), *Kildare: History and society* (Dublin: Geography Publications, 2006), pp. 97–128; Callan, *Sacred Sisters*, pp. 85–112.

32 Killaraght, associated with St Attracta (Athracht) may have been founded in the fifth century, due to her mention in Tirechan's *Life of St Patrick*; Gwynn and Hadcock, *Medieval Religious Houses*, pp. 320–1; L. Bieler (ed.), *The Patrician Texts in the Book of Armagh* (Dublin: The Institute for Advanced Studies, 1979); Ó Riain, *A Dictionary*, pp. 81–2; Callan, *Sacred Sisters*, pp. 164–7.

33 Killeedy was founded by the sixth century by St Íte (Íde); she died in 570–1; Gwynn and Hadcock, *Medieval Religious Houses*, p. 392; Ó Riain, *A Dictionary*, pp. 375–8; Callan, *Sacred Sisters*, pp. 113–34.

34 Killevy was founded in the early sixth century by St Monenna (Moninne, Darerca). She died in 517 or 519. Gwynn and Hadcock, *Medieval Religious Houses*, p. 321; I. Sperber, 'The Life of St Monenna or Darerca of Killevy'; Ó Riain, *A Dictionary*, pp. 495–7; Callan, *Sacred Sisters*, pp. 61–84.

35 Oughterard is thought to have been founded in the sixth or seventh century by St Brigit (but not of Kildare). Gwynn and Hadcock, *Medieval Religious Houses*, p. 400; Lalor, *Irish Round Tower*, pp. 164–5; Ó Riain, *A Dictionary*, p. 121.

36 Bitel, 'Women's Monastic Enclosures', p. 26; E. Bhreathnach, 'Abbesses, Minor Dynasties and Kings *in Clericatu*: Perspectives of Ireland 700–850', in M. Brown and C. Farr (eds), *Mercia: An Anglo-Saxon kingdom in Europe* (Leicester: Leicester University Press, 2001), pp. 113–25; E. Bhreathnach, 'The Genealogies of Leinster as a Source for Local Cults in Leinster', in J. Carey, M. Herbert and P. Ó Riain (eds), *Studies in Irish Hagiography: Saints and scholars* (Dublin: Four Courts Press, 2001), pp. 250–67; Swift, 'Brigid, Patrick and the Kings of Kildare', pp. 100–23. For the Annals online see https://celt.ucc.ie/publishd.html; http://www.irish-annals.cs.tcd.ie/. Accessed 15 September 2020.

37 R.A.S. Macalister, *The Memorial Slabs of Clonmacnoise, King's County* (Dublin: The Stationery Office, 1909); R.A.S. Macalister, 'Some Cross-Slabs in the Neighbourhood of Athlone', *Journal of the Royal Society of Antiquaries of Ireland*, vol. 42, 1912, pp. 27–31; H.S. Crawford, 'A Descriptive List of Early Cross Slabs and Pillars [3 parts]', *Journal of the Royal Society of Antiquaries of Ireland*, vol. 43, 1913, pp. 151–69, 261–5, 326–34, at p. 160; R.A.S. Macalister, *Corpus Inscriptionum Insularum Celticarum Volume I* (Dublin: The Stationery Office, 1945), pp. 18–19.

38 O'Kelly, 'St Gobnet's House'; Callan, *Sacred Sisters*, pp. 170–4.

39 Leask, *Irish Churches and Monastic Buildings*. The literature on early pre-Romanesque churches has expanded significantly since Leask first published; for example, R. Stalley, 'Ecclesiastical Architecture before 1169', in D. Ó Cróinín (ed.), *A New History of Ireland. Volume I: Prehistoric and Early Ireland* (Oxford: Oxford University Press, 2005), pp. 714–43; T. Ó Carragáin, 'Habitual Masonry Styles and the Local Organisation of Church Building in Early Medieval Ireland', *Proceedings of the Royal Irish Academy*, vol. 105C, 2005, pp. 99–149; C. Manning, 'A Suggested Typology for Pre-Romanesque Stone Churches in Ireland', in N. Edwards (ed.), *The Archaeology of the Early Medieval Celtic Churches* (Leeds: Maney, 2009), pp. 265–79; Ó Carragáin, *Churches in Early Medieval Ireland*, p. 223.

40 For St Patrick's writings, see https://confessio.ie/#. Accessed 15 September 2020.

41 Killabuonia (Cill Buaine), Co. Kerry, a putative female religious site, is interesting. There are two ecclesiastical sites in the townland, the larger, better-known one and a second, smaller ecclesiastical site, approximately 500m to the southwest. This arrangement is very similar to the satellite female religious houses mentioned. Ó Carragáin, *Churches in Early Medieval Ireland*, p. 311; Ó Riain, *A Dictionary*, pp. 133, 502.

42 Killanin and Duignan, *Shell Guide*, p. 87; M. Herity (ed.), *Ordnance Survey Letters Kildare: Letters containing information relative to the antiquities of the county of Kildare collected during the progress of the OS in 1837–1839* (Dublin: Four Masters, 2002), p. 21.

43 An early sixth-century foundation associated with St Lasair. Gwynn and Hadcock, *Medieval Religious Houses*, p. 372; A. Hamlin, *The Archaeology of Early Christianity in the North of Ireland. BAR British Series 460* (Oxford: Archaeopress, 2008), pp. 328–9; Ó Riain, *A Dictionary*, pp. 393–4; R. Ó Baoill, 'Excavations at Aghavea, Co. Fermanagh', in C. Corlett and M. Potterton (eds), *The Church in Early Medieval Ireland, in the Light of Recent Archaeological Excavations* (Dublin: Wordwell, 2014), pp. 159–72.

44 The precise date of this foundation is unclear. It is associated with St Cránaid. D. Power, S. Lane, E. Byrne, U. Egan and M. Sleeman, *Archaeological Inventory of County Cork. Volume 4: North Cork*, 2 parts (Dublin: The Stationery Office, 2000), p. 558; Johnston, 'Powerful Women or Patriarchal Weapons?'; Ó Riain, *A Dictionary*, pp. 228–9; P. MacCotter, 'Túath, Manor and Parish: Kingdom of Fır Maıge, cantred of Fermoy', *Peritia*, vol. 22, 2012, pp. 211–48; Ó Carragáin, 'The Archaeology of Ecclesiastical Estates in Early Medieval Ireland'.

45 Faughart is associated with Ss Brigid and Monenna. O'Connor, 'Faughart Investigation 1966'; Gwynn and Hadcock, *Medieval Religious Houses*, p. 384; D. Murphy, 'The Distribution of Early Christian Monastic Sites and Its Implications for Contemporary Settlement in County Louth', *County Louth Archaeological and Historical Journal*, vol. 22, 1992, pp. 364–86; T. Condit and V. Buckley, *Faughart, Co. Louth. Archaeology Ireland Heritage Guide No. 37* (Dublin: Wordwell, 2007); Ó Riain, *A Dictionary*, p. 123; Boazman, 'The Material Culture of Self-Promotion'.

46 Founded by St Brendan of Clonfert for his sister Brige. Gwynn and Hadcock, *Medieval Religious Houses*, p. 312; O. Alcock, K. de hÓra and P. Gosling, *Archaeological Inventory of County Galway. Volume II: North Galway* (Dublin: The Stationery Office, 1999), pp. 292–3.

47 Gwynn and Hadcock, *Medieval Religious Houses*, p. 310; C. Lynn, 'Excavations in 46–48 Scotch Street, Armagh, 1979–80', *Ulster Journal of Archaeology*, vol. 51, 1988, pp. 69–84. Temple na Ferta is also known as the Church of the Repository. For recent background context to Armagh's layout, see E. FitzPatrick, 'Rethinking Settlement Values in Gaelic Society: The case of cathedral centres', *Proceedings of the Royal Irish Academy*, vol. 119C, 2019, pp. 69–102, at pp. 84, 86–7.

48 The first written reference to nuns at Clonmacnoise dates to 1026 and it is likely that this foundation was much earlier than this. Gwynn and Hadcock, *Medieval Religious Houses*, p. 315; C. Manning, 'Some Early Masonry Churches and the Round Tower at Clonmacnoise', in H. King (ed.), *Clonmacnoise Studies*, vol. 2 (Dublin: The Stationery Office, 2003), pp. 63–95, at pp. 82–3.

49 A church at this site is associated with Mella (Mealla), the reputed mother of St Manchán of Lemanaghan and may have been founded in the seventh century. Gwynn and Hadcock, *Medieval Religious Houses*, p. 40; C. O'Brien and P.D. Sweetman, *Archaeological Inventory of County Offaly* (Dublin: Government of Ireland, 1997), p. 104; E. FitzPatrick and C. O'Brien, *The Medieval Churches of County Offaly* (Dublin: Government of Ireland, 1988), pp. 12–15; M. Quinlan and R. Moss, *Lemanaghan County Offaly Conservation Plan* (Kilkenny: The Heritage Council, 2007); Ó Carragáin, *Churches in Early Medieval Ireland*, p. 312; Ó Riain, *A Dictionary*, pp. 429–30.

50 The saint Maol Ruain is associated with the ecclesiastical sites of Finglas and Tallaght, known as the 'two eyes of Ireland'; see Ó Riain, *A Dictionary*, pp. 445–6. The ecclesiastical site of Tallaght dates to the eighth century and was the origin of the Céli

Dé movement. The foundation date of Finglas seems to be at the end of the sixth century. It is known from the *Customs of Tallaght* that female religious communities were present at Tallaght and Finglas and were considered a vital part of the ecclesiastical complexes there; E. Gwynn and W. Purton, 'The Monastery at Tallaght', *Proceedings of the Royal Irish Academy*, vol. 29C, 1911–12, pp. 115–79; Gwynn and Hadcock, *Medieval Religious Houses*, pp. 45, 384; Harrington, *Women in a Celtic Church*, pp. 107–8, 177, 187, 208; W. Follett, *Céli Dé in Ireland* (Woodbridge: Boydell, 2006).

51 The church of St Mary's (or Our Lady's) is thought to be the location of the female religious community at Glendalough. The upstanding church dates to the eleventh or early twelfth century. It is primarily on the basis of its name that it has been attributed to female religious. Gwynn and Hadcock, *Medieval Religious Houses*, pp. 37, 58, 80; Harrington, *Women in a Celtic Church*, pp. 198, 208, 227, 238, 317; Ó Carragáin, *Churches in Early Medieval Ireland*, p. 242–53; Doherty et al., *Glendalough: City of God*; M. Seaver, C. McDermott and G. Warren, 'A Monastery Among the Glens', *Archaeology Ireland*, vol. 32, no. 2, 2018, pp. 19–23.

52 It is reputed that in the seventh century a female community was at Lismore that was strictly separately from the men's monastery of St Carthach (Mochuda). Gwynn and Hadcock, *Medieval Religious Houses*, p. 397; S. Sanderlin, 'The Monastery of Lismore AD 638–1111', in W. Nolan and T. Power (eds), *Waterford: History & society* (Dublin: Geography Publications, 1992), pp. 27–48; Harrington, *Women and the Celtic Church*, pp. 109, 229; Ó Riain, *A Dictionary*, pp. 470–3.

53 This is a putative early community of female religious. St Gerald was placed in charge at Mayo by St Colmán, and was said to have been near Mayo at a place called 'Elitheria' when he heard that his sister Segresia and one hundred of her nuns and fifty of his disciples had died of a pestilence, and he went to mourn in the church at Mayo. The male and female group suggests a double (mixed/dual) house, although there is no known location or other reference to female religious at Mayo. There is a further local association with female religious at Rosslee Church in Rathnacreeva townland (MO090-093001-) and it has been suggested that this is where the female community dwelt. Knox, *History of County Mayo*; Gwynn and Hadcock, *Medieval Religious Houses*, p. 398; J. Hawkes, 'An Iconography of Identity? The cross-head from Mayo Abbey', in C. Hourihane (ed.), *From Ireland Coming: Irish art from the early Christian to the late Gothic period and its European context* (Princeton: Dept of Art and Archaeology, Princeton University, 2001), pp. 261–76; Ó Riain, *A Dictionary*, p. 190.

54 Killyon, County Offaly, founded by St Ciarán of Sierkieran for his mother Liadhain, is not considered close enough to Sierkieran itself to be considered a satellite female community and so in this discussion has been grouped with lesser sites; see Ó Riain, *A Dictionary*, pp. 171–3.

55 Lynn, 'Excavations in 46–48 Scotch Street, Armagh'.

56 Gwynn and Purton, 'The Monastery at Tallaght', pp. 149–50; Harrington, *Women in a Celtic Church*, pp. 182–4; Follett, *Céli Dé*, pp. 98–9.

57 Follett, *Céli Dé*, p. 4.

58 Harrington, *Women in a Celtic Church*, p. 108.

59 Ibid., p. 109.

60 Ibid., p. 229.

61 For Whitby, see https://historicengland.org.uk/listing/the-list/list-entry/1316347. Accessed 15 September 2020.

62 Gwynn and Hadcock, *Medieval Religious Houses*, p. 398; Ó Riain, *A Dictionary*, p. 190; Hawkes, 'An Iconography of Identity?', p. 263.

63 C. McCullough and W.H. Crawford, *Irish Historic Towns Atlas No. 18: Armagh* (Dublin: Royal Irish Academy, 2007), map 4.
64 Ó Carragáin, *Churches in Early Medieval Ireland*, p. 62.
65 FitzPatrick and O'Brien, *Medieval Churches of County Offaly*, pp. 13–15; Quinlan and Moss, *Lemanaghan*, pp. 28–9, 45.
66 D. Murphy, 'Excavation of an Early Monastic Enclosure at Clonmacnoise', in H. King (ed.), *Clonmacnoise Studies*, vol. 2 (Dublin: The Stationery Office, 2003), pp. 1–33, at p. 21.
67 Quinlan and Moss, *Lemanaghan*, p. 21.
68 R. Ó Floinn, '"The Market Cross" at Glendalough', in C. Doherty, L. Doran and M. Kelly (eds), *Glendalough: City of God* (Dublin: Four Courts Press, 2011), pp. 80–111, at p. 95; I. Elliott, C. McDermott and G. Warren, 'Geophysical Survey at Glendalough Monastic Site, Co. Wicklow', in *Glendalough Valley Archaeology Project Newsletter 3* (Dublin: UCD School of Archaeology, 2014), pp. 1–8, at p. 6; Seaver et al., 'A Monastery Among the Glens'.
69 Harrington, *Women in a Celtic Church*, p. 109.
70 Ó Carragáin, *Churches in Early Medieval Ireland*, pp. 263–8.
71 O'Sullivan, 'Excavation of an Early Church and a Women's Cemetery', pp. 327–65; M. Herbert, *Iona, Kells and Derry: The history and hagiography of the monastic familia of Columba* (Dublin: Four Courts Press, 1996).
72 J. O'Donovan, *Annála Ríoghachta Éireann: Annals of the kingdom of Ireland by the Four Masters from the earliest period to the year 1616*, 7 vols (Dublin: Hodges & Smith, 1854); B. Lacey, *Medieval and Monastic Derry: Sixth century to 1600* (Dublin: Four Courts Press, 2013), pp. 56, 89.
73 For example, Edwards, *Archaeology of Early Medieval Ireland*; O'Sullivan et al., *Early Medieval Ireland*.
74 Excavation was carried out at the possible early medieval female religious church at Kilteel; C. Manning, 'Excavation at Kilteel Church, Co. Kildare', *Journal of the Kildare Archaeological Society*, vol. 16, 1982, pp. 173–229. Geophysical survey has been undertaken at another possible site of early female religious; see S. Greene, 'Killeen Cormac Colbinstown: An ecclesiastical site on the Kildare–Wicklow border', *County Kildare Online Electronic History Journal*, 2011. Available at: http://www.kildare.ie/library/ehistory/2011/03/killeen_cormac_colbinstown_an.asp. Accessed 15 September 2020.
75 There has been excavation elsewhere at Clonmacnoise; see H. King (ed.), *Clonmacnoise Studies*, vol. 1 (Dublin: The Stationery Office, 1998); H. King (ed.), *Clonmacnoise Studies*, vol. 2 (Dublin: The Stationery Office, 2003). Of particular interest were two female burials excavated near the main ecclesiastical complex. They returned later medieval radiocarbon dates; see Murphy, 'Excavation of an Early Monastic Enclosure', pp. 8–13.
76 Mytum, 'Geophysical Survey at Clonmacnoise', pp. 42, 45. Other types of geophysical survey were attempted at this location but proved unsuccessful due to the underlying geology of the site.
77 Seaver et al., 'A Monastery Among the Glens'.
78 E.M. Fahy, 'Inishleena Abbey and Other Sites in the Lee Valley', *Journal of the Cork Historical and Archaeological Society*, vol. 62, 1957, pp. 65–76; O'Connor, 'Faughart Investigation 1966'.
79 O'Kelly, 'St Gobnet's House'; Edwards, *Archaeology of Early Medieval Ireland*, p. 87.
80 Ó Riain, *A Dictionary*, pp. 276, 278–9.
81 Ibid., p. 406.
82 Stokes, *The Tripartite Life of St Patrick*, p. 235.

83 Lynn, 'Excavations in 46–48 Scotch Street, Armagh', pp. 80–3; Ó Carragáin, *Churches in Early Medieval Ireland*, p. 64.
84 Ó Baoill, 'Excavations at Aghavea', p. 162.
85 M.J. O'Kelly, 'Church Island near Valentia, Co. Kerry', *Proceedings of the Royal Irish Academy*, vol. 59C, 1958, pp. 57–136, at pp. 132–3.
86 Harrington, *Women in a Celtic Church*, pp. 50–1.
87 Hamlin and Foley, 'A Women's Graveyard at Carrickmore'.
88 Leigh Fry, *Burial in Medieval Ireland*, p. 180.
89 Ó Carragáin, 'From Family Cemeteries to Community Cemeteries', p. 221.
90 Harrington, *Women in a Celtic Church*, p. 230.
91 E. O'Brien, *Mapping Death: Burial in late Iron Age and early medieval Ireland* (Dublin: Four Courts Press, 2020). See also http://www.mappingdeathdb.ie/. Accessed 15 September 2020.
92 These sites are accepted as ecclesiastical in this discussion but Collierstown is not universally accepted as such. N. Brannon, 'A Trial Excavation at St John's Point Church, Co. Down', *Ulster Journal of Archaeology*, vol. 43, 1980, pp. 59–64; D. Hurl, C. Sandes and L. Buckley, 'The Excavation of an Early Christian Cemetery at Solar, Co. Antrim', *Ulster Journal of Archaeology*, vol. 61, 2002, pp. 37–82; D.M. Waterman, 'The Early Christian Churches and Cemetery at Derry, Co. Down', *Ulster Journal of Archaeology*, vol. 30, 1967, pp. 49–52.
93 E. O'Brien, *Post-Roman Britain to Anglo-Saxon England: Burial practices reviewed. BAR, British Series 289* (Oxford: Archaeopress, 1999); E. O'Brien, 'Pagan or Christian? Burial in Ireland during the 5th to 8th centuries AD', in N. Edwards (ed.), *The Archaeology of the Early Medieval Celtic Churches* (Leeds: Maney, 2009), pp. 135–54, at p. 141; E. O'Brien, 'Excavation of a Multi-Period Burial Site at Ballymacaward, Ballyshannon, Co. Donegal', *Donegal Annual: Journal of the County Donegal Historical Society*, vol. 51, 1999, pp. 56–61.
94 Ó Carragáin, 'From Family Cemeteries to Community Cemeteries'.
95 H.F. McClintock, 'The Mantle of St Brigid at Bruges', *Journal of the Royal Society of Antiquaries of Ireland*, vol. 36, 1936, pp. 32–40.
96 R. Ó Floinn, *Irish Shrines and Reliquaries of the Middle Ages* (Dublin: Country House, 1994), p. 44.
97 Bitel, *Two Saints*, p. 199.
98 Ó Floinn, *Irish Shrines and Reliquaries*, p. 45.
99 M. MacDermott, 'The Crosiers of St Dympna and St Mel and Tenth-Century Irish Metal-Work', *Proceedings of the Royal Irish Academy*, vol. 58C, 1957, pp. 167–95.
100 Ó Floinn, *Irish Shrines and Reliquaries*, p. 30; Hall, *Women and the Church*, p. 117.
101 Ó Riain, *A Dictionary*, p. 368.
102 C. Swift, 'Sculptors and Their Customers: A study of Clonmacnoise grave slabs', in H. King (ed.), *Clonmacnoise Studies*, vol. 2 (Dublin: The Stationery Office, 2003), pp. 105–23, at p. 109.
103 Macalister, *Memorial Slabs of Clonmacnoise*, p. 10; R.A.S. Macalister, *Corpus Inscriptionum Insularum Celticarum*, vol. II (Dublin: The Stationery Office, 1949), p. 46; P. Lionard, 'Early Irish Grave Slabs', *Proceedings of the Royal Irish Academy*, vol. 61C, 1961, pp. 95–169, at p. 113.
104 It is noted that the prefix on this inscription is 'Mael', which is usually, though not exclusively, used for masculine names, so it may represent a priest associated with a female community. A date not earlier than the twelfth century has been proposed for the inscription. See O'Sullivan and Ó Carragáin, *Inishmurray*, pp. 99, 152.

105 E. Bhreathnach, 'The *Vita Apostolica* and the Origin of the Augustinian Canons and Canonesses in Medieval Ireland', in M. Browne and C. Ó Clabaigh (eds), *Households of God: The regular canons and canonesses of Saint Augustine and of Prémontré in medieval Ireland* (Dublin: Four Courts Press, 2019), pp. 1–27, at pp. 20–6.
106 The same is true of excavations abroad; see, for example, Van Hove et al., 'Dans La Clôture D'une Grande Abbaye'; G. Thomas, 'Life Before the Minster'.
107 Ní Ghrádaigh, 'Mere Embroiderers?', p. 104.
108 J. Sheehan, 'The Peacock's Tale: Excavations at Caherlehillan, Iveragh, Ireland', in N. Edwards (ed.), *The Archaeology of the Early Medieval Celtic Churches* (Leeds: Maney, 2009), pp. 191–206; Sheehan, 'Caherlehillan, Co. Kerry'; Ó Carragáin, 'Is There an Archaeology of Lay People', pp. 11–12.
109 https://monasticon.celt.dias.ie/. Accessed 15 September 2020. See also Ó Riain, *A Dictionary*.
110 Ó Carragáin, 'The Architectural Setting'; Ó Carragáin, *Churches in Early Medieval Ireland*, p. 226.
111 See Bhreathnach, 'The *Vita Apostolica*'.
112 Gwynn and Hadcock, *Medieval Religious Houses*; Harrington, *Women in a Celtic Church*, map 2; Ó Riain, *A Dictionary*, p. 124.
113 P. Ó Riain, *The Making of a Saint: Finnbarr of Cork 600–1200* (Dublin: Irish Texts Society, 1997); Ó Riain, *A Dictionary of Irish Saints*, pp. 332–4.
114 Bhreathnach, 'The Genealogies of Leinster'.
115 Harrington, *Women in a Celtic Church*, maps 1–4.
116 Callan, *Sacred Sisters*.
117 Johnston, 'Powerful Women or Patriarchal Weapons?', pp. 305–8; Ó Riain, *A Dictionary*, pp. 228–9.
118 MacCotter, 'Túath, Manor and Parish'; Ó Carragáin, 'The Archaeology of Ecclesiastical Estates in Early Medieval Ireland'.
119 Harrington, *Women in a Celtic Church*, p. 3.
120 For an overview, see A.I. Beach and A. Juganaru, 'The Double Monastery as a Historiographical Problem (Fourth to Twelfth Century)', in A.I. Beach and I. Cochelin (eds), *Medieval Monasticism in the Latin West*, 2 vols (Cambridge: Cambridge University Press, 2020), pp. 561–78.
121 F. Medioli, 'An Unequal Law: The enforcement of clausura before and after the Council of Trent', in C. Meek (ed.), *Women in Renaissance and Early Modern Europe* (Dublin: Four Courts Press, 2000), pp. 136–52, at p. 138; A. Diem, 'The Gender of the Religious Wo/Men and the Invention of Monasticism', in J. Bennett and R. Karras (eds), *The Oxford Handbook of Women and Gender in Medieval Europe* (Oxford: Oxford University Press, 2013), pp. 432–46.
122 J.T. Schulenburg, 'Strict Active Enclosure and Its Effects on the Female Monastic Experience (*ca* 500–1100)', in J.A. Nichols and L.T. Shank (eds), *Distant Echoes: Medieval religious women*, vol. 1 (Kalamazoo: Cistercian Publications, 1984), pp. 51–86, at p. 52.
123 Schulenburg, 'Strict Active Enclosure', p. 51; Smith, *Ordering Women's Lives*, p. 155.
124 Bitel, 'Women's Monastic Enclosures', p. 34.
125 Wemple, *Women in Frankish Society*, pp. 187–8; Schulenburg, 'Strict Active Enclosure', pp. 58, 70, 77–9; Schulenburg, 'Female Sanctity'.
126 Harrington, *Women in a Celtic Church*, p. 94.
127 Ibid., p. 71; Callan, *Sacred Sisters*, pp. 20–2.
128 Follett, *Céli Dé*, p. 28.

129 F. Griffiths, 'The Mass in Monastic Practice: Nuns and ordained monks, *c.*400–1200', in A.I. Beach and I. Cochelin (eds), *Medieval Monasticism in the Latin West*, 2 vols (Cambridge: Cambridge University Press, 2020), pp. 729–46.
130 Gwynn and Purton, 'The Monastery at Tallaght'.
131 D.A. Bray, *A List of Motifs in the Lives of the Early Irish Saints* (Helsinki: Academia Scientarum Fennica, 1992).
132 De Paor, *Saint Patrick's World*, pp. 207–24; P. Harbison, *The High Crosses of Ireland*, 3 vols (Bonn: Dr Rudolf Habelt, 1992), p. 353; C. Neuman de Vegvar, 'Romanitas and Realpolitick in Cogitosus' Description of the Church of St Brigit, Kildare', in M. Carver (ed.), *The Cross Goes North: Processes of conversion in northern Europe AD 300–1300* (Woodbridge: York Medieval Press, 2003), pp. 153–70; Follett, *Céli Dé*, p. 57; Bitel, 'Women's Monastic Enclosures', p. 24; Bitel, *Two Saints*, pp. 140–61; Ó Carragáin, *Churches in Early Medieval Ireland*, p. 172.
133 Harrington, *Women in a Celtic Church*, p. 99.
134 From *Hibernensis*, book 45, chap. 14, translated by Harrington, *Women in a Celtic Church*, p. 95. See also R. Flechner, *The* Hibernensis*: Studies in medieval and early modern canon law*, 2 vols (Washington DC: The Catholic University of America Press, 2019).
135 Harrington, *Women in a Celtic Church*, p. 95.
136 Smith, *Ordering Women's Lives*, pp. 120–1. See also A. Diem and P. Rousseau, 'Monastic Rules (Fourth to Ninth Century)', in A.I. Beach and I. Cochelin (eds), *Medieval Monasticism in the Latin West*, 2 vols (Cambridge: Cambridge University Press, 2020), pp. 162–94.
137 McNamara, *Sisters in Arms*, p. 143. Diem suggests that the earliest rules may have been for women, with men adopting those rules later; see Diem, 'The Gender of the Religious Wo/Men', p. 440.
138 For example, the saints' lives of Monenna and Brigit refer to monastery rules; see Harrington, *Women in a Celtic Church*, pp. 86–7, 167–8, 212; but those specific rules – if they ever existed in text form – remain unknown. See also Bhreathnach, 'Vita Apostolica', pp. 20–3.
139 Smith, *Ordering Women's Lives*, pp. 112–15; McNamara, *Sisters in Arms*, pp. 70–8.
140 G. Lawless, *Augustine of Hippo and His Monastic Rule* (Oxford: Clarendon Press, 1987).
141 M. McCarthy, *Rule for Nuns* (Washington DC: Catholic University of America Press, 1960); A. Diem '… *Ut Si Professus Fueit Se Omnia Impleturum, Tunc Excipiatur*: Observations on the rules for monks and nuns of Caesarius and Aurelianus of Arles', in V. Zimmerl-Panagl, L.J. Dorfbauer and C. Weidmann (eds), *Edition und Erforschung lateinischer patristischer Texte. 150 Jahre CSEL. Festschrift für Kurt Smolak zum 70* (Boston: De Gruyter, 2014), pp. 191–224.
142 Smith, *Ordering Women's Lives*, pp. 124–7; Wemple, *Women in Frankish Society*, p. 192; A. O'Hara (ed.), *Columbanus and the Peoples of Post-Roman Europe* (Oxford: Oxford University Press, 2018). Interestingly, Columbanus was influenced by women in his mission; see E. Johnston, 'Movers and Shakers? How women shaped the career of Columbanus', in A. O'Hara (ed.), *Columbanus and the Peoples of Post-Roman Europe* (Oxford: Oxford University Press, 2018), pp. 69–90.
143 L. Sherley-Price (trans.), *Bede. A History of the English Church and People* (Harmonsworth: Penguin, 1968).
144 O'Sullivan, 'Excavation of an Early Church and a Women's Cemetery'.
145 Smith, *Ordering Women's Lives*, pp. 133–41; Foot, *Veiled Women*, p. 2.
146 Schulenburg, 'Strict Active Enclosure', p. 51; M. Dunn, *The Emergence of Monasticism* (Oxford: Blackwell, 2000), pp. 124–5; Smith, *Ordering Women's Lives*, p. 7; E. Bhreathnach,

'Benedictine Influence in Ireland in the Late Eleventh and Early Twelfth Century: A reflection, *Journal of Medieval Monastic Studies*, vol. 1, 2012, pp. 46–105.

147 Etchingham, *Church Organisation in Ireland*, p. 66.

148 Schulenburg, 'Women's Monastic Communities 500–1100', p. 264; McNamara, *Sisters in Arms*, pp. 69–88; J.T. Schulenburg, *Forgetful of Their Sex: Female sanctity and society* ca *500–1100* (Chicago: University of Chicago Press, 1998); Dunn, *Emergence of Monasticism*; Lawrence, *Medieval Monasticism*. For hermits specifically, see K. Jasper and J. Howe, 'Hermitism in the Eleventh and Twelfth Centuries', in A.I. Beach and I. Cochelin (eds), *Medieval Monasticism in the Latin West*, 2 vols (Cambridge: Cambridge University Press, 2020), pp. 684–96.

149 Bitel, *Women in Early Medieval Europe*, p. 136; Bitel, *Two Saints*, p. 56.

150 Wemple, *Women in Frankish Society*, pp. 136–41; J. Gerchow, K. Bodwaré, S. Marti and H. Röckelein, 'Early Monasteries and Foundations (500–1200): An introduction', in J.F. Hamburger and S. Marti (eds), *Crown and Veil: Female monasticism from the fifth to the fifteenth centuries* (New York: Columbia University Press, 2008), pp. 13–40, at p. 14.

151 Schulenburg, 'Women's Monastic Communities', p. 264; Lawrence, *Medieval Monasticism*, p. 14. This same is true of early female religious houses in the east; for example, see C. Sniveley, 'Invisible in the Community? The evidence for early women's monasticism in the southern Balkan Peninsula', in S. McNally (ed.), *Shaping Community: The art and archaeology of monasticism*. *BAR International Series 941* (Oxford: Archaeopress, 2001), pp. 57–66, at pp. 58, 63–4.

152 K. Bodarwé, 'Frauenleben Zwischen Klosterleben und Luxus? Alltag in Frühmittelalterlichen Frauenklöstern', in H. Brandt and J. Koch (eds), *Königin, Klosterfrau, Bäuerin: Frauen im Frühmittelalterlichen* (Münster: LIT Verlag, 1997), pp. 117–43; Venarde, *Women's Monasticism*, pp. 190–210; Schulenburg, 'Women's Monastic Communities', pp. 265–7.

153 S. Wemple, 'Female Spirituality and Mysticism in Frankish Monasticism: Radegund, Balthild and Aldegund', in J. Nichols and L.T. Shank (eds), *Peace Weavers: Medieval religious women*, vol. 2 (Kalamazoo: Cistercian Publications, 1987), pp. 39–54; Schulenburg, 'Women's Monastic Communities', p. 261; W. Berschin, 'Radegundis and Brigit', in J. Carey, M. Herbert and P. Ó Riain (eds), *Studies in Hagiography: Saints and scholars* (Dublin: Four Courts Press, 2001), pp. 72–6; Gerchow et al., 'Early Monasteries and Foundations', p. 20; Bitel, *Women in Early Medieval Europe*, pp. 120, 123–4.

154 Schulenburg, 'Women's Monastic Communities', p. 267; Charles-Edwards, *Early Christian Ireland*, pp. 344–90; Lawrence, *Medieval Monasticism*, p. 41; C. Stancliffe, 'Jonas's Life of Columbanus and His Disciples', in J. Carey, M. Herbert and P. Ó Riain (eds), *Studies in Hagiography: Saints and scholars* (Dublin: Four Courts Press, 2001), pp. 189–220; Gerchow et al., 'Early Monasteries and Foundations', p. 16; Van Hove et al., 'Dans La Clôture D'une Grande Abbaye'; O'Hara, *Columbanus*; Johnston, 'Movers and Shakers?'

155 Schulenburg, 'Women's Monastic Communities', p. 291.

156 M. Skinner, 'Benedictine Life for Women in Central France 850–1100', in J. Nichols and L. Thomas Shank (eds), *Distant Echoes: Medieval religious women*, vol. 1 (Kalamazoo: Cistercian Publications, 1984), pp. 87–114, at pp. 87–8.

157 McNamara, 'Monasticism and Nuns', p. 582.

158 Schulenburg, 'Women's Monastic Communities', p. 285. For an overview of the reform process on the continent, see S. Vanderputten, *Monastic Reform as Process: Realities and representations in medieval Flanders 900–1100* (Ithaca: Cornell University Press, 2013); S. Vanderputten, *Dark Age Nunneries: The ambiguous identity of female monasticism,*

800–1050 (Ithaca: Cornell University Press, 2018); R. Kramer, 'Monasticism, Reform and Authority in the Carolingian Era', in A.I. Beach and I. Cochelin (eds), *Medieval Monasticism in the Latin West*, 2 vols (Cambridge: Cambridge University Press, 2020), pp. 432–49.

159 Jarrett, 'Power Over Past and Future'; Jarrett, *Rulers and Ruled in Frontier Catalonia*.

160 Skinner, 'Benedictine Life for Women in Central France', pp. 90–6.

161 Cartwright, *Feminine Sanctity*, pp. 70–91; N. Edwards, 'Introduction', in N. Edwards (ed.), *The Archaeology of the Early Medieval Celtic Churches: Proceedings of a conference on the archaeology of the early medieval Celtic churches, September 2004* (Leeds: Maney, 2009), pp. 1–18, at p. 13.

162 Bezant, *Medieval Welsh Settlement*, pp. 44–5, 51–3.

163 D. Hall, 'Monasticism and Nuns: Celtic', in M. Schaus (ed.), *Women and Gender in Medieval Europe: An encyclopedia* (London: Routledge, 2006), pp. 586–7, at p. 586.

164 R.A. McDonald, 'The Foundation and Patronage of Nunneries by Native Elites in Twelfth- and Early Thirteenth-Century Scotland', in E. Ewan and M. Meikle (eds), *Women in Scotland* c.*1100*–c.*1750* (East Linton: Tuckwell Press, 1999), pp. 3–15, at p. 11.

165 Schulenburg, 'Women's Monastic Communities', p. 264; Dunn, *Emergence of Monasticism*, p. 138.

166 Luecke, 'The Unique Experience of Anglo-Saxon Nuns', p. 55; S. Foot, 'What Was an Early Anglo-Saxon Monastery?', in J. Loades (ed.), *Monastic Studies: The continuity of tradition* (Bangor: Headstart History, 1990), pp. 48–57, at p. 54; Foot, *Veiled Women*, pp. 36–46; S. Foot, *Monastic Life in Anglo-Saxon England,* c.*600–900* (Cambridge: Cambridge University Press, 2006), p. 9; Smith, *Ordering Women's Lives*, pp. 124–7; B. Yorke, *Nunneries and the Anglo-Saxon Royal Houses* (London: Continuum, 2003), pp. 17–46; C.A. Jones, 'Minsters and Monasticism in Anglo-Saxon England', in A.I. Beach and I. Cochelin (eds), *Medieval Monasticism in the Latin West*, 2 vols (Cambridge: Cambridge University Press, 2020), pp. 502–41.

167 Schulenburg, 'Women's Monastic Communities', pp. 261–4; S. Foot, 'Unveiling Anglo-Saxon Nuns', in D. Wood (ed.), *Women and Religion in Medieval England* (Oxford: Oxbow, 2003), pp. 13–31, at p. 13; Yorke, *Nunneries and the Anglo-Saxon Royal Houses*; Thomas, 'Life Before the Minster'.

168 Foot, *Veiled Women*, p. 198; Foot, 'Unveiling Anglo-Saxon Nuns', p. 27.

169 Foot 'Unveiling Anglo-Saxon Nuns', pp. 13–17, 27.

170 Gilchrist, *Gender and Material Culture*, p. 25; Foot, *Veiled Women*, pp. 29, 101; Foot, 'Unveiling Anglo-Saxon Nuns', pp. 24–7; Foot, *Monastic Life*; Yorke, *Nunneries and the Anglo-Saxon Royal Houses*, pp. 4–11.

171 D. Parsons (ed.), *Tenth-Century Studies: Essays in commemoration of the millennium of the Council of Winchester and the* Regularis Concordia (London: Royal Historical Society, 1975); Yorke, *Nunneries and the Anglo-Saxon Royal Houses*, p. 85.

172 Gilchrist, *Gender and Material Culture*, p. 32.

173 Termonkeelin, Co. Roscommon might be added to the list based on its possible early medieval origins. Ballynagallagh, Co. Limerick and Grace Dieu, Co. Dublin are less likely but are possible cases due to the excavation of archaeological sites nearby that produced early medieval material. See R. Cleary, 'Excavations of an Early-Medieval Period Enclosure at Ballynagallagh, Lough Gur, Co. Limerick', *Proceedings of the Royal Irish Academy*, vol. 106C, 2008, pp. 1–66; Conway, 'Excavation at Gracedieu'.

174 M.E. Meredith-Lobay, 'Memory, Landscapes and the Early Historic Monasteries of Scotland', *Archaeological Review from Cambridge*, vol. 20, no. 1, 2005, pp. 97–110; M. Carver, 'Early Scottish Monasteries and Prehistory: A preliminary dialogue', *The*

Scottish Historical Review, vol. 88, 2009, pp. 332–51; S. Semple, 'A Fear of the Past: The place of the prehistoric burial mound in the ideology of middle and later Anglo-Saxon England', *World Archaeology*, vol. 30, no. 1, 1998, pp. 109–26; S. Semple, 'Sacred Spaces and Places in Pre-Christian and Conversion Period Anglo-Saxon England', in H. Hamerow, D. Hinton and S. Crawford (eds), *The Oxford Handbook of Anglo-Saxon Archaeology* (Oxford: Oxford University Press, 2011), pp. 742–63.

175 Healy, 'Two Royal Abbeys'; Ó Carragáin, *Churches in Early Medieval Ireland*, pp. 224, 302, 310.

176 C. Manning, 'The Adaptation of Early Masonry Churches in Ireland for Use in Later Medieval Times', in M. Meek (ed.), *The Modern Traveller to Our Past: Festschrift in honour of Ann Hamlin* (Belfast: DPK Publishing, 2006), pp. 243–8, at p. 247. For an overview of the importance of relics in early Ireland, see N. Wycherley, *The Cult of Relics in Early Medieval Ireland* (Turnhout: Brepols, 2015).

177 G. Carville, *The Occupation of Celtic Sites in Medieval Ireland by the Canons Regular of St Augustine and the Cistercians* (Kalamazoo: Cistercian Publications, 1982); D.M. Robinson, *The Geography of Augustinian Settlement*, 2 parts. *BAR British Series 80* (Oxford: British Archaeological Reports, 1980), p. 64; A. Abram, 'Augustinian Canons and the Survival of Cult Centres in Medieval England', in J. Burton and K. Stöber (eds), *The Regular Canons in the British Isles* (Turnhout: Brepols, 2011), pp. 79–96; K. Stöber and D. Austin, 'Culdees to Canons: The Augustinian houses of north Wales', in J. Burton and K. Stöber (eds), *Monastic Wales: New approaches* (Cardiff: University of Wales Press, 2013), pp. 41–54, at p. 40.

178 Bhreathnach, 'The *Vita Apostolica*'.

179 McDowell, 'Armagh 50–56 Scotch Street'.

180 Flanagan, *Transformation*, pp. 1–33.

181 T. Bolger and C. Moloney, 'Archaeological Excavations at Lorrha, Co. Tipperary', *Journal of Irish Archaeology*, vol. 21, 2012, pp. 114–37; T. Bolger and C. Moloney, 'Archaeological Excavations at Lorrha, Co. Tipperary', in C. Corlett and M. Potterton (eds), *The Church in Early Medieval Ireland in the Light of Recent Archaeological Excavations* (Dublin: Wordwell, 2104), pp. 13–22.

182 Annagh, Inishmaine and Templenagalliaghdoo (Errew), Co. Mayo; Clonfert, Co. Galway; Ardcarn, Cloonoghil and Roscommon, Co. Roscommon; Clonard, Duleek and Kells, Co. Meath; Durrow and Killeigh, Co. Offaly; Termonfeckin, Co. Louth; and Derry, Co. Derry.

183 Ó Carragáin, *Churches in Early Medieval Ireland*, pp. 156–7.

184 See Manning, 'Some Early Masonry Churches'.

185 There is little evidence of female religious communities in Ireland at this period using pre-existing secular sites, but see Chapter 7 for discussion.

186 Ten later medieval nunneries have associated holy wells. The presence of such wells could be considered to be a deliberate early medieval association, particularly with the sacrament of baptism, though it is acknowledged that holy wells have a very long tradition, which in many cases may not have been continuous. It is also possible that the wells became sacred sometime after their association with the later nunnery. See M.P. Carroll, *Irish Pilgrimage, Holy Wells and Popular Catholic Devotion* (Baltimore: Johns Hopkins University Press, 1999); Ó Carragáin, *Churches in Early Medieval Ireland*, pp. 197–208, esp. p. 199.

187 Bullauns are irregular stones with a hollow or hollows in their upper surfaces. They can be portable artefacts or present on earth-fast boulders. Ó Carragáin suggests that the original function of bullauns were grinding mortars rather than water

fonts; *Churches in Early Medieval Ireland*, p. 199. For example, the bullaun stone at the nunnery of Aghade, Co. Carlow has been described erroneously as a baptismal font; M. Comerford, *Collections from the Dioceses of Kildare and Leighlin*, 3 vols (Dublin: James Duffy & Sons, 1883–6), p. 117; Hall, *Women and the Church*, p. 174. Liam Price correctly identified this example as a bullaun; L. Price, 'Rock-Basins or "Bullauns" at Glendalough and Elsewhere', *Journal of the Royal Society of Antiquaries of Ireland*, vol. 89, 1959, pp. 161–88, at p. 166. See also B. Dolan, '"Mysterious Waifs of Time": Some thoughts on the function of Irish bullaun stones', *Journal of the Royal Society of Antiquaries*, vols 142–3, 2012–13, pp. 42–58.

CHAPTER 3. WOMEN AND RELIGIOUS LIFE IN LATER MEDIEVAL IRELAND: THE DOCUMENTARY AND MATERIAL EVIDENCE

1 K. Simms, 'Women in Norman Ireland', in M. MacCurtain and D. Ó Corráin (eds), *Women in Irish Society: The historical dimension* (Dublin: Arlen House, The Women's Press, 1978), pp. 14–25, at p. 23.

2 K. Nicholls, *Gaelic and Gaelicized Ireland in the Middle Ages* (Dublin: Lilliput Press, 2003), p. 81.

3 'Anglo-Norman' is the term used for the first generation and 'Anglo-Irish' for subsequent generations of this group throughout.

4 S. Ellis, '"More Irish that the Irish themselves?" The "Anglo-Irish" in Tudor Ireland', *History Ireland*, vol. 7, no. 1, 1999, pp. 22–6.

5 For example, Simms, 'Women in Norman Ireland'; K. Simms, 'Bards and Barons: The Anglo-Irish aristocracy and native culture', in R. Bartlett and A. MacKay (eds), *Medieval Frontier Societies* (Oxford: Oxford University Press, 1989), pp. 177–97; K. Nicholls, 'Worlds Apart? The Ellis two-nation theory on later medieval Ireland', *History Ireland*, vol. 7, no. 2, 1999, pp. 22–6; Kenny, *Anglo-Irish and Gaelic Women*, p. 9.

6 It has been suggested that the differences between the two societies in later medieval Ireland has been overplayed and there were areas of mixed customs over time; see Nicholls, *Gaelic and Gaelicized Ireland*. The material culture of this period also shows exchange and fusion and the identity of two cultures is certainly not clear-cut; Nicholls, 'Worlds Apart?', p. 26; R. Ó Floinn, 'Later Medieval Ireland, AD 1150–1550', in P.F. Wallace and R. Ó Floinn (eds), *Treasures of the National Museum of Ireland: Irish antiquities* (Dublin: Gill & Macmillan, 2002), pp. 257–300, at p. 258; Simms, 'Women in Norman Ireland', p. 14; J. Lydon, 'A Land of War', in A. Cosgrove (ed.), *A New History of Ireland. Volume II: Medieval Ireland 1169–1534* (Oxford: Oxford University Press, 1993), pp. 240–74, at p. 270; J.A. Watt, 'Gaelic Polity and Cultural Identity', in A. Cosgrove (ed.), *A New History of Ireland. Volume II: Medieval Ireland 1169–1534* (Oxford: Oxford University Press, 1993), pp. 314–51, at pp. 325–9.

7 J.A. Watt, 'The Anglo-Irish Colony Under Strain 1327–99', in A. Cosgrove (ed.), *A New History of Ireland. Volume II: Medieval Ireland 1169–1534* (Oxford: Oxford University Press, 1993), pp. 352–96, at pp. 386–90.

8 G. Kenny, 'Anglo-Irish and Gaelic Marriage Laws and Traditions in Late Medieval Ireland', *Journal of Medieval History*, vol. 32, 2006, pp. 27–42; Kenny, *Anglo-Irish and Gaelic Women*, p. 9.

9 Intermarriage between the two communities of Gaelic and Anglo-Irish was also fairly common in the early stages of conquest, but was subsequently not encouraged and by 1357, marriage between the communities was expressly prohibited. See Watt, 'The Anglo-Irish Colony', pp. 383–4; Kenny, *Anglo-Irish and Gaelic Women*, p. 85. This rule was relaxed in 1399, in part to facilitate peace; see Simms, 'Women in Norman Ireland', p. 20.

10 Watt, 'Gaelic Polity', p. 314; P.J. Duffy, D. Edwards and E. FitzPatrick (eds), *Gaelic Ireland: Land, lordship and settlement* c.*1250*–c.*1650* (Dublin: Four Courts Press, 2001); K. Simms, 'Gaelic Culture and Society', in B. Smith (ed.), *Cambridge History of Ireland. Volume 1, 600–1550* (Cambridge: Cambridge University Press, 2018), pp. 415–40; B. Cunningham and R. Gillespie, *Stories from Gaelic Ireland: Microhistories from the sixteenth-century Irish annals* (Dublin: Four Courts Press, 2003).
11 Watt, 'Gaelic Polity', pp. 317–18.
12 For example, F. Byrne, 'The Trembling Sod: Ireland in 1169', in A. Cosgrove (ed.), *A New History of Ireland. Volume II: Medieval Ireland 1169–1534* (Oxford: Oxford University Press, 1993), pp. 1–42; Nicholls, *Gaelic and Gaelicized Ireland*; Kenny, *Anglo-Irish and Gaelic Women*, pp. 67–76.
13 Kenny, *Anglo-Irish and Gaelic Women*, p. 34.
14 Ibid., pp. 34–6.
15 Ó Corráin, 'Women in Early Irish Society', p. 7; Kenny, *Anglo-Irish and Gaelic Women*, p. 35.
16 Kenny, *Anglo-Irish and Gaelic Women*, p. 35.
17 Simms, 'Women in Norman Ireland', p. 14.
18 K. Nicholls, 'Gaelic Society and Economy', in A. Cosgrove (ed.), *A New History of Ireland. Volume II: Medieval Ireland 1169–1534* (Oxford: Oxford University Press, 1993), pp. 397–438, at p. 433.
19 Nicholls, *Gaelic and Gaelicized Ireland*, pp. 91–5. For background context, see E. FitzPatrick, *Royal Inauguration in Gaelic Ireland* c.*1100–1600: A cultural landscape study* (Woodbridge: Boydell, 2004).
20 Nicholls, *Gaelic and Gaelicized Ireland*, p. 93.
21 Ibid., p. 92; E. FitzPatrick, 'The Landscape and Settlements of the Uí Dhálaigh Poets of Muinter Bháire', in S. Duffy (ed.), *Princes, Prelates and Poets in Medieval Ireland: Essays in honour of Katharine Simms* (Dublin: Four Courts Press, 2013), pp. 460–80.
22 Nicholls, *Gaelic and Gaelicized Ireland*, p. 94.
23 Kelly, *Guide to Early Irish Law*, p. 77.
24 Kenny, *Anglo-Irish and Gaelic Women*, p. 36.
25 Ibid., p. 40.
26 Watt, 'Gaelic Polity', p. 317.
27 Simms, 'Women in Norman Ireland', p. 14.
28 Ibid., p. 15.
29 Simms, 'Women in Norman Ireland'; Kenny, *Anglo-Irish and Gaelic Women*, pp. 77–81.
30 Kenny, *Anglo-Irish and Gaelic Women*, pp. 13–15, 18–19.
31 C. Lennon and J. Murray (eds), *The Dublin Franchise Roll, 1468–1512* (Dublin: Dublin Corporation, 1998), p. xxiii; Kenny, *Anglo-Irish and Gaelic Women*, pp. 21, 40. See also M. Murphy, 'The Economy', in B. Smith (ed.), *Cambridge History of Ireland. Volume 1: 600–1550* (Cambridge: Cambridge University Press, 2018), pp. 385–414.
32 Kenny, *Anglo-Irish and Gaelic Women*, p. 21.
33 G. Kenny, 'The Power of Dower: The importance of dower in the lives of medieval women in Ireland', in C. Meek and C. Lawless (eds), *Pawns or Players? Studies on medieval and early modern women* (Dublin: Four Courts Press, 2003), pp. 59–74.
34 S. Shahar, *The Fourth Estate: A history of women in the middle ages*, trans. Chaya Galai (London: Routledge, 2003), pp. 205–10; Kenny, *Anglo-Irish and Gaelic Women*, p. 17.
35 Kenny, *Anglo-Irish and Gaelic Women*, p. 16.
36 Ibid., p. 38; Gilchrist, *Medieval Life*, pp. 147–8.
37 Hall, *Women and the Church*, pp. 174–5.
38 Kenny, *Anglo-Irish and Gaelic Women*, p. 39.

39 For Ireland, see Flanagan, *Transformation*. Monastic reform began at earlier dates in Britain and the continent. See Vanderputten, *Monastic Reform as Process*; Vanderputten, *Dark Age Nunneries*; S. Vanderputten, 'Monastic Reform from the Tenth to the Early Twelfth Century', in A.I. Beach and I. Cochelin (eds), *Medieval Monasticism in the Latin West*, 2 vols (Cambridge: Cambridge University Press, 2020), pp. 599–617.

40 K. Nicholls, 'Rectory, Vicarage and Parish in the Western Dioceses', *Journal of the Royal Society of Antiquaries of Ireland*, vol. 101, 1971, pp. 53–84. It has been suggested that parish formation began much earlier in certain places, For example, P. MacCotter, 'Parish, Pastoral Care and Túath in the Diocese of Limerick, *c.*1201', *Journal of the Royal Society of Antiquaries of Ireland*, vols 142–3, 2012–13, pp. 86–99; P. MacCotter, 'The Medieval Rural Dean and Rural Deanery in Ireland', in E. Purcell, P. MacCotter, J. Sheehan and J. Nyhan (eds), *Clerics, Kings and Vikings* (Dublin: Four Courts Press, 2015), pp. 155–68. For a recent overview, see C. Ó Clabaigh, 'The Church 1050–1460', in B. Smith (ed.), *Cambridge History of Ireland. Volume 1: 600–1550* (Cambridge: Cambridge University Press, 2018), pp. 355–84; A. Empey, 'The Role of the Regular Canons of St Augustine in the Formation of the Parochial Network in Ireland', in M. Browne and C. Ó Clabaigh (eds), *Households of God: The regular canons and canonesses of Saint Augustine and of Prémontré in medieval Ireland* (Dublin: Four Courts Press, 2019), pp. 124–37.

41 Watt, *The Church*, p. 25.

42 Flanagan, *Transformation*, p. 246.

43 Hall, *Women and the Church*, p. 21; FitzPatrick and Gillespie (eds), *The Parish*.

44 C. Platt, *The Parish Churches of Medieval England* (London: Chancellor Press, 1995), pp. 1–12.

45 J.A. Watt, '*Ecclesia inter Anglicos et inter Hibernicos*: Confrontation and coexistence in the medieval diocese and province of Armagh', in J.F. Lydon (ed.), *The English in Medieval Ireland* (Dublin: Royal Irish Academy, 1984), pp. 46–64; K. Simms, 'Frontiers in the Irish Church: Regional and cultural', in T. Barry, R. Frame and K. Simms (eds), *Colony and Frontier in Medieval Ireland: Essays presented to J.F. Lydon* (London: The Hambledon Press, 1995), pp. 177–200, at p. 177; Kenny, *Anglo-Irish and Gaelic Women*, p. 13.

46 Simms, 'Frontiers', p. 184.

47 Ibid., pp. 177–8.

48 Simms, 'Frontiers'.

49 Ibid., p. 199; E. Bhreathnach, 'The *Seanchas* Tradition in Late Medieval Ireland', in E. Bhreathnach and B. Cunningham (eds), *Writing Irish History: The Four Masters and their world* (Dublin: Wordwell, 2007), pp. 19–26, at p. 19.

50 Simms, 'Frontiers', p. 199.

51 Gilchrist, *Medieval Life*, pp. 169–81.

52 Flanagan, *Transformation*, p. 203.

53 Hall, *Women and the Church*, p. 34; Kenny, *Anglo-Irish and Gaelic Women*, pp. 102–14, 116–20.

54 M. Wade Labarge, *Women in Medieval Life* (London: Penguin, 2001), p. 33.

55 Kenny, *Anglo-Irish and Gaelic Women*, p. 126.

56 Simms, 'Frontiers', p. 182; Kenny, *Anglo-Irish and Gaelic Women*, p. 121.

57 Kenny, *Anglo-Irish and Gaelic Women*, p. 126.

58 Hall, *Women and the Church*, p. 165.

59 A.M. Freeman (ed.), *Annála Connacht: The Annals of Connacht AD 1224–1544* (Dublin: Dublin Institute for Advanced Studies, 1944); Kenny, *Anglo-Irish and Gaelic Women*, pp. 123–4.

60 Kenny, *Anglo-Irish and Gaelic Women*, p. 124.

61 Ibid., pp. 122–5.

62 Simms, 'Frontiers', p. 180.
63 Hall, *Women and the Church*, p. 35; Kenny, *Anglo-Irish and Gaelic Women*, p. 159.
64 Kenny, *Anglo-Irish and Gaelic Women*, p. 162; S. Sweetinburgh, *The Role of the Hospital in Medieval England: Gift giving and the spiritual economy* (Dublin: Four Courts Press, 2004).
65 Kenny, 'The Power of Dower', pp. 59–74.
66 Kenny, *Anglo-Irish and Gaelic Women*, pp. 153, 156.
67 Hall, *Women and the Church*, p. 21; Flanagan, *Transformation*, p. 73.
68 Devotion to the Virgin Mary was created very early on in the Christian faith, eventually becoming dogma. Medieval texts in both Ireland and England show a devotion to Mary: for example, Gilchrist, 'Blessed Art Thou Among Women'; Hall, *Women and the Church*; Kenny, *Anglo-Irish and Gaelic Women*; Flanagan, *Transformation*, pp. 202–41.
69 Gilchrist, *Gender and Material Culture*, pp. 140–3; J. Pelikan, *Mary Through the Centuries: Her place in the history of culture* (New Haven: Yale University Press, 1996), pp. 13–21, 220–1; Hall, *Women and the Church*, p. 73; N. Morgan, 'Texts and Images of Marian Devotion in English Twelfth-Century Monasticism, and Their Influence on the Secular Church', in B. Thompson (ed.), *Harlaxton Medieval Studies. Volume VI: Monasteries and Society in Medieval Britain* (Stamford: Paul Watkins, 1999), pp. 117–36; M. O'Carroll, 'Our Lady in Early Medieval Ireland', in A. Smyth (ed.), *Seanchas: Studies in early and medieval Irish archaeology, history and literature in honour of Francis J. Byrne* (Dublin: Four Courts Press, 2000), pp. 178–81; M. Rubin, *Emotion and Devotion: The meaning of Mary in medieval religious cultures* (New York: Central European University Press, 2009); Harrington, *Women*, pp. 280–1; S. Boardman and E. Williamson (eds), *The Cult of Saints and the Virgin Mary in Medieval Scotland* (Suffolk: Boydell, 2010); D. Ó Laoghaire, 'Mary in Irish Spirituality', in M. Maher (ed.), *Irish Spirituality* (Dublin: Veritas Publications, 1981), pp. 47–56.
70 R. Lightbown, 'The Jewellery', in M. Hurley and O. Scully (eds), *Late Viking Age and Medieval Waterford Excavations 1986–1992* (Waterford: Waterford Corporation, 1997), pp. 518–23, at p. 522.
71 K. Wiggins, 'An Early Medieval Ditched Enclosure with Burials and Cereal-Drying Kilns at Killeany, Co. Laois', in C. Corlett and M. Potterton (eds), *The Church in Early Medieval Ireland in the Light of Recent Archaeological Excavations* (Dublin: Wordwell, 2014), pp. 273–86, at pp. 280, 281, 285.
72 M. Hurley, 'Excavations at Grand Parade, Cork (part 2)', *Journal of the Cork Archaeological and Historical Society*, vol. 95, pp. 64–87, at p. 77; Lightbown, 'The Jewellery', pp. 520–2.
73 M. Hurley, 'Bone Artefacts', in E. FitzPatrick, M. O'Brien and P. Walsh (eds), *Archaeological Investigations in Galway City 1987–1998* (Dublin: Wordwell, 2004), pp. 463–76, at p. 464.
74 M. Hurley, 'The Bone and Antler Artefacts', in M. Hurley and C.A. Sheehan, *Excavations at the Dominican Priory: St Mary's of the Isle, Cork* (Cork: Cork Corporation, 1995), pp. 112–15.
75 https://celt.ucc.ie//book_lismore.html. Accessed 15 September 2020; D. Ó Corráin, Corpus Christianorum Clavis Litterarum Hibernensium: *Medieval Irish books and texts c.400–c.1600*, 3 vols (Turnhout: Brepols, 2017).
76 S. Ryan, 'Windows on Late Medieval Devotional Practice: Máire Ní Mháille's "Book of Piety" (1513) and the world behind the texts', in R. Moss, C. Ó Clabaigh and S. Ryan (eds), *Art and Devotion in Late Medieval Ireland* (Dublin: Four Courts Press, 2006), pp. 1–15.
77 Hall, *Women and the Church*, pp. 23–6, 40; Kenny, *Anglo-Irish and Gaelic Women*, pp. 92–5.

78 Hall, *Women and the Church*, pp. 26, 58, 176.
79 Gilchrist, *Gender and Material Culture*, pp. 34, 107, 117; Kenny, *Anglo-Irish and Gaelic Women*, p. 156; B. Golding, '"As for a nun": Corrodies, nunneries and the laity', in E. Jamroziak, J. Kerr and K Stöber (eds), *Monastic Life in the Medieval British Isles: Essays in honour of Janet Burton* (Cardiff: University of Wales Press, 2018), pp. 173–87.
80 Gilchrist, *Gender and Material Culture*, p. 177.
81 Kerr, *Religious Life for Women*, p. 101. Elsewhere it has been argued the issue was not that there were too many women in the general population in the later middle ages, but rather that there were too many to maintain in their proper class sphere; hence many upper-class women became nuns. See McNamara, *Sisters in Arms*, p. 261.
82 Flanagan, *Transformation*, p. 201.
83 For example, Power, *Medieval English Nunneries*, pp. 14–16; Oliva, *Convent and the Community*, p. 7.
84 Hall, *Women and the Church*, p. 33; Kenny, *Anglo-Irish and Gaelic Women*, pp. 165, 168.
85 B. Ó Dálaigh, 'Mistress, Mother and Abbess: Renalda Ní Bhriain, *c.*1447–1510', *North Munster Antiquarian Journal*, vol. 32, 1990, pp. 50–63; Hall, *Women and the Church*, p. 38; Kenny, *Anglo-Irish and Gaelic Women*, p. 168.
86 D. Webb, *Medieval European Pilgrimage* (Basingstoke: Palgrave, 2002); L. Nugent, *Journeys of Faith: Stories of pilgrimage from medieval Ireland* (Dublin: Columba Press, 2020).
87 P. Harbison, *Pilgrimage in Ireland* (Dublin: Irish Academic Press, 1991); O'Sullivan and Ó Carragáin, *Inishmurray*, pp. 316–48; Nugent, *Journeys of Faith*; L. Nugent, 'Medieval Pilgrims' Tokens and Other Souvenirs in Ireland: A review of the archaeological and historical evidence', in J. Higgins, A. Conneely and M. Gibbon (eds), *Irish Maritime Heritage: Proceedings of the 3rd Galway International Heritage Conference, 2013* (Galway: Crows Rock Publishing, 2013), pp. 23–46.
88 R. Stalley, 'Sailing to Santiago: Medieval pilgrimage to Santiago de Compostela and its artistic influence in Ireland', in J. Bradley (ed.), *Settlement and Society: Studies presented to F.X. Martin OSA* (Kilkenny: Boethius, 1988), pp. 397–420; P. Halpin, 'Anglo-Saxon Women and Pilgrimage', *Anglo-Norman Studies: Proceedings of the Battle Conference*, vol. 19, 1996, pp. 97–122; S. Schein, 'Bridget of Sweden, Margery Kempe and Women's Jerusalem Pilgrimages in the Middle Ages', *Mediterranean Historical Review*, vol. 14, no. 1, 1999, pp. 44–58; S. Morrison, *Women Pilgrims in Late Medieval England: Private piety as public performance* (London: Routledge, 2000); Hall, *Women and the Church*, p. 29.
89 Kenny, *Anglo-Irish and Gaelic Women*, p. 101; B. Cunningham, *Medieval Irish Pilgrims to Santiago de Compostela* (Dublin: Four Courts Press, 2018).
90 K. Rudy, *Virtual Pilgrimages in the Convent: Imagining Jerusalem in the late middle ages* (Turnhout: Brepols, 2011).
91 Ó Clabaigh, *Franciscans in Ireland*, p. 63; Kenny, *Anglo-Irish and Gaelic Women*, p. 98.
92 Flanagan, *Transformation*, p. 200.
93 Hall, *Women and the Church*, pp. 45–59.
94 Ibid., p. 42.
95 Ibid., pp. 43, 57; Kenny, *Anglo-Irish and Gaelic Women*, p. 94.
96 M. Burrows, 'Fifteenth-Century Irish Provincial Legislation and Pastoral Care', in W.J. Sheils and D. Woods (eds), *The Churches, Ireland and the Irish* (Oxford: Basil Blackwell, 1989), pp. 55–67, at p. 65.
97 Hall, *Women and the Church*, p. 27.
98 Ibid., pp. 27–8.
99 H. King, 'Late Medieval Crosses in County Meath, *c.*1470–1635', *Proceedings of the Royal Irish Academy*, vol. 84C, 1984, pp. 79–116.

100 Power, *Medieval English Nunneries*, pp. 25–41.
101 For example, Evangelisti, *Nuns*, pp. 13–39.
102 Freeman, *Annals of Connacht*; Ó Dálaigh, 'Mistress, Mother and Abbess', pp. 50–63.
103 Shahar, *Fourth Estate*, p. 39; Kenny, *Anglo-Irish and Gaelic Women*, p. 170.
104 Shahar, *Fourth Estate*, p. 39.
105 Kenny, *Anglo-Irish and Gaelic Women*, p. 169; A.I. Beach, *Women as Scribes: Book production and monastic reform in twelfth-century Bavaria* (Cambridge: Cambridge University Press, 2004); Hamburger and Marti, *Crown and Veil.*
106 Moran, *Monasticon Hibernicum*, vol. II, p. 258; Kenny, *Anglo-Irish and Gaelic Women*, pp. 28, 178.
107 C. Baswell, 'Heloise', in C. Dinshaw and D. Wallace (eds), *The Cambridge Companion to Medieval Women's Writing* (Cambridge: Cambridge University Press, 2003), pp. 161–71; G. Macy, 'Heloise, Abelard and the Ordination of Abbesses', *Journal of Ecclesiastical History*, vol. 57, 2006, pp. 16–32.
108 J. Fleming, *Gille of Limerick c.1070–1145: Architect of a medieval church* (Dublin: Four Courts Press, 2001), pp. 38, 98; M. Holland, 'Gille (Gilbert) of Limerick', in S. Duffy (ed.), *Medieval Ireland: An encyclopedia* (New York: Routledge, 2005), pp. 198–9, at p. 198; M. Holland, 'Malachy (Máel-Máedóic)', in S. Duffy (ed.), *Medieval Ireland: An encyclopedia* (New York: Routledge, 2005), pp. 312–14.
109 For a brief overview of the earlier church reform in England, which did include several female figures, see P. Stafford, 'Queens, Nunneries and Reforming Churchmen: Gender, religious status and reform in tenth- and eleventh-century England', *Past and Present*, vol. 163, 1999, pp. 3–35; Collins, 'Transforming Women Religious?'
110 Holland, 'Gille', p. 199; See also E. Bhreathnach, 'The World of Bishops in Religious Orders in Medieval Ireland', in K. Stöber, J. Kerr and E. Jamroziak (eds), *Monastic Life in the Medieval British Isles: Essays in honour of Janet Burton* (Cardiff: University of Wales Press, 2018), pp. 71–88.
111 Flanagan, *Transformation*, p. 55; Ó Carragáin, *Churches in Early Medieval Ireland*, p. 12.
112 Fleming notes that there was not agreement among canonists regarding the number of clerical grades in the local church, which varied from seven to nine. The traditional seven grades were: priest, deacon, sub-deacon, acolyte, exorcist, lector and porter. The additional two were bishop and psalmist. Gille used the seven-grade system; Fleming, *Gille of Limerick*, p. 90. The lower clerical grades of door-keepers, lectors, exorcists and acolytes mentioned by Gille could be married; Flanagan, *Transformation*, p. 70.
113 Fleming, *Gille of Limerick*, p. 88.
114 Fleming provides full particulars of the extant manuscripts of Gille's writing; Ibid., pp. 119–42. See also Flanagan, *Transformation*, p. 70, n. 182.
115 Flanagan, *Transformation*, p. 70.
116 Flanagan noted, in the *Life of St Malachy*, that women did not feature prominently, and when they did, they were portrayed as hindrances. However, this may be considered an illustration of the views of the writer, Cistercian monk Bernard of Clairvaux, rather than of Malachy himself; Flanagan, *Transformation*, p. 149.
117 Holland, 'Malachy', p. 314.
118 A. Halpin and C. Newman, *Ireland: An Oxford archaeological guide* (Oxford: Oxford University Press, 2006), p. 320.
119 Dunning, 'The Arroasian Order', pp. 300, 304; M.T. Flanagan, 'St Mary's Abbey, Louth and the Introduction of the Arroasian Observance into Ireland', *Clogher Record*, vol. 10, pp. 223–34, at p. 227; Flanagan, *Transformation*, p. 139; Holland, 'Malachy', p. 314.

120 Flanagan, *Transformation*, p. 137; Bhreathnach, 'The *Vita Apostolica*'.
121 Watt, *The Church*, p. 46.
122 Flanagan, *Transformation*, p. 151.
123 Thompson, *Women Religious*, p. 151.
124 J.M. Picard and Y. de Pontfarcy, *The Vision of Tnugdal* (Dublin: Four Courts Press, 1989); Flanagan, *Transformation*, p. 123, n. 32, p. 150.
125 Bhreathnach, 'The *Vita Apostolica*'.
126 This decree highlights the seemingly common practice of non-affiliation of many nunneries to a distinct order or rule. This was an issue not only in Ireland but throughout the Roman church where a nunnery claimed to be following a particular rule but was not actually officially incorporated into that order. This can pose particular problems for historians, who tend to study male monastic houses according to order but cannot apply the same rules for nunneries. For Ireland, the Benedictines, Cistercians, Augustinians, Arroasians and Franciscans (the Poor Clares) are orders linked to later medieval nunneries in Ireland yet there is no contemporary historical official documentation of incorporation or affiliation of any Irish nunnery to any particular order. See Burton, *Monastic and Religious Orders*, p. 86.
127 Kilcreevanty, Co. Galway is an example. See Berman, 'Medieval Monasticisms', p. 380.
128 Hall, *Women and the Church*, pp. 160–1.
129 Lawrence, *Medieval Monasticism*, pp. 220–1.
130 D. Luscombe, *The Letter Collection of Peter Abelard and Heloise* (Oxford: Oxford Medieval Texts, 2013).
131 Schulenburg, 'Strict Active Enclosure', pp. 60–2.
132 Lawrence, *Medieval Monasticism*, p. 222.
133 Schulenburg, 'Strict Active Enclosure', p. 79.
134 Ibid., pp. 59, 70; Schulenburg, 'Female Sanctity', p. 115.
135 E. Makowski, *Canon Law and Cloistered Women: Periculoso and its commentators 1298–1545* (Washington DC: The Catholic University of America Press, 1997). Brundage and Makowski provide an English translation of the decree as an appendix. See J.A. Brundage and E. M. Makowski, 'Enclosure of Nuns: The decretal *Periculoso* and its commentators', *Journal of Medieval History*, vol. 20, 1994, pp. 143–55.
136 Medioli, 'An Unequal Law', pp. 137–8.
137 Brundage and Makowski, 'Enclosure of Nuns', p. 143.
138 D. Hall, 'Necessary Collaborations: Religious women and lay communities in medieval Ireland c.1200–1540', in A. Hayes and D. Urquhart (eds), *Irish Women's History* (Dublin: Irish Academic Press, 2004), pp. 15–28, at p. 18.
139 Flanagan, *Transformation*, pp. 244–5.
140 G. Daichman, *Wayward Nuns in Medieval Literature* (Syracuse: Syracuse University Press, 1986); C. Knudsen, 'Naughty Nuns and Promiscuous Monks: Monastic sexual misconduct in late medieval England', unpublished PhD thesis, Centre for Medieval Studies, University of Toronto, 2012; C. Knudsen, 'Promiscuous Monks and Naughty Nuns: Poverty, sex, and apostasy in later medieval England', in A. Scott and C. Kosso (eds), *Poverty and Prosperity: The rich and the poor in the middle ages and Renaissance* (Belgium: Turnhout, 2012), pp. 75–91. Kilculliheen, Inishlounaght, Molough, Killone, Downpatrick, Termonfeckin and St Catherine's are associated with various scandals recorded in the historical sources.
141 Brundage and Makowski, 'Enclosure of Nuns', pp. 145–9.
142 C. Neel, 'The Origins of the Beguines', *Signs*, vol. 14, 1989, pp. 321–41; Gilchrist, *Gender and Material Culture*, pp. 170–2; D. Elliott, *Proving Woman: Female spirituality and*

inquisitional culture in the later middle ages (Princeton: Princeton University Press, 2004), pp. 47–84.

143 Neel, 'Origins of the Beguines', p. 324; More, *Fictive Orders*.

144 Brundage and Makowski, 'Enclosure of Nuns', p. 157.

145 D. Chart (ed.), *The Register of John Swayne, Archbishop of Armagh 1418–1439, with Some Entries of Earlier and Later Archbishops* (Belfast: Her Majesty's Stationery Office Northern Ireland, 1935).

146 D. Keeping, 'Life and Death in English Nunneries: A biocultural study of variations in the health of women during the later medieval period 1066–1540', unpublished PhD thesis, University of Bradford, 2000, p. 183.

147 Schulenburg, 'Strict Active Enclosure', p. 51; Gilchrist, *Gender and Material Culture*, p. 152; Brundage and Makowski, 'Enclosure of Nuns', p. 143.

148 McNamara, *Sisters in Arms*, p. 290.

149 E. Makowski, 'Monastic Enclosure', in M. Schaus (ed.), *Women and Gender in Medieval Europe: An encyclopedia* (London: Routledge, 2006), pp. 575–6.

150 Power, *Medieval English Nunneries*, p. 345.

151 Brundage and Makowski, 'Enclosure of Nuns', p. 156.

152 Kerr, *Religious Life for Women*, pp. 3–4. Bugyis rightly points out that the care of nuns extended to themselves also and the officers in the nunnery community carried out such tasks as hospitality, counsel, instruction, healing, absolution and intercession; K. Bugyis, *The Care of Nuns: The ministries of Benedictine women during the central middle ages* (Oxford: Oxford University Press, 2019).

153 Thompson, 'The Problem of the Cistercian Nuns'; Burton, *Monastic and Religious Orders*, p. 101.

154 Skinner, 'Benedictine Life for Women in Central France', p. 95; Burton, *Monastic and Religious Orders*, pp. 100–8; Burton, 'Looking for Medieval Nuns'; Burton, 'Moniales and *Ordo Cisterciensis*'; Degler-Spengler, 'Incorporation of Cistercian Nuns'; Berman, 'Were There Twelfth-Century Cistercian Nuns?'; Berman, *Cistercian Evolution*; Berman, 'Medieval Monasticisms'; E. Freeman, 'Nuns', in M.B. Bruun (ed.), *The Cambridge Companion to the Cistercian Order* (Cambridge: Cambridge University Press, 2013), pp. 100–11, at pp. 100–1; Jamroziak, *Cistercian Order*, pp. 124–55; Berman, *The White Nuns*.

155 Berman, 'Medieval Monasticisms', p. 388.

156 Kerr, *Religious Life for Women*, p. 1; Berman, 'Medieval Monasticisms', pp. 389–90.

157 Freeman, 'Nuns'.

158 Berman, 'Medieval Monasticisms', p. 378.

159 McNamara, *Sisters in Arms*, pp. 290, 295; E.A. Matter, 'Influence of Jerome', in M. Schaus (ed.), *Women and Gender in Medieval Europe: An encyclopaedia* (London: Routledge, 2006), pp. 421–3, at p. 422.

160 B. Golding, 'Bishops and Nuns: Forms of the *cura monialium* in twelfth- and thirteenth-century England', in J. Burton and K. Stöber (eds), *Women in the Medieval Monastic World* (Turnhout: Brepols, 2015), pp. 97–122.

161 McNamara, *Sisters in Arms*, p. 299.

162 Ibid., pp. 295, 298.

163 Brundage and Makowski, 'Enclosure of Nuns', p. 147; Golding, *Gilbert of Sempringham*, pp. 444–7; Lawrence, *Medieval Monasticism*, pp. 222–7.

164 Kerr, *Religious Life for Women*, pp. 4, 47–8. Kerr has argued that because of the nature of the organisation of Fontevraud, it should not be considered a double house but rather a female order with an integrated male element. The term 'double house' is so

broad – in that it covers diverse arrangements between men and women religious – as to deem it unuseful.

165 Kerr, *Religious Life for Women*, p. 45.

166 McNamara, *Sisters in Arms*, p. 296. Gwynn and Hadcock cite 1141 for this dissolution and note that Premonstratensian nuns should be a league away from canons: Gwynn and Hadcock, *Medieval Religious Houses*, p. 202.

167 Lawrence, *Medieval Monasticism*, p. 224.

168 It has been suggested that Killeentrynode, Co. Mayo was a Premonstratensian nunnery. This has been discounted by Gwynn and Hadcock, *Medieval Religious Houses*, p. 205; and by Dr Miriam Clyne, personal communication.

169 M. Clyne, 'Medieval Irish Premonstratensian Monasteries and Their European Context', 2 vols, unpublished PhD thesis NUI Galway, 2010, pp. 39, 105–6; M. Clyne, 'The Monasteries of the Canons of Prémontré, *c.*1180–*c.*1607', in M. Browne and C. Ó Clabaigh (eds), *Households of God: The regular canons and canonesses of Saint Augustine and of Prémontré in medieval Ireland* (Dublin: Four Courts Press, 2019), pp. 62–86.

170 S.A. Wolbrink, 'Women in the Premonstratensian Order of Northwestern Germany 1120–1250', *The Catholic Historical Review*, vol. 89, 2003, pp. 287–408.

171 There is currently no evidence of Beguines from later medieval Ireland either.

172 Lawrence, *Medieval Monasticism*, p. 228; Freeman, 'Nuns', p. 102; Jamroziak, *Cistercian Order*, p. 128.

173 Lawrence, *Medieval Monasticism*, pp. 227–8.

174 Freeman, 'Nuns', p. 102; Jordan, *Women, Power and Religious Patronage*; Jordan, 'Gender Concerns'.

175 McNamara, *Sisters in Arms*, p. 301; Berman, 'Medieval Monasticisms', p. 380.

176 Lawrence, *Medieval Monasticism*, pp. 229–30.

177 McNamara, *Sisters in Arms*, pp. 304–9.

178 J. Mueller, 'Clare of Assisi', in M. Schaus (ed.), *Women and Gender in Medieval Europe: An encyclopedia* (London: Routledge, 2006), pp. 144–5; M. Lehmijoki-Gardner, 'Dominican Order', in M. Schaus (ed.), *Women and Gender in Medieval Europe: An encyclopedia* (London: Routledge, 2006), pp. 223–5; M. Robson, *The Franciscans in the Middle Ages* (Woodbridge: Boydell, 2006), pp. 53–4.

179 McNamara, *Sisters in Arms*, p. 309; C.M. Mooney, *Clare of Assisi and the Thirteenth-Century Church: Religious women, rules and resistance* (Philadelphia: University of Pennsylvania Press, 2016).

180 N.B. Warren, 'Monastic Rules', in M. Schaus (ed.), *Women and Gender in Medieval Europe: An encyclopedia* (London: Routledge, 2006), pp. 576–8.

181 The liturgy of hours (*liturgia horarum*), work of God (*Opus Dei*) and the canonical hours are synonymous with the divine office (*officium divinum*). The divine office has been used here throughout.

182 Warren, 'Monastic Rules', p. 576. For a comprehensive history of the liturgy used in different contexts, see R. Pfaff, *The Liturgy in Medieval England: A history* (Cambridge: Cambridge University Press, 2009).

183 When Abelard was compiling a rule for Heloise's community at Paraclete, she requested that the 'gender-less' Benedictine rule be modified. This modified version made changes targeted on women's bodily differences from men: see Warren, 'Monastic Rules', p. 577.

184 Power, *Medieval English Nunneries*, pp. 285–314.

185 Flanagan, *Transformation*, p. 123.

186 Berman, *Cistercian Evolution*, p. 236; Berman, 'Medieval Monasticisms'.

187 O'Keeffe, *An Anglo-Norman Monastery*, pp. 15–17; Browne and Ó Clabaigh, *Households of God*.
188 Warren, 'Monastic Rules', p. 577; Mooney, *Clare of Assisi*.
189 Bourdillon, *Order of Minoresses*, pp. 1–9.
190 There is an extant seventeenth-century copy of the rule of St Clare translated into Irish: see E. Bhreathnach and B. Cunningham (eds), *Writing Irish History: The Four Masters and their world* (Dublin: Wordwell, 2007), pp. 112–13.
191 Hall, *Women and the Church*, p. 136. See also an Irish later medieval treatise on the monastic life by a spiritual advisor likely to a religious woman: J. MacKechnie, *Instructio Pie Vivendi et Superna Meditandi*, vol. 29 (Dublin: Irish Texts Society, 1934).
192 For example, kitchen accounts, which are available for the male Augustinian Priory at Kells, Co. Kilkenny: see Clyne, *Kells Priory*, pp. 10–1.
193 For example, Power, *English Medieval Nunneries*; McNamara, *Sister in Arms*, pp. 233–82; Kerr, *Religious Life for Women*; Evangelisti, *Nuns*.
194 B. Harvey, *Living and Dying in England 1100–1540: The monastic experience* (Oxford: Clarendon Press, 1993), p. 210.
195 H.F. Berry (ed.), *Register of Wills and Inventories of the Diocese of Dublin* (Dublin: Royal Society of Antiquaries of Ireland, special volume 211, 1898), p. 176.
196 The offices were: Matins (night office during night or at midnight); Lauds (dawn prayer, at dawn or approx. 3 a.m.); Prime (early morning prayer, first hour, approx. 6 a.m.); Terce (mid-morning prayer, third hour, approx. 9 a.m.); Sext (midday prayer, sixth hour, 12 noon); None (mid-afternoon prayer, ninth hour, approx. 3 p.m.), Vespers (evening prayer, approx. 6 p.m. or at the 'lighting of the lamps') and Compline (night prayer before retiring, approx. 9 p.m.). https://www.newadvent.org/cathen/11219a.htm. Accessed 15 September 2020.
197 A. O'Donoghue, 'Mendicant Cloisters in Munster', in R. Stalley (ed.), *Limerick and South-West Ireland: Medieval art and architecture* (Leeds: Maney, 2011), pp. 111–31, at p. 126.
198 Ó Clabaigh, *The Friars in Ireland*, pp. 170–1.
199 K.A. Smith, 'Books of Hours', in M. Schaus (ed.), *Women and Gender in Medieval Europe: An encyclopaedia* (London: Routledge, 2006), pp. 89–92; E. Duffy, *Marking the Hours: English people and their prayers 1240–1570* (Yale: Yale University Press, 2007).
200 Bruzelius and Berman, 'Introduction', p. 73.
201 Nunneries associated with early medieval male sites are: Addrigoole, Co. Laois, Clonard, Co. Meath, Clonfert, Co. Galway, Derry, Co. Derry, Duleek, Co. Meath, Durrow, Co. Offaly, Inishmaine, Co. Mayo, Kells, Co. Meath, Killcigh, Co. Offaly, Lusk, Co. Dublin, Roscommon, Co. Roscommon, Templenagalliaghdoo, Co. Mayo, and Termonfeckin, Co. Louth.
202 This graveslab is now located in Clonfert Cathedral. I am grateful to Dr Christy Cunniffe who identified it, and who remembers the graveslab being moved from the nunnery site. See C. Cunniffe, 'The Canons and Canonesses of St Augustine at Clonfert', in M. Browne and C. Ó Clabaigh (eds), *Households of God: The regular canons and canonesses of Saint Augustine and of Prémontré in medieval Ireland* (Dublin: Four Courts Press, 2019), pp. 103–23.
203 A full catalogue of all nunneries cited in this book can be accessed online at DOI: http://doi.org/10.5281/zenodo.5035404. See Table 3.1 for modern county locations of nunneries.
204 A stone head from Grace Dieu, recorded by Archdall in the eighteenth century, was at Turvey House (now unlocated), though Turvey House is not on the site of the nunnery as has been suggested, in Hall, *Women and the Church*, p. 116, n. 91. A second

stone head from Grace Dieu is in the National Museum of Ireland (see Figure 7.38). No possible nunnery fragments were found from excavations at Dublin Castle according to the excavator: Conleth Manning, personal communication.

205 A non-exhaustive list of these nunneries can be accessed at DOI: http://doi.org/10.5281/zenodo.5035404. For example, Jamestown, Co. Leitrim; Coolnagranshy near Boyle, and Moor, Co. Roscommon; Baldongan, Brunswick Street North, and St Mary Le Dam, Co. Dublin; Russagh, Kilbride and Coolcor, Co. Offaly; and a second nunnery at Cork city. Many of these sites were Franciscan Third Order houses.

206 Gwynn and Hadcock's *Medieval Religious Houses* remains an important source but it is not without problems. It is based largely on antiquarian accounts which have not been subjected to modern scholarly scrutiny. It has been noted, however, that it was intended as a first-search resource in a largely pre-computer world, and was not meant to be relied upon without recourse to the cited sources; see Flanagan, *Transformation*, p. 137.

207 Hadcock, 'Origin of the Augustinian Order', p. 127; Gwynn and Hadcock, *Medieval Religious Houses*, pp. 344–57; see also G. Lee, *Leper Hospitals in Medieval Ireland* (Dublin: Four Courts Press, 1996); Sweetinburgh, *The Role of the Hospital*.

208 Gwynn and Hadcock, *Medieval Religious Houses*, pp. 209, 219, 263–6, 309.

209 Gilchrist, *Gender and Material Culture*, pp. 36–50; Gilchrist, *Contemplation and Action*.

210 The Augustinian canons (OSA) were not monastic as they were clerics living under a rule (regular), rather than monks; this was the only order of clerics recognised by Rome at that time. Dunning noted in 1945 that there was no adequate history written for Augustinian canons and that earlier works were inclined to attribute all Irish foundations to the canons regular. At a later date, about 1256–9, the Augustinian Friars (Austin Friars) were established, known as the Order of Hermits of St Augustine (OESA). See Dunning, 'Arroasian Order', p. 299; Gwynn and Hadcock, *Medieval Religious Houses*, pp. 146, 293–4; Ó Clabaigh, *The Friars in Ireland*, pp. 18–21; Browne and Ó Clabaigh, *Households of God*.

211 Dunning, 'Arroasian Order', p. 309; Hadcock, 'Origin of the Augustinian Order', p. 124; Gwynn and Hadcock, *Medieval Religious Houses*, p. 146; Bhreathnach, 'The *Vita Apostolica*'.

212 Hall, *Women and the Church*, p. 67.

213 B.W. Dwyer, *Stephen of Lexington: Letters from Ireland 1228–1229* (Kalamazoo: Cistercian Publications, 1982); Stalley, *Cistercian Monasteries*.

214 Kilcreevanty is considered Augustinian of Arroasian observance in this book.

215 H.J. de Varebeke, 'The Benedictines in Medieval Ireland', *Journal of the Royal Society of Antiquaries of Ireland*, vol. 80, 1950, pp. 92–6, at p. 92; Gwynn and Hadcock, *Medieval Religious Houses*, p. 102; Ó Carragáin, *Churches in Early Medieval Ireland*, pp. 250, 289; Bhreathnach, 'Benedictine Influence in Ireland'.

216 C. Mooney, 'Franciscan Architecture in Pre-Reformation Ireland [part 1]', *Journal of the Royal Society of Antiquaries of Ireland*, vol. 85, 1955, pp. 133–73; C. Mooney, 'Franciscans in Ireland', *Terminus*, vol. 11, 1955, p. 131; C. Mooney, 'The Franciscans in County Mayo', *Journal of the Galway Archaeological and Historical Society*, vol. 28, 1958–9, pp. 42–69, at p. 57; C. Mooney, 'Franciscan Architecture in Pre-Reformation Ireland [part 2]', *Journal of the Royal Society of Antiquaries of Ireland*, vol. 86, 1956, pp. 125–69; C. Mooney, 'Franciscan Architecture in Pre-Reformation Ireland [part 3]', *Journal of the Royal Society of Antiquaries of Ireland*, vol. 87, 1957, pp. 1–38, 103–24. This is considered too early a date by some, who put forward a later date of 1224–6. See Gwynn and Hadcock, *Medieval Religious Houses*, p. 236; Ó Clabaigh, *The Friars in Ireland*, pp. 11–14.

217 The medieval female branch of the Franciscan Order is commonly called Poor Clares or Poor Nuns of St Francis in Ireland – Ó Clabaigh, *The Friars in Ireland*, p. 310; Minoresses in England – Bourdillon, *Order of Minoresses*; or Clarissans on continental Europe – Bruzelius, 'Hearing is Believing'; Mooney, *Clare of Assisi*.
218 Gwynn and Hadcock, *Medieval Religious Houses*, p. 309. There are now four Franciscan (Poor Clare) houses known: Carrick-on-Suir, Co. Tipperary; Fooran, Co. Westmeath; Galway city; Youghal, Co. Cork.
219 Mooney, 'Franciscans in County Mayo', p. 57; Ó Clabaigh, *The Friars in Ireland*, pp. 310–11.
220 A. Clapham, 'The Priory and Manor House of Dartford', *Archaeological Journal*, vol. 83, 1926, pp. 67–85.
221 A. Knox, 'Her Book-Lined Cell: Irish nuns and the development of texts, translation and literacy in late medieval Spain', in V. Blanton, V. O'Mara and P. Stoop (eds), *Nuns' Literacies in Medieval Europe: The Kansas City dialogue* (Turnhout: Brepols, 2015), pp. 67–86, at p. 67.
222 Gilchrist has estimated 153 nunneries, eighteen double houses, six nuns' cells attached to male houses and four quasi double houses in medieval England; Gilchrist, *Gender and Material Culture*, p. 36.
223 Curran has estimated fifteen nunneries in medieval Scotland; Curran, 'Religious Women', p. 38.
224 In regard to nunneries in medieval Wales there are only three long-standing communities. They are: Llanllŷr in Ceredigion founded in 1197, Llanllugan in Cydewain (now Powy) founded between 1170 and 1190. Both these houses were Cistercian. The third was Benedictine, founded at Usk in 1135 and confirmed in 1330. Other supposed houses in Wales appear to be erroneous; see Cartwright, *Feminine Sanctity*, pp. 177–8; Bezant, *Medieval Welsh Settlement*, p. 44.
225 Gilchrist, *Gender and Material Culture*, p. 61.
226 Power, *Medieval English Nunneries*, pp. 285–314.
227 For example, Jordan, 'Gender Concerns'; Jordan, '*Pro remedio anime sue*'; Cariboni, 'Cistercian Nuns in Northern Italy'; McGuire, 'Cistercian Nuns in Twelfth- and Thirteenth-Century Denmark'.
228 Bruzelius, 'Nuns in Space'; Jornet-Benito, 'Female Mendicant Spirituality in Catalan Territory'.
229 Gilchrist, *Gender and Material Culture*, p. 40.
230 Stalley, *Cistercian Monasteries*; O'Keeffe, *An Anglo-Norman Monastery*; M. Clyne, 'Archaeological Excavations at Holy Trinity Abbey, Lough Key, Co. Roscommon', *Proceedings of the Royal Irish Academy*, vol. 105C, 2005, pp. 23–98; Clyne, *Kells Priory*; Clyne, 'Monasteries of the Canons of Prémontré'; Y. McDermott, 'Patronage and Observance: The Franciscan and Dominican friaries in the Connacht lordships of the Mac William Burkes 1350–1550', unpublished PhD thesis, NUI Galway, 2012; A. Lafaye, 'Spiritual Renewal and Changing Landscapes: The mendicant orders in Ireland, thirteenth–sixteenth century', in J. Lyttleton and M. Stout (eds), *Church and Settlement in Ireland* (Dublin: Four Courts Press, 2018), pp. 119–41.
231 T. Collins, 'An Archaeology of Augustinian Nuns in Medieval Ireland', in M. Browne and C. Ó Clabaigh (eds), *Households of God: The regular canons and canonesses of Saint Augustine and of Prémontré in medieval Ireland* (Dublin: Four Courts Press, 2019), pp. 87–102.
232 Burton, *Monastic and Religious Orders*, pp. 85–108.
233 Gilchrist, *Gender and Material Culture*, p. 61; Berman, 'Medieval Monasticisms'.

234 Burton, *Monastic and Religious Orders*, p. 86.
235 Gilchrist, *Gender and Material Culture*, pp. 36–50.
236 Gwynn and Hadcock, *Medieval Religious Houses*, pp. 202, 218–19, 282–4.
237 Ibid., pp. 327–42; M. Browne and C. Ó Clabaigh (eds), *Soldiers of Christ: The Knights Hospitaller and the Knights Templar in medieval Ireland* (Dublin: Four Courts Press, 2016).
238 Golding, *Gilbert of Sempringham*; Kerr, *Religious Life for Women*, pp. 64–80; T. Nyberg, *Birgittinische Klostergründungen des Mittelalters* (Lund: C.W.K. Gleerup, 1965). Ware recorded Plary as a Gilbertine house, but this has been discounted; see Hadcock, 'Origin of the Augustinian Order', p. 130.
239 Hall has identified four waves of nunnery foundation: early medieval foundations, twelfth-century reform foundations, first-generation Anglo-Norman foundations, and those of the fifteenth-century reform movement in Gaelic Ireland; see Hall, *Women and the Church*, pp. 63–95.
240 Nunneries without a known foundation date: Addrigoole, Co. Laois, Buttevant, Co. Cork, Carricknahorna, Co. Sligo, Inishlounaght, Co. Tipperary, Jerpoint, Co. Kilkenny, Mellifont, Co. Louth, Templenagalliaghdoo, Co. Mayo, and Tisrara, Co. Roscommon.
241 Stalley, *Cistercian Monasteries*, p. 239.
242 Ibid., pp. 45–6.
243 Caltragh, Derrane, Duleek, Durrow, Kells, Kilbride, Lusk, Roscommon, Skreen and Termonfeckin.
244 Others were: Calliaghstown, Grace Dieu and Killeigh.
245 Picard and de Pontfarcy, *Vision*; Flanagan, *Transformation*, p. 123, n. 32; p. 150.
246 Kilcreevanty and Graney, 1200; Derry and Plary, 1218; Inishmaine, 1223 and possibly Killaraght; Lismullin, 1240; Ballynagallagh, 1283; and Cork city, 1297.
247 Wardell, 'The History and Antiquities of St Catherine's'; Collins, 'Unveiling Female Monasticism'.
248 Fooran, Youghal and Carrick-on-Suir.
249 Gilchrist, *Gender and Material Culture*, pp. 37, 61.
250 Ibid., p. 41; Hall, *Women and the Church*, p. 81.
251 A locality was defined as approximately 10km radius of the nunnery.
252 Gwynn and Hadcock, *Medieval Religious Houses*, pp. 321–2; Ó Dálaigh, 'Mistress, Mother and Abbess', pp. 50–8.
253 Gwynn and Hadcock, *Medieval Religious Houses*, p. 130; Stalley, *Cistercian Monasteries*, p. 244.
254 In the case of the ten nunneries that were early medieval establishments and were re-used or re-occupied in the later period, the later medieval founder (if known) has been considered in this part of the discussion.
255 A king in this instance relates to a regional ruler and not a king of all Ireland or the high king.
256 L. Lydon, 'The Expansion and Consolidation of the Colony 1215–54', in A. Cosgrove (ed.), *A New History of Ireland. Volume II: Medieval Ireland 1169–1534* (Oxford: Oxford University Press, 1993), pp. 157–78, at pp. 162–4; F. Verstraten, 'Ua Conchobair', in S. Duffy (ed.), *Medieval Ireland: An encyclopedia* (London: Routledge, 2005), pp. 464–6.
257 Diarmait Mac Murchada (1110–1171) originated in Ferns, Co. Wexford, later becoming king of Leinster, and led a most interesting if violent life; he was pivotal to the Anglo-Norman invasion of Ireland. See Byrne, 'The Trembling Sod', pp. 22–3; P. Crooks, 'Mac Murchada, Diarmait', in S. Duffy (ed.), *Medieval Ireland: An encyclopedia* (London: Routledge, 2005), pp. 299–302.

258 King of Oriel (Airgialla, now broadly contiguous with the diocese of Clogher), Donchad O'Carroll (Ua Cerbaill) had his power centre in Louth. See F. Byrne, *Irish Kings and High Kings* (Dublin: Four Courts Press, 2001), pp. 127–8; C. Doherty, 'Airgialla', in S. Duffy (ed.), *Medieval Ireland: An encyclopedia* (London: Routledge, 2005), pp. 13–14.

259 He died in 1153; F.X. Martin, 'Allies and an Overlord 1169–72', in A. Cosgrove (ed.), *A New History of Ireland. Volume II: Medieval Ireland 1169–1534* (Oxford: Oxford University Press, 1993), pp. 67–97, at p. 96.

260 Bréga was a portion of Co. Meath; Byrne, 'The Trembling Sod', p. 19; Gwynn and Hadcock, *Medieval Religious Houses*, pp. 173, 314.

261 She died in 1193 at Mellifont. She is also noted in history for being abducted by the king of Leinster, Mac Murchada. See Nicholls, 'Gaelic Society and Economy', p. 436; Martin, 'Allies and an Overlord', pp. 49–50.

262 Manning has made a strong case that Temple Finghin was the second nunnery at Clonmacnoise. His argument has been accepted and it has been considered as a nunnery in this book. Manning, 'Mystery of the Second Nunnery at Clonmacnoise'; Nicholls, 'Towards a new *Monasticon Hibernicum*'.

263 He has been credited with the establishment of St Peter's Cell, Clare Abbey and Killone. Hall explains that this is based on a foundation charter which was thought by Westropp and others to be dated to the thirteenth century. This charter is now considered to be a fifteenth-century copy and so the charter which claims Donal as founder is not authentic; Hall *Women and the Church*, pp. 74–5; T.J. Westropp, 'Foundation Charter of Forgy Abbey, Co. Clare', *Journal of the Royal Society of Antiquaries of Ireland*, vol. 22, 1892, pp. 78–9. Nevertheless, he continues to be cited as the founder: for example, L. McInerney, 'A 1555 Papal Bulla for Clare Abbey', *Journal of the Royal Society of Antiquaries of Ireland,* vol. 141, 2011, pp. 128–48, at p. 133.

264 Ó Dálaigh, 'Mistress, Mother and Abbess', pp. 50–63.

265 He was an important Gaelic lord, who also founded Kilcrea Abbey and built a number of castles including Blarney and Dripsey (Carrignamuck), all in County Cork.

266 The Lynches were a prominent merchant family in Galway; see W. Childs and T. O'Neill, 'Overseas Trade', in A. Cosgrove (ed.), *A New History of Ireland. Volume II: Medieval Ireland 1169–1534* (Oxford: Oxford University Press, 1993), pp. 492–524, at p. 505; E. FitzPatrick and P. Walsh, 'Buildings and Architecture', in E. FitzPatrick, M. O'Brien and P. Walsh (eds), *Archaeological Investigations in Galway City 1987–1998* (Dublin: Wordwell, 2004), pp. 337–55, at pp. 340–2.

267 Walter de Burgo (de Burgh or Burke) was the third lord of Lower Connacht and viscount of Mayo; T.W. Moody, F.X. Martin and F.J. Byrne (eds), *A New History of Ireland. Volume IX: Maps, Genealogies, Lists. A Companion to Irish History, Part II* (Oxford: Clarendon Press, 1984), p. 171.

268 Also known as lord of Norragh or Norrach; Gwynn and Hadcock, *Medieval Religious Houses*, p. 325.

269 Also known as Walter de Ridelesford, who died in 1226; see Carville, 'St Mary's Abbey, Graney', p. 40.

270 David Fitz Milo was the second baron of Overke, his father Milo Fitz David was one of Strongbow's supporters; Martin, 'Allies and an Overlord', p. 97.

271 The Barnewalls were a prominent Anglo-Norman family who later were granted Grace Dieu at the dissolution; see C. Culleton, 'From Barrow Boy to Viscount: The story of Matthew Barnewell', *History Ireland*, vol. 7, 1999, pp. 5–6.

272 Gwynn and Hadcock, *Medieval Religious Houses*, p. 321.

273 The de Lacys controlled much of the Meath and Westmeath lordships; see Moody et al., *A New History of Ireland. Volume IX: Maps*, p. 173.

274 The Butler family became earls and later dukes of Ormond; see Moody et al., *A New History of Ireland. Volume IX: Maps*, p. 169. It is not known which family member established the nunnery.

275 Collins, 'Unveiling Female Monasticism'. See also G. O'Carroll, *The Earls of Desmond: The rise and fall of a Munster lordship* (Limerick: self-published, 2013), pp. 2, 66.

276 Malachy's perceived influence comes from his prominent position as prime instigator of the church's reform and this remains the traditional meta narrative. Scholars are beginning to question this view; see Flanagan, *Transformation*; Bhreathnach, 'The *Vita Apostolica*'.

277 J. Bradley, A. Halpin and H. King, 'Urban Archaeology Survey for Cork' (unpublished report for OPW Dublin, 1985), p. 92.

278 Hall, *Women and the Church*, p. 60.

279 Hicks, *Religious Life in Normandy*, pp. 7–9; Stöber, *Late Medieval Monasteries*, p. 206.

280 Thompson, *Women Religious*, pp. 162–3.

281 Another Irish woman, Aífe daughter of Diarmait Mac Murchada, and wife of Strongbow, earl of Pembroke, patronised Ickleton nunnery in Cambridgeshire, England; see M.T. Flanagan, *Irish Society, Anglo-Norman Settlers, Angevin Kingship: Interactions in Ireland in the late twelfth century* (Oxford: Oxford University Press, 1989), pp. 124–6.

282 Flanagan, *Transformation*, p. 201.

283 Another example: Affreca de Courcy founded the Cistercian house at Grey Abbey, Co. Down in 1193, and she was 'even buried there'; see Leigh Fry, *Burial in Medieval Ireland*, p. 176.

284 He also records female anchorites at male religious houses, for example at the Premonstratensian house at Trinity Island, Co. Roscommon: C. Ó Clabaigh, 'Anchorites in Late Medieval Ireland', in L. Herbert McAvoy (ed.), *Anchoritic Traditions of Medieval Europe* (Woodbridge: Boydell, 2101), pp. 153–77, at pp. 167–8.

285 Hall, *Women and the Church*, p. 60.

286 For women as patrons of male religious houses, see ibid., pp. 59–62; Flanagan, *Transformation*, pp. 200–2.

287 Female founders are much more numerous in England: Thompson, *Women Religious*, pp. 167–77; Burton, *Monastic and Religious Orders*, pp. 91–3; Gilchrist, *Gender and Material Culture*, pp. 50–60; J.C. Ward, 'English Noblewomen and the Local Community in the Later Middle Ages', in D. Watt (ed.), *Medieval Women in Their Communities* (Cardiff: University of Wales Press, 1997), pp. 186–203, at pp. 192–3. However, the general trend is the same – women founders are less numerous than men: Stöber, *Late Medieval Monasteries*, pp. 209–49.

288 Cartwright, *Feminine Sanctity*, pp. 203–4.

289 Thompson, *Women Religious*, pp. 182–3; Flanagan, *Transformation*, p. 202.

290 Burton, *Yorkshire Nunneries*, p. 2; Johnson, *Equal in Monastic Profession*, p. 232; G. Muschiol, 'Time and Space: Liturgy and rites in female monasteries', in J. Hamburger and S. Marti (eds), *Crown and Veil: Female monasticism from the fifth to the fifteenth centuries* (New York: Columbia University Press, 2008), pp. 191–204, at p. 195; Flanagan, *Transformation*, p. 202.

291 Hall, *Women and the Church*, p. 60.

292 Thompson, *Women Religious*, pp. 183–7.

293 Stöber, *Late Medieval Monasteries*. Her extensive study of patronage included houses of Benedictine, Cluniac, Cistercian and Carthusian monks, Augustinian and

Premonstratensian canons, Gilbertine canons and double houses, Fontevraud and Birgittine orders, the Order of Grandmont, Houses of Bonhommes, the Order of Tiron, Trinitarians, Benedictine, Cluniac, and Cistercian nuns, Augustinian and Premonstratensian canonesses, Franciscan and Dominican nuns. She did not include houses of friars.

294 Stöber, *Late Medieval Monasteries*, pp. 28–33, 206. She notes that the monastic patronage in England and Wales reached its peak by 1300 and had begun to grind to a halt immediately after this date. Thompson's earlier study made similar conclusions. She noted a word of caution when researching founders, highlighting a tendency for later tradition to re-assign the role of founder to a person whose rank or prestige had caused their help to be sought. These would be later benefactors rather than initial founders. This occurrence can affect the results of any study; Thompson, *Women Religious*, pp. 163–4.

295 Stöber, *Late Medieval Monasteries*, p. 6. Stöber notes that this change, while universally accepted, has never been studied as to *how* the changes in relationships between founder and foundation actually changed in the later medieval period.

296 Stöber, *Late Medieval Monasteries*, pp. 207–8.

297 Gilchrist, *Gender and Material Culture*; Thompson, *Women Religious*.

298 Stöber, *Late Medieval Monasteries*, p. 208.

299 Hall, *Women and the Church*, pp. 60–1.

300 Thompson, *Women Religious*, p. 177.

301 Hall, *Women and the Church*, p. 60–2.

302 Thompson, *Women Religious*, p. 181.

303 Stalley, *Cistercian Monasteries*, pp. 35–6. The site was Dunbrody, Co. Wexford, which was initially rejected as unsuitable for foundation, though later became a prosperous monastery.

304 C. Jäggi and U. Lobbedey, 'Church and Cloister: The architecture of female monasticism in the middle ages', in J.F. Hamburger and S. Marti (eds), *Crown and Veil: Female monasticism from the fifth to the fifteenth centuries* (New York: Columbia University Press, 2008), pp. 109–31, at pp. 118–19; Freeman, 'Nuns', p. 101; Berman, 'Medieval Monasticisms', p. 380.

305 H. Röckelein, 'Founders, Donors and Saints: Patrons of nuns' convents', in J.F. Hamburger and S. Marti (eds), *Crown and Veil: Female monasticism from the fifth to the fifteenth centuries* (New York: Columbia University Press, 2008), pp. 207–24.

306 Gilchrist, *Gender and Material Culture*, p. 139.

307 Ibid., pp. 128–43. This analysis depended on a sample of sixty-one nunneries (34.4% of total sample, twenty-one with northern cloisters and forty with southern cloisters) where the orientation of the cloister relative to the church could be established.

308 Gilchrist, *Gender and Material Culture*, pp. 152–60.

309 Ibid., p. 187. In these dedications it has been assumed that it was Mary, mother of Jesus, that is being invoked. There were two other important Marys in the Bible – Mary of Bethany, sister of Lazarus and Martha, and Mary Magdalene. Gilchrist has noted that Mary Magdalene was linked to healing due to her association with anointing, particularly at the Resurrection, and she was a popular dedication for hospitals and leper hospitals in the medieval period. Interestingly, Mary Magdalene was a very rare dedication for English nunneries, which were most frequently dedicated to the Virgin Mary. The two Marys – the Virgin and Magdalene – became icons for the respective contemplative and active roles of religious women in the medieval period.

310 Flanagan, *Transformation*, p. 131.

311 Stalley, *Cistercian Monasteries*, p. 40. He noted that the additional dedication to St Benedict caused much confusion in earlier scholarship, where it has been assumed in error that these houses were Benedictine and not Cistercian. He has listed Jerpoint, Kilkenny, Newry, Monasterevin, Kilcooly and Holycross, where this confusion took place.

312 Brady, 'Nunnery at Clonard', p. 5; Hadcock, 'Origin of the Augustinian Order', p. 125.

313 Extensive church doctrine and dogma had grown up around the personage of Mary. See Pelikan, *Mary Through the Centuries*, for full discussion.

314 Brigit is recognised as one of the three patron saints of Ireland. Her birth place was Faughart, Co. Louth although there is another tradition that she originated in west Leinster. Her feast day is 1 February. She is sometimes associated with a pagan deity. Her ecclesiastical centre was at Kildare. See Harrington, *Women in a Celtic Church*, p. 315; Bitel, *Two Saints*, pp. 138–94; Ó Riain, *A Dictionary*, pp. 123–5; Boazman, 'The Material Culture of Self-Promotion', pp. 327–50; Kissane, *Saint Brigid of Kildare*; Callan, *Sacred Sisters*, pp. 85–112.

315 Gwynn and Hadcock, *Medieval Religious Houses*, p. 323.

316 A. Spears, *The Cult of Saint Catherine of Alexandria in Ireland* (Rathmullen: Rathmullen District Local History Society, 2006), pp. 8, 27; K.J. Lewis, *The Cult of St Catherine of Alexandria in Late Medieval England* (Woodbridge: Boydell, 2000). There are a number of Catherines in the medieval Christian calendar; the most popular being St Catherine of Alexandria (d. early fourth century) and St Catherine of Siena (d. 1380). It is generally accepted that the cult of St Catherine arrived in Ireland with the Anglo-Norman invasion and spread throughout the country. The two nunnery dedications to St Catherine at Portrane, Co. Dublin and Old Abbey, Co. Limerick refer to St Catherine of Alexandria.

317 John the Baptist was cousin to Jesus and son of Elizabeth. In the medieval period, John the Baptist was considered, along with the Virgin Mary, as an important intercessor on behalf of humankind; G. Buzwell, *Saints in Medieval Manuscripts* (London: The British Library, 2005), p. 56.

318 St Anne was the mother of the Virgin Mary.

319 St Peter (Simon Peter) was the principal apostle and had an important role in the early church as head of the church on earth. The keys of the kingdom of heaven were promised to him.

320 The Holy Trinity or tripersonal God is the Father, the Son and the Holy Spirit (Ghost); see G. O'Collins, *Catholicism: A very short introduction* (Oxford: Oxford University Press, 2008), pp. 57–62. The motif of the Trinity is commonly found in medieval sculpture and metalwork. Two depictions are known from wall paintings at Abbeyknockmoy, Co. Galway, and now no longer extant, St Audeon's church, Dublin. These depictions have been categorised as the Throne of Grace in medieval figurative art, where Christ is supported by God and the Holy Spirit represented as a dove above Christ's head; K. Morton, 'Aspects of Image and Meaning in Irish Medieval Wall Paintings', in R. Moss, C. Ó Clabaigh and S. Ryan (eds), *Art and Devotion in Late Medieval Ireland* (Dublin: Four Courts Press, 2006), pp. 51–71, at pp. 55–8.

321 Hall, *Women and the Church*, p. 71. The cult of the Virgin Mary continued strongly; C. Tait, 'Art and the Cult of the Virgin Mary in Ireland, *c.*1500–1660', in R. Moss, C. Ó Clabaigh and S. Ryan (eds), *Art and Devotion in Late Medieval Ireland* (Dublin: Four Courts Press, 2006), pp. 163–83.

322 Cartwright, *Feminine Sanctity*, p. 8.

323 St John the Baptist and St John the Evangelist are two distinct personages. The nunneries of Killone, Cork and Buttevant were dedicated to St John the Baptist; see Gwynn and Hadcock, *Medieval Religious Houses*, pp. 315, 321–2, 326. However, the Cork nunnery was named once as St John the Evangelist which is very unusual for a nunnery and possibly a mistake; see Hall, *Women in the Church*, p. 174; Smith, *County and City of Cork*, p. 383.

324 Locally, the nunnery is believed to be named after St Cailchín. Interestingly, the nuns there celebrated his feast day on 10 February; see Ó Riain, *A Dictionary*, p. 134.

CHAPTER 4. SITUATING NUNNERIES IN LATER MEDIEVAL IRELAND

1 For a summary of this chapter, see Collins, 'Isolated in the Wilderness?'

2 Carlow, Clare, Derry, Down, Kilkenny, Laois, Waterford, Wexford and Wicklow.

3 Armagh, Kildare, Limerick, Louth, Tipperary and Westmeath.

4 Hall, *Women and the Church*, p. 93.

5 J. Cuppage, *Dingle Peninsula Archaeological Survey* (Ballyferriter: Oidhreacht Chorca Dhuibhne, 1996), pp. 257–346, 360–9; A. O'Sullivan and J. Sheehan, *Archaeological Survey of the Iveragh Peninsula* (Cork: Cork University Press, 1996), pp. 246–322, 262–381; Ó Carragáin, 'A Landscape Converted'; Ó Carragáin, *Churches in Early Medieval Ireland*; F. Byrne, W. Jenkins, G. Kenny and C. Swift, *Historical Knowth and Its Hinterland: Excavations at Knowth*, vol. 4 (Dublin: Royal Irish Academy, 2008); and several other counties such as Cavan: see P. O'Donovan, *Archaeological Inventory of County Cavan* (Dublin: The Stationery Office, 1995), pp. 191–216.

6 B. Lacy, *Archaeological Survey of County Donegal* (Lifford: Donegal County Council, 1983), pp. 240–300, 326–49.

7 C. Foley and R. McHugh, *An Archaeological Survey of County Fermanagh*, 2 vols (Belfast: Department of the Environment, 2014).

8 M.J. Moore, *Archaeological Inventory of County Leitrim* (Dublin: The Stationery Office, 2003), pp. 171–93.

9 A. Brindley, *Archaeological Inventory of County Monaghan* (Dublin: The Stationery Office, 1986), pp. 85–9.

10 Gilchrist, *Gender and Material Culture*, p. 50; Hicks, *Religious Life in Normandy*, pp. 151–2; Stöber, *Late Medieval Monasteries*, p. 206.

11 Hall, *Women and the Church*, pp. 70–95.

12 In the Archaeological Survey of Ireland and the Northern Ireland Sites and Monuments Record.

13 The Archaeological Survey of Ireland in its Sites and Monuments Record uses the following classifications for nunneries: Religious House Augustinian Nuns; Religious House Arroasian Nuns; Religious House Benedictine Nuns; Religious House Cistercian Nuns; Religious House Franciscan Nuns. In instances where the affiliation of the nunnery is unknown, the nunnery appears in the Religious House Unclassified category.

14 Clonard, Lusk, the Nuns' Church, Portrane, Skreen, Temple Finghin, and Tisrara.

15 Annaghdown, Clonfert, Annagh, Termonkeelin, Aghade, Lismullin, Killeigh, Killone, Ballymacdane, St Peter's Cell, St Catherine's, and Molough.

16 Inishmaine, Ardcarn, Cloonoghil, Derrane, Drumalgagh, Killinmulrooney, St Mary de Hogges, Grace Dieu, Kildare, Timolin, Graney, Kellystown, Taghmon, and Kilculliheen.

17 Addrigoole, Ballynagallagh, Buttevant, Carricknahorna, Templenagalliaghdoo, Killaraght, and Killeenatrava.

18 Burton and Stöber, *Women in the Medieval Monastic World*, p. 3.
19 Beach and Juganaru, 'The Double Monastery as a Historiographical Problem'; Golding, *Gilbert of Sempringham*; F. Griffiths, 'The Cross and the *Cura Monialium*: Robert of Arbrissel, John the Evangelist, and the pastoral care of women in the age of reform', *Speculum*, vol. 83, no. 2, 2008, pp. 303–30; Kerr, *Religious Life for Women*; Venarde, 'Robert of Arbrissel'.
20 Flanagan, *Transformation*, p. 150.
21 W.T. St John Hope, 'The Ground Plan of Watton in the East Riding of Yorkshire', *Yorkshire Archaeological Journal*, vol. 58, 1901, pp. 1–34.
22 Carter, 'Silk Purse or Sow's Ear?'
23 Hicks, *Religious Life in Normandy*, pp. 19–20, 136–9.
24 Annaghdown, Ardcarn, Clonard, Clonfert, Clonmacnoise, Derrane, Duleek, Durrow, Kells, Roscommon, and Termonfeckin.
25 T. Collins, 'The Materiality of Female Religious Reform in Twelfth-Century Ireland: The case of co-located religious houses', in J. Hotchin and J. Thibaut (eds), *Engendered Perspectives on Monastic Reform* (Woodbridge: Boydell, forthcoming).
26 It has been stated that the new continental orders did not establish at Clonmacnoise; see C. Manning, *Clonmacnoise* (Dublin: The Office or Public Works, Government of Ireland, 1994), p. 14; though Augustinian canons are historically recorded there, as a separate entity to the cathedral, but it remains unknown precisely where they were located or how their religious complex would have been arranged: see Gwynn and Hadcock, *Medieval Religious Houses*, p. 165.
27 J. Morrin (ed.), *Calendar of the Patent and Close Rolls of Chancery in Ireland from the 18th to the 45th of Elizabeth*, vol. II (Dublin: Alex Thom & Sons for Her Majesty's Stationery Office, 1862), p. 267.
28 Gibson and George, 'Geophysical Investigation'; P.J. Gibson, 'Seeing Beneath the Ground: Using geophysics at the former ecclesiastical site of Clonard, Co. Meath', *Ríocht na Mídhe, Records of the Meath Archaeological and Historical Society*, vol. 20, 2009, pp. 69–79.
29 Hall, *Women and the Church*, pp. 146–7.
30 The precise location of the nunnery at Skreen is unknown. As a medieval settlement there are several possible locations. This nunnery appeared to be a short-lived house, as Lismullin was established close by. It was suggested that Skreen nunnery may have actually been at Calliaghstown, in the parish of Tara: see Gywnn and Hadcock, *Medieval Religious Houses*, p. 324.
31 Bradley et al., 'Urban Archaeology Cork', p. 92.
32 Carville, 'Cistercian Nuns in Medieval Ireland'.
33 O'Dywer, *Stephen of Lexington*. There is some ambiguity over the identification of Jerpoint as one of the houses and some have suggested that it was actually Graiguenamanagh: see J. Bradley and C. Manning, 'Excavations at Duiske Abbey, Graiguenamanagh, Co. Kilkenny', *Proceedings of the Royal Irish Academy*, vol. 81C, 1981, pp. 16–426, at pp. 398–9; Stalley, *Cistercian Monasteries*, p. 45.
34 Stalley, *Cistercian Monasteries*, p. 6; Gilchrist, *Gender and Material Culture*, p. 68.
35 C. Foley, 'Excavation at a Medieval Settlement Site in Jerpointchurch Townland, County Kilkenny', *Proceedings of the Royal Irish Academy*, vol. 89C, 1989, pp. 71–126; Oxford Archaeology, *Newtown Jerpoint, County Kilkenny. Heritage Conservation Plan No. 11* (Kilkenny: The Heritage Council, 2007), pp. 40–1.
36 Carter, 'Silk Purse or Sow's Ear?', p. 258.
37 Carville, 'Cistercian Nuns in Medieval Ireland', p. 62.

38 De Paor, 'Excavations at Mellifont Abbey'. However, this structure is a much later addition to the complex and has been described as a regular fifteenth- or sixteenth-century tower house, whose vaulted ground-floor walls were later removed to give a false impression of a gate house: see Halpin and Newman, *Ireland*, p. 321.
39 Stout, 'Settlement on Mellifont Abbey's Monastic Estate', pp. 160–1.
40 T. Dolan, 'Writing in Ireland', in D. Wallace (ed.), *The Cambridge History of Medieval English Literature* (Cambridge: Cambridge University Press, 1999), pp. 208–28.
41 Although Flanagan has suggested that the church would not have been shared due to a prohibition of the Lateran Council in 1139 which forbade nuns and canons or monks coming together in choir for the singing of the divine office; see Flanagan, *Transformation*, p. 151. However, in continental examples male and female groups used the same church at slightly different times to overcome this, for example at the Poor Clare house at Königsfelden, Switzerland: see Jäggi, 'Eastern Choir or Western Gallery?', p. 85; Untermann, 'The Place of the Choir', pp. 346–7.
42 Collins, 'The Materiality of Female Religious Reform'.
43 For example, Aston, *Monasteries in the Landscape*; Bond, *Monastic Landscapes*; Hall, *Scottish Monastic Landscapes*; B. Waites, *Monasteries and Landscape of the North York Moors and Wolds* (Stroud: Tempus, 2007).
44 Robinson, *Geography of Augustinian Settlement*.
45 Coppack, 'How the Other Half Lived'.
46 G. Astill, 'Monastic Research Designs: Bordesley and the Avon Valley', in R. Gilchrist and H. Mytum (eds), *The Archaeology of Rural Monasteries. BAR British Series 203* (Oxford: British Archaeological Reports, 1989), pp. 277–94; S. Hirst and S. Wright, 'Bordesley Abbey Church: A long-term research excavation', in R. Gilchrist and H. Mytum (eds), *The Archaeology of Rural Monasteries. BAR British Series 203* (Oxford: British Archaeological Reports, 1989), pp. 295–312.
47 Brown, *Stanley Abbey*.
48 Bezant, *Medieval Welsh Settlement*; Bezant, 'The Medieval Grants to Strata Florida Abbey'; D. Austin, 'The Archaeology of Monasteries in Wales and the Strata Florida Project', in J. Burton and K. Stöber (eds), *Monastic Wales: New approaches* (Cardiff: University of Wales Press, 2013), pp. 3–37.
49 Stalley, *Cistercian Monasteries*; Carville, *Occupation of Celtic Sites*; Carville, 'Cistercian Nuns in Medieval Ireland'; G. Carville, *The Impact of the Cistercians on the Landscape of Ireland* (Wicklow: KB Publications, 2002); Lynch, *A Monastic Landscape*. But see as exceptions, Lafaye, 'Spiritual Renewal and Changing Landscapes'; A. Lafaye, 'Mendicant Friaries and the Changing Landscapes of Late Medieval Ireland: The foundations of the Augustinian friars in counties Mayo and Sligo', in N. Brady and C. Theune (eds), *Settlement Change Across Medieval Europe: Old paradigms and new vistas (Ruralia XII)* (Leiden: Sidestone Press, 2019), pp. 223–32.
50 Power, *Medieval English Nunneries*, pp. 341–4.
51 One league is three statute miles or approximately 4.9km.
52 D.H. Williams, 'Cistercian Nunneries in Medieval Wales', *Citeaux Commentarii Cistercienses*, vol. 26, 1975, pp. 155–74, at p. 155; Gilchrist, *Gender and Material Culture*, p. 68.
53 Bond, 'Medieval Nunneries in England and Wales', p. 53.
54 Gilchrist, *Gender and Material Culture*, p. 68; Burton, *Monastic and Religious Orders*, pp. 96–101.
55 Gilchrist, *Contemplation and Action*, p. 115.
56 Friaries in Ireland could not be established within about a mile from any another religious house; Ó Clabaigh, *The Friars in Ireland*, p. 204.

57 Carville, *Occupation of Celtic Sites*; Carville, *Impact of the Cistercians*; Stalley, *Cistercian Monasteries*, p. 31; O'Keeffe, *An Anglo-Norman Monastery*, pp. 31–42; Ó Clabaigh, *Friars in Ireland*, pp. 207–11.

58 A. Stott, 'The Ring of Gullion', in F.H.A. Aalen, K. Whelan and M. Stout (eds), *Atlas of the Irish Rural Landscape*, 1st edn (Cork: Cork University Press, 1997), pp. 316–28.

59 These demesne landscapes are post-medieval or early modern in date and clearly later than the medieval nunneries. However, nunneries situated within them at Durrow, Kilbride and Lismullin are interesting as although there is no supporting evidence it is possible that land holdings of the nunneries may have become foci for later demesne estates, as occurred at several male religious houses. This demesne land would be considered of good quality. Some ten nunneries are included in dissolution surveys; see White, *Extents*. For example, it is likely that the holdings of the important nunnery of Lismullin formed the basis of the later Lismullin House and demesne: see D. Hall, 'The Nuns of the Medieval Convent of Lismullin'.

60 Two nunneries are located adjacent to the ecclesiastical complex at Clonmacnoise, which was not specifically urban, but would have been a large settlement nevertheless.

61 Hall, *Women and the Church*, p. 94.

62 Thompson, 'Why English Nunneries Had No History', p. 133.

63 Thompson, 'Why English Nunneries Had No History'; Thompson, *Women Religious*, p. 12; Gilchrist, *Gender and Material Culture*, p. 67.

64 Gilchrist, *Gender and Material Culture*, pp. 36–44, 67–8; Ó Clabaigh, *Friars in Ireland*, pp. 203–4.

65 The statutes of Citeaux in 1098 stated that monasteries should not be built in cities, castles or towns, but rather far from the conversation of men. Ireland, due to its small, dispersed population, would have been perfect for such seclusion; Stalley, *Cistercian Monasteries*, p. 31. Having said this, the Cistercians' craving for isolation may have been exaggerated as in some cases they chose sites that had already been occupied or were abandoned: see Carville, *Occupation of Celtic Sites*. In many cases, they also chose sites near major rivers which were routeways for commerce; Stalley, *Cistercian Monasteries*, p. 31.

66 Stalley, *Cistercian Monasteries*, pp. 31, 38.

67 The land use and agricultural regions considered are modern designations, but are likely broadly reflective of earlier times.

68 These areas include the marginal poor lands of the western seaboard of Mayo and Galway; the southwestern portion of Kerry and Cork; Donegal and areas of Antrim.

69 Browne and Ó Clabaigh (eds), *Households of God*.

70 Ó Clabaigh, *Friars in Ireland*.

71 Carville, *Occupation of Celtic Sites*, pp. 8–17; Carville, *Impact of the Cistercians*; O'Keeffe, *An Anglo-Norman Monastery*.

72 O'Keeffe, *An Anglo-Norman Monastery*, p. 36.

73 Stöber, *Late Medieval Monasteries*, pp. 21–5.

74 Stalley, *Cistercian Monasteries*, p. 31.

75 Power, *Medieval English Nunneries*, pp. 96–130; Hall, *Women and the Church*, p. 137.

76 Gilchrist, *Gender and Material Culture*, pp. 85–90.

77 Ibid., p. 90.

78 Johnson, *Equal in Monastic Profession*, pp. 107, 208; Gilchrist, *Gender and Material Culture*, p. 85; Kerr, *Religious Life for Women*, pp. 143–6; Lawrence, *Medieval Monasticism*, p. 221. Although perhaps up to the fourteenth century, nunneries may have worked their own demesne lands in England; Gilchrist, *Gender and Material Culture*, p. 86.

79 Power, *Medieval English Nunneries*, pp. 131–60; Hall, *Women and the Church*, p. 133.
80 Johnson, *Equal in Monastic Profession*, p. 212.
81 Household accounts of an urban English nunnery of St Helen's, Bishopsgate in the 1500s showed that it was heavily in debt to a brewer, a corn man, two fishmongers and a butcher; see Power, *Medieval English Nunneries*, p. 109.
82 J. Bond, 'Water Management in the Rural Monastery', in R. Gilchrist and H. Mytum (eds), *The Archaeology of Rural Monasteries. BAR British Series 203* (Oxford: British Archaeological Reports, 1989), pp. 83–111, at p. 83; J. Bond, 'Water Management in the Urban Monastery', in R. Gilchrist and H. Mytum (eds), *Advances in Monastic Archaeology. BAR British Series 227* (Oxford: Tempus Reparatum Archaeological and Historical Associates, 1993), pp. 43–78, at pp. 43–50, 74; J.P. Greene, *Medieval Monasteries* (London: Continuum, 1992), pp. 109–32; G. Coppack, *Abbeys and Priories* (Stroud: Tempus, 2006), pp. 143–66.
83 Stalley, *Cistercian Monasteries*, p. 31.
84 Some of the water sources near nunneries have changed significantly, due to hedgerow and boundary removal, drainage and other reclamation works. In assessing the various possible water sources for the nunneries in this study, the first-edition six-inch Ordnance Survey maps were taken into consideration (dating from the 1830s to 1840s). For six nunneries, pinpointing their water sources is now difficult, and Derrane, Kells, Kellystown, Plary, Skreen and Youghal do not have obvious water sources. It is likely that they used springs or wells which are now no longer extant. It is possible that the nunneries of Kells and St Anne's, Youghal may have used the public water supplies, as occurred at several urban friaries. The two upland nunneries Carricknahorna and Killevy likely used mountain streams or springs.
85 Ó Clabaigh, *Friars in Ireland*, pp. 208–11.
86 Thomas, *The Walled Towns*, vol. 2, pp. 200–10; M. Murphy, A. Connon and J. Galloway, 'Waterford and Its Hinterland: An historical overview', in J. Eogan and E. Shee Twohig (eds), *Cois tSiuire: Nine thousand years of human activity in the lower Suir Valley* (Dublin: National Roads Authority, 2011), pp. 217–44, at pp. 230–1, 237–8. The northern suburb of Waterford was not apparently walled in the medieval period; see Thomas, *Walled Towns*, vol. 2, pp. 202–10. The nearest contemporary bridge crossing of the river Suir was upstream at Carrick-on-Suir some 30kms to the northwest of Waterford city.
87 P. O'Keeffe and T. Simington, *Irish Stone Bridges* (Dublin: Irish Academic Press, 1991), p. 172.
88 Post-medieval wells are known from Kildare; Andrews, *Historic Towns Atlas: Kildare*; Thomas, *Walled Towns*, vol. 2, pp. 123–5. Armagh had two nunneries. Excavations carried out at Market Street in 1975 showed there had once been a lake on the site which may have been artificially created in the medieval period. At Scotch Street two stone-lined wells were revealed; see Lynn, 'Excavations in 46-48 Scotch Street, Armagh', p. 69.
89 R.H. Buchanan and A. Wilson, *Irish Historic Towns Atlas No. 8: Downpatrick* (Dublin: Royal Irish Academy, 1997), pp. 1–2.
90 O'Keeffe, *An Anglo-Norman Monastery*, pp. 71, 75.
91 Excavated by F. Coyne. www.excavations.ie/report/2008/Clare/0019134/. Accessed 15 September 2020.
92 Ó Clabaigh, *Friars in Ireland*, p. 209.
93 Gilchrist, 'Gender, Ideology and Material Culture in Later Medieval England, *c.*1050–1550', unpublished PhD thesis, university of York, 1990, p. 52.
94 Ó Riain, *A Dictionary*, pp. 151–2.
95 A. Moloney, 'From East to West: Crossing the bogs at Clonmacnoise', in H. King (ed.), *Clonmacnoise Studies*, vol. 1 (Dublin: Government of Ireland, 1998), pp. 7–10; E. Shee

Twohig, 'Context and Chronology of the Carved Stone at Clonfinlough, County Offaly', *Journal of the Royal Society of Antiquaries of Ireland*, vol. 132, 2002, pp. 99–113.

96 A. O'Sullivan and D. Boland, *The Clonmacnoise Bridge: An early medieval river crossing in County Offaly. Heritage Guide No. 11* (Bray: Wordwell, 2000).

97 L. Doran, 'Medieval Communication Routes through Longford and Roscommon and Their Associated Settlements', *Proceedings of the Royal Irish Academy*, vol. 104C, 2004, pp. 57–80, at pp. 72, 79.

98 A perch is 5.5 imperial yards. An Irish perch measures 21 feet or 7 yards; about 6.4m.

99 Moorhouse, 'Monastic Estates', p. 59.

100 Bond, *Monastic Landscapes*, pp. 294–309.

101 Gilchrist, *Gender and Material Culture*, p. 67.

102 L.A.S. Butler, 'Medieval Urban Religious Houses', in J. Scofield and R. Leech (eds), *Urban Archaeology in Britain* (London: Council for British Archaeology, 1987), pp. 167–76, at p. 168; Gilchrist, 'Gender, Ideology and Material Culture', p. 51; Bond, 'Medieval Nunneries in England and Wales', p. 54.

103 Gilchrist, *Contemplation and Action*, p. 116.

104 K.D. O'Conor, *The Archaeology of Medieval Rural Settlement in Ireland. Discovery Programme Monographs 3* (Dublin: Royal Irish Academy, 1998), pp. 41–57; N. Brady and C. Theune (eds), *Settlement Change Across Medieval Europe: Old paradigms and new vistas (Ruralia XII)* (Leiden: Sidestone Press, 2019).

105 N. Brady, 'Rural Settlement in Later Medieval Ireland Through the Lens of Deserted Settlements', in N. Brady and C. Theune (eds), *Settlement Change Across Medieval Europe: Old paradigms and new vistas (Ruralia XII)* (Leiden: Sidestone Press, 2019), pp. 137–46.

106 Archaeological classification is set by the Archaeological Survey of Ireland; see www.archaeology.ie. A historical discussion of the terms vill and its English equivalent, village, and their uses in medieval Ireland is provided by MacCotter, *Medieval Ireland*, pp. 58–87.

107 Gilchrist, *Gender and Material Culture*, p. 69; C. Dyer, 'Making Sense of Town and Country', in K. Giles and C. Dyer (eds), *Town and Country in the Middle Ages: Contrast, contacts and interconnections 1100–1500. SMA Monograph 22* (Leeds: Maney, 2007), pp. 313–21; McCullough, and Crawford, *Irish Historic Towns Atlas: Armagh*; E. O'Flaherty, *Irish Historic Towns Atlas No. 21: Limerick* (Dublin: Royal Irish Academy, 2010); Thomas, *Walled Towns*, vol. 2, pp. 60–7, 142–53, 200–10, 222.

108 Gilchrist, 'Gender, Ideology and Material Culture', pp. 51–2.

109 Gilchrist, *Gender and Material Culture*, pp. 52, 69; Bond, 'Medieval Nunneries in England and Wales', p. 54.

110 Gilchrist, 'Gender, Ideology and Material Culture', pp. 51–2.

111 Oliva, *Convent and the Community*, pp. 22–4.

112 Gilchrist, *Contemplation and Action*, p. 115.

113 Burton, *Yorkshire Nunneries*; Coppack, 'How the Other Half Lived'.

114 Venarde, *Women's Monasticism*, p. 143.

115 Hicks, *Religious Life in Normandy*, p. 19.

116 Usk in Wales was also sited near a town for protection; see Bond, 'Medieval Nunneries in England and Wales', p. 54.

117 For the purpose of this analysis these nunneries are either within the wall of the historic town itself or outside the town but within a radius of 1km. There are further nunnery settlements discussed later which are outside this 1km limit.

118 Hall, *Women and the Church*, p. 93.

119 T. Collins, F. Coyne, N. Darmody, D. Humphreys, L. Lynch and B. O'Mahony, 'Limerick City Walls Conservation and Management Plan' (unpublished report for Limerick City Council and the Heritage Council, 2008); O'Flaherty, *Irish Historic Towns Atlas: Limerick*, pp. 2–4.

120 Canons were present at St Mary's Cathedral in this period and it is likely that they were of the Augustinian Order; G.J. Hand, 'Medieval Chapter of St Mary's Cathedral, Limerick', in J.A. Watt, J.B. Morrall and F.X. Martin (eds), *Medieval Studies Presented to Aubrey Gwynn* (Dublin: Four Candles, 1961), pp. 74–89; Gwynn and Hadcock, *Medieval Religious Houses*, pp. 90–1; K. Nicholls, 'Medieval Irish Cathedral Chapters', *Archivium Hibernicum*, vol. 31, 1973, pp. 102–11. The nuns of St Peter's Cell were also Augustinian and were affiliated with the other O'Brien foundation at Killone, Co. Clare; see Ó Dálaigh, 'Mistress, Mother and Abbess'.

121 This is a similar location to one of the few urban nunneries in England at St Mary's, Winchester where it is described as being within the monastic quarter of the town and within its episcopal precincts; see Bond, 'Medieval Nunneries in England and Wales', p. 54.

122 Monastic foundations at Limerick included Franciscan, Dominican, *Fratres Cruciferi* (Augustinian hospital) and Knights Templar. The foundation date of St Peter's Cell predates these male religious houses; O'Flaherty, *Irish Historic Towns Atlas: Limerick*, pp. 2–3.

123 L. Simpson, 'The Priory of All Hallows and Trinity College, Dublin: Recent archaeological discoveries', *Medieval Dublin*, vol. III, 2002, pp. 195–236, at pp. 199–202.

124 An area of Waterford is still referred to as 'Ferry Bank', preserving the probable medieval use of a ferry across the river Suir. The nearest contemporary bridge crossing of the river Suir was upstream at Carrick-on-Suir some 30km to the northwest of Waterford.

125 Murphy et al., 'Waterford and Its Hinterland', pp. 230–3.

126 R. Buchanan, 'The Lecale Peninsula, County Down', in F.H.A. Aalen, K. Whelan and M. Stout (eds), *Atlas of the Irish Rural Landscape* (Cork: Cork University Press, 1997), pp. 277–86, at p. 280.

127 Gwynn and Hadcock, *Medieval Religious Houses*, p. 316. Thomas noted that Downpatrick is unusual. Its parish church has a rare dedication for the period to St Margaret, and its cathedral lies well outside the town walls and is unique in Ireland in being the only cathedral not to be parochial; Thomas, *Walled Towns*, vol. 2, p 71. Nick Brannon, archaeologist, who has excavated at Downpatrick, does not consider the cathedral to be the location of the nunnery (personal communication).

128 The post-medieval Poor Clare nunnery at Galway was founded on Nuns' Island outside the town walls. It is still in operation as an enclosed community. The land was first granted to the community by Galway Corporation, provided the nuns created access (a bridge) to Nuns' Island and an adjacent island. This is not thought to be the location of Lynch's earlier community, which he founded for his daughter. There is evidence in the post-medieval period that nuns in Galway used town houses within the walled town. It is also possible that this occurred in the later medieval period and so it is suggested that Lynch's 1511 foundation was likely somewhere within the walled town; see P. Walsh, 'Galway: A summary history', in E. FitzPatrick, M. O'Brien and P. Walsh (eds), *Archaeological Investigations in Galway City 1987–1998* (Dublin: Wordwell, 2004), pp. 269–91; J. Prunty and P. Walsh, *Irish Historic Towns Atlas No. 28: Galway/ Gaillimh* (Dublin: Royal Irish Academy, 2016).

129 Ó Clabaigh, *Friars in Ireland*, pp. 97–8; A. Lafaye, 'Medieval Mendicant Communities in East Munster: History, archaeology, landscapes', unpublished PhD thesis, University College Dublin, 2012.

130 O'Conor, *Archaeology of Medieval Rural Settlement*, pp. 41–57.

131 Thomas, *The Walled Towns*, vol. 2, p. 154; A. Thomas, *Irish Historic Towns Atlas No. 15: Derry-Londonderry* (Dublin: Royal Irish Academy, 2005), p. 2. The *Annals of the Four Masters* for the year 1162 describe that a 'separation of the houses from the church at Doire [Derry] was caused by a successor of Colum-Cille, Flaithbertach Ua Brolcháin [abbot of Derry] and by Muirceartach Ua Lochlainn, King of Ireland; and they removed eighty houses, or more, from the place where they were. And the Caiseal an Urlair was erected by the successor of Colum-Cille, who pronounced a curse against anyone who should come over it'. The Caiseal an Urlair has been interpreted as a boundary wall to separate the secular and religious parts of Derry in the twelfth century; see O'Donovan, *Annála Ríoghachta Éireann*; R. Ó Baoill, *Island City: The archaeology of Derry-Londonderry* (Derry: NIEA and Derry City Council, 2013), p. 58. The Cistercian nunnery was founded at Derry in 1218 and its location is considered to be some 200m to the northeast of the site of the religious centre. On this basis, the Cistercian nunnery was outside the Caiseal an Urlair and as such within the unenclosed part of the settlement at Derry. There may have been nuns in Derry earlier. In 1134 the death of banairchinnech (female monastic steward) Bé Bhinn Mac Conchaille was recorded, and it has been suggested that she was almost certainly an abbess. Her community may have been within the Caiseal an Urlair but this remains speculation. Lacey, *Medieval and Monastic Derry*, pp. 56, 88–9.

132 FitzPatrick and O'Brien, *Medieval Churches of County Offaly*, p. 84.

133 Ó Baoill, *Island City*, p. 63.

134 Without the benefit of archaeological excavation, the precise time period and chronology of these smaller settlement clusters cannot be fully known. However, it is suggested that where historical and/or extant archaeological evidence are suggestive of a later medieval date, it is accepted that the settlement at least for a time may have been in use at the same time as the nunnery.

135 Foley, 'Excavation at a Medieval Settlement'; Oxford Archaeology, *Newtown Jerpoint*.

136 Hurcle is located in County Meath across the river Mattock from Mellifont.

137 Carville discussed the strategic siting of the Cistercian nunnery near the motte and bailey at Ballymore on the shores of Lough Sewdy; 'Cistercian Nuns in Medieval Ireland', p. 69. The monastery of Plary, however, is now considered an Augustinian canons' house, according to the Archaeological Survey of Ireland. The nunnery was located further to the southeast, where Carville has marked 'Augustinian monastery'. Despite this, her general discussion of the relationship of the nunnery with contemporary settlement in the locality remains valid. See also Y. Seale, '*De Monasterio Desolato*: Patronage and politics in a frontier Irish convent', *Journal of Medieval Monastic Studies*, vol. 4, 2015, pp. 21–45.

138 The townland to the north of Clonard Old is Monagalliagh, translated as 'meadow of the nuns', which further records their presence; Brady, 'Nunnery at Clonard', p. 6; Gwynn and Hadcock, *Medieval Religious Houses*, p. 314; Hall, *Women and the Church*, pp. 70–5. A previous excavation at Clonard uncovered human remains, interpreted as being post-medieval in date, though it is possible that they may be earlier. P.D. Sweetman, 'Excavation of Medieval Field Boundaries at Clonard, Co. Meath', *Journal of the Royal Society of Antiquaries of Ireland*, vol. 108, 1978, pp. 10–22.

139 For example, J. Bradley, 'The Monastic Town of Clonmacnoise', in H. King (ed.), *Clonmacnoise Studies*, vol. 1 (Dublin: The Stationery Office, 1998), pp. 42–55; Swift, 'Sculptors and Their Customers'.

140 K.D. O'Conor and C. Manning, 'Clonmacnoise Castle', in H. King (ed.), *Clonmacnoise Studies*, vol. 2 (Dublin: The Stationery Office, 2003), pp. 137–65, at p. 137.

141 C. Manning, 'Clonmacnoise Cathedral', in H. King (ed.), *Clonmacnoise Studies*, vol. 1 (Dublin: The Stationery Office, 1998), pp. 57–86.

142 O'Conor and Manning, 'Clonmacnoise Castle'.

143 H. Mytum, 'Surface and Geophysical Survey at Clonmacnoise: Defining the extent of intensive monastic settlement', in H. King (ed.), *Clonmacnoise Studies*, vol. 2 (Dublin: The Stationery Office, 2003), pp. 35–58.

144 Mytum, 'Geophysical Survey at Clonmacnoise', p. 55.

145 T.J. Westropp, 'On Certain Typical Earthworks and Ringwalls in County Limerick, parts I and II', *Proceedings of the Royal Irish Academy*, vol. 33C, 1916–17, pp. 9–42, at p. 35; pp. 444–92.

146 Barry, *Medieval Archaeology*, pp. 37–71; T.B. Barry, '"The People of the Country … Dwelt Scattered": The pattern of rural settlement in Ireland in the later middle ages', in J. Bradley (ed.), *Settlement and Society in Medieval Ireland* (Kilkenny: Boethius Press, 1988), pp. 345–60; O'Keeffe, *Medieval Irish Buildings*, pp. 184–306.

147 T.B. Barry, 'Medieval Moated Sites in Ireland: Some new conclusions on their chronology and function', in G. MacNiocaill and P.F. Wallace (eds), *Keimelia: Studies in memory of Tom Delaney* (Galway: Galway University Press, 1988), pp. 524–35.

148 For an outline of this more traditional view, see P.D. Sweetman, *Castles in Ireland* (Cork: The Collins Press, 1999); T.B. Barry, 'Rural Settlement in Medieval Ireland', in T.B. Barry (ed.), *A History of Settlement in Ireland* (London: Routledge, 2000), pp. 110–23.

149 For example, Barry, *Medieval Archaeology*, pp. 37–71.

150 O. Creighton and T.B. Barry, 'Seigneurial and Elite Sites in the Medieval Landscape', in N. Christie and P. Stamper (eds), *Medieval Rural Settlement: Britain and Ireland AD 800–1600* (Oxford: Windgather Press, 2012), pp. 63–80; Doran, 'Medieval Communication Routes', p. 73; Duffy et al., *Gaelic Ireland*; A. Horning, 'Ireland: Medieval identities, settlement and land use', in N. Christie and P. Stamper (eds), *Medieval Rural Settlement: Britain and Ireland AD 800–1600* (Oxford: Windgather Press, 2012), pp. 172–85, at pp. 175–6; O'Conor, *Archaeology of Medieval Rural Settlement*, pp. 109–11; K.D. O'Conor, 'The Ethnicity of Irish Moated Sites', *Ruralia*, vol. 3, 2000, pp. 92–102; K.D. O'Conor, 'Gaelic Lordly Settlement in 13th and 14th Century Ireland', in I. Holm, S. Innselet and I. Oye (eds), *Utmark: The outfield as industry and ideology in the Iron Age and the middle ages* (Bergen: University of Bergen, 2005), pp. 209–21, at p. 211; O'Keeffe, *Medieval Ireland*, pp. 15–33; O'Keeffe, *Medieval Irish Buildings*, pp. 184–7, 255–76.

151 Horning, 'Ireland: Medieval identities', pp. 182–4.

152 T. Collins and A. Cummins, *Excavation of a Ringwork at Ballysimon, Co. Limerick* (Limerick: Aegis Archaeology Limited, 2001); K.D. O'Conor, 'Housing in Later Medieval Gaelic Ireland', *Ruralia*, vol. 4, 2002, pp. 201–10; N. Bermingham, F. Coyne, G. Hull, F. Reilly and K. Taylor, *River Road: The archaeology of the Limerick Southern Ring Road. NRA Monograph 14* (Dublin: National Roads Authority, 2013), pp. 94–6, 110–14.

153 F. Ryan, '2007:1573 – Ballintotty, Tipperary'. Available at: www.excavations.ie/report/2007/Tipperary/0018562/. Accessed 15 September 2020; P. MacCotter, 'The M7 Motorway Historical Landscape: Studies in the history of Ormond', *Tipperary Historical Journal*, 2018, pp. 66–87.

154 Gilchrist, *Gender and Material Culture*, p. 69.

155 Hall, *Women and the Church*, p. 95.

156 For the purposes of this discussion the classification of castles by the Archaeological Survey of Ireland has been adopted. Castles are usually considered a later medieval phenomenon in Ireland; see T. McNeill, *Castles in Ireland: Feudal power in a Gaelic*

world (London: Routledge, 1997); T. O'Keeffe, *Ireland Encastellated AD 950–1550: Insular castle-building in its European context* (Dublin: Four Courts Press, 2021); Sweetman, *Castles*. All castle types have been listed. Fortified houses have been excluded. Only those enclosures positively identified as moated sites by the Archaeological Survey of Ireland have been included. It is suggested that this is a minimum number and many of those monuments labelled 'enclosure' in the sites and monuments record may, with future survey and investigation, be classified as moated sites. Castles and moated sites have been chosen as it is supposed – without the benefit of excavation – that at least some of these monuments would have been contemporary with the nunneries.

157 These are typologically earlier than masonry-built castles, but may be considered contemporary in some regions; see Sweetman, *Castles*; O'Keeffe, *Medieval Irish Buildings*.

158 It is acknowledged that tower houses are late in the sequence of castle building in Ireland, though there would have been some chronological overlap with nunneries that lasted until the dissolution.

159 O'Conor, *Archaeology of Medieval Rural Settlement*, pp. 89–94; A. O'Sullivan, 'Crannógs in Late Medieval Gaelic Ireland, *c.*1350–*c.*1650', in P.J. Duffy, D. Edwards and E. FitzPatrick (eds), *Gaelic Ireland: Land, lordship and settlement* c.*1250*–c.*1650* (Dublin: Four Courts Press, 2001), pp. 397–417; Carville, *Impact of the Cistercians*, pp. 45–54; M. Comber, *The Economy of the Ringfort and Contemporary Settlement in Early Medieval Ireland. BAR International Series 1773* (Oxford: Archaeopress, 2008); E. FitzPatrick, 'Native Enclosed Settlement and the Problem of the Irish "Ringfort"', *Medieval Archaeology*, vol. 53, 2009, pp. 271–307; Horning, 'Ireland: Medieval identities'; O'Sullivan et al., *Early Medieval Ireland*, p. 333.

160 For example, Stalley, *Cistercian Monasteries*; Lafaye, 'Mendicant Friaries'.

161 For example, O'Conor, *Archaeology of Medieval Rural Settlement*; T.B. Barry (ed.), *A History of Settlement in Ireland* (London: Routledge, 2000); N. Christie and P. Stamper (eds), *Medieval Rural Settlement: Britain and Ireland AD 800–1600* (Oxford: Windgather Press, 2012).

162 For a European perspective, see C.H. Berman, 'Men's Houses, Women's Houses: The relationship between the sexes in twelfth-century monasticism', in A. MacLeish (ed.), *The Medieval Monastery* (St Cloud, Minnesota: North Star Press, 1988), pp. 43–52.

163 J. Burton, '*Moniales* and *Ordo Cisterciensis*', p. 379.

164 M. Potterton, *Medieval Trim: History and archaeology* (Dublin: Four Courts Press, 2005), p. 298.

165 McNamara, *Sisters in Arms*, pp. 260–88, esp. pp. 263, 287.

166 Carville, 'Cistercian Nuns in Medieval Ireland', pp. 78–81; Carville, *Impact of the Cistercians*, p. 246.

167 Gwynn and Hadcock, *Medieval Religious Houses*, p. 323.

168 O'Flaherty, *Irish Historic Towns Atlas: Limerick*, p. 3.

169 Murphy et al., 'Waterford and Its Hinterland', pp. 217–44.

170 The associations and networks between religious houses and the masons they employed have been shown through a detailed survey; C. Hourihane, *The Mason and His Mark: Mason's marks in the medieval Irish archbishoprics of Cashel and Dublin. BAR British Series 294* (Oxford: Archaeopress, 2000).

171 Ní Ghrádaigh, '"But What Exactly Did She Give?"; C. Manning, 'Mystery of the Second Nunnery at Clonmacnoise'.

172 Kalkreuter, *Boyle Abbey*.

173 Wardell, 'The History and Antiquities of St Catherine's', p. 43; Westropp, 'On Certain Typical Earthworks', pp. 35–6.

174 Power, *Medieval English Nunneries*, p. 483.
175 J. MacCaffrey, *The Black Book of Limerick: Studies on the diocese of Limerick based principally upon the manuscript known as the Black Book of Limerick* (Germany: Albert-Ludwigs-Universität, 1906), p. lxxvii; Hand, 'Medieval Chapter', pp. 74–89; Nicholls, 'Medieval Irish Cathedral Chapters', p. 103.
176 Visitations by bishops and archbishops were recorded in episcopal registers. Many of these visitations still exist for English nunneries and contain very valuable information. The nature of visitations meant that problems encountered were recorded and positive points of individual houses were not and so they are inherently biased. See Burton, 'Looking for Medieval Nuns', p. 123. Ireland has very few references to visitations of nunneries. An undated visitation of St Catherine's, Co. Limerick is recorded which is thought to date to the early fifteenth century; Wardell, 'The History and Antiquities of St Catherine's', p. 45. However, the earliest documents copied in the *Black Book* date to 1362 and so the entry could be earlier than suggested, MacCaffrey, *Black Book of Limerick*, p. xii. A visitation was carried out at St Mary de Hogges on 27 April 1468 when the male Augustinian house of All Hallows Priory was also visited by Archbishop Tregury. Records of the nunnery visitation are sparse but it was recorded that the abbess owed 12s 8d. On 6 May 1468 Grace Dieu was visited by Robert Waren on behalf of the archbishop – six nuns are named in that visitation record; Berry (ed.), *Register of Wills*, pp. xl, 69, 175–7.
177 Hall, *Women and the Church*, pp. 146–7.
178 W.H. Bliss (ed.), *Calendar of Entries in the Papal Registers Relating to Great Britain and Ireland: Papal Letters, Vol. I, AD 1198–1304* (London: His Majesty's Stationery Office, 1893), pp. viii, 400–1.
179 Andrews, *Irish Historic Towns Atlas: Kildare*, p. 2; Buchanan and Wilson, *Irish Historic Towns Atlas: Downpatrick*, p. 2.
180 Bond, 'Medieval Nunneries in England and Wales', p. 54.
181 Gilchrist, *Contemplation and Action*, p. 155.
182 Bond, 'Medieval Nunneries in England and Wales', p. 54.
183 Hall, *Women and the Church*, p. 94.
184 Ó Clabaigh, *The Friars in Ireland*, pp. 205–6.
185 Ibid., pp. 206–7.
186 J.J. O'Meara (ed.), *The History and Topography of Ireland by Giraldus Cambrensis* (Dublin: Dolmen Press, 1942, rep. 1982), p. 154. I am grateful to Prof. M.T. Flanagan for drawing these references to my attention.
187 Gilchrist, *Contemplation and Action*, p. 116.
188 The water management of the streams at Grace Dieu and St Catherine's are suggestive of moats. Those at Grace Dieu cannot now be fully traced. Those at St Catherine's only border its southern side. Both have upstanding bridges to facilitate access across the watercourses.
189 Gilchrist, *Contemplation and Action*, p. 155.
190 Gilchrist, *Gender and Material Culture*, pp. 39–40.
191 Kenny, *Anglo-Irish and Gaelic Women*, pp. 169–84.
192 Dunning, 'Arroasian Order'; Brady, 'The Nunnery at Clonard'; Hadcock, 'Origin of the Augustinian Order'.
193 Ó Dálaigh, 'Mistress, Mother and Abbess'.
194 Hall, *Women and the Church*, pp. 70–8.
195 Burton, *Monastic and Religious Orders*, p. 85; Burton, 'Looking for Medieval Nuns'; Burton and Stöber (eds), *Women in the Medieval Monastic World*.

196 For example, Thompson, *Women Religious*; Gilchrist, *Gender and Material Culture*; Gilchrist, *Contemplation and Action*; Oliva, *Convent and the Community*; Venarde, *Women's Monasticism*; Lee, *Nunneries, Learning and Spirituality*; Spear, *Leadership*; Stöber, *Late Medieval Monasteries*.

197 Gilchrist, *Gender and Material Culture*, p. 36.

198 Ibid., p. 39; Curran, 'Religious Women', p. 38.

199 Cartwright, *Feminine Sanctity*, p. 177.

200 Collins, 'Transforming Women Religious?'

201 A.B. Scott and F.X. Martin, Expugnatio Hibernica*: The Conquest of Ireland by Giraldus Cambrensis* (Dublin: Royal Irish Academy, 1978); Martin, 'Allies and an Overlord', pp. 67–97.

202 Mohn, *Mittelalterliche Klosteranlagen der Zisterzienserinnen*, p. 444; J. Hamburger, P. Marx and S. Marti, 'The Time of the Orders 1200–1500', in J. Hamburger and S. Marti (eds), *Crown and Veil: Female monasticism from the fifth to the fifteenth centuries* (New York: Columbia University Press, 2008), pp. 41–75; Burton and Stöber, *Women in the Medieval Monastic World*.

203 Johnson, *Equal in Monastic Profession*; Venarde, *Women's Monasticism*, pp. 187–210; J. Hamburger and R. Suckale, 'Between this World and the Next: The art of religious women in the middles ages', in J. Hamburger and S. Marti (eds), *Crown and Veil: Female monasticism from the fifth to the fifteenth centuries* (New York: Columbia University Press, 2008), pp. 76–108, at pp. 76–8.

204 Hamburger et al., 'The Time of the Orders', p. 41; Jordan, 'Gender Concerns'.

205 Scheepsma, *Medieval Religious Women in the Low Countries*; Jordan, *Women, Power and Religious Patronage*.

CHAPTER 5. NUNNERY ENCLOSURE AND LAYOUT

1 Certeau, *The Practice of Everyday Life*; Cassidy-Welch, 'Space and Place in Medieval Contexts'.

2 Müller, 'Presenting Identity in the Cloister'; A. Müller, 'Interpretations of Claustral Spaces with Special Reference to Dormitories', in J. Burton and K. Stöber (eds), *Monastic Wales: New Approaches* (Cardiff: University of Wales Press, 1013), pp. 229–45; Müller, 'Symbolic Meanings of Space'.

3 Kerr, *Life in the Medieval Cloister*.

4 There is surviving male material from Ireland. For example, TCD MS 97 contains a copy of the *Liber Ordinis* of the Victorine canons which gives very detailed instructions on how to behave in various parts of the house (Dr Colmán Ó Clabaigh OSB, personal communication). See also MacKechnie, *Instructio Pie Vivendi*. I am grateful to Dr Ó Clabaigh for drawing these references to my attention.

5 V.I.J. Flint, 'Space and Discipline in Early Modern Europe', in B.A. Hanawalt and M. Kobialka (eds), *Medieval Practices of Space* (London: University of Minnesota Press, 2000), pp. 149–66, at p. 149.

6 Cassidy-Welch, *Monastic Spaces and Their Meanings*; J. Burton and J. Kerr, *The Cistercians in the Middle Ages* (Woodbridge: Boydell Press, 2011), pp. 56–81.

7 J.T. Schulenberg, 'Space, Sacred and Gender', in M. Schaus (ed.), *Women and Gender in Medieval Europe: An encyclopedia* (London: Routledge, 2006), pp. 771–3.

8 Smith, *Ordering Women's Lives*, p. 155.

9 Gilchrist, 'Community and Self', p. 55; G. Signori, 'Wanderers between Worlds: Visitors, letters, wills and gifts as means of communication in exchanges between cloister and the world', in J.F. Hamburger and S. Marti (eds), *Crown and Veil: Female*

monasticism from the fifth to the fifteenth centuries (New York: Columbia University Press, 2008), pp. 259–73; C. Schleif and V. Schier, *Katerina's Windows: Donation and devotion, art and music, as heard and seen through the writings of a Birgittine nun* (Philadelphia: Penn State University Press, 2009).

10 Hall, *Women and the Church*, pp. 16–19.

11 De Paermentier, 'Experiencing Space', pp. 59–64.

12 E. de Paermentier, 'Architecturale Ruimte en Beweginsvrijheid Van De Vrouw in Laatmiddeleeuwse Gentse Religieuze en Caritatieve Instellingen', *Handelingen der Maatschappij voor Geschiedenis en Oudheidkunde te Gent*, vol. 51, 1997, pp. 77–113, at pp. 77–111; De Paermentier, 'Experiencing Space', p. 60.

13 Stalley, *Cistercian Monasteries*, p. 174; Ó Clabaigh, *The Friars in Ireland*, p. 201; Cassidy-Welch, *Imprisonment*.

14 Flint, 'Space and Discipline', p. 164.

15 Foucault, *Discipline and Punish*.

16 Cassidy-Welch, *Monastic Spaces and Their Meanings*, p. 8.

17 There is no medieval nunnery in Ireland which is still used for its original purpose. There are modern enclosed nunneries in operation, for example the Poor Clares (Franciscan) Galway and Glencairn (Cistercian), Co. Waterford.

18 Gilchrist, 'Community and Self'. She interviewed and discussed with the Anglican nuns their use of space within their nunnery and how medieval nuns may have used those same spaces. She supplemented her study with plans and historical documentation. Burnham Abbey was suitable for such a study as much of its medieval layout is still used as a nunnery.

19 Ibid., p. 57.

20 I am grateful to Robin Turk for discussing his archaeological study of contemporary Cistercian monks and nuns with me.

21 Kerr, *Religious Life for Women*, pp. 137–43.

22 Ibid., p. 152.

23 Gilchrist, 'Community and Self', p. 56.

24 Kerr, *Life in the Medieval Cloister*, pp. 25–37.

25 B. Sloane, 'Tenements in London's Monasteries *c.*1450–1540', in D. Gaimster and R. Gilchrist (eds), *The Archaeology of Reformation 1480–1580* (Leeds: Maney, 2003), pp. 290–8; Sloane, *Augustinian Nunnery of St Mary Clerkenwell*, p. 144.

26 W. Horn, 'On the Origin of the Medieval Cloister', *Gesta*, vol. 12, 1973, pp. 13–52; R. Stalley, *Early Medieval Architecture* (Oxford: Oxford University Press, 1999), pp. 184–9; J. McNeill, 'The Continental Context [of medieval cloisters]', *Journal of the British Archaeological Association*, vol. 159, 2006, pp. 1–47, at pp. 1–6.

27 Gilchrist, *Gender and Material Culture*, p. 121; McNamara, *Sisters in Arms*, pp. 262, 290; O'Keeffe, *An Anglo-Norman Monastery*, pp. 107–45; Coppack, *Abbeys and Priories*, pp. 105–6; Jäggi and Lobbedey, 'Church and Cloister', pp. 118–19.

28 Gilchrist, *Gender and Material Culture*, p. 152.

29 For a discussion of space in dormitories in male Cistercian houses in Wales, see Müller, 'Interpretations of Claustral Spaces'.

30 Signori, 'Wanderers between Worlds', p. 268; Signori, 'Cell or Dormitory?'

31 Signori, 'Wanderers between Worlds', pp. 270–1.

32 Hamburger et al., 'The Time of the Orders', p. 61; Müller, 'Presenting Identity in the Cloister', pp. 177–9.

33 Kerr, *Life in the Medieval Cloister*, pp. 82–99.

34 De Paermentier, 'Experiencing Space', p. 63.

35 Gilchrist, 'Community and Self', p. 58.

36 A. Lynch, *Tintern Abbey, Co. Wexford: Cistercians and Colcloughs. Excavations 1982–2007* (Dublin: Government of Ireland, 2010), pp. 66–71. Or the collation bay at Jerpoint, Co. Kilkenny; Stalley, *Cistercian Monasteries*, p. 161.
37 Rudy, *Virtual Pilgrimages*, p. 216.
38 Hamburger et al., 'Time of the Orders', p. 59.
39 E.C. Rae, 'The Sculpture of the Cloister of Jerpoint Abbey', *Journal of the Royal Society of Antiquaries of Ireland*, vol. 96, 1966, pp. 59–91; Stalley, *Cistercian Monasteries*, pp. 189–93.
40 There are a few exceptions; see O'Donoghue, 'Mendicant Cloisters in Munster'.
41 Medioli, 'An Unequal Law'; Hamburger et al., 'Time of the Orders', pp. 44–5; S. Corbellini, 'Mapping the Spiritual Life: A spatial approach to later medieval spirituality', *Anuario de Estudios Medievales*, vol. 44, 2014, pp. 81–100.
42 Smith, *Ordering Women's Lives*, p. 178.
43 Ibid.
44 Schulenburg, 'Strict Active Enclosure', p. 79; Brundage and Makowski, 'Enclosure of Nuns', p. 153.
45 Smith, *Ordering Women's Lives*, p. 163.
46 De Paermentier, 'Experiencing Space', p. 58.
47 Modern enclosed contemplative nunnery communities consider it in this way.
48 Hamburger et al., 'Time of the Orders', p. 61.
49 Schulenburg, 'Strict Active Enclosure', pp. 63, 69.
50 P.D. Johnson, 'The Cloistering of Medieval Nuns: Release or repression, reality or fantasy?', in D.O. Helly and S.M. Reverby (eds), *Gendered Domains: Rethinking public and private in women's history* (New York: Ithaca, 1992), pp. 27–39, at p. 36.
51 Johnson, 'The Cloistering of Medieval Nuns', p. 37; C. Fowler, *The Archaeology of Personhood* (London: Routledge, 2004), p. 157.
52 Makowski, 'Monastic Enclosure', p. 575.
53 Hall, *Women and the Church*, pp. 159–90.
54 Ibid., pp. 191–200; Hall, 'Necessary Collaborations'.
55 Ó Dálaigh, 'Mistress, Mother and Abbess'; Kenny, *Anglo-Irish and Gaelic Women*, p. 183.
56 Berman, 'Men's Houses, Women's Houses'; J. Hamburger, 'Art, Enclosure and the *Cura Monialium*: Prolegomena in the guise of a postscript', *Gesta*, vol. 31, no. 2, 1992, pp. 108–34, at p. 110.
57 McNamara, *Sisters in Arms*, p. 290.
58 Hamburger et al., 'Time of the Orders', p. 44.
59 There is some historical evidence for vowesses and consecrated widows in medieval Ireland; see Hall, *Women and the Church*, p. 187. There is also a rite for the consecration of a vowess in a pontifical from County Meath (Dr Colmán Ó Clabaigh OSB, personal communication).
60 E. Makowski, *A Pernicious Sort of Woman: Quasi-religious women and canon lawyers in the later middle ages* (Washington DC: The Catholic University of America Press, 2005), p. 139.
61 Neel, 'Origins of the Beguines'; E. Makowski, '*Mulieres Religiosae*, Strictly Speaking: Some fourteenth-century canonical opinions', *The Catholic Historical Review*, vol. 85, 1999, pp. 1–14, at p. 2; Makowski, *A Pernicious Sort of Woman*, pp. 139–41; More, *Fictive Orders*.
62 Jenkins, *Holy, Holier, Holiest*; Ó Carragáin, *Churches in Early Medieval Ireland*, pp. 8–9, 57–60; Dey and Fentress, *Western Monasticism* Ante Litteram.
63 Gilchrist, *Gender and Material Culture*, p. 152. Terminology in regard to the monastic precinct and inner and outer courts can vary. Gilchrist's terminology that uses 'inner

court' to describe the claustral area itself, and 'outer court' for the area used for the service and subsidiary buildings, has been used in this book, see Gilchrist, *Gender and Material Culture*, p. 73.

64 Everson and Stocker, 'St Leonard's at Kirkstead', p. 230.
65 Moorhouse, 'Monastic Estates', p. 41; Clyne, *Kells Priory*, p. 52.
66 L.A.S. Butler, 'The Archaeology of Rural Monasteries in England and Wales', in R. Gilchrist and H. Mytum (eds), *The Archaeology of Rural Monasteries. BAR British Series 203* (Oxford: British Archaeological Reports, 1989), pp. 1–28, at p. 15.
67 Aston, *Monasteries in the Landscape*, pp. 101–24.
68 G. Coppack, 'Thornholme Priory: The development of a monastic outer court', in R. Gilchrist and H. Mytum (eds), *The Archaeology of Rural Monasteries. BAR British Series 203* (Oxford: British Archaeological Reports, 1989), pp. 185–222.
69 Brown, *Stanley Abbey*, pp. 45–8.
70 Ibid., p. 72; M. Carter, *Hailes Abbey* (London: English Heritage, 2017).
71 Hall, *Scottish Monastic Landscapes*, p. 82.
72 Bond, 'Medieval Nunneries in England and Wales', p. 70.
73 Coppack, 'How the Other Half Lived', pp. 276–7.
74 Ibid., pp. 296–7.
75 Bull et al., *Holywell Priory*, p. 37.
76 Sloane, *St Mary Clerkenwell*, p. 146.
77 J. Schofield, 'Building in Religious Precincts in London at the Dissolution and After', in R. Gilchrist and H. Mytum (eds), *Advances in Monastic Archaeology. BAR British Series 227* (Oxford: Tempvs Reparatvm, 1993), pp. 29–41, at p. 30.
78 Ward, *Excavations at Chester*, p. 9; S. Ward, 'The Monastic Topography of Chester', in R. Gilchrist and H. Mytum (eds), *Advances in Monastic Archaeology. BAR British Series 227* (Oxford: Tempvs Reparatvm, 1993), pp. 113–26, at p. 115.
79 Clapham, 'Priory and Manor House of Dartford'; Lee, *Nunneries, Learning and Spirituality*, p. 18.
80 J. Burnett-Brown, *Lacock Abbey, Wiltshire* (The National Trust: Beckenham, 1974), p. 10.
81 Bond, 'Medieval Nunneries in England and Wales', p. 76.
82 Gilchrist, *Gender and Material Culture*, p. 112.
83 Aston, *Monasteries in the Landscape*, p. 114.
84 P. Everson, 'Rural Monasteries within the Secular Landscape', in R. Gilchrist and H. Mytum (eds), *The Archaeology of Rural Monasteries. BAR British Series 203* (Oxford: British Archaeological Reports, 1989), pp. 141–5, at pp. 143–4.
85 Gilchrist, *Gender and Material Culture*, p. 70.
86 D. Ganz, 'The Buildings of Godstow Nunnery', *Oxoniensia*, vol. 37, 1972, pp. 150–7, at plate xvi; Bond, 'Medieval Nunneries in England and Wales', p. 71.
87 D. Baker, 'Excavations at Elstow Abbey, 1968–1970, Third Interim Report', *Bedfordshire Archaeological Journal*, vol. 6, 1971, pp. 55–64; D. Baker and E. Baker, 'Research Designs: Timbers phases and outbuildings with special reference to Elstow Abbey and Grove Priory, Bedfordshire and a note about the availability of information', in R. Gilchrist, and H. Mytum (eds), *The Archaeology of Rural Monasteries BAR British Series 203* (Oxford: British Archaeological Reports, 1989), pp. 261–75, at p. 267; Gilchrist, *Gender and Material Culture*, p. 110.
88 Bond 'Medieval Nunneries in England and Wales', p. 72.
89 O. Sharkey, *Fore and Its Ancient Buildings* (Mullingar: Magpie Publications, 1999), p. 4; T. O'Keeffe, *Medieval Fore: An archaeological wonder in the Westmeath landscape. Heritage Guide No. 28* (Dublin: Wordwell, 2004); Masterson, *Medieval Fore*, pp. 44–51.

90 Stalley, *Cistercian Monasteries*, pp. 175–6.
91 R. Stalley, 'Mellifont Abbey: A study of its architectural history', *Proceedings of the Royal Irish Academy*, vol. 80C, pp. 263–354, at pp. 272, 314.
92 R. Stalley, 'Corcomroe Abbey: Some observations on its architectural history', *Journal of the Royal Society of Antiquaries of Ireland*, vol. 105, pp. 21–46.
93 Lynch, *Tintern Abbey*, pp. 190–1.
94 Stalley, *Cistercian Monasteries*, p. 237.
95 P.D. Sweetman, 'Archaeological Excavations at Abbeyknockmoy, Co. Galway', *Proceedings of the Royal Irish Academy*, vol. 87C, 1987, pp. 1–12, at pp. 9–11.
96 Bradley and Manning, 'Excavations at Duiske Abbey', p. 424.
97 Stalley, *Cistercian Monasteries*, p. 177.
98 D. Doggett, 'The Medieval Monasteries of the Augustinian Canons Regular', *Archaeology Ireland*, vol. 10, 1996, pp. 31–3; O'Keeffe, *An Anglo-Norman Monastery*, pp. 108, 112–13; M. O'Neill, 'Christ Church Cathedral as a Blueprint for Other Augustinian Buildings in Ireland', in J. Bradley, A.J. Fletcher and A. Simms (eds), *Dublin in the Medieval World: Studies in honour of Howard B. Clarke* (Dublin: Four Courts Press, 2009), pp. 168–87, at p. 168.
99 Bradley, 'Precinct of St John's Priory'.
100 C. Walsh, 'Archaeological Excavations at the Abbey of St Thomas the Martyr, Dublin', *Medieval Dublin*, vol. I, 2000, pp. 185–202, at pp. 190–2, 201; C. Duddy, 'The Role of St Thomas's Abbey in the Early Development of Dublin's Western Suburb', *Medieval Dublin*, vol. IV, 2003, pp. 79–97.
101 T. Drew, 'On Evidences of the Plan of the Cloister Garth and Monastic Buildings of the Priory of the Holy Trinity, Now Known as Christ Church Cathedral, Dublin', *Proceedings of the Royal Irish Academy*, vol. 2, 1879–88, pp. 214–18; S. Kinsella 'Mapping Christ Church Cathedral, Dublin *c.*1028–1608: An examination of the western cloister', in J. Bradley, A.J. Fletcher and A. Simms (eds), *Dublin in the Medieval World: Studies in honour of Howard B. Clarke* (Dublin: Four Courts Press, 2009), pp. 143–67.
102 Simpson, 'Priory of All Hallows and Trinity College', p. 218; R. Moss, 'Reduce, Reuse, Recycle: Irish monastic architecture *c.*1540–1640', in R. Stalley (ed.), *Irish Gothic Architecture: Construction, decay and reinvention* (Dublin: Wordwell, 2012), pp. 115–59, at p. 124.
103 O'Keeffe, *An Anglo-Norman Monastery*, p. 48.
104 Fanning, 'Excavations at Clontuskert Priory', pp. 121–2.
105 Clyne, *Kells Priory*, pp. 52–3.
106 M. Quinlan, *Athassel Augustinian Priory, County Tipperary: Conservation plan* (Dublin: Office of Public Works, 2009), p. 27.
107 O'Keeffe, *An Anglo-Norman Monastery*, pp. 134–5; Clyne, *Kells Priory*, p. 54.
108 Ó Clabaigh, *Friars in Ireland*, p. 135.
109 Mooney, 'Franciscan Architecture [part 1]'; Mooney, 'Franciscans in Ireland', p. 131; Mooney, 'Franciscans in County Mayo'; C. Mooney, 'Franciscan Architecture in Pre-Reformation Ireland [part 2]', *Journal of the Royal Society of Antiquaries of Ireland*, vol. 86, 1956, pp. 125–69; C. Mooney, 'Franciscan Architecture in Pre-Reformation Ireland [part 3]', *Journal of the Royal Society of Antiquaries of Ireland*, vol. 87, 1957, pp. 1–38; M. O'Neill, 'Irish Franciscan Architecture: Late medieval and early modern', in E. Bhreathnach, J. MacMahon and J. McCafferty (eds), *The Irish Franciscans 1534–1990* (Dublin: Four Courts Press, 2009), pp. 305–27, at p. 305.
110 M. Hurley and C. Sheehan, *Excavations at the Dominican Priory: St Mary's of the Isle, Cork* (Cork: Cork Corporation, 1995).

111 A. Halpin and L. Buckley, 'Archaeological Excavations at the Dominican Priory, Drogheda, Co. Louth', *Proceedings of the Royal Irish Academy*, vol. 95C, 1995, pp. 175–253, at p. 176.
112 S. Duffy and L. Simpson, 'The Hermits of St Augustine in Medieval Dublin: Their history and archaeology', in J. Bradley, A. Fletcher and A. Simms (eds), *Dublin in the Medieval World: Studies in honour of Howard B. Clarke* (Dublin: Four Courts Press, 2009), pp. 202–48, at pp. 211–13, 234–7.
113 Collins et al., 'Limerick City Walls', pp. 81–4.
114 A number of nunneries in Ireland have walls around their perimeters, but these are later additions for the purpose of surrounding a modern graveyard or suchlike, and do not represent precinct walls. For example, Aghade, Annaghdown, Ballynagallagh, Derrane, Kilcreevanty, Killaraght, Killevy, Killone, Molough, the Nuns' Church, Portrane, and Tisrara. The wall at St Catherine's is of later date and related to Old Abbey House. The wall contains a few medieval architectural fragments.
115 Flanagan, 'St Mary's Abbey Louth'; Flanagan, *Transformation*, p. 153.
116 I am grateful to Dr Brian Golding for supplying this translation pre-publication. B. Golding, *Giraldus Cambrensis*' Speculum Ecclesie (translation) (Oxford: Oxford Medieval Texts, Clarendon Press, forthcoming).
117 Bradley, *Natural Places*, pp. 33–44.
118 K. Villiers-Tuthill, 'The Irish Benedictine Nuns: From Ypres to Kylemore', in M. Browne and C. Ó Clabaigh (eds), *The Irish Benedictines: A history* (Dublin: The Columba Press, 2005), pp. 122–39, at p. 136.
119 Errew is additionally 'enclosed' – if the two were contemporary – by the proximity of a male Augustinian house, founded in 1413, further inland on the same peninsula. It is known that there was a monastery here in the twelfth century and possibly before. There are no definite remains of this earlier establishment. It remains unclear at what date a community of nuns was established. Knox, *History of the County of Mayo*, p. 97; T. Ó Carragáin, 'Pre-Romanesque Churches in Ireland', 2 vols, unpublished PhD thesis, University College Cork, 2002. Inishmaine is also thought to have been once an island location; see, Healy, 'Two Royal Abbeys'.
120 Collins, 'Unveiling Female Monasticism'.
121 McCullough and Crawford, *Irish Historic Towns Atlas: Armagh*; Ó Carragáin, *Churches in Early Medieval Ireland*, pp. 56, 62.
122 FitzPatrick and O'Brien, *Medieval Churches of County Offaly*, p. 84.
123 Murphy, 'Excavation of an Early Monastic Enclosure', p. 21; Ó Carragáin, *Churches in Early Medieval Ireland*, p. 216.
124 Smith, *Ordering Women's Lives*, p. 178; Hall, *Women and the Church*, pp. 151–8; Kenny, *Women in Ireland*, pp. 175–81.
125 Jäggi and Lobbedey, 'Church and Cloister', p. 120.
126 De Paermentier, 'Experiencing Space', pp. 57, 59–64.
127 For example, Jäggi, *Fraunenkloster im Spatmittelalter*; C. Mohn, *Mittelalterliche Klosteranlagen der Zisterzienserinnen*; M. Mersch, *Das Ehemalige Zisterzienserinnenkloster Vallis Dei in Brenkhausen im 13. Und 14. Jahrhundert* (Mainz: Denkmalpflege und Forschung, 2007); Mersch, 'Programme, Pragmatism and Symbolism'.
128 Coppack, 'How the Other Half Lived'.
129 Bond, 'Medieval Nunneries in England and Wales', p. 76.
130 De Paermentier, 'Experiencing Space', p. 57.
131 Gilchrist, *Gender and Material Culture*, p. 152.
132 Smith, *Ordering Women's Lives*, pp. 178–80.

133 De Paermentier, 'Experiencing Space', p. 57.
134 Hamburger et al., 'Time of the Orders', p. 48; Frings, *Krone und Schleier*, p. 48.
135 C. Walker Bynum, *Holy Feast and Holy Fast: The religious significance of food to medieval women* (London: University of California Press, 1987), p. 296.
136 Gilchrist, *Gender and Material Culture*, p. 73; Coppack, *Abbeys and Priories*, p. 109.
137 Gilchrist, *Gender and Material Culture*, p. 73.
138 Dunn, *Emergence of Monasticism*, pp. 124–5.
139 Gilchrist, *Gender and Material Culture*, p. 90.
140 R.W. Morant, *The Monastic Gatehouse* (Lewes: The Book Guild, 1995), pp. 12–13.
141 Gilchrist, *Gender and Material Culture*, p. 73. There are the remains of about 230 monastic gate houses in Britain; see Morant, *Monastic Gatehouse*.
142 There are several gatehouses extant at male religious houses in Ireland, for example Athassel, Co. Tipperary (Augustinian), Corcomroe, Co. Clare and Mellifont, Co. Louth (both Cistercian), although the latter has been re-interpreted as a tower house; see Halpin and Newman, *Ireland*, p. 321.
143 Gilchrist, *Gender and Material Culture*, p. 73; Morant, *Monastic Gatehouses*, pp. 61–5. The Franciscan friary at Adare, Co. Limerick, although a later foundation (1465), has both a wide and narrow entrance feature extant, confirming the existence of such an arrangement in Ireland.
144 There are fifty-five dovecotes known in Ireland and some of this number relate to post-medieval examples.
145 The location of a dovecote is important. It must be away from trees and sheltered from the prevailing winds. A southern aspect is favourable. An abundant water source is also important for the birds for drinking and washing. The dovecote at St Catherine's is to the south of the nunnery complex, adjacent to a fast-flowing stream. P. Hansell and J. Hansell, *Dovecotes* (Aylesbury: Shire Publications, 1988), p. 10.
146 Ibid., p. 10.
147 Ibid., pp. 3–6. There is historical and pictorial evidence of pigeons acting as messenger birds in the fifteenth century, due to their strong homing instinct; see Hansell and Hansell, *Dovecotes*, p. 2. I have not found any reference to this function in medieval Ireland, though it is possible the birds were used this way.
148 Ó Clabaigh, *Friars in Ireland*, pp. 132–3.
149 From fieldwork at St Catherine's it appears that two streams were deliberately joined by a diversion channel which originally ran along the eastern side of the entrance causeway. Although now silted up, Westropp's drawing clearly shows a flow of water towards the southern side of the nunnery. Even today, both these streams are very fast-flowing with a surprising volume of water for such a low-lying site. Field survey did not identify any remains of a mill, which might be expected at a site like this.
150 The majority of this information derives from post-dissolution surveys; see White, *Extents*. Surveys from eleven nunneries are included: St Mary de Hogges, Grace Dieu, Graney, Kildare, Timolin, Kilculliheen, St Peter's Cell, Termonfeckin, Lismullin, Odder, and Molough. The descriptions of the precincts are sparse. At St Mary de Hogges all the buildings had already been demolished and the material moved to Dublin Castle for repairs. At Kilculliheen, the survey merely recorded 'all other buildings within the precincts are suitable for the farmer and are worth 40 s', and Odder 'all the buildings in the precinct are still standing as at the dissolution'. St Peter's Cell is described as ruinous, and at Termonfeckin, 'sites with houses and gardens, yards *etc*. On the site, containing 2 acres and is of no value above repairs'.
151 MacCurtain, 'Late Medieval Nunneries', p. 139.

152 There is a nineteenth-century mill to the east of Grace Dieu. There are some *ex situ* fragments in this mill that may have originated in the nunnery.
153 The nunnery at Lismullin must have had access to very large quantities of grain, as in addition to the water mill in its precinct it also owned two more at the vills of Blondeston and Betaghton; White, *Extents*, p. 256.
154 White, *Extents*, pp. 171, 255. The Cistercian house of Inishlounaght had two water mills adjacent and one mill in County Waterford. It is probable that the last example was on the opposite bank of the river Suir which lies in County Waterford. The fording point of the Suir at Inishlounaght would have facilitated easy access. It is not known if any of these mills might be related to the nunnery community there.
155 C.K. Currie, 'The Role of Fishponds in the Monastic Economy', in R. Gilchrist and H. Mytum (eds), *The Archaeology of Rural Monasteries. BAR British Series 203* (Oxford: British Archaeological Reports, 1989), pp. 147–72, at pp. 153–4; J. Bond, *Monastic Landscapes* (Stroud: Tempus, 2004), pp. 183–7.
156 Bond, *Monastic Landscapes*, p. 184.
157 Bond, 'Water Management in the Urban Monastery', p. 71.
158 Currie, 'Role of Fishponds', pp. 147, 150.
159 Westropp recorded this feature as a fishpond on his plan of 1902; see Westropp, 'The Conventual Buildings', p. 51.
160 Its modern dimensions are 5m in width (north–south) by *c.*20m in length. It is about 1m in depth.
161 Contrary to the popular belief that fishponds at monastic houses in Britain were commercial enterprises, fishponds only supplied the monastic houses' needs and were unlikely to ever produce an annual surplus suitable for sale. Fresh fish was probably only used on special feast days and for visitors. Everyday fish fare was dried and salted; Currie, 'Role of Fishponds', pp. 152, 154–6, 159–60.
162 At Kellystown, Co. Louth there is no trace of the nunnery, nor was it shown on early historic mapping. It is interesting to note, however, that on the mapping just to the south of the nunnery's supposed location is a long rectangular feature labelled 'pond'. It lies near a 'Kellystown house'. While this cannot be proven, it can be tentatively suggested that this may be a fishpond relating to the nunnery. At Baldongan, Co. Dublin, a church and castle that is a supposed nunnery and also associated with the Knights Templars has a fishpond close by.
163 White, *Extents*, p. 336.
164 Ibid., p. 338.
165 The townland boundaries shown on the first-edition Ordnance Survey six-inch map (sheet 5) at St Peter's Cell location suggest that the nunnery's precinct stretched beyond the town wall and reached the right (southern) bank of the Abbey river. It is recorded that St Saviour's Dominican Priory (male house), just to the north of St Peter's Cell, owned weirs on the Shannon; S. Spellissy, *The History of Limerick City* (Limerick: The Celtic Bookshop, 1998), p. 154.
166 O'Keeffe and Simington, *Irish Stone Bridges*, pp. 171–2.
167 Bond, 'Medieval Nunneries in England and Wales', pp. 72, 84, 85.
168 Nunneries also had estates beyond their immediate precincts. In some cases, this land may have been at quite a remove from the nunnery itself. These are considered separately in Chapter 9.
169 Hall, *Women and the Church*, p. 96.
170 O'Keeffe, *An Anglo-Norman Monastery*, pp. 112–13.
171 For example, Champneys, *Irish Ecclesiastical Architecture*, pp. 157–98; Leask, *Irish Churches and Monastic Buildings*.

172 Horn, 'On the Origin'. Lorsh was accepted as an early cloister based on a *villa rustica* in 1973, but in 2006 this interpretation was under review; see J. McNeill, 'Continental Context', p. 5.

173 Horn, 'On the Origin', pp. 47–8; Stalley, *Early Medieval Architecture*, p. 189; McNeill, 'Continental Context', p. 1.

174 Stalley, *Early Medieval Architecture*, pp. 184–8.

175 Ibid., p. 51.

176 B.W. Braunfels, *Monasteries of Western Europe: The architecture of the orders* (London: Thames & Hudson, 1972); T. Coomans, *Life Inside the Cloister: Understanding monastic architecture* (Leuven: Leuven University Press, 2018).

177 See J. Ashbee, 'Cloisters in English Palaces in the Twelfth and Thirteenth Centuries', *Journal of the British Archaeological Association*, vol. 159, 2006, pp. 71–90; J. Montague, 'The Cloister and Bishop's Palace at Old Sarum with Some Thoughts on the Origins and Meaning of Secular Cathedral Cloisters', *Journal of the British Archaeological Association*, vol. 159, 2006, pp. 48–70; T. Tatton-Brown, 'The Two Mid-Twelfth-Century Cloister Arcades at Canterbury Cathedral Priory', *Journal of the British Archaeological Association*, vol. 159, 2006, pp. 91–104.

178 Bruzelius and Berman, 'Introduction', p. 73.

179 From the archaeological evidence at Ballymacdane, it is highly likely that it too had a claustral plan. In this case, now only the church survives (see Chapter 6). The remains at Killcreevanty are unclear. The Archaeological Survey of Ireland recorded a claustral layout – it was heavily overgrown at time of survey – and now is no longer visible, being covered by modern burials. There are also free-standing structure platforms around the church area also; Alcock et al., *Archaeological Inventory of County Galway*, p. 315.

180 J.P. Greene, *Norton Priory: The archaeology of a medieval religious house* (Cambridge: Cambridge University Press, 1989).

181 Collins, 'Unveiling Female Monasticism', p. 143.

182 Baker, 'Excavations at Elstow Abbey'; Baker and Baker, 'Research Designs', p. 265.

183 Ganz, 'Godstow Nunnery'; Bond, 'Medieval Nunneries in England and Wales', p. 69.

184 O'Donovan, *Annála Ríoghachta Éireann*, vol. V; W.M. Hennessy and B. MacCarthy (eds), *Annala Uladh: Annals of Ulster, otherwise Annala Senait, Annals of Senat: A chronicle of Irish affairs from AD 431 to AD 1540*, 4 vols (Dublin: HMSO by A. Thom & Co., 1887–1901), vol. III; Ó Clabaigh, *Friars in Ireland*, p. 70.

185 Their construction spans a period of about 130 years if the 1320s date postulated for Molough is correct.

186 They also have different post-dissolution histories. Killone is a national monument in state ownership (national monument 176) and was first conserved in 1894–5. Burial has continued at the site to the present day. St Catherine's is a recorded monument and place. There is no tradition of modern (post-1700) burial at the site. Molough is a recorded monument and place, and is still used for burial.

187 While all three nunneries have a basic claustral layout, the function of some of the rooms cannot be clearly identified. For instance, none of the three examples show clear evidence for a chapter house, which was an important room in contemporary male houses. St Catherine's appears never to have had a chapter house and Molough's eastern range is no longer extant so it is impossible to say if it had such a room. Killone may have had a chapter house, possibly indicated by the twin ogee-headed light in the east wall of its eastern range. This is a later fifteenth-century insertion, however, which has been conserved in modern times. It is now impossible to identify from the masonry if a doorway would have led into this room from the cloister.

188 Westropp, 'Augustinian Houses', p. 129.
189 Lynch, *Tintern Abbey*, p. 61.
190 The walls of both the east and south ranges of Killone have been extensively re-built. Westropp's description appears to pre-date the re-building and he does not describe any features that would constitute the remains of a cloister ambulatory, arcade or lean-to roof either; see Westropp, 'Augustinian Houses', p. 132.
191 Modern burial is still taking place at Molough, in most parts of the interior of the nunnery complex and in the small graveyard to the south.
192 For a detailed description, see Collins, 'Unveiling Female Monasticism', pp. 107–22.
193 It cannot now be known if the different corbels represent different building phases or contemporary use of different profiles, although I would suggest the latter.
194 Westropp, 'The Conventual Buildings', p. 60.
195 Collins, 'Unveiling Female Monasticism', pp. 124–9.
196 Westropp first suggested this building sequence; see 'The Conventual Buildings'. The church is late in the building sequence at St Catherine's. This is considered unusual.
197 This wall would have separated the ambulatories (walkways) from the central garth. Collins, 'Unveiling Female Monasticism', pp. 124–9, 144–6.
198 Ibid., pp. 124–9, 144–6.
199 C. Ó Conbhuidhe, *The Cistercian Abbeys of Tipperary* (Dublin: Four Courts Press, 1999), pp. 164–275.
200 Lynch, *Tintern Abbey*, p. 62.
201 Westropp, 'The Conventual Buildings', p. 55. This fragment, along with several other fragments identified by Westropp, are now lost.
202 Leask, *Irish Churches and Monastic Buildings*, vol. 3, p. 135 for drawing of Athassel cloister details; Leask, *Irish Churches and Monastic Buildings*, vol. 2, pp. 139–40 for examples in timber. For an overview, see O'Donoghue, 'Mendicant Cloisters in Munster'.
203 O'Keeffe, *An Anglo-Norman Monastery*, pp. 74–6, 144. The shrine in the south transept of Holy Cross Abbey, Co. Tipperary has similar, though much looser, spiral decoration on the shafts of its arcades. This feature dates to the fifteenth century; see Leask, *Irish Churches and Monastic Buildings*, vol. 3, plate VII.
204 Leask, *Irish Churches and Monastic Buildings*, vol. 3, p. 144, plate XXa.
205 Tintern, Co. Wexford; Bective, Co. Meath; Kilcooly, Co. Tipperary; and Jerpoint, Co. Kilkenny. See Lynch, *Tintern Abbey*, pp. 63, 73; Stalley, *Cistercian Monasteries*, p. 55.
206 Hurley and Sheehan, *St Mary's of the Isle*, pp. 47–53.
207 Gilchrist, *Gender and Material Culture*, pp. 128–33.
208 For a comprehensive overview of this tradition, see Gilchrist, *Gender and Material Culture*, pp. 133–43; R. Gilchrist, *Gender and Archaeology*, pp. 109–45; Raguin and Stanbury, *Women's Space*.
209 M. Spurrell, *The Symbolism of Medieval Churches: An introduction* (London: Routledge, 2020).
210 M. Aston, 'Segregation in Church', in J. Sheils and D. Wood (eds), *Women in the Church: Studies in church history*, vol. 27 (Oxford: Blackwell, 1990), pp. 237–81; K. French, 'The Seat under Our Lady: Gender and seating in late medieval English parish churches', in V.C. Raguin and S. Stanbury (eds), *Women's Spaces: Patronage, place and gender in the medieval church* (New York: State University of New York Press, 2005), pp. 141–60; K. French, *The Good Women of the Parish: Gender and religion after the Black Death* (Philadelphia: University of Pennsylvania Press, 2007); C. Schleif, 'Men on the Right, Women on the Left: (A)symmetrical spaces and gendered places', in V.C. Raguin and S. Stanbury (eds), *Women's Space: Patronage, place and gender in the medieval church* (New York: State University of New York Press, 2005), pp. 207–49.

211 Gilchrist, *Gender and Material Culture*, pp. 133–5.
212 Ó Carragáin, *Churches in Early Medieval Ireland*, pp. 171–2.
213 Stalley, *Cistercian Monasteries*, p. 58.
214 O'Keeffe, *An Anglo-Norman Monastery*, pp. 112–13.
215 Collins, *Killone, Co. Clare.*
216 There is no clearly defined chapter house at any nunnery in Ireland. A single chapter house is mentioned in a 1586 description of St Mary de Hogges, Dublin; H.B. Clarke, *Irish Historic Towns Atlas No. 11: Dublin, Part I, to 1610* (Dublin: Royal Irish Academy, 2002), p. 19. The doorway at St Catherine's would be of similar dimensions to chapter house doorways at contemporary male Augustinian houses, for example the doorway excavated at Clontuskert, Co. Galway which measured almost 2m in width; or to the dimensions and style of the chapter house doorway at Cong Abbey, Co. Mayo; see Fanning, 'Excavations at Clontuskert Priory', p. 115.
217 Westropp, 'Augustinian Houses', p. 132.
218 Westropp noted that this blocked doorway had the 'upper socket stone' (probably a hanging eye feature) of an older door built into it, upside down. This is no longer identifiable. He suggested that this door led to a building to the north of the church and 'now quite levelled'. There is now no evidence of such a structure and it was not identified in geophysical survey or the excavations. Westropp, 'The Conventual Buildings', p. 59, note 5.
219 A very similar-looking mortar spread (F10) was found during excavations carried out at the Holy Trinity Augustinian friary at Fownes Street Upper and Cecilia Street, Dublin in 1995. There it was interpreted as a spread of mortar possibly related to the construction of the northern precinct wall of the monastery. This monastic house was founded some time after 1265; Duffy and Simpson, 'The Hermits of St Augustine', pp. 239–41.
220 Collins, 'Unveiling Female Monasticism', pp. 143–4.
221 The Augustinian church at Ballybeg, Co. Cork is located partially along the northern side of its cloister, and the majority of the church projects beyond the line of the eastern range. This is clearly not the same as St Catherine's arrangement but is the closest parallel that can be identified; see M. Shine, 'Ballybeg', *Mallow Field Club Journal*, vol. 11, 1993, pp. 84–112; O'Keeffe, *An Anglo-Norman Monastery*, p. 113. There is no topographical reason why the church at St Catherine's was placed in this location.
222 Westropp, 'The Conventual Buildings', p. 54.
223 Ibid., p. 61.
224 Further evidence that the vaults may be an alteration is the numerous blockings of opes, suggestive of a refurbishment. There is no evidence that the upper floor may have been supported on joists, as the location of such evidence is now obscured by the vaulting itself.
225 A corrodian was a lay person who paid, or was sponsored, to lodge in private accommodation within a monastic precinct. Often this arrangement was permanent and served as a form of pension. See Golding, '"As for a Nun": Corrodies, nunneries'.
226 This interpretation is based on the measurements of the vaults. The two extant vaults are similar in dimension. If it is supposed that the third vault was of similar dimension, this leaves enough space to accommodate a stairwell at the northern end of the range. This stair was not placed directly at the junction of the west range and the north cloister wall at this point as this wall is intact. It may have been located *c.*1.5m to the south of this junction. See Chapter 7 for further discussion.
227 O'Keeffe suggests that St Catherine's had a first-floor refectory, based on Westropp's record of an upper-floor window, now no longer visible; O'Keeffe, *Medieval Irish*

Buildings, p. 151. However, based on the ground-floor reader's recess, the relatively long lancet windows in the south wall and the lack of joist holes or corbels to support an upper floor, I suggest that St Catherine's did have a ground-floor refectory. The upper-floor window may have lit the ground floor, or garret space and not a first floor proper; see Collins, 'Unveiling Female Monasticism', pp. 146–8.

228 This is suggested, as Westropp noted smaller jambs at the base of this breach, now no longer visible. A lavabo feature might be expected near to the refectory doorway, the removal of which would certainly cause a weakening of the wall and its subsequent collapse, as had occurred here. The location of the lavabo here also fits with how the nuns may have traversed and used the claustral space (see Chapter 7).

229 Five lancets are suggested. The breach which remains to the east of the extant windows is wide enough to contain three further windows if the spacing is constant. The breach is splayed at either side, which suggests further windows. These three windows would have been shorter than the extant examples, as they accommodated the reader's recess beneath. It is recorded that at least one of these windows was removed and inserted into the summer house feature to the west of the fishpond, which is upstanding; Westropp, 'The Conventual Buildings', p. 62.

230 While there is no evidence now, it is postulated that the recess had a series of steps to a higher platform that was accommodated in such a return. This arrangement can be seen in modern examples. The use of the reader's recess in the rule and liturgy of the nuns is explored in Chapter 7.

231 Collins, 'Unveiling Female Monasticism', pp. 130–1.

232 The refectory is an important room in any religious house. The refectory at St Catherine's would appear to be of its primary phase, without features that would suggest it ever functioned as a kitchen. A separate kitchen would have been required from the earliest phases of the nunnery. A kitchen structure would be located close to the water source and the refectory. It may be that an earlier kitchen structure existed here (perhaps in timber, though fire was always a hazard) which was then replaced with the current structure in stone.

233 A door and two unglazed slits were recorded in this wall; they are no longer visible. Westropp, 'The Conventual Buildings', p. 62. He also recorded a possible return at the southeast corner of this kitchen which he suggested was a garderobe/reredorter (toilet). Although no longer visible, I would reject this suggestion on the basis that this would place the garderobe directly upstream of the kitchen. This arrangement would have been avoided as it would have resulted in water contamination. I suggest that the garderobe was at the junction of the west and south ranges and was likely in timber.

234 Collins, 'Unveiling Female Monasticism', pp. 131–2.

235 It is suggested that Ballymacdane, Cork, Grace Dieu, Graney, Kilcreevanty, Kilculliheen, Lismullin, St Mary de Hogges, St Peter's Cell, Wicklow, and perhaps Timolin and Buttevant, did have a claustral plan for which now no trace survives. It is not known what type of accommodation was used by the Cistercian nuns for example at Plary, Derry, Inishlounaght, Mellifont or Jerpoint.

236 This assumption is based on available historical descriptions and dissolution surveys.

237 White, *Extents*, p. 255.

238 Ibid., pp. 336–7.

239 Alcock et al., *Archaeological Inventory of County Galway*, p. 315.

240 O'Brien and Sweetman, *Archaeological Inventory of County Offaly*, p. 101; Fitzpatrick and O'Brien, *Medieval Churches of County Offaly*, pp. 82–8, plate 13.

241 A 1590 inquisition describes Ardcarn nunnery as a church and two houses of stone.

242 The site of the nunnery at Killinmulrooney, Co. Roscommon was levelled through land improvement. It was upstanding in 2009 when inspected by the Archaeological Survey of Ireland. This description has been relied upon.

243 J. Fenlon, *Ormond Castle Visitor's Guide* (Dublin: Government of Ireland OPW, 2008); C. Corlett and F. O'Mahony, *Ormond Castle: Ireland's Tudor rose. Heritage Guide No. 80* (Dublin: Wordwell, 2018).

244 MacCurtain, 'Late Medieval Nunneries'. This is no longer visible due to overgrowth.

245 Another example is Killogeenaghan, recorded as the site of an unclassified castle, which appeared on the seventeenth-century Down Survey map. The townland is associated as a grange with the Nuns' Church at Clonmacnoise. It is possible that this castle was related to the nunnery's grange there; Nicholls, 'Towards a New *Monasticon Hibernicum*', p. 332.

246 The nuns' accommodation at Portrane is also described as a small dwelling which they shared with their chaplain, while celebrating the divine office in the parish church. This implies that the west tower at Portrane was not used for their accommodation at least; Rev. Moran (ed.), *Monasticon Hibernicum*, vol. II, p. 86; MacCurtain, 'Late Medieval Nunneries', p. 140.

247 White, *Extents*, pp. 163, 171.

248 Stalley, *Cistercian Monasteries*, pp. 152, 176.

249 Halpin and Newman, *Ireland*, p. 321.

250 Healy, 'Two Royal Abbeys', pp. 7–8.

251 Alcock et al., *Archaeological Inventory of County Galway*, p. 292. It is thought that this church was later used by male Premonstratensians. In this book, it is considered a nunnery church following its designation as such on the first-edition Ordnance Survey six-inch map. There are no obvious alterations, though the structure itself has been conserved as part of the National Monument complex at Annaghdown.

252 The history of the church at Tisrara is somewhat confused. The excavator concluded that the buildings themselves included a nunnery, which may have also been a hostelry, hospital and place for pilgrims; Higgins, *Tisrara Medieval Church*, p. 12. Tisrara is considered a nunnery in this book and also by Ronan, 'Irish Nunneries: Spatial dimensions and gender implications', unpublished MA thesis, University College Cork, 1997, p. 135.

253 Higgins, *Tisrara Medieval Church*, pp. 24–30.

254 Clapham, 'Priory and Manor House at Dartford', p. 78, note 1.

255 Bond, 'Medieval Nunneries in England and Wales', p. 86.

256 Burton, *Monastic and Religious Orders*, p. 106.

257 Baker and Baker, 'Research Designs'.

258 J.P. Allen, 'Devon: Polsoe Priory', *Medieval Archaeology*, vol. 23, 1979, pp. 250–1.

259 Baker and Baker, 'Research Designs', p. 265; Baker, *La Grava*.

260 J. Blair and J.M. Steane, 'Investigations at Cogges, Oxfordshire 1978–1981: The priory and parish church', *Oxoniensia*, vol. 47, 1982, pp. 37–125.

261 H. Brakspear, 'Excavations at Some Wiltshire Monasteries', *Archaeologia*, vol. 73, 1922–3, pp. 225–52.

262 Gilchrist, *Gender and Material Culture*, p. 111.

263 P.A. Rahtz and E. Greenfield, *Excavations at Chew Valley Lake, Somerset. DoE Archaeological Report No. 8* (London: Her Majesty's Stationery Office, 1977), p. 326.

264 Bond, 'Medieval Nunneries in England and Wales', p. 68.

265 Ganz, 'Godstow Nunnery'.

266 Coppack, 'How the Other Half Lived', p. 293.

267 Gilchrist, *Gender and Material Culture*, p. 124.
268 M. Reddan and A.W. Clapham, *Survey of London. Volume 9: The Parish of St Helen, Bishopsgate*, part 1 (London: London County Council, 1924).
269 P.J. Tester, 'A Plan and Architectural Description of the Medieval Remains of Davington Priory', *Archaeologia Cantiana*, vol. 95, 1980, pp. 205–12.
270 Bond, 'Medieval Nunneries in England and Wales', pp. 69–70.
271 Nyberg, 'On Female Monasticism'.
272 Jäggi and Lobbedey, 'Church and Cloister', p. 119.
273 Barrière, 'Cistercian Convent of Coyroux', p. 77; B.K. Young, 'Archaeology in an Urban Setting: Excavations at Saint-Pierre-de-Monmartre, Paris, 1975–1977', *Journal of Field Archaeology*, vol. 5, 1978, pp. 319–29; Berman, *The White Nuns*.
274 Desmarchelier, 'L'architecture des Églises de Moniales Cisterciennes'.
275 For a comprehensive catalogue of German nunneries including phased plans, see Mohn, *Mittelalterliche Klosteranlagen*.
276 Jäggi and Lobbedey, 'Church and Cloister', p. 128.
277 Signori, 'Cell or Dormitory?'
278 Jäggi and Lobbedey, 'Church and Cloister', p. 119.
279 Barrière, 'Cistercian Convent of Coyroux', pp. 76–82; Burton and Kerr, *Cistercians*, pp. 28, 52.
280 Hicks, *Religious Life in Normandy*, pp. 155, 196, 197.
281 Golding, *Gilbert of Sempringham*, pp. 7–26; Kerr, *Religious Life for Women*, pp. 15–46; Griffiths, 'The Cross and the *Cura Monialium*'; Venarde, 'Robert of Arbrissel'.
282 McNamara, *Sisters in Arms*, pp. 270, 295; Hamburger et al., 'Time of the Orders', p. 44. Four medieval nunneries in Ireland have no recorded affiliation, which may mean they were either non-affiliated or that their affiliation has been lost to history. This is not an unusual occurrence; see Freeman, 'Nuns'.
283 C.A. Bruzelius, 'Architecture, Ecclesiastical', in M. Schaus (ed.), *Women and Gender in Medieval Europe: An encyclopaedia* (London: Routledge, 2006), pp. 30–1; C.A. Bruzelius, 'Architecture, Monastic', in M. Schaus (ed.), *Women and Gender in Medieval Europe: An encyclopaedia* (London: Routledge, 2006), pp. 31–5; Garí, 'Sacred Space of Meditation'.
284 Hall, 'Necessary Collaborations', p. 23.
285 C. McNeill (ed.), *Calendar of Archbishop Alen's Register* c.*1172–1534* (Dublin: Royal Society of Antiquaries of Ireland, 1950), p. 180.
286 Collins, 'Unveiling Female Monasticism', pp. 120–2; 139–43. For hall-houses, see: McNeill, *Castles in Ireland*, p. 151; Sweetman, *Castles*, p. 89; P.D. Sweetman, 'The Hall-House in Ireland', in J.R. Kenyon and K. O'Conor (eds), *The Medieval Castle in Ireland and Wales* (Dublin: Four Courts Press, 2003), pp. 121–32; O'Keeffe, *Medieval Irish Buildings*, pp. 222–7; K. Dempsey, 'Rectangular Chamber Towers and Their Medieval Halls: A recent look at buildings formerly described as "hall houses"', *Château Gaillard*, vol. 27, 2016, pp. 113–19; K. Dempsey, 'Understanding "Hall-Houses": Debating seigneurial buildings in Ireland in the thirteenth century', *Medieval Archaeology*, vol. 61, 2017, pp. 372–99.
287 A hall house at Rathumney, County Wexford was part of a grange complex associated with the male Cistercian house at Tintern, County Wexford; Lynch, *Tintern Abbey*, pp. 192. For clasping pilasters, see T. O'Keeffe, 'Building Lordship in Thirteenth-Century Ireland: The donjon of Coonagh Castle, Co. Limerick', *Journal of the Royal Society of Antiquaries of Ireland*, vol. 141, 2011, pp. 91–127.
288 T.J. Westropp, 'A Survey of Ancient Churches in the County of Limerick', *Proceedings of the Royal Irish Academy*, vol. 25, 1904–5, pp. 327–480; T.J. Westropp, 'The Ancient

Castles of the County of Limerick, North-Eastern Baronies and Western Baronies', *Proceedings of the Royal Irish Academy*, vol. 26, 1906–7, pp. 55–108, 143–268.

289 Collins, 'An Archaeology of Augustinian Nuns'.

290 The rule was not specifically written by St Augustine but was based on his letters. It is divided into eight chapters: Purpose and basis of common life; prayer; moderation and self denial; safeguarding chastity and fraternal correction; the care of community goods and treatment of the sick; asking pardon and forgiving offences; governance and obedience; and observance of the rule. See Robinson, *Geography of Augustinian Settlement*, pp. 5–11; E.A. Matter, 'Influence of Augustine', in M. Schaus (ed.), *Women and Gender in Medieval Europe: An encyclopaedia* (London: Routledge, 2006), pp. 51–3.

291 Browne and Ó Clabaigh, *Households of God*.

292 Dunning, 'Arroasian Order', p. 308; Nicholls, 'Medieval Irish Cathedral Chapters'; O'Keeffe, *An Anglo-Norman Monastery*, p. 17; L.B. Green, 'Unveiling the Cloisters: Augustinian nunneries in twelfth-century Ireland', *History Studies, UL History Society Journal*, vol. 2, 2000, pp. 37–49; Flanagan, *Transformation*; Collins, 'The Materiality of Female Religious'.

293 Dunning, 'Arroasian Order', p. 315; Hall, *Women and the Church*, p. 67.

294 Hall, *Women and the Church*, pp. 161–3.

295 Flanagan, *Transformation*, p. 152. The Arroasian constitutions were consulted in this regard and nothing specific was noted. See L. Milis (ed.), *Constitvtiones Canonicorvm Regvlarivm Ordinis Arroasiensis* (Turnhout: Brepols, 1970).

296 Flanagan, *Transformation*; Bhreathnach, 'The *Vita Apostolica*'.

297 Carville, *Occupation of Celtic Sites*. Site re-use has been noted elsewhere: see Stöber and Austin, 'Culdees to Canons', pp. 40–1; Abram, 'Augustinian Canons and the Survival of Cult Centres'.

298 For Ireland: O'Keeffe, *An Anglo-Norman Monastery*; O'Keeffe, 'Augustinian Regular Canons'; O'Keeffe, *Medieval Irish Buildings*, pp. 103–4, 147–80; Browne and Ó Clabaigh, *Households of God*. For Britain: Knowles, *Religious Orders in England*, vol. 1, pp. 28–31; Robinson, *Geography of Augustinian Settlement*, part 1, pp. 22–73; D.M. Robinson, 'The Augustinian Canons in England and Wales: Architecture, archaeology and liturgy 1100–1540', *Monastic Research Bulletin*, vol. 18, 2012, pp. 2–29, at pp. 11–25; Coppack, 'Thornholme Priory'; Coppack, *Abbeys and Priories*, p. 12; K. Stöber, 'The Regular Canons in Wales', in J. Burton and K. Stöber (eds), *The Regular Canons in the Medieval British Isles* (Turnout: Brepols, 2011), pp. 97–114; Stöber and Austin, 'Culdees to Canons', pp. 41–6.

299 Robinson, 'Augustinian Canons', pp. 25–8.

300 O'Keeffe, 'Augustinian Regular Canons', p. 479.

301 O'Keeffe, *An Anglo-Norman Monastery*, p. 12.

302 Collins, 'An Archaeology of Augustinian Nuns'.

303 O'Keeffe, 'Augustinian Regular Canons', p. 483. For the Romanesque and Augustinian sites specifically: O'Keeffe, *Romanesque Ireland*. See also: C. Ó Clabaigh, 'Monasticism, Colonization, and Ethnic Tension in Late Medieval Ireland', in A.I. Beach and I. Cochelin (eds), *Medieval Monasticism in the Latin West*, 2 vols (Cambridge: Cambridge University Press, 2020), pp. 901–21.

304 Golding, *Gilbert of Sempringham*, pp. 71–101; Burton, *Monastic and Religious Orders*, pp. 100–8; Gilchrist, *Gender and Material Culture*, pp. 39–41, 61.

305 Bond, Medieval Nunneries in England and Wales', p. 86.

306 Gilchrist, *Contemplation and Action*, pp. 151–5; Bruzelius, 'Architecture, Monastic', pp. 32–3; Burton and Stöber, *Women in the Medieval Monastic World*.

CHAPTER 6. CHURCH FORM AND RITUAL PRACTICE

1 Coppack, *Abbeys and Priories*, p. 37.
2 Hayes, *Body and Sacred Place*, pp. 11–17. While the church was the centre of the consecration rite, other parts of the complex could also be consecrated to facilitate burial. At Adare Friary, Co. Limerick, consecrated in 1466, consecration included the whole circuit of the cloisters, inside and outside, both sacristies and the cemetery, excepting a portion set aside for those who died without the right to a Christian burial; see C. Ó Clabaigh, 'Patronage, Prestige and Politics: The Observant Franciscans at Adare', in J. Burton and K. Stöber (eds), *Monasteries and Society in the British Isles in the Later Middle Ages* (Woodbridge: Boydell, 2008), pp. 71–82, at p. 76.
3 The significance of the consecration ritual at Adare is heightened as it is accompanied by rare archaeological evidence – three consecration crosses are still visible in the nave. I am grateful to Dr Ó Clabaigh OSB for showing these to me. For detail of the concentration ceremony, see C. Manning, 'Consecration Crosses at Castlemartyr', *Archaeology Ireland*, vol. 27, 2013, pp. 40–2.
4 Ardcarn, Graney and Taghmon have low register earthworks, which are not interpreted as churches and cannot be accurately measured. A stretch of wall at Derrane cannot now be confirmed as a church. The nunnery at Skreen remains unlocated. Kildare and Downpatrick are cathedral churches and are unlikely to represent the nunnery churches.
5 Tisrara has been described as a nave and chancel church although 'there is no division between nave and chancel'; Higgins, *Tisrara Medieval Church*, p. 21.
6 Kelly's description of Kilcreevanty's church in 1901 as T-shaped suggested that it had transepts, although this cannot now be confirmed; R.J. Kelly, 'Notes on the Round Tower at Kilbannon and on Kilcreevanty, County Galway', *Journal of the Royal Society of Antiquaries of Ireland*, vol. 31, 1901, pp. 379–84, at pp. 381–2. In 1988 it was described as having a rectangular area to the south of the church which was interpreted as the cloister. Wall footings could be seen which contained door and window opes interpreted as being consistent with ranges. The platforms were described as being the foundations of part of a domestic range; O. Alcock et al., *Archaeological Inventory of County Galway*, p. 315.
7 Alcock et al., *Archaeological Inventory of County Galway*, pp. 292–3.
8 Hamlin, *Archaeology of Early Christianity*, pp. 60, 239.
9 Alcock et al., *Archaeological Inventory of County Galway*, p. 315.
10 Higgins, *Tisrara Medieval Church*, pp. 73–4.
11 The bellcote at Killone is for a single bell and was placed over the apex of the gabled roof. Molough has a double bellcote and seems to have been set under the apex of the gabled roof. This feature shows the influence of the earls of Ormond (the Butlers) who founded this nunnery in the fourteenth century as this architectural feature is noted in areas of their influence like Adare, Co. Limerick (Dr Ó Clabaigh OSB, personal communication). The bellcote at St Catherine's is not currently visible. Westropp remarked that 'the west gable [of the church] is capped with a bell-chamber, I believe of one arch, but too thickly ivied to be clearly seen (even at the time of my visit in 1875)': Westropp 'The Conventual Buildings', p. 58.
12 Corneville is interesting as the bishop instructed the canons to create a partition in the bell tower so that both religious community and parish could ring their bells and avoid undue contact; Hicks, *Religious Life in Normandy*, pp. 154, 171.
13 G. Webb, *Architecture in Britain: The middle ages*, 2nd edn (Middlesex: Penguin, 1965), pp. 82, 120–1; Stalley, *Early Medieval Architecture*, pp. 116–19; O'Keeffe, *Medieval Irish Buildings*, pp. 89–93.

14 Ó Carragáin, *Churches in Early Medieval Ireland*, pp. 111–12.
15 Clyne, *Kells Priory*, pp. 487–90.
16 Stalley, *The Cistercian Monasteries*, pp. 68–75.
17 O'Keeffe, *An Anglo-Norman Monastery*, pp. 102–5; A.J. Lafaye, 'Kilmallock Borough and Dominican Priory: Planning, patronage and urban life in medieval Ireland', in M.A. Bevivino, E. Bhreathnach and L. Shine (eds), *A Research Miscellany* (Discovery Programme Reports, 9) (Dublin: The Discovery Programme, 2018), pp. 67–90, at p. 78.
18 Ó Carragáin, *Churches in Early Medieval Ireland*, pp. 110–13, 230; Stalley, *Cistercian Monasteries of Ireland*, p. 68.
19 Stalley, *Early Medieval Architecture*, p. 119; G. Bandmann, *Early Medieval Architecture: As bearer of meaning*, trans. K. Wallis (New York: Columbia University Press, 2005).
20 This section discusses better-preserved features. Those that only have remaining opes without dressed stone, or have been heavily conserved and re-built, have not been included. For full descriptions, see online nunnery catalogue at DOI: http://doi.org/10.5281/zenodo.5035404.
21 This doorway was in fragments when described at the beginning of the twentieth century: Westropp, 'Augustinian Houses', p. 131. It has since been reconstructed. From the fragments it appears to be of fifteenth-century date with quatrefoils in its cavetto mouldings.
22 Westropp, 'The Conventual Buildings', p. 58.
23 A local legend was attached to the hag's head, that those who visited and kissed the face would have good luck. Westropp also recorded a mason's mark on the door's northern side and its eastern face, near the capital. He described it as a letter A. This mark is no longer visible. Westropp, 'The Conventual Buildings', p. 58.
24 The insertion of this doorway is peculiar. The masons blocked a window immediately to the east of where the doorway was inserted but made no effort to re-use the window. In Westropp's time the door was intact. Westropp, 'The Conventual Buildings', p. 57.
25 This doorway is a very small example. It is known from excavation in the church that the original ground surface is *c.*0.10m lower than at present. This suggests that the doorway is only 1.2m in maximum height and only 0.50m in width. This is clearly an insertion, as is the space it accesses. Westropp suggests this was a sacristy. While this function is possible, the door is very small for this function. Having a sacristy at the west end of the church is also unusual.
26 Westropp, 'The Conventual Buildings', p. 55. The drawing of this doorway by Westropp corresponds to one now used as a gateway nearby.
27 The exterior of this wall cannot be examined at present due to vegetation and cement render. The west end of Molough Church and the adjoining wall of its west range was used as a handball alley. The southeast corner of St Catherine's cloister was also used as a handball alley in the nineteenth century.
28 This doorway was described in 1840 as being scattered on the ground. Externally it has a wide semi-circular arch with an outer cavetto and two inner roll mouldings. The doorway is predominantly limestone, though has three jamb stones that are sandstone, which show evidence of weathering. The inner face of the door has a flat arch above of sandstone and limestone voussoirs, which relates to its reconstruction. Another relieving arch is noted higher above the doorway, although it is likely that much of this wall has been re-built. The dating of this door is difficult. Its limestone fabric would suggest a fifteenth-century date, though it does maintain three sandstone jambs. The fact that it is an insertion also points to this later date. However, as the date of the founding of the nunnery is the fourteenth century, it is possible that the door dates

to sometime in the latter half of that period. An earlier west door was present in the church and it is possible that the door in question could have been moved from its original location in the west wall.

29 This is relatively large and elaborate for a mason's mark, but there is a similar (but not the same) large mason's mark at the Augustinian male house at Cahir Abbey, Co. Tipperary.

30 Hamlin, *Archaeology of Early Christianity*, p. 239.

31 Kalkreuter, *Boyle Abbey*; O'Keeffe, *Romanesque Ireland*; T. O'Keeffe, 'Built Environment of Local Community Worship', p. 142; O'Keeffe, *Medieval Irish Buildings*, p. 37.

32 Westropp compared the lozenge band to that at Killaloe Cathedral dated to 1182. He noted that the glazing bar holes are in an unusual position, being placed along a flat edge and not in the reveal or a channel as is more common; Westropp, 'Augustinian Houses', p. 131. O'Keeffe has noted while the windows would fit with the 'School of the West', the intramural passage which runs through that window has trefoil-headed openings, which are considered considerably later, well into the thirteenth century; O'Keeffe, *Romanesque Ireland*, p. 118.

33 Westropp, 'The Conventual Buildings', p. 55. He further noted that the window embrasure of the east window and that of a window in the south wall of the church both showed evidence for plank centring, though this is no longer extant and cannot be confirmed. Plank centring is usually indicative of a thirteenth-century date; see O'Keeffe, *Irish Medieval Buildings*, p. 82.

34 Higgins, *Tisrara Medieval Church*, pp. 17–18.

35 Hayes, *Body and Sacred Place*, pp. 17–23.

36 At Killone, the church itself is higher than its southern cloister, due to a natural slope. There are four steps up from the cloister to the church's nave. The church's south wall is not extant and the north wall has been substantially re-built.

37 For examples elsewhere, see Hayes, *Body and Sacred Place*, p. 19.

38 Freeman, 'Nuns', p. 103; B. Garí, 'The Sacred Space of Meditation', p. 75.

39 Coppack, *Abbeys and Priories*, pp. 72–4.

40 Collins, 'Unveiling Female Monasticism'.

41 Desmarchelier, 'L'architecture des Églises de Moniales Cisterciennes', p. 80–1.

42 C. Mohn, *Mittelalterliche Klosteranlagen der Zisterzienserinnen*, p. 28.

43 Johnson, *Equal in Monastic Profession*, pp. 225–6.

44 For example, Berman, 'Medieval Monasticisms', p. 378. See also Berman, *The Cistercian Evolution*.

45 Scott, 'Romsey Abbey', p. 156; For Germany, see Mohn, *Mittelalterliche Klosteranlagen der Zisterzienserinnen*, p. 109; For France, see Desmarchlier, 'L'architecture des Églises de Moniales Cisterciennes', pp. 97, 101.

46 J.H. Martin, 'Ordination of Women as Priests', in M. Schaus (ed.), *Women and Gender in Medieval Europe: An encyclopedia* (London: Routledge, 2006), pp. 624–6. Some studies have suggested that in the early church some women may have been ordained; for example, K. Torjesen, *When Women Were Priests* (New York: Harper Collins, 1995); K. Madigan and C. Osiek (eds), *Ordained Women in the Early Church* (Baltimore: The Johns Hopkins University Press, 2005); Macy, 'Heloise, Abelard and the Ordination of Abbesses'; G. Macy, *The Hidden History of Women's Ordination: Female clergy in the medieval West* (Oxford: Oxford University Press, 2008). There is no concrete evidence that women were ordained in medieval Ireland, though some have suggested that St Brigid was, though Ó Riain describes her as 'a bishop in all but name'; Ó Riain, *A Dictionary*, p. 124. For a recent comprehensive study of Brigid in all her facets, see Kissane, *Saint Brigid of Kildare*; Callan, *Sacred Sisters*, pp. 85–112.

47 Johnson, *Equal in Monastic Profession*, pp. 225–6.
48 Berman, 'Medieval Monasticisms', p. 378; Berman, *The White Nuns*.
49 Bruzelius, 'Hearing Is Believing'.
50 Garí, 'The Sacred Space of Meditation', pp. 76–7.
51 Those times commencing at daybreak but without strictly set times, were: Matins (also called Vigil, during night), Lauds (dawn prayer), Prime (early morning), Terce (mid-morning), Sext (midday), Nones (mid-afternoon prayer), Vespers (evening prayer), and Compline (night prayer). See Kerr, *Life in the Medieval Cloister*, pp. 151–2.
52 For example, Grace Dieu, Clonard, Odder and Termonfeckin; White, *Extents*, pp. 77, 235, 262; Hall, *Women and the Church*, p. 131.
53 Kerr, *Life in the Medieval Cloister*, pp. 86–7.
54 O'Keeffe, 'The Built Environment of Local Community Worship', p. 145.
55 J.P. McAleer, 'The Tradition of Detached Bell Towers at Cathedrals and Monastic Churches in Medieval England and Scotland 1066–1539', *Journal of the British Archaeological Association*, vol. 154, 2002, pp. 54–85, at pp. 66–7.
56 Garí, 'The Sacred Space of Meditation', p. 88.
57 C.P. Graves, 'Sensing and Believing: Exploring worlds of difference in pre-modern England. A contribution to the debate opened by Kate Giles', *World Archaeology*, vol. 39, 2007, pp. 515–31, at p. 527.
58 Ó Carragáin, *Churches in Early Medieval Ireland*, p. 165.
59 White, *Extents*, pp. 75, 77, 203, 206, 260, 262.
60 Ibid., p. 336.
61 Ibid., pp. 235, 260.
62 Domestic accommodation attached to churches or perhaps free-standing from the church structure is usually interpreted as priests' accommodation. See Westropp, 'The Augustinian Houses', pp. 128–9; H. Bermingham, 'Priests' Residences in Later Medieval Ireland', in E. FitzPatrick and R. Gillespie (eds), *The Parish in Medieval and Early Modern Ireland: Community, territory and building* (Dublin: Four Courts Press, 2006), pp. 168–85. Where churches are associated with nuns, this could represent priests' accommodation or equally feasible is that the accommodation was used by a small female religious community themselves, especially if their numbers were small or they required separate quarters for the abbess.
63 Potterton, *Medieval Trim*, pp. 298–9.
64 Gilchrist, *Gender and Material Culture*, pp. 159–60.
65 Westropp, 'The Conventual Buildings'; but see further below and Collins, 'Unveiling Female Monasticism' for an alternative interpretation of this feature.
66 Bruzelius, 'Hearing Is Believing'; K. Giles, 'Seeing and Believing: Visuality and space in pre-modern England', *World Archaeology*, vol. 39, 2007, pp. 105–21, at p. 115.
67 Graves, 'Sensing and Believing', p. 520.
68 C. Grössinger, 'At the Uttermost Ends of the Earth', in R. Stalley (ed.), *Limerick and South-West Ireland: Medieval art and architecture* (Leeds: Maney, for the British Archaeological Association, 2011), pp. 243–52; J. Cherry, 'The Misericords in St Mary's Cathedral, Limerick: An additional note', in R. Stalley (ed.), *Limerick and South-West Ireland: Medieval art and architecture* (Leeds: Maney, for the British Archaeological Association, 2011), pp. 253–8.
69 P. Dirsztay (ed.), *Church Furnishings* (London: Routledge & Keegan Paul, 1978), p. 229.
70 Collins, 'Unveiling Female Monasticism', pp. 122–4.
71 Higgins, *Tisrara Medieval Church*, p. 19.
72 J. Bradley, A. Halpin and H. King, 'Urban Archaeology Survey for County Westmeath' (Dublin: OPW unpublished report, 1985), p. 69. These piscinas are no longer visible.

73 White, *Extents*, p. 206.

74 FitzPatrick and Gillespie, *The Parish*; Gilchrist, *Medieval Life*, pp. 169–81; K. French, *The People of the Parish: Community life in a late medieval English diocese* (Philadelphia: University of Pennsylvania Press, 2000); Moss, 'Irish Parish Churches'.

75 A. Empey, 'The Layperson in the Parish: The medieval inheritance 1169–1536', in R. Gillespie and W.G. Neely (eds), *The Laity and the Church of Ireland 1000–2000: All sorts and conditions* (Dublin: Four Courts Press, 2002), pp. 7–48, at p. 13. See also P.S. Barnwell, 'The Laity, the Clergy, and the Divine Presence: The use of space in smaller churches of the eleventh and twelfth centuries', *Journal of the British Archaeological Association*, vol. 157, 2004, pp. 41–60; P.S. Barnwell, 'The Universal Church in the Local Community: English parochial churches, *c.*1130–1350', in P.S. Barnwell (ed.), *Places of Worship in Britain and Ireland, 1150–1350* (Donington: Shaun Tyas, 2018), pp. 188–213.

76 Flanagan, *Transformation*, pp. 206–9.

77 T. Ó Carragáin, 'Archaeology of Early Medieval Baptism at St Mullin's, Co. Carlow', *Peritia*, vol. 21, 2010, pp. 285–302.

78 Fleming, *Gille of Limerick*, pp. 154–5, 160–1.

79 E. FitzPatrick, 'The Material World of the Parish', in E. FitzPatrick and R. Gillespie (eds), *The Parish in Medieval and Early Modern Ireland: Community, territory and building* (Dublin: Four Courts Press, 2006), pp. 62–78, at p. 63.

80 O'Keeffe, 'The Built Environment of Local Community Worship', p. 127.

81 FitzPatrick, 'The Material World', p. 70.

82 For example, M. O'Neill, 'The Medieval Parish Churches of County Meath', *Journal of the Royal Society of Antiquaries of Ireland*, vol. 132, 2002, pp. 1–56.

83 Empey, 'The Layperson in the Parish', p. 12.

84 FitzPatrick 'The Material World', p. 72.

85 Gilchrist, *Gender and Material Culture*, p. 124.

86 Scott, 'Romsey Abbey'.

87 Ganz, 'Godstow Nunnery', pp. 150–7.

88 P.G. Stone, *An Exact Account of the Church and Priory at Goring in the County of Oxford* (Goring: Henry L. Smith, 1893).

89 Sloane, *Augustinian Nunnery of St Mary Clerkenwell.*

90 St John Hope, 'Ground Plan of Watton', pp. 1–34.

91 Gilchrist, *Gender and Material Culture*, p. 94; D.A. Bussell and J.M. McNamara, 'Barking Abbey: A GIS map of a medieval nunnery', *Peregrinations Journal of Medieval Art and Architecture*, vol. 4, 2013, pp. 173–89, at p. 177.

92 Mohn, *Mittelalterliche Klosteranlagen der Zisterzienserinnen*, pp. 33–5.

93 Lee, *Nunneries, Learning and Spirituality*, p. 101.

94 Oliva, *Convent and the Community*, p. 154.

95 Flanagan, *Transformation*, pp. 243–8; P. MacCotter, 'The Origins of the Parish in Ireland', *Proceedings of the Royal Irish Academy*, vol. 119C, 2019, pp. 37–67.

96 For example, the Poor Clare nunnery of Santa Chiara in Naples; C.A. Bruzelius, *Le Pietre di Napoli: L'architectura Religiosa Nell'Italia Angioina, 1266–1342* (Rome: Viella, 2005), pp. 140–75.

97 Garí, 'The Sacred Space of Meditation', p. 77; Untermann, 'The Place of the Choir'.

98 Mohn, *Mittelalterliche Klosteranlagen der Zisterzienserinnen.*

99 Untermann, 'The Place of the Choir', p. 348.

100 Mohn, *Mittelalterliche Klosteranlagen der Zisterzienserinnen*, pp. 22–35.

101 French, 'The Seat under Our Lady'; Schleif, 'Men on the Right, Women on the Left'.

102 Aston, 'Segregation in Church'; French, 'The Seat under Our Lady', p 141; French, *Good Women of the Parish.*

103 Gilchrist, *Gender and Material Culture*, p. 124. Various arrangements are recorded: see, for example, Reddan and Clapham, *Survey of London*, vol. 9, pp. 31–5; Golding, *Gilbert of Sempringham*, pp. 129–32; L.E. Webster and J. Cherry, 'Medieval Britain in 1978', *Medieval Archaeology*, vol. 23, 1979, pp. 234–78, at pp. 250–1; Sloane, *Augustinian Nunnery of St Mary Clerkenwell*, pp. 34–6, 103.

104 Gilchrist, *Gender and Material Culture*, pp. 96, 108. St Radegund's, Cambridge; Lacock, Wiltshire; Aconbury, Herfordshire; and Marrick, Yorkshire all used various types of galleries to segregate the nuns. T. Dinham Atkinson, *Cambridge Described and Illustrated* (London: Macmillan & Co., 1897); L.F. Salzman (ed.), *A History of the County of Cambridge and the Isle of Ely*, vol. 2 (London: Victoria County History, 1948), pp. 218–19; H. Brakspear, 'Lacock Abbey, Wiltshire', *Archaeologia*, vol. 57, 1900, pp. 125–58, at pp. 132–5; J.H. Tillotson, *Marrick Priory: A nunnery in late medieval Yorkshire* (York: Borthwick Institute, University of York, 1989).

105 Sloane, *Augustinian Nunnery of St Mary Clerkenwell*, pp. 101–3.

106 C. Tabraham (ed.), *Iona Abbey and Nunnery* (Edinburgh: Historic Scotland, 2004), pp. 26–7.

107 For example, J.M. Jeep, 'Wienhausen', in J.M. Jeep (ed.), *Medieval Germany: An encyclopedia* (London: Routledge, 2001), pp. 812–13; J.L. Mecham, 'A Northern Jerusalem: Transforming the spatial geography of the convent of Wienhausen', in S. Hamilton and A. Spicier (eds), *Defining the Holy: Sacred space in medieval and early modern Europe* (Aldershot: Ashgate, 2005), pp. 139–60; Coester, *Die Einschiffigen Cistercienserinnenkloster*, p. 275; Mohn, *Mittelalterliche Klosteranlagen der Zisterzienserinnen*; Untermann, 'The Place of the Choir'; Jäggi, 'Eastern Choir or Western Gallery?', p. 82; Scheepsma, *Medieval Religious Women in the Low Countries*, pp. 52–3; H.K. Kristensen, *Middelalderbyen Viborg*, vol. 4 (Denmark: Centrum, 1987), p. 127; R. Gilyard-Beer, *Abbeys: An introduction to the religious houses of England and Wales* (London: Her Majesty's Stationery Office, 1959), p. 44; T. Nyberg, 'On Female Monasticism', p. 190; Wessex Archaeology, 'Syon House, Syon Park, Hounslow: An archaeological evaluation of a Birgittine abbey and an assessment of the results. Ref: 52568.05' (Salisbury: unpublished report, 2003); Desmarchelier, 'L'architecture des Églises de Moniales', pp. 81–6; Dimier, 'L'architecture des Églises de Moniales Cisterciennes', pp. 8–13.

108 M. Rubin, *Corpus Christi: The Eucharist in late medieval culture* (Cambridge: Cambridge University Press, 1991), p. 55; Garí, 'The Sacred Space of Meditation', p. 78.

109 Jäggi and Lobbedey, 'Church and Cloister', p. 121.

110 Kalkreuter, *Boyle Abbey*, p. 73.

111 See Moss, 'Irish Parish Churches'.

112 Gilchrist, *Gender and Material Culture*, p. 99. For background, see J. Harper, 'The Space Enriched: Liturgy, ritual and music, 1150–1350', in P. Barnwell (ed.), *Places of Worship in Britain and Ireland, 1150–1350* (Donington: Shaun Tyas, 2018), pp. 10–23. Books of Augustinian use are known from the nunneries of Campsey, Harrold, and Lacock in England, and Iona in Scotland.

113 Platt, *Parish Churches of Medieval England*, pp. 13–47; O'Keeffe, 'The Built Environment of Local Community Worship', p. 130; Barnwell, 'The Laity, the Clergy and the Divine Presence', pp. 51–2.

114 O'Keeffe, 'The Built Environment of Local Community Worship', p. 136.

115 Ibid., pp. 139–41.

116 Hayes, *Body and Sacred Space*, pp. 19, 53–69.

117 Gilchrist, *Gender and Material Culture*, pp. 123–7; Gilchrist, *Contemplation and Action*, pp. 151–5.

118 O'Keeffe, 'The Built Environment of Local Community Worship', p. 145.

119 C.P. Graves, *The Form and Fabric of Belief: An archaeology of the lay experience of religion in medieval Norfolk and Devon. BAR British Series 311* (Oxford: John & Erica Hedges Ltd, 2000), pp. 157, 161.

120 E. Duffy, *The Stripping of the Altars: Traditional religion in England 1400–1580* (New Haven: Yale University Press, 1992); R. Marks, *Image and Devotion in Late Medieval England* (Phoenix Mill: Sutton, 2004).

121 Clapham, 'Priory and Manor House of Dartford', pp. 75, 77–8.

122 Mohn, *Mittelalterliche Klosteranlagen der Zisterzienserinnen*, pp. 277, 360, 430.

123 Jäggi and Lobbedey, 'Church and Cloister', p. 120.

124 Graves, *The Form and Fabric of Belief*; Graves, 'Sensing and Believing'; Giles, 'Seeing and Believing'; Gilchrist, 'Magic for the Dead?'; Gilchrist, *Medieval Life*, pp. 169–75.

125 Westropp, 'The Conventual Buildings', pp. 55–6.

126 Ibid., p. 56.

127 Collins, 'Unveiling Female Monasticism', pp. 122–39, 151–4.

128 Only the outer frame of this window is now visible.

129 It has also been suggested that buttresses, a stretch of wall base batter at the eastern end of the north wall, along with some re-building of the east wall itself, was undertaken at this time. While it is possible that these features were added in the fifteenth century, modern inspection does not clearly establish that they are later additions and I suggest that they are original, dating to the thirteenth century.

130 The insertion of this feature is dependent on Westropp's account as it is no longer visible.

131 Westropp, 'The Conventual Buildings'.

132 Graves, *The Form and Fabric of Belief*, p. 151.

133 The ship is described and its significance discussed in Chapter 7, Figure 7.51.

134 T. Collins, 'Missing the Boat ...', *Archaeology Ireland*, vol. 24, 2010, pp. 9–11.

135 Stalley, *Cistercian Monasteries*, p. 199; Ó Clabaigh, *The Friars in Ireland*, pp. 244–5. There is no modern publication on later medieval altars in Ireland to date. Altars dating to the Romanesque period (*c.* 1050–1200) have been most recently discussed; G. Murray, 'Altars in Ireland 1050–1200: A survey', *Journal of Irish Archaeology*, vol. XIX, 2010, pp. 101–12.

136 A piscina might be expected to be associated with an altar as a drain for the ablutions or rinsing of the chalice. However, since the fourteenth century ablutions were consumed by the priest and so a piscina would not be required in the fifteenth century; see L.E. Jones, *Old English Churches* (London: Frederick Warne & Co., 1969), p. 160.

137 M. Gardiner, 'Graffiti and Their Use in Late Medieval England', in J. Klapste and P. Sommer (eds), *Arts and Crafts in Medieval Rural Environment (Ruralia VI)* (Prague: Institute of Archaeology, 2007), pp. 265–76, at pp. 267–8.

138 Barrière, 'Cistercian Convent of Coyroux', p. 80. Ronan was the first to identify the painted plaster at Molough; see 'Irish Nunneries,' pp. 53–6.

139 Jones, *Old English Churches*, p. 157; Barnwell, 'The Universal Church in the Local Community', pp. 208–9.

140 Ó Clabaigh, 'Anchorites', p. 158.

141 A. Mulder-Bakker, *Lives of the Anchoresses: The rise of the urban recluse in medieval Europe* (Philadelphia: University of Pennsylvania Press, 2005); L. Herbert McAvoy (ed.), *Anchoritic Traditions of Medieval Europe* (Woodbridge: Boydell, 2010).

142 R. Gilchrist, 'Unsexing the Body: The interior sexuality of medieval religious women', in R.A. Schmidt and B.L. Voss (eds), *Archaeologies of Sexuality* (London:

Routledge, 2000), pp. 89–103, at p. 90. I have used the term anchorite to denote a religious person living in seclusion, whether male or female.

143 White, *Extents*, p. 8.

144 Hall, *Women and the Church*, p. 187. Hall notes that this is a reference from a manuscript in the British Library: Egerton MS 1774, f.152 (M. Archdall *Monasticon Hibernicon* with notes by M. Mason). Moran's *Monasticon Hibernicum* does not make reference to the anchorite.

145 Masterson, *Medieval Fore*, p. 11.

146 Ó Clabaigh, 'Anchorites', p. 162.

147 Clay, *Hermits and Anchorites*, p. 76.

148 Mulder-Bakker, *Lives of the Anchoresses*, pp. 1–2.

149 Ó Clabaigh, *The Friars in Ireland*, p. 199.

150 Clyne, 'Archaeological Excavations at Holy Trinity Abbey'.

151 Ó Clabaigh, 'Anchorites', p. 155.

152 Collins, 'Unveiling Female Monasticism', pp. 132–8, 151–4.

153 Clay, *Hermits and Anchorites*; A.K. Warren, *Anchorites and Their Patrons in Medieval England* (Berkeley: University of California Press, 1985). For a list of anchorholds in England, which are also called hermitages, anchorites' cells, or anchorages, see: http://www.pastscape.org.uk/SearchResults.aspx?a=0&type=ANCHORITE%20 CELL&class1=11&period=1066|1540|MEDIEVAL|26|0&county=None&parish=None &district=None&place=&rational=a&rtype=&rnumber=&yearfrom=1066&yearto= 1540&recordsperpage=10&source=text&sort=2&p=1&nor=25&recfc=0&move=n. Accessed 15 September 2020.

154 D. Knowles and R.N. Hadcock, *Medieval Religious Houses of England and Wales* (London: Longman, 1971), pp. 259, 276.

155 In the Republic of Ireland, these features are generally classified as hermitages, of which there are seventeen examples, mostly related to early medieval saints. None is associated with a religious house, http://webgis.archaeology.ie/historicenvironment/. Accessed 15 September 2020.

156 Clay, *Hermits and Anchorites*, p. 83.

157 Gilchrist, 'Unsexing the Body', p. 95.

158 B. Millett, *Ancrene Wisse / Guide for Anchoresses: A translation* (Exeter: Exeter University Press, 2009); B. Millett, 'The Origins of the *Ancrene Wisse*: New answers, new questions', *Medium Aevum*, vol. 61, 1992, pp. 206–28; B. Millett, '*Ancrene Wisse* and the Life of Perfection', *Leeds Studies in English*, vol. 33, 2002, pp. 53–76; B. Millett, 'Can There Be Such a Thing as an Anchoritic Rule?', in C. Innes-Parker and N. Kukita Yoshokawa (eds), *Anchoritism in the Middle Ages: Texts and traditions* (Cardiff: University of Wales Press, 2013), pp. 11–30. It has been recently postulated that this manual was written in the thirteenth century at the Augustinian house of Haughmond Abbey, Shropshire, England; see J. West and N. Palmer, *Haughmond Abbey: Excavation of a twelfth-century cloister in its historical and landscape context* (London: Historic England, 2014).

159 For example, C. Roman, 'Anchoritism and the Everyday: The sacred-domestic discourse in the *Ancrene Wisse*', *Florilegium*, vol. 23, no. 2, 2006, pp. 99–122. For a case study of a female anchorite, see M. Rubin, 'An English Anchorite: The making, unmaking and remaking of Christine Carpenter', in R. Horrox and S. Rees Jones (eds), *Pragmatic Utopias: Ideas and communities 1200–1630* (Cambridge: Cambridge University Press, 2011), pp. 204–23.

160 Gilchrist, *Gender and Material Culture*, p. 179.

161 Westropp made a detailed record; Westropp, 'The Conventual Buildings', p. 59.
162 Clay, *Hermits and Anchorites*, pp. 79, 138.
163 Ibid., p. 73.
164 Ibid., p. 113.
165 Roman, 'Anchoritism and the Everyday', p. 102.
166 Gilchrist, 'Unsexing the Body', p. 94.
167 Empey, 'The Layperson in the Parish', p. 13.
168 Walker Bynum, *Holy Feast and Holy Fast*; Rubin, *Corpus Christi*.

CHAPTER 7. DAILY LIFE AND IDENTITY FORMATION

1 For an overview, see T. Collins, 'Space and Place: Archaeologies of monasticism in later medieval Ireland', in V. Blud, D. Heath and E. Klafter (eds), *Gender in Medieval Places, Spaces and Thresholds* (London: University of London Institute of Historical Research, 2019), pp. 25–44.
2 Kenny, *Anglo-Irish and Gaelic Women*, p. 169.
3 Power, *Medieval English Nunneries*, pp. 25–41.
4 Johnson, *Equal in Monastic Profession*, p. 229.
5 The term 'bride of Christ' is multi-faceted. In the first instance it relates to the church as bride to Christ, a biblical metaphor from St John (21:9–10). This was coupled in the middle ages with the love song in the Song of Songs between the bride and her groom. Second, 'bride of Christ' could relate to Mary as a heavenly bride and representative of the church. Third, nuns were also referred to as brides of Christ, as a variation of a sacred marriage found in other religions, and the phrase 'bride of Christ' was used in their consecration liturgy. See U. Wiethaus, 'Bride of Christ Imagery', in M. Schaus (ed.), *Women and Gender in Medieval Europe: An encyclopedia* (London: Routledge, 2006), pp. 94–5. For background, see C. Walker Bynum, *Jesus as Mother: Studies in the spirituality of the high middle ages* (Berkeley: University of California Press, 1982).
6 Hicks, *Religious Life in Normandy*, pp. 127–52.
7 Röckelein, 'Founders, Donors and Saints', p. 212.
8 De Paermentier, 'Experiencing Space'.
9 For an interesting view of monastic stability, see R. Irvine, 'The Architecture of Stability: Monasteries and the importance of place in a world of non-places', *Etnofoor*, vol. 23, no. 1, 2011, pp. 29–49.
10 De Paermentier, 'Experiencing Space', p. 55.
11 For example, Ó Dalaigh, 'Mistress, Mother and Abbess'; Hall, *Women and the Church*, pp. 176–90; Signori, 'Wanderers Between Worlds'; Schleif and Schier, *Katerina's Windows*.
12 For example, Schleif and Schier, *Katerina's Windows*.
13 N. Bradley Warren, 'The Ritual for the Ordination of Nuns', in M. Rubin (ed.), *Medieval Christianity in Practice* (Princeton: Princeton University Press, 2009), pp. 318–23; J. Hotchin, 'Emotions and the Ritual of a Nun's Coronation in Late Medieval Germany', in M.L. Bailey and K. Barclay (eds), *Emotion, Ritual and Power in Europe, 1200–1920: Family, state and church* (New York: Palgrave Macmillan, 2017), pp. 171–92.
14 D. Rives, 'Taking the Veil: Clothing and the transformation of identity (trans. by C.E. Harrison)', *Proceedings of the Western Society for French History*, vol. 33, 2005, pp. 465–86, at p. 465.
15 There are examples of medieval nuns' finger rings from England, for example St Cross nunnery, Somerset and Holywell Priory, London. See Gilchrist, *Gender and Material Culture*, p. 185; Bull, et al., *Holywell Priory*, p. 121. There are no known examples of

medieval finger rings associated with nuns from Ireland as yet, but there is a post-medieval example, see Figure 7.1.

16 Hicks, *Religious Life in Normandy*, pp. 29–30.
17 Muschiol, 'Time and Space', pp. 196–7; C. Walker Bynum, 'Foreword', in J. Hamburger and S. Marti (eds), *Crown and Veil: Female monasticism from the fifth to the fifteenth centuries* (New York: Columbia University Press, 2008), pp. xiii–xviii, at p. xiii.
18 Gilchrist, 'Unsexing the Body', p. 91.
19 D. Watt, 'Introduction', in D. Watt (ed.), *Medieval Women in Their Communities* (Cardiff: University of Wales Press, 1997), pp. 1–19, at pp. 2–4.
20 Curran, 'Religious Women', p. 1.
21 Watt, 'Introduction', p. 16.
22 Hall, *Women and the Church*, pp. 69–70.
23 Thompson, *Women Religious*; Gilchrist, *Gender and Material Culture*; Oliva, *Convent and the Community*; Hall, *Women and the Church*; Curran, 'Religious Women', pp. 104–73; Stöber, *Late Medieval Monasteries*; Cartwright, *Feminine Sanctity*; K. Perkins-Curran, '"Quhat Say Ye Now"'.
24 Curran, 'Religious Women', p. 108.
25 Hall, 'Towards a Prosopography'; Hall, *Women and the Church*, pp. 211–20.
26 The practice of name-changing at profession appears to have been a late post-medieval or modern phenomenon; see Rives, 'Taking the Veil', pp. 478–85.
27 Burton, *Monastic and Religious Orders*, p. 86.
28 Bradley Warren, 'Monastic Rules'; Mooney, *Clare of Assisi*.
29 Collins, 'Isolated in the Wilderness?'
30 Schulenburg, 'Strict Active Enclosure'; Gilchrist, *Gender and Material Culture*, p. 151.
31 Kleinschmidt, *Understanding the Middle Ages*, p. 33.
32 Smith, *Ordering Women's Lives*, p. 179.
33 De Paermentier, 'Experiencing Space', p. 65.
34 Ibid., p. 56.
35 Hall, *Women and the Church*, pp. 159–90; Hicks, *Religious Life in Normandy*, p. 127.
36 Curran, 'Religious Women', pp. 150–73.
37 Hall, 'Towards a Prosopography'; Hall, *Women and the Church*; MacCurtain, 'Late Medieval Nunneries; Hicks, *Religious Life in Normandy*, pp. 128–35; Kenny, *Women in Ireland*, p. 169.
38 Gilchrist, 'Community and Self', p. 64.
39 Power, *Medieval English Nunneries*, pp. 315–40.
40 Ibid., p. 317.
41 De Paermentier, 'Experiencing Space', p. 61.
42 Gilchrist, 'Community and Self', p. 59.
43 S. Rees Jones, 'Women's Influence on the Design of Urban Homes', in M.C. Erler and M. Kowaleski (eds), *Gendering the Master Narrative: Women and power in the middle ages* (Ithaca: Cornell University Press, 2003), pp. 190–211, at pp. 210–11.
44 C. Walker Bynum, 'Patterns of Female Piety in the Later Middle Ages', in J.F. Hamburger and S. Marti (eds), *Crown and Veil: Female monasticism from the fifth to the fifteenth centuries* (New York: Columbia University Press, 2008), pp. 172–90, at pp. 172, 175.
45 G. Signori, 'Cell or Dormitory?', p. 42.
46 Hall, *Women and the Church*, pp. 159–76.
47 Kerr, *Life in the Medieval Cloister*, pp. 37–42.
48 Gilchrist, 'Community and Self', p. 58.

49 Gilchrist, 'Community and Self', pp. 62–3; Coppack, *Abbeys and Priories*, p. 50; G. Coppack, 'Make Straight in the Desert a Highway for Our God': The Carthusians and community in late medieval England', in J. Burton and K. Stöber (eds), *Monasteries and Society in the British Isles in the Later Middle Ages* (Woodbridge: Boydell, 2008), pp. 168–79; Y. McDermott, 'Kinalehin, Co. Galway: A history of Ireland's only Carthusian priory and its conversion to a Franciscan friary', *Journal of the Royal Society of Antiquaries of Ireland*, vols 142–3, 2012–13, pp. 100–13.

50 Kleinschmidt, *Understanding the Middle Ages*, p. 33.

51 Perkins-Curran, '"Quhat Say Ye Now".

52 MacKechnie's *Instructio Pie Vivendi*, translated from Latin to Irish in the fifteenth-century, is thought to have been created for an unnamed nun or nunnery community, and gives an important insight into what the nuns should be reading (Dr Colmán Ó Clabaigh OSB, personal communication). For what friars were reading in Ireland, see C. Ó Clabaigh, 'Friar Maurice Hanlan, his books and the Franciscan *studium* in Medieval Youghal', in P. Harbison and V. Hall (eds), *Carnival of Learning: Essays in honour of George Cunningham* (Roscrea: Cistercian Press, 2012), pp. 133–42

53 A comprehensive corpus of scholarly works on nuns' literacy is emerging, suggesting that at least some nuns were more literate than has been thought previously. See V. Blanton, V. O'Mara and P. Stoop (eds), *Nuns' Literacies in Medieval Europe: The Hull dialogue* (Turnhout: Brepols, 2013); V. Blanton, V. O'Mara and P. Stoop (eds), *Nuns' Literacies in Medieval Europe: The Kansas City dialogue* (Turnhout: Brepols, 2015); V. Blanton, V. O'Mara and P. Stoop (eds), *Nuns' Literacies in Medieval Europe: The Antwerp dialogue* (Turnhout: Brepols, 2018). For examples from Germany, see Hamburger et al., 'The Time of the Orders', p. 71. For regional Spain, see B. Garí, 'What Did Catalan Nuns Read? Women's literacy in the female monasteries of Catalonia, Majorca and Valencia', in V. Blanton, V. O'Mara and P. Stoop (eds), *Nuns' Literacies in Medieval Europe: The Antwerp dialogue* (Turnhout: Brepols, 2018), pp. 125–48; For England, see D.N. Bell, *What Nuns Read: Books and libraries in medieval English nunneries* (Kalamazoo: Cistercian publications, 1995); S. Powell, *The Birgittines of Syon Abbey: Preaching and print* (Turnhout: Brepols, 2017).

54 Lee, *Nunneries, Learning and Spirituality*, pp. 136–8. But see also: M. Oliva, 'Rendering Accounts: The pragmatic literacy of nuns in late medieval England', in V. Blanton, V. O'Mara and P. Stoop (eds), *Nuns' Literacies in Medieval Europe: The Hull dialogue* (Turnhout: Brepols, 2013), pp. 51–68; V. O'Mara, 'The Late Medieval English Nun and Her Scribal Activity: A complicated quest', in V. Blanton, V. O'Mara and P. Stoop (eds), *Nuns' Literacies in Medieval Europe: The Hull dialogue* (Turnhout: Brepols, 2013), pp. 69–96; V. O'Mara, 'Nuns and Writing in Late Medieval England: The quest continues', in V. Blanton, V. O'Mara and P. Stoop (eds), *Nuns' Literacies in Medieval Europe: The Kansas City dialogue* (Turnhout: Brepols, 2015), pp. 123–49; V. O'Mara, 'Scribal Engagement and the Late Medieval English Nun: The quest concludes?', in V. Blanton, V. O'Mara and P. Stoop (eds), *Nuns' Literacies in Medieval Europe: The Antwerp dialogue* (Turnhout: Brepols, 2018), pp. 187–208.

55 Sloane, *Augustinian Nunnery of St Mary Clerkenwell*, p. 160. In certain cases, however, nuns had high levels of literacy: see, for example, C. Taylor Jones, *Ruling the Spirit: Women, liturgy and Dominican reform in late medieval Germany* (Philadelphia: University of Pennsylvania Press, 2017); Bugyis, *The Care of Nuns*.

56 Kenny, *Women in Ireland*, p. 39. Three medieval continental nunneries – Rupertsberg (where Hildegard of Bingen was founder and abbess), Helfta, and Unterlinden – each produced significant bodies of religious writing in Latin; see B. Newman, 'The

Visionary Texts and Visual Worlds of Religious Women', in J. Hamburger and S. Marti (eds), *Crown and Veil: Female monasticism from the fifth to the fifteenth centuries* (New York: Columbia University Press, 2008), pp. 151–71, at p. 154; U. Wiethaus, 'Collaborative Literacy and the Spiritual Education of Nuns at Helfta', in V. Blanton, V. O'Mara and P. Stoop (eds), *Nuns' Literacies in Medieval Europe: The Kansas City dialogue* (Turnhout: Brepols, 2015), pp. 27–46.

57 Oliva, *Convent and the Community*, pp. 65–72.

58 A martyrology is a list of martyrs, usually with a longer account and dates on which they are remembered. The twelfth-century date is interesting as it significantly predates the recorded foundation of the community at Lismullin in 1240; and tantalising as it suggests that the community there is earlier than is currently thought. See S. Ryan, '"I too am Christian": Early martyrs and their lives in the late medieval and early modern Irish manuscript tradition', *Studies in Church History*, vol. 47, 2001, pp. 193–207, at p. 202.

59 K. Rudy, *Virtual Pilgrimages*.

60 Kerr, *Life in the Medieval Cloister*, pp. 81–2.

61 Ibid., p. 51. In an Irish context, the Augustinian Victorine constitutions of St Thomas the Martyr in Dublin had an entire section on sign language: see H.F. Berry, 'On the Use of Signs in the Ancient Monasteries with Special Reference to a Code Used by the Victorine Canons at St Thomas's Abbey Dublin', *Journal of the Royal Society of Antiquaries of Ireland*, vol. 2, 1892, pp. 107–25; A. Gwynn, 'The Early History of St Thomas's Abbey, Dublin', *Journal of the Royal Society of Antiquaries of Ireland*, vol. 84, 1954, pp. 1–35. I am grateful to Dr Colmán Ó Clabaigh OSB for drawing these references to my attention.

62 Kleinschmidt, *Understanding the Middle Ages*, p. 33.

63 Hall, *Women and the Church*.

64 For example, Schulenburg, 'Strict Active Enclosure'.

65 Gilchrist, *Gender and Material Culture*, p. 152.

66 Ibid., pp. 152–9.

67 Garí, 'Sacred Space of Meditation'.

68 Hillier and Hanson, *Social Logic of Space*. See also O'Keeffe, *Medieval Irish Buildings*, pp. 81–7. In this type of analysis, despite the name, access *and* egress are important considerations, and it can equally be applied to religious and secular structures.

69 Gilchrist, 'Spatial Archaeology of Gender Domains'; Gilchrist, 'Community and Self'; Gilchrist, *Gender and Material Culture*, pp. 160–7.

70 Gilchrist chose eight nunneries and eight male religious houses for her spatial analysis. Her chosen sample was dictated by the relatively small number of fully extant or excavated sites. She selected a wide range of nunnery types, including a double house, Watton; a wealthy Cistercian house, Roche; a modest Augustinian house, Lanercost; a Benedictine abbey, Chester; a Benedictine priory with hermitage origins, Finchale; a southern Cistercian house, Waverley; a rural mendicant monastery, Walsingham; and a Premonstratensian house, Leiston. Gilchrist, 'Gender, Ideology and Material Culture', pp. 125–33.

71 This idea has been successfully expanded in an Irish context by Hall in her historical discussion of what she terms the 'permeable cloister'. See Hall, *Women and the Church*, pp. 159–76.

72 Carville published Graney, Co. Kildare, on which she superimposed an 'ideal Augustinian canonesses nunnery' on the site; Carville, 'St Mary's Abbey, Graney', p. 51. She acknowledged that the site requires archaeological investigation. The extant

earthwork remains on the site bear no relationship to the superimposed plan. While it is certainly possible that Graney was claustrally planned, there is currently no upstanding archaeological evidence to confirm this.

73 Gilchrist, 'Gender, Ideology and Material Culture', pp. 125–9.

74 P. Power, 'Placenames of the Decies', *Journal of the Waterford and South-East of Ireland Archaeological Society*, vol. 11, 1908, pp. 1–34, at pp. 32–3.

75 Ronan, 'Irish Nunneries', p. 209.

76 These opes are where wall fabric was robbed and they do not appear to ever have been proper doorways.

77 For the possible earlier origin of the west range as a secular structure, see Chapter 5.

78 Westropp, 'The Conventual Buildings', pp. 60–2.

79 Ronan, 'Irish Nunneries', p. 228.

80 This interpretation must remain conjecture as it cannot be verified by upstanding evidence, but is plausible based on dimensions. A stair in a similar location is at the Augustinian friary, Adare, Co. Limerick. This was founded later than St Catherine's in 1325. Its stone stair leads from the cloister ambulatory to a first-floor refectory situated in the south range.

81 Similar arrangements can be seen at many male religious houses, for example Lislaughtin Friary, Co. Kerry; see Ó Clabaigh, *Friars in Ireland*, pp. 224–6. Nunnery community sizes in later medieval Ireland are unknown. There is some indirect evidence. In a visitation record to Grace Dieu in 1468, six nuns are named. It is possible that this constituted the entire community there. Dr Colmán Ó Clabaigh suggests that the visitation records are probably accurate, as this is the number that later received pensions at the dissolution (personal communication). H.F. Berry (ed.), *Register of Wills and Inventories of the Diocese of Dublin* (Dublin: Royal Society of Antiquaries of Ireland, 1898), p. 175.

82 Signori, 'Cell or Dormitory?', p. 28.

83 Signori has suggested that the individualisation of male monastic dormitory space was an attempt to return to the eremitical life of the desert fathers, rather than a move towards privatisation. The individualisation of space at nunneries was a much slower process: Signori, 'Cell or Dormitory?', pp. 41–2.

84 It is acknowledged that in all cases each have ranges of which little can be known without excavation.

85 Garí, 'The Sacred Space of Meditation', p. 75.

86 For detail on what occurred in a Cistercian context, see Stalley, *Cistercian Monasteries*, p. 162; for Augustinians, see C. Ó Clabaigh, 'Community, Commemoration and Confraternity: The chapter office and chapter books in Irish Augustinian foundations', in M. Browne and C. Ó Clabaigh (eds), *Households of God: The regular canons and canonesses of Saint Augustine and of Prémontré in medieval Ireland* (Dublin: Four Courts Press, 2019), pp. 235–51. For a more general overview of control and obedience in a monastery, see Kerr, *Life in the Medieval Cloister*, pp. 113–30.

87 Stalley, *Cistercian Monasteries of Ireland*, pp. 162–6; Ó Clabaigh, *Friars in Ireland*, pp. 222–4.

88 M. Seaborn, 'The Chapter House, Jesus College, Cambridge: Elements of a twelfth-century nunnery revealed', *Donald Insall Associates Newsletter*, vol. 38, 2011, pp. 4–5.

89 Mohn, *Mittelalterliche Klosteranlagen der Zisterzienserinnen*, pp. 72–5, 230–4.

90 Müller, 'Presenting Identity in the Cloister', p. 179.

91 Ibid., pp. 177–8.

92 Barrière, 'Cistercian Convent of Coyroux', p. 79.

93 There is one historical reference in 1536 in the *Calendar for Exchequer Inquisitions* to a nunnery chapter house which was located at St Mary de Hogges: see H.B. Clarke, *Irish*

Historic Towns Atlas No. 11: Dublin, Part I, to 1610 (Dublin: Royal Irish Academy, 2002), p. 19.

94 This is based on the lack of archaeological evidence. Dr Colmán Ó Clabaigh OSB has also noted in visitation records for religious houses in Dublin that male houses had designated 'chapter houses' mentioned. For nunneries, the visitation took place in the 'accustomed place' (personal communication). See Berry, *Register of Wills*.

95 Gilchrist, *Gender and Material Culture*, pp. 116–17, 125; Garí, 'The Sacred Space of Meditation', p. 84.

96 Robinson, 'Augustinian Canons', pp. 23–4.

97 P. Fergusson, 'The Refectory at Easby Abbey: Form and iconography', *Art Bulletin*, vol. 71, 1989, pp. 334–51.

98 Stalley, *Cistercian Monasteries of Ireland*, p. 169.

99 O'Keeffe proposes a first-floor refectory at St Catherine's: O'Keeffe, *Medieval Irish Buildings*, p. 151. Although alternatively I suggest it was probably on the ground floor; see Collins, 'Unveiling Female Monasticism', pp. 146–8.

100 For a good parallel for this feature, see the *in situ* lavabo at Kells, Co. Kilkenny; Clyne, *Kells Priory*, p. 129; or Adare Augustinian friary, Co. Limerick.

101 There is now no evidence of these features, though Westropp recorded a 'water table' which may have been for the lavabo basin: Westropp, 'The Conventual Buildings', p. 55.

102 Coppack, *Abbeys and Priories*, pp. 72, 149–54.

103 R. Stalley, 'Decorating the Lavabo: Late Romanesque sculpture from Mellifont Abbey', *Proceedings of the Royal Irish Academy*, vol. 98C, 1996, pp. 237–64, at pp. 252–4.

104 P. Christie and J. Coad, 'Excavations at Denny Abbey', *Archaeological Journal*, vol. 137, 1980, pp. 138–79; Coppack, *Abbeys and Priories*, p. 99.

105 Kerr, *Life in the Medieval Cloister*, p. 85.

106 Hurley and Sheehan, *St Mary's of the Isle*, p. 54.

107 Christie and Coad, 'Excavations at Denny Abbey'.

108 Collins, 'Unveiling Female Monasticism'.

109 Lynch, *Tintern Abbey*, pp. 62, 66–9.

110 Clyne, *Kells Priory*, p. 128.

111 Sloane, *St Mary Clerkenwell*, pp. 37, 110–18, 183–4.

112 C. Noble, 'Spiritual Practice and the Designed Landscape: Monastic precinct gardens', *Studies in the History of Gardens and Designed Landscapes: An International Quarterly*, vol. 20, 2000, pp. 197–205, at pp. 197, 200, 202; Müller, 'Presenting Identity in the Cloister', p. 180.

113 L. Herbert McAvoy, 'The Medieval *Hortus Conclusus*: Revisiting the pleasure garden', *Medieval Feminist Forum*, vol. 50, 2014, pp. 5–10.

114 Collins, 'Unveiling Female Monasticism', pp. 144–6.

115 P. Murphy and R.G. Scaife, 'The Environmental Archaeology of Gardens', in A.E. Brown (ed.), *Garden Archaeology*, CBA, Research Report 78 (London: Council for British Archaeology, 1991), pp. 87–8; Scott, 'Romsey Abbey', pp. 150–60.

116 Bull et al., *Holywell Priory*, p. 37.

117 Sloane, *St Mary Clerkenwell*, p. 13.

118 Ward, *Excavations at Chester*, pp. 5–6.

119 Bhreathnach, 'The *Vita Apostolica*'.

120 Golding, *Gilbert of Sempringham*, pp. 191–262; Kerr, *Life in the Medieval Cloister*, pp. 41–2.

121 Mohn, *Mittelalterliche Klosteranlagen der Zisterzienserinnen*, pp. 67–9. Dr Colmán Ó Clabaigh makes the point that modern monasteries are built over many years.

The final layout may be entirely different to that originally conceived (personal communication).

122 Garí, 'The Sacred Space of Meditation', pp. 90–1.

123 Higgins, *Tisrara Medieval Church*, pp. 24–30.

124 Healy, 'Two Royal Abbeys', p. 7.

125 Moran, *Monasticon Hibernicum*, vol. II, p. 86.

126 Manning, *Clonmacnoise*, p. 33.

127 Mytum, 'Geophysical Survey at Clonmacnoise', p. 45.

128 Alcock et al., *Archaeological Inventory of County Galway*, p. 315.

129 White, *Extents*, pp. 171, 234.

130 Archdall, *Monasticon Hibernicum*, p. 815.

131 White, *Extents*, p. 255.

132 Ibid., p. 336.

133 Curran, 'Religious Women'.

134 Cartwright, *Feminine Sanctity and Spirituality*.

135 Webster and Cherry, 'Medieval Britain in 1978', p. 250; Gilchrist, *Gender and Material Culture*, p. 154.

136 Bull et al., *Holywell Priory*.

137 Sloane, *St Mary Clerkenwell*.

138 E. Eames and T. Fanning, *Irish Medieval Tiles* (Dublin: Royal Irish Academy, 1988), pp. 89, 90, 122, 124. There are fifteen medieval tiles from Kildare Cathedral, both two colour and line impressed, which were found in the foundations of the north and east walls during restoration in the nineteenth century. It cannot be verified if these tiles were from the nunnery, however; see Eames and Fanning, *Irish Medieval Tiles*, p. 67. Interestingly, one is of the same design as one of the tiles from St Mary de Hogges.

139 Frings, *Krone und Schleier*; Hamburger and Marti, *Crown and Veil*; Schleif and Schier, *Katerina's Windows*; Garí, 'The Sacred Space of Meditation', p. 85.

140 J. Hamburger, *Nuns as Artists: The visual culture of a medieval convent* (Berkeley: University of California Press, 1997); Beach, *Women as Scribes*; Marks, *Image and Devotion*; Hamburger and Suckale, 'Between this World and the Next', pp. 76–108; A. Radini, M. Tromp, A. Beach, E. Tong, C. Speller, M. McCormick, J.V. Dudgeon, M.J. Collins, F. Rühli, R. Kröger and C. Warinner, 'Medieval Women's Early Involvement in Manuscript Production Suggested by Lapis Lazuli Identification in Dental Calculus', *Science Advances*, vol. 5, 2019, pp. 1–8.

141 Hamburger, *Nuns as Artists*.

142 J. Hamburger, 'The Use of Images in the Pastoral Care of Nuns: The case of Heinrich Suso and the Dominicans', *The Art Bulletin*, vol. 71, 1989, pp. 20–46; J. Hamburger, 'The Visual and the Visionary: The image in late medieval monastic devotion', *Viator*, vol. 20, 1989, pp. 161–82.

143 Hall, *Women and the Church*, pp. 117–18.

144 C. MacLeod, 'Medieval Wooden Figure Sculptures in Ireland: Medieval madonnas in the west', *Journal of the Royal Society of Antiquaries of Ireland*, vol. 75, 1945, pp. 167–82. These statues are not exclusively associated with nunneries, for example the Kilcorban Madonna, or the Madonna and Child from the Franciscan friary, Askeaton, Co. Limerick; see Ó Clabaigh, *Friars in Ireland*, plate 8. The Athlone Madonna is currently at the Poor Clare enclosed nunnery at Nun's Island, Galway. It is still venerated. C. MacLeod, 'The Statue of Our Lady of Limerick: A gift in reparation', in E. Rynne (ed.), *North Munster Studies: Essays in commemoration of Monsignor Michael Moloney* (Limerick: Thomond Archaeological Society, 1967), pp. 266–75.

145 Rubin, *Emotion and Devotion*, p. 85; A. Rudloff Stanton, 'Devotional Art', in M. Schaus (ed.), *Women and Gender in Medieval Europe: An encyclopaedia* (London: Routledge, 2006), pp. 200–4, at p. 201.
146 C. MacLeod, 'Some Medieval Wooden Figure Sculptures in Ireland: Statues of Irish saints', *Journal of the Royal Society of Antiquities of Ireland*, vol. 76, 1946, pp. 155–70, at pp. 164–8; Ó Riain, *A Dictionary*, p. 368; Callan, *Sacred Sisters*, pp. 170–4.
147 J. Bradley, 'The Ballyhale Madonna', in E. Rynne (ed.), *Figures from the Past: Studies on figurative art in Christian Ireland in honour of Helen M. Roe* (Dublin: Glendare Press for the Royal Society of Antiquaries of Ireland, 1987), pp. 258–77. This devotion continued into the early modern period; see Tait, 'Art and the Cult of the Virgin Mary'.
148 Rubin, *Emotion and Devotion*, pp. 82–7.
149 Pelikan, *Mary Through the Centuries*; Rubin, *Emotion and Devotion*, p. 86.
150 J. Bradley, 'A Medieval Figure at Calliaghstown, County Meath', *Journal of the Royal Society of Antiquaries of Ireland*, vol. 110, 1980, pp. 149–52. Bradley has suggested that this fragment came from the nunnery at Calliaghstown. Hall thought this unlikely as the nunnery was probably never very large. She conceded that it may have been donated by a wealthy patron or that it came from elsewhere such as Odder, or a male house, and made its way to Calliaghstown in the post-medieval period: Hall, *Women and the Church*, p. 117; but there is no reason to doubt that it originated at Calliaghstown.
151 The Magi are found on a canopied tomb at Strade Abbey, Co. Galway and the other figures on this tomb are suggestive of pilgrimage, perhaps specifically referencing Cologne Cathedral and its reliquary the Shrine of the Three Kings. See R. Stalley, 'The End of the Middle Ages: Gothic survival in sixteenth-century Connacht', *Journal of the Royal Society of Antiquaries of Ireland*, vol. 133, 2003, pp. 5–23, at pp. 17–19.
152 Gilchrist, *Gender and Material Culture*, p. 146; Gilchrist, *Contemplation and Action*, pp. 143–4.
153 Gilchrist, *Gender and Material Culture*, pp. 143–8.
154 D.H. Williams, *Catalogue of Seals in the National Museum of Wales. Volume I: Seal Dies, Welsh Seals, Papal Bullae* (Cardiff: National Museum of Wales. 1993), cat. no. W188; D.H. Williams, *Catalogue of Seals in the National Museum of Wales. Volume II: Ecclesiastical, Monastic and Collegiate Seals with a Supplement Concerning Wales* (Cardiff: National Museum and Galleries of Wales, 1998); E. New, 'The Seals in the Medieval Wales Project and Its Potential for Monastic and Ecclesiastical History', *Monastic Research Bulletin*, vol. 17, 2011, pp. 2–4. I am grateful to Dr Elizabeth New for drawing this example and references to my attention. See https://exploringmedievalseals.wordpress.com. Accessed 15 September 2020.
155 Hall records the use of seals at nunneries in the documentary evidence, for example at Graney, Lismullin, and nuns' seals of Renalda and Catherine from Killone. None of these seals is extant; Hall, *Women and the Church*, p. 118.
156 Ibid. She noted that similar images have been used on other monastic seals, such as the priory at Athlone.
157 Ibid., p. 119.
158 This head was reputedly taken to the library offices in Tullamore, Co. Offaly in 1978; Hall, *Women and the Church*, p. 116.
159 This head is located in the garden of Mr and Mrs Guiney, Old Abbey, Co. Limerick. They recall that it was brought to their house by a man from New Zealand who was a descendant of the Greens of Old Abbey House. I am grateful to Mr Guiney for drawing this feature to my attention. This head is in addition to the lost one recorded by Westropp.

160 P. Bates, *Donabate and Portrane: A history* (Dublin: self-published, 1988), p. 28; Hall, *Women and the Church*, p. 116, n. 91. This head is now lost.
161 The second stone head from Grave Dieu is in the National Museum of Ireland, reg. no. 2012:82.
162 This head is in Limerick Museum. J. Hunt, 'Romanesque Head from Peter's Cell', *North Munster Antiquarian Journal*, vol. 6, 1949, pp. 16–18.
163 Westropp, 'The Conventual Buildings'.
164 Ó Crualaoich, *Book of the Cailleach*.
165 M. Verling (ed.), *Beara Women Talking: Folklore from the Beara Peninsula* (Cork: Mercier Press, 2003); Callan, 'Líadain's *Lament*'; Callan, *Sacred Sisters*, pp. 174–86.
166 Hall, *Women and the Church*, p. 116; J.P. Hayes, 'Ballymacdane Abbey, Co. Cork', *Journal of the Cork Historical and Archaeological Society*, vol. 3, 1894, pp. 141–3, at p. 141; Anon, 'Ballymacdane Abbey', *Journal of the Cork Historical and Archaeological Society*, vol. 3, p. 173; D. Power, *Archaeological Inventory of County Cork. Volume 3: Mid Cork* (Dublin: The Stationery Office, 1997), pp. 374–5.
167 Ní Ghrádaigh, '"But What Exactly Did She Give?"', pp. 180–205; R. Moss, 'A Twelfth-Century Renaissance? Irish Romanesque sculpture and the insular tradition', in R. Moss (ed.), *Making and Meaning in Insular Art* (Dublin: Four Courts Press, 2007), pp. 126–41, at p. 128.
168 Healy, 'Two Royal Abbeys'; Kalkreuter, *Boyle Abbey*, p. 71.
169 This is a common motif particularly associated with St Francis and his support of the church, after a dream of Pope Innocent III where he dreamt Francis was physically supporting the Lateran Basilica in Rome, preventing its collapse. I am grateful to Dr Colmán Ó Clabaigh OSB for drawing this parallel to my attention.
170 Garí, 'The Sacred Space of Meditation', p. 85.
171 The church of Kilcatherine (thought to be a nunnery by some) and the church at Ballyvourney, both in County Cork, also have early carved stone heads. In addition, Ballyvourney has a sheela-na-gig over the west door.
172 Brady, 'Nunnery at Clonard'.
173 C. Baker, *Antiquities of Old Fingal: The archaeology of north County Dublin* (Dublin: Wordwell, 2010), p. 105.
174 R. Moss, 'The Material Culture of the Canonical Movement in Medieval Ireland', in M. Browne and C. Ó Clabaigh (eds), *Households of God: The regular canons and canonesses of St Augustine and of Premontré in medieval Ireland* (Dublin: Four Courts Press, 2019), pp. 191–206.
175 D. Maher, *Medieval Grave Slabs of County Tipperary 1200–1600* AD. *BAR British Series 262* (Oxford: John & Erica Hedges, 1997).
176 Nunneries with visible later medieval graveslabs are: Clonfert, Killone, Cloonoghil, Grace Dieu, Graney and possibly Timolin. There are some co-located sites, for instance Roscommon, Duleek and Skreen, that have extant graveslabs but it is impossible to know if they were related to the nunneries there. It is likely that nunneries with attached graveyards such as Ballynagallagh may also retain some unrecorded graveslabs, though none was located during this study. One graveslab recorded by Westropp at St Catherine's is now lost. In England, other forms of funerary monument such as brasses are known from nunneries; see Gilchrist, *Contemplation and Action*, p. 150.
177 I am grateful to Dr Christy Cunniffe for identifying the nunnery graveslab from several others in the cathedral. See Cunniffe, 'Canons and Canonesses of St Augustine at Clonfert'.
178 Maher, *Medieval Grave Slabs*, pp. 28–41.

179 Stalley, *Cistercian Monasteries*, p. 205. Medieval graveslabs are known from the Cistercian monasteries of Jerpoint, Mellifont and Inishlounaght. None has any evidence that might associate it with a nunnery. As the precise locations of the nunneries are unknown at these locations, these slabs have not been considered here.

180 Gilchrist, *Gender and Material Culture*, p. 20. Gilchrist further noted that symbols for nuns on graveslabs might be less easy to identify than those for priests, as nuns did not have a recognised liturgical identity. She notes that medieval priests' burials regularly have a chalice depicted, and so if a chalice is noted on a slab, it is always denoted a male. However, some nuns in England acted as sacristans or chaplains, and she suggests that the many slabs at nunneries that have a chalice may be actually related to these nuns.

181 For a full description, parallels and references for this effigy, see J. Hunt, *Irish Medieval Figure Sculpture 1200–1600*, 2 vols (Dublin: Irish University Press, 1974), p. 164, plate 1.

182 There is a graveslab possibly depicting a nun at St John's Cemetery, Kells, Co. Meath. This was the site of a Fratres Cruciferi religious house and hospital. See B. Mc Cabe, 'Survey of St John's Graveyard, Kells', *Ríocht na Mídhe: Records of the Meath Archaeological and Historical Society*, vol. 18, 2007, pp. 136–50.

183 J. Bradley, 'The Medieval Tombs of St Canice's', in A. Empey (ed.), *A Worthy Foundation: The cathedral church of St Canice, Kilkenny* (Mountrath: Dolmen Press, 1985), pp. 49–103; Hall, *Women and the Church*, pp. 191–200; J. Bradley, 'Death, Art and Burial: St Canice's Cathedral Kilkenny in the sixteenth century', in C. Hourihane (ed.), *Irish Art Historical Studies in Honour of Peter Harbison* (Dublin: Four Courts Press, 2004), pp. 210–18.

184 E.C. Rae, 'Irish Sepulchral Monuments of the Later Middle Ages', *Journal of the Royal Society of Antiquaries of Ireland*, vol. 100, 1970, pp. 1–38, at p. 4; Hunt, *Irish Medieval Figure Sculpture*; M. Phelan, 'An Unidentified Tomb in St Canice's Cathedral, Kilkenny', *Old Kilkenny Review: Journal of the Kilkenny Archaeological Society*, vol. 48, 1996, pp. 40–4, at p. 43; P. Harbison, 'Sculpture', in S. Duffy (ed.), *Medieval Ireland: An encyclopedia* (London: Routledge, 2005), pp. 424–5, at p. 424; R. Moss (ed.), *Art and Architecture of Ireland. Volume 1: Medieval, c.400–c.1600* (Dublin: Royal Irish Academy, 2015), pp. 497–502, 548–9.

185 Rae, 'Irish Sepulchral Monuments', p. 22.

186 There are two male and six female figures represented on the front and side panels. This ratio in favour of females may indeed be indicative of a woman's tomb, but because of the reconstruction no firm conclusions can be made.

187 Rae has suggested that this is Mary Magdalene, based on the hair arrangement and her container of ointment. He noted that this woman is regularly mistaken for St Barbara and her tower; but she is usually associated with a tower that is battlemented or shows loopholes, a book and a crown, all of which are lacking here. He further commented that at his time of writing there was no figure of St Barbara on funerary sculpture in an Irish context; Rae, 'Irish Sepulchral Monuments', p. 30.

188 Hunt suggested that this was an unidentified female saint; Hunt, *Irish Medieval Figure Sculpture*, p. 191.

189 Rae, 'Irish Sepulchral Monuments', pp. 22, 30; Hunt, *Irish Medieval Figure Sculpture*, pp. 190–1.

190 Rae 'Irish Sepulchral Monuments', p. 30.

191 Ibid., pp. 4, 31; Hunt, *Irish Medieval Figure Sculpture*, p. 191; Phelan, 'An Unidentified Tomb'.

192 Bradley, 'Death, Art and Burial', p. 215.

193 Rae, 'Irish Sepulchral Monuments'.
194 This mirrors the design of the church's west doorway, where each of its capitals is of different design.
195 The baptismal font previously recorded at Aghade is a bullaun stone.
196 I think that it is unlikely that this is the original location of the stoup.
197 H. Roe, *The Medieval Fonts of Meath* (Meath: Meath Archaeological and Historical Society, 1964), pp. 28–35.
198 Gilchrist, *Gender and Material Culture*; Hamburger and Marti, *Crown and Veil*.
199 Morton, 'Aspects of Image and Meaning', pp. 51–71.
200 The dimensions of the individual ashlar blocks depicted in paint were 0.18m in height by varying widths of 0.80m, 0.10m, 0.30m. These were recorded by Ronan, 'Irish Nunneries', p. 208.
201 I am grateful to Dr Barra O'Donnabhain, who first noticed the incised lines in the plaster: see Collins, 'Missing the Boat'.
202 K. Brady and C. Corlett, 'Holy Ships: Ships on plaster at medieval ecclesiastical sites in Ireland', *Archaeology Ireland*, vol. 18, 2004, pp. 28–31; K. Brady and C. Corlett, 'Ships on Plaster: Evidence for ships in medieval Ireland', in C. Manning (ed.), *From Ringforts to Fortified Houses: Studies on castles and other monuments in honour of David Sweetman* (Dublin: Wordwell, 2007), pp. 309–34. I am grateful to Karl Brady of the Underwater Unit, National Monuments Service, for identifying the ship type.
203 Brady and Corlett, 'Holy Ships'.
204 Gardiner, 'Graffiti and Their Use'.
205 Brady and Corlett, 'Ships on Plaster'.
206 Ó Floinn, *Irish Shrines and Reliquaries*, p. 44; Bitel, *Two Saints*, p. 198.
207 McClintock, 'The Mantle of St Brigid at Bruges'; Bitel, *Two Saints*, p. 198.
208 R. Ó Floinn, 'The Norman Conquest and the Later Middle Ages 1169 AD–*ca* 1500 AD', in M. Ryan (ed.), *Treasures of Ireland: Irish art 3000 BC–1500 AD* (Dublin: Royal Irish Academy, 1983), pp. 70–3, at pp. 70–1; Ó Floinn, *Irish Shrines and Reliquaries*, p. 45; R. Ó Floinn, 'Goldsmiths' Work in Ireland 1200–1400', in C. Hourihane (ed.), *From Ireland Coming* (Princeton: Dept of Art and Archaeology, Princeton University, 2001), pp. 289–312, at p. 295; R. Ó Floinn, 'Later Medieval Ireland, AD 1150–1550', in P.F. Wallace and R. Ó Floinn (eds), *Treasures of the National Museum of Ireland: Irish antiquities* (Dublin: Gill & Macmillan, 2002), pp. 257–300, at p. 262; Hamlin, *Archaeology of Early Christianity*, pp. 329, 375; Ó Riain, *A Dictionary*, p. 393; Ó Baoill, 'Excavations at Aghavea', p. 160.
209 Macalister, *Corpus Inscriptionum Insularum Celticarum*, vol. II, p. 127. Máire MacDermott provides a full description of the crosier: MacDermott, 'The Crosiers' pp. 169–75.
210 MacDermott, 'The Crosiers', p. 175.
211 This crosier is in the British Museum, BM No. 1859-2-21/1. MacDermott, 'The Crosiers', p. 191.
212 There are other forms of crosiers in Ireland, such as the Tau, volute, and the rare knop-headed staff forms; see R. Ó Floinn, 'Bishops, Liturgy and Reform: Some archaeological and art historical evidence', in D. Bracken and D. Ó Riain-Raedel (eds), *Ireland and Europe in the Twelfth Century: Reform and renewal* (Dublin: Four Courts Press, 2006), pp. 218–38; G. Murray, 'Insular-Type Crosiers: Their construction and characteristics', in R. Moss (ed.), *Making and Meaning in Insular Art* (Dublin: Four Courts Press, 2007), pp. 79–94; G. Murray, 'Insular Crosiers: An independent tradition?', in C. Newman, M. Mannion and F. Gavin (eds), *Islands in a Global Context: Proceedings of the Seventh International Conference on Insular Art* (Dublin: Four Courts Press, 2017), pp. 167–77.

213 Murray, 'Insular-Type Crosiers', pp. 82, 88. Murray has recently dated St Dympna's crosier. Radiocarbon dating of its wooden core indicates that the crosier was reconstructed sometime at the end of the medieval and beginning of the early modern period (personal communication).
214 Ó Floinn, 'Bishops, Liturgy and Reform', pp. 221.
215 R. Ó Floinn, 'A Crosier Head from Clonard', in T. Condit and C. Corlett (eds), *Above and Beyond: Essays in memory of Leo Swan* (Dublin: Wordwell, 2005), pp. 333–42.
216 Ó Floinn, *Irish Shrines and Reliquaries*, p. 30; Hall, *Women and the Church*, p. 117.
217 Ó Floinn *Irish Shrines and Reliquaries*, p. 30.
218 Higgins, *Tisrara Medieval Church*, pp. 83–105.
219 The stratigraphic reports on the excavations at Grace Dieu stated that due to the distance from the nunnery, 'none can be related to the nunnery with certainty'. I am grateful to Margaret Gowen for providing the reports. For a summary, see www.excavations.ie/report/1999/Dublin/0004132/. Accessed 15 September 2020.
220 Collins, 'Unveiling Female Monasticism', pp. 161–2.
221 C. McCutcheon, 'Medieval Pottery', in T. Collins, 'Unveiling Female Monasticism in Later Medieval Ireland: Survey and excavation at St Catherine's, Shanagolden, Co. Limerick', *Proceedings of the Royal Irish Academy*, vol. 119C, 2019, pp. 162–5.
222 Collins, 'Unveiling Female Monasticism', p. 161.
223 Hamburger, *Nuns as Artists*; Beach, *Women as Scribes*; Hamburger and Marti, *Crown and Veil*.
224 C. O'Brien, *The History of the Poor Clares* (Galway: Connacht Tribune, 1992), pp. 22, 23.
225 These are in Galway City Museum, https://www.galwaycitymuseum.ie/collections-medieval-post-medieval/. Accessed 15 September 2019.
226 T. Collins, 'Kenmare Lace', in J. Crowley and J. Sheehan (eds), *The Cultural Atlas of the Iveragh Peninsula* (Cork: Cork University Press, 2009), pp. 224–5.
227 E. Spearing (ed.), *Medieval Writings on Female Spirituality* (London: Penguin, 2002).
228 Newman, 'Visionary Texts and Visual Worlds', p. 151. Hildegard of Bingen: A.J. Dickens, *The Female Mystic: Great women thinkers of the middle ages* (London: I.B. Tauris, 2009), pp. 25–38; T. Thurston, *Gloria: An introduction to 1,000 years of European sacred music* (Dublin: Associated Editions, 2011), p. 18. Christina of Markyate: Against her parents' wishes declined marriage and eventually became prioress of a female community at Markyate near St Alban's; Spearing, *Medieval Writings*, pp. 27–45. Julian of Norwich: A female anchorite at St Julian's church, Norwich, in the late fourteenth to early fifteenth centuries; N. Watson, 'Julian of Norwich', in C. Dinshaw and D. Wallace (eds), *The Cambridge Companion to Medieval Women's Writing* (Cambridge: Cambridge University Press, 2003), pp. 210–21; Dickens, *The Female Mystic*, pp. 133–47. The pilgrim Margery Kempe: C. Dinshaw, 'Margery Kempe', in C. Dinshaw and D. Wallace (eds), *The Cambridge Companion to Medieval Women's Writing* (Cambridge: Cambridge University Press, 2003), pp. 222–39; Dickens, *The Female Mystic*, pp. 163–77.
229 J. Gerchow and S. Marti, '"Nuns' Work", "Caretaker Institutions" and "Women's Movements": Some thoughts about a modern historiography of medieval monasticism', in J. Hamburger and S. Marti (eds), *Crown and Veil: Female monasticism from the fifth to the fifteenth centuries* (New York: Columbia University Press, 2008), pp. 132–50, at p. 133.
230 Hamburger, *Nuns as Artists*.
231 Hamburger et al., 'The Time of the Orders', p. 70.

232 P. Stoop, 'The Convent of Jericho in Brussels and Its Literary Network', *Anuario de Estudios Medievales*, 2014, vol. 44, pp. 381–412, at p. 406. See also Taylor Jones, *Ruling the Spirit*.

233 Beach, *Women as Scribes*, pp. 120, 128–34; Radini et al., 'Medieval Women's Early Involvement in Manuscript Production'; J. Oliver, *Singing with Angels: Liturgy, music and art in the gradual of Gisela Von Kerssenbrock* (Turnhout: Brepols, 2007); Hamburger et al., 'The Time of the Orders', p. 70; Hamburger and Suckale, 'Between this World and the Next', p. 91.

234 F. Griffiths, 'Like the Sister of Aaron: Medieval religious women as makers and donors of liturgical textiles', in G. Melville and A. Müller (eds), *Female Vita Religiosa between Late Antiquity and the High Middle Ages: Structures, developments and spatial contexts* (Zürich: Lit Verglag, 2011), pp. 343–74; V.J. Moessner, 'The Medieval Embroideries of Convent Wienhausen', in M.P. Lillich (ed.), *Studies in Cistercian Art and Architecture*, 13 (Kalamazoo: Cistercian Publications, 1987), pp. 161–77; Hamburger et al., 'The Time of the Orders', pp. 72–3.

235 For example, Gilchrist, *Medieval Life*.

CHAPTER 8. LIVING AND DYING

1 Walker Bynum, *Holy Feast and Holy Fast*; Rubin, *Corpus Christi*.

2 R. Bertelsen, 'Food in Northern Europe from the Thirteenth to the Sixteenth Century', in M. Carver and J. Klápště (eds), *The Archaeology of Medieval Europe. Volume 2: Twelfth to Sixteenth Centuries* (Aarhus: Aarhus University Press, 2011), pp. 126–32, at p. 126.

3 T. Waldron, 'Nutrition and the Skeleton', in C. Woolgar, D. Serjeantson and T. Waldron (eds), *Food in Medieval England: Diet and nutrition* (Oxford: Oxford University Press, 2006), pp. 254–66, at p. 254.

4 While there is little direct evidence of foodstuffs in medieval Ireland comparable with England, there is some indirect evidence in some manorial accounts; see M. Murphy, 'Manor Centres, Settlement and Agricultural Systems in Medieval Ireland, 1250–1350', in M. Murphy and M. Stout (eds), *Agricultural and Settlement in Ireland* (Dublin: Four Courts Press, 2015), pp. 69–100. But as an exception, see specialist reports on fish, bird and environmental remains, in Stout and Stout, *Bective Abbey Project*, pp. 126–99. There is a European-funded project looking at food culture from the post-medieval period in Ireland, 1550–1650 led by Dr Susan Flavin: see https://foodcult.eu/project-details/. Accessed 15 September 2020.

5 For example, S. Bassett (ed.), *Death in Towns: Urban responses to the dying and the dead, 100–1600* (Leicester: Leicester University Press, 1992); Gilchrist, 'Christian Bodies and Souls', pp. 101–18; P. Binski, *Medieval Death: Ritual and representation* (London: British Museum Press, 1996); C. Dyer, *Standards of Living in the Later Middle Ages: Social change in England* c.*1200–1520* (Cambridge: Cambridge University Press, 1998); C. Dyer, *Everyday Life in Medieval England* (London: Hambledon & London, 2000); C. Dyer, *Making a Living in the Middle Ages: The people of Britain 850–1520* (London: Penguin, 2003); Bertelsen, 'Food in Northern Europe'; Gilchrist, *Medieval Life*; Gilchrist and Sloane, *Requiem*, pp. 207–13; B. Harvey, *Living and Dying in England 1100–1540: The monastic experience* (Oxford: Clarendon Press, 1993); Keeping, 'Life and Death in English Nunneries'; C. Woolgar, D. Serjeantson and T. Waldron (eds), *Food in Medieval England: Diet and nutrition* (Oxford: Oxford University Press, 2006), pp. 3–7.

6 Woolgar et al., *Food in Medieval England*, p. 13.

7 It has been suggested that in medieval England from the mid thirteenth to the fifteenth century there was a transformation in food consumption from a diet based

predominantly on cereal to one with a higher meat content. This change broadly corresponded with the Black Death, but this was not the only cause of the change; Dyer, *Everyday Life*, pp. xi, 95–8.

8 Ibid., pp. 39–40, 113–31.

9 D. Serjeantson and C. Woolgar, 'Fish Consumption in Medieval England', in C. Woolgar et al., *Food in Medieval England: Diet and nutrition* (Oxford: Oxford University Press, 2006), pp. 102–30.

10 Dyer, *Everyday Life*, pp. 101, 109.

11 N. Sykes, 'From *Cu* to *Sceap* to *Beffe* and *Motton*', in C. Woolgar et al., *Food in Medieval England: Diet and nutrition* (Oxford: Oxford University Press, 2006), pp. 56–71; U. Albarella, 'Pig Husbandry and Pork Consumption in Medieval England', in C. Woolgar et al., *Food in Medieval England: Diet and nutrition* (Oxford: Oxford University Press, 2006), pp. 72–87; C. Woolgar, 'Meat and Dairy Products in Late Medieval England', in C. Woolgar et al., *Food in Medieval England: Diet and nutrition* (Oxford: Oxford University Press, 2006), pp. 88–101.

12 D. Stone, 'The Consumption and Supply of Birds in Late Medieval England', in C. Woolgar et al., *Food in Medieval England: Diet and nutrition* (Oxford: Oxford University Press, 2006), pp. 148–61.

13 Sykes, 'From *Cu* to *Sceap* to *Beffe* and *Motton*'; N. Sykes, 'The Impact of the Normans on Hunting Practices in England', in C. Woolgar et al., *Food in Medieval England: Diet and nutrition* (Oxford: Oxford University Press, 2006), pp. 162–75; N. Sykes, 'Hunting and Venison in Medieval England', in M. Carver and J. Klápště (eds), *The Archaeology of Medieval Europe. Volume 2: Twelfth to Sixteenth Centuries* (Aarhus: Aarhus University Press, 2011), pp. 132–6, at p. 132; D. Serjeantson, 'Birds: Food and a mark of status', in C. Woolgar et al., *Food in Medieval England: Diet and nutrition* (Oxford: Oxford University Press, 2006), pp. 131–47. For Ireland, see F. Beglane, 'The Social Significance of Game in the Diet of Later Medieval Ireland', *Proceedings of the Royal Irish Academy*, vol. 115C, 2015, pp. 1–30.

14 Dyer, *Everyday Life*, pp. 77–99; C. Woolgar, 'Group Diets in Late Medieval England', in C. Woolgar et al., *Food in Medieval England: Diet and nutrition* (Oxford: Oxford University Press, 2006), pp. 191–200, at p. 191; G. Mülder and M. Richards, 'Diet in Medieval England: The evidence from stable isotopes', in C. Woolgar et al., *Food in Medieval England: Diet and nutrition* (Oxford: Oxford University Press, 2006), pp. 228–38, at pp. 234–7.

15 P. Schofield, 'Medieval Diet and Demography', in C. Woolgar et al., *Food in Medieval England: Diet and nutrition* (Oxford: Oxford University Press, 2006), pp. 239–53, at pp. 252–3.

16 C. Dyer, 'Seasonal Patterns in Food Consumption in the Later Middle Ages', in C. Woolgar et al., *Food in Medieval England: Diet and nutrition* (Oxford: Oxford University Press, 2006), pp. 201–14.

17 Woolgar, 'Group Diets', pp. 191–6.

18 Lent is a solemn religious observance in the Christian liturgical calendar that begins on Ash Wednesday and ends approximately six weeks later, before Easter Sunday. The dates of Lent are defined by the date of Easter, which is a moveable feast, meaning that it falls on a different date each year. Lent starts on Ash Wednesday and its observance lasts for forty days, mirroring the forty days that Jesus spent fasting in the wilderness before starting his ministry, and also the forty hours that Jesus spent in the tomb prior to His Resurrection. There are actually forty-six days, however, as the Lenten fast starts on Ash Wednesday and ends on Holy Saturday, the day before Easter Sunday,

but does not include the six Sundays within the period which are not fast days (Sundays are always feast days in the Christian calendar) and therefore not counted in the forty days of Lent. See B. Sloane and G. Malcolm, *Excavations at the Priory of the Order of the Hospital of St John of Jerusalem* (London: Museum of London Archaeology Service, 2004), p. 208; Kerr, *Life in the Medieval Cloister*, pp. 46–55; Ó Clabaigh, *The Friars in Ireland*, pp. 125–35.

19 Woolgar, 'Group Diets', pp. 192–3.

20 B. Harvey, 'Monastic Pittances in the Middle Ages', in C. Woolgar et al., *Food in Medieval England: Diet and nutrition* (Oxford: Oxford University Press, 2006), pp. 215–27, at p. 215.

21 Sloane, *Augustinian Nunnery of St Mary Clerkenwell*, p. 155.

22 For example, Harvey, *Living and Dying in England*; Woolgar et al., *Food in Medieval England*; P. Slavin, *Bread and Ale for the Brethren: The provisioning of Norwich Cathedral Priory 1260–1536* (Hatfield: University of Hertfordshire Press, 2012).

23 A. Empey, 'The Augustinian Priory at Kells: An historical introduction', in M. Clyne, *Kells Priory, Co. Kilkenny: Archaeological excavations by T. Fanning and M. Clyne* (Dublin: The Stationery Office, 2007), pp. 1–11, at pp. 10–11; N.B. White, *Irish Monastic and Episcopal Deeds AD 1200–1600* (Dublin: Irish Manuscripts Commission, 1936), pp. 10–11.

24 Harvey, *Living and Dying in England*, pp. 34–71.

25 Slavin, *Bread and Ale for the Brethren*, p. 140.

26 This was referred to at other places as white bread, *panis albus*, or wastel bread. This best bread was reserved for the monks and unusually the priory cooks. Slavin concluded that the priory cooks must have been highly valued within the community to warrant the best bread; Slavin, *Bread and Ale for the Brethren*, pp. 147–8, 158.

27 Ibid., pp. 146–7, 159, 173–87.

28 Slavin, *Bread and Ale for the Brethren*, p. 160. Ale consumption would have been in tandem with wine. Where there was an orchard, cider was made, but this was normally a drink of the poorer classes; C. Dyer, 'Gardens and Garden Produce in the Later Middle Ages', in C. Woolgar et al., *Food in Medieval England: Diet and nutrition* (Oxford: Oxford University Press, 2006), pp. 27–40, at pp. 36–7, 40. The differences in the ale types remain unclear. It may have been the strength of the same ale type, or perhaps the quality of its ingredients; for example, wheat ale was rare and was considered a luxury, as ale was usually brewed with barley malt, but oat malt was also used. See Slavin, *Bread and Ale for the Brethren*, pp. 161–2.

29 White, *Extents*, p. 203.

30 K. Nicholls, *Irish Fiants, Henry, Edward, Philip and Mary and Elizabeth I*, 3 vols (Dublin: Irish Manuscripts Commission, 1994), vol. II, p. 160.

31 Gilchrist and Sloane, *Requiem*, p. 207.

32 Ibid., p. 210; Ó Clabaigh, *Friars in Ireland*, p. 125.

33 Gilchrist, Unsexing the Body', p. 100.

34 The male Cistercian house at Bective, Co. Meath has been considered in this regard; Stout and Stout, *Bective Abbey Project*. There are some publications on health from male religious houses, for example L. Buckley, 'Health Status in Medieval Dublin: Analysis of the skeletal remains from the abbey of St Thomas the Martyr', *Medieval Dublin*, vol. IV, 2003, pp. 98–126. Leigh Fry uses archaeological evidence in her study of burial in medieval Ireland but it is primarily an historical account; Leigh Fry, *Burial in Medieval Ireland*.

35 No human remains were included in the published report; Sloane, *St Mary Clerkenwell*.

36 Ibid., pp. 155–7, 160.

37 Ibid., p. 196.
38 Bull et al., *Holywell Priory*, pp. 136–7.
39 Sloane, *St Mary Clerkenwell*, pp. 1–2.
40 Gilchrist and Sloane, *Requiem*, pp. 238, 245, 246–7; R. Dobson and S. Donaghey, *The History of Clementhorpe Nunnery: Archaeology of York* (York: York Archaeological Trust, 1984).
41 Bull et al., *Holywell Priory*.
42 Wessex Archaeology, 'Syon House'.
43 S. Clough, 'Human Remains Report on Priory Hotel, Grenoble Road, Littlemore, Oxford' (Archaeological Burials Company, unpublished report for John Moore Heritage Services, 2015).
44 Bezant, *Medieval Welsh Settlement*, pp. 44–50.
45 I am grateful to Dr Jemma Bezant for discussing the excavations with me. The evaluation phase of works was carried out with Fran Murphy of Dyfed Archaeological Trust. (Dr J. Bezant personal communication.)
46 Ward, *Excavations at Chester*, pp. 3–13.
47 A.J.E. Cave, 'Human Bones I 1939', in S. Ward, *Excavations at Chester: The lesser medieval religious houses sites investigated 1964–1983* (Chester: Chester City Council Department of Leisure Services, 1990), pp. 16–21.
48 D. Goose, 'Human Bones II 1964', in S. Ward, *Excavations at Chester: The lesser medieval religious houses sites investigated 1964–1983* (Chester: Chester City Council Department of Leisure Services, 1990), pp. 21–2.
49 Paget's disease is a chronic disorder that results in enlarged and misshapen bones. It is typically localised and affects one or a few bones, unlike osteoporosis which usually affects all the bones. (Dr Linda G. Lynch, personal communication.)
50 I am grateful to the excavation director Paul Murray then of John Moore Heritage Services for supplying me with his unpublished excavation data and specialist reports.
51 Keeping, 'Life and Death in English Nunneries', pp. 177–83.
52 Ibid., p. 187.
53 Ibid., pp. 188–90.
54 Ibid., pp. 128, 202.
55 Gilchrist and Sloane, *Requiem*, p. 213.
56 Keeping, 'Life and Death in English Nunneries', p. 203.
57 Ibid., p. 202.
58 C. Mullins, 'Appendix II. A Report on the Human Remains from Graney East, Castledermot, Co. Kildare', in M. Byrne, 'Graney East, Castledermot, Co. Kildare: Report on archaeological monitoring and testing 99E0052' (Kildare: Byrne, Mullins & Associates, unpublished report, 2001); B. O'Donnabhain, 'Human Remains', in T. Collins, 'Unveiling Female Monasticism in Later Medieval Ireland: Survey and excavation at St Catherine's, Shanagolden, Co. Limerick', *Proceedings of the Royal Irish Academy*, vol. 119C, 2019, pp. 166–71.
59 M.E. Byrne, 'Graney East, Castledermot, Co. Kildare: Report on archaeological monitoring and testing 99E0052' (Kildare: Byrne, Mullins & Associates, unpublished report, 2001). I am grateful to Martin Byrne for providing me with his unpublished report on the monitoring and testing at Graney East, Co. Kildare and the specialist report on the human remains.
60 Ibid., p. 12.
61 Following consultation with the regulatory bodies it was agreed that a buffer zone *c.*25m diameter was created around these skeletons and they remained *in situ*. Strong grass was sown to aid consolidation of the burials; Ibid., p. 10.

62 Mullins, 'A Report on the Human Remains'.

63 The remains of burial 1 comprised skull fragments, fragment of left mandible (jaw) and a number of loose teeth, vertebrae, sternum, fragments of sacrum and ilia, right and left legs, incomplete right arm and fragmentary left arm, and partially represented hands and feet; Mullins, 'A Report on the Human Remains'.

64 Although the sex was indeterminate, fragments of the pelvis displayed a well-developed pre-auricular sulcus which suggested to the osteoarchaeologist that it was female: 'the weight of evidence would suggest that this individual was female but the evidence is by no means conclusive'; Mullins, 'A Report on the Human Remains'.

65 This height is about 5' 6". The female average stature in the medieval period in Ireland is between the range 5' 2" and 5' 3". If the burial is a male, Mullins estimated stature at 174.63cm or 5' 7" which coincides with the average estimated medieval average for males.

66 This is a small osteochondritis dessicans lesion of the distal articular surface of the right tibia, whereby a fragment of the articular surface of the joint fractures and becomes separated from the rest of the joint. This condition can lead to osteoarthritis in later life; Mullins, 'A Report on the Human Remains'.

67 The changes noted are concentrated in the lower thoracic and lumbar region. The pattern of changes was considered reliable as the vertebral column was well represented in this individual. Schmorl's node development was identified on the upper lumbar and lower thoracic bodies as well as slight osteophyte development on T11, T12, L5 and S1. Some arthritic changes of the costal facets of the ribs were noted; Mullins, 'A Report on the Human Remains'.

68 The remains of burial 2 comprised fragments of skull, two loose teeth, well-represented thoracic and lumbar vertebrae, complete sacrum, fragmentary pelvis, well-represented limbs, hands and feet; Mullins, 'A Report on the Human Remains'.

69 This height is about 5' 2".

70 The left knee was moderately arthritic with osteophytic lipping on the distal femur and pitting and surface breakdown of the patella. The right hip, right elbow and wrist were mildly arthritic. The left wrist was moderately to severely arthritic. The medial end of the left clavicle (collarbone) was mildly arthritic. The vertebral column was only mildly arthritic in comparison with the remainder of the skeleton. Mild lipping was noted on the lower thoracic vertebrae and on the superior body surface of L5. Generalised mild arthritis was evident on the posterior and costal facets of the thoracic vertebrae, together with generalised mild arthritis of the ribs. The lumbar vertebrae were generally healthy. A genetic variation was present in the vertebral column, the presence of six lumbar vertebrae instead of five. This condition is associated with a downward shift in the number of thoracic vertebrae. Deviations such as this are thought to occur in about 10 per cent of the population. L6 was partially sacralised, that is the transverse processes articulate with the ala of the sacrum and some evidence of an early fusion on the right side of these two bones was noted. The condition would not have put any great strain on the spinal column; Mullins, 'A Report on the Human Remains'.

71 Trauma was noted at the lateral end of the left clavicle, where its curve was unnaturally angled and there was some abnormality of the lateral articular surface; Mullins, 'A Report on the Human Remains'.

72 A first step in monastic population comparison has been taken in Ireland with Dr Elise Alonzi's research into mobility in monastic populations: 'Peregrini: A comparative study of mobility among medieval ecclesiastics and nuns in Ireland and Wales'. See E. Alonzi, N. Daly, G. Gordon, R.E. Scott and K.J. Knudson, 'Travelling Monastic

Paths: Mobility and religion at medieval Irish monasteries', *Journal of Anthropological Archaeology*, vol. 55, 2019, pp. 1–24.

73 These occur when the compression of the intervertebral disc causes its jelly-like core to herniate and the bone of the endplate resorbs around the extruded material. As the core solidifies in adulthood, herniation of the disc can be interpreted as adolescent girls undertaking heavy physical labour.

74 This is a joint disorder where the cartilage or bone in a joint is inflamed which can lead to cracks forming in the articular cartilage and the underlying bone. It usually causes pain and swelling of the affected joint which may catch and lock during movement.

75 This is a crack or stress fracture in one of the vertebrae. The injury most often occurs in children and adolescents who in a modern context participate in sports that involve repeated stress on the lower back, such as gymnastics, football and weight lifting. In a medieval context it may be caused by physical labour.

76 Evangelisti, *Nuns*, pp. 13–15; Kenny, *Anglo-Irish and Gaelic Women*, p. 169; Burton, 'Looking for Medieval Nuns', p. 117; Cartwright, 'Abbess Agnes and the Ape', p. 203.

77 Keeping, 'Life and Death in English Nunneries', p. 201.

78 B. Harris, 'A New Look at the Reformation: Aristocratic women and nunneries 1450–1540', *The Journal of British Studies*, vol. 32, 1993, pp. 89–113, at pp. 91–3.

79 Oliva, 'Aristocracy or Meritocracy?', pp. 198–201; Oliva, *Convent and the Community*, pp. 52–61.

80 Collins, 'Unveiling Female Monasticism'.

81 C. McCutcheon, 'Medieval Pottery', in T. Collins, 'Unveiling Female Monasticism in Later Medieval Ireland: Survey and excavation at St Catherine's, Shanagolden, Co. Limerick', *Proceedings of the Royal Irish Academy*, vol. 119C, 2019, pp. 162–5.

82 Ibid.

83 The chosen locations of the trenches had a bearing on the amount of archaeological material retrieved. The excavation by design was limited in extent and so the material culture recovered must be considered a small representative sample. It may highlight the deliberately low sanitation standards of nunneries noted by Gilchrist as a deliberate expression of piety and humility: see Gilchrist, 'Unsexing the Body', p. 100; but the sample here is too small for firm conclusions to be drawn.

84 C. McCutcheon, 'Appendix III. A Note on Some Pottery from Graney East, Castledermot, Co. Kildare', in M. Byrne, 'Graney East, Castledermot, Co. Kildare: Report on archaeological monitoring and testing 99E0052' (Kildare: Byrne, Mullins & Associates, unpublished report, 2001).

85 P. Geary, *Living with the Dead in the Middle Ages* (Ithaca: Cornell University Press, 1994), p. 2.

86 Ibid., p. 44.

87 Binski, *Medieval Death*, pp. 33–50.

88 N.F. Blake, 'Ars Moriendi', in J.R. Strayer (ed.), *Dictionary of the Middle Ages*, vol. 1 (New York: Charles Scribner's Sons, 1982), pp. 547–8.

89 Gilchrist and Sloane. *Requiem*, p. 71.

90 Gilchrist, *Medieval Life*, p. 190.

91 Binski, *Medieval Death*, pp. 50–8.

92 Gilchrist, *Medieval Life*, p. 191–2.

93 Cassidy-Welch, *Monastic Spaces and Their Meanings*, pp. 237–9.

94 Kerr, *Life in the Medieval Cloister*, pp. 167–8; Cassidy-Welch, *Monastic Spaces and Their Meanings*, pp. 219–23, 226–32.

95 Kerr, *Life in the Medieval Cloister*, pp. 159–62, 168.

96 Ó Clabaigh, 'Patronage, Prestige and Politics', pp. 71–82.

97 Gilchrist and Sloane, *Requiem*, pp. 56–7.

98 For example, de Paor, 'Excavations at Mellifont Abbey'; Fanning, 'Excavations at Clontuskert Priory'; K. Power, 'The Burials: A medieval demographic sample', in M. Hurley and C. Sheehan, *Excavations at the Dominican Priory: St Mary's of the Isle, Cork* (Cork: Cork Corporation, 1995), pp. 66–83; Halpin and Buckley, 'Archaeological Excavations at the Dominican Priory, Drogheda'; O'Sullivan et al. 'Ennis Friary, Co. Clare', pp. 25, 29; Buckley, 'Health Status in Medieval Dublin'; Clyne, 'Archaeological Excavations at Holy Trinity Abbey', pp. 31–62; J. Higgins, 'The Funerary Monuments', in M. Clyne, *Kells Priory, Co. Kilkenny: Archaeological excavations by T. Fanning and M. Clyne* (Dublin: Government of Ireland, 2007), pp. 453–67; M. Delaney, 'The Human Remains', in M. Clyne, *Kells Priory, Co. Kilkenny: Archaeological excavations by T. Fanning and M. Clyne* (Dublin: Government of Ireland, 2007), pp. 467–76; C. Manning, 'The Grave Slabs', in A. Lynch, *Tintern Abbey, Co. Wexford: Cistercians and Colcloughs excavations 1982–2007* (Dublin: Government of Ireland, 2010), pp. 103–5; B. O'Donnabhain, 'The Human Remains', in A. Lynch, *Tintern Abbey, Co. Wexford: Cistercians and Colcloughs excavations 1982–2007* (Dublin: Government of Ireland, 2010), pp. 105–25.

99 Earlier excavations in Ireland did not appear to publish full details of excavated burials. For example, published excavations at the Cistercian house of Mellifont, Co. Louth noted burials, but provided no detail on the majority; see de Paor, 'Excavations at Mellifont Abbey'. At the Augustinian monastery at Clontuskert, Co. Galway, burials were removed and reinterred; see Fanning, 'Excavations at Clontuskert Priory', p. 105 n. 46. This is not unique to earlier Irish excavations. Early excavations at Glastonbury, England 'must have encountered medieval graves but these were of relatively little interest to the early excavators': R. Gilchrist, 'Conclusions', in R. Gilchrist and C. Green, *Glastonbury Abbey: Archaeological excavations 1904–1979* (London: Society of Antiquaries of London, 2015), pp. 415–35, at p. 425. At the Dominican house of St Mary's of the Isle, Cork, 164 burials were excavated, of which sixty-three were male, forty were female and the remainder were unidentified or juveniles; see Power, 'The Burials', pp. 66–83. At the Dominican priory in Drogheda, sixty-one individuals were excavated, of which thirty-two were male, fourteen were female, eleven were juvenile and four were unidentified; see Halpin and Buckley, 'Archaeological Excavations at the Dominican Priory, Drogheda', p. 196. Human remains excavated from the abbey of St Thomas the Martyr, Dublin totalled eighteen burials, of which four were juveniles, eight were male and six were female; see Buckley, 'Health Status in Medieval Dublin', p. 98. At Holy Trinity, Loughkey, Co. Roscommon, a Premonstratensian male house, four females and twelve children were buried in the church, several men and children and women were also buried in what the excavator interpreted as the sacristy. Only men were buried in the conventual buildings. In the burial ground, situated to the northeast of the east range, one woman and one child were excavated: see Clyne, 'Archaeological Excavations at Holy Trinity Abbey', pp. 48–55. At the Augustinian house of Kells, Co. Kilkenny, female burials were found in the chancel and the north transept. None was found in the cloister areas: see Delaney, 'The Human Remains', pp. 467–76. At the Cistercian house of Tintern, Co. Wexford 106 burials were excavated and men, women and children were found throughout the church and the northern ambulatory: see O'Donnabhain 'The Human Remains'.

100 Golding, *Gilbert of Sempringham*, pp. 334–42; Ó Clabaigh, 'Patronage, Prestige and Politics', p. 76; Ó Clabaigh, *Friars in Ireland*, pp. 107–110, 219.

101 Cassidy-Welch, *Monastic Spaces and Their Meanings*, p. 228.
102 Gilchrist, *Medieval Life*, p. 200.
103 For example, see discussion of burial in Yorkshire Cistercian houses: Cassidy-Welch, *Monastic Spaces and Their Meanings*, pp. 232–7.
104 Affreca de Courcy was buried at the Cistercian house of Grey Abbey, Co. Down, which she founded in 1193; Desideria, daughter of Gerald FitzMaurice, was buried at the Franciscan abbey of Ardfert, Co. Kerry in 1345; and in 1353 Gormlaith O'Donnell was buried with her brothers at Armagh. Joan de Burgh, wife of Thomas earl of Kildare, was buried at Kildare with her husband in 1357; see Leigh Fry, *Burial in Medieval Ireland*, p. 175. Seven women made their own requests to be buried at the Cistercian house of Fountains Abbey in Yorkshire, England between 1132 and 1300. A further two women were included in their husband's requests for burial: see Cassidy-Welch, *Monastic Spaces and Their Meanings*, pp. 232–3.
105 Leigh Fry, *Burial in Medieval Ireland*, p. 121. Leigh Fry commented that such a quick translation of a body to a relic is unusual in any circumstances. Mór's status at Killone is also unclear. Was she a widow who had retired there as a vowess or corrodian? The only record of a death of a man who may have been her husband occurs ten years after her own death, suggesting that she was not a widow when she died; Leigh Fry, *Burial in Medieval Ireland*, p. 122; Hall, *Women and the Church*, p. 173.
106 Gilchrist and Sloane, *Requiem*, p. 65.
107 T. Dyson, M. Samuel, A. Steele and S. Wright, *The Cluniac Priory and Abbey of St Saviour Bermondsey, Surrey: Excavations 1984–95* (London: Museum of London Archaeology, 2011).
108 P. Miller and D. Saxby, *The Augustinian Priory of St Mary Merton, Surrey: Excavations 1976–90* (London: Museum of London Archaeology Services, 2007).
109 G. Coppack, *Fountains Abbey* (London: Batsford, for English Heritage, 1993).
110 Renalda was an O'Brien of Thomond; first she became the mistress of Sir John Ormond at an early age when he was quite her senior. She bore him a son, James (Sir James of Ormond), and later she became wife of Richard Butler. When the political climate deteriorated between the Butlers and the O'Brien's, she returned to her home of Thomond and settled at Killone. Much is known of her political connections due to her will of 1510; see Ó Dálaigh, 'Mistress, Mother and Abbess'. She is also somewhat infamous in that she has been identified as having an incestuous relationship with her father and bore him two sons. It is possible that a third son may have been born by another relative, a bishop. These events have been recorded as the sons later became clerics and required papal dispensations due to the perceived defect of their births. By tracking the events chronologically, though with some speculation, Renalda has been identified as the mother of these clerics; see Hall, *Women and the Church*, pp. 166–7; Kenny, *Anglo-Irish and Gaelic Women*, p. 183, for fuller explanation.
111 Ó Dálaigh, 'Mistress, Mother and Abbess', p. 61.
112 Phelan, 'An Unidentified Tomb'.
113 Gilchrist and Sloane, *Requiem*, p. 64.
114 For example, Hamlin and Foley, 'A Women's Graveyard at Carrickmore'.
115 Leigh Fry, *Burial in Medieval Ireland*, pp. 176–80.
116 Hall, *Women and the Church*, pp. 172–4.
117 Archaeological excavations near the nunneries of Armagh and Grace Dieu have produced human remains but these dated to the early medieval period.
118 Maher, *Medieval Grave Slabs*, pp. 40, 66–7, 91.
119 Gilchrist, *Medieval Life*, pp. 196–200.

120 Rae, 'Irish Sepulchral Monuments', p. 22; Hunt, *Irish Medieval Figure Sculpture*, p. 191; Phelan, 'An Unidentified Tomb'; Hall, *Women and the Church*, pp. 191–200.
121 Cassidy-Welch, *Monastic Spaces and Their Meanings*, p. 106.
122 T. O'Keeffe, 'Buttevant Friary and Its Crypt', *Archaeology Ireland*, vol. 26, 2012, pp. 23–5.
123 O'Donoghue, 'Mendicant Cloisters in Munster', p. 128.
124 O'Sullivan et al., 'Ennis Friary, Co. Clare', pp. 27–31.
125 Gilchrist and Sloane, *Requiem*, p. 57.
126 Müller, 'Presenting Identity in the Cloister', pp. 170–1, 173–4.
127 A. Kehnel and M. Mencej, 'Representing Eternity: Circular movement in the cloister, round dancing, winding-staircases and dancing angels', in A. Müller and K. Stöber (eds), *Self-Representation of Medieval Religious Communities: The British Isles context* (Berlin: LIT Verlag, 2009), pp. 67–97, at p. 88.
128 Collins, 'Space and Place'.
129 Kehnel and Mencej, 'Representing Eternity', pp. 86–8.
130 Gilchrist and Sloane, *Requiem*, pp. 58–9.
131 Jäggi, 'Eastern Choir or Western Gallery?', p. 82.
132 For example, in advance of drainage works: Sweetman, 'Medieval Field Boundaries at Clonard'. In advance of quarrying works: Byrne, 'Graney East, Co. Kildare'.
133 Higgins, *Tisrara Medieval Church*, p. 59.
134 Ibid., p. 82. As well as the excavation of the church and attached accommodation at Tisrara, a record of all the graveyard inscriptions was made. No medieval funerary monuments were found. The earliest graveslab recorded was dated to 1721; Higgins, *Tisrara Medieval Church*, pp. 101–38.
135 I. Hagen, '2022:0648 – Portraine, Dublin', in https://excavations.ie/report/2002/Dublin/0007964/. Accessed 15 September 2019.
136 Cunniffe, 'Canons and Canonesses of St Augustine at Clonfert'.
137 In the SMR file for this putative nunnery (KD027-025---), Martin E. Byrne noted that a number of cottages were built on site in the 1950s and people in the area remembered human remains and skeletal material being revealed. It appears that the parish priest sent school children onto the site to collect the skeletal material which was subsequently interred in the old graveyard at Nurney (KD027-027---). A plaque now marks this burial plot. Byrne undertook testing in an area adjacent to the nunnery location in 1997. Nothing of an archaeological nature was found during those investigations (M.E. Byrne, '1997:289 – Walterstown, Kildare', in https://excavations.ie/report/1997/Kildare/0002838/. Accessed 15 September 2020). Similarly, Opie's investigations after geophysical survey of a site near the nunnery did uncover medieval features but no human remains; H. Opie, '2002:0972 – Nurney, Kildare', in https://excavations.ie/report/2002/Kildare/0008289/. Accessed 15 September 2020.
138 G. O'Grady, 'History and Antiquities of the District of Rathcoole and Saggart', *Journal of the Kildare Archaeological Society*, vol. 5, 1906, pp. 75–8, at p. 78. He recorded that 'human bones were found which in the opinion of a medical man were those of females'. This possible site is not recorded as a nunnery; see Gwynn and Hadcock, *Medieval Religious Houses*. It is marked on the Ordnance Survey first-edition six-inch map as the site of a monastery and is described as such by F.E. Ball, *A History of County Dublin*, 6 vols (Dublin: A. Thom, 1905); P. Healy, *Third Report on Monuments and Sites of Archaeological Interest in County Dublin: Northern section*, vol. 3 (Dublin: An Foras Forbartha Teoranta, 1975), pp. 1-30. Investigations close by did not uncover anything of an archaeological nature; M.E. Byrne, '2005:525 – Coolmine, Saggart, Dublin', in https://excavations.ie/report/2005/Dublin/0013529/. Accessed 15 September 2020.

139 At St Catherine's, for instance, there is a legend of an earl of Desmond fleeing an assault on nearby Shanid Castle with his lady, who gets injured with an arrow in the mêlée. He arrives at the gate of the nunnery only to find that she is dead. She is quickly buried at the east end of the church, though had unfortunately been buried alive and so continues to haunt the nunnery.
140 Gilchrist and Sloane, *Requiem*, p. 68.
141 Ibid., p. 204.
142 Gilchrist, *Gender and Material Culture*, p. 59; Gilchrist and Sloane, *Requiem*, p. 68.
143 Gilchrist and Sloane, *Requiem*, p. 60.
144 Coppack, *Abbeys and Priories*, p. 78.
145 Gilchrist, *Gender and Material Culture*, p. 59.
146 Cassidy-Welch, *Monastic Spaces and Their Meanings*, pp. 232–7; Gilchrist and Sloane, *Requiem*, p. 56–60; Ó Clabaigh, *Friars in Ireland*, pp. 107–10, 219–20.
147 Gilchrist and Sloane, *Requiem*, p. 81.
148 Bull et al., *Holywell Priory*, p. 130.
149 Collins, 'Unveiling Female Monasticism'.
150 Wardell, 'The History and Antiquities of St Catherine's', pp. 51–2.
151 Gilchrist noted that while accompanying grave goods were never common in later medieval cemeteries, 'the pararitual of placing grave goods with the corpse' is a strong indicator of local practice in burial which can be identified in virtually every excavated churchyard; Gilchrist, *Medieval Life*, p. 210. See also Gilchrist, 'Magic for the Dead?'; R. Gilchrist, 'Magic and Archaeology: Ritual residues and "odd" deposits', in S. Page and C. Rider (eds), *The Routledge History of Medieval Magic* (Routledge: Abingdon, 2019), pp. 383–401.
152 These numbers prefixed with a C (context) relate to numbers allocated to the burials upon excavation. This burial was (C160).
153 Gilchrist and Sloane, *Requiem*, p. 131.
154 For example, J. Rugg, 'Constructing the Grave: Competing burial ideas in nineteenth-century England, *Social History*, vol. 38, no. 3, 2013, pp. 328–45; J. Rugg, F. Sterling and A. Clayden, 'Churchyard and Cemetery in an English Industrial City', *Urban History*, vol. 41, no. 4, 2014, pp. 627–46.
155 C909; C114.
156 C908; C917; C112; C128; C160.
157 C914.
158 I am grateful to Dr Barra O'Donnabhain for analysing the human remains; see B. O'Donnabhain, 'The Human Remains'.
159 C128 and C917.
160 C908.
161 C112; C160.
162 O'Donnabhain, 'The Human Remains', pp. 105–25.
163 Delaney, 'The Human Remains', pp. 472–3.
164 An Inca bone is an extra ossicle that can occur in the occipital bone in the region of the lambdoid suture. A metopic suture is located in the midline of the frontal area of the skull and is normally fused in the first five years of life; O'Donnabhain, 'The Human Remains', pp. 168–9.
165 Gilchrist and Sloane, *Requiem*, p. 223.
166 A. Young and D. Lunt, 'Human Bone', in *Perthshire Society of Natural Science* (eds), *Pitmiddle Village and Elcho Nunnery: Research and excavation on Tayside* (Perth: Perthshire Society of Natural Science, 1988), pp. 60–6, at pp. 64–5.

167 For example, Power, *Medieval English Nunneries*, pp. 436–74; Kenny, *Anglo-Irish and Gaelic Women*, pp. 181–4.
168 Hall, *Women and the Church*, pp. 174–5.
169 This symbolism is rare even in a male context. There is a single graveslab in Ireland depicting a crosier thought to designate a male monastic burial at Boyle, Co. Roscommon (Cistercian).
170 C23; this individual was not radiocarbon dated.
171 Four individuals were fully excavated and a fifth adult was partially exposed in the foundation cut of the north wall of the church. It was dated to AD 1280–1320 or AD 1340–90. There was no archaeological evidence to suggest that this location was intensively used for burial.
172 Collins, 'Unveiling Female Monasticism', pp. 151–2.
173 Gilchrist and Sloane, *Requiem*, p. 32.
174 Ibid., p. 184.
175 Cassidy-Welch, *Monastic Spaces and Their Meanings*, p. 224.
176 For material culture relating to visibility and commemoration of graves, see Gilchrist and Sloane, *Requiem*, pp. 184–94.
177 Cassidy-Welch, *Monastic Spaces and Their Meanings*, p. 217.

CHAPTER 9. ESTATES: NUNNERIES IN A WIDER LANDSCAPE CONTEXT

1 For example, O'Conor, *Archaeology of Medieval Rural Settlement*; Barry, *A History of Settlement*; C. Corlett and M Potterton (eds), *Rural Settlement in Medieval Ireland in the Light of Recent Archaeological Excavation* (Dublin: Wordwell, 2009).
2 O'Conor, *Archaeology of Medieval Rural Settlement*.
3 Stalley, *Cistercian Monasteries*; O'Keeffe, *An Anglo-Norman Monastery*; Ó Clabaigh, *The Friars in Ireland*; Browne and Ó Clabaigh, *Soldiers of Christ*; Browne and Ó Clabaigh, *Households of God*.
4 McNeill, *Castles in Ireland*; Sweetman, *Castles*.
5 FitzPatrick and Gillespie, *The Parish*.
6 J. Lyttleton and T. O'Keeffe (eds), *The Manor in Medieval and Early Modern Ireland* (Dublin: Four Courts Press, 2005).
7 Duffy et al., *Gaelic Ireland*; E. FitzPatrick, *Royal Inauguration in Gaelic Ireland*.
8 M. Murphy and M. Stout (eds), *Agriculture and Settlement in Ireland* (Dublin: Four Courts Press, 2015).
9 But see E. Campbell, E. FitzPatrick and A. Horning (eds), *Becoming and Belonging in Ireland AD c.1200–1600: Essays in identity and cultural practice* (Cork: Cork University Press, 2018).
10 The work of the Group for the Study of Historic Irish Settlement, the Irish Historic Towns Atlas, the Discovery Programme and the annual Space and Settlement Conference held at Trinity College Dublin is acknowledged. Each has produced a number of publications. For an excellent synthetic regional study of medieval Dublin and its hinterland, which could be replicated elsewhere, sources permitting, see Murphy and Potterton, *The Dublin Region*.
11 For example, Gaimster and Gilchrist, *Archaeology of Reformation*; K. Giles and C. Dyer (eds), *Town and Country in the Middle Ages* (Leeds: Maney, 2007); Gilchrist, *Medieval Life*; C. Gerrard and A. Gutierrez (eds), *The Oxford Handbook of Later Medieval Archaeology in Britain* (Oxford: Oxford University Press, 2018).
12 C. Baker, 'Tullykane, Co. Meath: A medieval rural settlement', in C. Corlett and M. Potterton (eds), *Rural Settlement in Medieval Ireland in the Light of Recent Archaeological*

Excavation (Dublin: Wordwell, 2009), pp. 1–17, at pp. 6–9; T. Barry, 'Foreword', in C. Corlett and M. Potterton (eds), *Rural Settlement in Medieval Ireland in the Light of Recent Archaeological Excavation* (Dublin: Wordwell, 2009), pp. viii–x, at p. viii.

13 As suggested by A. Simms, 'Perspectives on Irish Settlement Studies', in T. Barry (ed.), *A History of Settlement in Ireland* (London: Routledge, 2000), pp. 228–47, at pp. 237–43.

14 For example, Campbell et al., *Becoming and Belonging*; FitzPatrick, 'Rethinking Settlement Values in Gaelic Society'.

15 Johnson, *Equal in Monastic Profession*, pp. 248–53.

16 For a recent comprehensive overview of the discourse on monastic landscape history and archaeology, see Austin, 'The Archaeology of Monasteries', pp. 3–20.

17 Lee, *Nunneries, Learning and Spirituality*, pp. 57–8; Kenny, *Anglo-Irish and Gaelic Women*, p. 170.

18 Lee, *Nunneries, Learning and Spirituality*, pp. 57–108; Curran, 'Religious Women'; Perkins-Curran, '"Quhat Say Ye Now"'.

19 Power, *Medieval English Nunneries*, pp. 203–12; Oliva, 'Aristocracy or Meritocracy?'

20 Knowles, *Religious Orders in England*.

21 For example, Burton, *Yorkshire Nunneries*, pp. 17–27; J. Burton, 'Looking for Medieval Nuns'; Bond, 'Medieval Nunneries in England and Wales'; Jamroziak, *Cistercian Order*, pp. 124–55; Berman, 'Medieval Monasticisms'.

22 Stöber, *Late Medieval Monasteries*, pp. 1–8.

23 Gilchrist, *Gender and Material Culture*, p. 44.

24 Ibid., pp. 65–9; Bond, 'Medieval Nunneries in England and Wales', pp. 53–4.

25 A.E. Lester, 'Making the Margins in the Thirteenth Century: Suburban space and religious reform between the Low Countries and the county of Champagne', *Parergon*, vol. 27, 2010, pp. 59–87, at pp. 85–6.

26 Fredengren, *Crannógs*.

27 Moorhouse, 'Monastic Estates', p. 60.

28 Bond, *Monastic Landscapes*, pp. 25–9; Stöber, *Late Medieval Monasteries*; Stout, 'The Cistercian Grange', pp. 28–30; H. Röckelein, 'Monastic Landscapes', in A.I. Beach and I. Cochelin (eds), *Medieval Monasticism in the Latin West*, 2 vols (Cambridge: Cambridge University Press, 2020), pp. 816–30.

29 Power, *Medieval English Nunneries*, p. 100; Greene, *Medieval Monasteries*, p. 133; Moorhouse, 'Monastic Estates', p. 39; Golding, *Gilbert of Sempringham*, pp. 302–8; Hall, *Women and the Church*, pp. 135–7.

30 Bezant, 'Revising the Monastic "Grange"', p. 57.

31 Oliva, *Convent and the Community*, p. 75.

32 There are some difficulties in using the term 'estate' to describe many monastic holdings. Not least because an estate suggests a consolidation of a number of manors, which many of the smaller religious houses never actually possessed. In the meagre evidence available for nunnery estates in Ireland, a few are recorded as possessing manors; see Hall, *Women and the Church*, pp. 372–5.

33 Monastic house income is commonly described as temporalities and spiritualities. Temporalities relate to income from rents from lands and houses, perquisites or grants of courts, fairs, mills, woods and other manorial perquisites, issues of the manor, such as sale of farm produce and miscellaneous payments from boarders, gifts, etc. Spiritualities comprise tithes from appropriated benefices such as alms, mortuaries and other spiritual services. Power noted for the English evidence at least that the distinction between the two income sources was a technical one, although temporal income was usually the greater; Power, *English Nunneries*, p. 100.

34 Bond, 'Nunneries in England and Wales', p. 77; D.A. Hinton, *Archaeology, Economy and Society: England from the fifth to the fifteenth century* (London: Routledge, 1990), pp. 165–213; S.H. Rigby, *English Society in the Later Middle Ages: Class, status and gender* (London: Macmillan, 1995), pp. 17–144.

35 K. Down, 'Colonial Society and Economy', in A. Cosgrave (ed.), *A New History of Ireland. Volume II: Medieval Ireland 1169–1534* (Oxford: Clarendon Press, 1993), pp. 439–91; Murphy, 'The Economy'.

36 The Statute of Mortmain (1279) imposed penalties for alienation – the right to transfer land – to monastic houses (as they were considered corporate bodies that could not die, marry or be in a minority). Where land was transferred to monastic houses, the crown was denied its entitlement of income in these transactions, so the imposition of the statute permitted the crown to then receive an entitlement. Monastic institutions managed to evade this statute by taking an action of recovery through the courts. For discussion, see P. Brand, 'King, Church and Property: The enforcement of restrictions on alienations into Mortmain in the lordship of Ireland in the later middle ages', *Peritia*, vol. 3, 1984, pp. 481–502; P. Brand, 'The Licensing of Mortmain Alienations in the Medieval Lordship of Ireland', *Irish Jurist*, vol. 21, 1986, pp. 125–44. There are several occurrences in the Irish records which refer to the Statute of Mortmain. For example, the nuns of Timolin were granted land in Armacrenan by the archbishop of Dublin in the later twelfth century and they purchased more there in 1291. This purchase was deemed contrary to the Statute of Mortmain and was confiscated; Hall, *Women and the Church*, p. 144; McNeill, *Archbishop Alen's Register*. The church of Molyngar (?Mullingar) in the possession of St Mary de Hogges came into the possession of Queen Elizabeth, as a result of this statute; see Nicholls, *Irish Fiants*, vol. 2, p. 752. In 1596–7 the Statute of Mortmain was enacted in relation to the rectory of Nuregare which was once the parcel of the monastery of St Mollins [sic] alias Timolin, and was granted to George Isham Brianstowne, a Wexford gent; Nicholls, *Irish Fiants*, vol. 3, p. 277.

37 Hall, 'The Nuns of the Medieval Convent of Lismullin'; Hall, *Women and the Church*, p. 137. Brady identified these locations as Collinstown, Co. Westmeath, Kilmessan, Co. Meath and near Tara, Co. Meath respectively; Brady, 'Nunnery at Clonard', p. 6. This was obviously a genuine petition, which was taken seriously, as the fees incurred due to the petition were waived for the abbess on account of her poverty; Hall, *Women and the Church*, p. 137.

38 Hall, *Women and the Church*, p. 133. Gilchrist has suggested that nunneries in England did maintain and defend their estates but did not actively seek to extend their landholdings through land purchase, like some contemporary male houses. Many nunneries there appear not to have gained substantial parcels of land after their initial grant at their foundation; Gilchrist, *Gender and Material Culture*, pp. 71–3; Bond, 'Medieval Nunneries in England and Wales', p. 79.

39 Curran 'Religious Women', pp. 39–103; Perkins Curran, '"Quhat Say Ye Now"', p. 125.

40 Burke, 'Nunnery of Kilculliheen', p. 11; Hall, *Women and the Church*, p. 140.

41 Hall, *Women and the Church*, pp. 140–51.

42 Ibid., pp. 151–7.

43 Bond, *Monastic Landscapes*, pp. 34–9.

44 M. Jurkowski, N. Ramsey and S. Renton (eds), *English Monastic Estates 1066–1540: A list of manors, churches and chapels*, 3 vols (Kew: List and Index Society, 2007).

45 Hall, *Women and the Church*, pp. 129, 136.

46 Rectories, vicarages and tithes were benefices that nunneries (and others) were entitled to. They were usually bestowed by local lords or the bishop; see Flanagan, *Transformation*, pp. 85–91.

47 Hall, *Women and the Church*, pp. 122–32.
48 Moorhouse, 'Monastic Estates', p. 32; Gilchrist, *Gender and Material Culture*, p. 69.
49 Gilchrist, *Gender and Material Culture*, p. 90; Bond, 'Medieval Nunneries in England and Wales', p. 77.
50 Bond, *Monastic Landscapes*, pp. 68–86.
51 Gilchrist, *Gender and Material Culture*, pp. 68, 90.
52 Bond, 'Medieval Nunneries in England and Wales', p. 86.
53 S. Bond and C. Maines, 'The Archaeology of Monasticism: A survey of recent work in France', *Speculum*, vol. 63, 1988, pp. 794–825; Barrière, 'Cistercian Convent of Coyroux'.
54 Jordan, *Women, Power and Religious Patronage*, p. 78.
55 Bond, *Monastic Landscapes*, pp. 87–100.
56 Hall, *Women and The Church*, pp. 137–40.
57 Gywnn and Hadcock, *Medieval Religious Houses*, p. 166; Hogan, *Priory of Llanthony Prima and Secunda in Ireland*; A. Hogan, 'The Settlement of the Augustinian Canons of Llanthony Prima and Secunda in Ireland 1172–1541', in M. Browne and C. Ó Clabaigh (eds), *Households of God: The regular canons and canonesses of Saint Augustine and of Prémontré in medieval Ireland* (Dublin: Four Courts Press, 2019), pp. 138–55; A. Simms, 'The Geography of Irish Manors: The example of the Llanthony cells of Duleek and Colp, County Meath', in J. Bradley (ed.), *Settlement and Society in Medieval Ireland: Studies presented to F.X. Martin* (Kilkenny: Boethius Press, 1988), pp. 291–315, at pp. 305–12.
58 D. Hall, 'Women and Religion in Late Medieval Ireland', unpublished PhD thesis, University of Melbourne, 2000, pp. 372–75. I am very grateful to Dr Hall for making her thesis available to me, including data that did not appear in her subsequent publications.
59 Carville, 'St Mary's Abbey, Graney', pp. 48–9.
60 Nicholls, 'Rectory, Vicarage and Parish'.
61 Empey, 'The Layperson in the Parish'; Hall, *Women and the Church*, p. 145.
62 There have been several studies of male religious house estates and economy in Britain, and to a lesser extent in Ireland. It should be noted that the surviving evidence of all medieval monastic and religious estates in Ireland is much less than Britain; for an overview, see B.J. Graham, *Medieval Irish Settlement: A review* (Lancaster: Historical Geography Group, 1980), pp. 26–7. For Britain, see: Robinson, *Geography of Augustinian Settlement*, pp. 308–48; Brown, *Stanley Abbey*; G. Astill, S. Hirst and S. Wright, 'The Bordesley Abbey Project Reviewed', *Archaeological Journal*, vol. 161, 2004, pp. 106–58; D. Austin, 'Strata Florida and Its Landscape Archaeology', *Archaeologia Cambrensis*, vol. 153, 2004, pp. 192–201; Austin, 'The Archaeology of Monasteries', pp. 3–37; Bezant, *Medieval Welsh Settlement*; Bezant, 'The Medieval Grants to Strata Florida'; Bezant, 'Revising the Monastic "Grange"'; J. Bond, 'The Estates of Evesham Abbey: A preliminary survey of their medieval topography', *Vale of Evesham Historical Society Research Papers*, vol. 4, 1973, pp. 1–62; J. Bond, 'The Reconstruction of the Medieval Landscape: The estates of Abingdon Abbey', *Landscape History*, vol. 1, 1979, pp. 59–75; J. Burton, 'The Estates and Economy of Rievaulx Abbey in Yorkshire', *Citeaux Commentarii Cistercienses*, vol. 49, 1998, pp. 29–94; B. Harrison, 'Field Systems and Demesne Farming on the Wiltshire Estates of St Swithun's Priory, Winchester', *Agricultural History Review*, vol. 43, 1995, pp. 1–18. For Ireland, see: Simms, 'The Geography of Irish Manors'; Hogan, *The Priory of Llanthony Prima and Secunda in Ireland*; Lynch, *A Monastic Landscape*; Stout, 'St Mary's Abbey, Dublin'; Stout, 'The Cistercian Grange'; Ó Clabaigh, *Friars in Ireland*, pp. 125–42.

63 For example, Power, *Medieval English Nunneries*; Burton, *Yorkshire Nunneries*; Coldicott, *Hampshire Nunneries*; Gilchrist, *Gender and Material Culture*; Kerr, *Religious Life for Women*; Lee, *Nunneries, Learning and Spirituality*; Bond, 'Medieval Nunneries in England and Wales', pp. 77–86; Spear, *Leadership*.
64 Hall, *Scottish Monastic Landscapes*, pp. 105, 115, 173–4, 192, 194–5, 198, 202; Perkins-Curran, '"Quhat Say Ye Now"', pp. 126–9.
65 Bond and Maines, 'Archaeology of Monasticism'; Johnson, *Equal in Monastic Profession*; L.N. Simmons, 'The Abbey Church at Fontevraud in the Later Twelfth Century: Anxiety, authority and architecture in the female spiritual life', *Gesta*, vol. 31, 1992, pp. 99–107; Venarde, *Women's Monasticism*.
66 Bezant, *Medieval Welsh Settlement*; Bezant, 'The Medieval Grants to Strata Florida Abbey'.
67 Strata Florida was described by Bezant as the 'mother house' of the nunnery, but it remains unclear if a male religious house could be considered a 'mother house' of a nunnery.
68 Bezant, *Medieval Welsh Settlement*, pp. 44–53, 117–18.
69 Ibid., p. 52.
70 J. Otway Ruthven, 'The Medieval Church Lands of County Dublin', in J.A. Watt, J.B. Worrall and F.X. Martin (eds), *Medieval Studies Presented to Aubrey Gwynn* (Dublin: Three Candles, 1961), pp. 54–73.
71 Carville, *Impact of the Cistercians*, pp. 245–50.
72 Hall, *Women and the Church*, pp. 148–9, 153; Carville, 'St Mary's Abbey, Graney', pp. 41, 49.
73 Collins, 'Timolin'.
74 A messuage is a dwelling house with associated outbuildings and land assigned to its use.
75 White, *Extents*, p. 171.
76 Hall tracked all holdings of twenty-three nunneries through the Irish historical documents. None is complete and many nunneries have no extant records; Hall, 'Women and Religion', pp. 357–83. For an overview of the problems regarding the scarcity of Irish sources, see Chapter 1.
77 Moorhouse, 'Monastic Estates', p. 29; Bond, *Monastic Landscapes*, pp. 13–22.
78 Moorhouse, 'Monastic Estates', pp. 29, 67; Bond, *Monastic Landscapes*, pp. 22–4.
79 Stout, 'The Cistercian Grange', p. 28.
80 Bezant, 'Revising the Monastic "Grange"', pp. 59, 62, 63.
81 Stout, 'The Cistercian Grange', p. 58; G. Conroy, 'Hartwell Castle and Bawn: A monastic grange?', in C. Manning (ed.), *From Ringforts to Fortified Houses: Studies on castles and other monuments in honour of David Sweetman* (Dublin: Wordwell, 2007), pp. 187–93.
82 Moorhouse, 'Monastic Estates', pp. 45–9; Bond, *Monastic Landscapes*, pp. 43–67; G. Coppack, *Abbeys and Priories* (Stroud: Tempus, 2006), p. 141.
83 Austin, 'The Archaeology of Monasteries in Wales', pp. 14–15; Bezant, 'Revising the Monastic "Grange"'.
84 Bezant, 'Revising the Monastic "Grange"', pp. 57–9, 67.
85 C. Platt, *The Monastic Grange in Medieval England* (London: Macmillan, 1969); Greene, *Medieval Monasteries*, p. 134; Coppack, *Abbeys and Priories*, p. 138.
86 Brown, *Stanley Abbey*, pp. 71–92.
87 Greene, *Medieval Monasteries*, p. 143.
88 P. Mayes, *Excavations at a Templar Preceptor: South Witham, Lincolnshire 1965–67* (Leeds: Society for Medieval Archaeology, 2002).

89 Coppack, *Abbeys and Priories*, pp. 138–40.
90 Colfer, *The Hook Peninsula*, pp. 52, 65.
91 E. FitzPatrick, 'Aughris Headland, Co. Sligo', in F.H.A. Aalen, K. Whelan and M. Stout (eds), *Atlas of the Irish Rural Landscape*, 2nd edn (Cork: Cork University Press, 2011), pp. 352–67.
92 J. Fenwick, 'Geophysical Survey at Knowth', in G. Eogan, *Excavations at Knowth. Volume 5: The Archaeology of Knowth in the First and Second Millennia AD* (Dublin: Royal Irish Academy, 2012), pp. 832–40.
93 Stout, 'The Medieval Grange', p. 59.
94 Ibid., pp. 50, 53–7.
95 M. Stephens, 'Home on the Grange', *Archaeology Ireland*, vol. 23, 2009, pp. 31–3.
96 G. Kenny, 'Late Medieval Brugh na Bóinne, 1142–1541', in F.J. Byrne, W. Jenkins, G. Kenny and C. Swift (eds), *Historical Knowth and Its Hinterland: Excavations at Knowth*, vol. 4 (Dublin: Royal Irish Academy, 2008), pp. 133–71; Stout, 'Settlement on Mellifont Abbey's Monastic Estate'.
97 Foley, 'Excavation at a Medieval Settlement Site'.
98 For a summary, see A. Hayden, '2003:1974 – Site 1, Kilbeggan, Co. Westmeath', in https://excavations.ie/report/2003/Westmeath/0011006/. Accessed 15 September 2020.
99 G. Stout, *Newgrange and the Bend of the Boyne* (Cork: Cork University Press, 2002), pp. 87–8; G. Eogan, *Excavations at Knowth. Volume 5: The Archaeology of Knowth in the First and Second Millennia AD* (Dublin: Royal Irish Academy, 2012), p. 179; Stout, 'Settlement on Mellifont Abbey's Monastic Estate', pp. 157–9.
100 Stout and Stout, *Bective Abbey Project*.
101 D.H. Williams, *Atlas of Cistercian Lands in Wales* (Cardiff: Cardiff University Press, 1990); D.H. Williams, *The Welsh Cistercians* (Leominister: Gracewing, 2001).
102 Bezant, *Medieval Welsh Settlement*, pp. 42, 44; Bezant, 'Revising the Monastic "Grange"'; Austin, 'The Archaeology of Monasteries in Wales', p. 15.
103 Bezant, *Medieval Welsh Settlement*, p. 45.
104 Ibid., pp. 56–60.
105 Ibid., p. 40.
106 They are North Berwick, Eccles, Haddington, Manuel, Elcho (all Cistercian) and Lincluden (Benedictine); see Hall, *Scottish Monastic Landscapes*, pp. 95, 194–5, 202.
107 Bond, *Monastic Landscapes*, pp. 101–23, 126–53.
108 Collins, 'Timolin', pp. 65–9.
109 Nicholls, 'Towards a New *Monasticon Hibernicum*', p. 332; Manning, 'Mystery of the Second Nunnery at Clonmacnoise', p. 24.
110 Moorhouse, 'Monastic Estates', pp. 64–5. Stephen Moorhouse has suggested that many upland monastic landscapes may actually be misidentified as pre-historic landscapes. Discussion at International Medieval Congress, Leeds University, 10 July 2012; personal communication.
111 Bond, 'Medieval Nunneries in England and Wales', pp. 79–81.
112 Williams, *Cistercian Lands in Wales*, p. 16.
113 C. Rynne, *Technological Change in Anglo-Norman Munster* (Kinsale: Barryscourt Trust with Cork County Council, 1998), p. 91; C. Rynne, 'Milling of Cereals in Gaelic and Anglo-Norman Ireland *c.*1200–1500: Technology and cultural choice', in E. Campbell, E. FitzPatrick and A. Horning (eds), *Becoming and Belonging in Ireland AD c.1200–1600* (Cork: Cork University Press, 2018), pp. 45–68.
114 Greene, *Medieval Monasteries*, pp. 126–8, 145; C. Rynne, 'The Development of Milling Technology in Ireland, *c.*600–1875', in A. Bielenberg (ed.), *Irish Flour Milling: A history*

600–2000 (Dublin: Lilliputt Press, 2003), pp. 11–38, at pp. 19–22; Coppack, *Abbeys and Priories*, p. 139; Murphy, 'Manor Centres', pp. 92–4.

115 Moorhouse, 'Monastic Estates', pp. 52–3.

116 Bond, *Monastic Landscapes*, pp. 310–24.

117 Ibid., p. 323.

118 G. Astill, S. Hirst and S. Wright, 'The Bordesley Abbey Project: Watermills, 2008', at http://www.reading.ac.uk/bordesley/. Accessed 15 September 2020.

119 White, *Extents*, pp. 77, 171, 255–60.

120 J. Farrelly and C. O'Brien, *Archaeological Inventory of North Tipperary* (Dublin: The Stationery Office, 2002), p. 345; B. Ó Dálaigh, *Irish Historic Towns Atlas No. 25: Ennis* (Dublin: Royal Irish Academy, 2012), pp. 4, 14, 16.

121 Moorhouse, 'Monastic Estates', p. 62.

122 Stalley, *Cistercian Monasteries*, p. 175.

123 O'Keeffe, *Medieval Fore*.

124 O'Keeffe, *Medieval Irish Buildings*, p. 63; Hansell and Hansell, *Dovecotes*, pp. 6–10.

125 Greene, *Medieval Monasteries*, pp. 124–5; Bond, *Monastic Landscapes*, pp. 183–210.

126 Bond, *Monastic Landscapes*, pp. 186–7.

127 Moorhouse, 'Monastic Estates', p. 64.

128 Bond, *Monastic Landscapes*, pp. 180–2.

129 T. Williamson, *The Archaeology of Rabbit Warrens* (Princes Risborough: Shire Publications, 2006).

130 Nine rabbit warrens are recorded by the Archaeological Survey of Ireland; five in Co. Westmeath, one in Cork, one in Dublin, one in Kildare and one in Laois. The examples from the townlands of Monksland, Co. Westmeath and Greatconnell, Co. Kildare are associated with religious houses, https://webgis.archaeology.ie/historicenvironment/. Accessed 15 September 2020.

131 Murphy et al., 'Waterford and Its Hinterland', p. 229.

132 I am grateful to Con Manning for drawing to my attention this possible re-use of this site as a rabbit warren. While I think that this is a valid interpretation, I note that there is not universal agreement. For an image, see Westropp, 'On Certain Typical Earthworks', plate iv.

133 Moorhouse, 'Monastic Estates', p. 65.

134 Bond, *Monastic Landscapes*, pp. 174–9.

135 F. Beglane, *Anglo-Norman Parks in Medieval Ireland: 1169 – c.1350* (Dublin: Four Courts Press, 2015); Beglane, 'The Social Significance of Game in the Diet'.

136 Medieval deerparks in Ireland are only known to have belonged to bishops, rather than religious houses. Dr Fiona Beglane, personal communication.

137 H.W.L. Weir, 'Deerparks of Clare', *The Other Clare*, vol. 10, 1986, pp. 54–5.

138 Nicholls, *Irish Fiants*, vol. 1, p. 89.

139 Bond, 'Medieval Nunneries of England and Wales', p. 81.

140 Moorhouse, 'Monastic Estates', p. 54.

141 Greene, *Medieval Monasteries*, pp. 145–6; Bond, *Monastic Landscapes*, pp. 329–47.

142 Greene, *Medieval Monasteries*, p. 146; Bond, *Monastic Landscapes*, pp. 343–53.

143 Stout, 'The Cistercian Grange', p. 28.

144 Lynch, *A Monastic Landscape*, pp. 4–5.

145 Bond, 'Medieval Nunneries in England and Wales', p. 79; Hall, *Scottish Monastic Landscapes*.

146 Noble, 'Spiritual Practice and the Designed Landscape'; Herbert McAvoy, 'The Medieval *Hortus Conclusus*'.

147 Moorhouse, 'Monastic Estates', p. 55.
148 Collins, 'Timolin', p. 72. For Gowran, see Thomas, *The Walled Towns*, vol. 2, pp. 113–15.
149 A tenement in this context was likely a piece of land held rather than a house divided and let as separate residences.
150 Kelly, 'Notes on the Round Tower at Kilbannon and on Kilcreevanty'; White, *Extents*, pp. 69–71, 73, 336–7.
151 Ó Clabaigh, *Friars in Ireland*, pp. 129–35.
152 M. Murphy and K. O'Conor, 'Castles and Deerparks in Ireland', *Eolas*, vol. 2006, pp. 1; 53–70, at p. 53; Murphy, 'Manor Centres'.
153 O'Conor, *Archaeology of Medieval Rural Settlement*, p. 109; Barry, 'Rural Settlement in Medieval Ireland', pp. 112–18; N. Brady, 'Rural Settlement in Later Medieval Ireland Through the Lens of Deserted Settlements', in N. Brady and C. Theune (eds), *Settlement Change Across Medieval Europe: Old paradigms and new vistas (Ruralia XII)* (Leiden: Sidestone Press, 2019), pp. 137–46.
154 J. Otway-Ruthven, 'The Medieval County of Kildare', *Irish Historical Studies*, vol. 11, 1959, pp. 181–99; O'Conor, *Archaeology of Medieval Rural Settlement*, pp. 17–39.
155 O'Conor, *Archaeology of Medieval Rural Settlement*, pp. 57–71; Brady, 'Rural Settlement in Later Medieval Ireland'.
156 White, *Extents*.
157 Moorhouse, 'Monastic Estates', p. 65.
158 Collins, 'Timolin', pp. 62–3.
159 Stout, 'The Cistercian Grange', pp. 28–30; Collins, 'Space and Place', pp. 38–42.
160 Ní Dhonnchadha, 'Caillech and Other Terms for Veiled Women'; Ó Crualaoich, *The Book of the Cailleach*, pp. 81–2. It might also be translated as relating to a woman who is no longer sexually active (Dr Kelly Fitzgerald, personal communication), which would neatly cover both older women and female religious.
161 Bhreathnach, 'The *Vita Apostolica*', p. 21.
162 Interestingly in this case, 'Hagstown' was chosen as a possible translation by John O'Donovan of the Ordnance Survey, rather than nun; see Westropp, 'Augustinian Houses'; M. McMahon, 'The Charter of Clare Abbey and the Augustinian "Province" in Co. Clare', *The Other Clare*, vol. 17, 1993, pp. 21–8.
163 https://www.logainm.ie/34779.aspx. Accessed 15 September 2020. In this case, John O'Donovan translated this as the 'town of the ferry' on the basis that *caladh* is the Irish for a landing place for boats.
164 https://www.logainm.ie/42835.aspx. Accessed 15 February 2019.
165 https://www.logainm.ie/39033.aspx. Accessed 15 September 2020.
166 http://www.placenamesni.org/resultdetails.php?entry=789. Accessed 15 September 2020.
167 http://www.placenamesni.org/resultdetails.php?entry=13916. Accessed 15 September 2020.
168 https://www.logainm.ie/16749.aspx. Accessed 15 September 2020.
169 https://www.logainm.ie/38031.aspx. Accessed 15 September 2020; J. Otway Ruthven, 'Parochial Development in the Rural Deanery of Skreen', *Journal of the Royal Society of Antiquaries of Ireland*, vol. 94, 1964, pp. 112–22. Otway Ruthven noted that this townland is located in the parish of Skreen but was originally in the parish of Odder. It is assumed that the nunnery was in the townland of Odder.
170 Collins, 'Unveiling Female Monasticism'.
171 Westropp, 'On Certain Typical Earthworks'.

172 J. Wardell, 'The History and Antiquities of St Catherine's'.
173 Hall, 'Women and Religion', pp. 377–8.
174 P. MacCotter, 'The Church Lands of the Diocese of Limerick: Reconstruction and history', *North Munster Antiquarian Journal*, vol. 53, 2013, pp. 99–122. See also P. MacCotter, 'Parish, Pastoral Care and Túath in the Diocese of Limerick, *c.*1201', *Journal of the Royal Society of Antiquaries of Ireland*, vols 142–3, 2012–13, pp. 86–99.
175 MacCotter, 'Church Lands of the Diocese of Limerick, pp. 99–122.
176 Begley, *Diocese of Limerick*, p. 375; Hall, *Women and the Church*, p. 156.
177 MacCotter, 'Church Lands of the Diocese of Limerick', p. 109.
178 Hamburger and Suckale, 'Between this World and the Next', pp. 104–6.
179 MacCotter, 'Church Lands of the Diocese of Limerick', p. 109.
180 C. Peyton, *The Peyton and Desmond Survey* (PROIM 5039, 1586), part II, p. 84. Available at https://celt.ucc.ie//published/E580000-001/index.html. Accessed 15 September 2020. These land parcels are in addition to Hall's list in 'Women and Religion'.
181 I am grateful to Dr Paul MacCotter for drawing this reference to my attention.
182 Collins, 'Timolin'.
183 It is possible that some of the enclosures recorded in St Catherine's holdings were either re-used or constructed as animal pounds, and some features might be a source for rabbits. Without the benefit of archaeological excavation, however, this must remain conjecture.
184 This occurred at other nunneries. For example, Timolin nunnery was granted the benefices of churches in Norraghmore and Crookstown by its founder. Later they were re-granted to St Patrick's Cathedral, Dublin by the archbishop. It is unclear if the benefices ever returned to Timolin. Grace Dieu was also granted rectories in Dublin by the archbishop only for them to be redistributed by his successor; Hall, *Women and the Church*, pp. 147–8.
185 A monument LI028-139--- is located in this townland. It is no longer upstanding. It is classified as a designed landscape feature and probable tree ring. However, there are no country houses in the feature's immediate vicinity with which it might be associated and, on this basis, it is suggested here that it may have been an enclosure.
186 Power, *English Nunneries*.
187 Wardell, 'The History and Antiquities of St Catherine's', p. 44; Hall, *Women and the Church*, p. 127.
188 Begley, *Diocese of Limerick*, p. 376. Begley noted that in 1428 'St Catherine de O'Conill' was described as being in 'the first year of the parochial church'. In Peyton's *Survey* dated 1586, Monasternegellegh is described as a parish. The full extent of this parish is not known. Dr Paul MacCotter has suggested that it probably included the townlands of Old Abbey and Aughinish at a minimum; personal communication.
189 Wardell, 'The History and Antiquities of St Catherine's', p. 46; T.J. Culhane, *The Barony of Shanid Incorporating Connello Lower* (Limerick: Mount Pleasant Publications, 2003), p. 22. Begley suggested that in 1428 its church was 'vacant by the suppression of the order of nuns': *Diocese of Limerick*, p. 376, perhaps due to it being described as 'parochial' at this time. Hall repeats this date: *Women and the Church*, p. 210. I suggest that the nunnery continued to function at this time. Alterations to its fabric, such as the northern doorway into the cloister, and the narrowing of the west doorway of the church suggests its continued use by nuns.
190 Power, *English Medieval Nunneries*, pp. 203–36.
191 Walker Bynum, *Holy Feast and Holy Fast*, p. 8; Johnson, *Equal in Monastic Profession*, p. 242.

192 MacCotter, 'Church Lands in the Diocese of Limerick', p. 109.

193 MacCotter, *Medieval Ireland*, pp. 186–7.

194 Westropp, 'On Certain Typical Earthworks', p. 27.

195 There is some confusion in the published sources about the name of the founder. Begley named him as John Fitzmaurice: Begley, *Diocese of Limerick*, p. 375; and a more recent study of the earls of Desmond stated his name as John FitzThomas: O'Carroll, *The Earls of Desmond*, p. 2. I have used the latter source. He is named as John Fitzgerald and John of Callan by Gwynn and Hadcock, *Medieval Religious Houses*, p. 230.

196 The first reference to St Catherine de O'Conyl was made in 1298 in an inquisition relating to the manor of Shanid: 'whereform are substracted 8s. paid yearly to the Bishop of Limerick for land which his grandfather [John FitzThomas] granted to the nuns of O'Konyl and 26s 8d paid to the same Bishop to acquit land of demesne which Sir Thomas held of him there', cited in Begley, *Diocese of Limerick*, p. 375. This reference suggests that the patron of the nunnery was paying a yearly rent for cross (church) land from the bishop of Limerick on which he built the nunnery. Furthermore, John FitzThomas founded Holy Cross Priory (Dominican) in 1243 in Tralee, Co. Kerry and was buried there with his son Maurice in 1261, after the Battle of Callan; O'Carroll, *The Earls of Desmond*, pp. 2–3.

197 O'Carroll, *Earls of Desmond*, p. 2. For background, see: M. MacCurtain, 'A Lost Landscape: The Geraldine castles and tower houses of the Shannon estuary', in J. Bradley (ed.), *Settlement and Society in Medieval Ireland: Studies presented to F.X. Martin* (Kilkenny: Boethius Press, 1988), pp. 429–44, at p. 430; P. MacCotter, 'The Subinfeudation and Descent of the Fitzstephen/Carew Moiety of Desmond, Part I', *Journal of the Cork Historical and Archaeological Society*, vol. 101, 1996, pp. 64–80; P. MacCotter, 'The Subinfeudation and Descent of the Fitzstephen/Carew Moiety of Desmond, Part II', *Journal of the Cork Historical and Archaeological Society*, vol. 102, 1997, pp. 89–106; M. Keegan, 'The Archaeology of Manorial Settlement in West County Limerick in the Thirteenth Century', in J. Lyttleton and T. O'Keeffe (eds), *The Manor in Medieval and Early Modern Ireland* (Dublin: Four Courts Press, 2005), pp. 17–39; P. MacCotter, 'The Rise of Meic Carthaig and the Political Geography of Desmumu', *Journal of the Cork Historical and Archaeological Society*, vol. 111, 2006, pp. 59–76.

198 M. Taylor, 'Early Anglo-Norman Settlement Patterns in Co. Limerick', *North Munster Antiquarian Journal*, vol. 53, 2013, pp. 123–33.

199 O'Carroll, *Earls of Desmond*, pp. 2–4; Taylor, 'Early Anglo-Norman Settlement'.

200 It is possible that there was an earlier foundation date for St Catherine's nunnery or the religious house at Rathkeale. Ó Riain has noted several indications of possible Augustinian influence in the life of the County Limerick saint, Íte of Killeedy, which had been written by the final quarter of the twelfth century; Ó Riain, *A Dictionary*, pp. 376–7.

201 A locality for the purpose of this discussion is 10km radius from St Catherine's. Rathkeale Priory is 10.6kms from St Catherine's.

202 Gwynn and Hadcock, *Medieval Religious Houses*, p. 190.

203 Westropp recorded an old road associated with a deserted settlement situated to the northwest of the nunnery: Westropp, 'On Certain Typical Earthworks', p. 34, plate iv.

204 Shanagolden belonged to the diocese of Limerick and functioned as an episcopal manor; J. Bradley, A. Halpin and H. King, 'Urban Archaeology Survey for County Limerick', 2 vols (Dublin: unpublished report for the OPW, 1989), p. 228. The bishop of Limerick was involved with the nunnery at Old Abbey, being paid yearly sums, in the thirteenth century at least; Begley, *Diocese of Limerick*, p. 375.

205 Johnson, 'The Cloistering of Medieval Nuns', p. 35.
206 Dunn, *Emergence of Monasticism*, pp. 12–13.
207 Makowski, *Canon Law and Cloistered Women*.
208 Johnson, 'The Cloistering of Medieval Nuns', p. 38.
209 Ibid.; Cassidy-Welch, 'Space and Place in Medieval Contexts'; Cassidy-Welch, *Imprisonment*. See also Berman, 'How Much Space Did Medieval Nuns Have or Need?'
210 Johnson, *Equal in Monastic Profession*, p. 246.
211 M. Wiesner, *Women and Gender in Early Modern Europe* (Cambridge: Cambridge University Press, 2000), pp. 13–47.
212 These sources were clearly biased and Burton notes, 'visitation returns note not the good but the bad and the ugly'; Burton, 'Looking for Medieval Nuns', p. 123. See also Power, *Medieval English Nunneries*, pp. 29–31, 436–74; Burton, *Yorkshire Nunneries*, pp. 29–36; Burton, *Monastic and Religious Orders*, pp. 106–8; Hall, *Women and the Church*, pp. 159–200; Kenny, *Anglo-Irish and Gaelic Women*, pp. 181–4; Knudsen, 'Promiscuous Monks and Naughty Nuns'.
213 Gilchrist, *Gender and Archaeology*, p. 143.
214 Ibid., pp. 16, 109–13, 122, 142, 144.
215 A. Dronzek, 'Private and Public Spheres', in M. Schaus (ed.), *Women and Gender in Medieval Europe: An encyclopedia* (London: Routledge, 2006), pp. 670–1, at p. 670.
216 M. McAuliffe, 'The Lady in the Tower: The social and political role of women in tower houses', in C. Meek and M.K. Simms (eds), *The Fragility of Her Sex? Medieval Irish women in their European context* (Dublin: Four Courts Press, 1996), pp. 153–62. For a recent synthesis of tower houses in Ireland, see V.L. McAlister, *The Irish Tower House: Society, economy and environment* c.*1300–1650* (Manchester: Manchester University Press, 2019).
217 McAuliffe, 'The Lady in the Tower'.
218 Gilchrist, *Gender and Archaeology*, pp. 109–45. Karen Dempsey considers castles and other structures from engendered perspectives in Ireland and Britain: see Dempsey, 'Gender and Medieval Archaeology'; Dempsey, 'Planting New Ideas'; Dempsey, 'Home is Where the Heart(h) is'; Dempsey et al., 'Beyond the Martial Façade'.
219 Gilchrist, *Gender and Archaeology*, p. 144.
220 Johnson, 'The Cloistering of Medieval Nuns', p. 27.
221 Johnson, *Equal in Monastic Profession*, pp. 231–2, 234.
222 D.J. Meltzer, 'Lessons in Landscape Learning', in M. Rockman and J. Steele (eds), *Colonisation of Unfamilar Landscapes: The archaeology of adaptation* (London: Routledge, 2003), pp. 222–41, at pp. 223–5.
223 Wardell, 'The History and Antiquities of St Catherine's', pp. 52–3.
224 Foot, 'What Was an Early Anglo-Saxon Monastery?'; R. Bradley, *The Significance of Monuments: On the shaping of human experience in Neolithic and Bronze Age Europe* (London: Routledge, 1998); Semple, 'A Fear of the Past'; Semple, 'Sacred Spaces and Places'; S. Semple, *Perceptions of the Prehistoric in Anglo-Saxon England: Religion, ritual and rulership in the landscape* (Oxford: Oxford University Press, 2013); S. Driscoll, 'Picts and Prehistory: Cultural resource management in early medieval Scotland', *World Archaeology*, vol. 30, 1998, pp. 142–58; H. Williams (ed.) *Archaeologies of Remembrance: Death and memory in past societies* (London: Springer, 2003); Meredith-Lobay, 'Memory, Landscapes'; Carver, 'Early Scottish Monasteries and Prehistory'; Ó Carragáin, *Churches in Early Medieval Ireland*, pp. 143–9, 156–7; Bhreathnach, *Ireland in the Medieval World*, pp. 131–48.
225 Ó Carragáin, *Churches in Early Medieval Ireland*, pp. 62, 157.

226 Murphy, 'Distribution of Early Christian Monastic Sites', p. 368; Condit and Buckley, *Faughart, Co. Louth*, p. 3; Boazman, 'The Material Culture of Self-Promotion'.
227 T. O'Keeffe, 'Religious Buildings', in J. Graham-Campbell (ed.), *The Archaeology of Medieval Europe. Volume 1: Eighth to Twelfth Centuries AD* (Aarhus: Aarhus University Press, 2007), pp. 398–419.
228 Ó Carragáin, 'Skeuomorphs and Spolia'; Ó Carragáin, *Churches in Early Medieval Ireland*, pp. 156–8.
229 Fredengren, *Crannógs*, p. 140.
230 Carville, *The Occupation of Celtic Sites*.
231 Semple, 'A Fear of the Past'; Semple, *Perceptions of the Prehistoric in Anglo-Saxon England*.
232 Ó Carragáin, *Churches in Early Medieval Ireland*, p. 157.
233 R. Bradley, 'Time Regained: The creation of continuity', *Journal of the British Archaeological Association*, vol. 140, 1987, pp. 1–17; Bradley, *The Past in Prehistoric Societies*; R. Bradley, 'Time in Translation', in S. Alcock and R. Van Dyke (eds), *Archaeologies of Memory* (Oxford: Blackwell, 2003), pp. 221–7; S. Alcock, *Archaeologies of the Greek Past: Landscape, monuments and memories* (Cambridge: Cambridge University Press, 2002).
234 Tuan, *Space and Place*, p. 187.
235 FitzPatrick, 'Native Enclosed Settlement'. FitzPatrick has suggested a later use of enclosures in the Burren region of County Clare. Most of the enclosures around St Catherine's are no longer visible and cannot now be verified on the ground. Interestingly, many were recorded by Westropp, who specifically remarked on their similarity with the Burren region: see Westropp, 'On Certain Typical Earthworks', p. 31. See also M. Comber and G. Hull, 'Excavations at Caherconnell Cashel, the Burren, Co. Clare: Implications for cashel chronology and Gaelic settlement', *Proceedings of the Royal Irish Academy*, vol. 110C, 2010, pp. 133–212.
236 Westropp, 'On Certain Typical Earthworks', p. 34.
237 Meltzer, 'Lessons in Landscape Learning', pp. 226–7.
238 Tuan, *Space and Place*, pp. 149, 153, 158.
239 Ibid., p. 159.
240 H. Flora, *The Devout Belief of the Imagination: The Paris* Meditationes Vitae Christi *and female Franciscan spirituality in Trecento, Italy* (Turnhout: Brepols, 2009); Rudy, *Virtual Pilgrimages*.
241 Ó Dálaigh, 'Mistress, Mother and Abbess'.
242 O'Carroll, *Earls of Desmond*, p. 3; McAuliffe, 'The Lady in the Tower', p. 158.
243 Berman, 'Medieval Monasticisms', p. 381.
244 Hall, *Women and the Church*, p. 192.
245 Bradley et al., *Urban Archaeology Survey for County Limerick*, pp. 228–33; MacCotter, 'Church Lands in the Diocese of Limerick', p. 107.
246 Bond, 'Medieval English Nunneries in England and Wales', p. 54.
247 Collins, 'Isolated in the wilderness?'
248 Hall, *Women and the Church*; Jordan, 'Gender Concerns', p. 92.
249 Johnson, *Equal in Monastic Profession*, p. 235.
250 O'Carroll, *Earls of Desmond*.
251 Thomas, *The Walled Towns*, vol. 2, p. 222.
252 Ibid., p. 236.
253 Ibid., p. 244.
254 Ibid., pp. 2–3.
255 For example, Hall, 'The Nuns of the Medieval Convent of Lismullin'.
256 Wardell, 'The History and Antiquities of St Catherine's', pp. 43–9; Begley, *Diocese of Limerick*, pp. 374–7.

257 Gwynn and Hadcock, *Medieval Religious Houses*, p. 162.
258 Ibid., pp. 190–1.
259 Ibid., p. 191.
260 Begley, *Diocese of Limerick*, pp. 366–70.
261 Gwynn and Hadcock, *Medieval Religious Houses*, pp. 242–3, 295.
262 Contemporary secular buildings would also be of use. For other regions, see Hourihane, *The Mason and His Mark*.
263 For a similar discussion on Cistercian houses, see Burton, '*Moniales* and *Ordo Cisterciensis*', pp. 379–80.
264 Hicks, *Religious Life in Normandy*, pp. 153–61.

CHAPTER 10. CONCLUSIONS

1 Gilchrist, 'A Research Design', p. 251. See also K. Curran, 'Looking for Medieval Female Religious in Britain and Ireland: Sources, methodologies and pitfalls', in K. Stöber, J. Kerr and E. Jamroziak (eds), *Monastic Life in the Medieval British Isles: Essays in honour of Janet Burton* (Cardiff: University of Wales Press, 2018), pp. 161–72.
2 For example, Berman, 'Medieval Monasticisms'; Beach and Cochelin, *Medieval Monasticism in the Latin West*; Vanderputten, *Medieval Monasticisms*.
3 Milis, *Constitvtiones*.
4 Browne and Ó Clabaigh, *Households of God*.
5 Collins, 'Unveiling Female Monasticism'.
6 Boazman, 'The Material Culture of Self-Promotion'.
7 Ó Carragáin, 'The Archaeology of Ecclesiastical Estates in Early Medieval Ireland'.
8 Stöber and Austin, 'Culdees to Canons'.
9 Gilchrist, 'A Research Design', p. 255.
10 Ibid., p. 253; Gilchrist, *Gender and Material Culture*, pp. 128–43.
11 Collins, 'Unveiling Female Monasticism', pp. 139–43.
12 Killone has been conserved and the ogee-headed double-light window which appears to mark the chapter house has been entirely re-built, so it is unclear if this was its original location. For St Mary de Hogges, see Clarke, *Irish Historic Towns Atlas: Dublin, Part I*, p. 2.
13 Mohn, *Mittelalterliche Klosteranlagen der Zisterzienserinnen*, p. 443.
14 Gilchrist, *Gender and Material Culture*, pp. 155–60.
15 Golding, *Gilbert of Sempringham*, pp. 129–32.
16 It is to be remembered that Augustinian, and Augustinian of Arroasian observance nunneries may have actually followed so-called 'secular' liturgical forms, such as those used in parish churches and strictly non-monastic religious houses such as friaries. Harper, 'The Space Enriched', pp. 10–23.
17 Collins, 'Archaeologies of Female Monasticism in Ireland'.
18 See Bugyis, *The Care of Nuns*.
19 For example, Kerr, *Religious Life for Women*, p. v.
20 Keeping, 'Life and Death in English Nunneries', p. 201.
21 Oliva, 'Aristocracy or Meritocracy?'; Harris, 'A New Look at the Reformation'.
22 An Irish Research Council funded project led by Dr Elise Alonzi at the School of Archaeology, University College Dublin is a first step. She is primarily investigating the origins of religious people but information on status may also emerge, '*Peregrini*: A comparative study of mobility among medieval ecclesiastics and nuns in Ireland and Wales'; personal communication. The human remains excavated at St Catherine's form part of this research assemblage. See Alonzi et al., 'Travelling Monastic Paths'.

23 Collins, 'Isolated in the Wilderness?'

24 M.A. Lyons, 'Revolt and Reaction: The Geraldine rebellion and monastic confiscation in Co. Kildare', *Journal of the County Kildare Archaeological Society*, vol. 18, 1992–3, pp. 39–60; Collins, 'Timolin'.

25 For example, Gilchrist, 'A Research Design'; Gilchrist, *Sacred Heritage*, pp. 178–217; J.P. Greene, 'Strategies for Future Research and Site Investigation', in G. Keevil, M. Aston and T. Hall (eds), *Monastic Archaeology* (Oxford: Oxbow, 2001), pp. 4–8; Curran, 'Looking for Medieval Female Religious'; G. Thomas, A. Pluskowshi, R. Gilchrist, G. Garcia-Contreras Ruiz, A. Andren, A. Augenti, G. Astill, J. Staecker and H. Valk, 'Religious Transformations in the Middle Ages: Towards a new archaeological agenda', *Medieval Archaeology*, vol. 61, no. 2, 2017, pp. 300–29.

26 Collins, 'Unveiling Female Monasticism'.

27 For example, McDermott, 'Patronage and Observance'.

28 Murphy and Potterton, *The Dublin Region*.

29 Hicks, *Religious Life in Normandy*.

30 Stout's work is an excellent start; see Stout, 'St Mary's Abbey, Dublin'; Stout, 'The Cistercian Grange'; Stout, 'Settlement on Mellifont Abbey's Monastic Estate'; Stout and Stout, *Bective Abbey Project*; G. Stout, R. Loeber and K. O'Brien, 'Mellifont Abbey, Co. Louth: A study of its post-dissolution architecture 1540–1727', *Proceedings of the Royal Irish Academy*, vol. 116C, 2016, pp. 191–226. Research by John Bradley is also important in this regard; Bradley, 'Precinct of St John's Priory'.

31 Ó Carragáin, 'Archaeology of Ecclesiastical Estates in Early Medieval Ireland'; MacCotter, 'Túath, Manor and Parish'.

32 MacCotter, 'Parish, Pastoral Care and Túath', pp. 92, 95; MacCotter, 'Church Lands of the Diocese of Limerick'.

33 See, for example, Bhreathnach, 'The Saintly Mothers and Virgins of Early Ireland'.

34 Identified during fieldwork by Frank Coyne; personal communication.

35 Ó Clabaigh, *The Friars in Ireland*, p. 311.

36 There has been relatively very little archaeological work done on Third Order houses, but see Y. McDermott, 'Rosserk Friary: A house of the Franciscan Third Order Regular', *Journal of the Galway Archaeological and Historical Society*, vol. 63, 2011, pp. 57–70; Y. McDermott, 'Killeenbrenan Friary: Flag-ship house of the Franciscan Third Order in Ireland?', *Cathair na Mart: Journal of the Westport Historical Society*, vol. 30, 2012, pp. 42–58; Y. McDermott, 'Kilcorban Friary, Co. Galway: Ireland's only house of the Dominican Third Order Regular', *History Ireland*, vol. 22, 2014, pp. 16–18.

37 Ó Clabaigh, 'Anchorites'.

38 Millett, *Ancrene Wisse*; Millett, 'Can There Be Such a Thing as an Anchoritic Rule?'

39 At the time of writing, there are seventy-one monuments classified as medieval hospitals by the Archaeological Survey of Ireland in the Republic of Ireland, http://webgis.archaeology.ie/historicenvironment/. Accessed 15 September 2020.

40 For example, Gilchrist, *Contemplation and Action*, pp. 8–61; Sweetinburgh, *The Role of the Hospital*.

41 For example, U. Wiethaus, *Maps of Flesh and Light: The religious experience of medieval women mystics* (Syracuse: Syracuse University Press, 1993); Dickens, *The Female Mystic*; Spearing, *Female Spirituality*; C. Dinshaw and D. Wallace (eds), *The Cambridge Companion to Medieval Women's Writing* (Cambridge: Cambridge University Press, 2003).

42 Gaimster and Gilchrist, *Archaeology of Reformation*; Sloane, 'Tenements in London's Monasteries'; Sloane, *Augustinian Nunnery of St Mary Clerkenwell*, pp. 169–94. Investigation of post-dissolution uses of medieval buildings in Ireland is beginning; see,

for example, R. Stalley (ed.), *Irish Gothic Architecture: Construction, decay and reinvention* (Dublin: Wordwell, 2012); Y. McDermott, 'Post Medieval Developments at Moyne Friary, Co. Mayo, *c.*1540–*c.*1700, *Cathair na Mart: Journal of the Westport Historical Society*, vol. 32, 2014, pp. 23–40; Stout et al., 'Mellifont Abbey'.

43 For example, C. Van Whye (ed.), *Female Monasticism in Early Modern Europe: An interdisciplinary view* (Aldershot: Ashgate, 2008); M.L. Coolahan, 'Archipelagic Identities in Europe: Irish nuns in English convents', in C. Bowden and J. Kelly (eds), *The English Convents in Exile, 1600–1800: Communities, culture and identity* (London: Taylor & Francis, 2013), pp. 211–28; M.L. Coolahan, 'Nuns' Writing: Translation, textual mobility and transnational networks', in P. Phillippy (ed.), *A History of Early Modern Women's Writing* (Cambridge: Cambridge University Press, 2018), pp. 257–75; B. McShane, 'Negotiating Religious Change and Conflict: Female religious communities in early modern Ireland 1530–1641', *British Catholic History*, vol. 33, 2017, pp. 357–82; B. McShane, 'Visualising the Reception and Circulation of Early Modern Nuns' Letters', *Journal of Historical Network Research*, vol. 2, 2018, pp. 1–25; D. Raftery, 'The Next "Wave" is Digital: Researching women religious in the twenty-first century', *American Catholic Studies*, vol. 128, 2017, pp. 29–50; J. Kelly, *English Convents in Catholic Europe* c.*1600–1800* (Cambridge: Cambridge University Press, 2020); C.M. Mangion, *Contested Identities: Catholic women religious in nineteenth-century England and Wales* (Manchester: Manchester University Press, 2008); C.M. Mangion, *Catholic Nuns and Sisters in a Secular Age: Britain 1945–90* (Manchester: Manchester University Press, 2020). See also www.historyofwomenreligious.org, for regularly updated bibliographies on all periods of female religious. Accessed 15 September 2020.

44 For example, S. Hoy and M. MacCurtain, *From Dublin to New Orleans: The journey of Nora and Alice* (Dublin: Attic Press, 1994); Knox, 'Her Book-Lined Cell'.

45 M.A. Lyons and T. O'Connor (eds), *Strangers to Citizens: The Irish in Europe 1600–1800* (Dublin: Wordwell, 2008), pp. 84–5.

46 For example, D. Raftery, C. Delaney and C. Nowlan-Roebuck, *Nano Nagle: The Irish life and the legacy* (Dublin: Irish Academic Press, 2018).

47 Collins, 'Kenmare Lace'.

Bibliography

Abram, A., 'Augustinian Canons and the Survival of Cult Centres in Medieval England', in J. Burton and K. Stöber (eds), *The Regular Canons in the British Isles* (Turnhout: Brepols, 2011), pp. 79–96

Albarella, U., 'Pig Husbandry and Pork Consumption in Medieval England', in C. Woolgar, D. Serjeantson and T. Waldron (eds), *Food in Medieval England: Diet and nutrition* (Oxford: Oxford University Press, 2006), pp. 72–87

Alcock, O., K. De hÓra and P. Gosling, *Archaeological Inventory of County Galway. Volume II: North Galway* (Dublin: The Stationery Office, 1999)

Alcock, S., *Archaeologies of the Greek Past: Landscape, monuments and memories* (Cambridge: Cambridge University Press, 2002)

Alemand, L., *Historie Monastique D'Irlande* (Paris: Louis Lucas, 1690)

Allen, J.P., 'Devon: Polsoe Priory', *Medieval Archaeology*, vol. 23, 1979, pp. 250–1

Alonzi, E., N. Daly, G. Gordon, R.E. Scott and K.J. Knudson, 'Travelling Monastic Paths: Mobility and religion at medieval Irish monasteries', *Journal of Anthropological Archaeology*, vol. 55, 2019, pp. 1–24

Andrews, J.H., *Irish Historic Towns Atlas No. 1: Kildare* (Dublin: Royal Irish Academy, 1986)

Anon., 'Ballymacdane Abbey', *Journal of the Cork Historical and Archaeological Society*, vol. 3, 1894, p. 173

Archdall, M., *Monasticon Hibernicum* (Dublin: Luke White, 1786)

Ashbee, J., 'Cloisters in English Palaces in the Twelfth and Thirteenth Centuries', *Journal of the British Archaeological Association*, vol. 159, 2006, pp. 71–90

Ashmore, W., 'Social Archaeologies of Landscape', in L. Meskell and R.W. Preucel (eds), *A Companion to Social Archaeology* (Oxford: Blackwell, 2007), pp. 255–71

Astill, G., 'Monastic Research Designs: Bordesley and the Avon Valley', in R. Gilchrist and H. Mytum (eds), *The Archaeology of Rural Monasteries. BAR British Series 203* (Oxford: British Archaeological Reports, 1989), pp. 277–94

Astill, G., S. Hirst and S. Wright, 'The Bordesley Abbey Project Reviewed', *Archaeological Journal*, vol. 161, 2004, pp. 106–58

Astill, G., S. Hirst and S. Wright, 'The Bordesley Abbey Project: Watermills, 2008.' Available at http://www.reading.ac.uk/bordesley/. Accessed 15 September 2020

Aston, M., 'Segregation in Church', in J. Sheils and D. Wood (eds), *Women in the Church* (Oxford: Blackwell, 1990), pp. 237–81

Aston, M., *Monasteries in the Landscape* (Stroud: Tempus, 2000)

Austin, D., 'Strata Florida and its Landscape Archaeology', *Archaeologia Cambrensis*, vol. 153, 2004, pp. 192–201

Austin, D., 'The Archaeology of Monasteries in Wales and the Strata Florida Project', in J. Burton and K. Stöber (eds), *Monastic Wales: New approaches* (Cardiff: University of Wales Press, 2013), pp. 3–37

Baker, C., 'Tullykane, Co. Meath: A medieval rural settlement', in C. Corlett and M. Potterton (eds), *Rural Settlement in Medieval Ireland in the Light of Recent Archaeological Excavation* (Dublin: Wordwell, 2009), pp. 1–17

Baker, C., *Antiquities of Old Fingal: The archaeology of north County Dublin* (Dublin: Wordwell, 2010)

Baker, D., 'Excavations at Elstow Abbey, 1968–1970, Third Interim Report', *Bedfordshire Archaeological Journal*, vol. 6, 1971, pp. 55–64

Baker, D. and E. Baker, 'Research Designs: Timbers phases and outbuildings with special reference to Elstow Abbey and Grove Priory, Bedfordshire and a note about the availability of information', in R. Gilchrist and H. Mytum (eds), *The Archaeology of Rural Monasteries. BAR British Series 203* (Oxford: British Archaeological Reports, 1989), pp. 261–75

Baker, E., *La Grava Blair: The Archaeology and history of a royal manor and alien priory of Fontevrault* (York: Council for British Archaeology, 2013)

Ball, F.E., *A History of County Dublin*, 6 vols (Dublin: A. Thom, 1905)

Bandmann, G., *Early Medieval Architecture: As bearer of meaning*, trans. K. Wallis (New York: Columbia University Press, 2005)

Barnwell, P.S., 'The Laity, the Clergy, and the Divine Presence: The use of space in smaller churches of the eleventh and twelfth centuries', *Journal of the British Archaeological Association*, vol. 157, 2004, pp. 41–60

Barnwell, P.S., 'The Universal Church in the Local Community: English parochial churches, *c.* 1130–1350', in P.S. Barnwell (ed.), *Places of Worship in Britain and Ireland, 1150–1350* (Donington: Shaun Tyas, 2018), pp. 188–213

Barrett, J.C., 'Chronologies of Landscape', in P. Ucko and R. Layton (eds), *The Archaeology and Anthropology of Landscape* (London: Routledge, 1999), pp. 21–30

Barrett, J.C., 'Agency, the Duality of Structure and the Problem of the Archaeological Record', in I. Hodder (ed.), *Archaeological Theory Today* (Cambridge: Polity, 2001), pp. 140–64

Barrière, B., 'The Cistercian Convent of Coyroux in the Twelfth and Thirteenth Centuries', *Gesta*, vol. 31, 1992, pp. 76–82

Barry, T., *The Medieval Archaeology of Ireland* (London: Routledge, 1987)

Barry, T., '"The People of the Country … Dwelt Scattered": The pattern of rural settlement in Ireland in the later middle ages', in J. Bradley (ed.), *Settlement and Society in Medieval Ireland* (Kilkenny: Boethius Press, 1988), pp. 345–60

Barry, T., 'Medieval Moated Sites in Ireland: Some new conclusions on their chronology and function', in G. Mac Niocaill and P.F. Wallace (eds), *Keimelia: Studies in memory of Tom Delaney* (Galway: Galway University Press, 1988), pp. 524–35

Barry, T. (ed.), *A History of Settlement in Ireland* (London: Routledge, 2000)

Barry, T., 'Rural Settlement in Medieval Ireland', in T. Barry (ed.), *A History of Settlement in Ireland* (London: Routledge, 2000), pp. 110–23

Barry, T., 'Foreword', in C. Corlett and M. Potterton (eds), *Rural Settlement in Medieval Ireland in the Light of Recent Archaeological Excavation* (Dublin: Wordwell, 2009), pp. viii–x

Bassett, S. (ed.), *Death in Towns: Urban responses to the dying and the dead, 100–1600* (Leicester: Leicester University Press, 1992)

Baswell, C., 'Heloise', in C. Dinshaw and D. Wallace (eds), *The Cambridge Companion to Medieval Women's Writing* (Cambridge: Cambridge University Press, 2003), pp. 161–71

Bates, P., *Donabate and Portrane: A history* (Dublin: Self-published, 1988)

Bateson, M., 'The Origin and Early History of Early Double Monasteries', *Transactions of the Royal Historical Society*, vol. 13, 1899, pp. 137–98

Beach, A.I., *Women as Scribes: Book production and monastic reform in twelfth-century Bavaria* (Cambridge: Cambridge University Press, 2004)

Beach, A.I., 'Review article: *Female* Vita Religiosa *between Late Antiquity and the High Middle Ages: Structures, developments and spatial contexts* (ed. G. Meville and A. Müller)', *Journal of Medieval Monastic Studies*, vol. 2, 2013, pp. 186–7

Beach, A.I., 'Review article: "Inventing Sempringham: Gilbert of Sempringham and the origins of the role of master (K. Sykes)"', *Journal of Medieval Monastic Studies*, vol. 2, 2013, pp. 189–90

Beach A.I. and I. Cochelin (eds), *Medieval Monasticism in the Latin West*, 2 vols (Cambridge: Cambridge University Press, 2020)

Beach, A.I. and A. Juganaru, 'The Double Monastery as a Historiographical Problem (Fourth to Twelfth Century)', in A.I. Beach and I. Cochelin (eds), *Medieval Monasticism in the Latin West*, 2 vols (Cambridge: Cambridge University Press, 2020), pp. 561–78

Beglane, F., 'The Social Significance of Game in the Diet of Later Medieval Ireland', *Proceedings of the Roya Irish Academy*, vol. 115C, 2015, pp. 1–30

Beglane, F., *Anglo-Norman Parks in Medieval Ireland: 1169–c.1350* (Dublin: Four Courts Press, 2015)

Begley, J., *The Diocese of Limerick Ancient and Medieval*, 3 vols (Dublin: Browne & Nolan, 1906)

Bell, D.N., *What Nuns Read: Books and libraries in medieval English nunneries* (Kalamazoo: Cistercian Publications, 1995)

Bennett, J.M., 'Medievalism and Feminism', in N. Partner (ed.), *Studying Medieval Women* (Cambridge, MA: The Medieval Academy of America, 1993), pp. 7–29

Berman, C.H., 'Medieval Agriculture, the Southern French Countryside and the Early Cistercians: A study of forty-three monasteries', *Transactions of the American Philosophical Society*, vol. 76, no. 5 1986, pp. 1–179

Berman, C.H., 'Men's Houses, Women's Houses: The relationship between the sexes in twelfth-century monasticism', in A. MacLeish (ed.), *The Medieval Monastery* (St Cloud, Minnesota: North Star Press, 1988), pp. 43–52

Berman, C.H., 'Were There Twelfth-Century Cistercian Nuns?' *Church History*, vol. 68, no. 4, 1999, pp. 824–64

Berman, C.H., 'How Much Space Did Medieval Nuns Have or Need?' in S. McNally (ed.), *Shaping Community: The art and archaeology of monasticism. BAR International Series 941* (Oxford: Archaeopress, 2001), pp. 100–16

Berman, C.H., *The Cistercian Evolution: The invention of a religious order in twelfth-century Europe* (Philadelphia: University of Pennsylvania, 2010)

Berman, C.H., 'Medieval Monasticisms', in J. Arnold (ed.), *The Oxford Handbook of Medieval Christianity* (Oxford: Oxford University Press, 2014), pp. 337–95

Berman, C.H., *The White Nuns: Cistercian abbeys for women in medieval France* (Philadelphia: University of Pennsylvania, 2018)

Bermingham, H., 'Priests' Residences in Later Medieval Ireland', in E. FitzPatrick and R. Gillespie (eds), *The Parish in Medieval and Early Modern Ireland: Community, territory and building* (Dublin: Four Courts Press, 2006), pp. 168–85

Bermingham, N., F. Coyne, G. Hull, F. Reilly and K. Taylor, *River Road: The archaeology of the Limerick southern ring road* (Dublin: National Roads Authority, 2013)

Berry, H.F., 'On the Use of Signs in the Ancient Monasteries with Special Reference to a Code Used by the Victorine Canons at St Thomas's Abbey, Dublin', *Journal of the Royal Society of Antiquaries of Ireland*, vol. 2, 1892, pp. 107–25

Berry, H.F. (ed.), *Register of Wills and Inventories of the Diocese of Dublin* (Dublin: Royal Society of Antiquaries of Ireland special volume 211, 1898)

Berschin, W., 'Radegundis and Brigit', in J. Carey, M. Herbert and P. Ó Riain (eds), *Studies in Hagiography: Saints and scholars* (Dublin: Four Courts Press, 2001), pp. 72–6

Bertelsen, R., 'Food in Northern Europe from the Thirteenth to the Sixteenth Century', in M. Carver and J. Klápště (eds), *The Archaeology of Medieval Europe. Volume 2: Twelfth to Sixteenth Centuries* (Aarhus: Aarhus University Press, 2011), pp. 126–32

Bezant, J., *Medieval Welsh Settlement and Territory: Archaeological evidence from a Teifi landscape. BAR British Series 487* (Oxford: Archaeopress, 2009)

Bezant, J., 'The Medieval Grants to Strata Florida Abbey: Mapping the agency of lordship', in J. Burton and K. Stöber (eds), *Monastic Wales: New approaches* (Cardiff: University of Wales Press, 2013), pp. 73–87

Bezant, J., 'Revising the Monastic "Grange": Problems at the edge of the Cistercian world', *Journal of Medieval Monastic Studies*, vol. 3, 2014, pp. 51–70

Bhreathnach, E., 'Review: Medieval Irish history at the end of the twentieth century, unfinished work', *Irish Historical Studies*, vol. 32, 2000, pp. 260–71

Bhreathnach, E., 'Abbesses, Minor Dynasties and Kings *in Clericatu*: Perspectives of Ireland 700–850', in M. Brown and C. Farr (eds), *Mercia: An Anglo-Saxon kingdom in Europe* (Leicester: Leicester University Press, 2001), pp. 113–25

Bhreathnach, E., 'The Genealogies of Leinster as a Source for Local Cults in Leinster', in J. Carey, M. Herbert and P. Ó Riain (eds), *Studies in Irish Hagiography: Saints and scholars* (Dublin: Four Courts Press, 2001), pp. 250–67

Bhreathnach, E., 'The *Seanchas* Tradition in Late Medieval Ireland', in E. Bhreathnach and B. Cunningham (eds), *Writing Irish History: The Four Masters and their world* (Dublin: Wordwell, 2007), pp. 19–26

Bhreathnach, E., 'Benedictine Influence in Ireland in the Late Eleventh and Early Twelfth Century: A reflection', *Journal of Medieval Monastic Studies*, vol. 1, 2012, pp. 46–105

Bhreathnach, E., *Ireland in the Medieval World* AD *400–1000: Landscape, kingship and religion* (Dublin: Four Courts Press, 2014)

Bhreathnach, E., 'The World of Bishops in Religious Orders in Medieval Ireland', in K. Stöber, J. Kerr and E. Jamroziak (eds), *Monastic Life in the Medieval British Isles: Essays in honour of Janet Burton* (Cardiff: University of Wales Press, 2018), pp. 71–88

Bhreathnach, E., 'The *Vita Apostolica* and the Origin of the Augustinian Canons and Canonesses in Medieval Ireland', in M. Browne and C. Ó Clabaigh (eds), *Households of God: The regular canons and canonesses of Saint Augustine and of Prémontré in medieval Ireland* (Dublin: Four Courts Press, 2019), pp. 1–27

Bhreathnach, E., 'The Saintly Mothers and Virgins of Early Ireland: A diverse group remembered in places, personal names and genealogies', in A. O'Hara, Å. Ommundsen and A. Tore Hommedal (eds), *Saint Sunniva: The Irish patron saint of western Norway 1170–2020* (Bergen: Bergen University Press, forthcoming)

Bhreathnach, E. and B. Cunningham (eds), *Writing Irish History: The Four Masters and their world* (Dublin: Wordwell, 2007)

Biddick, K., 'Decolonising the English Past: Readings in medieval archaeology', *Journal of British Studies*, vol. 32, 1993, pp. 1–23

Bieler, L. (ed.), *The Patrician Texts in the Book of Armagh* (Dublin: The Institute for Advanced Studies, 1979)

Binchy, D.A., 'The Legal Capacity of Women in Regard to Contracts', in R. Thurneysen, N. Power, M. Dillon, K. Mulchrone, D.A. Binchy, A. Knoch and J.S. Ryan (eds), *Studies in Early Irish Law* (Dublin: Royal Irish Academy, 1936), pp. 207–34

Binford, L., *An Archaeological Perspective* (New York: Seminar Press, 1972)

Binski, P., *Medieval Death: Ritual and representation* (London: British Museum Press, 1996)

Bitel, L., 'Women's Donations to the Churches in Early Ireland', *Journal of the Royal Society of Antiquaries of Ireland*, vol. 114, 1984, pp. 5–23

Bitel, L., 'Women's Monastic Enclosures in Early Ireland: A study of female spirituality and male monastic mentalities', *Journal of Medieval History*, vol. 12, 1986, pp. 15–36

Bitel, L., *Isle of Saints: Monastic settlement and Christian community in early Ireland* (Ithaca: Cornell University Press, 1990)

Bitel, L., *Land of Women* (Ithaca: Cornell University Press, 1996)

Bitel, L., *Women in Early Medieval Europe 400–1100* (Cambridge: Cambridge University Press, 2002)

Bitel, L., 'Ekphrasis at Kildare: The imaginative architecture of a seventh-century hagiographer', *Speculum*, vol. 79, 2004, pp. 605–27

Bitel, L., *Landscape with Two Saints* (Oxford: Oxford University Press, 2009)

Bitel, L., 'Monastic Identity in Early Medieval Ireland', in A.I. Beach and I. Cochelin (eds), *Medieval Monasticism in the Latin West*, 2 vols (Cambridge: Cambridge University Press, 2020), pp. 297–316

Blair, J. and J.M. Steane, 'Investigations at Cogges, Oxfordshire 1978–1981: The priory and parish church', *Oxoniensia*, vol. 47, 1982, pp. 37–125

Blake, N.F., 'Ars Moriendi', in J.R. Strayer (ed.), *Dictionary of the Middle Ages*, vol. 1 (New York: Charles Scribner's Sons, 1982), pp. 547–8

Blanton, V., V. O'Mara and P. Stoop (eds), *Nuns' Literacies in Medieval Europe: The Hull dialogue* (Turnhout: Brepols, 2013)

Blanton, V., V. O'Mara and P. Stoop (eds), *Nuns' Literacies in Medieval Europe: The Kansas City dialogue* (Turnhout: Brepols, 2015)

Blanton, V., V. O'Mara and P. Stoop (eds), *Nuns' Literacies in Medieval Europe: The Antwerp dialogue* (Turnhout: Brepols, 2018)

Bleier, R., 'Re-Examining the Function of St Patrick's Writings in the Early Medieval Tradition', *Proceedings of the Royal Irish Academy*, vol. 116C, 2016, pp. 95–117

Bliss, W.H. (ed.), *Calendar of Entries in the Papal Registers Relating to Great Britain and Ireland: Papal letters. Volume I: AD 1198–1304* (London: His Majesty's Stationery Office, 1893)

Boardman, S. and E. Williamson (eds), *The Cult of Saints and the Virgin Mary in Medieval Scotland* (Suffolk: Boydell, 2010)

Boazman, G., 'Theme and Variations: Christianity and regional landscapes in early medieval Ireland', unpublished PhD thesis, University College Cork, 2013

Boazman, G., 'The Material Culture of Self-Promotion: The Conaille Muirthemne kings and the ecclesiastical site of Faughart, County Louth', *County Louth Archaeological and Historical Journal*, vol. XXVIII, 2015, pp. 327–50

Bodarwé, K., 'Frauenleben Zwischen Klosterleben und Luxus? Alltag in Frühmittelalterlichen Frauenklöstern', in H. Brandt and J. Koch (eds), *Königin, Klosterfrau, Bäuerin: Frauen im Frühmittelalterlichen* (Münster: LIT Verlag, 1997), pp. 117–43

Bolger, T., 'Status Inheritance and Land Tenure: Some thoughts on early medieval settlement in the light of recent archaeological excavations', in C. Corlett and M. Potterton (eds), *Settlement in Early Medieval Ireland in the Light of Recent Archaeological Excavations* (Dublin: Wordwell, 2011), pp. 1–10

Bolger, T. and C. Moloney, 'Archaeological Excavations at Lorrha, Co. Tipperary', *Journal of Irish Archaeology*, vol. 21, 2012, pp. 114–37

Bolger, T. and C. Moloney, 'Archaeological Excavations at Lorrha, Co. Tipperary', in C. Corlett and M. Potterton (eds), *The Church in Early Medieval Ireland in the Light of Recent Archaeological Excavations* (Dublin: Wordwell, 2014), pp. 13–22

Bond, J., 'The Estates of Evesham Abbey: A preliminary survey of their medieval topography', *Vale of Evesham Historical Society Research Papers*, vol. 4, 1973, pp. 1–62

Bond, J., 'The Reconstruction of the Medieval Landscape: The estates of Abingdon Abbey', *Landscape History*, vol. 1, 1979, pp. 59–75

Bond, J., 'Water Management in the Rural Monastery', in R. Gilchrist and H. Mytum (eds), *The Archaeology of Rural Monasteries. BAR British Series 203* (Oxford: British Archaeological Reports, 1989), pp. 83–111

Bond, J., 'Water Management in the Urban Monastery', in R. Gilchrist and H. Mytum (eds), *Advances in Monastic Archaeology. BAR British Series 227* (Oxford: Tempus Reparatum Archaeological and Historical Associates, 1993), pp. 43–78

Bond, J., 'Medieval Nunneries in England and Wales: Buildings, precincts and estates', in D. Wood (ed.), *Women and Religion in Medieval England* (Oxford: Oxbow, 2003), pp. 46–90

Bond, J., *Monastic Landscapes* (Stroud: Tempus, 2004)

Bond, S. and C. Maines, 'The Archaeology of Monasticism: A survey of recent work in France', *Speculum*, vol. 63, 1988, pp. 794–82

Bourdieu, P., *Outline of a Theory of Practice* (Cambridge: Cambridge University Press, 1977)

Bourdieu, P., *Distinction: A social critique of the judgement of taste* (London: Routledge & Kegan Paul, 1979)

Bourdieu, P., *The Logic of Practice* (Cambridge: Polity Press, 1990)

Bourdillon, A., *The Order of Minoresses in England* (Manchester: Manchester University Press, 1926)

Bracken, D. and D. Ó Riain-Raedel (eds), *Ireland and Europe in the Twelfth Century: Reform and renewal* (Dublin: Four Courts Press, 2006)

Bradley Warren, N., 'Monastic Rules', in M. Schaus (ed.), *Women and Gender in Medieval Europe: An encyclopedia* (London: Routledge, 2006), pp. 576–7

Bradley Warren, N., 'The Ritual for the Ordination of Nuns', in M. Rubin (ed.), *Medieval Christianity in Practice* (Princeton: Princeton University Press, 2009), pp. 318–23

Bradley, J., 'A Medieval Figure at Calliaghstown, County Meath', *Journal of the Royal Society of Antiquaries of Ireland*, vol. 110, 1980, pp. 149–52

Bradley, J., 'The Medieval Tombs of St Canice's', in A. Empey (ed.), *A Worthy Foundation: The cathedral church of St Canice, Kilkenny* (Mountrath: Dolmen Press, 1985), pp. 49–103

Bradley, J., 'The Ballyhale Madonna', in E. Rynne (ed.), *Figures from the Past Studies on Figurative Art in Christian Ireland in Honour of Helen M. Roe* (Dublin: Glendare Press for the Royal Society of Antiquaries of Ireland, 1987), pp. 258–77

Bradley, J., 'The Monastic Town of Clonmacnoise', in H. King (ed.), *Clonmacnoise Studies*, vol. 1 (Dublin: The Stationery Office, 1998), pp. 42–55

Bradley, J., 'Death, Art and Burial: St Canice's Cathedral, Kilkenny in the sixteenth century', in C. Hourihane (ed.), *Irish Art Historical Studies in Honour of Peter Harbison* (Dublin: Four Courts Press, 2004), pp. 210–18

Bradley, J., 'The Precinct of St John's Priory, Kilkenny at the Close of the Middle Ages', *Peritia*, vols 22–3, 2011–12, pp. 317–45

Bradley, J. and C. Manning, 'Excavations at Duiske Abbey, Graiguenamanagh, Co. Kilkenny', *Proceedings of the Royal Irish Academy*, vol. 81C, 1981, pp. 397–426

Bradley, J., A. Halpin and H. King, 'Urban Archaeology Survey for Cork' (Dublin: OPW, unpublished report, 1985)

Bradley, J., A. Halpin and H. King, 'Urban Archaeology Survey for County Westmeath' (Dublin: OPW, unpublished report, 1985)

Bradley, J., A. Halpin and H. King, 'Urban Archaeology Survey for County Limerick', 2 vols (Dublin: OPW, unpublished report, 1989)

Bradley, R., 'Time Regained: The creation of continuity', *Journal of the British Archaeological Association*, vol. 140, 1987, pp. 1–17

Bradley, R., *The Significance of Monuments: On the shaping of human experience in Neolithic and Bronze Age Europe* (London: Routledge, 1998)

Bradley, R., *An Archaeology of Natural Places* (London: Routledge, 2000)

Bradley, R., *The Past in Prehistoric Societies* (London: Routledge, 2002)

Bradley, R., 'Time in Translation', in S. Alcock and R. Van Dyke (eds), *Archaeologies of Memory* (Oxford: Blackwell, 2003), pp. 221–7

Bradshaw, B., *The Dissolution of the Religious Orders in Ireland under Henry VIII* (Cambridge: Cambridge University Press, 1974)

Brady, J., 'The Nunnery at Clonard', *Ríocht na Midhe*: *Records of the Meath Archaeological and Historical Society*, vol. 2, 1960, pp. 4–7

Brady, K. and C. Corlett, 'Holy Ships: ships on plaster at medieval ecclesiastical sites in Ireland', *Archaeology Ireland*, vol. 18, 2004, pp. 28–31

Brady, K. and C. Corlett, 'Ships on Plaster: Evidence for ships in medieval Ireland', in C. Manning (ed.), *From Ringforts to Fortified Houses: Studies on castles and other monuments in honour of David Sweetman* (Dublin: Wordwell, 2007), pp. 309–34

Brady, N., 'Rural Settlement in Later Medieval Ireland Through the Lens of Deserted Settlements', in N. Brady and C. Theune (eds), *Settlement Change Across Medieval*

Europe: Old paradigms and new vistas (Ruralia XII) (Leiden: Sidestone Press, 2019), pp. 137–46

Brady, N. and C. Theune (eds), *Settlement Change Across Medieval Europe: Old paradigms and new vistas (Ruralia XII)* (Leiden: Sidestone Press, 2019)

Brakspear, H., 'Lacock Abbey, Wiltshire', *Archaeologia*, vol. 57, 1900, pp. 125–58

Brakspear, H., 'Excavations at Some Wiltshire Monasteries', *Archaeologia*, vol. 73, 1922–3, pp. 225–52

Brand, P., 'King, Church and Property: The enforcement of restrictions on alienation into mortmain in the lordship of Ireland in the later middle ages', *Peritia*, vol. 3, 1984, pp. 481–502

Brand, P., 'The Licencing of Mortmain Alienations in the Medieval Lordship of Ireland', *Irish Jurist*, vol. 21, 1986, pp. 125–44

Brannon, N., 'A Trial Excavation at St John's Point Church, Co. Down', *Ulster Journal of Archaeology*, vol. 43, 1980, pp. 59–64

Braunfels, B.W., *Monasteries of Western Europe: The architecture of the orders* (London: Thames & Hudson, 1972)

Bray, D.A., *A List of Motifs in the Lives of the Early Irish Saints* (Helsinki: Academia Scientarum Fennica, 1992)

Brindley, A., *Archaeological Inventory of County Monaghan* (Dublin: The Stationery Office, 1986)

Britnell, R.H., *Britain and Ireland 1050–1530: Economy and society* (Oxford: University Press, 2004)

Brown, G., *Stanley Abbey and its Estates 1151–c. 1640: A Cistercian monastery and its impact on the landscape. BAR British Series 566* (Oxford: Archaeopress, 2012)

Brown, J.N. and D. Alfano Bussell (eds), *Barking Abbey and Medieval Literary Culture: Authorship and authority in a female community* (Woodbridge: York Medieval Press, 2012)

Browne, M. and C. Ó Clabaigh (eds), *Soldiers of Christ: The Knights Hospitaller and the Knights Templar in medieval Ireland* (Dublin: Four Courts Press, 2016)

Browne, M. and C. Ó Clabaigh (eds), *Households of God: The regular canons and canonesses of Saint Augustine and of Prémontré in medieval Ireland* (Dublin: Four Courts Press, 2019)

Brück, J., 'Experiencing the Past? The development of a phenomenological archaeology in British prehistory', *Archaeological Dialogues*, vol. 12, 2005, pp. 45–72

Brumfiel, E.M., 'It's a Material World: History, artifacts and anthropology', *Annual Review of Anthropology*, vol. 32, 2003, pp. 205–23

Brundage J.A. and E. Makowski, 'Enclosure of Nuns: The decretal *Periculoso* and its commentators', *Journal of Medieval History*, vol. 20, 1994, pp. 143–55

Bruzelius, C.A., 'Hearing is Believing: Clarissan architecture *ca.* 1213–1340', *Gesta*, vol. 31, no. 2, 1992, pp. 83–91

Bruzelius, C.A., 'Nuns in Space: Strict enclosure and the architecture of Clarisses in the thirteenth century', in I. Peterson (ed.), *Clare of Assisi: A medieval and modern woman* (New York: The Franciscan Institute, 1996), pp. 53–74

Bruzelius, C.A., *Le Pietre di Napoli: L'architectura Religiosa Nell'Italia Angioina, 1266–1342* (Rome: Viella, 2005)

Bruzelius, C.A., 'Architecture, Ecclesiastical', in M. Schaus (ed.), *Women and Gender in Medieval Europe: An encyclopaedia* (London: Routledge, 2006), pp. 30–1

Bruzelius, C.A., 'Architecture, Monastic', in M. Schaus (ed.), *Women and Gender in Medieval Europe: An encyclopaedia* (London: Routledge, 2006), pp. 31–5

Bruzelius, C.A., 'The Architecture of the Mendicant Orders in the Middle Ages: An overview of recent literature', *Travaux*, vol. 2, 2012, pp. 365–86

Bruzelius, C.A., *Preaching, Building and Burying: Friars in the medieval city* (New Haven: Yale University Press, 2014)

Bruzelius, C.A. and C.H. Berman, 'Introduction', *Gesta*, vol. 31, no. 2, 1992, pp. 73–5

Buchanan, R., 'The Lecale Peninsula, County Down', in F.H.A. Aalen, K. Whelan and M. Stout (eds), *Atlas of the Irish Rural Landscape* (Cork: Cork University Press, 1997), pp. 277–86

Buchanan, R. and A. Wilson, *Irish Historic Towns Atlas No. 8: Downpatrick* (Dublin: Royal Irish Academy, 1997)

Buckley, L., 'Health Status in Medieval Dublin: Analysis of the skeletal remains from the abbey of St Thomas the Martyr', *Medieval Dublin*, vol. IV, 2003, pp. 98–126

Bugyis, K., *The Care of Nuns: The ministries of Benedictine women during the central middle ages* (Oxford: Oxford University Press, 2019)

Bull, R., S. Davis, H. Lewis and C. Phillpotts, with A. Birchenough, *Holywell Priory and the Development of Shoreditch to c. 1600: Archaeology from the London Overground East London Line* (London: Museum of London Archaeology Service, 2011)

Burke, W.P., 'The Nunnery of Kilculliheen', *Journal of the Waterford and Southeast Ireland Archaeological Society*, vol. 8, 1902, pp. 9–17

Burnett-Brown, J., *Lacock Abbey, Wiltshire* (The National Trust: Beckenham, 1974)

Burrows, M., 'Fifteenth-Century Irish Provincial Legislation and Pastoral Care', in W.J. Sheils and D. Woods (eds), *The Churches, Ireland and the Irish* (Oxford: Basil Blackwell, 1989), pp. 55–67

Burton, J., The *Yorkshire Nunneries in the Twelfth and Thirteenth Centuries* (York: Borthwick Institute, University of York, 1979)

Burton, J., *Monastic and Religious Orders in Britain 1000–1300* (Cambridge: Cambridge University Press, 1994)

Burton, J., 'The Estates and Economy of Rievaulx Abbey in Yorkshire', *Citeaux Commentarii Cistercienses*, vol. 49, 1998, pp. 29–94

Burton, J., 'Looking for Medieval Nuns', in J. Burton and K. Stöber (eds), *Monasteries and Society in the British Isles in the Later Middle Ages* (Woodbridge: Boydell, 2008), pp. 113–23

Burton, J., '*Moniales* and *Ordo Cisterciensis* in Medieval England and Wales', in G. Melville and A. Müller (eds), *Female* Vita Religiosa *between Late Antiquity and the High Middle Ages: Structures, developments and spatial contexts* (Berlin: LIT Verlag, 2011), pp. 375–89

Burton, J., 'Medieval Nunneries and Male Authority: Female monasteries in England and Wales', in J. Burton and K. Stöber (eds), *Women in the Medieval Monastic World* (Turnhout: Brepols, 2015), pp. 123–43

Burton, J. and J. Kerr, *The Cistercians in the Middle Ages* (Woodbridge: Boydell Press, 2011)

Burton, J. and K. Stöber (eds), *Women in the Medieval Monastic World* (Turnhout: Brepols, 2015)

Bussell, D.A. and J.M. McNamara, 'Barking Abbey: A GIS map of a medieval nunnery', *Peregrinations Journal of Medieval Art and Architecture*, vol. 4, 2013, pp. 173–89

Butler, J., *Gender Trouble: Feminism and the subversion of identity* (London: Routledge, 1990)

Butler, L.A.S., 'Medieval Urban Religious Houses', in J. Scofield and R. Leech (eds), *Urban Archaeology in Britain* (London: Council for British Archaeology, 1987), pp. 167–76

Butler, L.A.S., 'The Archaeology of Rural Monasteries in England and Wales', in R. Gilchrist and H. Mytum (eds), *The Archaeology of Rural Monasteries. BAR British Series 203* (Oxford: British Archaeological Reports, 1989), pp. 1–28

Buzwell, G., *Saints in Medieval Manuscripts* (London: The British Library, 2005)

Byrne, F., 'The Trembling Sod: Ireland in 1169', in A. Cosgrove (ed.), *A New History of Ireland. Volume II: Medieval Ireland 1169–1534* (Oxford: University Press, 1993), pp. 1–42

Byrne, F., *Irish Kings and High Kings* (Dublin: Four Courts Press, 2001)

Byrne, F., W. Jenkins, G. Kenny and C. Swift, *Historical Knowth and Its Hinterland: Excavations at Knowth*, vol. 4 (Dublin: Royal Irish Academy, 2008)

Byrne, M.E., '1997:289 – Walterstown Kildare'. Available at https://excavations.ie/report/1997/Kildare/0002838/. Accessed 15 September 2020

Byrne, M.E., '2005:525 – Coolmine, Saggart, Dublin'. Available at https://excavations.ie/report/2005/Dublin/0013529/. Accessed 15 September 2020

Byrne, M.E., 'Graney East, Castledermot, Co. Kildare: Report on archaeological monitoring and testing 99E0052' (Kildare: Byrne, Mullins & Associates, unpublished report, 2001)

Callan, M., 'Líadain's *Lament*, Darerca's *Life*, and Íte's *Ísucán*: Evidence for nuns' literacies in early Ireland', in V. Blanton, V. O'Mara and P. Stoop (eds), *Nuns' Literacies in Medieval Europe: The Kansas City dialogue* (Turnhout: Brepols, 2015), pp. 209–27

Callan, M., *Sacred Sisters: Gender, sanctity and power in medieval Ireland* (Amsterdam: Amsterdam University Press, 2020)

Campbell, E., E. FitzPatrick and A. Horning (eds), *Becoming and Belonging in Ireland AD c.1200–1600: Essays in identity and cultural practice* (Cork: Cork University Press, 2018)

Cariboni, G., 'Cistercian Nuns in Northern Italy: Variety of foundations and construction of an identity', in J. Burton and K. Stöber (eds), *Women in the Medieval Monastic World* (Turnhout: Brepols, 2015), pp. 53–74

Carroll, M.P., *Irish Pilgrimage, Holy Wells and Popular Catholic Devotion* (Baltimore: Johns Hopkins University Press, 1999)

Carter, M., 'Silk Purse or Sow's Ear? The art and architecture of the Cistercian nunnery of Swine, Yorkshire', in J. Burton and K. Stöber (eds), *Women in the Medieval Monastic World* (Turnhout: Brepols, 2015), pp. 253–78

Carter, M., *Hailes Abbey* (London: English Heritage, 2017)

Cartwright, J., 'The Desire to Corrupt: Convent and community in medieval Wales', in D. Watt (ed.), *Medieval Women in Their Communities* (Cardiff: University of Wales Press, 1997), pp. 20–48

Cartwright, J., *Feminine Sanctity and Spirituality in Medieval Wales* (Cardiff: University of Wales Press, 2008)

Cartwright, J., 'Abbess Agnes and the Ape', in J. Burton and K. Stöber (eds), *Monastic Wales: New approaches* (Cardiff: University of Wales Press, 2013), pp. 191–207

Carver, M., 'Early Scottish Monasteries and Prehistory: A preliminary dialogue', *The Scottish Historical Review*, vol. 88, 2009, pp. 332–51

Carville, G., *The Occupation of Celtic Sites in Medieval Ireland by the Canons Regular of St Augustine and the Cistercians* (Kalamazoo: Cistercian Publications, 1982)

Carville, G., 'Cistercian Nuns in Medieval Ireland: Plary Abbey, Ballymore, Co. Westmeath', in J.A. Nicols and L. Thomas Shank (eds), *Hidden Springs: Cistercian monastic women*. *Medieval Religious Women*, vol. 3 (Kalamazoo: Cistercian Publications, 1995), pp. 62–84

Carville, G., *The Impact of the Cistercians on the Landscape of Ireland* (Wicklow: KB Publications, 2002)

Carville, G., 'St Mary's Abbey, Graney: To live an apostolic life', *Journal of the Kildare Archaeological Society*, vol. XX, part 2, 2010, pp. 33–56

Casey, E.S., 'Place in Landscape Archaeology: A western philosophical prelude', in B. David and J. Thomas (eds), *Handbook of Landscape Archaeology* (California: Left Coast Press, 2008), pp. 44–50

Cassidy-Welch, M., *Monastic Spaces and Their Meanings: Thirteenth-century English Cistercian monasteries* (Turnhout: Brepols, 2001)

Cassidy-Welch, M., 'Space and Place in Medieval Contexts', *Parergon*, vol. 27, no. 2, 2010, pp. 1–12

Cassidy-Welch, M., *Imprisonment in the Medieval Religious Imagination,* c. *1150–1400* (London: Palgrave Macmillan, 2011)

Cave, A.J.E., 'Human Bones I, 1939', in S. Ward, *Excavations at Chester: The lesser medieval religious houses, sites investigated 1964–1983* (Chester: Chester City Council Department of Leisure Services, 1990), pp. 16–21

Caverno-Dominguez, G., 'Spanish Female Monasticism: Family monasteries and their transformation, eleventh to twelfth centuries', in J. Burton and K. Stöber (eds), *Women in the Medieval Monastic World* (Turnhout: Brepols, 2015), pp. 15–52

Champneys, A., *Irish Ecclesiastical Architecture* (London: G. Bell & Sons, 1910)

Charles-Edwards, T.M., *Early Irish and Welsh Kinship* (Oxford: Oxford University Press, 1993)

Charles-Edwards, T.M., *Early Christian Ireland* (Cambridge: Cambridge University Press, 2000)

Charles-Edwards, T.M., 'Early Irish Saints' Cults and Their Constituencies', Ériu, vol. 54, 2004, pp. 79–102

Charles-Edwards, T.M., 'Early Irish Law', in D. Ó Cróinín (ed.), *A New History of Ireland. Volume I: Prehistoric and Early Ireland* (Oxford: Oxford University Press, 2005), pp. 331–70

Chart, D. (ed.), *The Register of John Swayne, Archbishop of Armagh 1418–1439, with Some Entries of Earlier and Later Archbishops* (Belfast: Her Majesty's Stationery Office Northern Ireland, 1935)

Cherry, J., 'The Misericords in St Mary's Cathedral, Limerick: An additional note', in R. Stalley (ed.), *Limerick and South-West Ireland: Medieval art and architecture* (Leeds: Maney, for the British Archaeological Association, 2011), pp. 253–8

Childs, W. and T. O'Neill, 'Overseas Trade', in A. Cosgrove (ed.), *A New History of Ireland. Volume II: Medieval Ireland 1169–1534* (Oxford: Oxford University Press, 1993), pp. 492–524

Christie, N. and P. Stamper (eds), *Medieval Rural Settlement: Britain and Ireland* AD *800–1600* (Oxford: Windgather Press, 2012)

Christie, P. and J. Coad, 'Excavations at Denny Abbey', *Archaeological Journal*, vol. 137, 1980, pp. 138–79

Clapham, A., 'The Priory and Manor House of Dartford', *Archaeological Journal*, vol. 83, 1926, pp. 67–85

Clarke, D., *Analytical Archaeology* (London: Methuen, 1968)

Clarke, D., 'Archaeology: The loss of innocence', *Antiquity*, vol. 47, 1973, pp. 6–18

Clarke, H.B., *Irish Historic Towns Atlas No. 11: Dublin, Part I, to 1610* (Dublin: Royal Irish Academy, 2002)

Clay, R.M., *The Medieval Hospitals of England* (London: Methuen & Company, 1909)

Clay, R.M., *The Hermits and Anchorites of England* (London: Methuen, 1914)

Cleary, R., 'Excavations of an Early-Medieval Period Enclosure at Ballynagallagh, Lough Gur, Co. Limerick', *Proceedings of the Royal Irish Academy*, vol. 106C, 2008, pp. 1–66

Clough, S., 'Human Remains Report on Priory Hotel, Grenoble Road, Littlemore, Oxford' (England: Archaeological Burials Company, unpublished report for John Moore Heritage Services, 2015)

Clyne, M., 'Archaeological Excavations at Holy Trinity Abbey, Lough Key, Co. Roscommon', *Proceedings of the Royal Irish Academy*, vol. 105C, 2005, pp. 23–98

Clyne, M., *Kells Priory, Co. Kilkenny: Archaeological excavations by T. Fanning and M. Clyne* (Dublin: Government of Ireland, 2007)

Clyne, M., 'Medieval Irish Premonstratensian Monasteries and Their European Context', 2 vols, unpublished PhD thesis NUI Galway, 2010

Clyne, M., 'The Monasteries of the Canons of Prémontré, *c.*1180–*c.*1607', in M. Browne and C. Ó Clabaigh (eds), *Households of God: The regular canons and canonesses of Saint Augustine and of Prémontré in medieval Ireland* (Dublin: Four Courts Press, 2019), pp. 62–86

Coester, E., *Die Einschiffigen Cistercienserinnenkloster West- und Suddeutschlands von 1200–1350. Quellen und Abhandlungen zur mittelrheinischen Kirchengeschichte 46* (Mainz: Gesellschaft für Mittelrheinische Kirchenheschichte, 1984)

Coldicott, D.K., *Hampshire Nunneries* (Chichester: Phillimore, 1989)

Colfer, B., *The Hook Peninsula, County Wexford* (Cork: Cork University Press, 2004)

Collins, T., *The Other Monasticism: Killone Co. Clare. Heritage Guide No. 38* (Dublin: Wordwell, 2007)

Collins, T., 'Kenmare Lace', in J. Crowley and J. Sheehan (eds), *The Cultural Atlas of the Iveragh Peninsula* (Cork: Cork University Press, 2009), pp. 224–5

Collins, T., 'Missing the Boat …', *Archaeology Ireland*, vol. 24, 2010, pp. 9–11

Collins, T., 'Nunneries in Ireland in the Middle Ages: An archaeological overview', *The Kerry Magazine*, vol. 23, 2013, pp. 11–12

Collins, T., 'Timolin: A case study of a nunnery estate in later medieval Ireland', *Anuario de Estudios Medievales*, vol. 44, no. 1, 2014, pp. 51–80

Collins, T., 'An Archaeological Perspective on Female Monasticism in the Middle Ages in Ireland', in J. Burton and K. Stöber (eds), *Women in the Medieval Monastic World* (Turnhout: Brepols, 2015), pp. 229–51

Collins, T., 'Isolated in the Wilderness? An archaeological exploration of nunneries in the medieval landscape of Ireland', in J. Lyttleton and M. Stout (eds), *Landscape, Life and Legacy: Church and settlement in Ireland* (Dublin: Four Courts Press, 2018), pp. 142–56

Collins, T., 'Later Medieval Nunneries in Ireland: Form and function', in P. Barnwell (ed.), *Places of Worship in Britain and Ireland 1150–1350* (Donington: Shaun Tyas, 2018), pp. 168–87

Collins, T., 'Archaeologies of Female Monasticism in Ireland: Becoming and belonging *c.*1200–1600', in E. Campbell, E. FitzPatrick and A. Horning (eds), *Becoming and Belonging in Ireland 1200–1600 AD: Essays in identity and cultural practice* (Cork: Cork University Press, 2018), pp. 69–87

Collins, T., 'An Archaeology of Augustinian Nuns in Medieval Ireland', in M. Browne and C. Ó Clabaigh (eds), *Households of God: The regular canons and canonesses of Saint Augustine and of Prémontré in medieval Ireland* (Dublin: Four Courts Press, 2019), pp. 87–102

Collins, T., 'Unveiling Female Monasticism in Later Medieval Ireland: Survey and excavation at St Catherine's, Shanagolden, Co. Limerick', *Proceedings of the Royal Irish Academy*, vol. 119C, 2019, pp. 103–71

Collins, T., 'Space and Place: Archaeologies of female monasticism in later medieval Ireland', in V. Blud, D. Heath and E. Klafter (eds), *Gender in Medieval Places, Spaces and Thresholds* (London: Institute for Historical Research, 2019), pp. 25–44

Collins, T., 'Transforming Women Religious? Church reform and the archaeology of female monasticism in Ireland', in E. Bhreathnach, M. Kasnodębska-D'Aughton and K. Smith (eds), *Monastic Europe* (Turnhout: Brepols, 2019), pp. 277–301

Collins, T., 'The Materiality of Female Religious Reform in Twelfth-Century Ireland: The case of co-located religious houses', in J. Hotchin and J. Thibaut (eds), *Engendered Perspectives on Monastic Reform* (Woodbridge: Boydell, forthcoming 2021).

Collins, T., F. Coyne, N. Darmody, D. Humphreys, L. Lynch and B. O'Mahony, 'Limerick City Walls Conservation and Management Plan', unpublished report for Limerick City Council and the Heritage Council, 2008

Collins, T. and A. Cummins, *Excavation of a Ringwork at Ballysimon, Co. Limerick* (Limerick: Aegis Archaeology Limited, 2001)

Comber, M., *The Economy of the Ringfort and Contemporary Settlement in Early Medieval Ireland. BAR International Series 1773* (Oxford: Archaeopress, 2008)

Comber, M. and G. Hull, 'Excavations at Caherconnell Cashel, the Burren, Co. Clare: Implications for cashel chronology and Gaelic settlement', *Proceedings of the Royal Irish Academy*, vol. 110C, 2010, pp. 133–212

Comerford, M., *Collections from the Dioceses of Kildare and Leighlin*, 3 vols (Dublin: James Duffy & Sons, 1883–6)

Condit, T. and V. Buckley, *Faughart, Co. Louth. Archaeology Ireland Heritage Guide No. 37* (Dublin: Wordwell, 2007)

Conkey, M.W. and J. Gero, 'From Programme to Practice: Gender and feminism in archaeology', *Annual Review of Anthropology*, vol. 26, 1997, pp. 411–37

Conkey, M.W. and J. Spector, 'Archaeology and the Study of Gender', in K. Hays-Gilpin and D.S. Whitley (eds), *Reader in Gender Archaeology* (London: Routledge, 1998), pp. 12–45

Connolly, P., *Medieval Record Sources. Maynooth Research Guides for Irish History Number 4* (Dublin: Four Courts Press, 2002)

Connolly, S. and J.-M. Picard, 'Cogitosus's *Life of St Brigit*: Content and value', *Journal of the Royal Society of Antiquaries of Ireland*, vol. 117, 1987, pp. 5–27

Connon, A., 'The Banshenchas and the Uí Queens of Tara', in A.P. Smyth (ed.), *Seanchas: Studies in early and medieval Irish archaeology, history and literature, in honour of Francis J. Byrne* (Dublin: Four Courts Press, 2000), pp. 98–108

Conroy, G., 'Hartwell Castle and Bawn: A monastic grange?', in C. Manning (ed.), *From Ringforts to Fortified Houses: Studies on castles and other monuments in honour of David Sweetman* (Dublin: Wordwell, 2007), pp. 187–93

Conway, M., 'Excavation at Gracedieu'. Available at www.excavations.ie/report/1999/Dublin/0004132/. Accessed 15 September 2020

Coolahan, M.L., 'Archipelagic Identities in Europe: Irish nuns in English convents', in C. Bowden and J. Kelly (eds), *The English Convents in Exile, 1600–1800: Communities, culture and identity* (London: Taylor & Francis, 2013), pp. 211–28

Coolahan, M.L., 'Nuns' Writing: Translation, textual mobility and transnational networks', in P. Phillippy (ed.), *A History of Early Modern Women's Writing* (Cambridge: Cambridge University Press, 2018), pp. 257–75

Coomans, T., *Life Inside the Cloister: Understanding monastic architecture* (Leuven: Leuven University Press, 2018)

Cooney, G. and E. Grogan, *Irish Prehistory: A social perspective* (Dublin: Wordwell, 1994)

Coppack, G., *Fountains Abbey* (London: Batsford for English Heritage, 1993)

Coppack, G., 'Thornholme Priory: The development of a monastic outer court', in R. Gilchrist and H. Mytum (eds), *The Archaeology of Rural Monasteries. BAR British Series 203* (Oxford: British Archaeological Reports, 1989), pp. 185–222

Coppack, G., *Abbeys and Priories* (Stroud: Tempus, 2006)

Coppack, G., 'How the Other Half Lived: Cistercian nuns in early sixteenth-century Yorkshire', *Citeaux: Commentarii Cistercienses*, vol. 59, 2008, pp. 253–98

Coppack, G., '"Make Straight in the Desert a Highway for Our God": The Carthusians and community in late medieval England', in J. Burton and K. Stöber (eds), *Monasteries and Society in the British Isles in the Later Middle Ages* (Woodbridge: Boydell, 2008), pp. 168–79

Corbellini, S., 'Mapping the Spiritual Life: A spatial approach to later medieval spirituality', *Anuario de Estudios Medievales*, vol. 44, 2014, pp. 81–100

Corlett, C. and F. O'Mahony, *Ormond Castle: Ireland's Tudor rose. Heritage Guide No. 80* (Dublin: Wordwell, 2018)

Corlett, C. and M. Potterton (eds), *Rural Settlement in Medieval Ireland in the Light of Recent Archaeological Excavation* (Dublin: Wordwell, 2009)

Cosgrove, A. (ed.), *A New History of Ireland. Volume II: Medieval Ireland 1169–1534* (Oxford: Oxford University Press, 1993)

Cosgrove, A., 'The Emergence of the Pale 1399–1447', in A. Cosgrove (ed.), *A New History of Ireland. Volume II: Medieval Ireland 1169–1534* (Oxford: University Press, 1993), pp. 533–56

Cotter, E., 'Archaeological and Environmental Heritage at Buttevant, County Cork', unpublished report for Buttevant Heritage Group Cork, 2010

Coyne. F., '2008:120 – The Cloister Bar, Abbeybridge, Ennis, Clare'. Available at: www.excavations.ie/report/2008/Clare/0019134/. Accessed 15 September 2020

Crawford, H.S., 'A Descriptive List of Early Cross Slabs and Pillars [3 parts]', *Journal of the Royal Society of Antiquaries of Ireland*, vol. 43, 1913, pp. 151–69, 261–5, 326–34

Creighton, O. and T.B. Barry, 'Seigneurial and Elite Sites in the Medieval Landscape', in N. Christie and P. Stamper (eds), *Medieval Rural Settlement: Britain and Ireland AD 800–1600* (Oxford: Windgather Press, 2012), pp. 63–80

Crooks, P., 'Mac Murchada, Diarmait', in S. Duffy (ed.), *Medieval Ireland: An encyclopedia* (London: Routledge, 2005), pp. 299–302

Culhane, T.J., *The Barony of Shanid incorporating Connello Lower* (Limerick: Mount Pleasant Publications, 2003)

Culleton, C., 'From Barrow Boy to Viscount: The story of Matthew Barnewell', *History Ireland*, vol. 7, 1999, pp. 5–6

Cunniffe, C., 'The Canons and Canonesses of St Augustine at Clonfert', in M. Browne and C. Ó Clabaigh (eds), *Households of God: The regular canons and canonesses of Saint Augustine and of Prémontré in medieval Ireland* (Dublin: Four Courts Press, 2019), pp. 103–23

Cunningham, B., *Medieval Irish Pilgrims to Santiago de Compostela* (Dublin: Four Courts Press, 2018)

Cunningham, B. and R. Gillespie, *Stories from Gaelic Ireland: Microhistories from the sixteenth-century Irish annals* (Dublin: Four Courts Press, 2003)

Cuppage, J., *Dingle Peninsula Archaeological Survey* (Ballyferriter: Oidhreacht Chorca Dhuibhne, 1996)

Curran, K., 'Religious Women and Their Communities in Late Medieval Scotland', PhD thesis, University of Glasgow, 2005

Curran, K., 'Review article: *Anchorites, Wombs and Tombs: Intersections of Gender and Enclosure in the Middle Ages* (ed. L. Herbert McEvoy and M. Hughes-Edwards)', *Journal of Medieval Monastic Studies*, vol. 1, 2012, pp 155–6

Curran, K., 'Review article: *Feminine Sanctity and Spirituality in Medieval Wales* (J. Cartwright)', *Journal of Medieval Monastic Studies*, vol. 1, 2012, pp. 145–6

Curran, K., 'Looking for Medieval Female Religious in Britain and Ireland: Sources, methodologies and pitfalls', in K. Stöber, J. Kerr and E. Jamroziak (eds), *Monastic Life in the Medieval British Isles: Essays in honour of Janet Burton* (Cardiff: University of Wales Press, 2018), pp. 161–72

Currie, C.K., 'The Role of Fishponds in the Monastic Economy', in R. Gilchrist and H. Mytum (eds), *The Archaeology of Rural Monasteries. BAR British Series 203* (Oxford: British Archaeological Reports, 1989), pp. 147–72

Daichman, G., *Wayward Nuns in Medieval Literature* (Syracuse: Syracuse University Press, 1986)

De Beauvoir, S., *The Second Sex*, trans. H.M. Parshley (New York: Vintage Books, Random House, 1989)

De Certeau, M., *The Practice of Everyday Life* (Berkeley: University of California Press, 1984)

De Paermentier, E., 'Architecturale Ruimte en Beweginsvrijheid van de Vrouw in Laatmiddeleeuwse Gentse Religieuze en Caritatieve Instellingen', *Handelingen der Maatschappij voor Geschiedenis en Oudheidkunde te Gent*, vol. 51, 1997, pp. 77–113

De Paermentier, E., 'Experiencing Space through Women's Convent Rules: The Rich Clares in medieval Ghent (thirteenth to fourteenth centuries)', *Medieval Feminist Forum*, vol. 44, no. 1, 2008, pp. 53–68

De Paor, L., 'Excavations at Mellifont Abbey, Co. Louth', *Proceedings of the Royal Irish Academy*, vol. 68C, 1969, pp. 109–64

De Paor, L., *Saint Patrick's World* (Dublin: Four Courts Press, 1996)

De Varebeke, H.J., 'The Benedictines in Medieval Ireland', *Journal of the Royal Society of Antiquaries of Ireland*, vol. 80, 1950, pp. 92–6

Degler-Spengler, B., 'The Incorporation of Cistercian Nuns into the Order in the Twelfth and Thirteenth Century', in J. Nichols and L. Thomas Shank (eds), *Hidden Springs: Cistercian monastic women. Medieval Religious Women*, vol. 3 (Kalamazoo: Cistercian Publications, 1995), pp. 85–134

Delaney, M., 'The Human Remains', in M. Clyne, *Kells Priory, Co. Kilkenny: Archaeological excavations by T. Fanning and M. Clyne* (Dublin: Government of Ireland, 2007), pp. 467–76

Dempsey, K., 'Rectangular Chamber Towers and Their Medieval Halls: A recent look at buildings formerly described as "hall houses"', *Château Gaillard*, vol. 27, 2016, pp. 113–19

Dempsey, K., 'Understanding "Hall-Houses": Debating seigneurial buildings in Ireland in the thirteenth century', *Medieval Archaeology*, vol. 61, 2017, pp. 372–99

Dempsey, K., 'Gender and Medieval Archaeology: Storming the castle', *Antiquity*, vol. 93, 2019, pp. 772–88

Dempsey, K., 'Planting New Ideas: A feminist gaze on medieval castles', *Château Gaillard*, vol. 29, 2020, pp. 85–98

Dempsey, K., 'Home is Where the Heart(h) is: Investigating medieval houses in Ireland 1100–1600 AD', *Archaeology Ireland*, vol. 34, no. 1, 2020, pp. 49–51

Dempsey, K., R. Gilchrist, J. Ashbee, S. Sagrott and S. Stones, 'Beyond the Martial Façade: Gender, heritage and medieval castles', *International Journal of Heritage Studies*, vol. 26, no. 4, 2020, pp. 352–69

Desmarchelier, M., 'L'architecture des Églises de Moniales Cisterciennes, Essai de Classement des Différents Types de Plans (en guise de suite)', in B. Chauvin (ed.), *Mélanges á la Mémoire du Père Anselme Dimier. Tome III: Architecture Cistercienne; Vol. 5: Ordre, Fouilles* (Arbois: Pupillin, 1982), pp. 79–121

Dey, H. and E. Fentress (eds), *Western Monasticism* Ante Litteram: *The spaces of monastic observance in late antiquity and the early middle ages* (Turnhout: Brepols, 2011)

Días-Andreu, M. and M.L. Stig Sørensen, 'Excavating Women: Towards an engendered history of archaeology', in T. Murray and C. Evans (eds), *Histories of Archaeology: A reader in the history of archaeology* (Oxford: Oxford University Press, 2008), pp. 279–311

Dickens, A.J., *The Female Mystic: Great women thinkers of the middle ages* (London: I.B. Tauris, 2009)

Diem, A., 'The Gender of the Religious Wo/Men and the Invention of Monasticism', in J. Bennett and R. Karras (eds), *The Oxford Handbook of Women and Gender in Medieval Europe* (Oxford: Oxford University Press, 2013), pp. 432–46

Diem, A. '... Ut Si Professus Fueit Se Omnia Impleturum, Tunc Excipiatur: Observations on the rules for monks and nuns of Caesarius and Aurelianus of Arles', in V. Zimmerl-Panagl, L.J. Dorfbauer and C. Weidmann (eds), *Edition und Erforschung lateinischer patristischer Texte. 150 Jahre CSEL. Festschrift für Kurt Smolak zum 70* (Boston: De Gruyter, 2014), pp. 191–224

Diem, A. and P. Rousseau, 'Monastic Rules (Fourth to Ninth Century)', in A.I. Beach and I. Cochelin (eds), *Medieval Monasticism in the Latin West*, 2 vols (Cambridge: Cambridge University Press, 2020), pp. 162–94

Dimier, A., *Recueil de Plans D'églises Cisterciennes. Supplément* (Paris: Aiguebelle, 1967)

Dimier, A., 'L'architecture des Églises de Moniales Cisterciennes', *Cîteaux: Commentarii Cistercienses*, vol. 25, 1974, pp. 8–13

Dinham Atkinson, T., *Cambridge Described and Illustrated* (London: Macmillan & Co., 1897)

Dinshaw, C., 'Margery Kempe', in C. Dinshaw and D. Wallace (eds), *The Cambridge Companion to Medieval Women's Writing* (Cambridge: Cambridge University Press, 2003), pp. 222–39

Dinshaw, C. and D. Wallace (eds), *The Cambridge Companion to Medieval Women's Writing* (Cambridge: Cambridge University Press, 2003)

Dirsztay, P. (ed.), *Church Furnishings* (London: Routledge & Kegan Paul, 1978)

Dobson, R. and S. Donaghey, *The History of Clementhorpe Nunnery: Archaeology of York* (York: York Archaeological Trust, 1984)

Doggett, D., 'The Medieval Monasteries of the Augustinian Canons Regular', *Archaeology Ireland*, vol. 10, 1996, pp. 31–3

Doherty, C., 'Airgialla', in S. Duffy (ed.), *Medieval Ireland: An encyclopedia* (London: Routledge, 2005), pp. 13–14

Doherty, C., L. Doran and M. Kelly (eds), *Glendalough: City of God* (Dublin: Four Courts Press, 2011)

Dolan, B., '"Mysterious Waifs of Time": Some thoughts on the function of Irish bullaun stones', *Journal of the Royal Society of Antiquaries*, vols 142–3, 2012–13, pp. 42–58

Dolan, T., 'Writing in Ireland', in D. Wallace (ed.), *The Cambridge History of Medieval English Literature* (Cambridge: Cambridge University Press, 1999), pp. 208–28

Doran, L., 'Medieval Communication Routes through Longford and Roscommon and Their Associated Settlements', *Proceedings of the Royal Irish Academy*, vol. 104C, 2004, pp. 57–80

Down, K., 'Colonial Society and Economy', in A. Cosgrave (ed.), *A New History of Ireland. Volume II: Medieval Ireland 1169–1534* (Oxford: Clarendon Press, 1993), pp. 439–91

Drew, T., 'On Evidences of the Plan of the Cloister Garth and Monastic Buildings of the Priory of the Holy Trinity, Now Known as Christ Church Cathedral, Dublin', *Proceedings of the Royal Irish Academy*, vol. 2, 1879–88, pp. 214–18

Driscoll, S., 'Picts and Prehistory: Cultural resource management in early medieval Scotland', *World Archaeology*, vol. 30, 1998, pp. 142–58

Dronzek, A., 'Private and Public Spheres', in M. Schaus (ed.), *Women and Gender in Medieval Europe: An Encyclopedia* (London: Routledge, 2006), pp. 670–1

Duddy, C., 'The Role of St Thomas's Abbey in the Early Development of Dublin's Western Suburb', *Medieval Dublin*, vol. IV, 2003, pp. 79–97

Duffy, E., *The Stripping of the Altars: Traditional religion in England 1400–1580* (New Haven: Yale University Press, 1992)

Duffy, E., *Marking the Hours: English people and their prayers 1240–1570* (Yale: Yale University Press, 2007)

Duffy, P.J., D. Edwards and E. FitzPatrick (eds), *Gaelic Ireland: Land, lordship and settlement* c. *1250* – c. *1650* (Dublin: Four Courts Press, 2001)

Duffy, S. and L. Simpson, 'The Hermits of St Augustine in Medieval Dublin: Their history and archaeology', in J. Bradley, A. Fletcher and A. Simms (eds), *Dublin in the Medieval World: Studies in honour of Howard B. Clarke* (Dublin: Four Courts Press, 2009), pp. 202–48

Dumville, D.N., *Councils and Synods of the Gaelic Early and Central Middle Ages* (Cambridge: Cambridge University Press, 1997)

Dunn, M., *The Emergence of Monasticism* (Oxford: Blackwell, 2000)

Dunning, P.J., 'The Arroasian Order in Medieval Ireland', *Irish Historical Studies*, vol. 4, pp. 297–315

Dwyer, B.W., *Stephen of Lexington: Letters from Ireland 1228–1229* (Kalamazoo: Cistercian Publications, 1982)

Dyer, C., *Standards of Living in the Later Middle Ages: Social change in England* c.*1200–1520* (Cambridge: Cambridge University Press, 1998)

Dyer, C., *Everyday Life in Medieval England* (London: Hambledon & London, 2000)

Dyer, C., *Making a Living in the Middle Ages: The people of Britain 850–1520* (London: Penguin, 2003)

Dyer, C., 'Gardens and Garden Produce in the Later Middle Ages', in C. Woolgar et al. (eds), *Food in Medieval England: Diet and nutrition* (Oxford: Oxford University Press, 2006), pp. 27–40

Dyer, C., 'Seasonal Patterns in Food Consumption in the Later Middle Ages', in C. Woolgar et al. (eds), *Food in Medieval England: Diet and nutrition* (Oxford: Oxford University Press, 2006), pp. 201–14

Dyer, C., 'Making Sense of Town and Country', in K. Giles and C. Dyer (eds), *Town and Country in the Middle Ages: Contrast, contacts and interconnections 1100–1500. SMA Monograph 22* (Leeds: Maney, 2007), pp. 313–21

Dyson, T., M. Samuel, A. Steele and S. Wright, *The Cluniac Priory and Abbey of St Saviour Bermondsey, Surrey: Excavations 1984–95* (London: Museum of London Archaeology, 2011)

Eames, E. and T. Fanning, *Irish Medieval Tiles* (Dublin: Royal Irish Academy, 1988)

Eckenstein, L., *Women Under Monasticism 500–1500* (Cambridge: Cambridge University Press, 1896)

Edwards, N., *The Archaeology of Early Medieval Ireland* (London: Batsford, 1990)

Edwards, N., 'Early Medieval Munster: Summary and prospect', in M.A. Monk and J. Sheehan (eds), *Early Medieval Munster: Archaeology, history and society* (Cork: Cork University Press, 1998), pp. 200–5

Edwards, N., 'The Archaeology of Early Medieval Ireland, *c.*400–1169: Settlement and economy', in D. Ó Cróinín (ed.), *A New History of Ireland. Volume I: Prehistoric and Early Ireland* (Oxford: Oxford University Press, 2005), pp. 235–300

Edwards, N., 'Introduction', in N. Edwards (ed.), *The Archaeology of the Early Medieval Celtic Churches: Proceedings of a conference on the archaeology of the early medieval Celtic churches, September 2004* (Leeds: Maney, 2009), pp. 1–18

Edwards, N., R. Flechner and M. Ní Mhaonaigh (eds), *Transforming Landscapes of Belief in the Early Medieval Insular World and Beyond: Converting the isles, II* (Turnhout: Brepols, 2017)

Ehrenberg, M., *Women in Prehistory* (London: British Museum Publications, 1989)

Elkins, S.K., *Holy Women of Twelfth-Century England* (Chapel Hill: University of North Carolina Press, 1988)

Elliott, D. *Proving Woman: Female spirituality and inquisitional culture in the later middle ages* (Princeton: Princeton University Press, 2004)

Elliott, I., C. McDermott and G. Warren, 'Geophysical Survey at Glendalough Monastic Site, Co. Wicklow', in *Glendalough Valley Archaeology Project Newsletter 3* (Dublin: UCD School of Archaeology, 2014), pp. 1–8

Ellis, S. '"More Irish than the Irish Themselves?" The "Anglo-Irish" in Tudor Ireland', *History Ireland*, vol. 7, no. 1, 1999, pp. 22–6

Emerick, K., 'Whitby and Clonmacnoise', in H. King (ed.), *Clonmacnoise Studies*, vol. 2 (Dublin: The Stationery Office, 2003), pp. 209–21

Empey, A., 'The Layperson in the Parish: The medieval inheritance 1169–1536', in R. Gillespie and W.G. Neely (eds), *The Laity and the Church of Ireland 1000–2000: All sorts and conditions* (Dublin: Four Courts Press, 2002), pp. 7–48

Empey, A., 'The Augustinian Priory at Kells: An historical introduction', in M. Clyne, *Kells Priory, Co. Kilkenny: Archaeological excavations by T. Fanning and M. Clyne* (Dublin: The Stationery Office, 2007), pp. 1–11

Empey, A., 'The Role of the Regular Canons of St Augustine in the Formation of the Parochial Network in Ireland', in M. Browne and C. Ó Clabaigh (eds), *Households of God: The regular canons and canonesses of Saint Augustine and of Prémontré in medieval Ireland* (Dublin: Four Courts Press, 2019), pp. 124–37

Engelstad, E., 'Images of Power and Contradiction: Feminist theory and post-processual archaeology', *Antiquity*, vol. 65, 1991, pp. 502–14

Eogan, G., *Excavations at Knowth. Volume 5: The Archaeology of Knowth in the First and Second Millennia AD* (Dublin: Royal Irish Academy, 2012)

Eogan, J. and E. Shee-Twohig (eds), *Cois tSiuire: Nine thousand years of human activity in the lower Suir Valley. Archaeological Excavations on the N25 Waterford City Bypass* (Dublin: The National Roads Authority, 2011)

Etchingham, C., *Church Organisation in Ireland AD650 to 1000* (Maynooth: Laigin Publications, 1999)

Evangelisti, S., *Nuns: A history of convent life* (Oxford: Oxford University Press, 2008)

Everson, P., 'Rural Monasteries within the Secular Landscape', in R. Gilchrist and H. Mytum (eds), *The Archaeology of Rural Monasteries. BAR British Series 203* (Oxford: British Archaeological Reports, 1989), pp. 141–5

Everson, P. and D. Stocker, 'St Leonard's at Kirkstead, Lincolnshire: The landscape of the Cistercian monastic precinct', in M. Gardiner and S. Rippon (eds), *Medieval Landscapes* (Bollington: Windgather Press, 2007), pp. 215–30

Fahy, E.M., 'Inishleena Abbey and Other Sites in the Lee Valley', *Journal of the Cork Historical and Archaeological Society*, vol. 62, 1957, pp. 65–76

Fanning, T., 'Excavations at Clontuskert Priory, County Galway', *Proceedings of the Royal Irish Academy*, vol. 76C, 1976, pp. 97–169

Farrelly, J. and C. O'Brien, *Archaeological Inventory of North Tipperary* (Dublin: The Stationery Office, 2002)

Feder, E.K., 'Review: *Feminism, Foucault, and Embodied Subjectivity* (by M.A. McLaren)', *Foucault Studies*, vol. 6, 2009, pp. 131–5

Fenlon, J., *Ormond Castle: Visitor's guide* (Dublin: Government of Ireland, 2008)

Fenwick, J., 'Geophysical Survey at Knowth', in G. Eogan, *Excavations at Knowth. Volume 5: The Archaeology of Knowth in the First and Second Millennia AD* (Dublin: Royal Irish Academy, 2012), pp. 832–40

Fergusson, P., 'The Refectory at Easby Abbey: Form and iconography', *Art Bulletin*, vol. 71, 1989, pp. 334–51

Ferriter, D., *The Transformation of Ireland 1900–2000* (London: Profile Books, 2012)

Finlay, N., 'Outside of Life and Death: Traditions of infant burial in Ireland from cillín to cist', *World Archaeology*, vol. 31, 2000, pp. 407–22

Firey, A., 'Cross-examining the Witness: Recent research in Celtic monastic history', *Monastic Studies*, vol. 14, 1983, pp. 17–30

Fitzgerald, P. and J.J. McGregor, *History, Topography and Antiquities of the County and City of Limerick* (Dublin: McKern, 1826)

FitzPatrick, E., *Royal Inauguration in Gaelic Ireland* c.*1100–1600: A cultural landscape study* (Woodbridge: Boydell, 2004)

FitzPatrick, E., 'The Material World of the Parish', in E. FitzPatrick and R. Gillespie (eds), *The Parish in Medieval and Early Modern Ireland: Community, territory and building* (Dublin: Four Courts Press, 2006), pp. 62–78

FitzPatrick, E., 'Native Enclosed Settlement and the Problem of the Irish "Ringfort"', *Medieval Archaeology*, vol. 53, 2009, pp. 271–307

FitzPatrick, E., 'Aughris Headland, Co. Sligo', in F.H.A. Aalen, K. Whelan and M. Stout (eds), *Atlas of the Irish Rural Landscape*, 2nd edn (Cork: Cork University Press, 2011), pp. 352–67

FitzPatrick, E., 'The Landscape and Settlements of the Uí Dhálaigh Poets of Muinter Bháire', in S. Duffy (ed.), *Princes, Prelates and Poets in Medieval Ireland: Essays in honour of Katharine Simms* (Dublin: Four Courts Press, 2013), pp. 460–80

FitzPatrick, E., 'Rethinking Settlement Values in Gaelic Society: The case of cathedral centres', *Proceedings of the Royal Irish Academy*, vol. 119C, 2019, pp. 69–102

FitzPatrick, E. and C. O'Brien, *The Medieval Churches of County Offaly* (Dublin: Government of Ireland, 1988)

FitzPatrick, E. and R. Gillespie (eds), *The Parish in Medieval and Early Modern Ireland: Community, territory and building* (Dublin: Four Courts Press, 2006)

FitzPatrick, E. and P. Walsh, 'Buildings and Architecture', in E. FitzPatrick, M. O'Brien and P. Walsh (eds), *Archaeological Investigations in Galway City 1987–1998* (Dublin: Wordwell, 2004), pp. 337–55

Flanagan, M., 'Ordnance Survey Letters for County Limerick', 3 vols, unpublished typescript, 1927

Flanagan, M.T., 'St Mary's Abbey, Louth and the Introduction of the Arroasian Observance into Ireland', *Clogher Record*, vol. 10, 1980, pp. 223–34

Flanagan, M.T., *Irish Society, Anglo–Norman Settlers, Angevin Kingship: Interactions in Ireland in the late twelfth century* (Oxford: Oxford University Press, 1989)

Flanagan, M.T., *The Transformation of the Irish Church in the Twelfth Century* (Woodbridge: Boydell, 2010)

Flechner, R., *The* Hibernensis*: Studies in medieval and early modern canon law*, 2 vols (Washington DC: The Catholic University of America Press, 2019)

Fleming, J., *Gille of Limerick c. 1070–1145: Architect of a medieval church* (Dublin: Four Courts Press, 2001)

Flint, V.I.J., 'Space and Discipline in Early Modern Europe', in B.A. Hanawalt and M. Kobialka (eds), *Medieval Practices of Space* (London: University of Minnesota Press, 2000), pp. 149–66

Flora, H., *The Devout Belief of the Imagination: The Paris* Meditationes Vitae Christi *and female Franciscan spirituality in Trecento, Italy* (Turnhout: Brepols, 2009)

Florea, C., '"For They Wanted Us to Serve Them": Female monasticism in medieval Transylvania', in J. Burton and K. Stöber (eds), *Women in the Medieval Monastic World* (Turnhout: Brepols, 2015), pp. 211–27

Foley, C., 'Excavation at a Medieval Settlement Site in Jerpointchurch Townland, County Kilkenny', *Proceedings of the Royal Irish Academy*, vol. 89C, 1989, pp. 71–176

Foley, C. and R. McHugh, *An Archaeological Survey of County Fermanagh*, 2 vols (Belfast: Department of the Environment, 2014)

Follett, W., *Céli Dé in Ireland* (Woodbridge: Boydell, 2006)

Foot, S., 'What Was an Early Anglo-Saxon Monastery?', in J. Loades (ed.), *Monastic Studies: The continuity of tradition* (Bangor: Headstart History, 1990), pp. 48–57

Foot, S., *Veiled Women: The disappearance of nuns from Anglo-Saxon England*, 2 vols (Aldershot: Ashgate, 2000)

Foot, S., 'Unveiling Anglo-Saxon Nuns', in D. Wood (ed.), *Women and Religion in Medieval England* (Oxford: Oxbow, 2003), pp. 13–31

Foot, S., *Monastic Life in Anglo-Saxon England, c. 600–900* (Cambridge: Cambridge University Press, 2006)

Foot, S., *Æthelstan: The first king of England* (New Haven: Yale University Press, 2011)

Foucault, M., *Discipline and Punish: The birth of the prison* (New York: Random House, 1977)

Foucault, M., *The History of Sexuality. Volume 1: An Introduction* (Harmonsworth: Penguin, 1981)

Fowler, C., *The Archaeology of Personhood* (London: Routledge, 2004)

Frantzen, A.J., 'When Women Aren't Enough', in N. Partner (ed.), *Studying Medieval Women* (Cambridge, MA: The Medieval Academy of America, 1993), pp. 143–69

Frazer, S., 'The Public Forum and the Space Between: The materiality of social strategy in the Irish Neolithic', *Proceedings of the Prehistoric Society*, vol. 64, 1998, pp. 203–24

Fredengren, C., *Crannógs* (Bray: Wordwell, 2002)

Freeman, E., 'Nuns', in M.B. Bruun (ed.), *The Cambridge Companion to the Cistercian Order* (Cambridge: Cambridge University Press, 2013), pp. 100–11

Freeman, A.M. (ed.), *Annála Connacht: The Annals of Connacht AD 1224–1544* (Dublin: Dublin Institute for Advanced Studies, 1944)

French, K., *The People of the Parish: Community life in a late medieval English diocese* (Philadelphia: University of Pennsylvania Press, 2000)

French K., 'The Seat Under Our Lady: Gender and seating in late medieval English parish churches', in V.C. Raguin and S. Stanbury (eds), *Women's Spaces: Patronage, place and gender in the medieval church* (New York: State University of New York Press, 2005), pp. 141–60

French, K., *The Good Women of the Parish: Gender and religion after the Black Death* (Philadelphia: University of Pennsylvania Press, 2007)

Friedan, B., *The Feminine Mystique* (London: Norton & Company, 2001)

Frings, J. (ed.), *Krone und Schleier. Kunst aus Mittelalterlichen Frauenklöstern [museum exhibition catalogue]. Herausgegben von der Kunst- und Ausstellungshalle der Bundesrepublik Deutschland, Bonn und dem Ruhrlandmuseum Essen* (Munich: Hirmer Verlag, 2005)

Gaillard, G., 'Female Monasteries of the Early Middle Ages (Seventh to Ninth Century) in Northern Gaul: Between monastic ideals and aristocratic powers', in J. Burton and K. Stöber (eds), *Women in the Medieval Monastic World* (Turnhout: Brepols, 2015), pp. 75–96

Gaimster, D. and R. Gilchrist (eds), *The Archaeology of Reformation 1480–1580* (Leeds: Maney, 2003)

Ganz, D., 'The Buildings of Godstow Nunnery', *Oxoniensia*, vol. 37, 1972, pp. 150–7

Gardiner, M., 'Graffiti and Their Use in Late Medieval England', in J. Klapste and P. Sommer (eds), *Arts and Crafts in Medieval Rural Environment (Ruralia 6)* (Prague: Institute of Archaeology, 2007), pp. 265–76

Garí, B. (ed.), *Redes Femenias de Promoción Spiritual en los Reinos Peninsulares, s. xiii-xvi, Ircum-Medieval Cultures, 1* (Rome: Viella, 2013)

Garí, B. (ed.), *Anuario de Estudios Medievales, Temas Monograficos: Espacios de espiritualidad femenina en la Europa medieval. Una Mirada interdisciplinar*, vol. 44, 2014

Garí, B., 'The Sacred Space of Meditation: Nunneries and devotional performance in the territories of the Crown of Aragón (fourteenth–fifteenth centuries)', *Journal of Medieval Monastic Studies*, vol. 3, 2014, pp. 71–95

Garí, B., 'What Did Catalan Nuns Read? Women's literacy in the female monasteries of Catalonia, Majorca, and Valencia', in V. Blanton, V. O'Mara and P. Stoop (eds), *Nuns' Literacies in Medieval Europe: The Antwerp dialogue* (Turnhout: Brepols, 2018), pp. 125–48

Geary, P., *Living with the Dead in the Middle Ages* (Ithaca: Cornell University Press, 1994)

Geber, J., *Victims of Ireland's Great Famine: The bioarchaeology of mass burials at Kilkenny Union workhouse* (Gainsville: University Press of Florida, 2015)

Gerchow, J., K. Bodwaré, S. Marti and H. Röckelein, 'Early Monasteries and Foundations (500–1200): An introduction', in J. Hamburger and S. Marti (eds), *Crown and Veil: Female monasticism from the fifth to the fifteenth centuries* (New York: Columbia University Press, 2008), pp. 13–40

Gerchow, J. and S. Marti, '"Nuns' Work", "Caretaker Institutions", and "Women's Movements": Some thoughts about a modern historiography of medieval monasticism', in J. Hamburger and S. Marti (eds), *Crown and Veil: Female monasticism from the fifth to the fifteenth centuries* (New York: Columbia University Press, 2008), pp. 132–50

Gerrard, C. and A. Gutierrez (eds), *The Oxford Handbook of Later Medieval Archaeology in Britain* (Oxford: Oxford University Press, 2018)

Gibson, P.J., 'Seeing Beneath the Ground: Using geophysics at the former ecclesiastical site of Clonard, Co. Meath', *Ríocht na Mídhe: Records of the Meath Archaeological and Historical Society*, vol. 20, 2009, pp. 69–79

Gibson, P.J., 'Geophysical Investigation Around the Sites of the Former Monastic Settlement, Killeigh, Co. Offaly'. Report No. EGU 01/05 (Maynooth: unpublished report, 2015). Available at https://www.offaly.ie/eng/Services/Heritage/Archaeology/Monastic-Sites/Killeigh-Paul-Gibson-Geophys-2005.pdf. Accessed 15 September 2020.

Gibson, P.J. and D.M. George, 'Geophysical Investigation of the Site of the Former Monastic Settlement, Clonard, County Meath, Ireland', *Archaeological Prospection*, vol. 13, 2006, pp. 45–56

Giddens, A., *Central Problems in Social Theory* (London: Macmillan, 1979)

Gilchrist, R., 'The Spatial Archaeology of Gender Domains: A case study of medieval English nunneries', *Archaeological Review from Cambridge*, vol. 7, no. 1, 1988, pp. 21–8

Gilchrist, R., 'The Archaeology of Medieval English Nunneries: A research design', in R. Gilchrist and H. Mytum (eds), *The Archaeology of Rural Monasteries. BAR British Series 203* (Oxford: British Archaeological Reports, 1989), pp. 251–7

Gilchrist, R., 'Community and Self: Perceptions and use of space in medieval monasteries', *Scottish Archaeological Review*, vol. 6, 1989, pp. 55–64

Gilchrist, R., 'Gender, Ideology and Material Culture in Later Medieval England, *c.*1050–1550', unpublished PhD thesis, University of York, 1990

Gilchrist, R., 'Blessed Art Thou Among Women: The archaeology of piety', in P.J.P. Goldberg (ed.), *Woman is a Worthy Wight: Women in medieval English society 1200–1500* (Stroud: Alan Sutton, 1992), pp. 212–26

Gilchrist, R., 'Christian Bodies and Souls: The archaeology of life and death in later medieval hospitals', in S. Bassett (ed.), *Death in Towns: Urban responses to the dying and the dead 100–1600* (Leicester: Leicester University Press, 1992), pp. 101–18

Gilchrist, R., 'Medieval Bodies in the Material World: Gender, stigma and the body', in S. Kay and M. Rubin (eds), *Framing Medieval Bodies* (Manchester: Manchester University Press, 1994), pp. 43–61

Gilchrist, R., *Gender and Material Culture: The archaeology of religious women* (London: Routledge, 1994)

Gilchrist, R., *Contemplation and Action: The other monasticism* (London: Leicester University Press, 1995)

Gilchrist, R., 'Ambivalent Bodies: Gender and medieval archaeology', in J. Moore and E. Scott (eds), *Invisible People* (London: Leicester University Press, 1997), pp. 42–58

Gilchrist, R., 'Women's Archaeology? Political feminism, gender theory and historical revision', in K. Hays-Gilpin and D.S. Whitley (eds), *Reader in Gender Archaeology* (London: Routledge, 1998), pp. 48–56

Gilchrist, R., *Gender and Archaeology: Contesting the past* (London: Routledge, 1999)

Gilchrist, R., 'Landscapes of the Middle Ages', in J. Hunter and I. Ralston (eds), *The Archaeology of Britain* (London: Routledge, 1999), pp. 228–46

Gilchrist, R., 'Human Lifecycles', *World Archaeology*, vol. 31, 2000, pp. 325–8

Gilchrist, R., 'Unsexing the Body: The interior sexuality of medieval religious women', in R.A. Schmidt and B.L. Voss (eds), *Archaeologies of Sexuality* (London: Routledge, 2000), pp. 89–103

Gilchrist, R., *Norwich Cathedral Close: The evolution of the English cathedral landscape* (Woodbridge: Boydell, 2005)

Gilchrist, R., 'Archaeology and the Life Course: A time and age for gender', in L. Meskell and R.W. Preucel (eds), *A Companion to Social Archaeology* (Oxford: Blackwell, 2007), pp. 142–60

Gilchrist, R., 'Magic for the Dead? The archaeology of magic in later medieval burials', *Medieval Archaeology*, vol. 52, 2008, pp. 119–59

Gilchrist, R., 'Medieval Archaeology and Theory: A disciplinary leap of faith', in R. Gilchrist and A. Reynolds (eds), *Reflections: 50 years of medieval archaeology 1957–2007* (Leeds: Maney, 2009), pp. 385–408

Gilchrist, R., *Medieval Life: Archaeology and the life course* (Woodbridge: Boydell, 2012)

Gilchrist, R., 'Monastic and Church Archaeology', *Annual Review of Anthropology*, vol. 43, 2014, pp. 235–50

Gilchrist, R., 'Conclusions', in R. Gilchrist and C. Green, *Glastonbury Abbey: Archaeological excavations 1904–1979* (London: Society of Antiquaries of London, 2015), pp. 415–35

Gilchrist, R., 'Magic and Archaeology: Ritual residues and "odd" deposits', in S. Page and C. Rider (eds), *The Routledge History of Medieval Magic* (Routledge: Abingdon, 2019), pp. 383–401

Gilchrist, R., *Sacred Heritage: Monastic archaeology, identities, beliefs* (Cambridge: Cambridge University Press, 2020)

Gilchrist, R. and H. Mytum (eds), *The Archaeology of Rural Monasteries. BAR British Series 203* (Oxford: British Archaeological Reports, 1989)

Gilchrist, R. and M. Oliva, *Religious Women in Medieval East Anglia: History and archaeology* c.*1100–1540* (Norwich: Centre of East Anglian Studies, 1993)

Gilchrist, R. and B. Sloane, *Requiem: The medieval monastic cemetery in Britain* (London: Museum of London Archaeology Service, 2005)

Giles, K., 'Seeing and Believing: Visuality and space in pre-modern England', *World Archaeology*, vol. 39, 2007, pp. 105–21

Giles, K. and C. Dyer (eds), *Town and Country in the Middle Ages* (Leeds: Maney, 2007)

Gilyard-Beer, R., *Abbeys: An introduction to the religious houses of England and Wales* (London: Her Majesty's Stationery Office, 1959)

Gimbutas, M., *The Language of the Goddess* (London: Thames & Hudson, 1989)

Gleeson, P., 'Constructing Kingship in Early Medieval Ireland: Power, place and ideology', *Medieval Archaeology*, vol. 56, 2012, pp. 1–33

Golding, B., *Gilbert of Sempringham and the Gilbertine Order* c. *1130–1300* (Oxford: Oxford University Press, 1995)

Golding, B., 'Bishops and Nuns: Forms of the *cura monialium* in twelfth- and thirteenth-century England', in J. Burton and K. Stöber (eds), *Women in the Medieval Monastic World* (Turnhout: Brepols, 2015), pp. 97–122

Golding, B., '"As for a Nun": Corrodies, nunneries and the laity', in K. Stöber, J. Kerr and E. Jamroziak (eds), *Monastic Life in the Medieval British Isles: Essays in honour of Janet Burton* (Cardiff: University of Wales Press, 2018), pp. 173–87

Golding, B., *Giraldus Cambrensis'* Speculum Ecclesie (trans.) (Oxford: Oxford Medieval Texts/Clarendon Press, forthcoming 2021)

Goose, D., 'Human Bones II: 1964', in S. Ward, *Excavations at Chester: The lesser medieval religious houses, sites investigated 1964–1983* (Chester: Chester City Council Department of Leisure Services, 1990), pp. 21–2

Gowen, M., 'Excavations at Grace Dieu in Advance of a Gas Pipeline', unpublished draft text, Margaret Gowen & Company, 1988

Graham, B.J., *Medieval Irish Settlement: A review* (Lancaster: Historical Geography Group, 1980)

Graves, C.P., *The Form and Fabric of Belief: An archaeology of the lay experience of religion in medieval Norfolk and Devon. BAR British Series 311* (Oxford: John & Erica Hedges, 2000)

Graves, C.P., 'Sensing and Believing: Exploring worlds of difference in pre-modern England. A contribution to the debate opened by Kate Giles', *World Archaeology*, vol. 39, 2007, pp. 515–31

Graves, C.V., 'English Cistercian Nuns in Lincolnshire', *Speculum*, vol. 54, no. 3, 1979, pp. 492–9

Green, L.B., 'Unveiling the Cloisters: Augustinian nunneries in twelfth-century Ireland', *History Studies: UL History Society Journal*, vol. 2, 2000, pp. 37–49

Greene, J., *Norton Priory: The archaeology of a medieval religious house* (Cambridge: Cambridge University Press, 1989)

Greene, J.P., 'Strategies for Future Research and Site Investigation', in G. Keevil, M. Aston and T. Hall (eds), *Monastic Archaeology* (Oxford: Oxbow, 2001), pp. 4–8

Greene, J.P., *Medieval Monasteries* (London: Continuum, 1992)

Greene, S., 'Killeen Cormac Colbinstown: An ecclesiastical site on the Kildare–Wicklow border', *County Kildare Online Electronic History Journal*, 2011. Available at: http://www.kildare.ie/library/ehistory/2011/03/killeen_cormac_colbinstown_an.asp. Accessed 15 September 2020

Greene, S., 'Killeen Cormac: The archaeology and history of a significant early Christian foundation', *Journal of the Kildare Archaeological Society*, vol. XX, part 3, 2013, pp. 26–48

Griffiths, F., 'The Cross and the *Cura Monialium*: Robert of Arbrissel, John the Evangelist, and the pastoral care of women in the age of reform', *Speculum*, vol. 83, no. 2, 2008, pp. 303–30

Griffiths, F., 'Like the Sister of Aaron: Medieval religious women as makers and donors of liturgical textiles', in G. Melville and A. Müller (eds), *Female* Vita Religiosa *between Late Antiquity and the High Middle Ages: Structures, developments and spatial contexts* (Zürich: Lit Verglag, 2011), pp. 343–74

Griffiths, F., 'The Mass in Monastic Practice: Nuns and ordained monks, *c.* 400–1200', in A.I. Beach and I. Cochelin (eds), *Medieval Monasticism in the Latin West*, 2 vols (Cambridge: Cambridge University Press, 2020), pp. 729–46

Grössinger, C., 'At the Uttermost Ends of the Earth', in R. Stalley (ed.), *Limerick and South-West Ireland: Medieval art and architecture* (Leeds: Maney, for the British Archaeological Association, 2011), pp. 243–52

Gwynn, A., 'The Early History of St Thomas's Abbey, Dublin', *Journal of the Royal Society of Antiquaries of Ireland*, vol. 84, 1954, pp. 1–35

Gwynn, A. and R.N. Hadcock, *Medieval Religious Houses: Ireland* (Dublin: Irish Academic Press, 1970)

Gwynn, E. and W. Purton, 'The Monastery at Tallaght', *Proceedings of the Royal Irish Academy*, vol. 29C, 1911–12, pp. 115–79

Haarländer, S., 'Innumerabiles Populi de Utroque Sexu Confuentes ... Klöster für Männer und Frauen im Frühmittelalterlichen Irland', in G. Melville and A. Muller (eds), *Female* Vita Religiosa *between Late Antiquity and the High Middle Ages: Structures, developments and spatial contexts* (Zürich: LIT Verlag, 2011), pp. 137–50

Hadcock, N., 'The Origin of the Augustinian Order in Meath', *Ríocht na Midhe: Records of the Meath Archaeological and Historical Society*, vol. 3, 1964, pp. 124–31

Hagen, I., '2002:0648 – Portraine, Dublin'. Available at https://excavations.ie/report/2002/Dublin/0007964/. Accessed 15 September 2020

Hall, D., 'The Nuns of the Medieval Convent of Lismullin, County Meath and Their Secular Connections', *Ríocht na Midhe: Records of the Meath Archaeological and Historical Society*, vol. 10, 1999, pp. 58–70

Hall, D., 'Towards a Prosopography of Nuns in Medieval Ireland', *Archivium Hibernicum*, vol. 53, 1999, pp. 3–15

Hall, D., 'Women and Religion in Late Medieval Ireland', unpublished PhD thesis, University of Melbourne, 2000

Hall, D., *Women and the Church in Medieval Ireland* c. *1140–1540* (Dublin: Four Courts Press, 2003)

Hall, D., 'Necessary Collaborations: Religious women and lay communities in medieval Ireland *c.* 1200–1540', in A. Hayes and D. Urquhart (eds), *Irish Women's History* (Dublin: Irish Academic Press, 2004), pp. 15–28

Hall, D., 'Monasticism and Nuns: Celtic', in M. Schaus (ed.), *Women and Gender in Medieval Europe: An encyclopedia* (London: Routledge, 2006), pp. 586–7

Hall, D., *Scottish Monastic Landscapes* (Stroud: Tempus, 2006)

Halpin, A. and L. Buckley, 'Archaeological Excavations at the Dominican Priory, Drogheda, Co. Louth', *Proceedings of the Royal Irish Academy*, vol. 95C, 1995, pp. 175–253

Halpin, A. and C. Newman, *Ireland: An Oxford archaeological guide* (Oxford: Oxford University Press, 2006)

Halpin, P., 'Anglo-Saxon Women and Pilgrimage', *Anglo-Norman Studies: Proceedings of the Battle Conference*, vol. 19, 1996, pp. 97–122

Hamburger, J., 'The Use of Images in the Pastoral Care of Nuns: The case of Heinrich Suso and the Dominicans', *The Art Bulletin*, vol. 71, 1989, pp. 20–46

Hamburger, J., 'The Visual and the Visionary: The image in late medieval monastic devotion', *Viator*, vol. 20, 1989, pp. 161–82

Hamburger, J., 'Art, Enclosure and the *Cura Monialium*: Prolegomena in the guise of a postscript', *Gesta*, vol. 31, no. 2, 1992, pp. 108–34

Hamburger, J., *Nuns as Artists: The visual culture of a medieval convent* (Berkeley: University of California Press, 1997)

Hamburger, J. and S. Marti (eds), *Crown and Veil: Female monasticism from the fifth to the fifteenth centuries* (New York: Columbia University Press, 2008)

Hamburger, J., P. Marx and S. Marti, 'The Time of the Orders 1200–1500', in J. Hamburger and S. Marti (eds), *Crown and Veil: Female monasticism from the fifth to the fifteenth centuries* (New York: Columbia University Press, 2008), pp. 41–75

Hamburger, J. and R. Suckale, 'Between this World and the Next: The art of religious women in the middles ages', in J. Hamburger and S. Marti (eds), *Crown and Veil: Female monasticism from the fifth to the fifteenth centuries* (New York: Columbia University Press, 2008), pp. 76–108

Hamlin, A., *The Archaeology of Early Christianity in the North of Ireland. BAR British Series 460* (Oxford: Archaeopress, 2008)

Hamlin, A. and N. Brannon, 'Northern Ireland: The afterlife of monastic buildings', in D. Gaimster and R. Gilchrist (eds), *The Archaeology of Reformation 1480–1580* (Leeds: Maney, 2003), pp. 252–66

Hamlin, A. and C. Foley, 'A Women's Graveyard at Carrickmore, County Tyrone, and the Separate Burial of Women', *Ulster Journal of Archaeology*, vol. 46, 1983, pp. 41–6

Hanawalt, B.A. and M. Kobialka (eds), *Medieval Practices of Space* (London: University of Minnesota Press, 2000)

Hand, G.J., 'Medieval Chapter of St Mary's Cathedral, Limerick', in J.A. Watt, J.B. Morrall and F.X. Martin (eds), *Medieval Studies Presented to Aubrey Gwynn* (Dublin: Four Candles, 1961), pp. 74–89

Hansell, P. and J. Hansell, *Dovecotes* (Aylesbury: Shire Publications, 1988)

Harbison, P., *Pilgrimage in Ireland* (Dublin: Irish Academic Press, 1991)

Harbison, P., *The High Crosses of Ireland*, 3 vols (Bonn: Dr Rudolf Habelt, 1992)

Harbison, P., 'Sculpture', in S. Duffy (ed.), *Medieval Ireland: An encyclopedia* (London: Routledge, 2005), pp. 424–5

Harper, J., 'The Space Enriched: Liturgy, ritual and music 1150–1350', in P. Barnwell (ed.), *Places of Worship in Britain and Ireland, 1150–1350* (Donington: Shaun Tyas, 2018), pp. 10–23

Harrington, C., *Women in a Celtic Church: Ireland 450–1150* (Oxford: Oxford University Press, 2002)

Harris, A., 'Saint Gobnet, Abbess', *Journal of the Royal Society of Antiquaries of Ireland*, vol. 68, 1938, pp. 272–7

Harris, B., 'A New Look at the Reformation: Aristocratic women and nunneries 1450–1540', *The Journal of British Studies*, vol. 32, no. 2, 1993, pp. 89–113

Harris, W., *The Whole Works of Sir James Ware Concerning Ireland*, 2 vols (Dublin: S. Powell, 1739, 1745)

Harrison, B., 'Field Systems and Demesne Farming on the Wiltshire Estates of St Swithun's Priory, Winchester', *Agricultural History Review*, vol. 43, 1995, pp. 1–18

Harvey, B., *Living and Dying in England 1100–1540: The monastic experience* (Oxford: Clarendon Press, 1993)

Harvey, B., 'Monastic Pittances in the Middle Ages', in C. Woolgar et al. (eds), *Food in Medieval England: Diet and nutrition* (Oxford: Oxford University Press, 2006), pp. 215–27

Hawkes, J., 'An Iconography of Identity? The cross-head from Mayo Abbey', in C. Hourihane (ed.), *From Ireland Coming: Irish art from the early Christian to the late Gothic period and its European context* (Princeton: Dept of Art and Archaeology, Princeton University, 2001), pp. 261–76

Hayden, A., '2003:1974 – Site 1, Kilbeggan, Co. Westmeath', Available at https://excavations.ie/report/2003/Westmeath/0011006/. Accessed 15 September 2020

Hayes, D.M., *Body and Sacred Place in Medieval Europe 1100–1389* (London: Routledge, 2003)

Hayes, J.P., 'Ballymacdane Abbey, Co. Cork', *Journal of the Cork Historical and Archaeological Society*, vol. 3, 1894, pp. 141–3

Hays-Gilpin, K. and D.S. Whitley (eds), *Reader in Gender Archaeology* (London: Routledge, 1998)

Healy, P., *Third Report on Monuments and Sites of Archaeological Interest in County Dublin: Northern section*, vol. 3 (Dublin: An Foras Forbartha Teoranta, 1975)

Healy, Rev. D., 'Two Royal Abbeys by the Western Lakes (Cong and Inishmaine)', *Journal of the Royal Society of Antiquaries of Ireland*, vol. 35, 1905, pp. 1–20

Helvetius, A., 'L'organisation des Monastères Féminins à L'époque Mérovingienne', in G. Melville and A. Müller (eds), *Female* Vita Religiosa *between Late Antiquity and the High Middle Ages: Structures, developments and spatial contexts* (Berlin: LIT Verlag, 2011), pp. 151–69

Hennessy, W. M. and B. Mac Carthy (eds), *Annala Uladh: Annals of Ulster otherwise Annala Senait, Annals of Senat: A chronicle of Irish affairs from AD431 to AD1540*, 4 vols (Dublin: HMSO by A. Thom & Co., 1887–1901)

Herbert McAvoy, L. (ed.), *Anchoritic Traditions of Medieval Europe* (Woodbridge: Boydell, 2010)

Herbert McAvoy, L., 'The Medieval *Hortus Conclusus*: Revisiting the pleasure garden', *Medieval Feminist Forum*, vol. 50, 2014, pp. 5–10

Herbert, M., *Iona, Kells and Derry: The history and hagiography of the monastic familia of Columba* (Dublin: Four Courts Press, 1996)

Herity, M. (ed.), *Ordnance Survey Letters Kildare: Letters containing information relative to the antiquities of the county of Kildare collected during the progress of the OS in 1837–1839* (Dublin: Four Masters, 2002)

Hickey, H., 'Excavation of an Enclosure on Aughinish Island, Co. Limerick', *North Munster Antiquarian Journal*, vol.16, 1973–4, pp. 15–28

Hicks, L.V., *Religious Life in Normandy 1050–1300: Space, gender and social pressure* (Woodbridge: Boydell, 2007)

Higgins, J., *The Tisrara Medieval Church, Carrowntemple, Four Roads, Co. Roscommon: Its archaeology and history* (Ireland: Tisrara Heritage and Graveyard Restoration Committee, 1995)

Higgins, J., 'The Funerary Monuments', in M. Clyne, *Kells Priory, Co. Kilkenny: Archaeological excavations by T. Fanning and M. Clyne* (Dublin: Government of Ireland, 2007), pp. 453–67

Hillier, B. and J. Hanson, *The Social Logic of Space* (Cambridge: Cambridge University Press, 1984)

Hinton, D.A., *Archaeology, Economy and Society: England from the fifth to the fifteenth century* (London: Routledge, 1990)

Hirst, S. and S. Wright, 'Bordesley Abbey Church: A long-term research excavation', in R. Gilchrist and H. Mytum (eds), *The Archaeology of Rural Monasteries. BAR British Series 203* (Oxford: British Archaeological Reports, 1989), pp. 295–312

Hodder, I. (ed.), *Symbolic and Structural Archaeology* (Cambridge: Cambridge University Press, 1982)

Hodder, I., 'Archaeology in 1984', *Antiquity*, vol. 58, 1984, pp. 25–32

Hodder, I., *The Archaeology of Contextual Meanings* (Cambridge: Cambridge University Press, 1987)

Hodder, I., *Theory and Practice in Archaeology* (London: Routledge, 1995)

Hodder, I. (ed.), *Archaeological Theory Today* (Cambridge: Polity Press, 2002)

Hodder, I., 'The "Social" in Archaeological Theory', in L. Meskell and R.W. Preucel (eds), *A Companion to Social Archaeology* (Oxford: Blackwell, 2007), pp. 23–42

Hodder, I. and S. Hutson, *Reading the Past: Current approaches to interpretation in archaeology* (Cambridge: Cambridge University Press, 2003)

Hogan, A., *Kilmallock Dominican Priory* (Kilmallock: Kilmallock Historical Society, 1991)

Hogan, A., *The Priory of Llanthony Prima and Secunda in Ireland 1172–1541* (Dublin: Four Courts Press, 2007)

Hogan, A., 'The Settlement of the Augustinian Canons of Llanthony Prima and Secunda in Ireland 1172–1541', in M. Browne and C. Ó Clabaigh (eds), *Households of God: The regular canons and canonesses of Saint Augustine and of Prémontré in medieval Ireland* (Dublin: Four Courts Press, 2019), pp. 138–55

Hogan, E., *Onomasticon Goedelicum* (Dublin: Royal Irish Academy, 1910)

Holland, M., 'Gille (Gilbert) of Limerick', in S. Duffy (ed.), *Medieval Ireland: An encyclopedia* (New York: Routledge, 2005), pp. 198–9

Holland, M., 'Malachy (Máel-Máedóic)', in S. Duffy (ed.), *Medieval Ireland: An encyclopedia* (New York: Routledge, 2005), pp. 312–14

Hollis, S., *Anglo-Saxon Women and the Church* (Woodbridge: Boydell, 1992)

Horn, W., 'On the Origin of the Medieval Cloister', *Gesta*, vol. 12, 1973, pp. 13–52

Horning, A., 'Ireland: Medieval identities, settlement and land use', in N. Christie and P. Stamper (eds), *Medieval Rural Settlement: Britain and Ireland AD 800–1600* (Oxford: Windgather Press, 2012), pp. 172–85

Hotchin, J., 'Emotions and the Ritual of a Nun's Coronation in Late Medieval Germany', in M.L. Bailey and K. Barclay (eds), *Emotion, Ritual and Power in Europe, 1200–1920: Family, state and church* (New York: Palgrave Macmillan, 2017), pp. 171–92

Hourihane, C., *The Mason and His Mark: Mason's marks in the medieval Irish archbishoprics of Cashel and Dublin. BAR British Series 294* (Oxford: Archaeopress, 2000)

Hoy, S. and M. MacCurtain, *From Dublin to New Orleans: The journey of Nora and Alice* (Dublin: Attic Press, 1994)

Hughes, K., *The Church in Early Irish Society* (London: Cornell University Press, 1966)

Hughes, K., *Early Christian Ireland: Introduction to the sources* (London: Sources for History, 1972)

Hughes, K. and A. Hamlin, *The Modern Traveller to the Early Irish Church* (Dublin: Four Courts Press, 1997)

Hunt, J., 'Romanesque Head from Peter's Cell', *North Munster Antiquarian Journal*, vol. 6, 1949, pp. 16–18

Hunt, J., *Irish Medieval Figure Sculpture 1200–1600*, 2 vols (Dublin: Irish University Press, 1974)

Hurl, D., C. Sandes and L. Buckley, 'The Excavation of an Early Christian Cemetery at Solar, Co. Antrim', *Ulster Journal of Archaeology*, vol. 61, 2002, pp. 37–82

Hurley, M., 'Excavations at Grand Parade, Cork (part 2)', *Journal of the Cork Archaeological and Historical Society*, vol. 95, 1990, pp. 64–87

Hurley, M., 'The Bone and Antler Artefacts', in M. Hurley and C. Sheehan, *Excavations at the Dominican Priory: St Mary's of the Isle, Cork* (Cork: Cork Corporation, 1995), pp. 112–15

Hurley, M., 'Bone Artefacts', in E. FitzPatrick, M. O'Brien and P. Walsh (eds), *Archaeological Investigations in Galway City 1987–1998* (Dublin: Wordwell, 2004), pp. 463–76

Hurley, M. and C. Sheehan, *Excavations at the Dominican Priory: St Mary's of the Isle, Cork* (Cork: Cork Corporation, 1995)

Hutton, R., 'The Neolithic Great Goddess: A study in modern tradition', *Antiquity*, vol. 71, 1997, pp. 91–9

Irvine, R., 'The Architecture of Stability: Monasteries and the importance of place in a world of non-places', *Etnofoor*, vol. 23, no. 1, 2011, pp. 29–49

Jäggi, C., 'Eastern Choir or Western Gallery? The problem of the place of the nuns' choir in Koenigsfelden and other early mendicant nunneries', *Gesta*, vol. 40, no. 1, 2001, pp. 79–93

Jäggi, C., *Fraunenkloster im Spätmittelalter. Die Kirchen der Klarissen und Dominikanerinnen im 13 und 14 Jahrundert* (Petersburg: Imhof, 2006)

Jäggi, C. and U. Lobbedey, 'Church and Cloister: The architecture of female monasticism in the middle ages', in J.F. Hamburger and S. Marti (eds), *Crown and Veil: Female monasticism from the fifth to the fifteenth centuries* (New York: Columbia University Press, 2008), pp. 109–31

Jamroziak, E., *Survival and Success on Medieval Borders: Cistercian houses in medieval Scotland and Pomerania from the twelfth to late fourteenth century* (Turnhout: Brepols, 2011)

Jamroziak, E., *The Cistercian Order in Medieval Europe 1090–1500* (London: Routledge, 2013)

Jamroziak, E. and J. Burton (eds), *Religious and Laity in Northern Europe 1000–1400: Interaction, negotiation and power* (Turnhout: Brepols, 2007)

Jamroziak, E. and K. Stöber (eds) *Monasteries on the Borders of Medieval Europe: Conflict and cultural interaction* (Turnhout: Brepols, 2013)

Jarrett, J., 'Power Over Past and Future: Abbess Emma and the nunnery of Sant Joan de les Abadesses', *Early Medieval Europe*, vol. 12, no. 3, 2003, pp. 229–58

Jarrett, J., *Rulers and Ruled in Frontier Catalonia 880–1010: Pathways of power* (Woodbridge: Boydell, 2010)

Jasper, K. and J. Howe, 'Hermitism in the Eleventh and Twelfth Centuries', in A.I. Beach and I. Cochelin (eds), *Medieval Monasticism in the Latin West*, 2 vols (Cambridge: Cambridge University Press, 2020), pp. 684–96

Jeep, J.M., 'Wienhausen', in J.M. Jeep (ed.), *Medieval Germany: An encyclopedia* (London: Routledge, 2001), pp. 812–13

Jenkins, D., *Holy, Holier, Holiest: The sacred topography of the early medieval Irish church* (Turnhout: Brepols, 2010)

Johnson, M., 'Conceptions of Agency in Archaeological Interpretation', in J. Thomas (ed.), *Interpretive Archaeology: A reader* (London: Leicester University Press, 2000), pp. 211–27

Johnson, M., *Ideas of Landscape* (Oxford: Blackwell, 2007)

Johnson, M., *Archaeological Theory: An introduction* (Chichester: Wiley-Blackwell, 2010)

Johnson, P., *Equal in Monastic Profession: Religious women in medieval France* (Chicago: University of Chicago Press, 1991)

Johnson, P., 'The Cloistering of Medieval Nuns: Release or repression, reality or fantasy?', in D. Helly and S. Reverby (eds), *Gendered Domains: Rethinking public and private in women's history* (New York: Ithaca, 1992), pp. 27–39

Johnston, E., 'Transforming Women in Irish Hagiography', *Peritia*, vol. 9, 1995, pp. 197–220

Johnston, E., 'Íte: Patron of her people?' *Peritia*, vol. 14, 2000, pp. 421–8

Johnston, E., 'Powerful Women or Patriarchal Weapons? Two medieval Irish saints', *Peritia*, vol. 15, 2001, pp. 302–10

Johnston, E., *Literacy and Identity in Early Medieval Ireland* (Suffolk: Boydell & Brewer, 2013)

Johnston, E., 'Movers and Shakers? How women shaped the career of Columbanus', in A. O'Hara (ed.), *Columbanus and the Peoples of Post-Roman Europe* (Oxford: Oxford University Press, 2018), pp. 69–90

Jones, C.A., 'Minsters and Monasticism in Anglo-Saxon England', in A.I. Beach and I. Cochelin (eds), *Medieval Monasticism in the Latin West*, 2 vols (Cambridge: Cambridge University Press, 2020), pp. 502–41

Jones, L.E., *Old English Churches* (London: Frederick Warne & Co., 1969)

Jordan, E., 'Gender Concerns: Monks, nuns and patronage of the Cistercian Order in thirteenth-century Flanders and Hainaut', *Speculum*, vol. 87, 2006, pp. 62–94

Jordan, E., *Women, Power and Religious Patronage in the Middle Ages* (New York: Palgrave Macmillan, 2006)

Jordan, E., '*Pro Remedio Anime Sue:* Cistercian nuns and space in the Low Countries', in J. Burton and K. Stöber (eds), *Women in the Medieval Monastic World* (Turnhout: Brepols, 2015), pp. 279–98

Jornet-Benito, N., 'Female Mendicant Spirituality in Catalan Territory: The birth of the first communities of Poor Clares', in J. Burton and K. Stöber (eds), *Women in the Medieval Monastic World* (Turnhout: Brepols, 2015), pp. 185–210

Jurkowski, M., N. Ramsey and S. Renton (eds), *English Monastic Estates 1066–1540: A list of manors, churches and chapels*, 3 vols (Kew: List and Index Society, 2007)

Kalkreuter, B., *Boyle Abbey and the School of the West* (Dublin: Wordwell, 2001)

Keegan, M., 'The Archaeology of Manorial Settlement in West County Limerick in the Thirteenth Century', in J. Lyttleton and T. O'Keeffe (eds), *The Manor in Medieval and Early Modern Ireland* (Dublin: Four Courts Press, 2005), pp. 17–39

Keeping, D., 'Life and Death in English Nunneries: A biocultural study of variations in the health of women during the later medieval period 1066-1540', unpublished PhD thesis, University of Bradford, 2000

Kehnel, A. and M. Mencej, 'Representing Eternity: Circular movement in the cloister, round dancing, winding-staircases and dancing angels', in A. Müller and K. Stöber (eds), *Self-Representation of Medieval Religious Communities: The British Isles context* (Berlin: LIT Verlag, 2009), pp. 67–97

Kelly, D. and T. O'Keeffe, *Irish Historic Towns Atlas No. 27: Youghal* (Dublin: Royal Irish Academy, 2015)

Kelly, F., *A Guide to Early Irish Law* (Dublin: Institute for Advanced Studies, 1988)
Kelly, F., *Early Irish Farming* (Dublin: Institute for Advanced Studies, 1997)
Kelly, J., *English Convents in Catholic Europe c.1600–1800* (Cambridge: Cambridge University Press, 2020)
Kelly, R.J., 'Notes on the Round Tower at Kilbannon and on Kilcreevanty, County Galway', *Journal of the Royal Society of Antiquaries of Ireland*, vol. 31, 1901, pp. 379–84
Kenny, G., 'The Power of Dower: The importance of dower in the lives of medieval women in Ireland', in C. Meek and C. Lawless (eds), *Pawns or Players? Studies on medieval and early modern women* (Dublin: Four Courts Press, 2003), pp. 59–74
Kenny, G., 'Anglo-Irish and Gaelic Marriage Laws and Traditions in Late Medieval Ireland', *Journal of Medieval History*, vol. 32, 2006, pp. 27–42
Kenny, G., *Anglo-Irish and Gaelic Women in Ireland c.1170–1540* (Dublin: Four Courts Press, 2007)
Kenny, G., 'Late Medieval Brugh na Bóinne, 1142–1541', in F.J. Byrne, W. Jenkins, G. Kenny and C. Swift (eds), *Historical Knowth and Its Hinterland: Excavations at Knowth*, vol. 4 (Dublin: Royal Irish Academy, 2008), pp. 133–71
Kerr, B., *Religious Life for Women c.1100–c.1350: Fontevraud in England* (Oxford: Clarendon Press, 1999)
Kerr, J., *Life in the Medieval Cloister* (London: Continuum, 2009)
Killanin, Lord and M.V. Duignan, *The Shell Guide to Ireland*, 2nd edn (London: Ebury Press, 1967)
King, H., 'Late Medieval Crosses in County Meath, *c*.1470–1635', *Proceedings of the Royal Irish Academy*, vol. 84C, 1984, pp. 79–116
King, H. (ed.), *Clonmacnoise Studies*, vol. 1 (Dublin: The Stationery Office, 1998)
King, H. (ed.), *Clonmacnoise Studies*, vol. 2 (Dublin: The Stationery Office, 2003)
Kinsella, S., 'Mapping Christ Church Cathedral Dublin *c*.1028–1608: An examination of the western cloister', in J. Bradley, A.J. Fletcher and A. Simms (eds), *Dublin in the Medieval World: Studies in honour of Howard B. Clarke* (Dublin: Four Courts Press, 2009), pp. 143–67
Kissane, N., *Saint Brigid of Kildare: Life, legend and cult* (Dublin: Four Courts Press, 2017)
Kleinschmidt, H., *Understanding the Middle Ages: The transformation of ideas and attitudes in the medieval world* (London: Boydell, 2000)
Knapp, A.B., 'Boys Will Be Boys: Masculinist approaches to a gendered archaeology', in K. Hays-Gilpin and D. Whitley (eds), *Reader in Gender Archaeology* (London: Routledge, 1998), pp. 365–71
Knowles, D., *The Religious Orders in England*, 3 vols (Cambridge: Cambridge University Press, 1948, 1955, 1959)
Knowles, D. and R.N. Hadcock, *Medieval Religious Houses of England and Wales* (London: Longman, 1971)
Knox, A., 'Her Book-Lined Cell: Irish nuns and the development of texts, translation, and literacy in late medieval Spain', in V. Blanton, V. O'Mara and P. Stoop (eds), *Nuns' Literacies in Medieval Europe: The Kansas City dialogue* (Turnhout: Brepols, 2015), pp. 67–86
Knox, H.T., *The History of the County of Mayo to the Close of the Sixteenth Century* (Dublin: Hodges Figgis, 1908)

Knudsen, C., 'Naughty Nuns and Promiscuous Monks: Monastic sexual misconduct in late medieval England', unpublished PhD thesis, Centre for Medieval Studies, University of Toronto, 2012

Knudsen, C., 'Promiscuous Monks and Naughty Nuns: Poverty, sex, and apostasy in later medieval England', in A. Scott and C. Kosso (eds), *Poverty and Prosperity: The rich and the poor in the middle ages and Renaissance* (Belgium: Turnhout, 2012), pp. 75–91

Kramer, R., 'Monasticism, Reform and Authority in the Carolingian Era', in A.I. Beach and I. Cochelin (eds), *Medieval Monasticism in the Latin West*, 2 vols (Cambridge: Cambridge University Press, 2020), pp. 432–49

Kristensen, H.K., *Middelalderbyen Viborg*, vol. 4 (Denmark: Centrum, 1987)

Lacey, B., *Medieval and Monastic Derry: Sixth century to 1600* (Dublin: Four Courts Press, 2013)

Lackner, B., 'Cistercian Nuns in Medieval Hungary', in J. Nichols and L. Thomas Shank (eds), *Hidden Springs: Cistercian monastic women. Medieval Religious Women*, vol. 3 (Kalamazoo: Cistercian Publications, 1995), pp. 159–70

Lacy, B., *Archaeological Survey of County Donegal* (Lifford: Donegal County Council, 1983)

Lafaye, A., 'Medieval Mendicant Communities in East Munster: History, archaeology, landscapes', unpublished PhD thesis, University College Dublin, 2012

Lafaye, A., 'Spiritual Renewal and Changing Landscapes: The mendicant orders in Ireland, thirteenth–sixteenth century', in J. Lyttleton and M. Stout (eds), *Church and Settlement in Ireland* (Dublin: Four Courts Press, 2018), pp. 119–41

Lafaye, A., 'Kilmallock Borough and Dominican Priory: Planning, patronage and urban life in medieval Ireland', in M.A. Bevivino, E. Bhreathnach and L. Shine (eds), *A Research Miscellany* (Discovery Programme Reports, 9) (Dublin: The Discovery Programme, 2018), pp. 67–90

Lafaye, A., 'Mendicant Friaries and the Changing Landscapes of Late Medieval Ireland: The foundations of the Augustinian Friars in counties Mayo and Sligo', in N. Brady and C. Theune (eds), *Settlement Change Across Medieval Europe: Old paradigms and new vistas (Ruralia XII)* (Leiden: Sidestone Press, 2019), pp. 223–32

Lalor, B., *The Irish Round Tower* (Cork: The Collins Press, 1999)

Lawless, G., *Augustine of Hippo and His Monastic Rule* (Oxford: Clarendon Press, 1987)

Lawrence, C.H., *Medieval Monasticism*, 3rd edn (Harlow: Longman, 2001)

Leask, H.G., *Irish Churches and Monastic Buildings*, 3 vols (Dundalk: Dundalgan Press, 1955–60)

Leclercq, J., 'Solitude and Solidarity: Medieval women recluses', in J. Nichols and L. Thomas Shank (eds), *Peace Weavers: Medieval religious women*, vol. 2 (Kalamazoo: Cistercian Publications, 1987), pp. 67–84

Lee, G., *Leper Hospitals in Medieval Ireland* (Dublin: Four Courts Press, 1996)

Lee, P., *Nunneries, Learning and Spirituality in Late Medieval English Society: The Dominican Priory of Dartford* (York: York Medieval Press, 2001)

Lefebvre, H., *The Production of Space*, trans. D. Nicholson-Smith (Oxford: Blackwell, 1991)

Lehmijoki-Gardner, M., 'Dominican Order', in M. Schaus (ed.), *Women and Gender in Medieval Europe: An encyclopedia* (London: Routledge, 2006), pp. 223–5

Leigh Fry, S., *Burial in Medieval Ireland 900–1500* (Dublin: Four Courts Press, 1999)

Lennon, C. and J. Murray (eds), *The Dublin Franchise Roll, 1468–1512* (Dublin: Dublin Corporation, 1998)

Lester, A.E., 'Making the Margins in the Thirteenth Century: Suburban space and religious reform between the Low Countries and the county of Champagne', *Parergon*, vol. 27, 2010, pp. 59–87

Lewis, K.J., *The Cult of St Catherine of Alexandria in Late Medieval England* (Woodbridge: Boydell, 2000)

Lewis, S., *A Topographical Dictionary of Ireland* (London: Lewis & Sons, 1837)

Lightbown, R., 'The Jewellery', in M. Hurley and O. Scully (eds), *Late Viking Age and Medieval Waterford Excavations 1986–1992* (Waterford: Waterford Corporation, 1997), pp. 518–23

Lionard, P., 'Early Irish Grave Slabs', *Proceedings of the Royal Irish Academy*, vol. 61C, 1961, pp. 95–169

Luecke, J., 'The Unique Experience of Anglo-Saxon Nuns', in J. Nichols and L. Thomas Shank (eds), *Peace Weavers: Medieval religious women*, vol. 2 (Kalamazoo: Cistercian Publications, 1987), pp. 55–66

Luscombe, D., *The Letter Collection of Peter Abelard and Heloise* (Oxford: Oxford Medieval Texts, 2013)

Lydon, J., 'The Expansion and Consolidation of the Colony 1215–54', in A. Cosgrove (ed.), *A New History of Ireland. Volume II: Medieval Ireland 1169–1534* (Oxford: University Press, 1993), pp. 157–78

Lydon, J., 'A Land of War', in A. Cosgrove (ed.), *A New History of Ireland. Volume II: Medieval Ireland 1169–1534* (Oxford: University Press, 1993), pp. 240–74

Lynch, A., *Tintern Abbey, Co. Wexford: Cistercians and Colcloughs. Excavations 1982–2007* (Dublin: Government of Ireland, 2010)

Lynch, B., *A Monastic Landscape: The Cistercians in medieval Ireland* (Kilkenny: Xlibris, 2010)

Lynn, C., 'Excavations in 46–48 Scotch Street, Armagh, 1979–80', *Ulster Journal of Archaeology*, vol. 51, 1988, pp. 69–84

Lyons, M.A., 'Revolt and Reaction: The Geraldine rebellion and monastic confiscation in Co. Kildare', *Journal of the County Kildare Archaeological Society*, vol. 18, 1992–3, pp. 39–60

Lyons, M.A. and T. O'Connor (eds), *Strangers to Citizens: The Irish in Europe 1600–1800* (Dublin: Wordwell, 2008)

Lyttleton, J., *The Jacobean Plantations in Seventeenth-Century Offaly: An archaeology of a changing world* (Dublin: Four Courts Press, 2013)

Lyttleton, J. and T. O'Keeffe (eds), *The Manor in Medieval and Early Modern Ireland* (Dublin: Four Courts Press, 2005)

Macalister, R.A.S., *The Memorial Slabs of Clonmacnoise, King's County* (Dublin: The Stationery Office, 1909)

Macalister, R.A.S., 'Some Cross-Slabs in the Neighbourhood of Athlone', *Journal of the Royal Society of Antiquaries of Ireland*, vol. 42, 1912, pp. 27–31

Macalister, R.A.S., *Corpus Inscriptionum Insularum Celticarum*, vol. I (Dublin: The Stationery Office, 1945)

Macalister, R.A.S., *Corpus Inscriptionum Insularum Celticarum*, vol. II (Dublin: The Stationery Office, 1949)

MacCaffrey, J., *The Black Book of Limerick: Studies on the diocese of Limerick based principally upon the manuscript known as the Black Book of Limerick* (Germany: Albert-Ludwigs-Universität, 1906)

MacCotter, P., 'The Subinfeudation and Descent of the Fitzstephen/Carew Moiety of Desmond, Part I', *Journal of the Cork Historical and Archaeological Society*, vol. 101, 1996, pp. 64–80

MacCotter, P., 'The Subinfeudation and Descent of the Fitzstephen/Carew Moiety of Desmond, Part II', *Journal of the Cork Historical and Archaeological Society*, vol. 102, 1997, pp. 89–106

MacCotter, P., 'The Rise of Meic Carthaig and the Political Geography of Desmumu', *Journal of the Cork Historical and Archaeological Society*, vol. 111, 2006, pp. 59–76

MacCotter, P., *Medieval Ireland: Territorial, political and economic divisions* (Dublin: Four Courts Press, 2008)

MacCotter, P., 'Túath, Manor and Parish: Kingdom of Fir Maige, cantred of Fermoy', *Peritia*, vol. 22, 2012, pp. 211–48

MacCotter, P., 'Parish, Pastoral Care and Túath in the Diocese of Limerick, *c.*1201', *Journal of the Royal Society of Antiquaries of Ireland*, vol. 142–3, 2012–13, pp. 86–99

MacCotter, P., 'The Church Lands of the Diocese of Limerick: Reconstruction and history', *North Munster Antiquarian Journal*, vol. 53, 2013, pp. 99–122

MacCotter, P., 'The Medieval Rural Dean and Rural Deanery in Ireland', in E. Purcell, P. MacCotter, J. Sheehan and J. Nyhan (eds), *Clerics, Kings and Vikings* (Dublin: Four Courts Press, 2015), pp. 155–68

MacCotter, P., 'The M7 Motorway Historical Landscape: Studies in the history of Ormond', *Tipperary Historical Journal*, 2018, pp. 66–87

MacCotter, P., 'The Origins of the Parish in Ireland', *Proceedings of the Royal Irish Academy*, vol. 119C, 2019, pp. 37–67

MacCurtain, M., 'A Lost Landscape: The Geraldine castles and tower houses of the Shannon estuary', in J. Bradley (ed.), *Settlement and Society in Medieval Ireland: Studies presented to F.X. Martin* (Kilkenny: Boethius Press, 1988), pp. 429–44

MacCurtain, M., 'Late Medieval Nunneries of the Irish Pale', in H.B. Clarke, J. Prunty and M. Hennessy (eds), *Surveying Ireland's Past: Multidisciplinary essays in honour of Anngret Simms* (Dublin: Geography Publications, 2004), pp. 129–43

MacCurtain, M. and D. Ó Corráin (eds), *Women in Irish Society: The historical dimension* (Dublin: Arlen House, The Women's Press, 1978)

MacCurtain, M. and M. O'Dowd, *Women in Early Modern Ireland* (Dublin: Wolfhound Press, 1991)

MacCurtain, M., M. O'Dowd and M. Luddy, 'An Agenda for Women's History in Ireland, 1500–1900', *Irish Historical Studies*, vol. 28, 1992, pp. 1–37

MacDermott, M., 'The Crosiers of St Dympna and St Mel and Tenth-Century Irish Metal-Work', *Proceedings of the Royal Irish Academy*, vol. 58C, 1957, pp. 167–95

MacKechnie, J., *Instructio Pie Vivendi et Superna Meditandi*, vol. 29 (Dublin: Irish Texts Society, 1934)

MacLeod, C., 'Medieval Wooden Figure Sculptures in Ireland: Medieval madonnas in the west', *Journal of the Royal Society of Antiquaries of Ireland*, vol. 75, 1945, pp. 167–82

MacLeod, C., 'Some Medieval Wooden Figure Sculptures in Ireland: Statues of Irish saints', *Journal of the Royal Society of Antiquities of Ireland*, vol. 76, 1946, pp. 155–70

MacLeod, C., 'The Statue of Our Lady of Limerick: A gift in reparation', in E. Rynne (ed.), *North Munster Studies: Essays in commemoration of Monsignor Michael Moloney* (Limerick: Thomond Archaeological Society, 1967), pp. 266–75

Macy, G., 'Heloise, Abelard and the Ordination of Abbesses', *Journal of Ecclesiastical History*, vol. 57, 2006, pp. 16–32

Macy, G., *The Hidden History of Women's Ordination: Female clergy in the medieval West* (Oxford: Oxford University Press, 2008)

Madigan, K. and C. Osiek (eds), *Ordained Women in the Early Church* (Baltimore: The Johns Hopkins University Press, 2005)

Maher, D., *Medieval Grave Slabs of County Tipperary 1200–1600 AD. BAR British Series 262* (Oxford: John & Erica Hedges, 1997)

Makowski, E., *Canon Law and Cloistered Women: Periculoso and its commentators 1298–1545* (Washington DC: The Catholic University of America Press, 1997)

Makowski, E., '*Mulieres Religiosae*, Strictly Speaking: Some fourteenth-century canonical opinions', *The Catholic Historical Review*, vol. 85, 1999, pp. 1–14

Makowski, E., *A Pernicious Sort of Woman: Quasi-religious women and canon lawyers in the later middle ages* (Washington DC: The Catholic University of America Press, 2005)

Makowski, E., 'Monastic Enclosure', in M. Schaus (ed.), *Women and Gender in Medieval Europe: An encyclopedia* (London: Routledge, 2006), pp. 575–6

Mangion, C.M., *Contested Identities: Catholic women religious in nineteenth-century England and Wales* (Manchester: Manchester University Press, 2008)

Mangion, C.M., *Catholic Nuns and Sisters in a Secular Age: Britain 1945–90* (Manchester: Manchester University Press, 2020)

Manning, C., 'Excavation at Kilteel Church, Co. Kildare', *Journal of the Kildare Archaeological Society*, vol. 16, 1982, pp. 173–229

Manning, C., *Clonmacnoise* (Dublin: Government of Ireland, 1994)

Manning, C., 'Clonmacnoise Cathedral', in H. King (ed.), *Clonmacnoise Studies*, vol. 1 (Dublin: The Stationery Office, 1998), pp. 57–86

Manning, C., 'Some Early Masonry Churches and the Round Tower at Clonmacnoise', in H. King (ed.), *Clonmacnoise Studies*, vol. 2 (Dublin: The Stationery Office, 2003), pp. 63–95

Manning, C. 'Finghin MacCarthaigh, King of Desmond, and the Mystery of the Second Nunnery at Clonmacnoise', in D. Edwards (ed.), *Regions and Rulers in Ireland 1100–1650* (Dublin: Four Courts Press, 2004), pp. 20–6

Manning, C., 'The Adaptation of Early Masonry Churches in Ireland for Use in Later Medieval Times', in M. Meek (ed.), *The Modern Traveller to Our Past: Festschrift in honour of Ann Hamlin* (Belfast: DPK Publishing, 2006), pp. 243–8

Manning, C., 'A Suggested Typology for Pre-Romanesque Stone Churches in Ireland', in N. Edwards (ed.), *The Archaeology of the Early Medieval Celtic Churches* (Leeds: Maney, 2009), pp. 265–79

Manning, C., 'The Grave Slabs', in A. Lynch, *Tintern Abbey, Co. Wexford: Cistercians and Colcloughs. Excavations 1982–2007* (Dublin: Government of Ireland, 2010), pp. 103–5

Manning, C., 'Consecration Crosses at Castlemartyr', *Archaeology Ireland*, vol. 27, 2013, pp. 40–2

Marks, R., *Image and Devotion in Late Medieval England* (Stroud: Sutton, 2004)

Martin, F.X., 'Allies and an Overlord 1169–72', in A. Cosgrove (ed.), *A New History of Ireland. Volume II: Medieval Ireland 1169–1534* (Oxford: Oxford University Press, 1993), pp. 67–97

Martin, J.H., 'Ordination of Women as Priests', in M. Schaus (ed.), *Women and Gender in Medieval Europe: An encyclopedia* (London: Routledge, 2006), pp. 624–6

Massey, D., *Space, Place and Gender* (Minnesota: University of Minnesota Press, 1994)

Masterson, R., *Medieval Fore, County Westmeath* (Dublin: Four Court Press, 2014)

Matter, E.A., 'Influence of Augustine', in M. Schaus (ed.), *Women and Gender in Medieval Europe: An encyclopaedia* (London: Routledge, 2006), pp. 51–3

Matter, E.A., 'Influence of Jerome', in M. Schaus (ed.), *Women and Gender in Medieval Europe: An encyclopaedia* (London: Routledge, 2006), pp. 421–3

Mayes, P., *Excavations at a Templar Preceptor: South Witham, Lincolnshire 1965–67* (Leeds: Society for Medieval Archaeology, 2002)

McAleer, J.P., 'The Tradition of Detached Bell Towers at Cathedrals and Monastic Churches in Medieval England and Scotland 1066–1539', *Journal of the British Archaeological Association*, vol. 154, 2002, pp. 54–85

McAlister, V.L., *The Irish Tower House: Society, economy and environment c.1300–1650* (Manchester: Manchester University Press, 2019)

McAuliffe, M., 'The Lady in the Tower: The social and political role of women in tower houses', in C. Meek and M.K. Simms (eds), *The Fragility of her Sex? Medieval Irish women in their European context* (Dublin: Four Courts Press, 1996), pp. 153–62

McCabe, B., 'Survey of St John's Graveyard, Kells', *Ríocht na Mídhe: Records of the Meath Archaeological and Historical Society*, vol. 18, 2007, pp. 136–50

McCarthy, D.P., *The Irish Annals: Their genesis, evolution and history* (Dublin: Four Courts Press, 2008)

McCarthy, M., *Rule for Nuns* (Washington DC: Catholic University of America Press, 1960)

McClintock, H.F., 'The Mantle of St Brigid at Bruges', *Journal of the Royal Society of Antiquaries of Ireland*, vol. 36, 1936, pp. 32–40

McCullough, C. and W.H. Crawford, *Irish Historic Towns Atlas No. 18: Armagh* (Dublin: Royal Irish Academy, 2007)

McCutcheon, C., 'Appendix III. A Note on Some Pottery from Graney East, Castledermot, Co. Kildare', in M. Byrne, 'Graney East, Castledermot, Co. Kildare: Report on archaeological monitoring and testing 99E0052' (Kildare: Byrne, Mullins & Associates, unpublished report, 2001)

McCutcheon, C., 'Medieval Pottery', in T. Collins, 'Unveiling Female Monasticism in Later Medieval Ireland: Survey and excavation at St Catherine's, Shanagolden, Co. Limerick', *Proceedings of the Royal Irish Academy*, vol. 119C, 2019, pp. 162–5

McDermott, Y., 'Rosserk Friary: A house of the Franciscan Third Order Regular', *Journal of the Galway Archaeological and Historical Society*, vol. 63, 2011, pp. 57–70

McDermott, Y., 'Patronage and Observance: The Franciscan and Dominican friaries in the Connacht lordships of the Mac William Burkes 1350–1550', unpublished PhD thesis, NUI Galway, 2012

McDermott, Y., 'Killeenbrenan Friary: Flag-ship house of the Franciscan Third Order in Ireland?' *Cathair na Mart: Journal of the Westport Historical Society*, vol. 30, 2012, pp. 42–58

McDermott, Y., 'Kinalehin, Co. Galway: A history of Ireland's only Carthusian priory and its conversion to a Franciscan friary', *Journal of the Royal Society of Antiquaries of Ireland*, vol. 142–3, 2012–13, pp. 100–13

McDermott, Y., 'Post Medieval Developments at Moyne Friary, Co. Mayo: *c.*1540–*c.*1700', *Cathair na Mart: Journal of the Westport Historical Society*, vol. 32, 2014, pp. 23–40

McDermott, Y., 'Kilcorban Friary, Co. Galway: Ireland's only house of the Dominican Third Order Regular', *History Ireland*, vol. 22, 2014, pp. 16–18

McDonald, R.A., 'The Foundation and Patronage of Nunneries by Native Elites in Twelfth- and Early Thirteenth-Century Scotland', in E. Ewan and M. Meikle (eds), *Women in Scotland* c.*1100*–c.*1750* (East Linton: Tuckwell Press, 1999), pp. 3–15

McDowell, J.A., '50–56 Scotch Street, Armagh, Early Christian Cemetery and Medieval/Post-Medieval Settlement'. Available at www.excavations.ie/report/1985/Armagh/0000573/. Accessed 15 September 2020

McGuire, B.P., 'Cistercian Nuns in Twelfth- and Thirteenth-Century Denmark and Sweden: Far from the madding crowd', in J. Burton and K. Stöber (eds), *Women in the Medieval Monastic World* (Turnhout: Brepols, 2015), pp. 167–84

McInerney, L., 'A 1555 Papal Bulla for Clare Abbey', *Journal of the Royal Society of Antiquaries of Ireland*, vol. 141, 2011, pp. 128–48

McLaren, M.A., *Feminism, Foucault, and Embodied Subjectivity* (Albany, NY: SUNY Press, 2007)

McMahon, M., 'The Charter of Clare Abbey and the Augustinian "Province" in Co. Clare', *The Other Clare*, vol. 17, 1993, pp. 21–8

McNamara, J., *Sisters in Arms: Catholic nuns through two millennia* (Cambridge, MA: Harvard University Press, 1996)

McNamara, J., 'Monasticism and Nuns', in M. Schaus (ed.), *Women and Gender in Medieval Europe: An encyclopedia* (London: Routledge, 2006), pp. 579–85

McNeill, C. (ed.), *Calendar of Archbishop Alen's Register* c. *1172–1534* (Dublin: Royal Society of Antiquaries of Ireland, 1950)

McNeill, J., 'The Continental Context [of Medieval Cloisters]', *Journal of the British Archaeological Association*, vol. 159, 2006, pp. 1–47

McNeill, T., *Castles in Ireland: Feudal power in a Gaelic world* (London: Routledge, 1997)

McShane, B., 'Negotiating Religious Change and Conflict: Female religious communities in early modern Ireland 1530–1641', *British Catholic History*, vol. 33, 2017, pp. 357–82

McShane, B., 'Visualising the Reception and Circulation of Early Modern Nuns' Letters', *Journal of Historical Network Research*, vol. 2, 2018, pp. 1–25

Mecham, J.L., 'A Northern Jerusalem: Transforming the spatial geography of the convent of Wienhausen', in S. Hamilton and A. Spicier (eds), *Defining the Holy: Sacred space in medieval and early modern Europe* (Aldershot: Ashgate, 2005), pp. 139–60

Medioli, F., 'An Unequal Law: The enforcement of clausura before and after the Council of Trent', in C. Meek (ed.), *Women in Renaissance and Early Modern Europe* (Dublin: Four Courts Press, 2000), pp. 136–52

Meek, C. (ed.), *Women in Renaissance and Early Modern Europe* (Dublin: Four Courts Press, 2000)
Meek, C. and K. Simms (eds), *The Fragility of her Sex? Medieval Irish women in their European context* (Dublin: Four Courts Press, 1996)
Meek, C. and C. Lawless (eds), *Pawns or Players? Studies on medieval and early modern women* (Dublin: Four Courts Press, 2003)
Meek, C. and C. Lawless (eds), *Victims or Viragos? Studies on medieval and early modern women* (Dublin: Four Courts Press, 2005)
Meltzer, D.J., 'Lessons in Landscape Learning', in M. Rockman and J. Steele (eds), *Colonisation of Unfamilar Landscapes: The archaeology of adaptation* (London: Routledge, 2003), pp. 222–41
Melville, G., *The World of Medieval Monasticism: Its history and forms of life* (Minnesota: Cistercian Publications, 2016)
Melville, G. and A. Müller (eds), *Female* Vita Religiosa *between Late Antiquity and the High Middle Ages: Structures, developments and spatial contexts* (Berlin: LIT Verlag, 2011)
Meredith-Lobay, M.E., 'Memory, Landscapes and the Early Historic Monasteries of Scotland', *Archaeological Review from Cambridge*, vol. 20, no. 1, 2005, pp. 97–110
Mersch, M., *Das ehemalige Zisterzienserinnenkloster Vallis Dei in Brenkhausen im 13. Und 14. Jahrhundert* (Mainz: Denkmalpflege und Forschung, 2007)
Mersch, M., 'Programme, Pragmatism and Symbolism in Mendicant Architecture', in A. Müller and K. Stöber (eds), *Self-Representation of Medieval Religious Communities: The British Isles in context* (Berlin: LIT Verlag, 2009), pp. 143–66
Meskell, L., 'Goddesses, Gimbutas and "New Age" Archaeology', *Antiquity*, vol. 69, 1995, pp. 74–86
Meskell, L., 'Archaeologies of Identity', in I. Hodder (ed.), *Archaeological Theory Today* (Cambridge: Polity, 2001), pp. 187–213
Milis, L. (ed.), *Constitvtiones Canonicorvm Regvlarivm Ordinis Arroasiensis* (Turnhout: Brepols, 1970)
Miller, P. and D. Saxby, *The Augustinian Priory of St Mary Merton, Surrey: Excavations 1976–90* (London: Museum of London Archaeology Services, 2007)
Millett, B., 'The Origins of the *Ancrene Wisse*: New answers, new questions', *Medium Aevum*, vol. 61, 1992, pp. 206–28
Millett, B., '*Ancrene Wisse* and the Life of Perfection', *Leeds Studies in English*, vol. 33, 2002, pp. 53–76
Millett, B., *Ancrene Wisse / Guide for Anchoresses: A translation* (Exeter: Exeter University Press, 2009)
Millett, B. 'Can There Be Such a Thing as an Anchoritic Rule?', in C. Innes-Parker and N. Kukita Yoshokawa (eds), *Anchoritism in the Middle Ages: Texts and traditions* (Cardiff: University of Wales Press, 2013), pp. 11–30
Moessner, V.J., 'The Medieval Embroideries of Convent Wienhausen', in M.P. Lillich (ed.), *Studies in Cistercian Art and Architecture*, 13 (Kalamazoo: Cistercian Publications, 1987), pp. 161–77
Mohn, C., *Mittelalterliche Klosteranlagen der Zisterzienserinnen: Architektur der Frauenkloster im mitteldeutschen Raum. Berliner Beitrage zu Bauforschung und Denkmalpflege 4* (Petersberg: Michael Imhof Verlag, 2006)

Moloney, A., 'From East to West: Crossing the bogs at Clonmacnoise', in H. King (ed.), *Clonmacnoise Studies*, vol. 1 (Dublin: Government of Ireland, 1998), pp. 7–10

Monk, M.A. and J. Sheehan (eds), *Early Medieval Munster: Archaeology, history and society* (Cork: Cork University Press, 1998)

Montague, J., 'The Cloister and Bishop's Palace at Old Sarum with Some Thoughts on the Origins and Meaning of Secular Cathedral Cloisters', *Journal of the British Archaeological Association*, vol. 159, 2006, pp. 48–70

Moody, T.W., F.X. Martin and F.J. Byrne (eds), *A New History of Ireland. Volume III: Early Modern Ireland 1534–1691* (Oxford: Oxford University Press, 1976)

Moody, T.W., F.X. Martin and F.J. Byrne (eds), *A New History of Ireland. Volume IX: Maps, Genealogies, Lists. A Companion to Irish History, Part II* (Oxford: Clarendon Press, 1984)

Mooney, C., 'Franciscans in Ireland', *Terminus*, vol. 11, 1955, p. 131

Mooney, C., 'Franciscan Architecture in Pre-Reformation Ireland [part 1]', *Journal of the Royal Society of Antiquaries of Ireland*, vol. 85, 1955, pp. 133–73

Mooney, C., 'Franciscan Architecture in Pre-Reformation Ireland [part 2]', *Journal of the Royal Society of Antiquaries of Ireland*, vol. 86, 1956, pp. 125–69

Mooney, C., 'Franciscan Architecture in Pre-Reformation Ireland [part 3]', *Journal of the Royal Society of Antiquaries of Ireland*, vol. 87, 1957, pp. 1–38, 103–24

Mooney, C., 'The Franciscans in County Mayo', *Journal of the Galway Archaeological and Historical Society*, vol. 28, 1958–9, pp. 42–69

Mooney, C.M., *Clare of Assisi and the Thirteenth-Century Church: Religious women, rules and resistance* (Philadelphia: University of Pennsylvania Press, 2016)

Moore, M.J., *Archaeological Inventory of County Leitrim* (Dublin: The Stationery Office, 2003)

Moorhouse, S., 'Monastic Estates: Their composition and development', in R. Gilchrist and H. Mytum (eds), *The Archaeology of Rural Monasteries. BAR British Series 203* (Oxford: British Archaeological Reports, 1989), pp. 29–81

Moran, D., *Introduction to Phenomenology* (London: Routledge, 2000)

Moran, Rev. P.F. (ed.), *Monasticon Hibernicum or a History of the Abbeys, Priories and Other Religious Houses in Ireland, by Mervyn Archdall*, 2 vols (Dublin: W.B. Kelly, 1873, 1876)

Morant, R.W., *The Monastic Gatehouse* (Lewes: The Book Guild, 1995)

More, A., *Fictive Orders and Feminine Religious Identities 1200–1600* (Oxford: Oxford University Press, 2018)

Morgan, N., 'Texts and Images of Marian Devotion in English Twelfth-Century Monasticism, and Their Influence on the Secular Church', in B. Thompson (ed.), *Harlaxton Medieval Studies. Vol. VI: Monasteries and Society in Medieval Britain* (Stamford: Paul Watkins, 1999), pp. 117–36

Morrin, J. (ed.), *Calendar of the Patent and Close Rolls of Chancery in Ireland in the Reigns of Henry VIII, Edward VI, Mary and Elizabeth* (Dublin: Alex Thom & Sons, 1861)

Morrin, J. (ed.), *Calendar of the Patent and Close Rolls of Chancery in Ireland from the 18th to the 45th of Elizabeth*, vol. II (Dublin: Alex Thom & Sons for her Majesty's Stationery Office, 1862)

Morrison, S., *Women Pilgrims in Late Medieval England: Private piety as public performance* (London: Routledge, 2000)

Morton, K., 'Aspects of Image and Meaning in Irish Medieval Wall Paintings', in R. Moss, C. Ó Clabaigh and S. Ryan (eds), *Art and Devotion in Late Medieval Ireland* (Dublin: Four Courts Press, 2006), pp. 51–71

Moss, R., 'A Twelfth-Century Renaissance? Irish Romanesque sculpture and the insular tradition', in R. Moss (ed.), *Making and Meaning in Insular Art* (Dublin: Four Courts Press, 2007), pp. 126–41

Moss, R., 'Reduce, Reuse, Recycle: Irish monastic architecture *c*.1540–1640', in R. Stalley (ed.), *Irish Gothic Architecture: Construction, decay and reinvention* (Dublin: Wordwell, 2012), pp. 115–59

Moss, R. (ed.), *Art and Architecture of Ireland. Volume 1: Medieval,* c.*400* – c.*1600* (Dublin: Royal Irish Academy, 2015)

Moss, R., 'Irish Parish Churches: 1350–1550', in P. Barnwell (ed.), *Places of Worship in the British Isles 1350–1550* (Donington: Shaun Tyas, 2019), pp. 174–90

Moss, R., 'The Material Culture of the Canonical Movement in Medieval Ireland', in M. Browne and C. Ó Clabaigh (eds), *Households of God: The regular canons and canonesses of St Augustine and of Premontré in medieval Ireland* (Dublin: Four Courts Press, 2019), pp. 191–206

Mueller, J., 'Clare of Assisi', in M. Schaus (ed.), *Women and Gender in Medieval Europe: An encyclopedia* (London: Routledge, 2006), pp. 144–5

Mülder, G. and M. Richards, 'Diet in Medieval England: The evidence from stable isotopes', in C. Woolgar et al. (eds), *Food in Medieval England: Diet and nutrition* (Oxford: Oxford University Press, 2006), pp. 228–38

Mulder-Bakker, A., *Lives of the Anchoresses: The rise of the urban recluse in medieval Europe* (Philadelphia: University of Pennsylvania Press, 2005)

Müller, A., 'Presenting Identity in the Cloister: Remarks on Benedictine and Mendicant concepts of space', in A. Müller and K. Stöber (eds), *Self-Representation of Medieval Religious Communities: The British Isles in context* (Berlin: LIT Verlag, 2009), pp. 167–87

Müller, A., 'Interpretations of Claustral Spaces with Special Reference to Dormitories', in J. Burton and K. Stöber (eds), *Monastic Wales: New approaches* (Cardiff: University of Wales Press, 2013), pp. 229–45

Müller, A., 'Symbolic Meanings of Space in Female Monastic Tradition', in J. Burton and K. Stöber (eds), *Women in the Medieval Monastic World* (Turnhout: Brepols, 2015), pp. 299–326

Mullins, C., 'Appendix II. A Report on the Human Remains from Graney East, Castledermot, Co. Kildare', in M. Byrne, 'Graney East Castledermot, Co. Kildare. Report on Archaeological Monitoring and Testing 99E0052' (Kildare: unpublished report by Byrne, Mullins & Associates, 2001)

Murphy, D., 'The Distribution of Early Christian Monastic Sites and its Implications for Contemporary Settlement in County Louth', *County Louth Archaeological and Historical Journal*, vol. 22, 1992, pp. 364–86

Murphy, D., 'Excavation of an Early Monastic Enclosure at Clonmacnoise', in H. King (ed.). *Clonmacnoise Studies*, vol. 2 (Dublin: The Stationery Office, 2003), pp. 1–33

Murphy, M., 'Manor Centres, Settlement and Agricultural Systems in Medieval Ireland, 1250–1350', in M. Murphy and M. Stout (eds), *Agriculture and Settlement in Ireland* (Dublin: Four Courts Press, 2015), pp. 69–100

Murphy, M., 'The Economy', in B. Smith (ed.), *Cambridge History of Ireland. Volume 1: 600–1550* (Cambridge: Cambridge University Press, 2018), pp. 385–414

Murphy, M., A. Connon and J. Galloway, 'Waterford and Its Hinterland: An historical overview', in J. Eogan and E. Shee Twohig (eds), *Cois tSiuire: Nine thousand years of human activity in the lower Suir Valley. Archaeological Excavations on the N25 Waterford city bypass* (Dublin: National Roads Authority, 2011), pp. 217–44

Murphy, M. and K. O'Conor, 'Castles and Deerparks in Ireland', *Eolas: The Journal of the American Society for Irish Medieval Studies*, vol. 2006, pp. 53–70

Murphy, M. and M. Potterton, *The Dublin Region in the Middle Ages* (Dublin: Four Courts Press, 2010)

Murphy, M. and M. Stout (eds), *Agriculture and Settlement in Ireland* (Dublin: Four Courts Press, 2015)

Murphy, P. and R.G. Scaife, 'The Environmental Archaeology of Gardens', in A.E. Brown (ed.), *Garden Archaeology*, CBA Research Report 78 (London: Council for British Archaeology, 1991), pp. 83–99

Murray, G., 'Insular-Type Crosiers: Their construction and characteristics', in R. Moss (ed.), *Making and Meaning in Insular Art* (Dublin: Four Courts Press, 2007), pp. 79–94

Murray, G., 'Altars in Ireland 1050–1200: A survey', *Journal of Irish Archaeology*, vol. XIX, 2010, pp. 101–12

Murray, G., 'Insular Crosiers: An independent tradition?', in C. Newman, M. Mannion and F. Gavin (eds), *Islands in a Global Context: Proceedings of the Seventh International Conference on Insular Art* (Dublin: Four Courts Press, 2017), pp. 167–77

Murray, J., 'Femininity and Masculinity', in M. Schaus (ed.), *Women and Gender in Medieval Europe: An encyclopaedia* (London: Routledge, 2006), pp. 284–7

Murray, J., 'One Flesh, Two Sexes, Three Genders?', in L.M. Bitel and F. Lifshitz (eds), *Gender and Christianity in Medieval Europe: New perspectives* (Philadelphia: Penn State University Press, 2008), pp. 34–51

Murray, P., 'Archaeological Excavations at Littlemore Priory, Oxford' (John Moore Heritage Services, unpublished report, 2015)

Muschiol, G., 'Time and Space, Liturgy and Rites in Female Monasteries', in J. Hamburger and S. Marti (eds), *Crown and Veil: Female monasticism from the fifth to the fifteenth centuries* (New York: Columbia University Press, 2008), pp. 191–204

Mytum, H., 'Functionalist and Non-Functionalist Approaches in Monastic Archaeology', in R. Gilchrist and H. Mytum (eds), *The Archaeology of Rural Monasteries. BAR British Series 203* (Oxford: BAR, 1989), pp. 339–57

Mytum, H., *The Origins of Early Christian Ireland* (London: Routledge, 1992)

Mytum, H., 'Surface and Geophysical Survey at Clonmacnoise: Defining the extent of intensive monastic settlement', in H. King (ed.), *Clonmacnoise Studies*, vol. 2 (Dublin: The Stationery Office, 2003), pp. 35–58

Mytum, H. and R. Gilchrist (eds), *Advances in Monastic Archaeology. BAR British Series 227* (Oxford: Tempvs Reparatvm, 1993)

Neel, C., 'The Origins of the Beguines', *Signs*, vol. 14, 1989, pp. 321–41

Nelson, S.M., *Gender in Archaeology: Analyzing power and prestige* (California: AltaMira Press, 2004)

Neuman de Vegvar, C., 'Romanitas and Realpolitick in Cogitosus' Description of the Church of St Brigit, Kildare', in M. Carver (ed.), *The Cross Goes North: Processes of conversion in northern Europe AD 300–1300* (Woodbridge: York Medieval Press, 2003), pp. 153–70

New, E., 'The Seals in the Medieval Wales Project and its Potential for Monastic and Ecclesiastical History', *Monastic Research Bulletin*, vol. 17, 2011, pp. 2–4

Newman, B., 'The Visionary Texts and Visual Worlds of Religious Women', in J. Hamburger and S. Marti (eds), *Crown and Veil: Female monasticism from the fifth to the fifteenth centuries* (New York: Columbia University Press, 2008), pp. 151–71

Ní Dhonnchadha, M., '*Caillech* and Other Terms for Veiled Women in Medieval Irish Texts', Éigse, vol. 28, 1994, pp. 71–96

Ní Ghrádaigh, J., '"But What Exactly Did She Give?" Derbforgaill and the Nuns' Church at Clonmacnoise', in H. King (ed.), *Clonmacnoise Studies*, vol. 2 (Dublin: The Stationery Office, 2003), pp. 175–207

Ní Ghrádaigh, J., 'Temple Finghin and Two Unusual Voussoirs from Clonmacnoise', *Archaeology Ireland*, vol. 19, 2005, pp. 26–31

Ní Ghrádaigh, J., 'Mere Embroiderers? Women and art in early medieval Ireland', in T. Martin (ed.), *Reassessing the Roles of Women as Makers in Medieval Art and Architecture* (Leiden: Brill, 2012), pp. 93–128

Ní Ghrádaigh, J., 'Towards an Emotive Christ? Changing depictions of the Crucifixion on the Irish high cross', in J. Mullins, J. Ní Ghrádaigh and R. Hawtree (eds), *Envisioning Christ on the Cross: Ireland and the early medieval West* (Dublin: Four Courts Press, 2013), pp. 262–85

Nicholls, K., 'Rectory, Vicarage and Parish in the Western Dioceses', *Journal of the Royal Society of Antiquaries of Ireland*, vol. 101, 1971, pp. 53–84

Nicholls, K., 'A List of Monasteries in Connacht, 1577', *Journal of the Galway Archaeological and Historical Society*, vol. 33, 1972, pp. 28–43

Nicholls, K., 'Medieval Irish Cathedral Chapters', *Archivium Hibernicum*, vol. 31, 1973, pp. 102–11

Nicholls, K., 'Towards a New *Monasticon Hibernicum*', *Peritia*, vol. 3, 1984, pp. 330–3

Nicholls, K., 'Gaelic Society and Economy', in A. Cosgrove (ed.), *A New History of Ireland. Volume II: Medieval Ireland 1169–1534* (Oxford: Oxford University Press, 1993), pp. 397–438

Nicholls, K. (ed.), *The Irish Fiants of the Tudor Sovereigns during the Reigns of Henry VIII, Edward VI, Philip and Mary, and Elizabeth I*, 3 vols (Dublin: Irish Manuscripts Commission, 1994)

Nicholls, K., 'Worlds Apart? The Ellis two-nation theory on later medieval Ireland', *History Ireland*, vol. 7, no. 2, 1999, pp. 22–6

Nicholls, K., *Gaelic and Gaelicized Ireland in the Middle Ages* (Dublin: Lilliput Press, 2003)

Nichols, J.A., 'The Internal Organisation of English Cistercian Nunneries', *Cîteaux: Commentaria Cistercienses*, vol. 30, 1982, pp. 23–40

Nichols, J.A. and L. Thomas Shank (eds), *Distant Echoes: Medieval religious women*, vol. 1 (Kalamazoo: Cistercian Publications, 1984)

Nichols, J.A. and L. Thomas Shank (eds), *Peace Weavers: Medieval Religious Women*, vol. 2 (Kalamazoo: Cistercian Publications, 1987)

Nichols, J.A. and L. Thomas Shank (eds), *Hidden Springs: Cistercian monastic women. Medieval Religious Women*, vol. 3 (Kalamazoo: Cistercian Publications, 1995)

Noble, C., 'Spiritual Practice and the Designed Landscape: Monastic precinct gardens', *Studies in the History of Gardens and Designed Landscapes: An International Quarterly*, vol. 20, 2000, pp. 197–205

Norman, E.R. and J.K. St Joseph, *The Early Development of Irish Society: The evidence of aerial photography* (Cambridge: Cambridge University Press, 1969)

Nugent, L., 'Medieval Pilgrims' Tokens and Other Souvenirs in Ireland: A review of the archaeological and historical evidence', in J. Higgins, A. Connelly and M. Gibbons (eds), *Irish Maritime Heritage: Proceedings of the 3rd Galway International Heritage Conference, 2013* (Galway: Crows Rock Publishing, 2013), pp. 23–46

Nugent, L., *Journeys of Faith: Stories of pilgrimage from medieval Ireland* (Dublin: Columba Press, 2020)

Nyberg, T., *Birgittinische Klostergründungen des Mittelalters* (Lund: C.W.K. Gleerup, 1965)

Nyberg, T., 'On Female Monasticism and Scandinavia', *Medieval Scandinavia*, vol. 13, 2000, pp. 181–97

Ó Baoill, R., *Island City: The archaeology of Derry-Londonderry* (Derry: NIEA and Derry City Council, 2013)

Ó Baoill, R., 'Excavations at Aghavea, Co. Fermanagh', in C. Corlett and M. Potterton (eds), *The Church in Early Medieval Ireland, in the Light of Recent Archaeological Excavations* (Dublin: Wordwell, 2014), pp. 159–72

Ó Carragáin, T., 'Pre-Romanesque Churches in Ireland', 2 vols, unpublished PhD thesis, University College Cork, 2002

Ó Carragáin, T., 'A Landscape Converted: Archaeology and early church organisation on Iveragh and Dingle, Ireland', in M. Carver (ed.), *The Cross Goes North: Processes of conversion in northern Europe AD300–1300* (Woodbridge: York Medieval Press, 2003), pp. 127–52

Ó Carragáin, T., 'Habitual Masonry Styles and the Local Organisation of Church Building in Early Medieval Ireland', *Proceedings of the Royal Irish Academy*, vol. 105C, 2005, pp. 99–149

Ó Carragáin, T., 'Church Buildings and Pastoral Care in Early Medieval Ireland', in E. FitzPatrick and R. Gillespie (eds), *The Parish in Medieval and Early Modern Ireland: Community, territory and building* (Dublin: Four Courts Press, 2006), pp. 91–123

Ó Carragáin, T., 'Skeuomorphs and Spolia: The presence of the past in Irish pre-Romanesque architecture', in R. Moss (ed.), *Making and Meaning in Insular Art* (Dublin: Four Courts Press, 2007), pp. 95–109

Ó Carragáin, T., 'The Architectural Setting of the Mass in Early Medieval Ireland', *Medieval Archaeology*, vol. 53, 2009, pp. 119–54

Ó Carragáin, T., 'Archaeology of Early Medieval Baptism at St Mullin's, Co. Carlow, *Peritia*, vol. 21, 2010, pp. 285–302

Ó Carragáin, T., 'From Family Cemeteries to Community Cemeteries in Viking Age Ireland?' in C. Corlett and M. Potterton (eds), *Death and Burial in Early Medieval Ireland in the Light of Recent Archaeological Excavations* (Dublin: Wordwell, 2010), pp. 217–26

Ó Carragáin, T., *Churches in Early Medieval Ireland: Architecture, ritual, and memory* (New Haven: Yale University Press, 2010)

Ó Carragáin, T., 'The View from the Shore: Perceiving island monasteries in early medieval Ireland, *Hortus Artium Medievalium*, vol. 19, 2013, pp. 21–33

Ó Carragáin, T., 'The Archaeology of Ecclesiastical Estates in Early Medieval Ireland: A case study of the kingdom of Fir Maige', *Peritia*, vols 24–5, 2014, pp. 266–312

Ó Carragáin, T., 'Is There an Archaeology of Lay People at Early Irish Monasteries?' *Bulletin du Centre D'études Médiévales d'Auxerre BUCEMA*, vol. 8, 2015, pp. 2–17

Ó Carragáin, T. and J. Sheehan, 'Making Christian Landscapes: Settlement, society and regionality in early medieval Ireland', 2 parts (unpublished report for the Heritage Council, 2010). Available at: https://www.yumpu.com/en/document/view/22251522/ar01049-christian-landscapes-summary-report-10pdf-the-. Accessed 15 September 2020.

Ó Clabaigh, C., *The Franciscans in Ireland, 1400–1534: From reform to reformation* (Dublin: Four Courts Press, 2002)

Ó Clabaigh, C., 'Patronage, Prestige and Politics: The Observant Franciscans at Adare', in J. Burton and K. Stöber (eds), *Monasteries and Society in the British Isles in the Later Middle Ages* (Woodbridge: Boydell, 2008), pp. 71–82

Ó Clabaigh, C., 'Anchorites in Late Medieval Ireland', in L. Herbert McAvoy (ed.), *Anchoritic Traditions of Medieval Europe* (Woodbridge: Boydell, 2010), pp. 153–77

Ó Clabaigh, C., 'Friar Maurice Hanlan, His Books and the Franciscan *studium* in Medieval Youghal', in P. Harbison and V. Hall (eds), *Carnival of Learning: Essays in honour of George Cunningham* (Roscrea: Cistercian Press, 2012), pp. 133–42

Ó Clabaigh, C., *The Friars in Ireland 1224–1540* (Dublin: Four Courts Press, 2012)

Ó Clabaigh, C., 'The Church 1050–1460', in B. Smith (ed.), *Cambridge History of Ireland. Volume 1: 600–1550* (Cambridge: Cambridge University Press, 2018), pp. 355–84

Ó Clabaigh, C., 'Community, Commemoration and Confraternity: The chapter office and chapter books in Irish Augustinian foundations', in M. Browne and C. Ó Clabaigh (eds), *Households of God: The regular canons and canonesses of Saint Augustine and of Prémontré in medieval Ireland* (Dublin: Four Courts Press, 2019), pp. 235–51

Ó Clabaigh, C., 'Monasticism, Colonization, and Ethnic Tension in Late Medieval Ireland', in A.I. Beach and I. Cochelin (eds), *Medieval Monasticism in the Latin West*, 2 vols (Cambridge: Cambridge University Press, 2020), pp. 901–21

Ó Conbhuidhe, C., *The Cistercian Abbeys of Tipperary* (Dublin: Four Courts Press, 1999)

Ó Corráin, D., 'Women in Early Irish Society', in M. Mac Curtain and D. Ó Corráin (eds), *Women in Irish Society: The historical dimension* (Dublin: Arlen House, 1978), pp. 1–14

Ó Corráin, D., 'The Early Irish Churches: Some aspects of organisation', in D. Ó Corráin (ed.), *Irish Antiquity: Essays and studies presented to Professor M.J. O'Kelly* (Dublin: Four Courts Press, 1981), pp. 326–41

Ó Corráin, D., 'Women and the Law in Early Ireland', in M. O'Dowd and S. Wichert (eds), *Chattel, Servant or Citizen: Women's status in church, state and society* (Belfast: Institute of Irish Studies, Queen's University, 1995), pp. 45–57

Ó Corráin, D., *The Irish Church, its Reform and the English Invasion* (Dublin: Four Courts Press, 2017)

Ó Corráin, D., Corpus Christianorum Clavis Litterarum Hibernensium: *Medieval Irish books and texts c.400–c.1600*, 3 vols (Turnhout: Brepols, 2017)

Ó Cróinín, D., *Early Medieval Ireland* (London: Longman, 1995)

Ó Crualaoich, G., *The Book of the Cailleach: Stories of the wise-woman healer* (Cork: Cork University Press, 2003)

Ó Dálaigh, B., 'Mistress, Mother and Abbess: Renalda Ní Bhriain, *c.* 1447–1510', *North Munster Antiquarian Journal*, vol. 32, 1990, pp. 50–63

Ó Dálaigh, B., *Irish Historic Towns Atlas No. 25: Ennis* (Dublin: Royal Irish Academy, 2012)

Ó Floinn, R., 'The Norman Conquest and the Later Middle Ages, 1169AD–*ca.* 1500AD', in M. Ryan (ed.), *Treasures of Ireland: Irish art 3000 BC–1500 AD* (Dublin: Royal Irish Academy, 1983), pp. 70–3

Ó Floinn, R., *Irish Shrines and Reliquaries of the Middle Ages* (Dublin: Country House, 1994)

Ó Floinn, R., 'Goldsmiths' Work in Ireland 1200–1400', in C. Hourihane (ed.), *From Ireland Coming: Irish art from the early Christian to the late Gothic period and its European context* (Princeton: Dept of Art and Archaeology, Princeton University, 2001), pp. 289–312

Ó Floinn, R., 'Later Medieval Ireland, AD 1150–1550', in P.F. Wallace and R. Ó Floinn (eds), Treasures of the National Museum of Ireland: Irish antiquities (Dublin: Gill & Macmillan, 2002), pp. 257–300

Ó Floinn, R., 'A Crosier Head from Clonard', in T. Condit and C. Corlett (eds), *Above and Beyond: Essays in memory of Leo Swan* (Dublin: Wordwell, 2005), pp. 333–42

Ó Floinn, R., 'Bishops, Liturgy and Reform: Some archaeological and art historical evidence', in D. Bracken and D. Ó Riain-Raedel (eds), *Ireland and Europe in the Twelfth Century: Reform and renewal* (Dublin: Four Courts Press, 2006), pp. 218–38

Ó Floinn, R., '"The Market Cross" at Glendalough', in C. Doherty, L. Doran and M. Kelly (eds), *Glendalough: City of God* (Dublin: Four Courts Press, 2011), pp. 80–111

Ó Laoghaire, D., 'Mary in Irish Spirituality', in M. Maher (ed.), *Irish Spirituality* (Dublin: Veritas Publications, 1981), pp. 47–56

Ó Riain, P., *The Making of a Saint: Finnbarr of Cork, 600–1200* (Dublin: Irish Texts Society, 1997)

Ó Riain, P., *A Dictionary of Irish Saints* (Dublin: Four Courts Press, 2011)

O'Brien, C., *The History of the Poor Clares* (Galway: Connacht Tribune, 1992)

O'Brien, C. and P.D. Sweetman, *Archaeological Inventory of County Offaly* (Dublin: Government of Ireland, 1997)

O'Brien, E., *Post-Roman Britain to Anglo-Saxon England: Burial practices reviewed. British Archaeological Reports. BAR, British Series 289* (Oxford: Archaeopress, 1999)

O'Brien, E., 'Excavation of a Multi-Period Burial Site at Ballymacaward, Ballyshannon, Co. Donegal', *Donegal Annual: Journal of the County Donegal Historical Society*, vol. 51, 1999, pp. 56–61

O'Brien, E., 'Pagan or Christian? Burial in Ireland during the 5th to 8th centuries AD', in N. Edwards (ed.), *The Archaeology of the Early Medieval Celtic Churches* (Leeds: Maney, 2009), pp. 135–54

O'Brien, E., *Mapping Death: Burial in late Iron Age and early medieval Ireland* (Dublin: Four Courts Press, 2020)

O'Carroll, G., *The Earls of Desmond: The rise and fall of a Munster lordship* (Limerick: self-published, 2013)

O'Carroll, M., 'Our Lady in Early Medieval Ireland', in A. Smyth (ed.), *Seanchas: Studies in early and medieval Irish archaeology, history and literature in honour of Francis J. Byrne* (Dublin: Four Courts Press, 2000), pp. 178–81

O'Collins, G., *Catholicism: A very short introduction* (Oxford: Oxford University Press, 2008)

O'Connor, L., 'Faughart Investigation 1966', *County Louth Archaeological Journal*, vol. 17, 1966, pp. 125–9

O'Conor, K.D., *The Archaeology of Medieval Rural Settlement in Ireland. Discovery Programme Monographs* 3 (Dublin: Royal Irish Academy, 1998)

O'Conor, K.D., 'The Ethnicity of Irish Moated Sites', *Ruralia*, vol. 3, 2000, pp. 92–102

O'Conor, K.D., 'Housing in Later Medieval Gaelic Ireland', *Ruralia*, vol. 4, 2002, pp. 201–10

O'Conor, K.D., 'Gaelic Lordly Settlement in 13th and 14th Century Ireland', in I. Holm, S. Innselet and I. Oye (eds), *Utmark: The outfield as industry and ideology in the Iron Age and the middle ages* (Bergen: University of Bergen, 2005), pp. 209–21

O'Conor K.D. and C. Manning, 'Clonmacnoise Castle', in H. King (ed.), *Clonmacnoise Studies*, vol. 2 (Dublin: The Stationery Office, 2003), pp. 137–65

O'Donnabhain, B., 'The Human Remains', in A. Lynch, *Tintern Abbey, Co. Wexford: Cistercians and Colcloughs excavations 1982–2007* (Dublin: Government of Ireland, 2010), pp. 105–25

O'Donnabhain, B., 'Human Remains', in T. Collins, 'Unveiling Female Monasticism in Later Medieval Ireland: Survey and excavation at St Catherine's, Shanagolden, Co. Limerick', *Proceedings of the Royal Irish Academy*, vol. 119C, 2019, pp. 166–71

O'Donoghue, A., 'Mendicant Cloisters in Munster', in R. Stalley (ed.), *Limerick and South-West Ireland: Medieval art and architecture* (Leeds: Maney, for the British Archaeological Association, 2011), pp. 111–31

O'Donovan, J. (ed.), *Annála Ríoghachta Eireann: Annals of the Kingdom of Ireland by the Four Masters from the Earliest Period to the Year 1616*, 7 vols (Dublin: Hodges & Smith, 1854)

O'Donovan, P., *Archaeological Inventory of County Cavan* (Dublin: The Stationery Office, 1995)

O'Dywer, B., *Stephen of Lexington: Letters from Ireland 1228–1229* (Kalamazoo: Cistercian Publications, 1982)

O'Flaherty, E., *Irish Historic Towns Atlas No. 21: Limerick* (Dublin: Royal Irish Academy, 2010)

O'Grady, G., 'History and Antiquities of the District of Rathcoole and Saggart', *Journal of the Kildare Archaeological Society*, vol. 5, 1906, pp. 75–8

O'Hara, A. (ed.), *Columbanus and the Peoples of Post-Roman Europe* (Oxford: Oxford University Press, 2018)

O'Keeffe, P. and T. Simington, *Irish Stone Bridges* (Dublin: Irish Academic Press, 1991)

O'Keeffe, T., *An Anglo-Norman Monastery: Bridgetown Priory and the architecture of the Augustinian canons regular in Ireland* (Cork: Cork County Council and Gandon Editions, 1999)

O'Keeffe, T., *Medieval Ireland: An archaeology* (Stroud: Tempus, 2000)

O'Keeffe, T., *Romanesque Ireland: Architecture and ideology in the twelfth century* (Dublin: Four Courts Press, 2003)

O'Keeffe, T., *Ireland's Round Towers* (Stroud: Tempus, 2004)

O'Keeffe, T., *Medieval Fore: An archaeological wonder in the Westmeath landscape. Heritage Guide No. 28* (Dublin: Wordwell, 2004)

O'Keeffe, T., 'The Built Environment of Local Community Worship Between the Later Eleventh and Early Thirteenth Centuries', in E. FitzPatrick and R. Gillespie (eds), *The Parish in Medieval and Early Modern Ireland* (Dublin: Four Courts Press, 2006), pp. 124–46

O'Keeffe, T., 'Religious Buildings', in J. Graham-Campbell (ed.), *The Archaeology of Medieval Europe. Volume 1: Eighth to Twelfth Centuries AD* (Aarhus: Aarhus University Press, 2007), pp. 398–419

O'Keeffe, T., 'Augustinian Regular Canons in Twelfth- and Thirteenth-Century Ireland: History, architecture and identity', in J. Burton and K. Stöber (eds), *The Regular Canons in the Medieval British Isles* (Turnhout: Brepols, 2011), pp. 469–84

O'Keeffe, T., 'Building Lordship in Thirteenth-Century Ireland: The donjon of Coonagh Castle, Co. Limerick', *Journal of the Royal Society of Antiquaries of Ireland*, vol. 141, 2011, pp. 91–127

O'Keeffe, T., 'Buttevant Friary and Its Crypt', *Archaeology Ireland*, vol. 26, 2012, pp. 23–5

O'Keeffe, T., *Medieval Irish Buildings 1100–1600* (Dublin: Four Courts Press, 2015)

O'Keeffe, T., 'Theory and Medieval Archaeology in Ireland and Beyond: The narrative tradition and the archaeological imagination', *Journal of Irish Archaeology*, vol. XXVII, 2018, pp. 99–116

O'Keeffe, T., *Ireland Encastellated AD 950–1550: Insular castle-building in its European context* (Dublin: Four Courts Press, 2021)

O'Kelly, M.J., 'St Gobnet's House, Ballyvourney, Co. Cork', *Journal of the Cork Historical and Archaeological Society*, vol. 57, 1952, pp. 18–40

O'Kelly, M.J., 'Church Island Near Valentia, Co. Kerry', *Proceedings of the Royal Irish Academy*, vol. 59C, 1958, pp. 57–136

O'Mara, V., 'The Late Medieval English Nun and Her Scribal Activity: A complicated quest', in V. Blanton, V. O'Mara and P. Stoop (eds), *Nuns' Literacies in Medieval Europe: The Hull dialogue* (Turnhout: Brepols, 2013), pp. 69–96

O'Mara, V., 'Nuns and Writing in Late Medieval England: The quest continues', in V. Blanton, V. O'Mara and P. Stoop (eds), *Nuns' Literacies in Medieval Europe: The Kansas City dialogue* (Turnhout: Brepols, 2015), pp. 123–49

O'Mara, V., 'Scribal Engagement and the Late Medieval English Nun: The quest concludes?', in V. Blanton, V. O'Mara and P. Stoop (eds), *Nuns' Literacies in Medieval Europe: The Antwerp dialogue* (Turnhout: Brepols, 2018), pp. 187–208

O'Meara, J.J. (ed.), *The History and Topography of Ireland by Giraldus Cambrensis* (Dublin: Dolmen Press, 1942, rep. 1982)

O'Neill, M., 'The Medieval Parish Churches of County Meath', *Journal of the Royal Society of Antiquaries of Ireland*, vol. 132, 2002, pp. 1–56

O'Neill, M., 'Christ Church Cathedral as a Blueprint for Other Augustinian Buildings in Ireland', in J. Bradley, A.J. Fletcher and A. Simms (eds), *Dublin in the Medieval World: Studies in honour of Howard B. Clarke* (Dublin: Four Courts Press, 2009), pp. 168–87

O'Neill, M., 'Irish Franciscan Architecture: Late medieval and early modern', in E. Bhreathnach, J. MacMahon and J. McCafferty (eds), *The Irish Franciscans 1534–1990* (Dublin: Four Courts Press, 2009), pp. 305–27

O'Sullivan, A., 'Crannógs in Late Medieval Gaelic Ireland, *c.*1350–*c.*1650', in P.J. Duffy, D. Edwards and E. FitzPatrick (eds), *Gaelic Ireland: Land, lordship and settlement c.1250–c.1650* (Dublin: Four Courts Press, 2001), pp. 397–417

O'Sullivan, A. and D. Boland, *The Clonmacnoise Bridge: An early medieval river crossing in County Offaly. Heritage Guide No. 11* (Bray: Wordwell, 2000)

O'Sullivan, A., F. McCormack, T. Kerr and L. Harney, *Early Medieval Ireland AD 400–1100: The evidence from archaeological excavations* (Dublin: Royal Irish Academy, 2014)

O'Sullivan, A. and J. Sheehan, *Archaeological Survey of the Iveragh Peninsula* (Cork: Cork University Press, 1996)

O'Sullivan, J., 'Excavation of an Early Church and a Women's Cemetery at St Ronan's Medieval Parish Church, Iona', *Proceedings of the Society of Antiquaries of Scotland*, vol. 124, 1994, pp. 327–65

O'Sullivan, J., 'Nationalists, Archaeologists and the Myth of the Golden Age', in M.A. Monk and J. Sheehan (eds), *Early Medieval Munster: Archaeology, history and society* (Cork: Cork University Press, 1998), pp. 178–89

O'Sullivan, J. and T. Ó Carragáin, *Inishmurray: Monks and pilgrims in an Atlantic landscape. Volume 1: Archaeological Survey and Excavations 1997–2000* (Cork: The Collins Press, 2008)

O'Sullivan, J., J. Roberts and S. Halliday, 'Archaeological Excavation of Medieval, Post-Medieval and Modern Burial at Ennis Friary, Co. Clare', *North Munster Antiquarian Journal*, vol. 43, 2003, pp. 21–42

Oliva, M., 'Aristocracy or Meritocracy? Office Holding Patterns in Late Medieval English Nunneries', *Studies in Church History*, vol. 27, 1990, pp. 197–208

Oliva, M., 'The Convent and Community in the Diocese of Norwich from 1350–1540', unpublished PhD dissertation, Fordham University, 1991

Oliva, M., *The Convent and the Community in Late Medieval England: Female monasteries in the diocese of Norwich 1359–1540* (Woodbridge: Boydell, 1998)

Oliva, M., 'Rendering Accounts: The pragmatic literacy of nuns in late medieval England', in V. Blanton, V. O'Mara and P. Stoop (eds), *Nuns' Literacies in Medieval Europe: The Hull dialogue* (Turnhout: Brepols, 2013), pp. 51–68

Oliver, J., *Singing with Angels: Liturgy, music and art in the gradual of Gisela von Kerssenbrock* (Turnhout: Brepols, 2007)

Opie, H., '2002:0972 – Nurney, Kildare'. Available at https://excavations.ie/report/2002/Kildare/0008289/. Accessed 15 September 2020

Otway-Ruthven, J., 'The Medieval County of Kildare', *Irish Historical Studies*, vol. 11, 1959, pp. 181–99

Otway Ruthven, J., 'The Medieval Church Lands of County Dublin', in J.A. Watt, J.B. Worrall and F.X. Martin (eds), *Medieval Studies Presented to Aubrey Gwynn* (Dublin: Three Candles, 1961), pp. 54–73

Otway Ruthven, J., 'Parochial Development in the Rural Deanery of Skreen', *Journal of the Royal Society of Antiquaries of Ireland*, vol. 94, 1964, pp. 112–22

Oxenham, H., *Perceptions of Femininity in Early Irish Society* (Woodbridge: Boydell, 2016)

Oxford Archaeology, *Newtown, Jerpoint, County Kilkenny. Heritage Conservation Plan No. 11* (Kilkenny: The Heritage Council, 2007)

Parsons, D. (ed.), *Tenth-Century Studies: Essays in commemoration of the millennium of the Council of Winchester and the* Regularis Concordia (London: Royal Historical Society, 1975)

Partner, N.F., 'No Sex, No Gender', in N. Partner (ed.), *Studying Medieval Women* (Cambridge, MA: The Medieval Academy of America, 1993), pp. 117–41

Pelikan, J., *Mary Through the Centuries: Her place in the history of culture* (New Haven: Yale University Press, 1996)

Perkins-Curran, K., '"Quhat Say Ye Now, My Lady Priores? How Have Ye Usit Your Office, Can Ye Ges?": Politics, power and realities of the office of a prioress in her community in late medieval Scotland', in J. Burton and K. Stöber (eds), *Monasteries and Society in the British Isles in the Later Middle Ages* (Woodbridge: Boydell, 2008), pp. 124–41

Petrie, G., *The Ecclesiastical Architecture of Ireland* (Dublin: Hodges & Smith, 1845)

Peyroux, C.R., 'Abbess and Cloister: Double monasteries in the early medieval west', unpublished dissertation, Princeton University, 1990

Peyton, C., *The Desmond Survey* (PROIM 5039, 1586). Available at https://celt.ucc.ie//published/E580000-001/index.html. Accessed 15 September 2020.

Pfaff, R., *The Liturgy in Medieval England: A history* (Cambridge: Cambridge University Press, 2009)

Phelan, M., 'An Unidentified Tomb in St Canice's Cathedral, Kilkenny', *Old Kilkenny Review: Journal of the Kilkenny Archaeological Society*, vol. 48, 1996, pp. 40–4

Picard, J.M. and Y. de Pontfarcy, *The Vision of Tnugdal* (Dublin: Four Courts Press, 1989)

Platt, C., *The Monastic Grange in Medieval England* (London: Macmillan, 1969)

Platt, C., *The Parish Churches of Medieval England* (London: Chancellor Press, 1995)

Pochin Mould, D., *The Irish Saints* (Dublin: Clonmore & Reynolds, 1964)

Potterton, M., *Medieval Trim: History and archaeology* (Dublin: Four Courts Press, 2005)

Powell, S., *The Birgittines of Syon Abbey: Preaching and print* (Turnhout: Brepols, 2017)

Power, D., *Archaeological Inventory of County Cork. Volume 2: East and South Cork* (Dublin: The Stationery Office, 1994)

Power, D., *Archaeological Inventory of County Cork. Volume 3: Mid Cork* (Dublin: The Stationery Office, 1997)

Power, D., S. Lane, E. Byrne, U. Egan and M. Sleeman, *Archaeological Inventory of County Cork. Volume 4: North Cork*, 2 parts (Dublin: The Stationery Office, 2000)

Power, E., *Medieval English Nunneries* c. *1275 to 1535* (Cambridge: Cambridge University Press, 1922)

Power, K., 'The Burials: A medieval demographic sample', in M. Hurley and C. Sheehan, *Excavations at the Dominican Priory: St Mary's of the Isle, Cork* (Cork: Cork Corporation, 1995), pp. 66–83

Power, P., 'Placenames of the Decies', *Journal of the Waterford and South-East of Ireland Archaeological Society*, vol. 11, 1908, pp. 1–34

Preucel, R.W. and I. Hodder (eds), *Contemporary Archaeology in Theory: A reader* (Oxford: Blackwell, 1996)

Preucel, R.W. and L. Meskell, 'Knowledges', in L. Meskell and R.W. Preucel (eds), *A Companion to Social Archaeology* (Oxford: Blackwell, 2007), pp. 3–22

Price, L., 'Rock-Basins or "Bullauns" at Glendalough and Elsewhere', *Journal of the Royal Society of Antiquaries of Ireland*, vol. 89, 1959, pp. 161–88

Prunty, J. and P. Walsh, *Irish Historic Towns Atlas No. 28: Galway/Gaillimh* (Dublin: Royal Irish Academy, 2016)

Quinlan, M., *Athassel Augustinian Priory, County Tipperary: Conservation plan* (Dublin: Office of Public Works, 2009)

Quinlan, M. and R. Moss, *Lemanaghan, County Offaly: Conservation plan* (Kilkenny: The Heritage Council, 2007)

Radini, A., M. Tromp, A. Beach, E. Tong, C. Speller, M. McCormick, J.V. Dudgeon, M.J. Collins, F. Rühli, R. Kröger and C. Warinner, 'Medieval Women's Early Involvement in Manuscript Production Suggested by Lapis Lazuli Identification in Dental Calculus', *Science Advances*, vol. 5, 2019, pp. 1–8.

Rae, E.C., 'Irish Sepulchral Monuments of the Later Middle Ages', *Journal of the Royal Society of Antiquaries of Ireland*, vol. 100, 1970, pp. 1–38

Rae, E.C., 'The Sculpture of the Cloister of Jerpoint Abbey', *Journal of the Royal Society of Antiquaries of Ireland*, vol. 96, 1966, pp. 59–91

Raftery, D., 'The Next "Wave" is Digital: Researching women religious in the twenty-first century', *American Catholic Studies*, vol. 128, no. 2, 2017, pp. 29–50

Raftery, D., C. Delaney and C. Nowlan-Roebuck, *Nano Nagle: The Irish life and the legacy* (Dublin: Irish Academic Press, 2018)

Raguin, V.C. and S. Stanbury (eds), *Women's Space: Patronage, place and gender in the medieval church* (New York: State University of New York Press, 2005)

Rahtz, P. and E. Greenfield, *Excavations at Chew Valley Lake, Somerset. DoE Archaeological Report No. 8* (London: Her Majesty's Stationery Office, 1977)

Ralegh Radford, C.A., 'The Earliest Irish Churches', *Ulster Journal of Archaeology*, vol. 40, 1977, pp. 1–11

Ranft, P., *Women and the Religious Life in Premodern Europe* (New York: St Martin's Press, 1996)

Rapetti, A., 'Women and Monasticism in Venice in the Tenth to Twelfth Centuries', in J. Burton and K. Stöber (eds), *Women in the Medieval Monastic World* (Turnhout: Brepols, 2015), pp. 145–66

Reddan, M. and A.W. Clapham, *Survey of London. Volume 9: The Parish of St Helen, Bishopsgate, Part 1* (London: London County Council, 1924)

Rees Jones, S., 'Women's Influence on the Design of Urban Homes', in M.C. Erler and M. Kowaleski (eds), *Gendering the Master Narrative: Women and power in the middle ages* (Ithaca: Cornell University Press, 2003), pp. 190–211

Reeves, W., 'The Ancient Churches of Armagh, Part 1', *Ulster Journal of Archaeology*, vol. 2, 1896, pp. 194–204

Reeves, W., 'The Ancient Churches of Armagh, Appendix', *Ulster Journal of Archaeology*, vol. 6, 1900, pp. 24–33

Rigby, S.H., *English Society in the Later Middle Ages: Class, status and gender* (London: Macmillan, 1995)

Rives, D., 'Taking the Veil: Clothing and the transformation of identity' (trans. C.E. Harrison), *Proceedings of the Western Society for French History*, vol. 33, 2005, pp. 465–86

Roberts, C., 'A Critical Approach to Gender as a Category of Analysis in Archaeology', in H. du Cros and L. Smith (eds), *Women in Archaeology: A feminist critique* (Canberra: Dept of Prehistory, Occasional Papers in Prehistory 23, 1993), pp. 16–21

Robinson, D.M., *The Geography of Augustinian Settlement*, 2 parts. BAR British Series 80 (Oxford: British Archaeological Reports, 1980)

Robinson, D.M., 'The Augustinian Canons in England and Wales: Architecture, archaeology and liturgy 1100–1540', *Monastic Research Bulletin*, vol. 18, 2012, pp. 2–29

Robson, M., *The Franciscans in the Middle Ages* (Woodbridge: Boydell, 2006)

Röckelein, H., 'Founders, Donors and Saints: Patrons of nuns' convents', in J. Hamburger and S. Marti (eds), *Crown and Veil: Female monasticism from the fifth to the fifteenth centuries* (New York: Columbia University Press, 2008), pp. 207–24

Röckelein, H., 'Frauen im Umkreis der Benediktinischen Reformen des 10 bis 12 Jahrhunderts. Gorze, Cluny, Hirsau, St. Blasien und Siegburg', in G. Melville and A. Müller (eds), *Female* Vita Religiosa *between Late Antiquity and the High Middle Ages: Structures, developments and spatial contexts* (Berlin: LIT Verlag, 2011), pp. 275–327

Röckelein, H., 'FemMoData: A database of medieval female monasteries in Europe', in J. Burton and K. Stöber (eds), *Women in the Medieval Monastic World* (Turnhout: Brepols, 2015), pp. 355–64

Röckelein, H., 'Monastic Landscapes', in A.I. Beach and I. Cochelin (eds), *Medieval Monasticism in the Latin West*, 2 vols (Cambridge: Cambridge University Press, 2020), pp. 816–30

Rockley, J., *Antiquarians and Archaeology in Nineteenth-Century Cork. BAR 454* (Oxford: Archaeopress, 2008)

Roe, H., *The Medieval Fonts of Meath* (Meath: Meath Archaeological and Historical Society, 1964)

Roman, C., 'Anchoritism and the Everyday: The sacred–domestic discourse in the *Ancrene Wisse*', *Florilegium*, vol. 23, no. 2, 2006, pp. 99–122

Ronan, S., 'Irish Nunneries: Spatial dimensions and gender implications', unpublished MA thesis, University College Cork, 1997

Rubin, M., *Corpus Christi: The Eucharist in late medieval culture* (Cambridge: Cambridge University Press, 1991)

Rubin, M., *Emotion and Devotion: The meaning of Mary in medieval religious cultures* (New York: Central European University Press, 2009)

Rubin, M., 'An English Anchorite: The making, unmaking and remaking of Christine Carpenter', in R. Horrox and S. Rees Jones (eds), *Pragmatic Utopias: Ideas and communities 1200–1630* (Cambridge: Cambridge University Press, 2011), pp. 204–23

Rubin, M., 'Presentism's Useful Anachronisms', *Past and Present*, vol. 234, 2017, pp. 236–44

Rudloff Stanton, A., 'Devotional Art', in M. Schaus (ed.), *Women and Gender in Medieval Europe: An encyclopaedia* (London: Routledge, 2006), pp. 200–4

Rudy, K., *Virtual Pilgrimages in the Convent: Imagining Jerusalem in the late middle ages* (Turnhout: Brepols, 2011)

Rugg, J., 'Constructing the Grave: Competing burial ideas in nineteenth-century England, *Social History*, vol. 38, no. 3, 2013, pp. 328–45

Rugg, J., F. Sterling and A. Clayden, 'Churchyard and Cemetery in an English Industrial City', *Urban History*, vol. 41, no. 4, 2014, pp. 627–46

Ryan, F., '2007:1573 – Ballintotty, Tipperary'. Available at: www.excavations.ie/report/2007/Tipperary/0018562/. Accessed 15 September 2020

Ryan, J., *Irish Monasticism: Origins and early development* (London: Longmans, Green & Co., 1931)

Ryan, S., '"I too am Christian": Early martyrs and their lives in the late medieval and early modern Irish manuscript tradition', *Studies in Church History*, vol. 47, 2001, pp. 193–207

Ryan, S., 'Windows on Late Medieval Devotional Practice: Máire Ní Mháille's "Book of Piety" (1513) and the world behind the texts', in R. Moss, C. Ó Clabaigh and S. Ryan (eds), *Art and Devotion in Late Medieval Ireland* (Dublin: Four Courts Press, 2006), pp. 1–15

Rynne, C., *Technological Change in Anglo-Norman Munster* (Kinsale: Barryscourt Trust with Cork County Council, 1998)

Rynne, C., 'The Development of Milling Technology in Ireland, *c.*600–1875', in A. Bielenberg (ed.), *Irish Flour Milling: A history, 600–2000* (Dublin: Lilliputt Press, 2003), pp. 11–38

Rynne, C., 'Milling of Cereals in Gaelic and Anglo-Norman Ireland *c.* 1200–1500: Technology and cultural choice', in E. Campbell, E. FitzPatrick and A. Horning (eds), *Becoming and Belonging in Ireland* AD *c.1200–1600: Essays in identity and cultural practice* (Cork: Cork University Press, 2018), pp. 45–68

Salzman, L.F. (ed.), *A History of the County of Cambridge and the Isle of Ely*, vol. 2 (London: Victoria County History, 1948)

Sanderlin, S., 'The Monastery of Lismore AD 638–1111', in W. Nolan and T. Power (eds), *Waterford: History & society* (Dublin: Geography Publications, 1992), pp. 27–48

Schaus, M. (ed.), *Women and Gender in Medieval Europe: An encyclopaedia* (London: Routledge, 2006)

Scheepsma, W., *Medieval Religious Women in the Low Countries: The modern devotion, the canonesses of Windsheim and their writings*, trans. D.F. Johnson (Woodbridge: Boydell, 2004)

Schein, S., 'Bridget of Sweden, Margery Kempe and Women's Jerusalem Pilgrimages in the Middle Ages', *Mediterranean Historical Review*, vol. 14, no. 1, 1999, pp. 44–58

Schleif, C., 'Men on the Right – Women on the Left: (A)symmetrical spaces and gendered places', in V.C. Raguin and S. Stanbury (eds), *Women's Space: Patronage, place and gender in the medieval church* (New York: State University of New York Press, 2005), pp. 207–49

Schleif, C. and V. Schier, *Katerina's Windows: Donation and devotion, art and music, as heard and seen through the writings of a Birgittine nun* (Philadelphia: Penn State University Press, 2009)

Schmidt, R.A. and B.L. Voss (eds), *Archaeologies of Sexuality* (London: Routledge, 2000)

Schofield, J., 'Building in Religious Precincts in London at the Dissolution and After', in R. Gilchrist and H. Mytum (eds), *Advances in Monastic Archaeology. BAR British Series 227* (Oxford: Tempvs Reparatvm, 1993), pp. 29–41

Schofield, P., 'Medieval Diet and Demography', in C. Woolgar et al. (eds), *Food in Medieval England: Diet and nutrition* (Oxford: Oxford University Press, 2006), pp. 239–53

Schulenburg, J.T., 'Strict Active Enclosure and Its Effects on the Female Monastic Experience (*ca.*500–1100)', in J.A. Nichols and L. Thomas Shank (eds), *Distant Echoes: Medieval religious women*, vol. 1 (Kalamazoo: Cistercian Publications, 1984), pp. 51–86

Schulenburg, J.T., 'Female Sanctity: Public and private roles *ca.*500–1100', in M. Erler and M. Kowaleski (eds), *Women and Power in the Middle Ages* (Athens: University of Georgia Press, 1988), pp. 102–25

Schulenburg, J.T., 'Women's Monastic Communities 500–1100: Patterns of expansion and decline', *Signs*, vol. 14, no. 2, 1989, pp. 261–92

Schulenburg, J.T., *Forgetful of Their Sex: Female sanctity and society* ca.*500–1100* (Chicago: University of Chicago Press, 1998)

Schulenberg, J.T., 'Gender, Celibacy and Proscriptions of Sacred Space: Symbol and practice', in V.C. Raguin and S. Stanbury (eds), *Women's Space: Patronage, place and gender in the medieval church* (Albany: State University of New York Press, 2005), pp. 185–205

Schulenberg, J.T., 'Space, Sacred and Gender', in M. Schaus (ed.), *Women and Gender in Medieval Europe: An encyclopedia* (London: Routledge, 2006), pp. 771–3

Scott, A.B. and F.X. Martin, Expugnatio Hibernica*: The Conquest of Ireland by Giraldus Cambrensis* (Dublin: Royal Irish Academy, 1978)

Scott, I.R., 'Romsey Abbey: Benedictine nunnery and parish church', in G. Keevil, M. Aston and T. Hall (eds), *Monastic Archaeology* (Oxford: Oxbow, 2001), pp. 150–60

Seaborn, M., 'The Chapter House, Jesus College, Cambridge: Elements of a twelfth-century nunnery revealed', *Donald Insall Associates Newsletter*, vol. 38, 2011, pp. 4–5

Seale, Y., '*De Monasterio Desolato*: Patronage and politics in a frontier Irish convent', *Journal of Medieval Monastic Studies*, vol. 4, 2015, pp. 21–45

Seaver, M., C. McDermott and G. Warren, 'A Monastery Among the Glens', *Archaeology Ireland*, vol. 32, no. 2, 2018, pp. 19–23

Semple, S., 'A Fear of the Past: The place of the prehistoric burial mound in the ideology of middle and later Anglo-Saxon England', *World Archaeology*, vol. 30, no. 1, 1998, pp. 109–26

Semple, S., 'Sacred Spaces and Places in Pre-Christian and Conversion Period Anglo-Saxon England', in H. Hamerow, D. Hinton and S. Crawford (eds), *The Oxford Handbook of Anglo-Saxon Archaeology* (Oxford: Oxford University Press, 2011), pp. 742–63

Semple, S., *Perceptions of the Prehistoric in Anglo-Saxon England: Religion, ritual and rulership in the landscape* (Oxford: Oxford University Press, 2013)

Serjeantson, D., 'Birds: Food and a mark of status', in C. Woolgar et al., *Food in Medieval England: Diet and nutrition* (Oxford: Oxford University Press, 2006), pp. 131–47

Serjeantson, D. and C. Woolgar, 'Fish Consumption in Medieval England', C. Woolgar et al., *Food in Medieval England: Diet and nutrition* (Oxford: Oxford University Press, 2006), pp. 102–30

Shahar, S., *The Fourth Estate: A history of women in the middle ages*, trans. Chaya Galai (London: Routledge, 2003)

Shanks, M., *Experiencing the Past* (London: Routledge, 1992)

Shanks, M. and C. Tilley, *Reconstructing Archaeology* (Cambridge: Cambridge University Press, 1987)

Shanks, M. and C. Tilley, *Social Theory and Archaeology* (Cambridge: Polity Press, 1987)

Shanks, M. and C. Tilley, *Studies in Archaeological Theory Practices* (Cambridge: Cambridge University Press, 1987)

Sharkey, O., *Fore and Its Ancient Buildings* (Mullingar: Magpie Publications, 1999)

Sharpe, R., 'Some Problems Concerning the Organisation of the Church in Early Medieval Ireland', *Peritia*, vol. 3, 1984, pp. 230–70

Sharpe, R., 'Churches and Communities in Early Ireland: Towards a pastoral model', in J. Blair and R. Sharpe (eds), *Pastoral Care Before the Parish* (Leicester: Leicester University Press, 1992), pp. 81–109

Shee Twohig, E., 'Context and Chronology of the Carved Stone at Clonfinlough, County Offaly', *Journal of the Royal Society of Antiquaries of Ireland*, vol. 132, 2002, pp. 99–113

Sheehan, J., 'Caherlehillan Co. Kerry: Ritual, domestic and economic aspects of a Corcu Duibne ecclesiastical site', in C. Corlett and M. Potterton (eds), *The Church in Early Medieval Ireland in the Light of Recent Archaeological Excavations* (Dublin: Wordwell, 2014), pp. 247–58

Sheehan, J., 'The Peacock's Tale: Excavations at Caherlehillan, Iveragh, Ireland', in N. Edwards (ed.), *The Archaeology of the Early Medieval Celtic Churches* (Leeds: Maney, 2009), pp. 191–206

Sherley-Price, L. (trans.), *Bede. A History of the English Church and People* (Harmondsworth: Penguin, 1968)

Shine, M., 'Ballybeg', *Mallow Field Club Journal*, vol. 11, 1993, pp. 84–112

Signori, G., 'Wanderers Between Worlds: Visitors, letters, wills and gifts as means of communication in exchanges between cloister and the world', in J.F. Hamburger and S. Marti (eds), *Crown and Veil: Female monasticism from the fifth to the fifteenth centuries* (New York: Columbia University Press, 2008), pp. 259–73

Signori, G., 'Cell or Dormitory? Monastic visions of space amidst the conflict of ideas', *Journal of Medieval Monastic Studies*, vol. 3, 2014, pp. 21–49

Simington, R.C., *Books of Survey and Distribution being Abstracts and Various Surveys and Instruments of Title 1636–1703, County Clare*, vol. 4 (Dublin: The Stationery Office, 1967)

Simmons, L.N., 'The Abbey Church at Fontevraud in the Later Twelfth Century: Anxiety, authority and architecture in the female spiritual life', *Gesta*, vol. 31, 1992, pp. 99–107

Simms, A., 'The Geography of Irish Manors: The example of the Llanthony cells of Duleek and Colp, County Meath', in J. Bradley (ed.), *Settlement and Society in Medieval Ireland: Studies presented to F.X. Martin* (Kilkenny: Boethius Press, 1988), pp. 291–315

Simms, A., *Irish Historic Towns Atlas No. 4: Kells* (Dublin: Royal Irish Academy, 1990)

Simms, A., 'Perspectives on Irish Settlement Studies', in T. Barry (ed.), *A History of Settlement in Ireland* (London: Routledge, 2000), pp. 228–47

Simms, K., 'Women in Norman Ireland', in M. MacCurtain and D. Ó Corráin (eds), *Women in Irish Society: The historical dimension* (Dublin: Arlen House, The Women's Press, 1978), pp. 14–25

Simms, K., 'Bards and Barons: The Anglo-Irish aristocracy and native culture', in R. Bartlett and A. MacKay (eds), *Medieval Frontier Societies* (Oxford: Oxford University Press, 1989), pp. 177–97

Simms, K., 'Frontiers in the Irish Church: Regional and cultural', in T. Barry, R. Frame and K. Simms (eds), *Colony and Frontier in Medieval Ireland: Essays presented to J.F. Lydon* (London: The Hambledon Press, 1995), pp. 177–200

Simms, K., *Medieval Gaelic Sources* (Dublin: Four Courts Press, 2009)

Simms, K., 'Gaelic Culture and Society', in B. Smith (ed.), *Cambridge History of Ireland. Volume 1: 600–1550* (Cambridge: Cambridge University Press, 2018), pp. 415–40

Simpson, L., 'The Priory of All Hallows and Trinity College, Dublin: Recent archaeological discoveries', *Medieval Dublin*, vol. III, 2002, pp. 195–236

Skinner, M., 'Benedictine Life for Women in Central France 850–1100', in J. Nichols and L. Thomas Shank (eds), *Distant Echoes: Medieval religious women*, vol. 1 (Kalamazoo: Cistercian Publications, 1984), pp. 87–114

Slavin, P., *Bread and Ale for the Brethren: The provisioning of Norwich Cathedral Priory 1260–1536* (Hatfield: University of Hertfordshire Press, 2012)

Sloane, B., 'Tenements in London's Monasteries *c.*1450–1540', in D. Gaimster and R. Gilchrist (eds), *The Archaeology of Reformation 1480–1580* (Leeds: Maney, 2003), pp. 290–8

Sloane, B., *The Augustinian Nunnery of St Mary Clerkenwell, London* (London: Museum of London Archaeology, 2012)

Sloane, B. and G. Malcolm, *Excavations at the Priory of the Order of the Hospital of St John of Jerusalem* (London: Museum of London Archaeology Service, 2004)

Smith, C., *The Ancient and Present State of the County and City of Cork*, 2 vols (Cork: Guy & Company, 1750)

Smith, J.A., *Ordering Women's Lives: Penitentials and nunnery rules in the early medieval West* (Aldershot: Ashgate, 2001)

Smith, J.A., '*Clausura Districta*: Conceiving space and community for Dominican nuns in the thirteenth century', *Parergon*, vol. 27, no. 2, 2010, pp. 13–36

Smith, K.A., 'Books of Hours', in M. Schaus (ed.), *Women and Gender in Medieval Europe: An encyclopaedia* (London: Routledge, 2006), pp. 89–92

Sniveley, C., 'Invisible in the Community? The evidence for early women's monasticism in the southern Balkan peninsula', in S. McNally (ed.), *Shaping Community: The art and archaeology of monasticism. BAR International Series 941* (Oxford: Archaeopress, 2001), pp. 57–66

Sorrentino, J., 'In Houses of Nuns, in Houses of Canons: A liturgical dimension to double monasteries', *Journal of Medieval History*, vol. 28, 2002, pp. 361–72

Spear, V.G., *Leadership in Medieval English Nunneries* (Woodbridge: Boydell, 2005)

Spearing, E. (ed.), *Medieval Writings on Female Spirituality* (London: Penguin, 2002)

Spears, A., *The Cult of Saint Catherine of Alexandria in Ireland* (Rathmullen: Rathmullen District Local History Society, 2006)

Spector, J.D., 'What This Awl Means: Toward a feminist archaeology', in R.W. Preucel and I. Hodder (eds), *Contemporary Archaeology in Theory: A reader* (Oxford: Blackwell, 1996), pp. 485–500

Spellissy, S., *The History of Limerick City* (Limerick: The Celtic Bookshop, 1998)

Sperber, I., 'The Life of St Monenna or Darerca of Killevy', in A.J. Hughes and W. Nolan (eds), *Armagh: History and society* (Dublin: Geography Publications, 2001), pp. 63–97

Spurrell, M., *The Symbolism of Medieval Churches: An introduction* (London: Routledge, 2020)

St John Hope, W.H., 'The Ground Plan of Watton in the East Riding of Yorkshire', *Yorkshire Archaeological Journal*, vol. 58, 1901, pp. 1–34

Stafford, P., 'Queens, Nunneries and Reforming Churchmen: Gender, religious status and reform in tenth- and eleventh-century England', *Past and Present*, vol. 163, 1999, pp. 3–35

Stalley, R., 'Corcomroe Abbey: Some observations on its architectural history', *Journal of the Royal Society of Antiquaries of Ireland*, vol. 105, 1975, pp. 21–46

Stalley, R., 'Mellifont Abbey: A study of its architectural history', *Proceedings of the Royal Irish Academy*, vol. 80C, 1980, pp. 263–354

Stalley, R., *The Cistercian Monasteries of Ireland: An account of the history, art and architecture of the White Monks in Ireland from 1142 to 1540* (London: Yale University Press, 1987)

Stalley, R., 'Sailing to Santiago: Medieval pilgrimage to Santiago de Compostela and its artistic influence in Ireland', in J. Bradley (ed.), *Settlement and Society: Studies presented to F.X. Martin* (Kilkenny: Boethius, 1988), pp. 397–420

Stalley, R., 'Decorating the Lavabo: Late Romanesque sculpture from Mellifont Abbey', *Proceedings of the Royal Irish Academy*, vol. 98C, 1996, pp. 237–64

Stalley, R., *Early Medieval Architecture* (Oxford: Oxford University Press, 1999)

Stalley, R., 'The End of the Middle Ages: Gothic survival in sixteenth-century Connacht', *Journal of the Royal Society of Antiquaries of Ireland*, vol. 133, 2003, pp. 5–23

Stalley, R., 'Ecclesiastical Architecture Before 1169', in D. Ó Cróinín (ed.), *A New History of Ireland. Volume I: Prehistoric and Early Ireland* (Oxford: Oxford University Press, 2005), pp. 714–43

Stalley, R. (ed.), *Irish Gothic Architecture: Construction, decay and reinvention* (Dublin: Wordwell, 2012)

Stancliffe, C., 'Jonas's *Life of Columbanus* and His Disciples', in J. Carey, M. Herbert and P. Ó Riain (eds), *Studies in Hagiography: Saints and scholars* (Dublin: Four Courts Press, 2001), pp. 189–220

Stephens, M., 'Home on the Grange', *Archaeology Ireland*, vol. 23, 2009, pp. 31–3

Stevens J. (ed.), *Monasticon Hibernicum* (London: William Mears, 1722)

Stig Sørensen, M.L., *Gender Archaeology* (Oxford: Polity Press, 2000)

Stig Sørensen, M.L., 'Gender Agenda? Review article' *Antiquity*, vol. 75, 2001, pp. 440–2

Stöber, K., *Late Medieval Monasteries and Their Patrons: England and Wales* c.*1300–1540* (Woodbridge: Boydell, 2007)

Stöber, K., 'The Regular Canons in Wales', in J. Burton and K. Stöber (eds), *The Regular Canons in the Medieval British Isles* (Turnout: Brepols, 2011), pp. 97–114

Stöber, K., 'Review article: *Redes Femenias de Promoción Spiritual en Los Reinos Peninsulares, s.xiii–xvi* (ed. B. Garí)', *Journal of Medieval Monastic Studies*, vol. 3, 2014, pp. 133–5

Stöber, K. and D. Austin, 'Culdees to Canons: The Augustinian houses of north Wales', in J. Burton and K. Stöber (eds), *Monastic Wales: New approaches* (Cardiff: University of Wales Press, 2013), pp. 41–54

Stokes, W. (ed.), Vita Tripartita*: The tripartite life of St Patrick and other documents relating to that saint*, 2 vols (London: Eyre & Spottiswoode, 1887)

Stone, D., 'The Consumption and Supply of Birds in Late Medieval England', in C. Woolgar et al., *Food in Medieval England: Diet and nutrition* (Oxford: Oxford University Press, 2006), pp. 148–61

Stone, P.G., *An Exact Account of the Church and Priory at Goring in the County of Oxford* (Goring: Henry L. Smith, 1893)

Stoop, P., 'Review article: *Barking Abbey and Medieval Literary Culture: Authorship and authority in a female community* (eds J.N. Brown and D. Alfano Bussell)', *Journal of Medieval Monastic Studies*, vol. 3, 2014, pp. 126–8

Stoop, P., 'The Convent of Jericho in Brussels and Its Literary Network', *Anuario de Estudios Medievales*, 2014, vol. 44, pp. 381–412

Stott, A., 'The Ring of Gullion', in F.H.A. Aalen, K. Whelan and M. Stout (eds), *Atlas of the Irish Rural Landscape*, 1st edn (Cork: Cork University Press, 1997), pp. 316–28

Stout, G., *Newgrange and the Bend of the Boyne* (Cork: Cork University Press, 2002)

Stout, G., 'St Mary's Abbey, Dublin and Its Medieval Farm Suppliers', *Medieval Dublin*, vol. XIV, 2015, pp. 146–62

Stout, G., 'The Cistercian Grange: A medieval farming system', in M. Murphy and M. Stout (eds), *Agriculture and Settlement in Ireland* (Dublin: Four Courts Press, 2015), pp. 28–68

Stout, G., 'Settlement on Mellifont Abbey's Monastic Estate in Cos Meath and Louth (1540–1)', in J. Lyttleton and M. Stout (eds), *Church and Settlement in Ireland* (Dublin: Four Courts Press, 2018), pp. 157–81

Stout, G. and M. Stout, *The Bective Abbey Project, Co. Meath: Excavations 2009–12* (Dublin: Wordwell, 2016)

Stout, G., R. Loeber and K. O'Brien, 'Mellifont Abbey, Co. Louth: A study of its post-dissolution architecture 1540–1727', *Proceedings of the Royal Irish Academy*, vol. 116C, 2016, pp. 191–226

Stout, M., *Early Medieval Ireland 431–1169* (Dublin: Wordwell, 2017)

Stuard, S.M., 'The Three-Decade Transformation: Medieval women and the course of history', in S.M. Stuard (ed.), *Considering Medieval Women and Gender* (Surrey: Ashgate, 2010), pp. 1–21

Stuard, S.M., 'The Annales School and Feminist History: Opening dialogue with the American stepchild', in S.M. Stuard (ed.), *Considering Medieval Women and Gender* (Surrey: Ashgate, 2010), part IX, pp. 135–43

Stuard, S.M., 'The Chase After Theory: Considering medieval women', in S.M. Stuard (ed.), *Considering Medieval Women and Gender* (Surrey: Ashgate, 2010), part XII, pp. 135–46

Stupecki, L. and M. Valor, 'Religions', in J. Graham-Campbell and M. Valor (eds), *The Archaeology of Medieval Europe. Volume 1: Eighth to Twelfth Centuries AD* (Aarhus: Aarhus University Press, 2007), pp. 366–93

Sweetinburgh, S., *The Role of the Hospital in Medieval England: Gift giving and the spiritual economy* (Dublin: Four Courts Press, 2004)

Sweetman, P.D., 'Excavation of Medieval Field Boundaries at Clonard, Co. Meath', *Journal of the Royal Society of Antiquaries of Ireland*, vol. 108, 1978, pp. 10–22

Sweetman, P.D., 'Excavations of a Moated Site at Rigsdale, County Cork 1977–8', *Proceedings of the Royal Irish Academy*, vol. 81C, 1981, pp. 103–205

Sweetman, P.D., 'Archaeological Excavations at Abbeyknockmoy, Co. Galway', *Proceedings of the Royal Irish Academy*, vol. 87C, 1987, pp. 1–12

Sweetman, P.D., *The Medieval Castles of Ireland* (Cork: The Collins Press, 1999)

Sweetman, P.D., 'The Hall-House in Ireland', in J.R. Kenyon and K. O'Conor (eds), *The Medieval Castle in Ireland and Wales* (Dublin: Four Courts Press, 2003), pp. 121–32

Swift, C., *Ogham Stones and the Earliest Irish Christians* (Maynooth: NUI Maynooth, 1997)

Swift, C., 'Sculptors and Their Customers: A study of Clonmacnoise grave slabs', in H. King (ed.), *Clonmacnoise Studies*, vol. 2 (Dublin: The Stationery Office, 2003), pp. 105–23

Swift, C., 'Brigid, Patrick and the Kings of Kildare AD 640–850', in W. Nolan and K. McGrath (eds), *Kildare: History and society* (Dublin: Geography Publications, 2006), pp. 97–128

Sykes, N., 'From *Cu* to *Sceap* to *Beffe* and *Motton*', in C. Woolgar et al., *Food in Medieval England: Diet and nutrition* (Oxford: Oxford University Press, 2006), pp. 56–71

Sykes, N., 'The Impact of the Normans on Hunting Practices in England', in C. Woolgar et al., *Food in Medieval England: Diet and nutrition* (Oxford: Oxford University Press, 2006), pp. 162–75

Sykes, N., 'Hunting and Venison in Medieval England', in M. Carver and J. Klápště (eds), *The Archaeology of Medieval Europe. Volume 2: Twelfth to Sixteenth Centuries* (Aarhus: Aarhus University Press, 2011), pp. 132–6

Tabraham, C. (ed.), *Iona Abbey and Nunnery* (Edinburgh: Historic Scotland, 2004)

Tait, C., 'Art and the Cult of the Virgin Mary in Ireland *c.* 1500–1660', in R. Moss, C. Ó Clabaigh and S. Ryan (eds), *Art and Devotion in Late Medieval Ireland* (Dublin: Four Courts Press, 2006), pp. 163–83

Tatton-Brown, T., 'The Two Mid-Twelfth-Century Cloister Arcades at Canterbury Cathedral Priory', *Journal of the British Archaeological Association*, vol. 159, 2006, pp. 91–104

Taylor Jones, C., *Ruling the Spirit: Women, liturgy and Dominican reform in late medieval Germany* (Philadelphia: University of Pennsylvania Press, 2017)

Taylor, M., 'Early Anglo-Norman Settlement Patterns in Co. Limerick', *North Munster Antiquarian Journal*, vol. 53, 2013, pp. 123–33

Tester, P.J., 'A Plan and Architectural Description of the Medieval Remains of Davington Priory', *Archaeologia Cantiana*, vol. 95, 1980, pp. 205–12

Thom, C., *Early Irish Monasticism: An understanding of its cultural roots* (London: T. & T. Clark, 2007)

Thomas, A., *The Walled Towns of Ireland*, 2 vols (Dublin: Irish Academic Press, 1992)

Thomas, A., *Irish Historic Towns Atlas No. 15: Derry-Londonderry* (Dublin: Royal Irish Academy, 2005)

Thomas, C., *The Early Christian Archaeology of North Britain* (London: Thames & Hudson, 1971)

Thomas, C., *Christianity in Roman Britain to AD 500* (Berkeley: University of California Press, 1981)

Thomas, C., *Christian Celts: Messages and images* (Stroud: Tempus, 1998)

Thomas, G., 'The Prehistory of Medieval Farms and Villages: From Saxons to Scandinavians', in N. Christie and P. Stamper (eds), *Medieval Rural Settlement: Britain and Ireland AD 800–1600* (Oxford: Windgather Press, 2012), pp. 43–62

Thomas, G., 'Life Before the Minster: The social dynamics of monastic foundation at Anglo-Saxon Lyminge, Kent', *The Antiquaries Journal*, vol. 93, 2013, pp. 109–45

Thomas, G., A. Pluskowshi, R. Gilchrist, G. Garcia-Contreras Ruiz, A. Andren, A. Augenti, G. Astill, J. Staecker and H. Valk, 'Religious Transformations in the Middle Ages: Towards a new archaeological agenda', *Medieval Archaeology*, vol. 61, no. 2, 2017, pp. 300–29

Thomas, J., 'Archaeologies of Place and Landscape', in I. Hodder (ed.) *Archaeological Theory Today* (Cambridge: Polity, 2001), pp. 165–86

Thomas, J., *Archaeology and Modernity* (London: Routledge, 2004)

Thompson, S., 'The Problem of the Cistercian Nuns in the Twelfth and Early Thirteenth Centuries', in D. Baker (ed.), *Medieval Women* (Oxford: Blackwell, 1978), pp. 227–52

Thompson, S., 'Why English Nunneries Had No History: A study of the problems of the English nunneries founded after the Conquest', in J.A. Nichols and L. Thomas Shank (eds), *Distant Echoes: Medieval religious women*, vol. 1 (Kalamazoo: Cistercian Publications, 1984), pp. 131–49

Thompson, S., *Women Religious: The founding of English nunneries after the Norman conquest* (Oxford: Clarendon Press, 1991)

Thurston, T., *Gloria: An introduction to 1,000 years of European sacred music* (Dublin: Associated Editions, 2011)

Tierney, M., 'Theory and Politics in Early Medieval Irish Archaeology', in M.A. Monk and J. Sheehan (eds), *Early Medieval Munster: Archaeology, history and society* (Cork: Cork University Press, 1998), pp. 190–9

Tilley, C., 'Phenomenology', in A.C. Renfrew and P. Bahn (eds), *Archaeology: The key concepts* (London: Routledge, 2005), pp. 201–7

Tillotson, J.H., *Marrick Priory: A nunnery in late medieval Yorkshire* (York: Borthwick Institute, University of York, 1989)

Torjesen, K., *When Women Were Priests* (New York: Harper Collins, 1995)

Trigger, B., *A History of Archaeological Thought* (Cambridge: Cambridge University Press, 1989)

Tuan, Y.F., *Space and Place: The perspective of experience* (London: Edward Arnold, 1977)

Untermann, M., *Architektur im Frühen Mittelalter* (Darmstadt: Wissenschaftliche Buchgesellschaft, 2006)

Untermann, M., 'Das Nonnenhaus: Traditionen eines klösterlichen bautyps', in R. Oldermann (ed.), *Gebaute Klausur: Function und architektur mittelalterlicher klosterräume* (Bielefeld: Verlag Regionalkultur, 2008), pp. 97–109

Untermann, M., 'The Place of the Choir in Churches of Female Convents in the Medieval German Kingdom', in J. Burton and K. Stöber (eds), *Women in the Medieval Monastic World* (Turnhout: Brepols, 2015), pp. 327–53

Van Hove, M., F. Chantinne and D. Willems, 'Dans La Clôture D'une Grande Abbaye: Premiers résultats des recherches archéologiques menées sur la place de Nivelles 2009–2011', *Medieval and Modern Matters*, vol. 3, 2012, pp. 165–210

Van Whye, C. (ed.), *Female Monasticism in Early Modern Europe: An interdisciplinary view* (Aldershot: Ashgate, 2008)

Vanderputten, S., *Monastic Reform as Process: Realities and representations in medieval Flanders 900–1100* (Ithaca: Cornell University Press, 2013)

Vanderputten, S., *Dark Age Nunneries: The ambiguous identity of female monasticism, 800–1050* (Ithaca: Cornell University Press, 2018)

Vanderputten, S., *Medieval Monasticisms: Forms and experiences of the monastic life in the Latin West* (Oldenbourg: De Gruyter, 2020)

Vanderputten, S., 'Monastic Reform from the Tenth to the Early Twelfth Century', in A.I. Beach and I. Cochelin (eds), *Medieval Monasticism in the Latin West*, 2 vols (Cambridge: Cambridge University Press, 2020), pp. 599–617

Venarde, B.L., *Women's Monasticism and Medieval Society: Nunneries in France and England 890–1215* (Ithaca: Cornell University Press, 1997)

Venarde, B.L., 'Robert of Arbrissel and Woman's *Vita Religiosa*: Looking back and ahead', in G. Melville and A. Müller (eds), *Female* Vita Religiosa *between Late Antiquity and the High Middle Ages: Structures, developments and spatial contexts* (Berlin: LIT Verlag, 2011), pp. 329–40

Verling, M. (ed.), *Beara Women Talking: Folklore from the Beara Peninsula* (Cork: Mercier Press, 2003)

Verstraten, F., 'Ua Conchobair', in S. Duffy (ed.), *Medieval Ireland: An encyclopedia* (London: Routledge, 2005), pp. 464–6

Villiers-Tuthill, K., 'The Irish Benedictine Nuns: From Ypres to Kylemore', in M. Browne and C. Ó Clabaigh (eds), *The Irish Benedictines: A history* (Dublin: The Columba Press, 2005), pp. 122–39

Voss, B.L., 'Feminisms, Queer Theories and the Archaeological Study of Past Sexualities', *World Archaeology*, vol. 32, 2000, pp. 180–92

Waddell, J., *Foundation Myths: The beginnings of Irish archaeology* (Dublin: Wordwell, 2005)

Wade Labarge, M., *Women in Medieval Life* (London: Penguin, 2001)

Waites, B., *Monasteries and Landscape of the North York Moors and Wolds* (Stroud: Tempus, 2007)

Waldron, T., 'Nutrition and the Skeleton', in C. Woolgar et al. (eds), *Food in Medieval England: Diet and nutrition* (Oxford: Oxford University Press, 2006), pp. 254–66

Walker Bynum, C., *Jesus as Mother: Studies in the spirituality of the high middle ages* (Berkeley: University of California Press, 1982)

Walker Bynum, C., *Holy Feast and Holy Fast: The religious significance of food to medieval women* (London: University of California Press, 1987)

Walker Bynum, C., 'Foreword', in J. Hamburger and S. Marti (eds), *Crown and Veil: Female monasticism from the fifth to the fifteenth centuries* (New York: Columbia University Press, 2008), pp. xiii–xviii

Walker Bynum, C., 'Patterns of Female Piety in the Later Middle Ages', in J. Hamburger and S. Marti (eds), *Crown and Veil: Female monasticism from the fifth to the fifteenth centuries* (New York: Columbia University Press, 2008), pp. 172–90

Walsh, C., 'Archaeological Excavations at the Abbey of St Thomas the Martyr, Dublin', *Medieval Dublin*, vol. I, 2000, pp. 185–202

Walsh, D., 'Bordesley Abbey Precinct: The definition and use of space in an English Cistercian abbey', in S. McNally (ed.), *Shaping Community: The art and archaeology of monasticism. BAR International Series 941* (Oxford: Archaeopress, 2001), pp. 91–9

Walsh, P., 'Galway: A summary history', in E. FitzPatrick, M. O'Brien and P. Walsh (eds), *Archaeological Investigations in Galway City 1987–1998* (Dublin: Wordwell, 2004), pp. 269–91

Ward, J.C., 'English Noblewomen and the Local Community in the Later Middle Ages', in D. Watt (ed.), *Medieval Women in Their Communities* (Cardiff: University of Wales Press, 1997), pp. 186–203

Ward, S., *Excavations at Chester: The lesser medieval religious houses, sites investigated 1964–1983* (Chester: Chester City Council, Department of Leisure Services, 1990)

Ward, S., 'The Monastic Topography of Chester', in R. Gilchrist and H. Mytum (eds), *Advances in Monastic Archaeology. BAR British Series 227* (Oxford: Tempvs Reparatvm, 1993), pp. 113–26

Wardell, J., 'The History and Antiquities of St Catherine's Old Abbey, County Limerick (with a description of the conventual buildings by T.J. Westropp)', *Journal of the Royal Society of Antiquaries of Ireland*, vol. 14, 1904, pp. 41–64

Ware, J., *De Hibernia et Antiqitatibus Ejus* (London: Crook & Thom, 1654)

Warren, A.K., *Anchorites and Their Patrons in Medieval England* (Berkeley: University of California Press, 1985)

Warren, N.B., 'Monastic Rules', in M. Schaus (ed.), *Women and Gender in Medieval Europe: An encyclopedia* (London: Routledge, 2006), pp. 576–8

Waterman, D.M., 'The Early Christian Churches and Cemetery at Derry, Co. Down', *Ulster Journal of Archaeology*, vol. 30, 1967, pp. 49–52

Watson, N., 'Julian of Norwich', in C. Dinshaw and D. Wallace (eds), *The Cambridge Companion to Medieval Women's Writing* (Cambridge: Cambridge University Press, 2003), pp. 210–21

Watt, D., 'Introduction', in D. Watt (ed.), *Medieval Women in Their Communities* (Cardiff: University of Wales Press, 1997), pp. 1–19

Watt, J.A., '*Ecclesia inter Anglicos et inter Hibernicos*: Confrontation and coexistence in the medieval diocese and province of Armagh', in J.F. Lydon (ed.), *The English in Medieval Ireland* (Dublin: Royal Irish Academy, 1984), pp. 46–64

Watt, J.A., 'Gaelic Polity and Cultural Identity', in A. Cosgrove (ed.), *A New History of Ireland. Volume II: Medieval Ireland 1169–1534* (Oxford: Oxford University Press, 1993), pp. 314–51

Watt, J.A., 'The Anglo-Irish Colony Under Strain, 1327–99', in A. Cosgrove (ed.), *A New History of Ireland. Volume II: Medieval Ireland 1169–1534* (Oxford: Oxford University Press, 1993), pp. 352–96

Watt, J.A., *The Church in Medieval Ireland*, 2nd edn (Dublin: UCD Press, 1998)

Webb, D., *Medieval European Pilgrimage* (Basingstoke: Palgrave, 2002)

Webb, G., *Architecture in Britain: The middle ages*, 2nd edn (Middlesex: Penguin, 1965)

Webster, L.E. and J. Cherry, 'Medieval Britain in 1978', *Medieval Archaeology*, vol. 23, 1979, pp. 234–78

Weir, H.W.L., 'Deerparks of Clare', *The Other Clare*, vol. 10, 1986, pp. 54–5

Wemple, S.F., *Women in Frankish Society: Marriage and the cloister 500–900* (Philadelphia: Penn, 1981)

Wemple, S.F., 'Female Spirituality and Mysticism in Frankish Monasticism: Radegund, Balthild and Aldegund', in J. Nichols and L. Thomas Shank (eds), *Peace Weavers: Medieval religious women*, vol. 2 (Kalamazoo: Cistercian Publications, 1987), pp. 39–54

Wessex Archaeology, 'Syon House, Syon Park Hounslow: An Archaeological evaluation of a Bridgettine abbey and an assessment of the results. Ref: 52568.05' (Salisbury: unpublished report, 2003)

West, J. and N. Palmer, *Haughmond Abbey: Excavation of a twelfth-century cloister in its historical and landscape context* (London: Historic England, 2014)

Westropp, T.J., 'Killone Abbey, Co. Clare', *Journal of the Royal Society of Antiquaries of Ireland*, vol. 1, 1891, pp. 409–10

Westropp, T.J., 'Foundation Charter of Forgy Abbey, Co. Clare', *Journal of the Royal Society of Antiquaries of Ireland*, vol. 22, 1892, pp. 78–9

Westropp, T.J., 'The Augustinian Houses of the County Clare: Clare, Killone and Inchicronan', *Journal of the Royal Society of Antiquaries of Ireland*, vol. 30, 1900, pp. 118–35

Westropp, T.J., 'The Conventual Buildings', in J. Wardell, 'The History and Antiquities of St Catherine's Old Abbey, County Limerick', *Journal of the Royal Society of Antiquaries of Ireland*, vol. 14, 1904, pp. 53–64

Westropp, T.J., 'A Survey of Ancient Churches in the County of Limerick', *Proceedings of the Royal Irish Academy*, vol. 25, 1904–5, pp. 327–480

Westropp, T.J., 'The Ancient Castles of the County of Limerick, North-Eastern Baronies and Western Baronies', *Proceedings of the Royal Irish Academy*, vol. 26, 1906–7, pp. 55–108, 143–268

Westropp, T.J., 'A Description of the Ancient Buildings and Crosses at Clonmacnois, King's County', *Journal of the Royal Society of Antiquaries of Ireland,* vol. 37, 1907, pp. 277–306

Westropp, T.J., 'On Certain Typical Earthworks and Ringwalls in County Limerick, Parts I and II', *Proceedings of the Royal Irish Academy*, vol. 33C, 1916–17, pp. 9–42, 444–92

White, N.B., *Irish Monastic and Episcopal Deeds AD 1200–1600* (Dublin: Irish Manuscripts Commission, 1936)

White, N.B., *Extents of Irish Monastic Possession 1540–'41: Manuscripts held in the Public Record Office London* (Dublin: Irish Manuscripts Commission, 1943)

Wiesner, M., *Women and Gender in Early Modern Europe* (Cambridge: Cambridge University Press, 2000)

Wiethaus, U., *Maps of Flesh and Light: The religious experience of medieval women mystics* (Syracuse: Syracuse University Press, 1993)

Wiethaus, U., 'Bride of Christ Imagery', in M. Schaus (ed.), *Women and Gender in Medieval Europe: An encyclopedia* (London: Routledge, 2006), pp. 94–5

Wiethaus, U., 'Collaborative Literacy and the Spiritual Education of Nuns at Helfta', in V. Blanton, V. O'Mara and P. Stoop (eds), *Nuns' Literacies in Medieval Europe: The Kansas City dialogue* (Turnhout: Brepols, 2015), pp. 27–46

Wiggins, K., 'An Early Medieval Ditched Enclosure with Burials and Cereal-Drying Kilns at Killeany, Co. Laois', in C. Corlett and M. Potterton (eds), *The Church in Early Medieval Ireland in the Light of Recent Archaeological Excavations* (Dublin: Wordwell, 2014), pp. 273–86

Williams, D.H., 'Cistercian Nunneries in Medieval Wales', *Citeaux: Commentarii Cistercienses*, vol. 26, 1975, pp. 155–74

Williams, D.H., *Atlas of Cistercian Lands in Wales* (Cardiff: Cardiff University Press, 1990)

Williams, D.H., *Catalogue of Seals in the National Museum of Wales. Volume I: Seal Dies, Welsh Seals, Papal Bullae* (Cardiff: National Museum of Wales, 1993)

Williams, D.H., *Catalogue of Seals in the National Museum of Wales. Volume II: Ecclesiastical, Monastic and Collegiate Seals with a Supplement Concerning Wales* (Cardiff: National Museum and Galleries of Wales, 1998)

Williams, D.H., *The Welsh Cistercians* (Leominister: Gracewing, 2001)

Williams, H. (ed.), *Archaeologies of Remembrance: Death and memory in past societies* (London: Springer, 2003)

Williamson, T., *The Archaeology of Rabbit Warrens* (Princes Risborough: Shire Publications, 2006)

Wolbrink, S.A., 'Women in the Premonstratensian Order of Northwestern Germany 1120–1250', *The Catholic Historical Review*, vol. 89, 2003, pp. 287–408

Wood, D. (ed.), *Women and Religion in Medieval England* (Oxford: Oxbow, 2003)

Woolgar, C., 'Meat and Dairy Products in Late Medieval England', in C. Woolgar et al., *Food in Medieval England: Diet and nutrition* (Oxford: Oxford University Press, 2006), pp. 88–101

Woolgar, C., 'Group Diets in Late Medieval England', in C. Woolgar et al., *Food in Medieval England: Diet and nutrition* (Oxford: Oxford University Press, 2006), pp. 191–200

Woolgar, C., D. Serjeantson and T. Waldron (eds), *Food in Medieval England: Diet and nutrition* (Oxford: Oxford University Press, 2006)

Wycherley, N., *The Cult of Relics in Early Medieval Ireland* (Turnhout: Brepols, 2015)

Wylie, A., 'Gender Theory and the Archaeological Record: Why is there no archaeology of gender?', in J.M. Gero and M.W. Conkey (eds), *Engendering Archaeology* (Oxford: Blackwell, 1991), pp. 31–54

Wylie, A., 'On "Heavily Decomposing Red Herrings": Scientific method in archaeology and the ladening of evidence with theory', in L. Embree (ed.), *Metaarchaeology* (Dordrecht: Kluwer, 1992), pp. 269–88

Wylie, A., 'The Interplay of Evidential Constraints and Political Interest: Recent archaeological research on gender', in K. Hays-Gilpin and D.S. Whitley (eds), *Reader in Gender Archaeology* (London: Routledge, 1998), pp. 57–84

Wylie, A., *Thinking from Things: Essays in the philosophy of archaeology* (Berkeley: University of California Press, 2002)

Yorke, B., *Nunneries and the Anglo-Saxon Royal Houses* (London: Continuum, 2003)

Young, A. and D. Lunt, 'Human Bone', in Perthshire Society of Natural Science (eds), *Pitmiddle Village and Elcho Nunnery Research and Excavation on Tayside* (Perth: Perthshire Society of Natural Science, 1988), pp. 60–6

Young, B.K., 'Archaeology in an Urban Setting: Excavations at Saint-Pierre-de-Monmartre Paris, 1975–1977', *Journal of Field Archaeology*, vol. 5, 1978, pp. 319–29

WEBSITES

http://historyofwomenreligious.org [History of Women Religious in Britain and Ireland network]
http://webgis.archaeology.ie/historicenvironment/ [Sites and Monuments Record database for Ireland]
http://www.bcn.cat/museuhistoria/Murals-sota-la-lupa-Monestir-Pedralbes/en/ [Conservation of paintings in St Michael's Chapel Monastery of Pedralbes, Spain]
http://downsurvey.tcd.ie/
http://www.heritagecouncil.ie
http://www.irish-annals.cs.tcd.ie/ [Irish Annals]
http://www.kildare.ie/library/ehistory/2011/03/killeen_cormac_colbinstown_an.asp.
http://www.limerickcity.ie/Library/LocalStudies/IrishTouristAssociationSurvey/
http://www.mappingdeathdb.ie/ [Database of burials and sites in Ireland first to eighth century AD]
http://www.pastscape.org.uk/ [Archaeological and architectural heritage in England]
http://www.placenamesni.org/ [Placenames database for Northern Ireland]
https://apps.communities-ni.gov.uk/NISMR-PUBLIC/Default.aspx [Northern Ireland's Sites and Monuments database]
https://arts.st-andrews.ac.uk/monasticmatrix/home [Monastic Matrix database]
https://celt.ucc.ie//book_lismore.html [Corpus of Electronic Texts, Book of Lismore]
https://celt.ucc.ie//published/E580000-001/index.html [Corpus of Electronic Texts, Desmond Survey]
https://chancery.tcd.ie/content/welcome-circle [A Calendar of Irish Chancery Letters *c.*1244–1509]
https://confessio.ie/# [St Patrick's writings]
https://cora.ucc.ie/ [Cork Open Research Archive, University College Cork]
https://excavations.ie/ [Database of Irish archaeological excavation reports]
https://exploringmedievalseals.wordpress.com [Medieval seals in Britain]
https://fmrsi.wordpress.com [Forum for Medieval and Renaissance Studies in Ireland]
https://foodcult.eu/project-details/ [Food Culture and Identity in Ireland *c.*1550–1650, ERC project]
https://historicengland.org.uk/
https://medieval.ie/ [Monastic Ireland project, database of religious houses in Ireland]
https://monasticon.celt.dias.ie/ [Database of early Christian ecclesiastical settlement in Ireland, fifth to twelfth centuries]
https://www.archaeology.ie/ [Portal of National Monuments Service Ireland]
https://www.galwaycitymuseum.ie
https://www.logainm.ie [Placenames database of Ireland]
https://www.monasticwales.org/ [Database of religious houses in Wales]
https://www.newadvent.org/cathen/ [Catholic encyclopedia]
https://www.ria.ie/irish-historic-towns-atlas-online
https://www.uni-goettingen.de/en/76297.html [FemMoData, female monasticism's database]
https://www.york.ac.uk/borthwick/publications/monastic-research-bulletin/
https://www.yumpu.com/en/document/view [Heritage Council documents]

Index

Illustrations are indicated by page numbers in **bold.**